Children's Hearings (Scotland) Act 2011

Children's Hearings (Scotland) Act 2011

Annotated by

Katy Macfarlane
Senior Teaching Fellow at the University of Edinburgh

Morag Driscoll
Retired Director of the Scottish Child Law Centre

Sheriff Brian Kearney
Retired Sheriff

Lindsey Anderson
Solicitor

W. GREEN

1st Edition 2018

ISBN 978-0414-03535-5

Published in 2018 by Thomson Reuters, trading as W. Green, 21 Alva Street, Edinburgh, EH2 4PS. Thomson Reuters is registered in England & Wales, Company No.1679046. Registered Office and address for service: 5 Canada Square, Canary Wharf, London, E14 5AQ.
For further information on our products and services, visit
http://www.sweetandmaxwell.co.uk/wgreen

Typeset by YHT Ltd, London
Printed and bound in the UK by CPI Group (UK) Ltd, Croydon, CR0 4YY

No natural forests were destroyed to make this product;
only farmed timber was used and replanted

A CIP catalogue record for this book is available from the British Library

Crown copyright material is reproduced with the permission of the Controller of HMSO and the Queen's Printer for Scotland.

All rights reserved. No part of this publication may be reproduced, or transmitted in any form, or by any means, or stored in any retrieval system of any nature, without prior written permission, except for permitted fair dealing under the Copyright, Designs and Patents Act 1988, or in accordance with the terms of a licence issued by the Copyright Licensing Agency in respect of photocopying and/or reprographic reproduction. Application for permission for other use of copyright material, including permission to reproduce extracts in other published works, should be made to the publishers. Full acknowledgement of the author, publisher and source must be given.

Thomson Reuters, the Thomson Reuters Logo and W. GREEN are trademarks of Thomson Reuters.

© 2018 Thomson Reuters (Professional) UK Limited

CONTENTS

	Page
Table of Cases	vii
Table of UK Statutes	xiii
Table of Scottish Statutes	xvii
Table of UK Statutory Instruments	xxv
Table of Scottish Statutory Instruments	xxvii
Children's Hearings (Scotland) Act 2011	1
Appendix: Lord Advocate's Guidelines	319
Index	323

This Act is reproduced from Mays, Scottish Social Work Legislation, *and reflects the looseleaf paragraph numbering*

TABLE OF CASES

A (A Child) (Disclosure of Third Party Information) Re [2012] UKSC 60; [2013] 2 A.C. 66; [2012] 3 W.L.R. 1484; [2013] 1 All E.R. 761; [2013] 1 F.L.R. 948; [2013] 1 F.C.R. 69; [2013] H.R.L.R. 11; [2013] B.L.G.R. 179; [2013] Fam. Law 269 .... C.455.5, C.557.4
A v Kennedy, 1993 S.C. 131; 1993 S.L.T. 1188; 1993 S.C.L.R. 107 .... C.446.6
AB and CD v AT. *See* B, Petitioner
AMI v Dunn [2012] HCJAC 108; 2013 J.C. 82; 2012 S.L.T. 983; 2012 S.C.L. 987; 2012 S.C.C.R. 673; 2012 G.W.D. 33-666 .... C.555.5
Application for a Child Protection Order, 2015 S.L.T. (Sh Ct) 9; 2015 Fam. L.R. 26; 2015 G.W.D. 1-22 .... C.421.3, C.421.4, C.422.2
Associated Provincial Picture Houses Ltd v Wednesbury Corp [1948] 1 K.B. 223; [1947] 2 All E.R. 680; (1947) 63 T.L.R. 623; (1948) 112 J.P. 55; 45 L.G.R. 635; [1948] L.J.R. 190; (1947) 177 L.T. 641; (1948) 92 S.J. 26 .... C.541.8
AU v Glasgow City Council and the Advocate General [2017] CSIH 12 .... C.503.2
AXA General Insurance Ltd v Lord Advocate [2011] UKSC 46; [2012] 1 A.C. 868; [2011] 3 W.L.R. 871; 2012 S.C. (U.K.S.C.) 122; 2011 S.L.T. 1061; [2012] H.R.L.R. 3; [2011] U.K.H.R.R. 1221; (2011) 122 B.M.L.R. 149; (2011) 108(41) L.S.G. 22 .... C.446.16, C.535.4
B Petitioner [2015] CSIH 25; 2015 S.C. 545; 2015 S.L.T. 269; 2015 S.C.L.R. 664; 2015 Fam. L.R. 58; 2015 G.W.D. 12-198 .... C.437.2, C.527.3, C.547.4
BC (A Minor) (Care Order: Appropriate Local Authority), Re [1995] 3 F.C.R. 598; (1996) 160 L.G. Rev. 13 .... C.545.2
C, Petitioner, 2002 Fam. L.R. 42 .... C.416.2, C.542.7
C v Miller, 2003 S.L.T. 1379; 2004 S.C.L.R. 55; 2003 G.W.D. 23-668 .... C.535.9, C.542.3
C (KJ) v HM Advocate, 1994 S.C.C.R. 560 .... C.555.7
Catto v Pearson, 1990 S.L.T. (Sh. Ct) 77; 1990 S.C.L.R. 267 .... C.409.2
CF v MF & GF and Scottish Reporter [2017] CSIH 44; 2017 S.L.T. 945; 2017 Fam. L.R. 83; 2017 G.W.D. 23-394... C.453.5, C.455.3, C.460.13, C.469.3, C.493.5, C.498.5, C.521.3, C.521.5, C.535.4, C.539.5, C.542.16
City of Edinburgh Council v MS; sub nom. City of Edinburgh Council v S, 2015 S.L.T. (Sh Ct) 69; 2015 S.C.L.R. 631; 2015 G.W.D. 11-190 .... C.446.20
Clarke v Edinburgh and District Tramways Co, 1919 S.C. (H.L.) 35; (1919) 1 S.L.T. 247 .... C.535.9
Constanda v M, 1997 S.C. 217; 1997 S.L.T. 1396; 1997 S.C.L.R. 510; 1997 G.W.D. 16-704 .... C.404.2, C.446.13, C.449.4, C.481.4, C.484.4, C.535.9
Cumbria CC, Petitioner [2016] CSIH 92; 2017 S.L.T. 34; 2017 Fam. L.R. 15; 2016 G.W.D. 40-703 .... C.510.8, C.569.3
Cunningham v M, 2005 S.L.T. (Sh Ct) 73; 2005 Fam. L.R. 14; 2004 G.W.D. 40-811 C.446.6
Cunninghame v J and S, 2000 Fam. L.B. 46–5 .... C.542.12
D (A Child) (Abduction) Re [2007] F.L.R. 242 .... C.406.5
D (Minors) (Adoption reports: confidentiality) Re [1996] A.C. 593; [1995] 3 W.L.R. 483; [1995] 4 All E.R. 385; [1995] 2 F.L.R. 687; [1996] 1 F.C.R. 205; [1996] Fam. Law 8; (1995) 145 N.L.J. 1612 .... C.455.5, C.557.4
D v H, 2004 S.L.T. (Sh Ct) 73; 2004 Fam. L.R. 41; 2004 G.W.D. 8-164 .... C.505.2
D v National Society for the Prevention of Cruelty to Children (NSPCC) [1978] A.C. 171; [1977] 2 W.L.R. 201; [1977] 1 All E.R. 589; 76 L.G.R. 5; (1977) 121 S.J. 119 .... C.443.2
D v Sinclair, 1973 S.L.T. (Sh. Ct) 47 .... C.535.4, C.535.5, C.535.9
D v South Tyneside Health Care NHS Trust [2003] EWCA Civ 878; [2004] P.I.Q.R. P12; [2004] M.H.L.R. 74 .... C.548.4
D, Appellant, 2014 Fam. L.R. 66; 2014 G.W.D. 21-405 .... C.511.2, C.517.6
DH v Scottish Children's Reporter, 2014 Fam. L.B. 130–6 .... C.458.2, C.460.5
Dosoo v Dosoo (No.1), 1999 S.L.T. (Sh Ct) 86; 1999 S.C.L.R. 905; 1999 Fam. L.R. 80; 1999 G.W.D. 13-586 .... C.557.2, C.557.4
E v United Kingdom (33218/96) [2003] 1 F.L.R. 348; [2002] 3 F.C.R. 700; (2003) 36 E.H.R.R. 31; [2003] Fam. Law 157 .... C.439.3
East Renfrewshire Council, Appellant [2016] SAC (Civ) 14; 2017 Fam. L.R. 23; 2016 G.W.D. 38-679 .... C.462.4, C.545.2, C.545.6, C.545.11, C.580.2
F (A Parent) v Kennedy (Reporter to the Children's Panel) (No.2), 1993 S.L.T. 1284; 1992 S.C.L.R. 750 .... C.552.6
F v Principal Reporter, 2014 Fam. L.R. 57; 2014 G.W.D. 13-235 ....

Falconer v Brown (1893) 1 Adam 96 .... C.460.5, C.460.13, C.498.5, C.521.3, C.521.5, C.521.6, C.539.5 C.554.3
Ferguson v S, 1992 S.C.L.R. 866 .... C.446.6
Finlayson, Applicant, 1989 S.C.L.R. 601 .... C.446.4
Flora v Wakom (Heathrow) Ltd (formerly Abela Airline Catering Ltd) [2006] EWCA Civ 1103; [2007] 1 W.L.R. 482; [2006] 4 All E.R. 982; [2007] P.I.Q.R. Q2; [2007] LS Law Medical 62; (2006) 156 N.L.J. 1289 .... C.535.4
Fraser v Mirza, 1993 S.C. (HL) 27; 1993 S.L.T. 527 .... C.443.2
G v Children's Reporter, 2016 S.L.T. 293 .... C.455.3, C.456.3
G v Scanlon, 1999 S.C. 226; 1999 S.L.T. 707; 2000 S.C.L.R. 1; 1998 Fam. L.R. 136; 1999 G.W.D. 8-365 .... C.404.2, C.534.7
Ghaidan v Godin-Mendoza [2004] UKHL 30; [2004] 2 A.C. 557; [2004] 3 W.L.R. 113; [2004] 3 All E.R. 411; [2004] 2 F.L.R. 600; [2004] 2 F.C.R. 481; [2004] H.R.L.R. 31; [2004] U.K.H.R.R. 827; 16 B.H.R.C. 671; [2004] H.L.R. 46; [2005] 1 P. & C.R. 18; [2005] L. & T.R. 3; [2004] 2 E.G.L.R. 132; [2004] Fam. Law 641; [2004] 27 E.G. 128 (C.S.); (2004) 101(27) L.S.G. 30; (2004) 154 N.L.J. 1013; (2004) 148 S.J.L.B. 792; [2004] N.P.C. 100; [2004] 2 P. & C.R. DG17 .... C.460.5, C.495.4
GM v MB and AS. *See* M v B
H v Harkness, 1998 S.C. 287; 1998 S.L.T. 1431; 1998 G.W.D. 12-584 .... C.446.4
H v Lees; D v Orr, 1993 J.C. 238; 1994 S.L.T. 908; 1993 S.C.C.R. 900 .... C.446.4, C.446.6
H v McGregor, 1973 S.C. 95; 1973 S.L.T. 110; 1973 S.L.T. (Notes) 5 .... C.533.2, C.533.6
H v Mearns, 1974 S.C. 152; 1974 S.L.T. 184 .... C.480.4, C.484.4, C.535.9
Harris v F, 1991 S.L.T. 242; 1991 S.C.L.R 124 .... C.481.4
HM Advocate v Bell (Jamie), 2002 S.L.T. 527; 2001 G.W.D. 13-472 .... C.538.6
Humphries v S, 1986 S.L.T. 683 .... C.405.3
Hyde Park Residence Ltd v Secretary of State for the Environment, Transport and the Regions (2000) 80 P. & C.R. 419; [2000] 1 P.L.R. 85; [2000] J.P.L. 936; [2000] E.G. 14 (C.S.); [2000] N.P.C. 7 .... C.574.2
J, Appellant, 2013 S.L.T. (Sh Ct) 18; 2013 Fam. L.R. 12; 2013 G.W.D. 1-31 .... C.467.2, C.533.9
J v M [2016] CSIH 52; 2016 S.C. 835; 2016 Fam. L.R. 124; 2016 G.W.D. 22-400 ... C.420.2
J and H v Lord Advocate, E v Lord Advocate, 2013 S.L.T. 27 .... C.416.2
JM v Taylor. *See* M v Locality Reporter Manager
JS v Childrens' Reporter; sub nom. S v Children's Reporter [2016] CSIH 74; 2017 S.C. 31; 2016 S.L.T. 1235; 2017 S.C.L.R. 539; 2016 Fam. L.R. 166; 2016 G.W.D. 31-547 .... C.555.7
JT v Stirling Council [2007] CSIH 52; 2007 S.C. 783; 2007 Fam. L.R. 88 ..... C.417.4, C.446.6, C.557.5
K v Gault (No.1) Paisley Sheriff Court 13 December 2000, Sheriff Principal Kerr QC C.446.7
K and F, Applicants, 2002 S.L.T. (Sh Ct) 38; 2002 S.C.L.R. 769; 2002 Fam. L.R. 44; 2002 G.W.D. 7-210 .... C.416.2, C.542.7
KA v Finland (27751/95) [2003] 1 F.L.R. 696; [2003] 1 F.C.R. 201; [2003] Fam. Law 230 .... C.415.3
Kennedy v A (A Child), 1986 S.L.T. 358 (IH) C.487.3, C.535.8, C.542.16
Kennedy v B (Change of Circumstances), 1972 S.C. 128; 1973 S.L.T. 38 .... C.535.5
Kennedy v Clark, 1970 J.C. 55; 1970 S.L.T. 260 .... C.446.18
Kennedy v M, 1995 S.C. 121; 1995 S.L.T. 717; 1995 S.C.L.R. 88 .... C.408.8
Kennedy v R's Curator ad litem, 1992 S.C. 300; 1993 S.L.T. 295; 1992 S.C.L.R. 546 .... C.446.6, C.446.7
Kennedy v S, 1986 S.C. 43; 1986 S.L.T. 679 .... C.446.4, C.446.9, C.470.5
Kerr (John) v HM Advocate, 1958 J.C. 14; 1958 S.L.T. 82 .... C.555.7
Kerseboom (Michel) v HM Advocate [2016] HCJAC 51; 2017 J.C. 47; 2016 S.C.L. 839; 2016 S.C.C.R. 386; 2016 G.W.D. 29-518 .... C.554.5
Kiely (Noel) v Lunn, 1983 J.C. 4; 1983 S.L.T. 207; 1982 S.C.C.R. 436 .... C.446.18
Kutzner v Germany (46544/99) [2003] 1 F.C.R. 249; (2002) 35 E.H.R.R. 25 .... C.407.2
L (A Child) (Care: Threshold Criteria) Re [2007] 1 F.L.R. 2050; [2007] Fam. Law 297 .... C.405.3, C.417.4, C.557.5
L, Petitioners (No.1) 1993 S.L.T. 130 .... C.488.7
L, Petitioners (No.2) (Children's Hearing) 1993 S.L.T. 1342 .... C.488.7, C.490.6
M, Appellant, 2014 Fam. L.B. 127-7 .... C.460.5, C.535.4
M v B, 2016 S.L.T. (Sh Ct) 279; 2016 Fam. L.R. 96; 2016 G.W.D. 16-294 ... C.555.3, C.564.4

Table of Cases

M v Constanda, 1999 S.C. 348; 1999 S.L.T. 494; 1999 S.C.L.R. 108; 1999 G.W.D. 1-3 .... C.450.5

M v HM Advocate (No.2) [2013] HCJAC 22; 2013 S.L.T. 380; 2013 S.C.C.R. 215, 2013 G.W.D. 8-170 .... C.554.5

M (C) v Kennedy, 1995 S.C. 61; 1995 S.L.T. 123; 1995 S.C.L.R. 15 .... C.535.9

M v Locality Reporter Manager [2014] CSIH 62; 2015 S.C. 71; 2015 S.C.L.R. 143; 2014 Fam. L.R. 102; 2014 G.W.D. 24-453 .... C.500.2, C.533.2, C.534.11, C.535.4, C.535.9, C.542.16, C.542.3, C.556.4

M v McClafferty [2007] CSIH 88; 2008 Fam. L.R. 22; 2008 G.W.D. 3-42 .... C.446.4

M v McGregor (Reporter to the Children's Panel), 1982 S.L.T. 41 .... C.446.4, C.487.3

M v Normand, 1995 S.L.T. 1284; 1995 S.C.C.R. 380 .... C.446.4, C.446.6

MA (Children) (Care Threshold) Re [2009] EWCA Civ 853; 2010 F.L.R. 431; [2010] F.C.R. 456; 2009 Fam. Law 1026 .... C.446.4

McGrath v McGrath, 1999 S.L.T. (Sh Ct) 90; 1999 S.C.L.R. 1121; 1999 Fam. L.R. 83; 1999 G.W.D. 20-915 .... C.557.2, C.557.4

McGregor v A, 1982 S.L.T. 45 .... C.535.9

McGregor v D (Francis), 1977 S.C. 330; 1977 S.L.T. 182 .... C.481.4

McGregor v H, 1983 S.L.T. 626 .... C.446.6, C.450.3, C.450.4, C.450.5

McGregor v L (J), 1983 S.L.T. (Sh. Ct) 7 .... C.480.4

McIntyre v Annan, 1991 S.C.C.R. 465 .... C.446.18

McKenzie v McKenzie [1971] P. 33; [1970] 3 W.L.R. 472; [1970] 3 All E.R. 1034; (1970) 114 S.J. 667 .... C.483.4

Macleay v Macdonald (No.1), 1928 S.C. 776; 1928 S.L.T. 463 .... C.536.2

McWilliams, Geraldine v Russell [2017] SC GLA 64 .... C.538.5

MB v Douglas Hill, Locality Reporter Manager [2017] SAC (Civ) 10 .... C.538.5

Meadow v General Medical Council [2006] EWCA Civ 1390; [2007] Q.B. 462; [2007] 2 W.L.R. 286; [2007] 1 All E.R. 1; [2007] I.C.R. 701; [2007] 1 F.L.R. 1398; [2006] 3 F.C.R. 447; [2007] LS Law Medical 1; (2006) 92 B.M.L.R. 51; [2007] Fam. Law 214; [2006] 44 E.G. 196 (C.S.); (2006) 103(43) L.S.G. 28; (2006) 156 N.L.J. 1686 .... C.490.4

MF and GF, Appellants. *See* F v Principal Reporter

Montgomery v Lanarkshire Health Board [2015] UKSC 11; [2015] A.C. 1430; [2015] 2 W.L.R. 768; [2015] 2 All E.R. 1031; 2015 S.C. (U.K.S.C.) 63; 2015 S.L.T. 189; 2015 S.C.L.R. 315; [2015] P.I.Q.R. P13; [2015] Med. L.R. 149; (2015) 143 B.M.L.R. 47; 2015 G.W.D. 10-179 .... C.565.3

MT and AG v Anne Gerry (Locality Reporter). *See* T v Locality Reporter

NJDB v JEG; sub nom. B v G [2012] UKSC 21; 2012 S.C. (U.K.S.C.) 293; 2012 S.L.T. 840; 2012 S.C.L.R. 428; 2012 Fam. L.R. 56; 2012 G.W.D. 19-387 ...... C.483.5, C.534.8 C.545.8, C.554.3

Northamptonshire CC v Islington LBC [2001] Fam. 364; [2000] 2 W.L.R. 193; [1999] 2 F.L.R. 881; [1999] 3 F.C.R. 385; [2000] B.L.G.R. 125; [1999] Fam. Law 687; (2000) 164 J.P.N. 166 .... C.545.2

O v Rae, 1993 S.L.T. 570; 1992 S.C.L.R. 318 .... C.446.18, C.578.3

O'Hagan v Rae, 2001 S.L.T. 30 .... C.446.18

P v D, Glasgow Sheriff Court, 20 July 2016, 2016 GWD 27-490 .... C.480.2

P (A Child) (Adoption: Unmarried Couples) Re [2008] UKHL 38; [2009] 1 A.C. 173; [2008] 3 W.L.R. 76; [2008] N.I. 310; [2008] 2 F.L.R. 1084; [2008] 2 F.C.R. 366; [2008] H.R.L.R. 37; [2008] U.K.H.R.R. 1181; 24 B.H.R.C. 650; [2008] Fam. Law 977; (2008) 105(25) L.S.G. 25 .... C.579.2

Principal Reporter v Glasgow City Council, 2011 Fam. L.R. 118 .... C.545.2

Principal Reporter v K [2010] UKSC 56; [2011] 1 W.L.R. 18; 2011 S.C. (U.K.S.C.) 91; 2011 S.L.T. 271; [2011] H.R.L.R. 8; 33 B.H.R.C. 352; 2011 Fam. L.R. 2; (2011) 108(1) L.S.G. 15; (2011) 161 N.L.J. 63; 2011 G.W.D. 3-112 .... C.379.6, C.422.3, C.427.5, C.458.2, C.460.5, C.484.4, C.487.6, C.495.4, C.496.3, C.505.2, C.539.5, C.540.2, C.542.17, C.543.2, C.544.6, C.554.5, C.579.2

R (Children) v Grant, 2000 S.L.T. 372; 2000 Fam. L.R. 2; 2000 G.W.D. 4-118 .... C.445.4, C.446.8

R. (on the application of Westminster City Council) v National Asylum Support Service [2002] UKHL 38; [2002] 1 W.L.R. 2956; [2002] 4 All E.R. 654; [2002] H.L.R. 58; [2003] B.L.G.R. 23; (2002) 5 C.C.L. Rep. 511; (2002) 146 S.J.L.B. 241 .... C.535.4

R. v Cannings (Angela) [2004] EWCA Crim 1; [2004] 1 W.L.R. 2607; [2004] 1 All
    E.R. 725; [2004] 2 Cr. App. R. 7; [2004] 1 F.C.R. 193; [2005] Crim. L.R. 126;
    (2004) 101(5) L.S.G. 27; (2004) 148 S.J.L.B. 114.. C.490.4
R. v Kennedy, 1993 S.C. 417; 1993 S.L.T. 910... C.488.7
R. v Lilley (Mark) (Appeal against Conviction) [2002] EWCA Crim 3115................. C.548.4
R. v Secretary for State for the Home Department Ex p. Venables [1998] A.C. 407;
    [1997] 3 W.L.R. 23; [1997] 3 All E.R. 97; [1997] 2 F.L.R. 471; (1997) 9 Admin.
    L.R. 413; [1997] Fam. Law 789; (1997) 94(34) L.S.G. 27; (1997) 147 N.L.J.
    955... C.561.6
R. v Secretary of State for Social Security ex p. Britnell [1991] 1 W.L.R. 198; [1991] 2
    All E.R. 726; (1991) 135 S.J. 412.. C.574.2
Ross v Kennedy (Reporter to the Children's Panel), 1995 S.C.L.R. 1160................... C.542.12
S v Miller (No.1), 2001 S.C. 977; 2001 S.L.T. 531; [2001] U.K.H.R.R. 514; 2001
    G.W.D. 13-458.. C.446.13, C.449.4
S v Proudfoot, 2002 S.L.T. 743; 2002 Fam. L.R. 92; 2002 G.W.D. 13-389... C.404.2, C.537.2,
                                                                                                            C.542.17
S v S [2012] CSIH 17; 2012 S.C.L.R. 361; 2012 Fam. L.R. 32; 2012 G.W.D. 11-209 C.406.5
S (G) v Kennedy, 1996 S.L.T. 1087.. C.446.5
S-B (Children) (Care Proceeding: Standard of Proof) Re [2009] UKSC 17; [2010] 1
    A.C. 678; [2010] 2 W.L.R. 238; [2010] 1 All E.R. 705; [2010] P.T.S.R. 456;
    [2010] 1 F.L.R. 1161; [2010] 1 F.C.R. 321; [2010] Fam. Law 231; (2009)
    153(48) S.J.L.B. 33.. C.430.2, C.480.2
Sahin v Germany (30943/96) [2002] 1 F.L.R. 119; [2002] 3 F.C.R. 321; (2003) 36
    E.H.R.R. 43; [2002] Fam. Law 94... C.406.5
Sharrat v Central London Bus Co Ltd (The Accident Group Test Cases) [2003]
    EWCA Civ 718; [2003] 1 W.L.R. 2487; [2003] 4 All E.R. 590; [2003] 3 Costs
    L.R. 423; (2003) 100(28) L.S.G. 30; (2003) 153 N.L.J. 920; (2003) 147 S.J.L.B.
    662... C.535.5
Shields v Shields, 2002 S.C. 246; 2002 S.L.T. 579; 2002 S.C.L.R. 334; 2002 Fam. L.R.
    37; 2002 G.W.D. 5-143.. C.406.5
Sloan (Reporter: Children's Hearings) v B (A Parent), 1991 S.C. 412; 1991 S.L.T.
    530... C.533.2, C.561.3
Stirling v D, 1995 S.C. 358; 1995 S.L.T. 1089; 1995 S.C.L.R. 460................ C.488.9, C.488.10,
                                                                                                            C.536.2
Sweet v Parsley [1970] A.C. 132; [1969] 2 W.L.R. 470; [1969] 1 All E.R. 347; (1969) 53
    Cr. App. R. 221; (1969) 133 J.P. 188; (1969) 113 S.J. 86................................. C.550.3
T v Locality Reporter [2014] CSIH 108; 2015 S.C. 359; 2015 Fam. L.R. 2; 2015
    G.W.D. 1-23..................... C.404.2, C.460.5, C.471.3, C.472.3, C.535.4, C.538.5,
                                                                          C.538.6, C.539.4, C.542.7, C.545.2
Templeton v E, 1998 S.C.L.R. 672.. C.398.2, C.446.6
Thomas v Thomas [1947] A.C. 484; [1947] 1 All E.R. 582; 1947 S.C. (H.L.) 45; 1948
    S.L.T. 2; 1947 S.L.T. (Notes) 53; 63 T.L.R. 314; [1948] L.J.R. 515; 176 L.T.
    498... C.535.9
Thomson (Blair Russell), Petitioner, 1998 S.C. 848; 1998 S.L.T. 1066; 1998 S.C.L.R.
    898; 1998 Fam. L.R. 84; 1998 G.W.D. 26-1285............................ C.533.8, C.533.13
V v Locality Reporter Manager, Stirling, 2013 Fam. L.R. 69........ C.458.4, C.460.5, C.460.6,
                                                                                                  C.505.2, C.542.9
W (an infant) Re [1971] A.C. 682; [1971] 2 W.L.R. 1011; [1971] 2 All E.R. 49; (1971)
    115 S.J. 286... C.446.17
W v C, 2013 Fam. L.R. 73; 2013 G.W.D. 26-531.............. C.458.2, C.458.4, C.460.5, C.579.2
W v Children's Reporter, 2013 S.L.T. (Sh Ct) 99; 2013 G.W.D. 27-549......... C.460.5, C.535.4
W v Schaffer, 2001 S.L.T. (Sh Ct) 86; 2000 G.W.D. 36-1348......... C.460.5, C.535.4, C.542.16
Walker v SC; sub. nom. Walker v C, 2003 S.C. 570; 2003 S.L.T. 293; 2003 G.W.D. 3-
    56.. C.446.13, C.481.3
Welsh v Richardson [2012] HCJAC 114; 2012 S.L.T. 1153; 2012 S.C.L. 1048; 2012
    S.C.C.R. 631; 2012 G.W.D. 30-614.. C.548.4, C.550.3
West Lothian Council v B [2017] UKSC 15; 2017 S.C. (U.K.S.C.) 67; 2017 S.L.T.
    319; 2017 Fam. L.R. 34; 2017 G.W.D. 8-114.. C.480.2
Wotherspoon v Procurator Fiscal, Glasgow [2017] HCJAC 17..................................... C.449.4
X (A Child) (Jurisdiction: Secure Accommodation), Re; sub nom. Y (A Child) In Re
    [2016] EWHC 2271 (Fam); [2017] Fam. 80; [2016] 3 W.L.R. 1718; [2017] 1
    F.C.R. 584; [2016] Fam. Law 1327... C.510.8, C.569.3
X, Appellants, 2013 S.L.T. (Sh Ct) 125; 2013 Fam. L.R. 100; 2013 G.W.D.
    30-600... C.460.5, C.535.4

Table of Cases

Y v Principal Reporter, Unreported, 24 April 1998, Wick Sheriff Court C.490.8
Young v National Coal Board, 1960 S.C. 6; 1959 S.L.T. (Notes) 77 .... C.555.7
ZH (Tanzania) v Secretary of State for the Home Department [2012] CSIH 17; 2012
    Fam. L.R. 32 .... C.406.5
ZM, AM v Locality Reporter [2016] SAC (Civ) 16 .... C.417.4, C.557.5

TABLE OF UK STATUTES

1937 Children and Young Persons (Scotland) Act (c.37)
- s.12 .... C.446.5
- s.15 .... C.446.5
- s.22 .... C.446.5
- s.33 .... C.446.5

1968 Firearms Act (c.27)
- s.51A C.450.2

1968 Social Work (Scotland) Act (c.49) C.439.2, C.534.7, C.535.8, C.542.16
- s.3 .... C.534.13
- s.37(2) C.415.5
- s.44(1) C.408.8
- s.49(2) C.535.4
  - (5) C.535.8
  - (b) C.535.8

1968 Law Reform (Miscellaneous Provisions) (Scotland) Act (c.70)
- s.10 .... C.450.4

1971 Misuse of Drugs Act (c.38)
- Sch.2 Pt 1 .... C.446.15
- Pt 2 .... C.446.15
- Pt 3 .... C.446.15

1971 Sheriff Courts (Scotland) Act (c.58) C.564.5, C.564.6
- s.32 .... C.564.3

1974 Rehabilitation of Offenders Act (c.53)
- s.3 .... C.379.19

1975 Children Act (c.72)
- s.66 .... C.409.02
- s.78 .... C.409.02

1978 Adoption (Scotland) Act (c.28)
- Pt IV C.579.2
- s.39 .... C.579.2

1980 Education (Scotland) Act (c.44)
- s.1(1) C.506.2
- s.14 .... C.506.6
  - (3) C.506.2, C.506.4
- s.31 .... C.446.18
- s.33 .... C.446.18
  - (1) C.446.18, C.578.3
  - (3)(a) C.578.3
  - (b) C.578.3
- s.35(2) C.506.4
- s.86 .... C.446.18
- s.135(1) C.441.7, C.506.2

1981 Matrimonial Homes (Family Protection) (Scotland) Act (c.59) C.441.6

1982 Civic Government (Scotland) Act (c.45)
- s.52 .... C.446.5
- s.52A C.446.5

1986 Law Reform (Parent and Child) (Scotland) Act (c.9)
- s.5 .... C.458.2

1986 Legal Aid (Scotland) Act (c.47) C.569.4
- ss.28B—28M C.569.4
- ss.28B—28S C.379.20, C.483.2
- s.28C C.569.4
- s.28D C.569.4
  - (3)(c) C.569.4
- s.33B C.569.4

1988 Civil Evidence (Scotland) Act (c.32)
- s.2 .... C.552.6, C.555.7
- s.9 .... C.555.7
  - (a) C.552.6

1989 Children Act (c.41) C.414.2
- Pt 1 .... C.458.2
- s.25 .... C.510.8, C.569.3
- s.31(1)(a) C.510.8
  - (b) C.510.8
- s.36(1) C.510.8
- s.53 .... C.547.5
- s.105(6) C.545.2

1990 Human Fertilisation and Embryology Act (c.37)
- ss.27—30 .... C.579.2

1991 Age of Legal Capacity (Scotland) Act (c.50)
- s.2(4) C.379.19, C.414.4, C.421.3, C.466.2, C.466.3, C.471.4, C.565.2, C.565.3
  - (4A).... C.427.4, C.533.3, C.533.4, C.569.4
  - (4B) C.533.3, C.533.4
  - (4C) C.569.4
- s.3 .... C.483.5

1994 Local Government etc. (Scotland) Act (c.39)
- ss.39—138 .... C.392.3
- s.128(5) C.399.2, C.401.2
- s.132 .... C.400.1, C.400.3
- s.134 .... C.402.1

1995 Children (Scotland) Act (c.36)... C.379.1, C.379.3, C.379.9, C.379.14, C.379.17, C.380.1, C.396.2, C.398.3, C.405.3, C.408.2, C.415.3, C.418.6, C.424.2, C.425.2, C.426.3, C.427.5, C.427.8, C.441.3, C.441.4, C.441.5, C.445.3, C.445.4, C.446.6, C.446.8, C.446.11, C.446.13, C.450.5, C.451.5, C.452.6—C.452.8, C.454.4, C.455.2, C.455.5, C.457.3, C.458.4, C.460.5, C.462.5, C.463.2, C.465.2, C.467.2, C.470.5, C.476.2, C.479.3, C.480.3, C.480.4, C.482.4, C.482.5, C.482.6,

	C.483.3, C.483.5, C.484.4,
	C.489.5, C.500.2, C.507.2,
	C.517.6, C.519.3, C.533.6,
	C.533.7, C.533.13, C.535.8,
	C.536.2, C.538.4, C.540.2,
	C.541.3, C.542.7, C.542.11,
	C.542.17, C.544.2, C.548.4,
	C.578.3
Pt I	C.379.1, C.458.2
Pt II	C.379.1
Ch 1	C.379.1
Ch 2	C.379.1
Ch 3	C.379.1
Ch 4	C.379.1
Pt III	C.379.1
Pt IV	C.379.1
Pt XIX	C.427.4
s.1	C.446.4, C.446.17, C.578.2
(1)	C.416.6, C.445.4
(d)	C.427.4, C.533.4
(2)(b)	C.578.2
s.2	C.446.4, C.446.17, C.578.2
(1)	C.416.6
(a)	C.462.6
(d)	C.427.4
s.4	C.579.2
s.4A	C.579.2
s.6	C.406.3
s.11	C.420.2, C.446.4, C.505.2, C.513.2
(2)	C.579.2
(b)	C.542.17
(d)	C.420.2, C.540.2
(7)	C.406.3
(a)	C.407.2
s.15(1)	C.579.2
(6)	C.427.4
s.16	C.403.2, C.408.2
(1)	C.534.7
(2)	C.406.3
(4)(b)	C.408.2
s.17	C.379.6, C.403.2, C.423.2, C.465.3
(c)	C.471.4
(6)	C.506.2
s.25	C.423.2, C.446.11, C.516.2
s.40	C.393.1, C.398.2
(2)	C.398.2
s.41	C.410.3, C.411.2
s.42(2)(e)—(g)	C.411.2
(6)	C.404.2
s.43	C.451.5
s.45	C.379.8, C.451.5, C.454.4
(2)(a)	C.452.5, C.452.6
(4)	C.407.3
(8)(b)	C.453.4
(9)	C.453.5
s.46(1)	C.455.2, C.455.3, C.456.2
(2)	C.455.2, C.455.5
s.51	C.535.4
(1)	C.533.8, C.541.3
(a)	C.533.2, C.533.13
(2)	C.534.3

(3)	C.440.4, C.534.3, C.534.7, C.534.14
(4)	C.535.3
(5)	C.533.2
(a)	C.533.8
(c)	C.535.4, C.535.8, C.535.9, C.535.11
(6)	C.535.3
(7)	C.538.3, C.538.4
(9)	C.537.2, C.537.3
(11)	C.542.15
(a)	C.542.4
(11)—(14)	C.542.2
(12)(a)	C.542.8
(b)	C.542.11
(14)	C.542.16
(15)(a)	C.542.2
s.52	C.446.2, C.446.9
(2)(l)	C.446.11
s.53(1)	C.439.2
(b)	C.439.2
(2)	C.443.2
(6)	C.442.2
s.54	C.441.3
(3)	C.441.3
s.55	C.414.2
(2)	C.415.4
s.56	C.445.3
(2)	C.447.2
(4)	C.447.2
(a)	C.447.5
(5)	C.447.2
s.57	C.427.3
(1)	C.418.2
(5)	C.427.7
(6)	C.437.2
(7)	C.423.2
ss.57—62	C.415.5
s.58	C.418.6, C.421.2
(1)	C.420.2
(4)	C.416.6, C.421.2
(5)	C.416.6
s.59(1)	C.424.2, C.425.2
(2)	C.424.2, C.425.2
(3)	C.424.2, C.425.2
(4)	C.426.2
(5)	C.424.2, C.425.2
s.60(1)	C.431.4
(3)	C.427.7, C.432.3
(7)	C.427.2, C.427.3
(d)	C.427.7
(9)	C.428.2
(10)	C.429.2
(11)—(13)	C.430.2
s.61	C.435.2
s.63(1)	C.444.2, C.451.2
(2)	C.451.2
(3)	C.444.2, C.444.3
(4)	C.444.2, C.451.2
s.64	C.404.2
s.65(9)	C.379.10
s.66	C.465.2, C.465.4, C.471.2
(1)	C.477.5
(3)(a)	C.477.4

Table of UK Statutes

(4)(a)	C.471.4	1995	Criminal Procedure (Scotland) Act (c.46)	C.447.4, C.555.4
(8)	C.477.4			
s.67	C.465.4			
(1)	C.478.1		s.41	C.481.2
(2)(a)	C.477.6		s.41A(1)	C.446.13
s.68	C.480.2, C.480.3		s.42	C.481.2
(2)	C.480.4		s.43(5)	C.444.3, C.445.6, C.447.4
(3)(a)	C.481.3			
(b)	C.481.4		s.44	C.511.3
(4)	C.482.2, C.483.2		s.49	C.446.13, C.450.2, C.450.3, C.489.4, C.509.2, C.542.4
(b)	C.482.3			
(5)	C.482.2		(1)	C.450.2, C.450.3
(6)	C.479.3, C.482.2, C.482.8		(a)	C.542.4
(7)	C.482.8		(2)—(7)	C.450.2
(8)	C.484.4		(3)	C.450.2
(10)	C.493.4, C.494.5		(5)	C.450.2
(b)	C.488.5		(6)	C.450.2
s.69	C.519.3, C.519.5		(c)	C.503.2
s.70	C.462.3, C.535.9		s.138(4)	C.468.2
(1)	C.379.10, C.470.5		s.262(3)	C.555.7
(2)	C.462.5		s.271	C.555.5
(3)(a)	C.462.6		s.274	C.552.2
(9)	C.541.3		s.275	C.552.2, C.554.5
s.71(1)	C.541.3		s.288F	C.555.3
s.73(6)	C.537.2		Sch.1	C.446.5, C.446.6, C.446.7, C.452.5, .483.4
(8)	C.538.3			
(9)	C.537.3		Sch.3	C.468.2
(b)	C.533.8	1997	Protection from Harassment Act (c.40)	C.441.6, C.446.9
s.76(1)	C.416.2			
(4)	C.403.2		s.8A	C.446.9
(8)	C.408.2, C.416.2	1998	Data Protection Act (c.29)	
ss.76—80	C.408.2		Sch.3	C.443.2
s.81	C.438.2	1998	Human Rights Act (c.42)	
s.85	C.488.7, C.492.2, C.493.4, C.493.5		s.3	C.579.2
			(1)	C.484.4, C.579.2
(2)	C.489.3		s.21(1)	C.460.5
(3)	C.490.2	2002	Adoption and Children Act (c.38)	C.460.5
(a)	C.490.7			
(b)	C.490.5	2003	Railways and Transport Safety Act (c.20)	
(c)	C.490.6			
(5)	C.490.2		s.24	C.435.3
(6)(a)	C.493.2	2004	Gender Recognition Act (c.7)	C.385.4
(b)	C.493.4, C.494.3, C.494.5	2006	Violent Crime Reduction Act (c.38)	
s.86	C.446.11			
ss.86—89	C.408.2		s.29	C.450.2
s.87(5)(b)	C.491.2	2008	Human Fertilisation and Embryology Act (c.22)	
s.89	C.550.4			
s.93(2)(b)	C.458.2, C.460.5, C.579.2		Pt 2	C.579.2
			s.35	C.579.2
(c)	C.458.2, C.460.5, C.579.2		s.36	C.579.2
			s.37	C.579.2
(5)	C.480.5, C.534.6		s.42	C.579.2
1995	Criminal Law (Consolidation) (Scotland) Act (c.39)		s.43	C.579.2
			s.44	C.579.2
			s.54(1)	C.579.2
Pt 1	C.446.5		s.55(1)	C.579.2

TABLE OF SCOTTISH STATUTES

Year	Act	Reference
2001	Protection from Abuse (Scotland) Act (asp 14)	
	s.7	C.446.9
2004	Vulnerable Witnesses (Scotland) Act (asp 3)	C.379.18, C.555.3
	s.11(1)	C.555.3
	s.12(1)	C.555.3, C.555.5
	(2)(a)	C.555.5
	s.13(1)(a)	C.555.5
	s.18(1)	C.555.5
	s.19	C.553.2
	s.22A	C.555.7, C.564.4
	(8)	C.555.7
	s.23	C.552.2
	s.24	C.534.9
2004	Education (Additional Support for Learning) (Scotland) Act (asp 4)	C.446.6
	s.1	C.506.2
	s.2(1)	C.417.4
	s.29(1)	C.506.2
2004	Antisocial Behaviour, etc. (Scotland) Act (asp 8)	C.445.3, C.449.2, C.449.3, C.449.4, C.507.2
	s.12	C.449.2, C.449.4
	(1)(b)	C.449.4
	s.102	C.379.13
	(3)	C.507.2
	(3)—(7)	C.507.2
	s.117	C.507.2
	s.143(1)	C.449.4
2005	Prohibition of Female Genital Mutilation (Scotland) Act (asp 8)	C.446.4, C.446.5
2005	Protection of Children and Prevention of Sexual Offences (Scotland) Act (asp 9)	
	s.1	C.446.5
	s.9	C.446.5
	s.10	C.446.5
	s.11	C.446.5
	s.12	C.446.5
2005	Licensing (Scotland) Act (asp 16)	
	s.105(1)	C.446.14
2007	Adoption and Children (Scotland) Act (asp 4)	C.408.2, C.460.5, C.540.2
	Pt I	C.579.2
	Ch 3	C.579.2
	Pt 2	C.408.2
	s.28	C.579.2
	(1)	C.579.2
	s.29	C.510.7, C.510.10, C.520.2, C.579.2
	s.30	C.510.7, C.510.10, C.520.2
	s.35(2)	C.579.2
	s.40	C.579.2
	s.80	C.379.16, C.446.12, C.505.2, C.516.2
	(2)	C.579.2
	ss.80–104	C.408.2
	s.82(2)	C.540.2
	s.87	C.579.2
	s.89	C.408.2
	(b)	C.510.6
	(c)	C.510.6
	s.90	C.408.2
	s.93(2)	C.557.7
	s.96	C.510.6
	s.106	C.510.7
	Sch.3 para.1	C.446.11
2007	Protection of Vulnerable Groups (Scotland) Act (asp 14)	C.411.
2009	Sexual Offences (Scotland) Act (asp 9)	C.446.5, C.446.10
	s.5	C.446.5
	s.6	C.446.5
	s.7	C.446.5
	s.8	C.446.5
	s.9	C.446.5
	s.18	C.446.5
	s.19	C.446.5
	s.20	C.446.5
	ss.21—26	C.446.5
	s.28	C.446.5
	s.29	C.446.5
	s.30	C.446.5
	ss.31—37	C.446.5
	s.42	C.446.5
	s.43(6)	C.446.5
2011	Children's Hearings (Scotland) Act (asp 1)	C.379.1, C.406.5, C.408.2, C.415.5, C.460.5, C.493.5, C.535.4, C.542.2, C.564.3, C.578.4
	Pt 2	C.379.3
	Pt 6	C.446.17
	Pt 7	C.451.5
	Pt 9	C.379.10
	Pt 10	C.410.3, C.498.2, C.502.2, C.519.7, C.555.3, C.555.4, C.564.4, C.569.4
	Pt 13	C.539.4
	Pt 15	C.410.3, C.470.5, C.564.4, C.569.4
	Pt 19	C.571.1
	s.1	**C.380**
	(c)	C.521.5
	s.2	**C.381**
	(4)(a)	C.465.3
	s.3	**C.382**
	(2)(a)	C.579.2
	(b)	C.579.2
	s.4	**C.383**
	(2)(b)	C.385.5
	s.5	**C.384**

s.6	**C.385**	ss.30—31	C.413.3
(1)	C.383.2	s.31	**C.410**, C.410.3, C.411.2, C.542.12
(3)(b)	C.383.2	(2)	C.409.2
(5)	C.384.1, C.458.2	s.32	**C.411**
s.7	**C.386**	s.33	**C.412**
s.8	**C.387**	(1)(a)	C.409.5
s.9	C.387.2, **C.388**, C.391.2	s.34	**C.413**
s.10	C.379.21, **C.389**	s.35	C.410.3, **C.414**, C.415.2, C.415.3, C.421.3, C.438.2
(1)(a)—(d)	C.577.1	(2)	C.565.2
(e)	C.576.1	(3)(b)	C.415.2, C.547.3
s.11	**C.390**	s.36	C.414.5, **C.415**
s.12	**C.391**, C.392.2	(1)	C.414.5
s.13	**C.392**	(2)	C.418.5
s.14	**C.393**, C.560.2	s.37	C.410.3, C.415.3, **C.416**, C.417.2, C.418.2, C.438.2, C.568.2
s.15	**C.394**		
s.16	C.392.3, **C.395**, C.408.2		
s.17	**C.396**, C.400.2, C.471.3		
s.18	C.379.21, **C.397**	(1)	C.414.3, C.417.2
(1)(a)—(d)	C.577.1	(a)	C.510.3
(e)	C.576.1	(2)(a)	C.432.3, C.432.4
s.19	**C.398**	(b)	C.431.3, C.432.3, C.432.4, C.547.3
s.20	**C.399**		
s.21	**C.400**	(c)	C.431.3, C.432.3, C.432.4, C.547.3
s.22	C.391.2, **C.401**, C.402.1		
s.23	**C.402**	(d)	C.416.6, C.419.2, C.432.3, C.432.4, C.565.2
s.24	**C.403**		
s.25	C.379.4, **C.404**, C.416.2, C.417.3, C.449.3, C.451.4, C.460.5, C.462.13, C.463.2, C.480.2, C.487.3, C.493.2, C.523.2, C.534.7, C.535.4, C.538.6, C.542.7, C.545.2, C.554.3, C.554.5	(3)	C.416.6, C.419.2, C.419.3, C.433.3
		(4)	C.416.6, C.419.2
		ss.37—59	C.415.5
		s.38	C.416.2, **C.417**, C.419.3, C.426.3, C435.4
(1)	C.403.2, C.406.4, C.427.5, C.480.2, C.535.4, C.541.8	(2)(a)	C.418.4, C.496.6, C.496.8
		(a)—(d)	C434.4
(2)	C.415.4, C.462.18	(3)	C.550.4
ss.25—29A	C.403.2	(4)	C.550.4
s.26	C.403.2, C.404.3, **C.405**, C.451.4, C.462.13, C.462.18, C.462.21, C.463.2, C.467.2	s.39	C.416.2, **C.418**, C.423.2, C.425.2, C.426.3, C.494.5
		(2)	C.416.3, C.432.3
(2)	C.463.2, C.541.3	(a)	C.415.3
s.27	C.379.4, **C.406**, C.449.3, C.495.5, C.496.4	(b)	C434.4, C435.3
		s.40	C.418.6, **C.419**, C.432.4, C.462.8
(1)	C.415.4		
(2)	C.415.4, C.416.2, C.417.3	ss.40—42	C.416.2, C.427.3
(3)	C.430.2, C.452.7	s.41	C.414.5, C.418.6, **C.420**, C.432.4
(4)	C.430.2		
s.28	**C.407**, C.408.2, C.462.13, C.477.6	(2)	C.416.6
		s.42	C.379.6, C.418.6, **C.421**, C.426.3, C.432.4
(1)	C.429.2, C.537.4		
(2)	C.379.4, C.510.4	(2)	C.416.6
s.29	**C.408**, C.449.3, C.495.5, C.496.4	(a)	C.419.3, C.426.3
		(b)	C.419.3
(1)(a)	C.414.2, C.415.4	s.43	C.416.2, **C.422**
(b)	C.416.2, C.417.3	(1)(b)	C.419.3
(2)	C.379.4, C.415.4	(c)	C.419.3
s.29A	C.408.5, C.462.12	(2)	C.379.6
(1)	C.462.15	s.44	C.379.6, C.416.2, **C.423**
s.30	C.379.16, **C.409**, C.410.3, C.411.2, C.533.6	s.45	C.416.2, C.418.6, C.420.2, **C.424**, C.425.2, C.426.2, C.427.2, C.431.5, C.432.5
(1)	C.409.2, C.542.12		
(2)(a)	C.435.3		
(3)	C.412.3	(3)	C.416.2
(4)	C.412.3	ss.45—47	C.416.2

Table of Scottish Statutes

s.46	C.416.2, C.418.6, **C.425**, C.426.2, C.427.2, C.432.5	(2)	C.432.3, C.439.4, C.441.3, C.444.3, C.446.2, C.448.2, C.451.3, C.468.2
(3)	C.416.2	(b)	C.446.13
s.47	**C.426**	(3)	C.447.3
(1)	C.416.2	(4)	C.447.2, C.447.3
s.48	C.416.2, C.418.6, C.421.5, **C.427**, C.432.5	s.67	C.379.7, C.379.11, C.379.21, C.441.4, **C.446**, C.447.3, C.448.3, C.449.4, C.460.6, C.468.2, C.542.12, C.542.13
(1)	C.410.3		
(a)	C.432.5		
(d)	C.547.4		
(f)	C.547.4	(2)	C.439.4, C.469.3, C.470.3, C.506.4, C.508.2, C.574.2
(3)	C.416.2		
(a)	C.430.2	(a)	C.484.4
(b)	C.430.2	(b)	C.452.6, C.484.4
ss.48—51	C.416.2	(c)	C.452.6, C.545.2
s.49	C.424.2, **C.428**	(g)	C.452.6, C.484.4
s.50	C.406.3, **C.429**	(h)	C.484.4
s.51	C.427.3, **C.430**, C.467.2	(i)	C.449.4
(5)(b)	C.421.5, C.427.3	(j)	C.379.7, C.379.18, C.441.4, C.449.4, C.468.2, C.481.4, C.487.3, C.489.4, C.508.2, C.509.4, C.542.4, C.552.6, C.555.5, C.555.7, C.564.4, C.569.4
s.52	C.426.2, **C.431**, C.433.3		
(2)	C.416.2		
ss.52—54	C.416.2		
s.53	C.416.2, C.424.2, C.425.2, C.426.2, C.427.7, C.431.5, **C.432**, C.433.3		
(1)	C.427.7	(l)	C.449.4
(2)	C.427.7	(m)	C.449.4, C.481.4, C.484.4, C.535.9
s.54	C.426.2, **C.433**, C.441.3	(n)	C.460.6, C.548.3
(1)(a)	C.416.2	(o)	C.445.4, C.503.2, C.506.4, C.578.3
(c)	C.416.2		
(d)	C.416.2	(p)	C.441.8, C.446.19, C.484.4
s.55	C.416.2, **C.434**, C.435.3, C.435.5, C.436.1, C.437.2, C.547.2, C.547.3, C.547.4, C.547.5, C.568.2		
		(q)	C.441.8, C.484.4
		(4)	C.379.21
		s.68	C.445.3, **C.447**
(1)(b)	C.547.3	(1)(a)	C.439.4
(c)	C.547.3	(2)	C.444.3
s.56	C.416.2, **C.435**, C.436.1, C.568.2	(3)	C.578.3
		(6)	C.439.4
s.57	C.416.2, **C.436**	s.69	C.445.3, **C.448**, C.451.2
s.58	C.416.2, C.416.6, **C.437**, C.547.2, C.547.4, C.547.5, C.547.6, C.548.7	(1)	C.432.3
		(2)	C.441.3, C.468.2
		(7)	C.467.2
s.59	C.416.2, **C.438**	(9)	C.467.2
(2)	C.538.5	s.70	**C.449**
(3)	C.450.2	s.71	C.441.3, C.445.3, **C.450**, C.509.2
s.60	**C.439**, C.443.2		
(1)	C.440.4	s.72	**C.451**
(3)	C.448.2	s.73	**C.452**, C.452.8, C.457.4, C.482.2, C.540.2
s.61	**C.440**		
(2)	C.448.2	(2)	C.458.5
s.62	C.379.7, **C.441**	(3)	C.458.3
(2)	C.448.2	(b)	C.457.3
s.63	**C.442**	(4)	C.457.4, C.474.3
s.64	C.379.7, C.441.4, **C.443**	s.74	C.452.4, **C.453**, C.454.1, C.455.2, C.472.6, C.487.6, C.540.2
(1)	C.441.6		
(2)	C.448.2		
s.65	**C.444**	(2)	C.452.3, C.457.3, C.458.5, C.487.6
(1)	C.451.3		
s.66	C.379.7, C.404.3, **C.445**, C.447.2, C.471.4, C.558.3, C.578.3	(3)	C.458.5, C.487.6
		(4)	C.458.5, C.469.3
		s.75	C.452.4, **C.454**, C.457.4, C.487.6, C.487.6
(1)	C.444.3, C.446.2		
(a)	C.578.3	(2)	C.474.3

s.76	**C.455**, C.456.2, C.457.4, C.457.8, C.460.5, C.469.3, C.472.6	(a)	C.477.5, C.488.4, C.515.2, C.547.3, C.569.3
(1)	C.487.6	(a)—(i)	C.477.5
(2)	C.379.1, C.453.3, C.457.3, C.458.5, C.487.6	(e)	C.477.5
		(d)	C.477.5
(3)	C.379.19, C.452.4, C.456.2, C.456.4	(f)	C.416.6, C.466.3, C.474.4, C.565.2
s.77	**C.456**, C.457.4, C.457.8, C.460.5, C.469.3, C.472.6	(g)	C.408.8, C.408.9, C.466.2, C.477.5, C.497.3
		(h)	C.565.2
(2)	C.457.3, C.487.6	(5)	C.466.4, C.467.4
s.78	C.379.8, C.455.2, C.456.2, C.456.4, **C.457**, C.458.5, C.501.3, C.561.3	(a)	C.519.6, C.530.6
		(6)	C.446.16, C.463.2, C.466.5, C.467.5, C.516.2, C.530.6, C.531.2
(1)(a)	C.482.7		
(c)	C.460.5, C.487.6	(c)	C.464.2
(d)	C.460.5	(7)	C.476.2, C.512.2
(f)	C.411.2	(a)	C.517.5
(2)	C.561.3	s.84	C.462.6, C.462.9, C.462.16, **C.463**, C.504.2
(7)	C.460.5		
s.79	C.452.3, C.452.4, **C.458**, C.459.3, C.460.5, C.579.2	s.85	C.452.2, C.462.6, **C.464**, C.465.2, C.530.2
(2)	C.460.5	s.86	C.407.3, C.452.2, **C.465**, C.471.2, C.474.3, C.488.4, C.499.2, C.535.9
(a)	C.427.5, C.457.3, C.460.5, C.521.4, C.539.6, C.543.6		
		(1)	C.477.5
(b)	C.521.4	(a)	C.547.3, C.565.2
(c)	C.411.2, C.533.3	(b)	C.488.4, C.522.2, C.545.2, C.580.2
(3)	C.521.4, C.533.3		
(b)	C.487.6	(2)	C.462.6, C.477.5, C.530.6, C.547.3, C.568.2
ss.79—81A	C.404.2		
ss.79—82	C.384.1	(3)	C.477.4, C.477.5, C.488.4
s.80	**C.459**	(a)—(e)	C.477.6
(3)	C.427.5, C.459.3, C.460.4, C.460.13, C.505.2, C.521.4, C.539.4, C.539.5, C.543.6	s.87	C.407.3, **C.466**, C.471.4, C.535.9
		(2)(a)	C.547.3
s.81	**C.460**	(b)	C.545.2, C.565.2, C.580.2
(3)	C.422.3, C.427.5, C.453.5, C.455.3, C.458.4, C.458.6, C.459.4, C.460.13, C.469.3, C.493.5, C.498.5, C.505.2, C.521.3, C.521.5, C.535.4, C.539.4, C.539.5, C.539.6, C.542.16		
		(3)	C.467.4
		(4)	C.467.5, C.530.6
		s.88	C.407.3, C.452.3, C.465.2, **C.467**, C.482.8, C.488.6, C.494.5, C.498.5, C.502.2, C.535.9
		(1)(a)	C.482.8
(4)	C.446.17, C.455.3, C.457.3, C.458.4, C.459.4, C.521.5, C.521.7, C.539.8, C.539.12, C.539.13	(2)	C.482.8
		(3)	C.530.6
		(4)(b)	C.482.8
		(c)	C.488.6
(f)	C.533.5, C.534.10, C.542.9, C.543.7	s.89	**C.468**, C.499.2
		(3)(a)	C.445.3
(h)	C.545.9	(b)	C.445.3
(5)	C.576.1	s.90	C.452.8, C.453.5, C.455.3, **C.469**, C.473.3
(7)	C.533.5, C.534.10		
s.81A	C.458.2, C.460.3, C.460.7, **C.460.8**, C.521.5, C.539.4	(1)	C.451.5, C.452.3, C.452.4
		(a)	C.473.3
(c)	C.460.5	s.91	**C.470**, C.477.2
s.82	C.409.2, **C.461**	(2)	C.533.6
(1)	C.411.2	(3)	C.498.4, C.517.6
s.83	**C.462**, C.523.2, C.535.9	(a)	C.517.5, C.541.4
(1)(b)	C.379.14, C.522.2, C.545.2, C.580.2	s.92	C.407.3, C.470.4, **C.471**, C.474.3, C.477.2
(2)	C.379.10, C.463.2, C.465.2, C.465.3, C.472.5, C.488.4, C.540.6	(2)	C.408.4, C.465.2, C.477.3
		(3)	C.379.10, C.466.2, C.541.4
		(4)(a)	C.493.2

s.93 .... C.379.18, C.470.4, C.471.2, **C.472**	
(1) C.441.3	
(2) C.462.2, C.477.2	
(a) C.408.4, C.412.3, C.465.5, C.473.4, C.479.2, C.486.2, C.487.2, C.533.3, C.533.6, C.552.2	
(3) C.471.3, C.475.3, C.541.4	
(a) C.462.2	
(4)(a) C.493.2	
(5) C.465.2, C.473.3, C.476.3, C.477.3, C.477.5, C.541.4	
s.94 ..... C.379.10, C.379.18, C.470.4, **C.473**	
(1) C.441.3	
(2) C.477.2	
(a) C.408.4, C.412.3, C.465.5, C.479.2, C.480.3, C.486.2, C.487.2, C.552.2	
(6) C.465.2	
s.95 .... C.470.4, **C.474**, C.510.6	
(2) C.467.2	
s.96 .... **C.475**, C.477.5, C.531.2	
(1) C.476.2	
(2) C.476.2	
(3) C.465.5, C.477.3, C.541.4	
(4) C.477.4	
s.97 .... **C.476**	
(5) C.541.4	
s.98 .... C.379.10, C.408.4, **C.477**, C.488.2, C.488.4, C.497.5, C.519.7, C.531.2, C.555.4	
(4) C.478.1	
s.99 .... C.379.10, C.408.4, C.477.6, **C.478**, C.488.2, C.488.4, C.497.5, C.519.7, C.531.2, C.555.4	
(2) C.477.6	
s.100 .... **C.479**, C.488.2, C.488.3, C.488.4, C.531.2, C.545.2, C.545.11	
(1)(b) C.497.3	
(2) C.477.2, C.479.3, C.497.3	
s.101 .... **C.480**, C.483.5, C.484.4, C.485.3, C.491.2	
(2) C.471.3	
(3) C.561.3	
s.102 .... **C.481**, C.484.4	
(2) C.471.3	
(3) C.446.13	
s.103 .... **C.482**	
(3) C.480.3	
(5) C.408.4, C.467.2, C.479.3, C.484.4, C.502.2	
(6) C.467.2	
(7) C.408.4, C.467.2, C.479.3	
s.104 .... C.457.4, **C.483**	
(2)—(4) C.533.12, C.541.6, C.542.10, C.542.12, C.545.8	
s.105 .... C.480.2, C.480.3, **C.484**, C.485.4, C.490.4	
(1) C.485.5	
(II) C.485.5	
(III) C.485.5	
(V) C.485.5	
(2) C.485.6, C.487.6	
s.106 .... C.480.3, **C.485**, C.490.4	
s.107 .... **C.486**	
(3) C.541.4	
s.108 .... **C.487**, C.488.8, C.489.3	
(2) C.408.4, C.493.2	
(4) C.493.2	
s.109 .... C.480.2, C.487.3, **C.488**	
(3) C.408.4	
(5) C.408.4	
(6) C.408.4	
s.110 ...... C.379.14, C.488.8, C.488.9, C.488.10, **C.489**, C.490.2, C.490.8, C.491.2, C.492.2, C.493.5, C.494.4, C.494.5, C.542.18	
(2) C.488.11, C.542.5, C.552.2	
ss.110—117 .... C.483.3	
ss.110—118 .... C.493.4, C.494.4	
s.111 .... **C.490**	
(4) C.493.2, C.493.5	
s.112 .... **C.491**	
(4) C.408.4	
s.113 .... **C.492**	
s.114 .... C.490.2, C.490.8, **C.493**	
(3) C.494.5	
(a) C.494.4	
s.115 .... C.491.2, **C.494**	
(3) C.545.2	
(4) C.408.4	
s.116 .... C.488.11, **C.495**	
s.117 .... C.379.11, C.379.14, C.413.2, C.491.2, **C.496**	
(4) C.408.4	
s.118 .... **C.497**	
(3) C.479.3	
(4) C.541.4	
s.119 .... **C.498**, C.499.2	
(1) C.541.4	
(2) C.458.5	
(3) C.517.6, C.541.4	
s.120 .... C.379.12, **C.499**	
(3) C.498.3	
(5) C.498.3, C.541.4	
(6) C.471.4, C.541.4	
s.121 .... C.379.13, C.452.7, **C.500**, C.556.4	
s.122 ...... C.379.13, C.457.4, C.483.4, **C.501**, C.585.1	
(2) C.483.4	
(4) C.576.1	
s.123 .... C.452.2, C.465.3, C.474.3, C.498.5, **C.502**, C.541.4	
s.124 .... **C.503**	
s.125 .... **C.504**	
(3) C.535.10	
s.126 .... C.379.13, C.462.12, **C.505**, C.511.2, C.514.2, C.540.2, C.544.2	
(2) C.540.2, C.544.5	
(b) C.540.4, C.544.6	
(3)(a) C.540.3, C.544.5	
(7) C.540.2	

s.127 .... C.379.13, **C.506**, C.563.2	(1) C.576.1
s.128 .... C.379.13, **C.507**	(a) C.463.2
s.129 .... **C.508**	(b) C.463.2
s.129—136 .... C.516.2	s.151 .... C.514.2, **C.530**
s.130 .... **C.509**	(3) C.541.3
(3) C.450.2	(4) C.514.2
s.131 .... **C.510**	(6) C.576.1
(2) C.522.2, C.569.3	ss.151—153 .... C.462.10, C.541.3
(a) C.514.2, C.530.6	s.152 .... **C.531**
(b) C.565.2	(1) C.576.1
(c) C.520.2	s.153 .... **C.532**
(d) C.520.2	(1) C.576.1
(e) C.520.2	(3) C.541.3
s.132 .... C.464.2, **C.511**, C.514.2,	s.154 ...... C.379.16, C.413.3, C.467.2,
C.537.2	C.475.3, C.476.2, **C.533**, C.534.8,
s.133 .... C.511.2, **C.512**	C.534.15, C.535.4, C.538.4,
s.134 .... C.511.2, **C.513**	C.541.3, C.542.16
s.135 .... C.379.14, C.462.10,	(2)(a) C.539.7
C.462.17, **C.514**	(c) C.411.2
s.136 .... C.462.10, C.511.2, **C.515**,	(3) C.534.4, C.535.9, C.537.2
C.516.2	(d) C.465.4
s.137 ...... C.510.3, C.510.9, C.510.10,	(e) C.465.4, C.535.7
C.516, C.520.2, C.569.3	(g) C.467.2
(3) C.515.2, C.569.3	(4) C.539.9, C.541.6, C.542.10
(3A) C.510.8	(5) C.540.7, C.542.14
s.138 .... C.497.4, **C.517**	ss.154—157 .... C.541.3
(2) C.533.6	s.155 .... C.480.2, **C.534**
(3) C.511.2, C.537.3	(3) C.561.3
(c) C.511.2	(5) C.535.9
(4) C.525.4	(f) C.541.8, C.545.6
s.139 .... **C.518**	(6) C.535.9, C.541.8, C.545.6
(3) C.463.2	(7) C.411.2
s.140 .... **C.519**	s.156 .... C.408.3, C.533.2, C.534.7,
(2) C.568.2	C.534.14, **C.535**, C.541.3,
(4) C.518.2	C.556.4
s.141 .... **C.520**	(1) C.533.2, C.534.7, C.534.14,
(2) C.406.3, C.510.6	C.535.9, C.538.5, C.539.10,
s.142 .... C.458.6, C.460.5, **C.521**	C.540.5, C.542.3, C.542.16
(1) C.460.5	(2) C.534.7, C.535.9
(c) C.460.5, C.460.13	(3) C.408.3, C.535.9
(2) C.460.5, C.539.4, C.539.5	(a) C.542.16
(3) C.460.5, C.539.5	(b) C.535.9
s.143 .... C.460.11, **C.522**	(b)—(e) C.542.15, C.544.8,
(2) C.515.2	C.545.5
s.144 ...... C.379.15, C.462.4, C.464.2,	(c) C.535.9
C.515.2, C.522.2, **C.523**	(d) C.535.9, C.545.2
(1) C.510.4	(e) C.408.4
(2) C.510.4	s.157 .... **C.536**, C.540.2, C.541.3
ss.144—148 .... C.545.2	(2) C.480.3, C.533.13
s.145 .... C.379.15, **C.524**	s.158 .... C.475.3, C.476.2, C.536.2,
s.146 ...... C.379.15, C.462.4, C.510.5,	**C.537**
C.523.2, **C.525**, C.563.2	s.159 .... **C.538**
(2) C.526.2, C.526.4	(1)(b) C.542.7, C.545.2
(3)(b) C.526.4	s.160 .... C.427.5, C.521.3, C.521.5,
(6) C.526.4	C.521.7, C.533.3, C.534.3,
(7) C.527.3	C.538.4, **C.539**, C.543.2
s.147 ...... C.379.15, C.462.4, C.525.5,	(1) C.536.2
C.525.7, **C.526**, C.559.2	(2) C.533.2
(1) C.542.2	(c) C.542.9
s.148 .... C.462.4, **C.527**, C.559.2	(4)(b) C.505.2
(1) C.526.5	s.161 ...... C.379.16, C.533.2, C.533.6,
(3) C.559.2	C.537.2, C.538.4, **C.540**,
s.149 .... **C.528**	C.544.2, C.544.6
s.150 .... C.462.9, **C.529**	(2) C.544.5

Table of Scottish Statutes

s.162	C.379.16, C.464.2, C.467.2, C.533.3, C.533.9, C.536.2, C.537.2, C.538.4, **C.541**
(1)	C.536.2
(3)	C.533.9, C.533.10, C.533.11, C.536.2
(4)(a)	C.533.9, C.533.10
(5)	C.542.10
(6)	C.540.2
(7)	C.576.1
s.163	C.427.5, C.533.2, **C.542**, C.543.2, C.544.2, C.546.2, C.546.8, C.556.4
(1)	C.414.2, C.415.2, C.416.2, C.427.5, C.543.3, C.543.4, C.544.3, C.544.4, C.546.3
(a)	C.430.2
(ii)	C.488.11
(2)	C.543.4, C.544.2, C.544.4
(3)(c)	C.411.2, C.543.5
(4)	C.543.5
(8)	C.543.8, C.544.7, C.546.5
(9)	C.543.9, C.544.8, C.546.6
(10)	C.543.10, C.544.9, C.546.7
(11)	C.543.11, C.544.10
ss.163—165	C.379.16, C.533.2
s.164	C.505.2, **C.543**, C.546.8
(c)	C.546.4
(3)	C.460.5, C.545.6
s.165	C.540.2, **C.544**, C.546.8
s.166	C.462.4, **C.545**, C.546.2, C.580.2
(1)	C.580.2
(2)	C.379.16, C.580.2
(4)	C.546.4
(6)	C.580.2
(7)	C.546.2
(8)	C.546.2
s.167	**C.546**
(7)	C.580.2
s.168	**C.547**
(2)(c)	C.548.7
(3)	C.379.17
s.169	**C.548**, C.549.3
(1)(b)	C.462.19, C.466.5, C.549.4, C.550.3
(2)	C.379.17
s.170	**C.549**
(2)	C.379.17
s.171	C.438.2, C.548.5, C.549.5, **C.550**
(3)	C.379.17
s.172	**C.551**
(2)	C.442.2
s.173	**C.552**, C.553.2, C.554.5, C.555.7, C.564.4
(2)	C.553.2, C.554.3
s.174	C.552.2, **C.553**
s.175	C.552.2, C.552.6, C.553.2, **C.554**
(2)(d)	C.411.2
(3)—(5)	C.552.4
s.176	C.379.18, **C.555**, C.564.4
(5)	C.379.18
s.177	C.457.5, C.533.2, C.534.5, **C.556**
(2)	C.452.3
(a)	C.458.5, C.533.3, C.576.1
(e)	C.576.1
(f)	C.576.1
(g)	C.576.1
(j)	C.576.1
(m)	C.576.1
s.178	C.379.19, C.451.5, C.455.5, C.456.4, C.457.9, C.472.6, C.487.6, C.556.4, **C.557**
(1)	C.462.8
s.179	C.457.9, **C.558**
s.180	C.457.9, **C.559**
s.181	**C.560**
(5)	C.561.3
s.182	C.379.19, C.457.8, **C.561**
(9)	C.379.19
s.183	**C.562**
s.184	**C.563**
s.185	**C.564**
(2)(c)	C.411.2
s.186	C.379.19, C.414.4, C.416.6, C.421.3, C.426.3, C.462.11, C.466.2, C.466.3, C.471.4, **C.565**
(3)	C.379.19
s.187	C.379.19, C.446.13, **C.566**, C.585.1
s.188	**C.567**, C.585.1
s.189	C.379.19, C.444.3, C.451.2, C.467.3, C.519.5, C.547.5, C.548.7, **C.568**
(2)	C.379.19, C.548.7
(3)	C.379.19, C.548.7
s.190	C.510.8, C.516.2, **C.569**
(1)	C.576.1
(2)	C.510.8, C.510.10
s.191	C.463.2, C.483.2, **C.570**
s.192	C.569.4, **C.571**
s.193	**C.572**, C.585.1
(2)	C.511.2, C.513.2
(3)	C.573.1
(b)	C.511.2, C.513.2
(4)	C.511.2, C.513.2
s.194	**C.573**
s.195	C.413.2, C.534.5, **C.574**, C.575.1, C.576.1, C.577.1
s.196	C.379.16, **C.575**, C.576.1
ss.196—198	C.574.2, C.574.3
s.197	C.379.21, **C.576**
s.198	C.379.21, C.576.1, **C.577**
s.199	C.379.21, C.404.3, C.445.4, C.446.19, C.495.5, C.503.2, C.530.6, **C.578**
(2)	C.446.18
(3)—(5)	C445.4
(6)	C446.5
(7)	C446.5, C.503.2
s.200	C.379.21, C.427.5, C.446.4, C.458.2, C.458.4, C.460.5,

C.460.6, C.521.3, C.521.7, C.539.8, **C.579**	
(g) C.458.2	
s.201 ...... C.379.21, C.462.4, C.471.3, C.545.2, **C.580**	
(1) C.545.2	
(g) C.576.1	
(2)(a) C.545.2	
s.202 .... C.379.19, C.379.21, **C.581**, C.585.1	
(1) C.409.3, C.519.5, C.534.13, C.540.7, C.547.5, C.548.7, C.568.2	
s.203 .... **C.582**, C.585.1	
s.204 .... C.576.1, **C.583**, C.585.1	
s.205 .... **C.584**, C.585.1	
s.206 .... **C.585**	
(2) C.574.3	
Sch.1 .... C.379.2, C.380.1, **C.586**	
para.10(1) C.545.7, C.559.2	
(2) C.560.2	
(6) C.386.2	
Sch.2 .... C.379.2, C.380.1, C.383.1, **C.587**	
(6) C.411.3	
Sch.3 .... C.392.3, C.394.1, C.395.1, **C.588**	
para.1(aa) C.379.19	
(ab) C.379.19	
paras 8–10 .... C.393.1	
para.8(6) C.393.1, C.401.1	
para.10 .... C.395.1, C.445.3, C.457.4	
(1) C.393.1, C.398.2, C.534.12	
(4) C.398.2	
Sch.4 .... C.403.1, **C.589**	
Sch.5 .... C.465.3, **C.590**	
para.2(3) C.403.2, C.408.2	

(4) C.403.2	
para.3 .... C.449.2	
para.9 .... C.408.2	
Sch.6 .... C.552.2, **C.591**	
Sch.8(8) C.391.2	
2011 Domestic Abuse (Scotland) Act (c.13) C.446.9	
2011 Forced Marriage etc (Protection and Jurisdiction) (Scotland) Act (asp 15) C.441.8	
s.1(1) C.446.20	
(6) C.446.20	
2012 Police and Fire Reform (Scotland) Act (asp 8)	
s.20(1) C440.6	
s.99 .... C435.3	
2014 Victims and Witnesses (Scotland) Act (asp 1)	
s.22 .... C.555.3	
2014 Children and Young People (Scotland) Act (asp 8).. C.458.6	
Pt 3 .... C.560.2	
Pt 16 .... C.379.1, C.460.7	
ss.7—18 .... C.560.2	
s.8(1) C.560.2	
s.21 .... C.445.6	
s.87 .... C.519.7	
2014 Courts Reform (Scotland) Act (asp 18)	
s.109 .... C.526.3, C.542.2, C.561.7	
(2) C.556.3	
(a) C.542.2	
(3) C.556.3, C.580.2	
(4) C.542.2	
s.136(1) C.542.2	
2016 Criminal Justice (Scotland) Act (asp 1)	
Sch. 2 para.24 .... C.548.5, C.549.5	

TABLE OF UK STATUTORY INSTRUMENTS

1975 Schools General (Scotland) Regulations (SI 1975/1135) C.506.4
    reg.4 .... C.506.2
1981 Act of Sederunt (Statutory Appeals) (SI 1981/1591) C.533.13
1993 Act of Sederunt (Sheriff Court Ordinary Cause Rules) (SI 1993/1956) .. C.483.5
    r.33.20 .... C.557.2
1993 Act of Sederunt (Sheriff Court Summary Application Rules) (SI 1993/3240) C.533.13
1994 Act of Sederunt (Rules of Court of Session 1994) (SI 1994/1443)
    Sch.2 para.41 .... C.542.2, C.561.3
1995 Children (Northern Ireland) Order (SI 1995/775)
    art.12(2) C.579.2
    art.50(1)(a) C.510.8
    (b) C.510.8
    art.55(1) C.510.8
1997 Act of Sederunt (Child Care and Maintenance Rules) (SI 1997/291) C.414.5, C.415.2, C.416.3, C.418.3, C.430.2, C.479.2, C.491.2, C.573.1
    Pt VI C.488.3
    Pt VII C.480.2
    Pt VIII C.534.3
    r.1.7.2 .... C.483.4
    rr.3.1—3.24 .... C.482.2
    r.3.3 .... C.482.3
    r.3.4 .... C.482.3
    r.3.5(2)(ca) C.483.5
    r.3.5A C.483.5
    r.3.7(1)(a) C.480.3
    r.3.13 .... C.536.2, C.572.1
    (2)(a) C.536.2
    r.3.19 .... C.556.3
    r.3.21 .... C.564.5
    (2) C.483.4
    (3) C.483.4
    r.3.22 .... C.480.2, C.555.5
    r.3.30 .... C.427.7
    r.3.31 .... C.427.3
    (2) C.427.3
    rr.3.31—3.33 .... C.416.2
    r.3.33 .... C.555.4
    (3) C.430.2
    (4) C.430.2, C.555.4
    (6) C.430.2
    r.3.33(3)—(6) C.427.3
    rr.3.39—3.43 .... C.415.5
    rr.3.44—3.52 .... C.480.2
    r.3.45 .... C.480.3, C.485.4
    (1) C.471.3, C.481.3
    (c) C.484.4
    (1B) C.471.3, C.481.3
    (3)—(9) C.485.3
    (4) C.480.3, C.485.4
    (5) C.480.3
    r.3.46(1) C.486.3, C.486.4
    (2) C.486.4
    (4) C.485.3, C.485.4
    r.3.46A C.480.2
    r.3.47(5) C.482.4
    (A1) C.484.4, C.485.4
    r.3.53(1A) C.533.3
    (c) C.533.3
    (1B) C.533.3
    (2) C.533.3
    (3) C.533.3
    r.3.54A C.545.5
    rr.3.53—3.58 .... C.534.3
    r.3.55 .... C.533.3, C.536.3
    r.3.58(2) C.535.3
    r.3.58B C.545.5, C.545.6
    (3) C.545.5
    r.3.59(1) C.542.3, C.556.3
    (2) C.542.3
    (3) C.542.3
    (4) C.542.3
    (5) C.542.3
    (6) C.542.3
    (7) C.542.3
    (b) C.542.3
    (11) C.542.2
    rr.3.59—3.61A C.542.3
    r.3.62 .... C.489.4
    r.3.62 .... C.489.4
    (b) C.492.3
    (1)(b) C.491.2
    rr.3.62—3.63 .... C.490.2
    r.3.63 .... C.491.2
    (1) C.492.3
    r.3.81A C.554.3
    r.13.1(3) C.415.2, C.416.2
    (4) C.430.2
    Sch.1 .... C.573.1
    Form 44A C.555.5
    Form 44B C.555.5
    Form 46 .... C.414.5
    Form 47 .... C.416.3, C.418.3, C.427.7
    Form 48 .... C.416.3, C.427.7
    Form 52 .... C.427.3
    Form 53 .... C.430.2
    Form 60 .... C.471.3, C.479.2
    Form 61 .... C.533.2, C.533.3, C.534.8
    Form 64A C.545.4, C.545.6, C.546.4
    Form 64B C.545.4, C.545.6, C.546.4
    Form 65 .... C.477.2
    Form 65A C.477.6
    Form 65B C.477.6
    Form 79 .... C.554.4

1999	Act of Sederunt (Summary Applications and Appeals etc.) Rules (SI 1999/929).......................... C.526.5	2013	Public Bodies Abolition of Administrative Justice and Tribunals Council Order (SI 2013/2042)... C.457.4

TABLE OF SCOTTISH STATUTORY INSTRUMENTS

2001 Panel of Persons to Safeguard the Interests of Children (Scotland) Regulations (SSI 2001/476) C.411.2
    reg.7(3) C.411.3
2003 Support and Assistance of Young People Leaving Care (Scotland) Regulations (SSI 2003/608) C.517.8
2011 Children's Hearings (Scotland) Act 2011 (National Convener Appeal against Dismissal) Regulations (SSI 2011/143) C.391.2
2011 Children's Hearings (Scotland) Act 2011 (Modification of Primary Legislation) Order (SSI 2013/211) C.379.1, C.494.3, C.458.2
    Sch.1 para.20(10) C.477.4
2012 Children's Hearings (Scotland) Act 2011 (Safeguarders Panel) Regulations (SSI 2012/54) .. C.411.2, C.411.3, C.564.6
    r.3 .... C.409.2
    r.4 .... C.409.2
    r.5 .... C.409.2
    reg.7 .... C.411.2, C.411.3
    reg.11 .... C.411.2
    (2) C.411.3
    (3) C.411.3
2012 Children's Hearings (Scotland) Act 2011 (Child Protection Emergency Measures) Regulations (SSI 2012/334) C.436.1
2012 Children's Hearings (Scotland) Act 2011 (Rights of Audience of the Principal Reporter) Regulations (SSI 2012/335) C.398.2, C.492.3
2012 Children's Hearings (Scotland) Act 2011 (Safeguarders: Further Provision) Regulations (SSI 2012/336) C.411.2, C.413.2, C.564.6
    reg.6 .... C.413.3, C.534.15
    reg.7 .... C.409.2, C.413.3
    reg.8 .... C.409.2, C.413.3
    reg.9 .... C.409.2, C.413.3

2013 Children's Hearings (Scotland) Act 2011 (Transfer of Children to Scotland— Effect of Orders made in England and Wales or Northern Ireland) Regulations (SSI 2013/99) C.510.8, C.510.9, C.510.10, C.569.3
    reg.2 .... C.510.8
    reg.3 .... C.510.8
    reg.4 .... C.510.8
    reg.5 .... C.510.8
    reg.6 .... C.510.8
    reg.7 .... C.510.8
    (3) C.569.3
    (4) C.569.3
2013 Children's Hearings (Scotland) Act 2011 (Compulsory Supervision Orders etc.: Further Provision) Regulations (SSI 2013/149) ....
    regs 6—9 .... C.462.6
2013 Act of Sederunt (Children's Hearings (Scotland) Act 2011) (Miscellaneous Amendments) (SSI 2013/172) ..C.414.5, C.415.2, C.415.5, C.416.2, C.416.3, C.418.3, C.427.3, C.430.2, C.471.3, C.477.6, C.480.2, C.480.3, C.481.3, C.483.4, C.485.3, C.485.4, C.489.4, C.491.2, C.533.2, C.534.3, C.536.3, C.542.2, C.554.3, C.554.4, C.555.4, C.556.3, C.564.5, C.572.1, C.573.1
    art.3(29) C.488.3, C.556.3
2013 Children's Hearings (Scotland) Act 2011 (Review of Contact Directions and Definition of Relevant Person) Order (SSI 2013/193) C.458.2
    art.2 .... C.505.2, C.540.2, C.540.4
    (2) C.540.2, C.544.6
    (a) C.579.3
    (b) C.579.2
    art.3 .... C.460.5, C.579.2
    (2)(a) C.460.5, C.579.2
2013 Children's Hearings (Scotland) Act 2011 (Rules of Procedure in Children's Hearings) Rules (SSI 2013/194) ..C.409.5, C.413.2, C.460.6, C.505.2, C.510.9, C.510.10, C.534.5
    Pts 6—11 .... C.451.5, C.468.2
    Pt 12 .... C.458.2

Pt 21	C.464.2	r.58(2)	C.556.4
r.6	C.474.3	r.59	C.469.3
(1)(b)	C.449.3	(1)	C.469.3
r.8	C.500.2, C.556.4	(2)	C.469.3
r.11	C.457.4	(4)	C.472.3
(1)	C.457.4	r.60	C.413.2, C.517.3
(2)	C.457.4	r.61(1)	C.470.4
r.14	C.468.2	r.62	C.497.4
r.15	C.462.8, C.500.2	(2)	C.534.11
(1)	C.557.7	(3)	C.534.11
(2)	C.557.7	r.63(3)	C.452.4
r.17	C.467.2	r.64	C.452.3, C.474.3
(2)	C.467.6	r.66	C.413.2
r.18	C.500.2	r.67	C.462.4
r.19	C.452.4, C.452.8, C.453.3, C.457.3, C.517.9, C.564.4	(1)	C.525.4
		(2)	C.525.5
(2)	C.452.6, C.458.5	r.70	C.413.2, C.424.2, C.425.2, C.426.2, C.534.5
r.20	C.457.5, C.561.3		
r.21(2)(b)	C.539.8	r.72	C.534.5
r.22	C.539.13	r.73	C.534.5
(2)(c)	C.460.5, C.539.13	r.74	C.505.2, C.534.5
r.23	C.452.3	r.75	C.450.2
r.26	C.412.3, C.534.5	r.77(7)	C.557.7
(2)	C.449.3	r.78	C.413.2, C.502.2
r.28	C.534.5	(1)	C.467.2
r.29	C.534.5	(2)	C.460.6, C.467.2
rr.29—47	C.412.3	(3)	C.460.6, C.467.3
r.30	C.534.5	r.79	C.387.2
r.32	C.534.5	(2)(c)	C.387.2
r.33	C.534.5	(d)	C.387.2
r.34	C.516.2	(5)	C.387.2
(1)(b)	C.556.4	r.80	C.534.5
(3)(b)	C.556.4	r.81	C.462.12
(f)	C.556.4	r.83	C.507.2
(6)	C.494.5	r.84	C.500.2
(b)	C.500.2, C.556.4	rr.84—87	C.462.8
r.35	C.516.2, C.534.5	r.85	C.413.2
r.36	C.515.2, C.534.5	(1)	C.413.2
r.38	C.534.5	r.86	C.413.2
r.39	C.424.2, C.425.2, C.534.5	rr.87—87	C.413.2
r.40	C.534.5	r.88	C.534.11
r.41	C.534.5	(3)(b)	C.387.2
r.42	C.505.2, C.534.5	rr.91—96	C.413.2
r.43	C.534.5	r.94	C.462.10, C.534.5
r.44	C.534.5	r.95	C.462.10, C.463.2
r.45	C.458.6	r.96	C.462.10, C.463.2
(1)	C.459.3	r.124	C.503.2
(2)(c)	C.458.4, C.460.5	2013 Children's Legal Assistance (Scotland) Regulations (SSI 2013/200)	C.569.4
(3)(b)	C.458.5		
r.46A	C.458.6		
r.47(3)	C.412.3	Pt 3	C.483.2
rr.48—49	C.412.3	Pt 4	C.483.2
r.49A	C.458.6	2013 Secure Accommodation (Scotland) Regulations (SSI 2013/205)	C.511.3, C.531.2, C.541.7
r.50	C.458.6		
(5)	C.413.2		
r.52	C.458.6, C.459.3, C.534.5		
(2)(e)	C.413.2	reg.4	C.514.2, C.516.2
r.53	C.413.2, C.534.5	reg.5	C.531.2
r.54	C.458.6	reg.7	C.531.2
r.55	C.539.4	(2)	C.531.2
(1)	C.539.5	(3)	C.531.2
r.56	C.409.2, C.413.2	(4)	C.531.2
(5)	C.412.3	(b)	C.511.3
r.57	C.413.2	(5)	C.511.3, C.516.2

regs 7—9	C.516.2	
reg.8	C.531.2	
(5)(b)	C.511.3	
(6)(a)	C.511.3	
(b)	C.511.3	
(c)	C.511.3	
(d)	C.511.3	
(e)	C.511.3	
(f)	C.511.3	
reg.9	C.516.2	
(5)(a)	C.511.3	
(b)	C.516.2	
reg.10(5)	C.516.2	
(6)	C.511.3, C.516.2	
reg.11	C.511.3	
(2)(b)	C.511.3	
reg.11A	C.531.2	
reg.12	C.511.3	
reg.13(1)(a)—(c)	C.511.3	
2013 Children's Hearings (Scotland) Act 2011 (Movement Restriction Conditions) Regulations (SSI 2013/210)	C.462.9, C.529.1	
reg.3	C.463.2	
reg.4(1)	C.463.2	
(2)(a)	C.463.2	
reg.6(1)	C.463.2	
(2)	C.463.2	
reg.7	C.463.2	
reg.8	C.463.2	
2013 Children's Hearings (Scotland) Act 2011 (Modification of Primary Legislation) Order (SSI 2013/211)		
art.20(10)	C.408.4	
Sch.1	C.408.2	
para.10(5)	C.450.3	
para.20(2)	C.458.2	
Sch.2	C.462.15	
2013 Children's Hearings (Scotland) Act 2011 (Implementation of Secure Accommodation Authorisation) (Scotland) Regulations (SSI 2013/212)	C.379.15, C.511.3, C.530.2, C.541.8	
reg.4	C.464.2	
(3)(a)	C.514.2, C.541.3	
(b)	C.514.2, C.541.3	
reg.5	C.541.3	
reg.6	C.464.2, C.530.4, C.541.3	
reg.7	C.464.2, C.511.3, C.541.3	
(3)	C.511.3	
(4)(d)	C.511.3	
reg.8	C.541.3	
(3)	C.464.2, C.511.3	
reg.9	C.464.2, C.511.3, C.541.3	
reg.10	C.530.6, C.530.7, C.541.3	
(1)—(3)	C.511.3	
(2)	C.530.6	
(3)	C.530.6	
reg.11	C.464.2, C.530.2	
(3)—(5)	C.541.8	
(4)	C.541.8	
(5)	C.541.8	
regs 11—14	C.511.3, C.541.8	
reg.12	C.464.2, C.530.2, C.541.8	
reg.13	C.464.2, C.530.2	
(1)	C.541.8	
(2)	C.541.8	
(3)	C.541.8	
(a)	C.511.3	
reg.14	C.530.2, C.530.6	
(1)	C.541.8	
(2)	C.541.8	
(3)	C.541.8	
(a)	C.511.3	
2013 Vulnerable Witnesses (Giving evidence in relation to the determination of Children's Hearing grounds: Authentication of Prior Statements) (Scotland) Regulations (SSI 2013/215)	C.555.7	
2013 Children's Hearings (Scotland) Act 2011 (Consequential Transitional Provisions and Savings Order (SI 2013/1465)	C.530.5	
art.7(1)	C.569.3	
(2)	C.569.3	
art.16(4)(b)	C.530.5	
(c)	C.530.5	
2014 Adoption and Children (Scotland) Act 2007 (Compulsory Supervision Order Reports in Applications for Permanence Orders) Regulations (SSI 2014/113)		
reg.3	C.520.2	
2015 Children's Hearings (Scotland) Act 2011 (Rules of Procedure in Children's Hearings) Amendment Rules (SSI 2015/21)		
r.5	C.469.3	
r.7	C.557.7	
r.8	C.557.7	
r.15	C.557.7	
2015 Act of Sederunt (Sheriff Appeal Court Rules) (SSI 2015/356)	C.542.2	
r.1.3	C.542.2	
r.2.1	C.542.2	
r.30.3	C.556.3	
r.30.5	C.542.7	
Form 30.5	C.542.7	

2015 Act of Sederunt (Rules of Court of Session, Sheriff Appeal Court Rules Amendment) (Sheriff Appeal Court) (SSI 2015/419)	C.542.2
2016 Children's Hearings (Scotland) Act 2011 (Safeguarders Panel) Amendment Regulations (SSI 2016/61)	C.411.3
reg.2	C.411.3
2016 Act of Sederunt (Sheriff Appeal Court Rules 2015 and Sheriff Court Rules Amendment) (Miscellaneous) (SSI 2016/194)	
r.4	C.556.3

CHILDREN'S HEARINGS (SCOTLAND) ACT 2011*

(asp 1)

INTRODUCTION AND GENERAL NOTE

The Children's Hearing (Scotland) Act 2011 (the Act) came into operation on 24 June 2013. Even though the Act changes and updates the current system, the Kilbrandon ethos remains intact, i.e. that all children will be treated using welfarist, and not punitive, principles. The welfare of the child generally remains the paramount consideration. In many ways, the effect of the Act is to clarify and strengthen the provisions of Pt 2, Chs 2 and 3, of the Children (Scotland) Act 1995 (the 1995 Act). Part I, Pt II, Chs 1 and 4, Pt III and Pt IV of the 1995 Act remain in force, subject to some minor and consequential changes. Substantial amendments have been effected by the Children's Hearings (Scotland) Act 2011 (Modification of Primary Legislation) Order 2013 (SSI 2013/211) and Pt 16 of the Children and Young People (Scotland) Act 2014. Some 25 pieces of subordinate legislation affecting the operation of the Act have been enacted.

C.379.1

The Act is intended to bring the Children's Hearings System into line with the European Convention on Human Rights, the United Nations Convention on the Rights of the Child and recent, relevant case law. In particular, there is now greater emphasis on support for the child and relevant persons, and for their participation during the process, along with a new definition of "relevant person" and the creation of "deemed" relevant person. In addition, the previous system of "business meetings" has been replaced by "pre-hearing panels", "supervision requirements" are now "compulsory supervision orders" (or CSOs), "warrants" are largely replaced with "interim compulsory supervision orders" (or ICSOs), the role of safeguarder has been strengthened and the "relevant local authority" is now the "implementation authority".

The Parts of the Act are summarised as follows:

Part 1—The National Convener and Children's Hearings Scotland

The Act has created a national organisation for panel members to be known as Children's Hearings Scotland (CHS), a non-departmental public body, under the leadership of a National Convener. Members of CHS are appointed by Scottish Ministers and they, in turn, have appointed (with the approval of Scottish Ministers) a National Convener. CHS has a "chairing member" appointed by Scottish Ministers. The roles and functions of the office bearers can be found in Sch.1 to the Act.

C.379.2

The recruitment process for panel members is arranged through the National Convener, who is also in charge of arranging for appropriate training of panel members. More information about this can be found in Sch.2 to the Act.

In practice, the "area support teams" (ASTs) have put in place arrangements for the selection of panel members to make up individual children's hearings.

Part 2—The Principal Reporter and the Scottish Children's Reporter Administration

The Act retains the Scottish Children's Reporter Administration (SCRA) and it remains largely unchanged. Part 2 clarifies the roles and functions of the Principal Reporter and SCRA. This Act, following the style of the 1995 Act, refers throughout to the "Principal Reporter" when referring to persons who exercise the functions delegated to them by the Principal Reporter, but in this commentary, the term "Reporter" will be used, except where the Principal Reporter him or herself is intended.

C.379.3

Part 3—General considerations

There is no change to the overarching principles, namely, the paramountcy of the welfare of the child principle (s.25); the duty of the children's hearing or a sheriff to have regard to the views of the child (s.27); and the minimum intervention principle (ss.28(2) and 29(2)).

C.379.4

Part 4—Safeguarders

A body known as the Safeguarders Panel has been established and is maintained by Scottish Ministers. Scottish Ministers have, by regulations, appointed Children 1st to coordinate, train and manage safeguarders in Scotland.

C.379.5

---

* Annotated by Katy Macfarlane, Senior Teaching Fellow at the University of Edinburgh, Morag Driscoll, retired Director of the Scottish Child Law Centre, Sheriff Brian Kearney, retired Sheriff and Lindsey Anderson, Solicitor.

Children's Hearings (Scotland) Act 2011

Part 5—Child Assessment and Child Protection Orders

C.379.6 This Part seeks to clarify rather than change the procedures that relate to an application for Child Assessment Orders and Child Protection Orders. Section 42 introduces a new Parental Responsibilities and Rights Direction that can be applied for at the same time as a Child Protection Order. Section 43(2) extends the list of persons to be notified of the order being made to include "any person (other than a relevant person in relation to the child) whom the Principal Reporter considers to have (or to recently have had) a significant involvement in the upbringing of the child". A further formulation was adopted in *Principal Reporter v K* [2010] UKSC 56; 2011 S.C. (U.K.S.C.) 91; 2011 S.L.T. 271; [2011] 1 W.L.R. 18 at [69], namely that persons to be notified of an application for an order should include "any person who appears to have established family life with the child with which the decision of a children's hearing may interfere".

Where a child is removed to a place of safety, s.44 retains the obligations (from s.17 of the 1995 Act) incumbent on the local authority as if the child were a "looked after child".

Part 6—Investigation and referral to Children's Hearing

C.379.7 The duties of the local authorities and the police to provide information to the Principal Reporter are retained with the addition of the s.62 provision that gives scope for a court to refer matters to the Principal Reporter, where the court considers that a s.67 ground (except s.67(2)(j)) might apply in relation to a child. "Other persons" who consider that a child is or might be in need of protection, guidance, treatment or control or that a compulsory supervision order might be necessary, continue to have the right to give all relevant information to the Principal Reporter (s.64). Section 66 clarifies the duties of the Principal Reporter on receiving such information.

The grounds for referral (now found in s.67) have been re-worded; the order changed and new grounds added (see annotations for s.67 for detail).

Part 7—Attendance at Children's Hearings

C.379.8 This part retains the obligations (in s.45 of the 1995 Act) imposed on a child and relevant person to attend the children's hearing and clarifies the powers of the children's hearing to proceed in the absence of a relevant person and to exclude a relevant person and/or his or her legal representative. Section 78 contains an extended list of the persons who have a right to attend a children's hearing.

Part 8—Pre-hearing panel

C.379.9 The "business meeting" (under the 1995 Act) has been replaced with the "pre-hearing panel". The purpose of this panel remains largely the same as that of the business meeting, i.e. to make determinations on procedural matters that relate to the child prior to the children's hearing itself. Such matters might be: whether or not to excuse the child and/or the relevant person from the children's hearing; whether the children's hearing is likely to make a compulsory supervision order that includes a secure accommodation authorisation; and whether an individual should be deemed or continue to be deemed a relevant person in relation to the child. A request for a pre-hearing panel may be made to the Principal Reporter by the child, relevant person or safeguarder, if one has been appointed. An individual wishing to be deemed a relevant person may also request a pre-hearing panel.

Part 9—Children's Hearings

C.379.10 The "supervision requirement" (under s.70(1) of the 1995 Act) has been replaced with the "compulsory supervision order" (CSO). Section 83(2) lists the "measures" that may be attached to a CSO.

The Act introduces an "interim compulsory supervision order" (ICSO). This substantially replaces the rather complex system of warrants. An ICSO may last for a period of 22 days and may be extended to a maximum continuous period of no more than 66 days. Any variation or extension, or further variation or extension may be granted by the sheriff under ss.98 and 99.

Section 94 extends the power of a children's hearing to direct the Principal Report to refer the matter to the sheriff to determine whether the ground is established, to include relevant persons who would not understand, or have not understood, the explanation of the ground(s) for referral. (Previously, s.65(9) of the 1995 Act referred to children only.)

Part 9 of the Act introduces a new "medical examination order" (MEO) that may be made by the children's hearing. The making of this type of order would serve to defer the final decision until further information was obtained (s.92(3)).

Part 10—Proceedings before sheriff

C.379.11 This Part clarifies and extends the powers of the sheriff. For example, where a sheriff reviews a ground established, s.117 empowers the sheriff to determine as established a s.67 ground that

Children's Hearings (Scotland) Act 2011

is not specified in the supporting statements that gives rise to the grounds determination, and to direct the Reporter to arrange a children's hearing for that purpose.

Part 11—Subsequent Children's Hearings
Section 120 provides clarification of the powers of the children's hearing where it considers it necessary to defer making a decision until a subsequent children's hearing. C.379.12

Part 12—Children's Hearings general
Section 121 introduces a new duty on the "chairing member" (formerly "panel chair") to ask the child if the documents/papers provided to him or her accurately reflect his or her views. The chairing member need not comply with this duty if he or she considers it inappropriate given the age and maturity of the child. C.379.13

Another new development is the duty on the chairing member to inform the child of the availability of children's advocacy services provided by regulations made by Scottish Ministers (s.122). This section has not yet been brought into force.

Where a children's hearing makes or varies a CSO, makes or varies an ICSO or makes a MEO that includes a "contact direction", s.126 allows for individuals who are not relevant persons and who are affected by the "contact direction" to request that the Reporter arranges to review the "contact direction" no later than five working days after the children's hearing (that included the "contact direction") was held.

Section 127 reiterates the power of the children's hearing to require the National Convener (previously the Principal Reporter) to make a referral to Scottish Ministers where an education authority has failed to comply with its duty to provide education during the period that the child is excluded from school. Where such a requirement is made, the National Convener must make the referral to Scottish Ministers and give a copy to the relevant education authority.

Section 128 extends the power of the children's hearing to make a "parenting order" under s.102 of the Antisocial Behaviour, etc. (Scotland) Act 2004. Previously, the Principal Reporter was required to apply for a parenting order to the sheriff court.

Part 13—Review of Compulsory Supervision Order
As in the 1995 Act, there are wide provisions allowing for, and in some instances requiring, the review of CSOs (formerly supervision requirements). This Part provides clarification of when a CSO must be reviewed on the initiative of the Principal Reporter; the "implementation authority" (the local authority that is responsible for giving effect to the CSO—see s.83(1)(b)) or at the instance of the child or relevant person. C.379.14

Section 135 introduces an obligation on the Reporter to initiate a review within three months where a secure accommodation authorisation has been made, continued or varied. A "review" under this Part is not to be confused with a "Review of sheriff's determination" under ss.110 to 117.

Part 14—Implementation of orders
This Part provides clarification of the duties of local authorities in the implementation of compulsory supervision orders. Section 144 reinforces the mandatory duty on the implementation authority to give effect to a CSO and to comply with any requirements that relate to the CSO. Where an order requires a child to reside in a certain place, s.145 reinforces the duty on the implementation authority to investigate, from time to time, that any conditions under the CSO are being complied with. Where the implementation authority fails to carry out its duty, s.146 empowers the children's hearing to direct the National Convener to enforce the authority's duty. Further, failure may result in the National Convener making an application to the relevant sheriff principal for an order to enforce the duty (s.147). C.379.15

The procedures regarding the implementation of secure accommodation authority are clarified. Detailed provision relating to this are contained in The Children's Hearings (Scotland) Act 2011 (Implementation of Secure Accommodation Authorisation) (Scotland) Regulations 2013 (SSI 2013/212).

Part 15—Appeals
This Part clarifies who may appeal to the sheriff court against the decision of a children's hearing. Section 154 lists the persons who may appeal, the decisions against which an appeal can be made and the time limits. A safeguarder (appointed under s.30) is now given the right to appeal against the decision of a children's hearing. C.379.16

Section 161 introduces the right of a person (other than a relevant person), for whom a contact order or permanence order (under s.80 of the Adoption and Children (Scotland) Act

2007) is in force in relation to the child, to appeal to the sheriff against a decision of the children's hearing that may affect the contact or permanence order.

Section 162 introduces a new right for the child or relevant person to appeal against a decision by the chief social worker to implement or not implement an order that includes a secure accommodation authorisation. This power also extends to appealing against a decision by the chief social worker to remove a child from secure accommodation.

Sections 163 to 165 deal with appeals to the sheriff principal (now the Sheriff Appeal Court) and the Court of Session.

Other changes may be made by way of the "negative procedure", which is defined in s.196.

As mentioned above much subordinate legislation, including the Rules and Regulations necessary for the practical operation of the Act, have been made. In this commentary we have not attempted to discuss each one of these many provisions, but have noted at appropriate places some of the most significant of these.

Under s.166(2), a local authority that is not satisfied that it is the implementation authority for the child is empowered to apply to the sheriff for a review of the decision and determine which local authority is the implementation authority for the child.

Part 16—Enforcement of orders

C.379.17   This Part refines and modifies, but does not substantially change, the provisions of the 1995 Act. It confirms that "officers of the law" may enforce specified orders (which are listed in s.168(3)), as well as arrest an absconding child and take him or her to the particular place in which he or she requires to be kept (s.169(2)), or to the authorised person (s.170(2)). It continues to be a summary offence to assist a child to abscond or prevent a child from returning to an authorised place or authorised person (s.171(3)).

Part 17—Proceedings under Part 10

C.379.18   This Part contains new provisions in relation to evidential aspects of procedures before the sheriff.

Section 176 amends the Vulnerable Witnesses (Scotland) Act 2004 to require that a child witness notice or a vulnerable witness application must be lodged before (or, on cause shown, after) the commencement of a sheriff court hearing.

Section 176(5) provides for evidence in chief, in cases where the ground for referral is under s.67(2)(j), to be given by means of a prior statement in any sheriff court hearing under s.93 (grounds not accepted) or s.94 (child or relevant person incapable of understanding grounds) of this Act.

Part 18—Miscellaneous

C.379.19   This Part contains a variety of provisions including those noted below.

Section 178 provides that a children's hearing need not disclose any information about a child to a person if disclosure would be likely to cause significant harm to the child. This power applies despite the requirement in s.76(3) for the children's hearing to explain to the relevant person (who has been excluded under s.76(2)) what has taken place in the relevant person's absence.

Section 182 reinforces the restrictions on publishing any "protected information" (defined in s.182(9), but not in s.202 (the Interpretation section)) that is intended, or is likely, to identify the child or his or her address or school.

Section 186 reinforces and clarifies the ability of a child, who has capacity under s.2(4) of the Age of Legal Capacity (Scotland) Act 1991, to consent, or refuse consent, to a medical examination arranged under the orders listed in s.186(3).

Section 187 amends the Rehabilitation of Offenders Act 1974 and repeals s.3 of that Act (i.e. where an offence ground has been accepted, established or deemed established that it will be treated as a conviction) and replaces it with new provisions under Sch.3 para.1(aa) and (ab) which limit the period after which the "alternative to prosecution" is spent, to three months from the day the compulsory supervision order is made, varied or continued; or three months from the date of discharge where the ground was accepted by the child and the relevant person; or three months from the date the grounds were established or deemed established. (NB: This is an amendment of UK legislation and cannot be brought into force until amended by the Westminster parliament. The reader is advised to check the status of the amendment at the time of reading.)

Section 189 restricts the use of a police station as a place of safety. Sections 189(2) and (3) requires that a child be kept in a police station for place of safety purposes *only* if it is not reasonable or practicable to detain the child elsewhere, and that steps must be taken to transfer the child to a place of safety that is not a police station *as soon as reasonably practicable*.

Part 19—Legal Aid and advice
This Part amends the Legal Aid (Scotland) Act 1986 by inserting ss.28B to 28S into that Act including provisions for "children's legal aid" to be available in proceedings before a children's hearing or pre-panel hearing in circumstances where secure accommodation may be necessary, and/or where the child has been arrested and is being detained in a place of safety.

Part 20—General
This Part contains Interpretation sections where "child", "relevant person" and "relevant local authority" are all defined in detail in ss.199, 200 and 201 respectively. Section 202 then goes on to define the full range of words and phrases used throughout the Act. It is a notable feature of this Act that it includes provisions enabling subordinate legislation to effect changes to the primary legislation, such as s.67(4) (grounds for referral), s.10 (power to change the functions of the National Convener) and s.18 (power to change the functions of the Principal Reporter), by way of, in the case of s.67, the "affirmative procedure" and, in the case of ss.10 and 18, by the "super-affirmative procedure". The "affirmative procedure" is defined in s.197 and the "super-affirmative procedure" is defined in s.198. There have been very few instances of this power being used by hearings. The National Convener, acting "in line with the general powers conveyed by this section", has published a *Practice and Procedure Manual*, which is provided to panel members and is up-dated from time to time. Amongst many other matters this clarifies the rôle of the Reporter at hearings, including, in para 2.8: "**2. Supporting fair process**. This can include offering a view to the hearing about a legal or procedural issue in the same way as any other hearing participant. This view can be offered in response to a question or on the Children's Reporter's initiative."

There are many people we must thank. We are most grateful to Professor Kenneth McK. Norrie for permission to quote from his works on the Children's Hearings system, which we have acknowledged at the appropriate places, and for many discussions on various issues over the years. We have also received valuable advice from Janys M. Scott, QC, Julian Aitken, Advocate, Sheriff Alan D. Miller, Alyson Evans of CHS and Gill Short of SCRA. The advice we have received has saved us from many errors and infelicities, but, needless to say, we alone are responsible for the final product. We are also most grateful to the editorial staff of W. Green for their technical guidance and patient forbearance over the long preparation period.

C.379.20

C.379.21

ARRANGEMENT OF SECTIONS

PART 1

THE NATIONAL CONVENER AND CHILDREN'S HEARINGS SCOTLAND

The National Convener and CHS

1. The National Convener
2. Children's Hearings Scotland
3. Further provision about National Convener and CHS

The Children's Panel

4. The Children's Panel

Children's hearings

5. Children's hearing
6. Selection of members of children's hearing
7. Holding of children's hearing
8. Provision of advice to children's hearing
9. Independence of children's hearing

Power to change National Convener's functions

10. Power to change National Convener's functions

Children's Hearings (Scotland) Act 2011

Functions of CHS

11. Provision of assistance to National Convener
12. Independence of National Convener
13. Directions

PART 2

THE PRINCIPAL REPORTER AND THE SCOTTISH CHILDREN'S REPORTER ADMINISTRATION

The Principal Reporter and SCRA

14. The Principal Reporter
15. The Scottish Children's Reporter Administration
16. Further provision about Principal Reporter and SCRA

The Principal Reporter

17. Duty as respects location of children's hearing
18. Power to change Principal Reporter's functions
19. Rights of audience

Functions of SCRA

20. Assisting Principal Reporter
21. Provision of accommodation for children's hearings
22. Independence of Principal Reporter
23. Directions

Transfer of staff, property etc.

24. Transfer of staff, property etc.

PART 3

GENERAL CONSIDERATIONS

25. Welfare of the child
26. Decisions inconsistent with section 25
27. Views of the child
28. Children's hearing: pre-condition for making certain orders and warrants
29. Sheriff: pre-condition for making certain orders and warrants
29A. Duty to consider including contact direction
30. Children's hearing: duty to consider appointing safeguarder
31. Sheriff: duty to consider appointing safeguarder

PART 4

SAFEGUARDERS

32. The Safeguarders Panel
33. Functions of safeguarder
34. Safeguarders: regulations

PART 5

CHILD ASSESSMENT AND CHILD PROTECTION ORDERS

Child assessment orders

35. Child assessment orders

36. Consideration by sheriff

Child protection orders

37. Child protection orders

Consideration of application by sheriff

38. Consideration by sheriff: application by local authority only
39. Consideration by sheriff: application by local authority or other person

Ancillary measures

40. Information non-disclosure directions
41. Contact directions
42. Parental responsibilities and rights directions

Notice of order

43. Notice of child protection order

Obligations of local authority

44. Obligations of local authority

Review by children's hearing of certain orders

45. Review by children's hearing where child in place of safety
46. Review by children's hearing where order prevents removal of child

Decision of children's hearing

47. Decision of children's hearing

Variation or termination of order by sheriff

48. Application for variation or termination
49. Notice of application for variation or termination
50. Children's hearing to provide advice to sheriff in relation to application
51. Determination by sheriff

Termination of order

52. Automatic termination of order
53. Power of Principal Reporter to terminate order
54. Termination of order after maximum of 8 working days

Other emergency measures

55. Application to justice of the peace
56. Constable's power to remove child to place of safety
57. Sections 55 and 56: regulations

Implementation of orders: welfare of child

58. Implementation of orders: welfare of child

Offences

59. Offences

Children's Hearings (Scotland) Act 2011

Part 6

Investigation and referral to children's hearing

Provision of information to Principal Reporter

60. Local authority's duty to provide information to Principal Reporter
61. Constable's duty to provide information to Principal Reporter
62. Provision of information by court
63. Provision of evidence from certain criminal cases
64. Provision of information by other persons
65. Provision of information by constable: child in place of safety

Investigation and determination by Principal Reporter

66. Investigation and determination by Principal Reporter
67. Meaning of "section 67 ground"
68. Determination under section 66: no referral to children's hearing
69. Determination under section 66: referral to children's hearing
70. Requirement under Antisocial Behaviour etc. (Scotland) Act 2004
71. Case remitted under section 49 of Criminal Procedure (Scotland) Act 1995
72. Child in place of safety: Principal Reporter's powers

Part 7

Attendance at children's hearing

73. Child's duty to attend children's hearing
74. Relevant person's duty to attend children's hearing
75. Power to proceed in absence of relevant person
76. Power to exclude relevant person from children's hearing
77. Power to exclude relevant person's representative from children's hearing
78. Rights of certain persons to attend children's hearing

Part 8

Pre-hearing panel

79. Referral of certain matters for pre-hearing determination
80. Determination of matter referred under section 79
81. Determination of claim that person be deemed a relevant person
81A. Determination that deeming of person as relevant person to end
82. Appointment of safeguarder

Part 9

Children's hearing

Key definitions

83. Meaning of "compulsory supervision order"
84. Meaning of "movement restriction condition"
85. Meaning of "secure accommodation authorisation"
86. Meaning of "interim compulsory supervision order"
87. Meaning of "medical examination order"
88. Meaning of "warrant to secure attendance"

Statement of grounds

89. Principal Reporter's duty to prepare statement of grounds

Grounds hearing

90. Grounds to be put to child and relevant person
91. Grounds accepted: powers of grounds hearing
92. Powers of grounds hearing on deferral
93. Grounds not accepted: application to sheriff or discharge
94. Child or relevant person unable to understand grounds
95. Child fails to attend grounds hearing

Children's hearing to consider need for further interim order

96. Children's hearing to consider need for further interim compulsory supervision order

Application of Part where compulsory supervision order in force

97. Application of Part where compulsory supervision order in force

PART 10

PROCEEDINGS BEFORE SHERIFF

Application for extension or variation of interim compulsory supervision order

98. Application for extension or variation of interim compulsory supervision order
99. Further extension or variation of interim compulsory supervision order

Power to make interim compulsory supervision order

100. Sheriff's power to make interim compulsory supervision order

Application to establish grounds

101. Hearing of application
102. Jurisdiction and standard of proof: offence ground
103. Child's duty to attend hearing unless excused
104. Child and relevant person: representation at hearing

Ground accepted before application determined

105. Application by virtue of section 93: ground accepted before determination
106. Application by virtue of section 94: ground accepted by relevant person before determination

Withdrawal of application: termination of orders etc.

107. Withdrawal of application: termination of orders etc. by Principal Reporter

Determination of application

108. Determination: ground established
109. Determination: power to make interim compulsory supervision order etc.

Review of sheriff's determination

110. Application for review of grounds determination
111. Sheriff: review or dismissal of application
112. Child's duty to attend review hearing unless excused
113. Child and relevant person: representation at review hearing
114. Sheriff's powers on review of grounds determination
115. Recall: power to refer other grounds

Children's Hearings (Scotland) Act 2011

116. Recall: powers where no grounds accepted or established
117. New section 67 ground established: sheriff to refer to children's hearing

Application of Part where compulsory supervision order in force

118. Application of Part where compulsory supervision order in force

PART 11

SUBSEQUENT CHILDREN'S HEARINGS

119. Children's hearing following deferral or proceedings under Part 10
120. Powers of children's hearing on deferral under section 119

PART 12

CHILDREN'S HEARINGS: GENERAL

Views of child

121. Confirmation that child given opportunity to express views before hearing

Children's advocacy services

122. Children's advocacy services

Warrants to secure attendance

123. General power to grant warrant to secure attendance

Child's age

124. Requirement to establish child's age

Compulsory supervision orders: review

125. Compulsory supervision order: requirement to review

Contact orders and permanence orders

126. Review of contact direction

Referral where failure to provide education for excluded pupil

127. Referral where failure to provide education for excluded pupil

Parenting order

128. Duty to consider applying for parenting order

PART 13

REVIEW OF COMPULSORY SUPERVISION ORDER

Requirement for review

129. Requirement under Antisocial Behaviour etc. (Scotland) Act 2004
130. Case remitted under section 49 of Criminal Procedure (Scotland) Act 1995
131. Duty of implementation authority to require review

132. Right of child or relevant person to require review
133. Principal Reporter's duty to initiate review
134. Duty to initiate review if child to be taken out of Scotland
135. Duty to initiate review: secure accommodation authorisation
136. Duty to initiate review where child transferred

Functions of Principal Reporter and children's hearing

137. Duty to arrange children's hearing
138. Powers of children's hearing on review
139. Powers of children's hearing on deferral under section 138
140. Interim variation of compulsory supervision order
141. Preparation of report in circumstances relating to permanence order or adoption

Review of relevant person determination

142. Review of determination that person be deemed a relevant person

PART 14

IMPLEMENTATION OF ORDERS

Power to transfer child in cases of urgent necessity

143. Transfers in cases of urgent necessity

Implementation of compulsory supervision order

144. Implementation of compulsory supervision order: general duties of implementation authority
145. Duty where order requires child to reside in certain place
146. Breach of duties imposed by sections 144 and 145
147. Application for order
148. Order for enforcement

Compulsory supervision orders etc.: further provision

149. Compulsory supervision orders etc.: further provision

Movement restriction conditions: regulations etc.

150. Movement restriction conditions: regulations etc.

Secure accommodation

151. Implementation of secure accommodation authorisation
152. Secure accommodation: placement in other circumstances
153. Secure accommodation: regulations

PART 15

APPEALS

Appeal against decision of children's hearing

154. Appeal to sheriff against decision of children's hearing
155. Procedure
156. Determination of appeal
157. Time limit for disposal of appeal against certain decisions

Children's Hearings (Scotland) Act 2011

Compulsory supervision order: suspension pending appeal

158. Compulsory supervision order: suspension pending appeal

Frivolous and vexatious appeals

159. Frivolous and vexatious appeals

Other appeals

160. Appeal to sheriff against relevant person determination
161. Appeal to sheriff against decision affecting contact or permanence order
162. Appeal to sheriff against decision to implement secure accommodation authorisation

Appeals to sheriff principal and Court of Session

163. Appeals to sheriff principal and Court of Session: children's hearings etc.
164. Appeals to sheriff principal and Court of Session: relevant persons
165. Appeals to sheriff principal and Court of Session: contact and permanence orders

Requirement imposed on local authority: review and appeal

166. Review of requirement imposed on local authority
167. Appeals to sheriff principal: section 166

Part 16

Enforcement of orders

168. Enforcement of orders
169. Child absconding from place
170. Child absconding from person
171. Offences related to absconding

Part 17

Proceedings under Part 10: evidence

172. Use of evidence obtained from prosecutor
173. Cases involving sexual behaviour: evidence
174. Cases involving sexual behaviour: taking of evidence by commissioner
175. Sections 173 and 174: application to sheriff for order as to evidence
176. Amendment of Vulnerable Witnesses (Scotland) Act 2004

Part 18

Miscellaneous

Children's hearings: procedural rules

177. Children's hearings: procedural rules

Disclosure of information

178. Children's hearing: disclosure of information
179. Sharing of information: prosecution
180. Sharing of information: panel members

Children's Hearings (Scotland) Act 2011

Implementation of compulsory supervision orders: annual report

181. Implementation of compulsory supervision orders: annual report

Publishing restrictions

182. Publishing restrictions

Mutual assistance

183. Mutual assistance
184. Enforcement of obligations on health board under section 183

Proceedings before sheriff under Act

185. Amendment of section 32 of Sheriff Courts (Scotland) Act 1971

Consent of child to medical examination or treatment

186. Consent of child to medical examination or treatment

Rehabilitation of offenders

187. Rehabilitation of Offenders Act 1974: treatment of certain disposals by children's hearings

Criminal record certificates

188. Criminal record certificates

Places of safety

189. Places of safety: restrictions on use of police stations

Orders made outwith Scotland

190. Effect of orders made outwith Scotland

PART 19

LEGAL AID AND ADVICE

191. Legal aid and advice
192. Power to make regulations about contracts for provision of children's legal aid

PART 20

GENERAL

Formal communications

193. Formal communications

Forms

194. Forms

Subordinate legislation

195. Subordinate legislation

196. Negative procedure
197. Affirmative procedure
198. Super-affirmative procedure

Interpretation

199. Meaning of "child"
200. Meaning of "relevant person"
201. Meaning of "relevant local authority"
202. Interpretation

General

203. Consequential amendments and repeals
204. Ancillary provision
205. Transitional provision etc.
206. Short title and commencement

    SCHEDULE 1—Children's Hearings Scotland
    SCHEDULE 2—The Children's Panel
    SCHEDULE 3—The Scottish Children's Reporter Administration
    SCHEDULE 4—Transfer of staff and property to CHS
    SCHEDULE 5—Minor and consequential amendments
    SCHEDULE 6—Repeals

The Bill for this Act of the Scottish Parliament was passed by the Parliament on 25th November 2010 and received Royal Assent on 6th January 2011

An Act of the Scottish Parliament to restate and amend the law relating to children's hearings; and for connected purposes.

PART 1

THE NATIONAL CONVENER AND CHILDREN'S HEARINGS SCOTLAND

The National Convener and CHS

The National Convener

C.380   **1.**—(1) There is to be an officer to be known as the National Convener of Children's Hearings Scotland (referred to in this Act as "the National Convener").

(2) The Scottish Ministers are to appoint a person as the first National Convener.

(3) The Scottish Ministers must take reasonable steps to involve persons who are under 21 years of age in the process for selection of a person for appointment under subsection (2).

(4) The period for which the person is appointed is 5 years.

(5) The terms and conditions on which the person holds and vacates office are to be determined by the Scottish Ministers.

GENERAL NOTE

C.380.1   This section creates a new organisation, Children's Hearings in Scotland (CHS) under the leadership of the National Convener. The National Convener is a new post with new powers. The intention is to ensure consistency in the recruitment, training and management of panel members, together with ensuring consistency in practice in hearings across Scotland. The remit also includes specific training for panel chairs (now called "chairing members"). More detailed provisions in relation to CHS and the National Convener are contained in Schs 1 and 2 to which the reader is referred.

Selection of members of children's hearing

Children's Hearings Scotland

2. There is established a body corporate to be known as Children's Hearings Scotland (referred to in this Act as "CHS").

GENERAL NOTE
A "body corporate" has legal personality which means it may perform actions such as entering into contracts and may sue and be sued in its own name.

Further provision about National Convener and CHS

3. Schedule 1 makes further provision about the National Convener and CHS.

GENERAL NOTE
This section is self-explanatory.

The Children's Panel

The Children's Panel

4.—(1) The National Convener must appoint persons to be members of a panel to be known as the Children's Panel.
(2) The National Convener must endeavour to ensure that—
(a) the number of persons that the National Convener considers appropriate is appointed, and
(b) the panel includes persons from all local authority areas.
(3) Schedule 2 makes further provision about the Children's Panel.

GENERAL NOTE
This section deals with the arrangements for the recruitment and management of panel members, including the functions of the National Convener in this regard. Some of the provisions in the statute are duplicated in Sch.2.

Subs.(2)(b)
Although CHS is a national body, the important local connection is maintained because children's hearings are composed of panel members from the local authority area concerned, as was the position under the Children (Scotland) Act 1995. However, when account is taken of the terms of s.6(1)(3)(b), discussed below, there is the possibility of "borrowing" a panel member from another area where this may be required.

Children's hearings

Children's hearing

5. A children's hearing consists of three members of the Children's Panel selected in accordance with section 6 for the purpose of carrying out functions conferred on a children's hearing by virtue of this Act or any other enactment.

GENERAL NOTE
This section defines the term "children's hearing". The Act has created the "pre-hearing panel" (PHP) which draws on the same pool of panel members but has different functions—see below ss.79–82. The Act generally makes clear which is being referred to—see, for example, below in relation to s.6(5).

Selection of members of children's hearing

6.—(1) This section applies where a children's hearing requires to be arranged by virtue of, or for the purposes of, this Act or any other enactment.

(2) The members of the children's hearing are to be selected by the National Convener.
(3) The National Convener must ensure that the children's hearing—
(a) includes both male and female members of the Children's Panel, and
(b) so far as practicable, consists only of members of the Children's Panel who live or work in the area of the local authority which is the relevant local authority for the child to whom the hearing relates.
(4) The National Convener may select one of the members of the children's hearing to chair the hearing.
[1] (5) In this section "children's hearing" includes a pre-hearing panel.

NOTE
C.385.1   1. Inserted by the Children's Hearings (Scotland) Act 2011 (Modification of Primary Legislation) Order 2013 (SSI 2013/211) Sch.1 para.20(2) (effective 24 June 2013).

DEFINITIONS
C.385.2   "area support teams": Sch.1 para.12(1).
"children's hearing": s.5.
"children's panel": s.4.
"National Convener": s.1.
"pre-hearing panel": s.79(2).
"relevant local authority": s.201.

GENERAL NOTE
This section provides, as before, that hearings must include both male and female members, and introduces the new provision that wherever practicable, hearings should comprise only persons from the local authority area of this child.

Subs.(2)
C.385.3   *By the National Convener.* This is a delegable function of the National Convener and, in practice, the "area support teams" (AST) have put in place arrangements for the selection of panel members to make up individual children's hearings.

Subs.(3)(a)
C.385.4   *Male and female.* In his *Children's Hearings in Scotland*, 3rd edn (Edinburgh: W. Green, 2013), para.2.03, fn.9, Professor Kenneth Norrie discusses the effect of the Gender Recognition Act 2004 and concludes:
"The end result of this is that for the purpose of satisfying the gender specific requirements for the makeup of an individual children's hearing, a panel member will be recognised in his or her new gender if either: (i) he or she has acquired a Gender Recognition Certificate under the 2004 Act to that effect or (ii) he or she has been living in the new gender and presents to the world (including the family and child attending the hearing) as a member of that gender".

Subs.(3)(b)
C.385.5   *So far as practicable.* As noted above under s.4(2)(b), the aim is to maintain the local connection, but this provision introduces a degree of flexibility.

Subs.(4)
C.385.6   In practice, it is the ASTs that decide which panel members sit at which hearings.

Holding of children's hearing

C.386   **7.** The National Convener must ensure that a children's hearing is held for the purpose of carrying out any function conferred on a children's hearing by virtue of this Act or any other enactment.

DEFINITIONS
C.386.1   "children's hearing": s.5.
"National Convener": s.1.

Provision of advice to children's hearing

GENERAL NOTE

Once again, it is the area support teams which in practice carry through the procedures incumbent on the National Convener by virtue of this section, although under Sch. 1 para.10(6), the National Convener may act personally.

C.386.2

Provision of advice to children's hearing

8.—(1) The National Convener may provide advice to children's hearings about any matter arising in connection with the functions conferred on children's hearings by virtue of this Act or any other enactment.
(2) The National Convener may in particular provide—
(a) legal advice,
(b) advice about procedural matters,
(c) advice about the consequences of decisions of the children's hearing,
(d) advice about how decisions of children's hearings are implemented.
(3) In this section, "children's hearing" includes pre-hearing panel.

C.387

DEFINITIONS
"children's hearing": s.5.
"National Convener": s.1.
"pre-hearing panel": s.79(2).

C.387.1

GENERAL NOTE

The aim of the present provision is to provide a formal procedure whereby the children's hearing may obtain legal and procedural advice that cannot be seen as other than independent and impartial. Note that the formal procedures apply equally to pre-hearing panels and children's hearings.

Where a question arises at a children's hearing or a pre-hearing panel which the hearing decides does not require to be referred to the National Convener, the chairing member may adjourn the hearing for a brief period to allow for the question to be discussed and for any written resources to be consulted. Before such adjournment the chairing member should ensure that those present understand the purpose of the adjournment and have been given an opportunity to express their views. After the adjournment, the chairing member should ensure that those present are given an explanation of what happened during the adjournment and the outcome of the hearings' deliberations. The resolution of the question, and the reasons should be covered in the statement of reasons (in effect required by r.88(3)(b) of the Children's Hearings (Scotland) Act 2011 (Rules of Procedure in Children's Hearings) Rules 2013 (SSI 2013/194) (the Procedural Rules).

In the event of the matter not being resolvable in this way the chairing member may defer making a decision until a subsequent hearing and apply formally for the advice of the National Convener under this section and r.79(2)(c) and (d) of the Procedural Rules (see below).

If a complex legal or procedural question arises during a hearing, the panel members may refer the question to the National Convener for advice. Where such a referral is made to the National Convener for advice, a formal procedure must be followed. (See r.79 of the Procedural Rules.) The request for advice must be made by the Reporter within 5 days and the National Convener must respond within 14 days. It is important to note that these deadlines are in calendar days and not working days. The Procedural Rules do not provide a time limit within which the continued hearing should be held, but good practice would require that it should be held as soon as is practicable. At the continued hearing, r.79(5) requires that the National Convener's advice must be given to all present at that hearing. The children's hearing is not bound to accept the advice and must make up its own mind (see s.9 below). There is no requirement that the information given should necessarily be provided in writing, although the substance of the advice should be included in the written reasons given by the hearing together with their reasons for accepting or rejecting all or part of the that advice. It should be reinforced that the advice provided by the National Convener is not binding upon the children's hearing whose independence in decision making is clearly stated in s.9 below. There have been very few instances of this power being used by hearings. The National Convener, acting "in line with the general powers conveyed by this section", has published a *Practice and Procedure Manual*, which is provided to panel members and is up-dated from time to time. Amongst many other matters this clarifies the rôle of the Reporter at hearings, including, in para 2.8: "**2. Supporting fair process.** This can include offering a view to the hearing about a legal or procedural issue in the same way as any other hearing participant. This view can be offered in response to a question or on the Children's Reporter's initiative."

C.387.2

Independence of children's hearings

C.388   **9.** Nothing in this Act authorises the National Convener or the Principal Reporter to direct or guide a children's hearing in carrying out the functions conferred on children's hearings by virtue of this Act or any other enactment.

DEFINITIONS
C.388.1   "children's hearing": s.5.
"National Convener": s.1.
"Principal Reporter": s.14 and Sch.3 paras 8–10.

GENERAL NOTE
C.388.2   This section reinforces that children's hearings are independent and have unfettered decision making powers. Any legal challenge is through the court process.

Power to change National Convener's functions

Power to change National Convener's functions

C.389   **10.**—(1) The Scottish Ministers may by order—
(a) confer additional functions on the National Convener,
(b) remove functions from the National Convener,
(c) transfer functions from another person to the National Convener,
(d) transfer functions from the National Convener to another person,
(e) specify the manner in which, or period within which, any function conferred on the National Convener by virtue of this Act is to be carried out.

(2) An order under this section is subject to the super-affirmative procedure (other than an order under subsection (1)(e), which is subject to the affirmative procedure).

DEFINITIONS
C.389.1   "affirmative procedure": s.197.
"National Convener": s.1.
"super-affirmative procedure": s.198.

GENERAL NOTE
C.389.2   These are very extensive provisions, potentially enabling fundamental changes to be effected without recourse to primary legislation. It is thought that they are unlikely to be used soon and will be kept in reserve to enable changes to be made to take account of future legal and social developments.

Functions of CHS

Provision of assistance to National Convener

C.390   **11.** CHS must—
(a) assist the National Convener in carrying out the functions conferred on the National Convener by virtue of this Act or any other enactment,
(b) facilitate the carrying out of those functions.

DEFINITIONS
C.390.1   "Children's Hearings Scotland": s.2.
"National Convener"': s.1.

GENERAL NOTE
C.390.2   This section defines the role of Children's Hearings Scotland (CHS) in assisting and facilitating the National Convener in the carrying out of his or her functions.

The Principal Reporter

Independence of National Convener

12.—(1) Nothing in this Act authorises CHS or any other person to direct C.391
or guide the National Convener in carrying out the functions conferred on
the National Convener by virtue of this Act or any other enactment.

(2) This section is subject to section 10(1)(e).

DEFINITIONS
"Children's Hearings Scotland": s.2. C.391.1
"National Convener": s.1.

GENERAL NOTE
This section gives statutory force to the right of the National Convener to carry out the C.391.2
functions of the National Convener as he or she sees fit, without interference from the
government.

Note that the wording of s.9 (Independence of children's hearings); s.12 (Independence of the
National Convener) and s.22 (Independence of the Reporter) are virtual mirror images and
reinforce the independence of all parts of the children's hearings system from direction or
influence. The relationship between the National Convener, the Reporter and their respective
boards must be carefully managed to avoid compromising their independence. The
independence of the National Convener is fortified by the entitlement of the National
Convener to appeal, under Sch.8(8), against dismissal by CHS. For the procedure in such an
appeal, see Children's Hearings (Scotland) Act 2011 (National Convener Appeal against
Dismissal) Regulations 2011 (SSI 2011/143).

Directions

13.—(1) The Scottish Ministers may give CHS general or specific C.392
directions about the carrying out of its functions.

(2) CHS must comply with a direction under subsection (1).

(3) The Scottish Ministers may vary or revoke a direction under
subsection (1) by giving a subsequent direction under that subsection.

DEFINITIONS
"Children's Hearings Scotland": s.2. C.392.1

GENERAL NOTE
It should be understood that a direction by Scottish Ministers to CHS (which must be C.392.2
complied with by CHS) does not refer to the exercising of the functions of the National
Convener. This cannot compromise the independence provided for in s.12 (above).

PART 2

THE PRINCIPAL REPORTER AND THE SCOTTISH CHILDREN'S REPORTER
ADMINISTRATION

GENERAL NOTE
This Part of the Act, along with the accompanying Sch.3 (enacted by s.16), outlines the mode C.392.3
of appointment, and the powers and functions of the Principal Reporter. The Act repeals ss.39
to 138 of the Local Government etc. (Scotland) Act 1994 but in general the new provisions
replicate existing enactments, but with changes which will be noted where applicable.

The Principal Reporter and SCRA

The Principal Reporter

14. There continues to be an officer known as the Principal Reporter. C.393

GENERAL NOTE
This Act, repeals, inter alia, s.40 of the Children (Scotland) Act 1995 which defines C.393.1
"Reporter" as the "Principal Reporter" or any officer of SCRA to whom the Principal
Reporter has delegated his or her functions, but Sch.3 para.10(1) of this Act in effect echoes this

by enacting that any function of the Principal Reporter, except that of making an annual report to Scottish Ministers, may be delegated to any person or class of persons authorised by the Principal Reporter. Note that the position of assistant Reporter has been introduced. These officers carry out some of the functions of the Reporter, but exercise no discretionary or decision-making functions and do not appear in court. The Act refers throughout to the "Principal Reporter" but in this commentary the term "Reporter" is used except where the Principal Reporter him or herself is intended. Further provisions in relation to the office of Principal Reporter can be found in Sch.3 paras 8–10 including the important provision in para.8(6) that the Principal Reporter may appeal to Scottish Ministers against dismissal by SCRA.

The Scottish Children's Reporter Administration

15. There continues to be a body corporate known as the Scottish Children's Reporter Administration (in this Act referred to as "SCRA").

GENERAL NOTE

A "body corporate" has legal personality which means it may perform actions such as entering into contracts and may sue and be sued in its own name. Further provisions are made in Sch.3, including certain rights to appeal to Scottish Ministers in the event of dismissal by SCRA.

Further provision about Principal Reporter and SCRA

16. Schedule 3 makes further provision about the Principal Reporter and SCRA.

GENERAL NOTE

Schedule 3 makes further provision about the Principal Reporter and SCRA including the provision, in para.10, enabling the Principal Reporter to delegate most of his or her functions, as specified in that paragraph.

The Principal Reporter

Duty as respects location of children's hearing

17. The Principal Reporter must ensure that, so far as practicable, a children's hearing takes place in the area of the relevant local authority for the child to whom the hearing relates.

DEFINITIONS

"relevant local authority": s.201.
"Principal Reporter": s.14 and Sch.3 paras 8–10.

GENERAL NOTE

The 1995 Act contained no explicit direction as to this matter, but the foregoing provisions of this Act reflect substantially what the practical position was under the 1995 Act.

Must ensure that, so far as practicable. This wording makes clear that a positive obligation is being imposed on the Reporter, qualified only by the provision that the obligation to ensure that a children's hearing takes place in the area of the relevant local authority for the child to whom the hearing relates, only attaches where this is practicable, and it is for the Reporter to decide what is "practicable'". It is thought that the Reporter's decision is unlikely to be challenged where it is founded on sound reasons which are consistent with the interests of the child and the interests of justice.

It is likely to be unusual for a hearing to take place outwith the area where the child resides. Likely reasons for holding the hearing elsewhere might include where the child is in a secure or therapeutic setting away from the area of his or her residence.

Power to change Principal Reporter's functions

18.—(1) The Scottish Ministers may by order—
(a) confer additional functions on the Principal Reporter,
(b) remove functions from the Principal Reporter,

Rights of audience

(c) transfer functions from another person to the Principal Reporter,
(d) transfer functions from the Principal Reporter to another person,
(e) specify the manner in which, or period within which, any function conferred on the Principal Reporter by virtue of this Act or the Criminal Procedure (Scotland) Act 1995 (c.46) is to be carried out.

(2) An order under this section is subject to the super-affirmative procedure (other than an order under subsection (1)(e), which is subject to the affirmative procedure).

DEFINITIONS
"affirmative procedure": s.197.
"Principal Reporter": s.14 and Sch.3 paras 8–10.
"super-affirmative procedure": s.198.

GENERAL NOTE
The conferring on Scottish Ministers by subs.(1)(a)–(d) the power to radically change or transfer the powers of the Reporter is, on the face of it, surprising and perhaps concerning in that it countenances basic change to primary legislation other than by further primary legislation. There are a number of similar empowering enactments in the Act. However, the requirement that the "super-affirmative" procedure has to be employed should ensure that parliamentary scrutiny is maintained. There have so far been no SSIs issued under this section.

Subs.(1)(e)
This provision, which is subject to the less exacting "affirmative procedure", will enable Scottish Ministers to make adjustments to the functions of the Principal Reporter as the system evolves.

Rights of audience

19.—(1) The Scottish Ministers may by regulations—
[1] (a) empower the Principal Reporter to conduct proceedings which by virtue of this Act require to be conducted before the sheriff, the sheriff principal or the Sheriff Appeal Court,
(b) prescribe qualifications or experience that must be acquired or training that must be undertaken by the Principal Reporter before conducting such proceedings.

(2) References in subsection (1) to the Principal Reporter include references to a person carrying out a function on behalf of the Principal Reporter by virtue of paragraph 10(1) of schedule 3.

NOTE
1. As amended by the Courts Reform (Scotland) Act 2014 (Consequential and Supplemental Provisions) Order 2015 (SSI 2015/402) Sch.1(1) para.7(2) (effective 1 January 2016).

DEFINITIONS
"Principal Reporter": s.14 and Sch.3 paras 8–10.
"Sheriff Appeal Court": Courts Reform (Scotland) Act s.9(3).

GENERAL NOTE
This section replaces s.40 of the 1995 Act and takes account of the conferring on the Sheriff Appeal Court of the appellate jurisdiction formerly vested in the Sheriff Principal. The Children's Hearings (Scotland) Act 2011 (Rights of Audience of the Principal Reporter) Regulations 2012 (SSI 2012/335) provide that the Principal Reporter (including persons carrying out the functions of the Principal Reporter by delegation by virtue of Sch.3 para.10(1) to the Act) may, where he or she has at least one year's experience, appear before the sheriff in proceedings under the Act and, where he or she has two years' experience, may appear before the Sheriff Principal (now the Sheriff Appeal Court)—thus putting to rest the doubt raised in *Templeton v E*, 1998 S.C.L.R. 672 at 679 B–D by Sheriff Principal D.J. Risk QC. These Regulations also provide that the "prescribed training" required by subs.(1)(b) is training in court skills and advocacy. The requirements as to experience do not apply where the Reporter is a member of the Faculty of Advocates or a solicitor, but the requirement as to prescribed

training does apply whether or not the Reporter is a member of the Faculty of Advocates or a solicitor. This section does not, as did s.40(2) of the 1995 Act, provide that Reporters shall not, without the consent of SCRA, be employed by a local authority. It is however enacted in Sch.3 para.10(4) that a function of the Principal Reporter may not be delegated to "a person who is employed by both SCRA *and* a local authority [emphasis added]" unless SCRA consents to the delegation.

Subs.(2)

C.398.3   There is no change here—this simply refers to the provision of this Act which, reflecting the 1995 Act, provides that all the Principal Reporter's functions, except that of producing an annual report, may be performed by persons authorised by him or her. As already mentioned, since, in the remainder of the Act, the term "Principal Reporter" is used to include those persons authorised by her or him we shall, for the sake of simplicity, generally refer to the "Reporter".

Functions of SCRA

Assisting Principal Reporter

C.399   **20.** SCRA must—
(a) assist the Principal Reporter in carrying out the functions conferred on the Principal Reporter by virtue of this Act or any other enactment, and
(b) facilitate the carrying out of those functions.

DEFINITIONS
C.399.1   "Principal Reporter": s.14 and Sch.3 paras 8–10.

Para.(a)
C.399.2   This substantially replicates s.128(5) of the Local Government etc. (Scotland) Act 1994.

Para.(b)
C.399.3   This is a new provision, but it is difficult to see what in practice "facilitate" here will add to "assist", in para.(a).

Provision of accommodation for children's hearings

C.400   **21.**—(1) SCRA must provide suitable accommodation and facilities for children's hearings.
(2) Accommodation and facilities must, so far as practicable, be provided in the area of each local authority.
(3) Accommodation and facilities must be dissociated from courts exercising criminal jurisdiction and police stations.

GENERAL NOTE
C.400.1   This replicates, with minor verbal refinements, s.132 of the Local Government etc. (Scotland) Act 1994.

Subs.(2)
C.400.2   *So far as practicable.* See Note to s.17, above.

Subs.(3)
C.400.3   *Must be dissociated.* As in s.132 of the Local Government etc. (Scotland) Act 1994, the dissociation from police stations and criminal courts is mandatory and not subject to practicability.

Independence of Principal Reporter

C.401   **22.**—(1) Nothing in this Act authorises SCRA or any other person to direct or guide the Principal Reporter in carrying out the functions

Transfer of staff, property etc.

conferred on the Principal Reporter by virtue of this Act or any other enactment.

(2) This section is subject to section 18(1)(e).

DEFINITIONS
"Principal Reporter": s.14 and Sch.3 paras 8–10.   C.401.1

GENERAL NOTE
This section asserts the independence of the Principal Reporter in carrying out his or her substantial duties. This independence is fortified by the provision in Sch.3 para.8(6) entitling the Principal Reporter to appeal to the Scottish Ministers against dismissal by SCRA.

Subs.(1)
This, obviously, re-affirms the independence of the Reporter. It is based on s.128(5) of the   C.401.2
Local Government etc. (Scotland) Act 1994, in relation to which the Minister of State said in the House of Lords that this provision contained:
> "a separation and an independence of quite crucial importance. We want to leave the principal reporter within the system in Scotland in a position wherein he can exercise his important professional decision-making independent of any interference" (*Hansard*, HL Vol.557, col.403).

The provisions of this section therefore limit how the Scottish Ministers are to exercise their powers, under the following section, to give SCRA general or specific directions about the carrying out of his or her functions and reflects the quasi-judicial functions of the Principal Reporter.

Directions

23.—(1) The Scottish Ministers may give SCRA general or specific   C.402
directions about the carrying out of its functions.

(2) SCRA must comply with a direction under subsection (1).

(3) The Scottish Ministers may vary or revoke a direction under subsection (1) by giving a subsequent direction under that subsection.

DEFINITIONS
"SCRA": s.15.

GENERAL NOTE
This substantially replicates s.134 of the Local Government etc. (Scotland) Act 1994. It must   C.402.1
be read with s.22, discussed above, which makes clear that Scottish Ministers are not empowered to direct the Reporter in relation to the execution of his or her professional duties.

Transfer of staff, property etc.

Transfer of staff, property etc.

24. Schedule 4 makes provision about the transfer of staff, property,   C.403
rights, liabilities and obligations to CHS.

DEFINITIONS
"CHS": s.2.

GENERAL NOTE
The reader is referred to the complex and detailed provisions of Sch.4.   C.403.1

Children's Hearings (Scotland) Act 2011

PART 3

GENERAL CONSIDERATIONS

PRELIMINARY GENERAL NOTE

C.403.2 Section 16 of Children (Scotland) Act 1995 enacted principles which were to apply to most decisions in relation to children which have to be made by courts and hearings under the provisions of that Act. These principles were not to be universal, because there exists decisions in relation to which not all of these principles apply, indeed, as we shall see:

(I) the paramountcy of the welfare of the child principle is expressly excluded in situations where the protection of the public from significant harm is an issue (see s.26 of the 2011 Act); and

(II) the paramountcy of the welfare of the child principle does not apply literally where a court, children's hearing or pre-hearing panel is determining an issue of fact or law see discussion below under s.25(1).

However, the principles in s.16 of the 1995 Act (now substantially ss.25 to 29A of the 2011 Act) may be regarded as encapsulating the welfare and child-centred philosophy of the children's hearings system. Professor Norrie has coined for them the term "overarching principles" and the present authors happily adopt this expression, always recalling the derogation contained in s.26. The present legislation (substantially following the 1995 Act) applies the first of the overarching principles, the paramountcy of the welfare of the child principle, to all decisions of courts and hearings, except where the protection of the public is at stake (and innovates by extending this principle to decisions of the pre-hearing panels); but in relation to the other two overarching principles, the "views of the child" principle and the "minimum intervention principle" (sometimes referred to as the "no non-beneficial order principle"), it applies them only to certain (various) specified circumstances.

The Act, in the "Minor and consequential amendments" contained in Sch.5 para.2(3), repeals almost all of s.16 of the 1995 Act in that it removes from it all references to decisions of children's hearings and removes references to decisions of sheriffs except, in Sch.5 para.2(4)(d), decisions where the sheriff is considering whether to make, vary or discharge an exclusion order made under s.76(4) of the 1995 Act (which remains in force). In other words, s.16 of the 1995 Act, in so far as still in force, applies the three overarching principles to decisions of sheriffs when considering whether to make, vary or discharge an exclusion order made under s.76(4) of the 1995 Act. The provisions as to the overarching principles, in relation to other decisions and determinations of children's hearings, pre-hearing panels and courts, under the 2011 Act, are now found in ss.25 to 29A of the Act, discussed below.

The overarching principles enacted in ss.25 to 29A apply in terms only to decisions and determinations of children's hearings, pre-hearing panels and courts, notwithstanding that the Act allows other persons and bodies to make decisions about children. Local authorities are, in relation to looked after children, subject to substantially the same principles by virtue of the (only formally amended) s.17 of the 1995 Act. On the other hand Reporters, who have many important decisions about children to make under the Act, are not mentioned in ss.25 to 29A as being subject to any of the overarching principles, but in practice Reporters aim to observe them: this makes sense since often enough decisions of Reporters result in proceedings before children's hearings, pre-hearing panels and courts, which are of course bound by the overarching principles.

Welfare of the child

C.404 **25.**—(1) This section applies where by virtue of this Act a children's hearing, pre-hearing panel or court is coming to a decision about a matter relating to a child.

(2) The children's hearing, pre-hearing panel or court is to regard the need to safeguard and promote the welfare of the child throughout the child's childhood as the paramount consideration.

DEFINITIONS
C.404.1 "child": s.199.
"children's hearing": s.5.
"pre-hearing panel": ss.79(2)(a), 202.

Welfare of the child

GENERAL NOTE
See Preliminary General Note, above.

Subs.(1)
"Business meetings" under s.64 of the 1995 Act were not formally bound by this overarching principle, presumably because their function was merely to give advice and therefore the substantive decision would be the responsibility of a hearing, which would be so bound (although in practice panel members at business meetings would inevitably have the child's welfare at the forefront of their minds). The new pre-hearing panels, however, are entitled to take operative decisions—see below for discussion of ss.79 to 81A—and are consequently subject to the paramountcy of the welfare of the child principle.

A matter relating to the child. These words are not to be taken literally. They can only refer to certain discretionary decisions which courts, hearings and pre-hearing panels may be called upon to make, such as whether to grant a child protection order, whether to grant, vary or terminate a compulsory supervision order, whether a child should be excused from attending a children's hearing and the like. The paramountcy of the welfare of the child principle does not apply to determinations of fact or law made by courts, children's hearings or pre-hearing panels. For example, a sheriff when considering if evidence was sufficient to find a ground for referral established could not legitimately invoke this principle in order, in a doubtful case, to allow his or her view as to where the interests of the child lay to tip the balance in favour of finding the ground established. An example of this is *Constanda v M*, 1997 S.C. 217 at 224F; 1997 S.C.L.R. 510 at 512D; 1997 S.L.T. 1396 at 1398C where there was evidence of a number of offences, but uncorroborated, and therefore not, by virtue of the requirement s.42(6) of the 1995 Act, provable as the offence by the child ground. The argument was advanced that these offences could be regarded as amounting to the ground for referral of being exposed to moral danger and Lord Rodger of Earlsferry, holding this to be illegitimate, said:

"To hold otherwise would be to deprive the child of the safeguard which Parliament provided in section 42(6). That cannot be allowed, even although the reporter may have acted with the best of intentions and may consider that in seeking to avoid the difficulties posed by section 42(6) she is trying to help the child."

Other examples of the non-applicability of the paramountcy of the welfare of the child principle are: jurisdictional decisions (*S v Proudfoot*, 2002 S.L.T. 743); and decisions of pre-hearing panels as to whether an individual should be deemed as a relevant person (*MT and AG v Anne Gerry (Locality Reporter)* [2014] CSIH 108, sub. nom. *T v Locality Reporter*, 2015 Fam. L.R. 2, IH, Extra Division). Certain procedural decisions may, however, have to have regard to the principle. For example in *G v Scanlon*, 2000 S.C.L.R. 1 the sheriff, whose decision was upheld by the Court of Session on appeal, while not referring to the paramountcy of the welfare of the child principle was apparently applying the essence of the principle when he decided, in relation to a child who had been held in a place of safety for a long time

"that it was of the utmost importance for the future of the child that a speedy decision be made as to whether the grounds were established or not"

and that therefore a motion for adjournment of the proof should be refused.

Subs.(2)
Throughout the child's childhood. For these purposes a child is a person who is under 16 or who otherwise qualifies as a child under s.199 (discussed below in the discussion of ss.66 and 199).

The paramount consideration. The "paramount" consideration for a court, children's hearing or pre-hearing panel in deciding a matter under the Act is the child's welfare. This does not mean that the child's interests are the sole relevant issue. Any doubt as to this has been removed by the incorporation into UK domestic law of the European Convention on Human Rights art.6, of which guarantees to all persons the right to a fair hearing in the determination of their civil rights and amongst these rights is the right to respect for private and family life, as enshrined in art.8. This right attaches to parents (and other family members) as well as to children and accordingly Reporters and panel members must take account of this. For further discussion of this issue see Kenneth McK. Norrie, *Children's Hearings in Scotland*, 3rd edn (Edinburgh: W. Green, 2013), para.1–09. Also circumstances can arise, as provided for in s.26 (discussed below) where the interests of the child may become a primary rather than the paramount consideration.

Decisions inconsistent with section 25

C.405   **26.**—[1] (1) A children's hearing or a court may make a decision that is inconsistent with the requirement imposed by section 25(2) if—
(a) the children's hearing, pre-hearing panel or court considers that, for the purpose of protecting members of the public from serious harm (whether physical or not), it is necessary that the decision be made, and
(b) in coming to the decision, the children's hearing, pre-hearing panel or court complies with subsection (2).

[1] (2) The children's hearing, pre-hearing panel or court is to regard the need to safeguard and promote the welfare of the child throughout the child's childhood as a primary consideration rather than the paramount consideration.

NOTE

C.405.1   1. As amended by the Children's Hearings (Scotland) Act 2011 (Modification of Primary Legislation) Order 2013 (SSI 2013/211) Sch.1 para.20(3) (effective 24 June 2013).

DEFINITIONS

C.405.2   "child": s.199.
"children's hearing": s.5.
"pre-hearing panel": ss.79(2)(a), 202.

GENERAL NOTE

See Preliminary General Note, above.

Subs.(1)

C.405.3   While the welfare of the child is otherwise the paramount consideration for courts and hearings, this section recognises that in certain situations the necessity of providing protection for others (impliedly from the child) will require a decision to be taken even where that decision is not in the best interests of the child. It may be necessary to place a child in secure accommodation and this may sometimes be regarded as not in the child's best interests (but not always—cf. the reasoning of the court in *Humphries v S*, 1986 S.L.T. 683 where, in the circumstances of that case, placement in secure accommodation was described as being "in his [the child's] own interest" to prevent him from offending), but such placement may be necessary to protect others.

Serious harm (whether physical or not). There is no change here from the 1995 Act. The harm from which members of the public are to be protected can be physical harm to person or property or emotional or psychological harm. However, in any case it must be *serious* harm. Serious harm is harm that is not trivial or transient, and is perhaps easier to recognise than define. In *Re L (A Child) (Care: Threshold Criteria)* [2007] 1 F.L.R. 2050; [2007] Fam. Law 297 Hedley J said that it would be unwise to attempt an all-embracing definition of "significant harm" since this was fact-specific and had to retain the breadth of meaning that human frailty required of it, adding that for significant harm there had to be more than human failure and inadequacy. We would suggest that it would be equally unwise to attempt an all-embracing definition of "serious harm" but would suggest that this subsection should not be invoked lightly either by the children's hearing or the sheriff. For a fuller discussion and definitions of "significant harm", see the Scottish Government's *National Guidance for Child Protection in Scotland* (2014), pp.13–14, paras 40–45.

Subs.(2)

C.405.4   Any decision made under subs.(1), while not governed by the paramountcy of the welfare of the child principle, must nevertheless regard the promotion of the welfare of the child as "a primary consideration". This accords with art.3(a) of the UN Convention on the Rights of the Child, ratified by the UK in December 1991, which makes this provision in relation to "all actions concerning children": it is notable that in Scotland, in all actions concerning children except under this section, the promoting and maintaining of the welfare of the child is the paramount consideration. It is interesting that in the Explanatory Notes (at para.28) the Scottish Government invokes the UN Convention in this connection. The practical effect of this provision is, it is submitted, that a hearing or sheriff, when giving reasons for a decision, should

Views of the child

27.—[1] (1) This section applies where by virtue of this Act a children's hearing, pre-hearing panel or the sheriff is coming to a decision about a matter relating to a child.

(2) This section does not apply where the sheriff is deciding whether to make a child protection order in relation to a child.

[1] (3) The children's hearing, pre-hearing panel or the sheriff must, so far as practicable and taking account of the age and maturity of the child—
(a) give the child an opportunity to indicate whether the child wishes to express the child's views,
(b) if the child wishes to do so, give the child an opportunity to express them, and
(c) have regard to any views expressed by the child.

(4) Without prejudice to the generality of subsection (3), a child who is aged 12 or over is presumed to be of sufficient age and maturity to form a view for the purposes of that subsection.

[1] (5) In this section "coming to a decision about a matter relating to a child", in relation to a children's hearing, pre-hearing panel includes—
(a) providing advice by virtue of section 50,
(b) preparing a report under section 141(2).

NOTE
1. As amended by the Children's Hearings (Scotland) Act 2011 (Modification of Primary Legislation) Order 2013 (SSI 2013/211) Sch.1 para.20(4) (effective 24 June 2013).

DEFINITIONS
"child": s.199.
"child protection order": ss.37, 202.
"children's hearing": s.5.
"pre-hearing panel": ss.79(2)(a), 202.

GENERAL NOTE
See Preliminary General Note, above. This section is based on s.16(2) of the Children (Scotland) Act 1995 and its provisions are of course crucial to the operating of the children's hearings system. The section simply applies its provisions to where a children's hearing or a sheriff is coming to a decision about "a matter" relating to a child, while making clear:

(I) that it applies to providing advice under s.50 (advising the sheriff on an application to vary or terminate a CPO) and providing a report under s.141(2) (advising an implementation authority or a court, in the context of applications concerning certain adoption procedures, as to the continuance or otherwise of a CSO), and

(II) that it does not apply where the sheriff is considering whether to make a CPO.

However, there is no exclusion from the views of the child principle where a hearing is considering the granting a medical examination order or a child assessment order. As with the (still in force) ss.6 and 11(7) of the 1995 Act this section keeps Scotland in compliance with art.12 of the UN Convention on the Rights of the Child.

Subs.(1)
A matter relating to the child. See above for discussion of these words in relation to s.25(1). The same considerations apply here.

Subss.(3) and (4)
Subsection (3) provides that regard must be paid to age and maturity of the child, and there is a presumption (i.e. regarded as true unless proved otherwise) that a child aged 12 or over is capable of forming and expressing a view. However, this should not be applied mechanically. It is possible that a child over the age of 12 might in particular circumstances be held as being not "mature" enough to form a view. And there have been, and will continue to be, children well under that age who are well able to do so. In *Sahin v Germany* (2003) 36 E.H.R.R. 43 at 765, the

European Court of Human Rights criticised the court below for not at least contemplating the possibility of making special arrangements to have direct contact with a child of four and for accepting the "vague statements" of an expert about the risks inherent in questioning such a child.

It is to be noted that the subs.(3) appears to envisage four stages:
- coming to a decision as to practicability, both in general and in relation to the age and maturity of the child;
- giving the child (when practicable) the opportunity to "indicate" whether he or she wishes to express views;
- if the child wishes to express views, giving him or her the opportunity to do so; and
- having regard to any views thus expressed.

It will generally be appropriate for sheriffs and hearings to make clear that these several steps are being taken and where necessary have this recorded. It hardly needs saying that "having regard to" does not mean accepting.

Should the court interview the child?

The Policy Document which accompanied the Bill quotes art.12(1) of the UN Convention on the Rights of the Child states:

"State[s] parties shall assure to the child who is capable of forming his or her own views the right to express those views freely in all matters affecting the child, the views of the child being given due weight in accordance with the age and maturity of the child",

and comments,

"The Bill reflects this stipulation across its provisions".

There are ample judicial dicta on this matter.

In *Shields v Shields*, 2002 S.C. 246; 2002 S.L.T. 579; 2002 S.C.L.R. 334 Lord Marnoch stated at 582 in the SLT report:

"Seeing a child in chambers is, of course, always open to the court but, in the case of a very young child, we do not discount the possibility that his or her views, or the lack of them, could properly be made known to the court through the agency of, for example, a private individual who is well known to the child or perhaps by a child psychologist. But, if, by one method or another, it is 'practicable' to give the child the opportunity of expressing his views, then, in our view, the only safe course is to employ that method."

In *Re D (A Child) (Abduction)* [2007] F.L.R. 242 Baroness Hale of Richmond observed: "Just as adults may have to do what the court decides whether they like it or not so may the child. But that is no more reason for failing to hear what the child has to say than it is for refusing to hear the parents' views."

In *ZH (Tanzania) v Secretary of State for the Home Department* [2012] CSIH 17; 2012 Fam. L.R. 32 the immigration authorities had not taken account of the interests or views of two children who appear to have been 9 and 7 years old at the time of their decision to deport their mother on grounds unconnected with any actings of the children. Allowing the mother's appeal the court stated:

"The immigration authorities must be prepared at least to consider hearing directly from a child who wishes to express a view and is old enough to do so."

However, in *S v S* [2012] CSIH 17; 2012 Fam. L.R. 32 a sheriff did not take steps to clarify the views of a six-year-old child, whose stance, in relation to a plan by the mother to emigrate, had been imperfectly conveyed in a report. On appeal by the father an Extra Division stated:

"At the material time he [the child] knew nothing of the relocation proposal, nor of its implications for his relationship with the defender [the father], nor indeed of the likely consequences if relocation did not take place. In such circumstances there was no reason to attach material significance to any views which B [the child] might be thought to have expressed and the sheriff in our view committed no error when he declined to do so".

S v S is, of course, not a case arising from the children's hearings system and, having regard to the enhanced emphasis in the 2011 Act on the listening to the child principle, this case should not be regarded as authority for any argument that the obligation to try to find out the views of the child can be side-stepped because the child, for one reason or another, is not aware of what is being proposed. It is submitted, on the contrary, that in a marginal case the attempt to find out the views of the child should be made. Note that SCRA has produced "All About Me" forms—one for under 12-year-olds and one for children aged 12 and over—to facilitate the expression of their views.

Children's hearing: pre-condition for making certain orders and warrants

C.407   **28.**—(1) Subsection (2) applies where a children's hearing is—
(a) considering whether to make a compulsory supervision order,

Children's hearing: pre-condition for making certain orders and warrants

(b) considering whether to vary or continue a compulsory supervision order,
(c) considering whether to make an interim compulsory supervision order,
(d) considering whether to make an interim variation of a compulsory supervision order,
(e) considering whether to make a medical examination order, or
(f) considering whether to grant a warrant to secure attendance.

(2) The children's hearing may make, vary or continue the order or interim variation or grant the warrant, only if the children's hearing considers that it would be better for the child if the order, interim variation or warrant were in force than not.

DEFINITIONS

"children's hearing": s.5.   C.407.1
"compulsory supervision order": s.83.
"interim compulsory supervision order": s.86.
"medical examination order": s.87.
"warrant to secure attendance": s.88.

GENERAL NOTE

See Preliminary General Note, above. This is the "minimum intervention principle" C.407.2 (sometimes also called the "no non-beneficial order principle"). This section reflects the terms of this principle as enacted in s.11(7)(a) of the Children (Scotland) Act 1995. The fundamental thrust of this principle is the almost self-evident proposition that if a proposed order is not likely to improve upon the child's situation either by promoting his or her welfare or getting rid of something which is harming his or her welfare then there is no point in the state intervening in the child's life for no apparent good reason. The principle accords with the principle of proportionality as imported by the jurisprudence of the European Convention: for example in *Kutzner v Germany* (2002) 35 E.H.R.R. 25 it was held not to be proportionate to remove a child from his parents and prohibit contact in order to address the child's special educational needs. The proportionality is with the needs of the child and not with the "gravity" of the original ground of referral and the principle does not entail imposing a "tariff" of disposals whereby the least invasive has to be tried first. For further discussion see Brian Kearney, *Children's Hearings and the Sheriff Court*, 2nd edn (Butterworths, 2000), paras 2.20, 25.12 and 25.13 and Kenneth McK. Norrie, *Children's Hearings in Scotland*, 3rd edn (Edinburgh: W. Green, 2013), para.9–18. The principle refers to intervention in the child's life and not minimum interference with orders already granted. The use of the formulation "no order principle" may tend to obscure this and we have not adopted it.

Subs.(1)

This specifies the individual circumstances (in relation to hearings) to which the principle C.407.3 applies. Paras (c) and (d) apply the principle to the making and varying of the "interim compulsory supervision order" (ICSO), explained more fully below, in the discussion of s.86 (definition of ICSO) and s.92 (powers of hearing on deferral). Paragraph (e) applies the principle to where the making of a "medical examination order", discussed at s.87, is under consideration. Paragraph (f) applies the principle to where a "warrant to secure attendance" is under consideration. This warrant, in relation to the attendance of a child, is defined in s.88, discussed below. Section 45(4) of the 1995 Act, empowered a hearing, on the motion of the Reporter, to grant such a warrant and a hearing's consideration of such a motion was not subject to the minimum intervention principle, although it required to be satisfied on cause shown that the granting of such a warrant was necessary to secure the child's attendance. Professor Norrie, in *Children's Hearings in Scotland*, 3rd edn (Edinburgh: W. Green, 2013), para.9–18, has pointed out that the requirement of establishing "necessity" would, under ECHR law, entail that the granting of such a warrant would have to constitute a proportionate response to the child's needs.

Subs.(2)

The children's hearing may make. Note that the powers here defined are conferred on C.407.4 children's hearings and not on pre-hearing panels which of course have none of the powers set out in subs.(1).

Sheriff: pre-condition for making certain orders and warrants

C.408   29.—(1) Subsection (2) applies where—
(a) the sheriff is considering making a child assessment order,
(b) the sheriff is considering making or varying a child protection order,
(c) by virtue of section 156(1)(b) or (2)(b), the sheriff is considering—
   (i) varying or continuing a compulsory supervision order,
   (ii) making or varying an interim compulsory supervision order or an interim variation of a compulsory supervision order,
   (iii) varying a medical examination order, or
   (iv) granting a warrant to secure attendance,
(d) the sheriff is otherwise considering—
   (i) making an interim compulsory supervision order or an interim variation of a compulsory supervision order, or
   (ii) granting a warrant to secure attendance, or
(e) the sheriff is considering extending or varying an interim compulsory supervision order under section 98 or 99.

(2) The sheriff may make, vary, continue or extend the order or interim variation or grant the warrant, only if the sheriff considers that it would be better for the child if the order, interim variation or warrant were in force than not.

DEFINITIONS

C.408.1   "child assessment order": s.35(2).
"child protection order" s.37(2).
"compulsory supervision order": s.83.
"interim compulsory supervision order": s.86.
"medical examination order": s.87.
"warrant to secure attendance": s.88.

GENERAL NOTE

C.408.2   See Preliminary General Note, above. This section specifies the circumstances in which the sheriff is bound by the minimum intervention principle. The section is based upon, but is far from precisely replicating, the provisions of s.16(4)(b) of the Children (Scotland) Act 1995. The operative passage of this section is in subs.(2), which refers to situations wherein the sheriff is deciding on whether to "make, vary or extend the order or interim order or grant warrant" and not (in this respect departing from some of the provisions of the 1995 Act) to any situation wherein the sheriff is considering the discharge of such order or warrant. This reflects the point made at the end of the General Note to s.28, above, that it is not minimisation of orders which is in question but avoidance of unnecessary and non-beneficial interference with a child's life: by definition the discharge of such orders or warrants (whatever the merit or otherwise of such a discharge) cannot logically be regarded as interference with the child's life.

Parental responsibilities orders and exclusion orders

It will be noted that these orders, mentioned in s.16 of the 1995 Act, are not mentioned here. The reason for this is that parental responsibilities orders have in effect been replaced by permanence orders which were enacted under Part 2 (ss.80–104) of the Adoption and Children (Scotland) Act 2007 (asp 4) and that exclusion orders remain subject to the provisions of the 1995 Act, which have not been repealed by the 2011 Act.

Exclusion orders and s.16(4)(b)(i) of the Children (Scotland) Act 1995

Most of the provisions of s.16 of the 1995 Act have been amended/repealed by Sch.5 para.2(3) of the 2011 Act and it is convenient to reproduce s.16 here in its amended form:

   "**Welfare of child and consideration of his views**

   16.—(1) Where under or by virtue of this Part of this Act a court determines any matter with respect to a child the welfare of that child throughout his childhood shall be its paramount consideration.

   (2) In the circumstances mentioned in subsection (4) below, the sheriff, taking account of the age and maturity of the child concerned, shall, so far as practicable—
      (a) give him an opportunity to indicate whether he wishes to express his views;
      (b) if he does so wish, give him an opportunity to express them; and

Sheriff: pre-condition for making certain orders and warrants

(c) have regard to such views as he may express;
and without prejudice to the generality of this subsection a child twelve years of age or more shall be presumed to be of sufficient age and maturity to form a view.

(3) In the circumstances mentioned in subsection (4) of this section, no order so mentioned shall be made with respect to the child concerned unless the sheriff considers, that it would be better for the child that the order be made than that none should be made at all.

(4) The circumstances to which subsection (2) refers are that the sheriff is considering whether to make, vary or discharge an exclusion order.

(5) If, for the purpose of protecting members of the public from serious harm (whether or not physical harm)—

(b) *[sic – this should, grammatically, be '(a)', but the amending provision does not take account of this]* a court considers it necessary to make a determination under or by virtue of Chapter 1 or 3 of this Part of this Act which (but for this paragraph) would not be consistent with its affording such paramountcy, it may make that determination."

The substantive provisions as to exclusion orders within the Children's Hearings System are contained in ss.76 to 80 of the 1995 Act, which, apart from consequential terminological changes to s.76(8) effected in Sch.5 para.9 of the 2011 Act, remain in force unchanged. Accordingly the extensive comments on these sections by Professor Norrie in his commentary *Children (Scotland) Act 1995* , 2nd edn (Edinburgh: W. Green, 2004), pp.167 to 179 are still applicable. The continuing in force of the (now much truncated) s.16 is the device employed to provide that the overarching principles apply to these exclusion orders.

Permanence Orders, replacing Parental Responsibilities Orders

Part 2 (ss.80–104) of the Adoption and Children (Scotland) Act 2007 introduces Permanence Orders and Sch.3 para.1 of that Act repeals the provisions as to Parental Responsibilities Orders enacted in ss.86–89 of the 1995 Act. The Explanatory Notes to the 2007 Act include this Background Note to Pt 2:

"Part 2 of this Act relates to permanence orders. These are designed to provide longterm security for children who cannot live with their family. A permanence order is also capable of including authority for a child to be adopted. Part 2 establishes the structure of a permanence order, including the provision for the distribution of parental responsibilities and parental rights, and also provides for its effect as regards supervision requirements and other types of order, and the variation and revocation of permanence orders. ... A permanence order is a new type of court order which will regulate the exercise of parental responsibilities and parental rights in respect of children who cannot reside with their parents but where contact or shared exercise of parental responsibilities and parental rights is or may be appropriate. A permanence order may remove some or all parental responsibilities and parental rights and grant them to other persons specified in the order."

Sections 89 and 90 of the Adoption and Children (Scotland) Act 2007, as terminologically amended by provisions in Sch.1 to the Children's Hearings (Scotland) Act 2011 (Modification of Primary Legislation) Order 2013 (SSI 2013/211), respectively provide: that where a permanence order is made and a compulsory supervision order is in force and the court is satisfied that the compulsory supervision order is no longer necessary, the court is to order the compulsory supervision order to cease; and that where a permanence order gives parental responsibilities and parental rights to a local authority that local authority must not act in a way which is incompatible with any court order, compulsory supervision order or interim compulsory supervision order which is in force.

Subs.(1)(c)

This refers to the situations wherein the sheriff, in an appeal from a decision of a children's hearing, is considering, when confirming or otherwise the decision of a hearing, what, if any, further steps to take under s 156(3). See the commentary on s.156 below for further discussion.

C.408.3

Subs.(1)(d), (e)

A children's hearing may, when deferring consideration of a child's case, make an interim compulsory supervision order (ICSO) under s.92(2) and the Reporter may apply to the sheriff for extension or variation of such an order under s.98 (as amended by the Children's Hearings (Scotland) Act 2011 (Modification of Primary Legislation) Order 2013 (SSI 2013/211) art.20(10)) and s.99. The sheriff may, in the course of dealing with a proof application under s.93(2)(a) or s.94(2)(a), make an ICSO. Where the sheriff sustains any ground for referral on a

C.408.4

proof application and directs the Reporter under s.108(2) to arrange a hearing to consider a compulsory supervision order (CSO), the sheriff may make an ICSO or a "further" ICSO by virtue of s.109(3) and (5). The occasions on which a sheriff may grant a warrant to secure attendance include those listed in the following: ss.103(5) and (7), 109(6), 112(4), 115(4), 117(4) and 156(3)(e). The effect of this section is that when considering making any of these orders or granting any of these warrants the sheriff must abide by the minimum intervention principle. The sheriff must also observe this principle where considering varying or extending an ICSO made by a hearing—see commentary on ss.98 and 99 below for further discussion.

Duty to consider including contact direction

C.408.5 [1] **29A.**—(1) A children's hearing must, when making, varying or continuing a compulsory supervision order in relation to a child, consider whether to include in the order a measure of the type mentioned in section 83(2)(g).

(2) A sheriff must, when varying or continuing a compulsory supervision order in relation to a child, consider whether to include in the order a measure of the type mentioned in section 83(2)(g).

NOTE
C.408.6 1. Inserted by the Children's Hearings (Scotland) Act 2011 (Modification of Primary Legislation) Order 2013 (SSI 2013/211) Sch.1 para.20(5) (effective 24 June 2013).

DEFINITIONS
C.408.7 "children's hearing": s.5.
"compulsory supervision order": s.83.

GENERAL NOTE
C.408.8 The obligation imposed on the children's hearing here is to consider a contact direction in terms of s.83(2)(g), i.e. not, necessarily, to make such a direction. The case of *Kennedy v M*, 1995 S.C. 121; 1995 S.L.T. 717, decided under s.44(1) of the Social Work (Scotland) Act 1968, where the decision of a hearing to leave the issue of access to the discretion of the social work department, indicates that the hearing has a wide discretion in the matter.

Subs.(1)
C.408.9 *A measure of the type mentioned in section 83(2)(g)*. Section 83(2)(g) of the Act reads: "a direction regulating contact between the child and a specified person or class of person". Thus, where the children's hearing is considering making, varying or continuing a compulsory supervision order (CSO) the hearing must consider whether to include a contact direction. The children's hearing will have to observe the three overarching principles, the European Convention principle of proportionality, and art. 8 of the European Convention (respect for private and family life). We suggest that the latter should incline the children's hearing to make a contact direction provided doing so does not expose the child to material risk of significant harm.

Subs.(2)
C.408.10 The same obligation is incumbent on the sheriff when considering making, varying or continuing a CSO and the same considerations apply.

Children's hearing: duty to consider appointing safeguarder

C.409 **30.**—(1) A children's hearing must consider whether to appoint a person to safeguard the interests of the child to whom the children's hearing relates (a "safeguarder").

(2) A children's hearing may appoint a safeguarder at any time when the children's hearing is still deciding matters in relation to the child.

(3) A children's hearing must record an appointment made under subsection (2).

(4) If a children's hearing appoints a safeguarder, it must give reasons for its decision.

Children's hearing: duty to consider appointing safeguarder

(5) Subsection (1) does not apply where a safeguarder has already been appointed.

DEFINITIONS
"child": s.199.
"children's hearing": s.5.
"pre-hearing panel": s.79.

C.409.1

GENERAL NOTE
This section requires a children's hearing to consider appointing a safeguarder unless a safeguarder has already been appointed. It does not apply to a pre-hearing panel (PHP); this is dealt with in s.82, which provides that a PHP may appoint a safeguarder for the child to whom the children's hearing relates and also provides that a safeguarder so appointed is to be treated as being appointed by a children's hearing under this section.

C.409.2

"Safeguarders" were introduced into the Scottish children's hearing system by ss.66 and 78 of the (English) Children Act 1975 but the provisions were not brought into force until 1985. The reason cited for a safeguarder to be appointed was to address a conflict that might arise in the proceedings between the child and his or her parent. (For a more detailed account of the growing involvement of safeguarders, see M. Hill, A. Lockyer, P. Morton, S. Batchelor and J. Scott, "The Role of Safeguarders in Scotland" (University of Glasgow: Centre for the Child & Society and Department of Politics, 2002) found at *http://www.gov.scot/resource/doc/46905/0024042.pdf* [Accessed 21 October 2015]). The management and operation of the Safeguarders Panel is under the authority of Scottish Ministers who have contracted with Children 1st to manage the day-to-day organisation. The role of Children 1st is to recruit, train, manage appointments, monitor performance of safeguarders and deal with any complaints.

Where a children's hearing or a sheriff takes a decision to appoint a safeguarder, that information is passed to Children 1st who then will allocate a safeguarder within two days of receiving the information. Allocation is carried out via the "taxi rank" system; a children's hearing or a sheriff cannot name a specific safeguarder.

Since their introduction there has been a general lack of guidance surrounding the criteria for the appointment of a safeguarder by a children's hearing or a sheriff. This gives the children's hearing and the sheriff great flexibility. It is no surprise then that this Act gives little guidance on the matters that should be considered by a children's hearing or a sheriff when arriving at a decision on whether to appoint a safeguarder, other than that in s.30(1) which states merely that a children's hearing "must consider whether to appoint a person to safeguard the interests of the child ..." and s.31(2) which states that a sheriff "must consider whether to appoint a safeguarder for the child". Further, r.56 of the Children's Hearings (Scotland) Act 2011 (Rules of Procedure in Children's Hearings) Rules 2013 (SSI 2013/194) makes no reference to criteria to be considered by a pre-hearing panel or children's hearing in deciding whether to appoint a safeguarder.

There is, however, extensive guidance on the termination of a safeguarder's appointment—see rr.3, 4 and 5 of the Children's Hearings (Scotland) Act 2011 (Safeguarders Panel) Regulations 2012 (SSI 2012/54). The thrust of these rules is to allow the safeguarder's appointment to continue until the completion of the procedural stage concerned including the period of appeal thus laying to rest the issue raised in *Catto v Pearson*, 1990 S.L.T. (Sh. Ct) 77; 1990 S.C.L.R. 267.

Guidance on some aspects of the role of the safeguarder has been addressed to some extent by the Children's Hearings (Scotland) Act 2011 (Safeguarders: Further Provision) Regulations 2012 (SSI 2012/336)—see rr.7, 8 and 9. Rule 7 imposes a duty on a safeguarder, as far as practicable, to take the views of the child and have regard to those views and include the child's views in his or her deliberations. It should be borne in mind, however, that the primary role of the safeguarder remains to "safeguard the *interest* of the child" (see subs.(1) below). It should be noted that a safeguarder might be appointed where a child has difficulty for whatever reason in expressing a view. It will generally be in the interest of the child for his or her views to be given to the children's hearing or the sheriff. The safeguarder must also include in the report to a children's hearing or a sheriff detail of the manner in which the views of the child were obtained. Rule 8 imposes a duty on a safeguarder to inform the child, relevant person or any other person of his or her functions and powers and to state clearly that the role of the safeguarder is to safeguard the interest of the child. Rule 9 imposes a duty on the Reporter to provide the safeguarder with any report prepared by another safeguarder and to provide copies of the reports that have been requested to the safeguarder, the child, relevant persons and the panel members.

For more detailed information about the role, responsibility and monitoring of safeguarders, see the Scottish Government's recent publications (Summer/Autumn 2015) "Practice Standards for Safeguarders" at http://www.children1st.org.uk/media/320615/FINAL-Practice-Standards-for-Safeguarders-JUNE-2015.pdf [Accessed 21 October 2015] and "Performance Support & Monitoring Framework for Safeguarders" a: http://www.children1st.org.uk/media/320611/FINAL-Performance-Support-and-Monitoring-Framework-for-Safeguarders-JULY-2015.pdf [Accessed 21 October 2015].

Subs.(1)

C.409.3 This gives the definition of a "safeguarder" to be used throughout the Act (as referred to in s.202(1)), as being "a person to safeguard the interests of the child to whom the children's hearing relates". No definition of "interests" is given, but the scope of the safeguarder's report will be guided by the remit given by the children's hearing and the independent status of the safeguarder reinforces that the focus will be on what is best for the child. It should be emphasised that, while the safeguarder must, where practicable, take the views of the child and include them in his or her report (see General Note above), the role of the safeguarder is not to advocate on behalf of the child (this is the role of the child's solicitor or the person providing advocacy services), but to make recommendations that are in the child's interests.

Subs.(2)

C.409.4 This subsection states that a decision to appoint a safeguarder by a children's hearing can take place at any time when the children's hearing is still deciding matters in relation to the child. In the event of the hearing, in the course of its discussion, considering that the appointment of a safeguarder is necessary, then the hearing will have to be continued and consideration given to the making of an interim compulsory supervision order or an interim variation of a compulsory supervision order. It would logically follow, strictly speaking, that, after the conclusion of discussions and once each panel member begins his or her formal decision, this cannot include the appointment of a safeguarder.

Subss.(3) and (4)

C.409.5 Once a decision has been taken to appoint a safeguarder, the decision must be recorded along with the reasons for the appointment. Where a safeguarder has not been appointed in a contentious situation it is good practice to state the reasons for not appointing a safeguarder. The "reasons" for the appointment of a safeguarder are, it is submitted, not the same as the "remit" of the safeguarder, although both may be based on the same issues. That said, there appears to be a blurring of these words so that the reasons that form the basis for the appointment of a safeguarder then become the remit of the safeguarder. At no place in the Act or the Children's Hearings (Scotland) Act 2011 (Rules of Procedure in Children's Hearings) Rules 2013 is there any mention of the hearing giving specific instructions to the safeguarder other than that stated at s.33(1)(a)—that the safeguarder must "prepare a report setting out anything that, in the opinion of the safeguarder, is relevant to the consideration of the matter before the children's hearing". It should be clearly understood that the independence of the safeguarder cannot be restricted to any specific agenda.

Sheriff: duty to consider appointing safeguarder

C.410 31.—(1) This section applies where—
   (a) proceedings are being taken before the sheriff under Part 10 or 15 in relation to a child, and
   (b) a safeguarder has not been appointed for the child in relation to proceedings under those Parts.
(2) The sheriff must consider whether to appoint a safeguarder for the child.
(3) The sheriff may appoint a safeguarder for the child.
[1] (4) A safeguarder appointed under this section is to be treated for the purposes of this Act (other than this section and section 33) as having been appointed by a children's hearing by virtue of section 30.
(5) An appointment under subsection (3) must be recorded.
(6) If the sheriff appoints a safeguarder, the sheriff must give reasons for the decision.

The Safeguarders Panel

NOTE

1. As amended by the Children's Hearings (Scotland) Act 2011 (Modification of Primary Legislation) Order 2013 (SSI 2013/211) Sch.1 para.20(6) (effective 24 June 2013).

C.410.1

DEFINITIONS
"child": s.199.
"safeguarder": s.202.

C.410.2

GENERAL NOTE

As noted in the General Note to s.30 in relation to the appointment of a safeguarder by a children's hearing, the sheriff, when appointing a safeguarder, does not name an individual but the matter is referred to Children 1st to appoint an individual. It should be noted that a sheriff's power to appoint a named curator *ad litem* is still in force.

The appointment of a safeguarder, by a children's hearing or by a sheriff, was contained in s.41 of the Children (Scotland) Act 1995. This decision has now been separated into two sections. This helps to clarify the circumstances under which a safeguarder may be appointed. Section 31 applies only where the matter is before the sheriff under Pt 10 proceedings (before the sheriff) or Pt 15 proceedings (appeals). A safeguarder cannot be appointed when the sheriff is making either a child assessment order (s.35) or a child protection order (s.37). However, where an application to the sheriff to vary or terminate a child protection order under s.48(1) has been made it would seem to be open to the sheriff to appoint a safeguarder or curator *ad litem*. Where s.31 applies, the sheriff must consider the appointment of a safeguarder to protect the interests of the child (see annotation to s.30 above). The sheriff must record his or her decision and give reasons for it. Again, there is no guidance on the criteria to be considered when deciding to appoint a safeguarder other than where it is considered necessary to safeguard the interests of the child. See General Note to s.30 (above) for a fuller discussion on this.

C.410.3

Subs.(1)

Where the decision taken by that sheriff is such that the case will not be returned to the hearing there will be no point in appointing a safeguarder.

C.410.4

PART 4

SAFEGUARDERS

The Safeguarders Panel

32.—(1) The Scottish Ministers must establish and maintain a panel of persons (to be known as the Safeguarders Panel) from which any appointment under this Act of a safeguarder is to be made.

(2) The Scottish Ministers may by regulations make provision for or in connection with—
  (a) the recruitment and selection of persons who may be appointed as members of the Safeguarders Panel,
  (b) the appointment and removal of members of the Safeguarders Panel,
  (c) qualifications to be held by members of the Safeguarders Panel,
  (d) the training of members and potential members of the Safeguarders Panel,
  (e) the payment of expenses, fees and allowances by the Scottish Ministers to members and potential members of the Safeguarders Panel,
  (f) the operation and management of the Safeguarders Panel.

(3) For the purpose of complying with the requirements imposed by subsection (1) and regulations under subsection (2), the Scottish Ministers may enter into arrangements (contractual or otherwise) with any person other than CHS or SCRA.

C.411

DEFINITIONS
"CHS": s.2.
"SCRA": s.15.
"safeguarder": s.202(1).

C.411.1

SUBORDINATE LEGISLATION UNDER THIS SECTION
Children's Hearings (Scotland) Act 2011 (Safeguarders Panel) Regulations 2012 (SSI 2012/54).
Children's Hearings (Scotland) Act 2011 (Safeguarders Panel) Amendment Regulations 2016 (SSI 2016/61).

GENERAL NOTE

C.411.2　See the General Note to ss.30 and 31 for a discussion of the legislative history and general justification of safeguarders.

This Part of the Act provides for the mode of appointment, and as to the powers and functions of the safeguarder. The Act repeals inter alia s.41 of the Children (Scotland) Act 1995, which made provision for safeguarders. The Act also repeals s.42(2)(e)–(g) of the 1995 Act by virtue of which the Panel of Persons to Safeguard the Interests of Children (Scotland) Regulations 2001 (SSI 2001/476) were enacted. The main primary and subordinate legislation as to safeguarders is contained respectively in: ss.30 and 31, above; this Part of the Act; and the new Regulations, specified above. Specific provisions in the Act in relation to safeguarders are contained in:

- s.78(f) (right of safeguarder to attend hearings);
- s.79(2)(c)(ii) (right of Reporter if requested by, inter alia, a safeguarder) to refer to a pre-hearing panel a specified matter (excusal of child/relevant person from attending a hearing; whether a secure accommodation authorisation is likely);
- s.82(1) (power of pre-hearing panel to appoint a safeguarder);
- s.154(2)(c) (right of safeguarder to appeal to the sheriff);
- s.155(7) (prescribing when a safeguarder requires to give a report to the sheriff in an appeal);
- s.163(3)(c) (right of a safeguarder to appeal to the Sheriff Principal (now the Sheriff Appeal Court—discussed below at C.542.2) or Court of Session);
- s.175(2)(d) (right of safeguarder to apply to sheriff for order regarding the taking of evidence); and
- s.185(2)(c) (empowering Court of Session to make rules in relation to the functions and rights of safeguarders appointed by the sheriff).

While the status and function of the safeguarder are, under the new Act and Regulations, recognisable as before, the new Act and Regulations introduce some new provisions and make some considerable clarifications. The Children's Hearings (Scotland) Act 2011 (Safeguarders Panel) Regulations 2012 (SSI 2012/54) make provisions for the recruitment of members of the Safeguarders Panel, including the prescription of qualification and training requirements. These provisions are self-explanatory and, except for those dealing with "Tenure of appointment and removal of members" (reg.7) and "Operation and Management of Safeguarders Panel" (reg.11) are merely referred to below. The provisions in relation to the duration and termination of the appointment of a safeguarder in relation to a particular child are enacted in the Children's Hearings (Scotland) Act 2011 (Safeguarders Further Provisions Regulations) 2012 (SSI 2012/336), which are discussed above in the General Note to ss.30 and 31.

Subs.(2)

C.411.3　The Children's Hearings (Scotland) Act 2011 (Safeguarders Panel) Regulations 2012 (SSI 2012/54) (the "2011 Regulations") include: provisions requiring Scottish Ministers to advertise for safeguarders, excluding persons connected with the system, such as members of CHS and SCRA, from eligibility for appointment as safeguarders; provisions excluding from eligibility for appointment as safeguarders any person barred from working with children under the Vulnerable Groups (Scotland) Act 2007; and provisions relating to the training and monitoring of safeguarders (with mention, amongst other methods of monitoring, of seeking the views of the child concerned and others as to the performance of the safeguarder).

Regulation 7 of the 2011 Regulations, as amended by the Children's Hearings (Scotland) Act 2011 (Safeguarders Panel) Amendment Regulations 2016 (SSI 2016/61) provides for tenure of office for the safeguarder of three years, with the obligation to re-appoint a safeguarder who so wishes for at least one and at most three years but only if the Scottish Ministers are satisfied that the person is fit to be a members of the Safeguarders Panel, that the Scottish Ministers may remove a member from the Panel if they consider he or she is not fit to be a member and that, in assessing whether he or she is fit, have regard to (a) the person's conduct, (b) whether the person concerned has failed to comply with any requirement in his or her letter of appointment or re-appointment, (c) and whether the person has been able and willing to operate in accordance with "Practice Standards", i.e. as defined in reg.2 of the amended Regulations, the *Practice Standards for Safeguarders* published by the Scottish Government in July 2015 (available at:

Functions of safeguarder

http://www.children1st.org.uk/media/320615/FINAL-Practice-Standards-for-Safeguarders-JUNE-2015.pdf [Accessed 21 October 2015]) There is no provision governing the mode of removing, or not re-appointing, a safeguarder. This contrasts with the position of the safeguarder under reg.7(3) of the Panel of Persons to Safeguard the Interests of Children (Scotland) Regulations 2001 (SSI 2001/476), which requires the agreement of the Children's Panel and the Sheriff Principal before removal can take place and with the position of a panel member under the present legislation, which, under Sch.2(6) of the Act, requires the consent of the Lord President for removal. The independence of the safeguarder is an important consideration and the fearless exercise of such a right is an important civil right under art.6 of the European Convention. Accordingly where the removal or non-re-appointment of a safeguarder is in contemplation, Scottish Ministers will be obliged to ensure that the decision is taken by "an independent and impartial tribunal established by law". In order for the "established by law" criterion to be achieved it may be that some further amendment of the Regulations will be necessary.

Regulation 11(2) of Children's Hearings (Scotland) Act 2011 (Safeguarders Panel) Regulations 2012 (SSI 2012/54) imposes on Scottish Ministers a duty to "ensure" that at all times the membership of the Safeguarders Panel is adequate and reg.11(3) requires Scottish Ministers to "endeavour to secure" that the Safeguarders Panel includes persons from all local authority areas. In practice it will generally be desirable for a safeguarder to be based within the local authority area where the child mainly resides and that, therefore, appropriate safeguarders should be available to effect this: these provisions reflect this but recognise that this may not always be practicable.

Functions of safeguarder

33.—(1) A safeguarder appointed in relation to a child by virtue of section 30 must—

[1] (a) except where subsection (2) or (3) applies, on being so appointed, prepare a report setting out anything that, in the opinion of the safeguarder, is relevant to the consideration of the matter before the children's hearing,
 (b) so far as reasonably practicable, attend the children's hearing, and
 (c) prepare any report that the safeguarder is required to prepare by a children's hearing.

(2) This subsection applies where the children's hearing directs the Principal Reporter under section 93(2)(a) or 94(2)(a) to make an application to the sheriff.

[2] (3) This subsection applies where the children's hearing was arranged under section 45, 46, 50, 96, 126 or 158.

NOTES
1. As amended by the Children and Young People (Scotland) Act 2014 (asp 8) Pt 16 s.82 (effective 26 January 2015).
2. Inserted by the Children and Young People (Scotland) Act 2014 (asp 8) Pt 16 s.82 (effective 26 January 2015).

DEFINITIONS
"CHS": s.2.
"children's hearing": s. 5.
"Principal Reporter: s.14, Sch.3 paras 8–10.
"safeguarder": s.202(1).

GENERAL NOTE
See General Note above.

Subs.(1)(a) and (c)
A report ... any report. It is clearly implied that these should be written reports: under r.56(5) of the Children's Hearings (Scotland) Act 2011 (Rules of Procedure in Children's Hearings) Rules 2013 (SSI 2013/194) it is provided that where a report is required under subs.(1)(a) then, within 35 days of being appointed, the safeguarder must prepare and give a report or interim report to the Reporter and that where an interim report is given there should be an explanation of the reasons for this, a note of the nature of the further investigations required and an estimation of the further time needed. As mentioned above in the note to s.30(3) and (4) the

independence of the safeguarder cannot be restricted to any specific agenda. Sections 93(2)(a) and 94(2)(a) deal with applications to the sheriff for proof and provide that in such proceedings it may not be necessary or practicable for a written report to be prepared—this will be a matter for the sheriff to decide. See below in discussion of these sections.

Safeguarders: regulations

C.413   **34.**—(1) The Scottish Ministers may by regulations make further provision about safeguarders.

(2) Regulations under this section may in particular make provision for or in connection with—
   (a) imposing additional requirements on safeguarders,
   (b) conferring additional powers (including rights of appeal) on safeguarders,
   (c) the termination of safeguarders' appointments.

DEFINITIONS

C.413.1   "safeguarder": s.202(1).

GENERAL NOTE

Subs.(2)(a) and (b)

C.413.2   Readers should be aware that there appears to be some element of duplication in that the Children's Hearings (Scotland) Act 2011 (Rules of Procedure in Children's Hearings) Rules 2013 (SSI 2013/194) (made "in exercise of the powers conferred by ss.177 and 195 of the Children's Hearings (Scotland) Act 2011 and all other powers enabling them [Scottish Ministers] to do so") contain many provisions as to safeguarders aimed at securing the effective participation of the safeguarder in children's hearings, pre-hearing panels and the proceedings generally—see the above mentioned Rules rr.26, 29–47, 48–49 (on the basis that, although the term "safeguarder" does not occur in these two regulations, it is clear from r.47(3) that a safeguarder who is able to attend at a pre-hearing panel may be present at and participate in a pre-hearing panel), see also 50(5), 52(2)(e), 53, 56, 57, 60, 66, 70, 78, 85 and 86 (on the basis that "any person" in r.85(1) must include a safeguarder), 87–88 and 91–96.

Subs.(2)(c)

C.413.3   The intricate provisions prescribing for the duration and termination of the office of safeguarder in the Children's Hearings (Scotland) Act 2011 (Safeguarders: Further Provision) Regulations 2012 (SSI 2012/336) are discussed in the General Note to ss.30–31 above, under the heading "*Duration and termination of office of safeguarder.*"

The 2012 Regulations also cover the following: reports by safeguarders in appeal proceedings under s.154 (reg.6); views of the child (reg.7); role of the safeguarder (reg.8); and access to reports of safeguarders (reg.9). It is particularly important for the safeguarder to ascertain where practicable the views of the child and include in the report the means by which the child's views were obtained.

PART 5

CHILD ASSESSMENT AND CHILD PROTECTION ORDERS

Child assessment orders

Child assessment orders

C.414   **35.**—(1) A local authority may apply to the sheriff for a child assessment order in respect of a child.

(2) A child assessment order is an order authorising an officer of a local authority or a person authorised by that officer to carry out (subject to section 186) an assessment of—
   (a) the child's health or development, or
   (b) the way in which the child has been or is being treated or neglected.
(3) An order may—

Child assessment orders

(a) require any person in a position to do so to produce the child to the officer,
(b) for the purpose of carrying out the assessment, authorise the taking of the child to any place and the keeping of the child at that place or any other place for a period specified in the order,
(c) where it contains an authorisation of the type mentioned in paragraph (b), include directions about contact between the child and any other person.

(4) A child assessment order must specify the period during which it has effect.

(5) That period must—
(a) begin no later than 24 hours after the order is granted, and
(b) not exceed 3 days.

DEFINITION
"child": s.199.
"local authority": Local Government etc. (Scotland) Act 1994 s.2.

C.414.1

GENERAL NOTE
One of the difficulties facing those engaged in child protection is that they may well have suspicions of abuse or neglect but lack evidence. This section, addressing this issue, substantially replicates s.55 of the Children (Scotland) Act 1995, which followed the model of the (English) Children Act 1989, in providing an order by which the court could procure an assessment of the child's condition even in the absence of consent by parent or guardian. For comment on the English legislation see R. Lavery, *The Child Assessment Order: A Reassessment* (1996) 8 Ch. Fam. L.Q. 41. In practice the order was not much used in England and the Scottish experience has been similar: whilst the use of the child protection order (CPO) is commonplace, the child assessment order (CAO) is rarely used. When considering whether to make a CAO the sheriff must have regard to the minimum intervention principle—see s.29(1)(a)—and art.8 of the European Convention on Human Rights. There is no provision (see s.163(1)) wherein the appeals available against decisions of the sheriff are listed for appeal from a decision of a sheriff making or refusing a child assessment order.

C.414.2

Subs.(1)
Only a local authority may apply for CAO. This contrasts with the position in relation to a CPO, which may be applied for by "a person" (see s.37(1) below). Application may be made by any department of a local authority, e.g. an education department or a housing department, but will generally be made by a social work services department.

C.414.3

Subs.(2)(a)
Medical examination of a child can be carried out only with the consent of the child where the child has the capacity to provide that consent. Capacity to consent is governed by s.2(4) of the Age of Legal Capacity (Scotland) Act 1991, which is specifically referred to in s.186 of the 2011 Act which provides that a CAO may only be carried out, in the case of a child having capacity under s.2(4) of the 1991 Act, where the child consents to this. It follows that those tasked with examination, including intimate medical examination of a child, must be scrupulous about ensuring, where the child is old and mature enough to give or withhold consent, that the appropriate consent has been given and continues to be given. It is to be noted that there is no mechanical age test.

C.414.4

Subss.(3), (4) and (5)
As mentioned above, the minimum intervention principle and art. 8 of the European Convention apply. These will require the sheriff, before granting an authorisation to take the child away from where he or she is staying, to be satisfied: that it is necessary to do so and, if so satisfied, to select as the time for removal a time, within the prescribed period of 24 hours, which is least disruptive of the child's family life; to restrict the duration of the CAO to the minimum necessary, up to three calendar days; and to allow reasonable contact with, for example, parents. The imposition of the 24 hours limitation will require the sheriff clerk to ensure that the time as well as the date of granting is noted on the face of the order. As to the possibility of a further CAO being made, it seems obvious that in the event of an application for a CAO having been refused on its merits then, on a change of circumstances, a fresh application would be competent. But could a fresh CAO on the same grounds be sought, where the original CAO had for some reason not been timeously implemented? It is thought that the scheme of the

C.414.5

Act, giving paramountcy to the promoting of the interests of the child, would suggest that this would be competent, but, in the event of a repeated application on the same grounds the sheriff will require to be addressed on why the original CAO was not timeously implemented. In the event of this being abused, the remedy, there being no provision for appeal, would be an application to the *nobile officium* of the Court of Session.

If the sheriff has concerns about the safety of the child in the place where he or she has been staying the sheriff should consider exercising the powers conferred by s.36(3) to make a CPO—see discussion of s.36 below.

Note that, under s.41, the sheriff must consider whether to include a contact direction in the CPO. The form of the CAO (Form 46 of the Act of Sederunt (Child Care and Maintenance Rules) 1997 (SI 1997/291) as amended by Act of Sederunt (Children's Hearings (Scotland) Act 2011) (Miscellaneous Amendments) 2013 (SSI 2013/172)) includes warrant to officers of law to take all lawful methods of execution, including inter alia searching for and apprehending the child and "so far as necessary, by breaking open shut and lockfast places".

Consideration by sheriff

C.415   **36.**—(1) This section applies where an application for a child assessment order in respect of a child is made by a local authority.
    (2) The sheriff may make the order if the sheriff is satisfied that—
      (a) the local authority has reasonable cause to suspect—
        (i) that the child has been or is being treated in such a way that the child is suffering or is likely to suffer significant harm, or
        (ii) that the child has been or is being neglected and as a result of the neglect the child is suffering or is likely to suffer significant harm,
      (b) an assessment of the kind mentioned in section 35(2) is necessary in order to establish whether there is reasonable cause to believe that the child has been or is being so treated or neglected, and
      (c) it is unlikely that the assessment could be carried out, or carried out satisfactorily, unless the order was made.
    (3) The sheriff may, instead of making a child assessment order, make a child protection order if the sheriff considers the conditions in section 38(2) are satisfied.

DEFINITIONS
C.415.1   "child": s.199.
        "child protection order": s.37.

GENERAL NOTE
C.415.2   This section sets out the factors which the sheriff must have regard to when considering making a child assessment order (CAO). As mentioned above in the General Note to s.35, there is no provision, either here or in s.163(1), wherein the appeals available against decisions of the sheriff are listed, for appeal from a decision of a sheriff making or refusing a CAO. Since there is no appeal against the making of a Child Protection Order (CPO) (see s.163(1)) it is perhaps unsurprising that there is no appeal against the making of a CAO, which is less intrusive than a CPO. However, the consideration that there is no right of appeal will, particularly where authorisation under s.35(3)(b) is sought, incline the sheriff to subject the application to particularly searching scrutiny. The proceedings before the sheriff are conducted in private: see Act of Sederunt (Child Care and Maintenance Rules) 1997 (SI 1997/291) as amended by Act of Sederunt (Children's Hearings (Scotland) Act 2011) (Miscellaneous Amendments) 2013 (SSI 2013/172), r.13.1 (3).

Subs.(2)
C.415.3   The sheriff is entitled to grant a CAO if satisfied that the four listed conditions are made out, i.e. the sheriff must be satisfied that:
- The local authority has reasonable cause to *suspect* [emphasis, here and elsewhere herein, supplied] that the child is as described in para.(a)(i) and consequently is or is likely to suffer significant harm; *or*
- The local authority has reasonable cause to suspect that the child is being or has been neglected with the result mentioned in para.(a)(ii) and consequently is or is likely to suffer significant harm; *and*

Consideration by sheriff

- An assessment as defined in s.35 is necessary to establish if this cause for suspicion amounts to a reasonable cause to *believe* these matters; *and*
- It is unlikely that a satisfactory assessment will be carried through unless a CAO is made.

This replicates the parallel provisions of the 1995 Act.

The sheriff may make. Even although the sheriff is satisfied on the foregoing matters the question is still a matter for his or her judgment. The sheriff's decision is governed by the overarching principles and by the European Convention principle of proportionality, which was discussed in *KA v Finland* [2003] 1 F.L.R. 696; [2003] 1 F.C.R. 201; [2003] Fam. Law 230 at [103]–[104] wherein the court stated:

"Any order relating to the public care of a child should, firstly, be capable of convincing an objective observer that the measure is based on a careful and unprejudiced assessment of all the evidence on file, with distinct reasons for the care measures being stated explicitly."

The sheriff is to decide on whether "reasonable cause to suspect" exists. This is a less demanding test than "reasonable grounds to believe" which is the test for a CPO, where a CPO is sought by a local authority or other person under s.39(2)(a), discussed below. Even information from an unnamed source, for example in relation to failure of a very young child to thrive, could, unless plainly spurious, be enough.

Significant harm. See discussion in commentary on s.37.

Subs.(3)

The sheriff may ... make. The parallel provision (s.55(2)) of the Children (Scotland) Act 1995 says "shall make", thereby suggesting the possibility, probably ill-founded, that the sheriff had no occasion to exercise his or her judgment here. The new wording clarifies the position. In the exercise of his or her judgment the sheriff must observe the paramountcy of welfare of the child principle (s.25(2)), the minimum intervention principle (s.29(1)(a) and (2)) and the European Convention principle of proportionality. In relation to the views of the child principle, s.27(1) applies this principle where "the sheriff is coming to a decision about a matter relating to a child", and making a decision as to a CAO is obviously a "decision about a matter relating to a child": accordingly any views expressed by the child must be taken into account here. Moreover, as noted above, s.27(2) provides specifically that the views of the child principle is not to apply where the granting of a child protection order is being considered, thus fortifying the conclusion that the views of the child principle does apply where a child assessment order is being considered.

C.415.4

Child protection orders

PRELIMINARY NOTE

The enactment of the child protection order (CPO) was precipitated by concerns as to the perceived inflexibility of the "place of safety" procedures under s.37(2) of the Social Work (Scotland) Act 1968, including the concerns expressed in Lord Clyde's *Report of the Inquiry into the Removal of Children from Orkney* (HMSO, 1992). As a result of these, and other, criticisms (see White Paper, *Scotland's Children: Proposals for Child Care Policy and Law* (Edinburgh: HMSO, 1993), Cm.2286, paras 5.8 to 5.18) the whole procedure for interim protection of the child was radically re-modelled, with the creation of the CPO which was designed:

(I) to last for the shortest period of time necessary to secure the safety and wellbeing of the child;

(II) to include a speedy review mechanism;

(III) to be more flexible than the old place of safety order; and

(IV) to have the conditions for its granting simplified and more clearly directed towards the immediate need to protect the child from imminent harm.

Moreover CPOs, unlike the former Place of Safety Orders, which were generally granted by Justices of the Peace, were to be granted by a sheriff except where this was impracticable. It is one of the paradoxes of this development that the Place of Safety Orders in the Orkney case were granted by Sheriff A.A. MacDonald, then the longest serving sheriff in Scotland. The main provisions as to CPOs were enacted in ss.57 to 62 of the Children (Scotland) Act 1995 and the regulations made thereunder. The 2011 Act repeals these sections and regulations. Sections 37 to 59 replace these sections and effect some relatively minor changes, which will be noted, however the broad picture remains the same. The rules for CPOs are contained in the Act of Sederunt (Care and Maintenance) Rules 1997 (SI 1997/291) rr.3.39 to 3.43 as amended by Act of Sederunt (Children's Hearings (Scotland) Act 2011) (Miscellaneous Amendments) 2013 (SSI 2013/172).

C.415.5

Child protection orders

37.—(1) A person may apply to the sheriff for a child protection order in respect of a child.

(2) A child protection order is an order doing one or more of the following—
  (a) requiring any person in a position to do so to produce the child to a specified person,
  (b) authorising the removal of the child by the specified person to a place of safety and the keeping of the child in that place,
  (c) authorising the prevention of the removal of the child from any place where the child is staying (whether or not the child is resident there),
  (d) authorising the carrying out (subject to section 186) of an assessment of—
    (i) the child's health or development, or
    (ii) the way in which the child has been or is being treated or neglected.

(3) A child protection order may also include any other authorisation or requirement necessary to safeguard or promote the welfare of the child.

(4) A child protection order may include an authorisation of the type mentioned in paragraph (d) of subsection (2) only if it also includes an authorisation of a type mentioned in paragraph (b) or (c) of that subsection.

(5) An application for a child protection order must—
  (a) identify the applicant,
  (b) in so far as is practicable, identify the child in respect of whom the order is sought,
  (c) state the grounds on which the application is made, and
  (d) be accompanied by supporting evidence, whether documentary or otherwise, sufficient to enable the sheriff to determine the application.

(6) In subsection (2), "specified" means specified in the order.

Definition

"child": s.199.
"place of safety": ss.202(1) and 189.

General Note

See Preliminary Note, above. The proceedings before the sheriff are conducted in private: see Act of Sederunt (Child Care and Maintenance Rules) 1997 (SI 1997/291) as amended by Act of Sederunt (Children's Hearings (Scotland) Act 2011) (Miscellaneous Amendments) 2013 (SSI 2013/172), r. 13.1 (3) (the "1997 Rules"). This section prescribes the essential features of a child protection order (CPO) and the content of an application therefor. Sections 38 and 39 make provision for the (different) matters which the sheriff must apply his or her mind to when considering, on the one hand, an application for a CPO by a local authority and, on the other hand, an application for such an order by a local authority or an "other person". Sections 40 to 42 deal with directions which can be attached to a CPO. Section 43 makes provision as to notification and s.44 enacts the obligations which are incurred by the local authority once a CPO has been granted. Sections 45 to 47 deal with the "second working day" hearings, following the implementation/making of a CPO. Sections 48 to 51 deal with the role of the sheriff in relation to dealing with applications to vary or terminate a CPO. Sections 52 to 54 prescribe various ways whereby CPOs may be terminated. Sections 55 and 56 deal with situations where it is not practicable to go to the sheriff for a CPO and provide emergency powers to Justices of the Peace and to the police. Section 57 empowers Scottish Ministers to make regulations in relation to ss.55 and 56. Section 58 makes provisions for how orders are to be implemented and s.59 creates offences for obstruction of the implementation of orders.

There are strict time limits to be adhered to throughout. The main features may be summarised as follows:

1. Once a CPO has been made the person given the task of implementing the order must attempt to implement it; if this person does not do so within 24 hours, then the order ceases to have effect (s.52(2)).

2. Once a CPO has been made (or, where removal of the child is ordered, implemented) the Reporter must, unless an appeal to the sheriff has been lodged and intimated under s.48,

Child protection orders

arrange a hearing to review the order, with power to terminate or continue it (s.47(1)). Where the CPO has required the removal of the child this hearing must take place on the second working day (hence "second working day hearing") after the removal has been effected (s.45(3)); where the order has authorised the prevention of removal of the child, then the "second working day hearing" must take place on the second working day after the day on which the child protection order was made (s.46(3)). Where a second working day hearing continues the CPO then (unless there is an appeal to the sheriff resulting in termination (see 3, below)) or a decision by the Reporter not to proceed (see 5, below) the case proceeds, with the CPO enduring until the "eighth working day hearing" (see 4, below).

3. In certain circumstances the making of a CPO may be challenged before the sheriff. Such a challenge takes the form of an application which may be lodged either before the beginning of a hearing arranged under s.45 or s.46, or, in the event of such a hearing having continued the CPO, within two working days after the making of the continuation (s.48(3)). The sheriff may confirm, vary or terminate the CPO. The sheriff must decide the matter within three working days of the application's being lodged. The CPO will cease to have effect if the sheriff terminates it or if the sheriff does not decide the matter within the prescribed three working days. If the sheriff confirms the CPO then (unless the Reporter terminates the order (see 5, below)) the case proceeds and the Reporter must arrange an eighth lawful day hearing (see 4, below).

4. Where the Reporter receives notice under s.43 that a CPO has been made he or she must consider:
   (i) whether the child might be in need of protection, guidance, treatment or control;
   (ii) whether a ground for referral of the child exists; *and* if so,
   (iii) whether a CPO is necessary.

If the answer to all three of these questions is "yes" the Reporter must fix a hearing (an "eighth working day hearing") within eight working days of (in the case of an order involving removal of the child) the date of the removal (s.54(1)(c)) or (in the case of an order not involving such removal) the date of the CPO (s.54(1)(d)). In this event the CPO expires at the beginning of the eighth working day hearing (s.54(1)(a)), and the child's case is now the direct responsibility of that hearing.

5. Except where a second working day hearing or proceedings before the sheriff for variation or termination have commenced the Reporter may terminate or vary the CPO (s.53).

Whatever happens, a CPO must come to an end at the latest on the eighth working day after it was made, or, in the case where removal of the child has been ordered, implemented. Before then the need for the order will have been reviewed at least once and conceivably twice (i.e. by the sheriff and/or a second working day hearing). It is perhaps because of these ample possibilities for review that there is no appeal from the granting of a CPO (s.163(1)). Interestingly, in the event of a CPO being refused, there is no appeal.

In deciding whether or not to grant a CPO the sheriff must observe the paramountcy of welfare principle (s.25) and the minimum intervention principle (s.29(1)(b)). The consulting the child principle does not apply (s.27(2)), no doubt because of the obvious impracticability of giving the child the opportunity to express a view in an emergency situation. However, those preparing an application for a CPO should, in the case of a sufficiently mature child, and where practicable, ascertain the child's view, since the consulting the child principle must be observed by a second working day hearing and by the sheriff in an application to vary or terminate. Also a sheriff, when considering an application for a CPO, although not bound by the consulting the child principle, may ask about the child's views, and it is as well to be prepared.

Section 76(8), as amended, of the Children (Scotland) Act 1995 provides that the sheriff, when considering an application for an exclusion order under s.76(1) of that Act, may in appropriate circumstances make a CPO under this present Act. The rules for this are 3.31 to 3.33 of the 1997 Rules.

Competency or otherwise of lodging a caveat against the lodging of a CPO

In *C Petitioner*, 2002 Fam. L.R. 42 Lord McCluskey held, in the circumstances of that case, that the lodging of a caveat against the lodging of a CSO was competent. In *K and F Appellants*, 2002 S.L.T. (Sh. Ct) 38; 2002 Fam.L. R. 42, Sheriff A.M. Bell, after close and comprehensive discussion, differed from Lord McCluskey. The issue was considered but not decided by Lord Brailsford in *J and H v Lord Advocate, E v Lord Advocate*, 2013 S.L.T. 27.

Subs.(1)

A CPO may be applied for by any person, but applications other than by a local authority are rare. Where an application is made by a person other than a local authority the sheriff has to be satisfied that there are reasonable grounds to *believe* (and not merely to suspect) that the child is at risk—see discussion below of s.39(2). The Forms of Application are: Form 47 (Application

C.416.3

Children's Hearings (Scotland) Act 2011

by local authority) and Form 48 (Application by a person other than a local authority) of the Act of Sederunt (Care and Maintenance) Rules 1997 (SI 1997/291), as amended.

Subs.(2)(b)

C.416.4 By the *specified person*. The use of the phrase "*the* [our emphasis] specified person" in this paragraph implies that the person to whom the child is to be delivered will be the same person as is responsible for removing the child and keeping her or him in a place of safety.

Subs.(2)(c)

C.416.5 *Removal of the child from any place*. Professor Norrie (in *Children's Hearings in Scotland*, 3rd edn (Edinburgh: W. Green, 2013), para.15–11) suggests that, since the purpose of the legislation is to protect children who need protection, "removal" here must be interpreted as including the situation where the child may seek to remove himself or herself from a place of safety. We agree with this. The place from which the child is not to be removed is expressly defined as being not necessarily the place where the child resides.

Subss.(2)(d), (3) and (4)

C.416.6 These provisions have some affinity with some of the provisions of s.58(4) and (5) of the Children (Scotland) Act 1995, which dealt with parental responsibilities and rights directions which may be sought as part of a CPO under that Act. The new substantive provisions as to parental responsibilities and rights directions are contained in s.42(2) of this Act and are discussed below in the commentary on that section.

Section 58(4) and (5) of the 1995 Act allowed the sheriff to secure that medical examination and/or treatment of a child subject to a CPO took place by in effect granting to the local authority the responsibility and right to do so, which originally vested in the parent by ss.1(1) and 2(1) of that Act, and then directing how that responsibility and right was to be exercised. On the face of it, s.37(2)(d), (3) and (4) permit, in the case of a CPO which requires a child to be removed to a place of safety or retained in a place, an explicit direction (under s.37(2)(d)) of a medical or other examination of the child in order to reveal his/her present condition and/or evidence of former mistreatment. Moreover s.37(3) permits "any other authorisation or requirement to safeguard or promote the welfare of the child". An example of an authorisation under this subsection would be an authorisation to perform a surgical intervention, which if not carried out immediately would result in permanent serious damage such as the manipulation under anaesthetic of a displaced bone—as mentioned above, the child with capacity would require to consent to this (see s.186). It would not, it is submitted, extend to the authorisation of a procedure such as a cochlear implant to the ear which, although in a particular case necessary for the future welfare of the child, and thus a possible requirement within a compulsory supervision order under s.83(2)(f)(ii), is not a matter of urgency. The implementation of a CPO, like that of a CAO, is governed by the provisions of s.58 of the Act to the effect that the steps taken must be believed to be necessary to safeguard or promote the welfare of the child. For the implications of this provision see below in the commentary on s.58. Of course the making or not of any authorisation or requirement under subs.(3) will be subject to the paramountcy of welfare of the child principle, the minimum intervention principle and the European Convention principle of proportionality. When making a CPO the sheriff must consider whether to include a contact direction—see below in discussion of s.41(2).

The form of the CPO (Form 49 of the 1997 Rules) includes warrant to officers of law to take all lawful methods of execution including, inter alia, searching for and apprehending the child and "so far as necessary, by breaking open shut and lockfast places".

Subs.(5)(d)

C.416.7 *Documentary or otherwise*. In practice the evidence will generally be in the form of reports. Those presenting the application to the sheriff will usually bring relevant social work records and be ready to supply the sheriff with further information: e.g. the sheriff may wish to know, where the removal of siblings to a place is being requested, that the place proposed is such that the siblings are able to be kept together.

Consideration of application by sheriff

Consideration by sheriff: application by local authority only

C.417 **38.**—(1) This section applies where an application for a child protection order in respect of a child is made by a local authority.

(2) The sheriff may make the order if the sheriff is satisfied that—

Consideration by sheriff: application by local authority only

    (a) the local authority has reasonable grounds to suspect that—
        (i) the child has been or is being treated in such a way that the child is suffering or is likely to suffer significant harm,
        (ii) the child has been or is being neglected and as a result of the neglect the child is suffering or is likely to suffer significant harm, or
        (iii) the child will be treated or neglected in such a way that is likely to cause significant harm to the child,
    (b) the local authority is making enquiries to allow it to decide whether to take action to safeguard the welfare of the child, or is causing those enquiries to be made,
    (c) those enquiries are being frustrated by access to the child being unreasonably denied, and
    (d) the local authority has reasonable cause to believe that access is required as a matter of urgency.

DEFINITIONS
"child": s.199.   C.417.1
"local authority": Local Government etc. (Scotland) Act 1994 s.2.

GENERAL NOTE
This section sets out the factors which must exist before the sheriff will be entitled to make a child protection order (CPO) when applied for by a local authority. As noted above in the General Note to s.37 and commentary on s.37(1), different considerations apply as between an application for a CPO by a local authority and an application by another person. The main distinction is that where a local authority makes an application it only has to have a reasonable suspicion that the child is at risk, whereas any other person must have reasonable grounds for believing this. In practice CPOs are generally applied for by a local authority.   C.417.2

Subs.(2)
The sheriff may make the order. By using the word "may" the Act provides that even where all the circumstances listed in paras (a) to (d) apply the sheriff requires to exercise his or her judgment. In doing so the sheriff will have to observe the paramountcy of the welfare of the child principle and the minimum intervention principle (see s.25 and s.29(1)(b)), but not the views of the child principle (see s.27(2)). The sheriff also, here as elsewhere, must observe the principle of proportionality under the European Convention. These principles allow for the possible situation wherein it may appear to the sheriff that the making of the order will more likely than not do more harm (perhaps psychological) to the child than good.   C.417.3

Subs.(2)(a)
A local authority may make application on the basis of mere suspicion of the existence of the factors listed in (i) to (iii). This is a lower standard than the "reasonable grounds to believe" standard, which applies where the application is made by an "other person" and this presumably reflects an acceptance that a local authority, with its wide sources of information and general responsibilities for the well-being of its citizens, should be allowed to act on this less exacting standard. It will, of course, be for the local authority to satisfy the sheriff that its suspicion is based on reasonable grounds.   C.417.4
Significant harm. This means harm which is not trivial. Minor or transient harm will not generally be enough, but each case must be decided on its own merits and what is "significant" will always be a matter for the judgment of the sheriff. In *JT v Stirling Council* [2007] CSIH 52; 2007 S.C. 783 the Court of Session, discussing "significant" in the context of the words "significant support" under s.2(1) of the Education (Additional Support for Learning) (Scotland) Act 2004, said that "significant" should be regarded as "importing more than 'not insignificant'". In *In Re L (A Child) (Care: Threshold Criteria)* [2007] 1 F.L.R. 2050; [2007] Fam. Law 297, Hedley J said that it would be unwise to attempt an all-embracing definition of "significant harm" because the concept was fact-specific and that for significant harm there had to be more than human failure and inadequacy. We would suggest that in the context of child protection the existence of a real possibility of harm to the child would be enough. It should also be noted that subparas (i) and (ii) include the child *having been* ill-treated or neglected.
In *ZM, AM v Locality Reporter* [2016] SAC (Civ) 16 the Sheriff Appeal Court discussed, at [10]–[12], the cognate concept of "significant contact".

Subs.(2)(b)

C.417.5 This paragraph is not qualified by any reference to "reasonable grounds to suspect", presumably because the sheriff is bound to accept the statement by the local authority that it is making enquiries. However, the sheriff must himself or herself be "satisfied", on the information presented to him or her, that it is more likely than not that the circumstances listed in these paragraphs exist.

Subs.(2)(c)

C.417.6 As in the preceding subsection there is no reference here to "reasonable grounds to suspect": accordingly the sheriff would seem simply have to be satisfied as to the matters mentioned.

Frustrated. This means "to render vain; to baffle, defeat, foil" with the consequence, as pointed out by Professor Norrie in his *Children's Hearings in Scotland*, 3rd edn (Edinburgh: W. Green, 2013), para.15–06, that the mere hampering or making difficult the local authority's enquiries will not of itself be enough; however, where there is reasonable cause to believe that access is required as a matter of urgency (as there must be under subs.(2)(d)) then that which might otherwise be regarded as merely hampering or making difficult may amount to frustrating.

Unreasonably denied. It is also difficult to figure a situation wherein, if the other criteria for granting the order were present, the denial of access could be categorised as "reasonable".

Subs.(2)(d)

C.417.7 As to the presence or not of "urgency", the test for the sheriff is here set as "reasonable cause to believe".

Consideration by sheriff: application by local authority or other person

C.418 39.—(1) This section applies where an application for a child protection order in respect of a child is made by a local authority or other person.

(2) The sheriff may make the order if the sheriff is satisfied that—
 (a) there are reasonable grounds to believe that—
  (i) the child has been or is being treated in such a way that the child is suffering or is likely to suffer significant harm,
  (ii) the child has been or is being neglected and as a result of the neglect the child is suffering or is likely to suffer significant harm,
  (iii) the child is likely to suffer significant harm if the child is not removed to and kept in a place of safety, or
  (iv) the child is likely to suffer significant harm if the child does not remain in the place at which the child is staying (whether or not the child is resident there), and
 (b) the order is necessary to protect the child from that harm or from further harm.

DEFINITIONS

C.418.1 "child": s.199.
 "local authority": Local Government etc. (Scotland) Act 1994 s.2.

GENERAL NOTE

C.418.2 This section, in so far as it deals with applications for a child protection order (CPO) by an "other person", substantially replicates and "unpacks" s.57(1) of the Children (Scotland) Act 1995. However, this section, unlike s.57(1), applies equally to applications made by the local authority. Given that a local authority can competently seek a CPO under s.37 of this present Act on the basis of "reasonable suspicion", it may be that the provisions in this section may, in relation to local authority applications, be regarded as surplusage.

Subs.(2)(a)

C.418.3 The standard of "reasonable grounds to believe" is more exacting than that "reasonable suspicion" and entails that the applicant must be able not only sufficiently to specify the grounds but also to justify the contention that a reasonable person, on being given the information on which this belief is founded, would think "this situation puts the child at risk of significant harm and cannot be allowed to continue". The term "grounds" here is not used in the technical sense of "ground for referral", but simply refers to the information on which the

Information non-disclosure directions

reasonable belief is said to be based, or grounded; however, the information should support the existence of one or more of the grounds for referral: Part 2 of the relevant Form (Form 47 of Act of Sederunt (Care and Maintenance) Rules 1997 (SI 1997/291), as amended) requires a statement of "GROUNDS FOR APPLICATION" and seems to indicate that it is good practice for a specific ground, or specific grounds, for referral to be mentioned. It should also be noted that subparas (i) and (ii) include the child *having been* ill-treated or neglected.

Subs.(2)(a)(i)
Significant harm. See commentary on s.38(2)(a) above.   C.418.4

Subs.(2)(b)
This paragraph, unlike sub-paragraphs (i) to (iv) within subs.(2)(a) is not qualified by any   C.418.5
reference to the sheriff's being satisfied that there are reasonable grounds to believe. Accordingly, this paragraph places a positive obligation on the sheriff to be satisfied on the information presented to him or her that it is more likely than not that the order is necessary to protect the child from the harm concerned or from further harm. Since the granting or not of a CPO is subject to the minimum intervention principle this provision may be regarded as re-enforcing that principle. By invoking the concept of necessity it also imports the European Convention principle of proportionality, discussed above under s.36(2), which would of course apply anyway.

Ancillary measures

PRELIMINARY NOTE
Sections 40, 41 and 42 concern the directions that the sheriff may include in a child protection   C.418.6
order (CPO). They replace the provisions of s.58 of the 1995 Act. The test of necessity which was used in that section of the 1995 Act is not repeated in these provisions. However, it is clear that the welfare principle will apply as well as the minimum intervention principle. It is essential that it be understood that these directions form part of the CPO and do not stand alone; thus they only endure while the CPO is in force.

Child protection orders are exceptional in that there is no requirement in these sections that the views of the child be provided to the sheriff or that any such views be taken into account. This is understandable in light of the urgent nature of the CPO. It will not often be practicable to obtain the child's view. However, it should be remembered that the child (amongst others) has the right to apply to the sheriff under s. 48 for variation or termination of the order. Also, when a CPO is reviewed by a children's hearing under ss.45 or 46, the views of the child, where these views can be obtained, will play an important part in the hearing's considerations. Thus it is entirely consistent that if the views of the child with regard to any directions are available at the time of application for the CPO, they should be provided to the sheriff at the time of application, and should form part of the sheriff's considerations. This may be particularly advisable where the child has a view about contact with one or more persons.

Information non-disclosure directions

40.—(1) This section applies where the sheriff makes a child protection   C.419
order in respect of a child.

(2) The sheriff must consider whether to include an information non-disclosure direction in the order.

(3) An information non-disclosure direction is a direction that—
 (a) the location of any place of safety at which the child is being kept, and
 (b) any other information specified in the direction relating to the child,
must not be disclosed (directly or indirectly) to any person or class of person specified in the direction.

(4) An information non-disclosure direction ceases to have effect when—
 (a) it is terminated by a children's hearing under section 47(1)(a)(ii) or the sheriff under section 51(5)(b), or
 (b) the child protection order in which it is included ceases to have effect.

DEFINITIONS
 "child": s.199.   C.419.1
 "child protection order": s.37.

Children's Hearings (Scotland) Act 2011

"children's hearing": s.5.

GENERAL NOTE
See Preliminary Note at para.C.418.6.

Subs.(2)

C.419.2 This imposes an obligation on the sheriff to consider whether the whereabouts of the child, or any other information about the child should be kept from a specified person or class of persons. There is no requirement that the sheriff be asked for the direction to be granted before he or she may consider it, thus the sheriff may make such a direction *ex proprio motu* (i.e. on his own initiative). If the applicant considers that a non-disclosure direction is necessary for the immediate welfare of the child, they should ask the sheriff to make it. (For discussion of sheriff's consideration, see annotation to s.37(2)(d), (3) and (4) above.) It should be noted that non-disclosure should be interpreted very strictly as provision for both direct and indirect disclosure is made. This will require the sheriff to be very precise in specifying what information is not to be disclosed, and those who have control of the information will need to exercise extreme care. Great care will have to be taken to ensure that the child understands the order.

Subs.(3)(b)

C.419.3 *Any other information specified*
While this is most likely to be information concerning details or location of any medical assessment, examination or treatment resulting from any order made under s.42(2)(a), it may also include information relating to "any other authorisation or requirement to safeguard or promote the welfare of the child" (see s.37(3) above). Section 42(2)(b) provides sufficient flexibility for other information to be restricted. However, there may also be matters that a child wishes to be kept from a person. The making of a child protection order has to be notified to various people, including the child and relevant persons (see s.43(1)(b) and (c)). It may be that specification of certain matters, for example as to the medical condition of a child, might be damaging to the child if disclosed. As with any information the test will be whether disclosure would be likely to cause significant harm to the child (see s.38 above), or potentially to another person.

Contact directions

C.420 **41.**—(1) This section applies where the sheriff makes a child protection order in respect of a child.
(2) The sheriff must consider whether to include a contact direction in the order.
(3) A contact direction is a direction—
(a) prohibiting contact between the child and a person mentioned in subsection (4),
(b) making contact between the child and such a person subject to any conditions which the sheriff considers appropriate to safeguard and promote the welfare of the child,
(c) making such other provision as the sheriff considers appropriate about contact between the child and such a person.
(4) The persons are—
(a) a parent of the child, person with parental responsibilities for the child or other person specified in the direction,
(b) a person falling within a class of person specified in the direction.
(5) A contact direction ceases to have effect when—
(a) it is terminated by a children's hearing under section 47(1)(a)(ii) or the sheriff under section 51(5)(b), or
(b) the child protection order in which it is included ceases to have effect.

DEFINITIONS
C.420.1 "child": s.199.
"child protection order": s.37.
"children's hearing": s.5.
"parental responsibilities": s.202(1) and the Children (Scotland) Act 1995 s.1(3).

Parental responsibilities and rights directions

GENERAL NOTE

This section imposes an obligation on the sheriff to consider whether to include a contact direction when granting a Child Protection Order, but does not oblige him or her to make such an order. This is compliant with the minimum intervention principle. This section replaces s.58(1) of the Children (Scotland) Act 1995 and clarifies the scope and duration of such a direction as well as the test that the sheriff must apply.

As with the non-disclosure direction it is not necessary for the sheriff to be asked to grant the direction, he or she can make the direction *ex proprio motu*, that is, if he or she decides it is appropriate to safeguard and promote the welfare of the child. This section should not be confused with an order for contact under s.11 of the 1995 Act; it forms part of the CPO and has the same limited duration as the CPO.

A contact direction will have the effect of suspending any order for contact made under s.11 for the duration of the CPO if the direction is in conflict with the order under s.11. Parental responsibilities and rights also remain intact, although, as with a supervision requirement, some or all will be, in effect, suspended for the duration of the CPO. With regard to directions regarding contact, the sheriff is given great scope to make any provision that he or she considers appropriate for the welfare of the child. The sheriff should ensure that contact directions are flexible, allowing for contact with a particular individual to be prevented, confirmed or regulated. It should be noted that these persons would have to be specified in the order.

Given that the CPO must be reviewed at the second working day after the child has been removed to a place of safety (see s.45 below) any contact direction will have a very limited life. Even so, it is clear that by including provision for a contact direction great importance is placed on not only preventing potentially harmful contact, but in protecting beneficial contact. This is entirely compatible with the paramountcy of welfare principle, but also the emphasis on the protection of family and the child's right to contact in both the ECHR and UNCRC. Thus s.41 places an obligation on the sheriff to ensure that beneficial contact is protected. However, in *J v M*, 2016 S.C. 835; 2015 Fam. L.R. 124 a father had made an application for contact under s.11(2)(d) of the Children (Scotland) Act 1995; the relationship between the parents was "appalling" and there were allegations, not proved but which "could not be ignored" against the father. The court rejected that a test of "necessity" had to be passed before refusing contact and refused contact since this was in the best interests of the child. Circumstances will dictate the level of detail as to the regulation of contact that the sheriff requires to specify. There is a clear obligation on any person with responsibilities under the CPO to ensure that they comply with any contact direction.

Subs.(4)

It is puzzling that the reference in subs.(4)(a) is to parental responsibilities only. We believe that the omission has no practical consequence.

The effect of this provision is to enable the sheriff to prohibit contact with *any* person including a parent with parental responsibilities (and rights) (PRRs), a parent who has never had PRRs and a parent who has had PRRs removed by a court.

Parental responsibilities and rights directions

42.—(1) A person applying to the sheriff for a child protection order in respect of a child may, at the same time, apply to the sheriff for a parental responsibilities and rights direction.

(2) A parental responsibilities and rights direction is a direction about the fulfilment of parental responsibilities or exercise of parental rights in relation to—
  (a) the treatment of the child arising out of any assessment authorised by the child protection order, or
  (b) any other matter that the sheriff considers appropriate.

(3) A parental responsibilities and rights direction ceases to have effect when—
  (a) it is terminated by a children's hearing under section 47(1)(a)(ii) or the sheriff under section 51(5)(b), or
  (b) the child protection order in which it is included ceases to have effect.

DEFINITIONS
  "child": s.199.
  "child protection order": s.37.

"children's hearing": s.5.
"parental responsibilities": s.202(1) and the Children (Scotland) Act 1995 s.1(3).

GENERAL NOTE

C.421.2 This section replaces s.58(4) of the Children (Scotland) Act 1995 and has much the same effect. As with that section, s.42 does not give parental responsibilities and rights (PRRs) to the applicant for the CPO or to any other person, rather it allows for a direction to be made concerning the fulfilling of PRRs in a specified manner. The practical effect is that the direction empowers the applicant to fulfil the PRRs in a manner limited to that specified in the order.

Where s.58 of the 1995 Act did not give the sheriff power to make an order *ex proprio motu*, s.42 is not so clear and is apparently self-contradictory. Subsection 1 of this present section states that the applicant for a CPO may apply to the sheriff for a parental responsibilities and rights direction, suggesting that the sheriff cannot make such an order *ex proprio motu*. However, subs.(2)(a) allows the sheriff to make a parental responsibilities and rights direction regarding any other matter that he or she thinks appropriate, giving the sheriff the power to make such a direction without the need for it to be requested by the applicant. It may be that in effect, once the sheriff is asked to grant the direction, he or she may grant it in such terms as he or she deems appropriate. In practice it is likely that this can be managed during the hearing of the application.

There is no sanction for failure to carry out the direction, as Professor Kenneth McK. Norrie points out although it is potentially a contempt of court (*Children's Hearings in Scotland*, 2nd edn (Edinburgh: W. Green, 2005), p.234). However, given that the situation in child protection matters can change with great rapidity, it is probably appropriate that there be no sanction as the direction may no longer be in the interests of the child, or necessary.

Subs.(2)(a)

C.421.3 This subsection makes it clear that the initial request for a parental responsibilities and rights direction can only arise where there has been an order for assessment attached to the CPO. Thus it can only be requested in that single circumstance. Sheriff Holligan in *Application for a Child Protection Order*, 2015 S.L.T. (Sh. Ct) 9; 2015 Fam. L.R. 26, refers to the direction as permitting "such emergency medical measures which are necessary to safeguard and promote the welfare of the child."

Any such assessment should not be confused with a Child Assessment Order granted under s.35. (See General Note for that section above.) A direction made under this section cannot over-ride the decision of a child who has the capacity to consent to or refuse medical treatment under s.2(4) of the Age of Legal Capacity (Scotland) Act 1991, which is confirmed in s.186.

Subs.(2)(b)

C.421.4 In addition to assessment, this section gives the sheriff a wide discretion to make a parental responsibilities and rights direction concerning any other matter he or she considers appropriate. This does not appear to be dependent on the sheriff having granted the original direction requested and does give a degree of flexibility. Given the nature and short duration of a CPO the sheriff must be satisfied that any direction fulfils the principles of necessity and minimum intervention, and is required as a matter of urgency. In the words of Sheriff Holligan in *Application for a Child Protection Order*, 2015 S.L.T. (Sh. Ct) 9; 2015 Fam. L.R. 26, "[a] CPO is not designed as a long term measure" therefore the directions attached to it answer an immediate need.

Subs.(3)

C.421.5 The duration of a parental responsibilities and rights order is brief. It can be terminated by the children's hearing at the second working day review or by a sheriff under s.51(5)(b) if an application for termination or variation of the order is made under s.48. Otherwise it will end when the CPO ceases to have effect.

Notice of order

Notice of child protection order

C.422 **43.**—(1) As soon as practicable after the making of a child protection order, the applicant must give notice to—
  (a) the person specified in the order under section 37(2)(a) (unless the person is the applicant),

Obligations of local authority

(b) the child in respect of whom it is made,
(c) each relevant person in relation to the child,
(d) the relevant local authority for the child (unless the local authority is the applicant),
(e) the Principal Reporter,
(f) any other person to whom the applicant is required to give notice under rules of court.

(2) Where the Principal Reporter receives notice under subsection (1)(e), the Principal Reporter must give notice of the making of the order to any person (other than a relevant person in relation to the child) who the Principal Reporter considers to have (or to recently have had) a significant involvement in the upbringing of the child.

DEFINITIONS
"child": s.199.
"child protection order" s.37.
"children's hearing": s.5.
"local authority": Local Government etc. (Scotland) Act 1994 s.2.
"looked after child": s.17 of the Children (Scotland) Act 1995.
"place of safety": s 202(1).
"Principal Reporter": s.14 and Sch 3 paras 8 to 10.
"relevant person": s. 200.
"relevant local authority": s. 201.

C.422.1

GENERAL NOTE
This section applies to the applicant, whether a local authority or an individual, and clarifies who should receive notification of the making of a child protection order. Given that CPOs are frequently applied for in haste, and in rapidly changing circumstances, subs.(1) acknowledges that it is not always possible to provide immediate notice to all who should receive it but it is clear that notice must be given as soon as possible. There is no requirement that notification be given to the relevant persons of an intention to apply for a CPO, and there is no requirement that they attend or be represented. Sheriff Holligan in *Application for a Child Protection Order*, 2015 S.L.T. (Sh. Ct) 9; 2015 Fam. L.R. 26 points out that there is no procedural mechanism to allow for notification of an intention to apply for a CPO or an opportunity for a parent to be heard at the first calling, there is also no power given to the sheriff to continue consideration to another hearing. In the event that a relevant person does appear, whether or not represented, it is competent for the sheriff to hear him or her.

C.422.2

Subs.(2)
This section goes some way to addressing the problem of those who may wish to be "deemed relevant persons" by requiring the Principal Reporter to give notice of the CPO to any person whom they consider has, or has recently had, significant involvement in the upbringing of the child, which is the same criteria used in s.81(3). It should be noted that subs.(2) places this obligation only on the Principal Reporter, not the applicant. The difficulties with the possible conflict between the definition of who may be deemed to be a relevant person and the decision in *Principal Reporter v K* [2010] UKSC 56; 2011 S.C. (U.K.S.C.) 91; 2011 S.L.T. 271; [2011] 1 W.L.R. 18 are examined at Pt 8 below.

C.422.3

Obligations of local authority

Obligations of local authority

44.—(1) This section applies where, by virtue of a child protection order, a child is removed to a place of safety provided by a local authority.

C.423

(2) Subject to the child protection order, the local authority has the same duties towards the child as the local authority would have by virtue of section 17 of the 1995 Act if the child were looked after by the local authority.

DEFINITIONS
"child": s.199.

C.423.1

"child protection order": ss.202(1) and 37.
"local authority": Local Government etc. (Scotland) Act 1994 s.2.
"place of safety": s.202(1).

GENERAL NOTE

C.423.2 This section replaces s.57(7) of the Children (Scotland) Act 1995. It applies where the child has been removed to a place of safety provided by a local authority. It gives the local authority the same duties towards the child that it would have if the child were a looked after child under s.17 of the 1995 Act, i.e. to safeguard and promote the welfare of the child. It does not apply in the case of a child who is in a place of safety provided by another person under s.39. However, it should be noted that if a child had been accommodated under s.25 of the 1995 Act the local authority will have similar duties.

Review by children's hearing of certain orders

Review by children's hearing where child in place of safety

C.424 **45.**—(1) This section applies where—
(a) a child protection order is in force in respect of a child,
(b) the child has been taken to a place of safety by virtue of the order, and
(c) the Principal Reporter has not received notice under section 49 of an application to the sheriff to terminate or vary the order.
(2) The Principal Reporter must arrange a children's hearing.
(3) The Principal Reporter must arrange for the children's hearing to take place on the second working day after the day on which the child is taken to the place of safety.

DEFINITIONS

C.424.1 "child": s.199.
"child protection order": s.37.
"children's hearing": s.5.
"place of safety: s.202(1).
"Principal Reporter": s.14 and Sch.3 paras 8–10.
"working day": s.202(1).

GENERAL NOTE

C.424.2 This section replaces s.59(1), (2), (3) and (5) of the 1995 Act with regard to a child who is subject to a child protection order who has been removed to a place of safety. It is triggered, not by the granting of the CPO, but by the removal of the child to a place of safety. The review must be held on the second working day after the child has been removed to a place of safety. As with the provision in the 1995 Act this is an absolute obligation unless prior to the second working day hearing an application has been made for variation or termination of the order. The Reporter has the power to terminate the CPO or vary a direction attached to it (see s.53 below). Thus, should the child be removed to a place of safety on a Friday, the second working day review will be held on the Tuesday of the next week. It is normal practice for the child to be removed on the same day as the CPO is granted. If, however, the Reporter is notified that an application has been made for termination or variation of the order under s.49 there is no need for a second working day review to be arranged as, in hearing the s.49 application, the sheriff will, in effect, review the CPO. Provision for who should be notified of the hearing by the Reporter, and what documents must be provided, are listed in r.39 of the Children's Hearings (Scotland) Act 2011 (Rules of Procedure in Children's Hearings) Rules 2013 (SSI 2013/194). The procedure at the hearing is governed by r.70.

Review by children's hearing where order prevents removal of child

C.425 **46.**—(1) This section applies where—
(a) a child protection order is in force in respect of a child,
(b) the order authorises the prevention of the removal of the child from a place, and
(c) the Principal Reporter has not received notice under section 49 of an application to the sheriff to terminate or vary the order.

Decision of children's hearing

(2) The Principal Reporter must arrange a children's hearing.
(3) The Principal Reporter must arrange for the children's hearing to take place on the second working day after the day on which the child protection order is made.

DEFINITIONS
"child": s.199.
"child protection order": s.37.
"children's hearing": s.5.
"Principal Reporter": s.14 and Sch.3 paras 8–10.
"working day": s.202(1).

C.425.1

GENERAL NOTE
This section replaces s.59(1), (2), (3) and (5) of the Children (Scotland) Act 1995 with regard to a child who is subject to a child protection order (CPO) which is in force and which prevents his or her removal from a place (see annotations to s.39). It is identical in effect to s.45. The review must be held on the second working day after the day on which the CPO was made. As with the provision in the 1995 Act this is an absolute obligation unless prior to the second working day hearing an application has been made for variation or termination of the order. The Reporter has the power to terminate the CPO or vary a direction attached to it (see s.53 below). However, the "trigger" will not be, as in s.45, the perceived need for removal of the child, but the perceived need for prevention of the removal of the child. Once notification has been made to the person or persons with the care and control of the child, the child protection order will have been implemented. Provision for who should be notified of the hearing by the Reporter, and what documents must be provided, are listed in r.39 of the Children's Hearings (Scotland) Act 2011 (Rules of Procedure in Children's Hearings) Rules 2013 (SSI 2013/194). Procedure at the hearing is governed by r.70.

C.425.2

Decision of children's hearing

Decision of children's hearing

47.—(1) A children's hearing arranged under section 45 or 46 may—
 (a) if it is satisfied that the conditions for making the order are met—
  (i) continue the order, or
  (ii) continue and vary the order (including by terminating, varying or including an information non-disclosure direction, a contact direction or a parental responsibilities and rights direction), or
 (b) if it is not satisfied that those conditions are met, terminate the order.
(2) In subsection (1), the "conditions for making the order" are—
 (a) where the order was made under section 38, the matters mentioned in subsection (2)(a) to (d) of that section,
 (b) where the order was made under section 39, the matters mentioned in subsection (2)(a) and (b) of that section.

C.426

DEFINITIONS
"child protection order": s.37.
"children's hearing": s.5.
"information non-disclosure direction": s.40(2).
"parental responsibilities and rights direction": s.42.

C.426.1

GENERAL NOTE
This replaces s.59(4) of the Children (Scotland) Act 1995, and clarifies the purpose of the second working day hearing held under ss.45 or 46. Sections 45 and 46 place an absolute obligation on the Reporter to arrange a second working day review unless he or she has used the powers contained in s.53 or the Principal Reporter has received notice that an application has been made to the sheriff to terminate or vary the order. Section 47 requires the hearing to do one of three things: continue, vary or terminate the order. Procedure at the hearing is governed by r.70 of the Children's Hearings (Scotland) Act 2011 (Rules of Procedure in Children's Hearings) Rules 2013 (SSI 2013/194). The duration of the order is contained in ss.52 and 54.

C.426.2

Subs.(1)
C.426.3   The hearing is given three options in reviewing a child protection order: continuation, variation or termination. The test to be applied is the same as that to be applied by the sheriff in ss.38 and 39. As the circumstances of the child can change rapidly, it is appropriate that this section continues the flexibility of the 1995 Act by allowing the hearing to vary the CPO, not just continue or terminate it. It is made very clear that the CPO can be varied to include a non-disclosure, contact and a parental responsibilities and rights direction. Any parental responsibilities and rights direction concerning medical treatment will be subject to the capacity of the child with regard to the medical treatment (see s.186 below). As with s.42(2)(a), s.47 does not give the local authority parental responsibilities and rights, but, in effect, removes the right of a person with parental responsibilities and rights to veto the decision (see s.42 above).

If the hearing is not satisfied that the conditions for making the order are met it may terminate the order. It should be noted that the word used in subs.(1) is *may*, thus there is no compulsion upon the hearing to terminate the order if it is not satisfied that the conditions are met. However, should they not terminate in circumstances where it would be appropriate to do so, it is likely that an appeal would succeed.

Variation or termination of order by sheriff

Application for variation or termination

C.427   **48.**—(1) An application may be made by any of the following persons to the sheriff to vary a child protection order—
   (a) the child in respect of whom the order is made,
   (b) a relevant person in relation to the child,
   (c) a person not falling within paragraph (b) who has (or recently had) a significant involvement in the upbringing of the child,
   (d) the person who applied for the child protection order,
   (e) the person specified in the child protection order under section 37(2)(a),
   (f) the Principal Reporter,
   (g) any other person prescribed by rules of court.
(2) An application may be made by any of the persons mentioned in subsection (1)(a) to (g) (other than the Principal Reporter) to the sheriff to terminate a child protection order.
(3) An application under this section may be made only—
   (a) before the commencement of a children's hearing arranged under section 45 or 46, or
   (b) if the children's hearing arranged under section 45 or 46 continues the child protection order (with or without variation), within 2 working days after the day on which the child protection order is continued.

DEFINITIONS
C.427.1   "child": s.199.
   "child protection order": s.37.
   "children's hearing": s.5.
   "Principal Reporter": s.14 and Sch.3 paras 8–10.
   "relevant person": s.200.
   "working day": s.202(1).

GENERAL NOTE
C.427.2   This section is based on s.60(7) of the Children (Scotland) Act 1995, and adds provisions which rationalise the procedure and take account of modifications introduced by this Act. The application to the sheriff to set aside or vary a child protection order (CPO) may be lodged before the commencement of any review hearing fixed under ss.45 or 46 of the Act—thus obviating the need for such a hearing. The application may only be made by or on behalf of the persons specified and not, for example, by a third party seeking to clear his or her name in relation to an allegation of abuse against the child. Subsection (1) lists the persons who may apply to vary the order; subs.(2) lists those who may apply to terminate it. Since the proceedings are, in effect, a review of and not an appeal against the initial decision to grant the child

Application for variation or termination

protection order there is no objection to the sheriff who granted the order being the sheriff presiding at the application.

It should be remembered that reference to the Principal Reporter in this section includes the Reporter or any other person to whom the Principal Reporter has delegated any of his or her powers.

Subs.(1)

An application may be made. Rule 3.33(1) and (2) of the Act of Sederunt (Child Care and Maintenance Rules) 1997 (SI 1997/291) as amended by the Act of Sederunt (Children's Hearings (Scotland) Act 2011) (Miscellaneous Amendments) 2013 (SSI 2013/172) provides that the application shall be made in Form 52 of these Rules and that a copy of the CPO must be lodged with the application. See r.3.33(3) to (6) for further procedural rules. **C.427.3**

Vary a child protection order. Section 60(7) of the 1995 Act refers to an application to set aside or vary a CPO made under s.57 of that Act "or a direction given under section 58" of that Act. The present provision does not separately refer to any power to vary directions (enacted in ss.40 to 42 of this Act). However, as noted below under s.51, the sheriff is accorded powers under s.51(5)(b) to vary directions. It therefore appears that "vary a child protection order" in effect means "vary a child protection order and any condition attached to it under sections 40 to 42 of this Act".

Subs.(1)(a)

The child. This section must be read with s.15(6) of the 1995 Act (still in force) which provides: **C.427.4**

"Where a child has a legal capacity to sue, or to defend, in any civil proceedings, he may nevertheless consent to be represented in those proceedings by a person who, had the child lacked that capacity, would have had the responsibility to act as his legal representative".

Accordingly a child who has legal capacity under s.2(4A) of the Age of Legal Capacity (Scotland) Act 1991 may elect for a person with parental responsibilities and rights (PRRs) to exercise his or her power under ss.1(1)(d) and 2(1)(d) of the 1995 Act to instruct a solicitor and make application to the court. Note that this *only* applies to persons with PRRs in relation to the child.

Note, also, that this does not remove the right of a child with legal capacity to instruct a solicitor under Part 19 of this Act.

Subs.(1)(b) and (c)

Relevant person. This will generally be a person having PRRs in relation to the child, but see definition of relevant person at s.200 of the Act and discussion in the commentary thereon. The provision in para.(c) extending the right to make this application to persons involved in the upbringing of the child exactly replicates the criterion, set out in s.81(3), which a pre-hearing panel (PHP) has to employ in determining whether an individual is to be "deemed" to be a relevant person. However where, in the circumstances of an application to the sheriff to vary or terminate it would not be feasible for a person claiming to comply with this criterion to go through the PHP procedure, it appears that the person claiming a significant involvement in the upbringing of the child may make an application to vary or terminate and be ready to justify his or her position and it will then be for the sheriff, on his or her own motion even if not invited to by any party, to consider whether the person is entitled to be heard. **C.427.5**

Whether the individual does meet the criterion will be a legal and not a discretionary decision for the sheriff and accordingly the overarching principles will not apply—see above for discussion of the meaning of "a matter" in s.25(1) of the Act. The sheriff will require to decide the issue on the information then available. In *Principal Reporter v K* [2010] UKSC 56; 2011 S.C. (U.K.S.C.) 91; 2011 S.L.T. 271; [2011] 1 W.L.R. 18; 2011 H.R.L.R. 8 the Supreme Court, in the context of a children's hearing having to decide if an unmarried father had established a family life with the child and thus have a right to appear at a children's hearing under the provisions of the 1995 Act, observed at [69]: "In a borderline case, it would be safer to include him and let others argue rather than leave him out". It may, where the decision to be made by the sheriff is a narrow one and the would-be applicant's claim does not appear mischievous, be preferable to include him in order to enable there to be a record of his views.

There is no provision for an appeal against any decision of a sheriff under this section—see s.163(1) of this Act. However, in the event of the proceedings continuing to an eighth working day hearing, a would-be relevant person (or the child or a relevant person) may require the Reporter to refer the "relevant person" issue to a PHP (s.79(2)(a)), which will decide the matter unless the arranging of a PHP is impracticable in which event the matter will be decided at the beginning of the children's hearing itself (s.80(3)). Moreover, where the Reporter becomes aware of an application being made by a would-be relevant person, it is best practice to convene a PHP *ex proprio motu*. As more fully discussed below in our discussions of ss.160 and 163, there is provision for appeal to the sheriff from the decision of a PHP or a hearing on a relevant person issue and the decision of the sheriff may be further appealed to the Sheriff Appeal Court and/or the Court of Session.

Subs.(1)(e)
C.427.6   *The person specified.* That is, the person who is specified in the CPO as the person to whom the child is to be produced.

Subss.(1)(f) and (2)
C.427.7   The Reporter is by subs.(1)(f) given the right to apply to the sheriff to vary a child protection order (meaning, as submitted above, a child protection order and any attached direction). However, the Reporter is specifically excluded, by subs.(2), from applying to the sheriff for termination of an order. The Reporter has in certain defined circumstances powers to terminate or vary a CPO—see below for commentary on s.53(1) and (2).

Section 60(7)(d) of the 1995 Act included amongst those entitled to apply for termination "any person to whom notice of the application for the order was given by virtue of rules". Forms 47 and 48 of the Act of Sederunt (Child Care and Maintenance Rules) 1997 (SI 1997/291) (as amended), prescribed by r.3.30 of these Rules, include the Reporter as a person who has to receive notice of the application—thus reflecting the obligation in s.57(5) of the 1995 Act to give notification to the Reporter. The specific exclusion of the Reporter from the list of those entitled to apply for termination of a child protection order is an innovation. Of course the Reporter possesses, under s.53(1) of this Act, the right to terminate the order if satisfied "that the conditions for making a child protection order in respect of a child are no longer satisfied". However, the words "no longer" may carry the implication that the Reporter may only terminate at his or her own hand in the event of a change of circumstances (as was the position under s.60(3) of the 1995 Act). For a further discussion of this see below in the commentary on s.53.

As noted above, Principal Reporter includes anyone to whom the Principal Reporter's powers have been delegated.

Subs.(3)
C.427.8   This sets out strict time-limits within which an application to the sheriff to set aside or vary the child protection order must be made. If application is not made within these limits it cannot be made later. There is no change here from the provisions of the 1995 Act.

Notice of application for variation or termination

C.428   49. A person applying under section 48 for variation or termination must, as soon as practicable after making the application, give notice of it to—
   (a) the person who applied for the child protection order (unless the person is the applicant),
   (b) the person specified in the child protection order under section 37(2)(a) (unless the person is the applicant),
   (c) the child (unless the child is the applicant),
   (d) each relevant person in relation to the child (unless the relevant person is the applicant),
   (e) the relevant local authority for the child (unless the local authority is the applicant),
   (f) the Principal Reporter (unless the Principal Reporter is the applicant), and
   (g) any other person to whom the applicant is required to give notice under rules of court.

DEFINITIONS
C.428.1   "child": s.199.
"child protection order": s.37.
"local authority": Local Government etc. (Scotland) Act 1994 s.2.
"Principal Reporter": s.14 and Sch.3 paras 8–10.
"relevant local authority": s.201.
"relevant person": s.200.

Determination by sheriff

GENERAL NOTE
This section refines and amplifies the provisions of s.60(9) of the 1995 Act. That section prescribed notification to the Reporter only, a requirement driven by the need for the Reporter to know of such an application, which would obviate the need for the Reporter to arrange a second working day hearing. The new provisions are aimed at ensuring that all interested parties are advised. The requirement to notify the relevant local authority is new. Of course, in most cases the relevant local authority will be the applicant, but this provision addresses the position wherein the applicant is an individual or a local authority other than the relevant local authority.

It should be remembered that reference to the Principal Reporter in this section includes the Reporter or any other person to whom the Principal Reporter has delegated any of his or her powers.

C.428.2

Para.(b)
The person specified. That is, the person who is specified in the CPO as the person to whom the child is to be produced.

C.428.3

So far no other person has been specified in any rule of court.

C.428.4

Children's hearing to provide advice to sheriff in relation to application

50. The Principal Reporter may arrange a children's hearing for the purpose of providing any advice the children's hearing may consider appropriate to assist the sheriff in the determination of an application under section 48.

C.429

DEFINITIONS
"children's hearing": s.5.
"Principal Reporter": s.14 and Sch.3 paras 8–10.

C.429.1

GENERAL NOTE
This substantially replicates s.60(10) of the Children (Scotland) Act 1995. It endows the Reporter with a discretion to arrange a children's hearing (to which the normal rules of attendance and procedure apply) where an application to the sheriff for variation or termination has been made. In deciding what advice to give to the sheriff, this children's hearing will be subject to the paramountcy of the welfare of the child principle and the views of the child principle. It will not be expressly subject to the minimum intervention principle (since this function does not appear in the list in s.28(1)), but as the sheriff will be subject to this principle, then this hearing will consequently have to have regard to it. The statute gives no guidance to the Reporter as to how and when to exercise his or her discretion to arrange this advice hearing and often the matter will be governed by the availability of time: this hearing does not interrupt the running of the three working days within which the sheriff must determine the application. In practice, constraints of time have meant that this sort of advice hearing is virtually unknown. However, the inclusion of this procedure and the possibility of the hearing giving advice to the sheriff is a recognition by the legislature of the primacy of the hearing.

C.429.2

Determination by sheriff

51.—(1) This section applies where an application is made under section 48 in relation to a child protection order.

(2) The sheriff must, before determining the application, give the following persons an opportunity to make representations—
   (a) the applicant,
   (b) the child in respect of whom the child protection order is made,
   (c) each relevant person in relation to the child,
   (d) any person not falling within paragraph (c) who the sheriff considers to have (or to recently have had) a significant involvement in the upbringing of the child,
   (e) the applicant for the child protection order,
   (f) the relevant local authority for the child (if the authority did not apply for the child protection order),
   (g) the Principal Reporter.

C.430

(3) The application must be determined within 3 working days after the day on which it is made.

(4) The child protection order ceases to have effect at the end of that period if the application is not determined within that period.

(5) The sheriff may—
  (a) terminate the child protection order if the sheriff is not satisfied of—
    (i) where the order was made under section 38, the matters mentioned in subsection (2)(a) to (d) of that section, or
    (ii) where the order was made under section 39, the matters mentioned in subsection (2)(a) and (b) of that section,
  (b) vary the child protection order (including by terminating, varying or including an information non-disclosure direction, a contact direction or a parental responsibilities and rights direction), or
  (c) confirm the child protection order.

(6) If the sheriff orders that the child protection order is to be terminated, the order ceases to have effect at the end of the hearing before the sheriff.

DEFINITIONS

C.430.1 "child": s.199.
"child protection order": s.37.
"children's hearing": s.5.
"contact direction": s.41(3).
"information non-disclosure direction": s.40(2).
"parental responsibilities and rights direction": s.42.
"Principal Reporter": s.14 and Sch.3 paras 8–10.
"relevant local authority": s.201.
"relevant person": s.200.
"working day" s.202(1).

GENERAL NOTE

C.430.2 This section refines and amplifies the provisions in s.60(11)–(13) of the Children (Scotland) Act 1995. It deals with the procedure in relation to the possible challenge which may be made to the granting of a child protection order (CPO) and/or directions made thereunder and constitutes what will be in nearly all cases by the first opportunity for the order and directions to be considered by a court which has the possibility of submissions from parties. The sheriff's deliberations here will throughout be subject to all three overarching principles and the European Convention principle of proportionality. The proceedings before the sheriff are conducted in private: see Act of Sederunt (Child Care and Maintenance Rules) 1997 (SI 1997/291) as amended by Act of Sederunt (Children's Hearings (Scotland) Act 2011) (Miscellaneous Amendments) 2013 (SSI 2013/172) (the "1997 Rules"), r.13.1 (4) The provisions in this section do not differentiate between an application to the sheriff under s.48(3)(a) of this Act (i.e. an application made in advance of, and therefore precluding, a second working day hearing) and an application under s.48(3)(b) of this Act (i.e. an application made after a children's hearing has continued a CPO). The decision of a sheriff under this section does not appear in the list of decisions which may competently be appealed to the sheriff principal (now the Sheriff Appeal Court) and/or the Court of Session under s.163(1)(a) of this Act.

The hearing before the sheriff of an application to vary or terminate may well be more comprehensive and more protracted than the proceedings before a children's hearing. It is an important and potentially pivotal stage in the consideration of the child's case. Of course there may well be much procedure and investigation still to come, but, as in hearings in other types of proceedings which determine the position *ad interim*, the result has the effect of settling the status quo, with potentially longer term effects. We refer to our discussion below in the General Note to s.101, including the distinction by Lady Hale in *Re S-B (Children) (Care Proceeding: Standard of Proof)* [2010] 1 A.C. 678 at 687/688, paras [18]/[19] between the social workers as "detectives" and the court as the decider of what facts have been made out. As already noted there is no appeal from the sheriff's determination. Accordingly, all parties must be well prepared and ready to address the court as fully as possible and the sheriff must be ready to explore matters *ex proprio motu* so far as necessary. For the first time all of the parties will have the opportunity to have their say (see r.33(3) and (4) of the 1997 Rules) and the local authority will have its opportunity to respond. Not least the views of the child may, subject to the child's age and maturity, be available and indeed the sheriff may wish to see the child in person (for discussion of the issue of when, if at all, the sheriff should "interview" the child in order to

Automatic termination of order

obtain the child's views, see commentary to s.27(3) and (4) under sub-heading "*Should the court interview the child?*"). Intimation of the granting or refusing of the application shall, where the sheriff so directs, be given by the applicant to such person as the sheriff shall direct (r.3.33(6) of the 1997 Rules).

Subs.(5)(b)
The form for varying a CPO (Form 53 of the 1997 Rules) includes warrant to officers of law to take all lawful methods of execution, including inter alia searching for and apprehending the child and "so far as necessary, by breaking open shut and lockfast places".

Termination of order

Automatic termination of order

52.—(1) This section applies where a child protection order contains an authorisation of the type mentioned in section 37(2)(b).

(2) The order ceases to have effect at the end of the period of 24 hours beginning with the making of the order if the person specified in the order under section 37(2)(a) has not attempted to implement it within that period.

(3) The order ceases to have effect at the end of the period of 6 days beginning with the making of the order if the child to whom the order relates has not been removed to a place of safety within that period.

DEFINITIONS
"child": s.199.
"child protection order": s.37.
"place of safety": ss.202(1) and 189.

GENERAL NOTE
As stated previously, where it is considered necessary for the welfare of the child, child protection measures are designed to provide immediate protection and last for the shortest time necessary. It is therefore logical that, where the order is not implemented immediately, the immediacy is, for whatever reason, no longer present and, consequently, the order should automatically terminate.

Subs.(1)
This subsection clarifies that automatic termination applies *only* where a child protection order has been made under s.37(2)(b) "authorising the removal of the child by a specified person to a place of safety and the keeping of the child in that place".

This automatic termination does not apply where the order has been made under s.37(2)(c) "authorising the prevention of the removal of the child from any place where the child is staying (whether or not the child is resident there)".

Subs.(2)
Person specified. Where the order which has been made was on the application of an individual, then it would be a logical inference that the individual would be named as the person specified and to whom the child is to be produced. On the other hand, where the order has been granted to a local authority it may, given the practicalities, not be feasible to name a specific individual. It is likely that it will be competent merely to specify an official or class of official.

This subsection mirrors s.60(1) of the Children (Scotland) Act 1995 and sets out the circumstances under which a child protection order will automatically cease to have effect. Where the person specified in the order has not attempted, for whatever reason, to implement the removal of the child within the 24 hours, starting when the order was granted, then the order will fall. Provided attempts have been made within the 24 hours, even if unsuccessful, then the order will not cease to have effect under this subsection, but see subs.(3) below.

Subs.(3)
Once a child protection order has been granted, the child has been removed to a place of safety and the Reporter has not received notice of any intention to make an application to vary or terminate the order, the Reporter *must* arrange for a hearing to take place on the second working day after the day on which the child was taken to the place of safety (see s.45 above), unless the Reporter has exercised his or her powers under s.53 of this Act.

However, where the specified person has made an attempt to implement the removal of the child to a place of safety as per the order, but, by the end of the period of six days beginning with the *making* of the order, the child has not been removed to a place of safety for whatever reason, then the order will cease to have effect at the end of that six-day period.

Power of Principal Reporter to terminate order

C.432   53.—(1) If the Principal Reporter is satisfied that the conditions for the making of a child protection order in respect of a child are no longer satisfied, the Principal Reporter may terminate the order by giving notice to—
(a) the person specified in the order under section 37(2)(a), or
(b) where there is no such person specified, the applicant for the order.

(2) If the Principal Reporter is satisfied that the conditions for including a relevant direction in a child protection order in respect of a child are no longer satisfied, the Principal Reporter may vary the child protection order so as to terminate the direction by giving notice to—
(a) the person specified in the order under section 37(2)(a), or
(b) where there is no such person specified, the applicant for the order.

(3) A relevant direction is—
(a) an information non-disclosure direction,
(b) a contact direction,
(c) a parental responsibilities and rights direction.

(4) The Principal Reporter may not terminate or vary the order if—
(a) a children's hearing arranged under section 45 or 46 has commenced, or
(b) proceedings before the sheriff in relation to an application under section 48 have commenced.

(5) Where the Principal Reporter terminates or varies a child protection order under subsection (1), the Principal Reporter must notify the sheriff who granted the order.

DEFINITIONS

C.432.1   "child": s.199.
"child protection order": s.37.
"contact direction": s.41.
"information non-disclosure direction": s.40(2).
"parental responsibilities and rights direction": s.42.
"Principal Reporter": s.14, Sch.3 paras 8–10.

GENERAL NOTE

C.432.2   One of the principles of child protection procedure is that no order or measure should remain in place for any longer than is necessary to ensure the safety of the child and, where possible, allow for provisions and support to be put in place that will allow for the child to return to his or her family home. This section reinforces that principle by empowering the Reporter to terminate or vary a child protection order (CPO) where evidence shows that the conditions for the making of the original order are no longer satisfied. It is puzzling that, where the Reporter terminates or varies the order, there is no obligation to notify the child or relevant person.

Subs.(1)

C.432.3   This subsection replaces s.60(3) of the Children (Scotland) Act 1995. Where the Reporter is "satisfied that the conditions for the making of a CPO in respect of a child are no longer satisfied", he or she must show that new evidence of a change in circumstances, or evidence that was not before the sheriff at the time the order was granted, has come to light to justify the decision to terminate the CPO. The decision to terminate cannot result from the fact that the Reporter disagrees with the decision of the sheriff who granted the order. The "conditions" are those set out in s.39(2).

Person specified. On the face of it, this means that the individual to whom the child is to be produced and the person authorised to remove the child should be identified by name. However, the authors understand that in some local authority areas this is interpreted as meaning a person nominated by the Chief Social Work Officer of the local authority without naming that person. The authors can envisage a challenge to this on the grounds that "specified" means "named".

Termination is effected and the authority to keep the child in a place of safety ceases when the Reporter gives notice of the decision to the person specified in s.37(2)(a) or (b), or to the applicant where there is no specified person (s.37(2)(c) and (d)).

Once terminated because the conditions are no longer satisfied, there remains neither reason nor authority for the child to continue residing in the place of safety and, as such, the child must be returned home—unless there is some other statutory reason why the child must not be returned. Although there is no longer a statutory obligation to do so, the Reporter may still arrange for a children's hearing to take place under s.69(1) when read with s.66(2).

Subs.(2)

The power of the Reporter to terminate a child protection order (CPO) is extended to cover the new specific directions that may accompany the order. These are: an information non-disclosure direction (s.40); a contact direction (s.41); and a parental responsibilities and rights direction (s.42). Where the Reporter can show that the specific directions included in the CPO are no longer appropriate, he or she may vary the CPO by terminating any or all of the directions.

As with termination of the CPO itself, variation by the termination of any or all of the directions comes into effect once the Reporter has notified the person specified in s.37(2)(a) or (b) or the applicant, where there is no specified person (s.37(2)(c) and (d)).

Subs.(4)

The Reporter cannot terminate or vary a CPO where a children's hearing arranged under ss.45 or 46 has commenced. (A s.45 hearing is one arranged to take place on the second working day after the day on which the child was taken into a place of safety. A s.46 hearing is one arranged to take place on the second working day after the day on which the CPO was made). When referring to a children's hearing, "commenced" means the beginning of the children's hearing. With regard to the application to the sheriff, it is thought that "commenced" means when the application has been lodged. The authors direct the reader's attention to Professor Norrie's *Children's Hearings in Scotland*, 3rd edn (Edinburgh: W. Green, 2013), para.15–40.

This prohibition on termination or variation of the order also extends to the situation where s.48 proceedings have commenced, i.e. an application to the sheriff to terminate or vary the CPO made by any of the persons listed in s.48(1)(a).

Termination of order after maximum of 8 working days

54. A child protection order in respect of a child ceases to have effect on the earliest of—
  (a) the beginning of a children's hearing arranged under section 69 in relation to the child,
  (b) the person specified in the order under section 37(2)(a) or, where there is no such person specified, the applicant for the order receiving notice under section 68(3) that the question of whether a compulsory supervision order should be made in respect of the child will not be referred to a children's hearing,
[1] (c) where the order contains an authorisation of the type mentioned in section 37(2)(b), the end of the period of 8 working days beginning on the day after the day on which the child was removed to a place of safety,
[1] (d) where the order does not contain such an authorisation, the end of the period of 8 working days beginning on the day after the day on which the order was made.

NOTE
  1. As amended by the Children and Young People (Scotland) Act 2014 (asp 8) Pt 16 s.83 (effective 26 January 2015).

DEFINITIONS
  "child": s.199.
  "child protection order": s.37.
  "children's hearing": s.5.

"compulsory supervision order": s.83.
"place of safety": ss.202(1) and 189.
"working day": s.202(1).

GENERAL NOTE

C.433.3 This section reinforces the principle that a child protection order (CPO) shall last for the minimum amount of time necessary by providing that if it has not been automatically terminated under s.52 (above) and has not been terminated by the Reporter under s.53 (above), it will cease to have effect on the earliest of the events listed in paras (a) to (d). Note, in relation to para.(c), that the date of removal to the place of safety may be different to the date on which the CPO was granted, where, for whatever reason, there was a delay in moving the child to a place of safety.

This section lists a range of reasons that will result in the termination of a CPO. The CPO will cease to exist on the date of the earliest occurrence of any one of the reasons. But, in any case, a CPO must come to an end at the latest on the eighth day after its implementation, after which all authorisation to do any authorised or required acts (under s.37(3)) ceases to exist. The CPO ends when the earliest of the events in paras (a) to (d) take place. It is interesting to note that in paras (c) and (d) the period of eight working days begins on the day *after* the child was removed to a place of safety or, as the case may be, the day after the order was made.

Other emergency measures

Application to justice of the peace

C.434 55.—(1) A person may apply to a justice of the peace for an order in respect of a child—
 (a) requiring any person in a position to do so to produce the child to a specified person,
 (b) authorising the removal of the child by the specified person to a place of safety and the keeping of the child in that place,
 (c) authorising the prevention of the removal of the child from any place where the child is staying.
(2) A justice of the peace may make an order under this section if—
 (a) the justice of the peace is satisfied of—
  (i) in a case where the applicant for the order is a local authority, the matters mentioned in section 38(2)(a) to (d), or
  (ii) in a case where the applicant for the order is a local authority or any other person, the matters mentioned in section 39(2)(a) and (b), and
 (b) the justice of the peace is satisfied that it is not practicable in the circumstances for an application for a child protection order to be made to or considered by the sheriff.
(3) As soon as practicable after the making of the order, the applicant must inform—
 (a) the Principal Reporter,
 (b) the person specified in the order under subsection (1)(a) (unless the person is the applicant).
(4) The order ceases to have effect at the end of the period of 12 hours beginning with the making of the order if—
 (a) where the order authorises the removal of the child to a place of safety, the child has not been taken, or is not being taken, to that place within that period,
 (b) where the order authorises the prevention of the removal of the child from a place where the child is staying, arrangements have not been made within that period to prevent that removal.
(5) Otherwise, the order ceases to have effect on the earlier of—
 (a) the end of the period of 24 hours beginning with the making of the order, or
 (b) the determination by the sheriff of an application to the sheriff for a child protection order in respect of the child.

Application to justice of the peace

(6) The Principal Reporter may, by giving notice to the applicant, terminate the order if—
   (a) the Principal Reporter is satisfied that the conditions for the making of an order under this section are no longer satisfied, or
   (b) the Principal Reporter is satisfied that it is no longer in the best interests of the child for the order to continue to have effect.

(7) In subsection (1), "specified" means specified in the order.

DEFINITIONS
"child": s.199.
"child protection order": s.37.
"place of safety": ss.202(1) and 189.
"Principal Reporter": s.14 and Sch.3 paras 8 to 10.

C.434.1

GENERAL NOTE

Situations may arise where a sheriff may not be available to grant a child protection order (CPO) and the urgency of the situation demands that the child is removed immediately from harm or it is necessary to prevent the removal of the child from a place. In such situations, the application to grant an order (see subs.(1) below) will be made to a justice of the peace. The justice of the peace must be satisfied that it has not been practicable to make the application to a sheriff. Note that an application to a justice of the peace is *not* an alternative to obtaining a CPO, but is a temporary emergency procedure until such time as a CPO can be obtained. As with a CPO (see discussion above) there is no obligation to notify the child or relevant persons prior to the application.

C.434.2

Subs.(1)

Applications for orders by a Justice of the Peace will rarely be made by persons other than a local authority, but this subsection makes clear that any "person" may make such an application. Where an application is made to a justice of the peace under this section, the application is not for a child protection order but for an order to authorise the carrying out of certain acts, namely those in s.55(1)(a), (b) and (c). It should be noted that there is no provision in this section for JP Orders to include a medical examination or treatment of the child.

C.434.3

Subs.(2)

Where an application is made by a local authority to a justice of the peace, the justice of the peace must be satisfied that the criteria under s.38(2)(a)–(d) have been met. (See our discussion above under s.38(2)(a)–(d) and s.39(2)(a) and (b).) The burden of proof that there are reasonable grounds for suspicion that the child has or will suffer significant harm will lie with the local authority.

C.434.4

Subs.(3)

It is incumbent on the applicant to inform the Reporter and the "specified person" in s.55(1)(a) and (b) that an order has been made. This is an important obligation, especially given the tight timescales that attach to the order.

C.434.5

Subs.(4)

This deals with the length of time for which the authorisation of certain acts under subs.(1)(a), (b) and (c) is valid. If the act that is authorised has not happened or is not happening within 12 hours of it being authorised, the order (and, therefore, the authorisation) to do so lapses and cannot be revived.

C.434.6

Subs.(5)

Where the acts have been carried out under subs.(4) above, the order ceases to have effect either 24 hours after it was made or on the disposal of an application to a sheriff for a CPO, whichever happens first.

Note that there is no requirement to make an application for a CPO after the making of an order by a justice of the peace under this section, but that will be the only way in which a child can be kept in a place of safety for longer than the periods provided for in this section.

C.434.7

Subs.(6)

An order under this section may be terminated by the Reporter before the expiry of the timescales where the Reporter is satisfied either that the criteria for the order no longer apply or that the best interests of the child will not be met if the order continues.

C.434.8

Children's Hearings (Scotland) Act 2011

Constable's power to remove child to place of safety

C.435   **56.**—(1) A constable may remove a child to a place of safety and keep the child there if—
    (a) the constable is satisfied—
        (i) of the matters mentioned in section 39(2)(a), and
        (ii) that the removal of the child is necessary to protect the child from the harm mentioned there or from further harm, and
    (b) it is not practicable in the circumstances for an application for a child protection order to be made to or considered by the sheriff.
    (2) As soon as practicable after a constable removes a child under this section, the constable must inform the Principal Reporter.
    (3) The child may not be kept in a place of safety under this section for a period of more than 24 hours.
    (4) The child may not be kept in a place of safety under this section if—
    (a) a child protection order is in force in respect of the child, or
    (b) an application has been made to the sheriff for a child protection order or to a justice of the peace for an order under section 55 on the basis of the facts before the constable and that application has been refused.
    (5) The Principal Reporter may, by giving notice to the constable, require the constable to release the child if—
    (a) the Principal Reporter is satisfied that the conditions for placing the child in a place of safety under this section are no longer satisfied, or
    (b) the Principal Reporter is satisfied that it is no longer in the best interests of the child to be kept in a place of safety.

DEFINITIONS

C.435.1   "child": s.199.
    "child protection order": s.37.
    "constable": Police and Fire Reform (Scotland) Act 1994 s.99.
    "place of safety": ss.202(1) and 189.
    "Principal Reporter": s.14 and Sch.3 paras 8 to 10.

GENERAL NOTE

C.435.2   This section, which was incorporated into s.61 of the Children (Scotland) Act 1995, now has its own section. It gives authority to police officers to remove a child to a place of safety and keep him or her for up to 24 hours.

Subs.(1)

C.435.3   *Constable.* This term is not defined in this Act but s.99 of the Police and Fire Reform (Scotland) Act 2012, which set up Police Scotland, defines "constable" as an officer of any rank, and includes a special constable and a temporary constable. Section 24 of the Railway and Transport Safety Act 2003 refers to the officers appointed by virtue of that Act as "constables". The Scottish Government is considering the possibility of amalgamating the police service provided for in that Act with Police Scotland. The constable must be satisfied that the criteria in s.30(2)(a) apply (note, not s.39(2)(b)). In addition to these criteria applying, such a removal by a constable will only take place if it is not practicable for a sheriff to consider the making of a child protection order (CPO). For whatever reason, no mention is made of the possible application to a justice of the peace under s.55 for an order authorising removal of the child. This suggests that the immediacy of the situation requires urgent action, for example, where the constable witnesses the child being beaten by family members or where a constable comes across a child in distress as a result of family issues.

Subss.(2) and (3)

C.435.4   Once removed from the source of harm by a constable, information about the removal must be given to the Reporter so that further action, if necessary, can be taken. The child may not be kept in the place of safety for more than 24 hours from the time of removal. If it is necessary to keep the child in the place of safety for longer, an application for a CPO must be made under s.38.

Implementation of orders: welfare of child

Subs.(4)
Where there is an order by a justice of the peace (under s.55) or a CPO, there is no need for the constable's power to keep the child in a place of safety and it is not lawful to keep a child in a place of safety under this section where a compulsory supervision order or a justice of the peace order on the same facts has been applied for and refused.   C.435.5

Subs.(5)
The Reporter has ultimate control over whether a child is to be kept in a place of safety under this section. The Reporter's decision will be based on his or her assessment as to whether the criteria for placing the child in a place of safety no longer exist, or it is no longer in the best interests of the child to remain in the place of safety.   C.435.6

Sections 55 and 56: regulations

57.—(1) The Scottish Ministers may by regulations make further provision in respect of a child removed to or kept in a place of safety—   C.436
(a) under an order under section 55,
(b) under section 56.
(2) In particular, the regulations may require notice to be given to a person specified in the regulations of—
(a) the removal of the child to the place of safety,
(b) the location of the place of safety,
(c) an order under section 55 ceasing to have effect by virtue of subsection (4) or (5) of that section.

SUBORDINATE LEGISLATION UNDER THIS SECTION
Children's Hearings (Scotland) Act 2011 (Child Protection Emergency Measures) Regulations 2012 (SSI 2012/334)

GENERAL NOTE
The above-mentioned have been enacted. These contain detailed additional requirements in relation to orders made under ss.55 and 56, including specific notification requirements and provisions aimed at ensuring that where a Justice of the Peace order has been made, the need to safeguard the interests of the child is regarded as paramount and that appropriate steps are taken to inform the child of the reason for the making of the order and to take account of the views of the child.   C.436.1

Implementation of orders: welfare of child

Implementation of orders: welfare of child

58.—(1) An applicant for (and any other person specified in) an order mentioned in subsection (2) may only take such steps to implement the order as the applicant (or other person) reasonably believes are necessary to safeguard or promote the welfare of the child.   C.437
(2) The orders are—
(a) a child assessment order,
(b) a child protection order,
(c) an order under section 55.

DEFINITIONS
"child": s.199.   C.437.1
"child assessment order": ss.202(1) and 35(2).
"child protection order": ss.202(1) and 37.

GENERAL NOTE
This replaces s.57(6) of the Children (Scotland) Act 1995 in respect of child protection orders and also covers orders made by a justice of the peace in terms of s.55. Such orders must not, as pointed out by Professor Kenneth McK. Norrie in his commentary *Children (Scotland) Act 1995*, 2nd edn (Edinburgh: W. Green, 2004), p.118, be enforced automatically or unthinkingly. The applicant (and any other person specified in the order such as the person to whom the child   C.437.2

is to be produced) is authorised or required to take steps to implement the order only where he reasonably believes that the doing of them is necessary to safeguard or promote the welfare of the child. If the applicant acts without this belief then he is acting without statutory authority and can be subject to liability therefor (e.g. for wrongful detention). Though it is likely to be difficult to establish lack of reasonable belief after an order has been granted, this is not impossible if, e.g. the original source of danger to the child has died or been imprisoned since the granting of the order.

It is submitted, however, that care must be taken when putting the provisions of this section into action. The section is aimed at those persons implementing the orders and, while governing the way in which the orders are to be implemented, its provisions do not take away from the implementers the obligation to carry through the orders according to their terms. For example, these provisions would generally not entitle, say, a social worker specified in a child protection order as the person authorised to remove a child from a place to refrain from removing the child because the social worker did not believe that doing so would safeguard or promote the welfare of the child, or because, which is substantially the same thing, the social worker had come to believe that taking this action would not be better for the child than taking no action at all. In *AB and CD v AT* [2015] CSIH 25; 2015 S.C. 545; sub nom. *B, Petitioner*, 2015 S.L.T. 269; sub nom. *AB, CD*, 2015 Fam. L.R. 58, the court had to consider the decision of a sheriff to hold that social workers had been in contempt of court for failing to implement a court order awarding contact to a parent. The Second Division, on the facts of the case, quashed the sheriff's finding of contempt, but, at [28], quoted, apparently with approval, the sheriff's observation that there could be

"an extreme situation when a social worker may believe it unsafe to comply with legal requirements. There may be an occasion when to comply would place a child at immediate risk of serious harm to life or limb".

It is difficult to figure circumstances wherein the implementation of a CPO, a CAO or a JP Order under s.55 would amount to such an extreme situation.

Offences

Offences

C.438 **59.**—(1) A person who intentionally obstructs—
(a) a person acting under a child assessment order,
(b) a person acting under a child protection order,
(c) a person acting under an order under section 55, or
(d) a constable acting under section 56(1),
commits an offence.

(2) A person guilty of an offence under subsection (1) is liable on summary conviction to a fine not exceeding level 3 on the standard scale.

DEFINITIONS
C.438.1 "child assessment order": ss.202(1) and 35(2).
"child protection order": ss.202(1) and 37(2).
"constable": Police and Fire Reform (Scotland) Act 2012 s.99 and the Railway and Transport Safety Act 2003 s.24, discussed above in our commentary on s.56(1).

GENERAL NOTE
C.438.2 This section mirrors s.81of the Children (Scotland) Act 1995. It is an offence, which attracts the stated penalty, to obstruct intentionally any person acting under a child assessment order made under s.35, a child protection order made under s.37, an order made by a justice of the peace when a sheriff is not available to make a child protection order, or to obstruct a constable removing a child to a place of safety and keeping him or her there. Other possible offences, e.g. knowingly assisting or inducing a child to abscond from a place or person, are contained in s.171, discussed below. The authors understand that there have been prosecutions in relation to these provisions but these are rare.

Local authority's duty to provide information to Principal Reporter

Part 6

Investigation and referral to children's hearing

Provision of information to Principal Reporter

Introductory Note to sections 60 to 65
In accordance with the general approach of the Act, these sections substantially separate out and sometimes modify provisions formerly compressed into a single section—in this case s.53—of the Children (Scotland) Act 1995.

Local authority's duty to provide information to Principal Reporter

60.—(1) If a local authority considers that it is likely that subsection (2) applies in relation to a child in its area, it must make all necessary inquiries into the child's circumstances.   C.439

(2) This subsection applies where the local authority considers—
 (a) that the child is in need of protection, guidance, treatment or control, and
 (b) that it might be necessary for a compulsory supervision order to be made in relation to the child.

(3) Where subsection (2) applies in relation to a child the local authority must give any information that it has about the child to the Principal Reporter.

Definitions
"child": s.199.   C.439.1
"compulsory supervision order": s.83.
"local authority": Local Government etc. (Scotland) Act 1994 s.2.
"Principal Reporter": s.14 and Sch.3 paras 8–10.

General Note
Section 53(1) of the Children (Scotland) Act 1995 made it a prerequisite that "information is   C.439.2 received by a local authority that compulsory measures of supervision may be necessary in respect of a child", whereas the wording here is "consider", without reference to any justifying factor. Section 53(1)(b) of the 1995 Act provided that the obligation to inform the Reporter would arise where it appeared to the local authority that "such measures" (i.e., compulsory measures of supervision) *may* [our emphasis] be required in respect of the child". This was generally interpreted as meaning, in spite of the "may", that the substantive decision as to whether compulsory measures were necessary was to be left to the Reporter. In the *Report of the Inquiry into Child Care Policies in Fife* (HMSO, 1992) ("the Fife Inquiry") it is stated at p.459:
 "We think the proper question to ask is whether a good reasoned case could be made for compulsory measures of care and that therefore the position can well arise when a [social] worker may be personally unconvinced that compulsory measures are appropriate but still be under obligation to send the information to the Reporter, together of course, with his views on the matter, but leaving the decision to the Reporter as to whether or not to place the matter before a hearing".
In *Children's Hearings in Scotland*, 3rd edn (Edinburgh: W. Green, 2013), Professor Norrie, at para.4–03, p.58, quotes Wilkinson and Norrie, *Parent and Child*, 3rd edn (Edinburgh: W. Green, 2013) at para.19.09:
 "... to the local authority is given the judgment, in cases in which it receives information, of whether there may be a need for a compulsory supervision order but not of whether there is an actual need. Accordingly, it is obliged to transmit information whenever the view that a compulsory supervision order is necessary could reasonably be entertained even if in its judgment alternative measures, or no action, would be preferable".
The authors of the Fife Inquiry Report (at p.461) accepted, under the parallel provisions of the Social Work (Scotland) Act 1968, "that social workers have a role in 'screening' cases so that children with no real prospect of having compulsory measures imposed are not referred to the Reporter". However, as noted below in relation to s.66(2) of this Act, the Reporter is the person vested with the statutory responsibility of determining whether "it is necessary for a compulsory supervision order to be made in respect of the child". It is accordingly submitted that, while the screening process may be used legitimately for "obvious non-starters", social work training should seek to ensure that social workers are able to identify these and also be

able to recognise situations where the decision not to inform the Reporter of information would amount to taking on the role of the Reporter. It is not the role of the local authority to identify a particular ground(s) for referral.

It is to be noted that, in Scots law, there is no general duty to report child abuse or ill treatment and, therefore, the obligations imposed under this section apply only to the departments of a local authority such as social work, education and housing.

Subs.(1)

Considers that it is likely

C.439.3 "Consider" means "to be of opinion that" (OED). Where a local authority is in possession of information suggesting, or giving it reasonable cause to suspect, that the child is in need of protection, guidance, treatment or control and may require a compulsory supervision order (CSO), then the local authority must make any necessary inquiries to follow this up. If those looking after the child obstruct these enquiries then a child assessment order (CAO) or a child protection order (CPO) may be applied for. A failure by a local authority to take appropriate action where circumstances may suggest that the child is being ill-treated or neglected might, if the mistreatment were serious enough, constitute a breach of the child's rights under art.3 (freedom from torture or inhuman or degrading treatment) of the European Convention—see *E v United Kingdom* [2003] 1 F.L.R. 348; [2002] 3 F.C.R. 700; (2003) 36 E.H.R.R. 31; [2003] Fam. Law 157.

Subss.(2) and (3)

C.439.4 Under s.66(2) of this Act, when read with other provisions such as s.68(1)(a) and s.68(6), it is clear that, at this stage, it is for the Reporter, and the Reporter only, to decide on (I) whether, on the available information, one or more of the s.67(2) grounds for referral apply to the child, (II) whether the child "might" be in need of protection, guidance, treatment or control and (III) that it "is" necessary for a CPO to be made for this child. The duty of the local authority under subs.(1) is to make "all necessary inquiries" into the child's circumstances where it considers it "likely" that the conditions set out in subs.(2) apply. These conditions are (a) that the child "is" in need of protection, guidance, treatment or control and (b) that it "might be" necessary for a CPO to be made. Where these conditions are satisfied the duty to pass information to the Reporter crystalises. These provisions seem to break down into these possible stages:

[1] The belief by the local authority that it is likely that the child is in need of protection, guidance, treatment or control.

[2] If the local authority thinks that this belief is well grounded and no further information is necessary, then it need make no further enquiries as to the need for protection, guidance, treatment or control and proceed to give the relevant information to the Reporter.

[3] If the local authority considers that further inquiries are necessary, then it must make these inquiries.

[4] If the further inquiries lead the local authority to conclude that the child does not require protection, guidance, treatment or control, then there is no duty to inform the Reporter under subs.(3).

[5] If the further inquiries lead the local authority to conclude that the child does require protection, guidance, treatment or control and the local authority considers if a CSO "might" be necessary for the child, then the local authority must give any information about the child to the Reporter.

Constable's duty to provide information to Principal Reporter

C.440 **61.**—(1) This section applies where a constable considers—
(a) that a child is in need of protection, guidance, treatment or control, and
(b) that it might be necessary for a compulsory supervision order to be made in relation to the child.

(2) The constable must give the Principal Reporter all relevant information which the constable has been able to discover in relation to the child.

[1] (3) If the constable makes a report under section 20(1)(d) of the Police and Fire Reform (Scotland) Act 2012 (asp 8) in relation to the child, the constable must also make the report to the Principal Reporter.

Provision of information by court

NOTE

1. As amended by the Police and Fire Reform (Scotland) Act 2012 (asp 8) Sch.7(1) para.44 (effective June 24, 2013: substitution came into force on 1 April 2013 but could not take effect until the commencement of 2011 asp 1 s.61(3) on 24 June 2013). **C.440.1**

DEFINITIONS

"child": s.199. **C.440.2**
"compulsory supervision order": s.83.
"constable": Police and Fire Reform (Scotland) Act 2012 s.99 and the Railway and Transport Safety Act 2003 s.24, discussed above at para.C.435.3.
"Principal Reporter": s.14 and Sch.3 paras 8–10.

GENERAL NOTE

Reports from the police constitute the main source of relevant information for the Reporter, both in relation to children allegedly involved in offending and children who may have been offended against. It should be noted that, of these referrals, only a small proportion relate to offending by children. Of the 15,858 referrals in 2014–15, 71.5 per cent (or 11,260) were from the police. Only 2,872 related to offence by the child ground (SCRA Annual Report 2014–15). This section provides the foundation for this. **C.440.3**

Subs.(1)

Considers. See discussion above of use of this term in s.60(1). Constables, unlike local authorities, do not amass records of children and families which may enable them to form the opinion that it is, in the words of s.60(1) of the present Act, "likely" that a child may require protection, guidance, treatment or control and a compulsory supervision order (CPO). Constables are more likely to become involved by coming upon, or being directed to, examples of children being ill-treated or neglected or seemingly being involved in offending. It therefore makes sense to infer that "consider'" here means, in the words of s.51(3) of the Children (Scotland) Act 1995, "has reasonable cause to believe". The constable may have little difficulty where he or she observes personally an event or events giving rise to belief, but the concept of "reasonable cause to believe" is capable of including evidence from a source or sources which the constable is prepared to regard as reliable. **C.440.4**

Subs.(2)

This obliges the constable who considers that the child is in need of protection, guidance, treatment or control and might require a CPO to be made, to inform the Reporter. Constables will not often possess background information which may be available to local authorities and their decisions will generally be founded only on what they have seen or heard in the course of investigating the incident concerned. **C.440.5**

Subs.(3)

Section 20(1) of the Police and Fire Reform (Scotland) Act 2012 provides that it is the duty of a constable **C.440.6**

"(d) to take such lawful measures and make such reports to the appropriate prosecutor, as may be needed to bring offenders with all due speed to justice".

The potential "offender" here may be the child or a person who has offended against the child. All the cases which would be covered by this subsection would appear also to be covered by subs.(2), but the provisions of this subsection focus clearly the obligation on the constable to make a report to the Reporter when reporting such cases to the Procurator Fiscal.

Provision of information by court

62.—(1) This section applies where, in the course of relevant proceedings, a court considers that a section 67 ground (other than the ground mentioned in section 67(2)(j)) might apply in relation to a child. **C.441**

(2) The court may refer the matter to the Principal Reporter.

(3) If the court refers the matter under subsection (2) it must give the Principal Reporter a section 62 statement.

(4) A section 62 statement is a statement—

(a) specifying which of the section 67 grounds the court considers might apply in relation to the child,

(b) setting out the reasons why the court considers that the ground might apply, and
(c) setting out any other information about the child which appears to the court to be relevant.

(5) In this section " relevant proceedings" means—
(a) an action for divorce,
(b) an action for separation,
(c) an action for declarator of marriage,
(d) an action for declarator of nullity of marriage,
(e) an action for dissolution of a civil partnership,
(f) an action for separation of civil partners,
(g) an action for declarator of nullity of a civil partnership,
(h) an action for declarator of parentage,
(i) an action for declarator of non-parentage,
(j) proceedings relating to parental responsibilities or parental rights,
(k) an application for an adoption order (as defined in section 28(1) of the Adoption and Children (Scotland) Act 2007 (asp 4)),
(l) an application for the making, variation or revocation of a permanence order (as defined in section 80(2) of the Adoption and Children (Scotland) Act 2007) in respect of a child who is not subject to a compulsory supervision order,
(m) proceedings relating to an offence under any of the following sections of the Education (Scotland) Act 1980 (c.44)—
(i) section 35 (failure by parent to secure regular attendance by child at a public school),
(ii) section 41 (failure to comply with attendance order),
(iii) section 42(3) (failure to permit examination of child),
[1] (n) an application for the making, variation, recall or extension of—
(i) a forced marriage protection order (as defined in section 1(6) of the Forced Marriage etc. (Protection and Jurisdiction) (Scotland) Act 2011 (asp 15)), or
(ii) an interim forced marriage protection order (as defined in section 5(2) of that Act),
[1] (o) civil proceedings in which a court makes an order such as is mentioned in sub-paragraph (i) or (ii) of paragraph (n) by virtue of section 4(1) of that Act (power to make order without application), or
[1] (p) proceedings relating to an offence under section 9(1) of that Act (offence of breaching order).

NOTE

C.441.1 1. Inserted by the Forced Marriage etc. (Protection and Jurisdiction) (Scotland) Act 2011 (asp 15) Pt 1 s.13(2) (effective 28 November 2011).

DEFINITIONS

C.441.2 "child": s.199.
"parental responsibilities": s.202(1) and Children (Scotland) Act 1995 s.1(3); see also s.42 of this Act.
"parental rights": s.202(1) and the Children (Scotland) Act 1995 s.2(4); see also s.42 of this Act.
"Principal Reporter": s.14 and Sch.3 paras 8–10.

GENERAL NOTE

C.441.3 This section reflects s.54 of the Children (Scotland) Act 1995, separating out some of the elements therein and adding additional categories in order to cover new statutory provisions. The big difference of principle from s.54 is the omission of any provision equivalent to the enactment in s.54(3) of the 1995 Act to the effect that the "condition" specified by the court was to constitute a "ground established", thus rendering unnecessary an admission or proof of the condition. Under this section the matter is simply referred to the Reporter who, if he or she thinks fit, under s.66(2), has to arrange a hearing under s.69(2) at which the ground may be admitted or denied, and, in the event of non-admission, the matter may be referred to the sheriff for proof, in terms of s.93(1) and s.94(1) of this Act. This represents an advance on the 1995 Act which, by allowing a ground to be established as a result of proceedings wherein this was not the main focus of concern and in which the child's interest was not necessarily represented, ran the risk of challenge under the "due process" provisions of art.6 of the European Convention. This risk was identified by Professor Kenneth McK. Norrie in his *Children's Hearings in Scotland*, 2nd edn (Edinburgh: W. Green, 2005), p.45 and is removed by the present section. The position where a criminal court is empowered to certify a "ground established" is different in respect that for such a court the commission or not or the offence(s) concerned is the main focus of concern. See below for our comments on s.71.

Subs.(1)

Considers that a s.67 ground ... might apply. In the parallel provision of the 1995 Act the court had to be "satisfied" as to the application of a condition of referral. The less demanding test imported by "might" seems to reflect the present provision that the court's reference no longer operates so as to create a ground established. This provision confirms the jurisdiction of the Reporter in deciding whether to bring a child to a hearing and upon which ground(s) for referral. **C.441.4**

Other than the ground mentioned in section 67(2)(j). The "offence by the child" ground (ground (j)) is excepted from this provision. This exception was particularly important under the 1995 Act wherein, for the reasons noted above, the consequence would have been that a child would have been held as being guilty of an offence without admission or proof. This is no longer the case, but the exception has remained. As will be suggested below in our comments on s.64, it would appear to be open to a sheriff or judge as a "person" to refer to the Reporter a child whom the court considered might be amenable to any s.67 ground, including ground (j).

In relation to a child. There is no limitation as to which child a court may refer. Typically the child will be the child at the centre of one of the family actions listed in subs.(5), but it is possible that information concerning a child not directly involved in a family litigation may come before the court, for example if in an adoption application in relation to one child, it is alleged that the biological parent who is withholding consent mistreated another child, the court might exercise its discretion in favour of referring the other child to the Reporter. In view of the considerations mentioned in the following paragraph, courts may be more inclined than before to make such a referral.

Subs.(2)

May refer. The expression of this as a discretion replicates the parallel provision of the 1995 Act. Under that Act some sheriffs, conscious that the consequence of such a referral would lead to a "ground established" were cautious of referring. As noted above this no longer obtains and sheriffs may be more ready to refer. In making a decision on this matter sheriffs and judges must apply the paramountcy of the welfare of the child principle and the views of the child principle; the no non-beneficial order principle does not specifically apply here, however the proportionality principle imported by the European Convention in effect supplies this. **C.441.5**

Subs.(5)

It should be noted that the list of relevant proceedings in subs.5 does not include actions for interdict and/or exclusions under the Matrimonial Homes (Family Protection) (Scotland) Act 1981 and the Protection from Harassment Act 1997. However, as we note below in our commentary on s.64(1), a judge or sheriff, as a "person", may make a referral, and this would cover such cases. **C.441.6**

Subs.(5)(m)(i)

Public school. This comprises all schools which children in Scotland attend under compulsory education provisions. English readers should be aware that this expression does not carry the same meaning as south of the border. It should be noted that "parent" relates to the wider definition under s.135(1) of the Education (Scotland) Act 1980. **C.441.7**

Subs.(5)(n), (o) and (p)

These sub-paragraphs, added by the Forced Marriage etc (Protection and Jurisdiction) (Scotland) Act 2011 deal with procedures under that Act. See below in discussion of s.67(2)(p) and (q) for consideration of some of the provisions of this Act. **C.441.8**

Provision of evidence from certain criminal cases

C.442 **63.**—(1) The Lord Advocate may direct that in any specified case or class of case evidence lawfully obtained in the investigation of a crime or suspected crime must be given to the Principal Reporter.

(2) The evidence must in that case, or in a case of that class, be given to the Principal Reporter even if the Principal Reporter has not made a request under section 172.

DEFINITION
C.442.1 "Principal Reporter": s.14 and Sch.3 paras 8–10.

GENERAL NOTE
C.442.2 Subject to some verbal refinements this exactly replicates s.53(6) of the Children (Scotland) Act 1995. In practice Procurators Fiscal generally routinely liaise with Reporters and share information in relation to alleged offences by and against children, subject to retention of evidence as provided for by s.172(4), discussed below under that section.

Provision of information by other persons

C.443 **64.**—(1) This section applies where a person considers—
  (a) that a child is in need of protection, guidance, treatment or control, and
  (b) that it might be necessary for a compulsory supervision order to be made in relation to the child.

(2) The person may give the Principal Reporter all relevant information which the person has in relation to the child.

DEFINITIONS
C.443.1 "child": s.199.
"compulsory supervision order": ss.202(1) and 83.
"Principal Reporter": s.14 and Sch.3 paras 8–10.

GENERAL NOTE

Subs.(1)
C.443.2 *A person.* There is no limitation on who has the right to invoke the intervention of the Reporter and it may be a judge, sheriff, medical practitioner, law enforcement officer, school teacher, youth group leader, neighbour, relative, child protection agency, social worker (as an individual as opposed to as an employee of the local authority) or even the child himself or herself.

A person considers. See the discussion in the first paragraph of the General Note to s.60. In s.53(2) of the Children (Scotland) Act 1995 it was a prerequisite for "any person" to have "reasonable cause to believe" that compulsory measures of supervision might be necessary before an entitlement to inform the Reporter arose. Read literally, the present provision appears to authorise contacting the Reporter on the basis of a "hunch" for which no tangible justification could be advanced. Perhaps that was the intention. A person maliciously reporting to the Reporter might, however, be liable for defamation—see *Fraser v Mirza*, 1993 S.C. (HL) 27; 1993 S.L.T. 527; but it may be that the Reporter would not be compelled by the court to reveal his or her source of information—see *D v NSPCC* [1978] A.C. 171; [1977] 2 W.L.R. 201; 1977 1 All E.R. 589.

All relevant information. A person providing information to the Reporter is entitled to provide "relevant" sensitive information. This is in accordance with Sch.3 of the Data Protection Act 1998. Care should be taken to ensure that only the relevant information is provided to the Reporter, but the consideration that such information is sensitive should not prevent its provision to the Reporter.

Provision of information by constable: child in place of safety

C.444 **65.**—(1) Subsection (2) applies where a constable informs the Principal Reporter under subsection (5) of section 43 of the Criminal Procedure (Scotland) Act 1995 (c.46) that—

Investigation and determination by Principal Reporter

    (a) a child is being kept in a place of safety under subsection (4) of that section, and
    (b) it has been decided not to proceed with the charge against the child.
(2) The Principal Reporter may direct—
    (a) that the child be released from the place of safety, or
    (b) that the child continue to be kept in the place of safety until the Principal Reporter makes a determination under section 66(2).

DEFINITIONS
"child": s.199.   C.444.1
"constable": Police and Fire Reform (Scotland) Act 2012 s.99 and the Railway and Transport Safety Act 2003 s.24, discussed above at para.C.435.3.
"place of safety": s.202(1).
"Principal Reporter": s.14 and Sch.3 paras 8–10.

GENERAL NOTE
This replicates, with the modification noted below, provisions within s.63(1), (3) and (4) of the Children (Scotland) Act 1995.   C.444.2

Subs.(2)(a)
Section 63(3) of the 1995 Act only authorised the Reporter to direct that the child should no longer be kept in the place of safety where he or she considered that the child did not require compulsory measures of supervision, but the present provision permits the Reporter to order release of the child even if he or she has decided that a compulsory supervision order may ultimately be necessary, or even where the Reporter has not decided the matter either way. Of course on receiving information from a constable under s.43(5) of the Criminal Procedure (Scotland) Act 1995 the Reporter must, under s.66(1) and (2), consider and decide as to the necessity for a compulsory supervision order and, if he or she decides against this, direct the release of the child under s.68(2). The provisions in the instant subsection enable the Reporter to release the child at once while keeping open the option of proceeding to refer the child. Where the place of safety concerned is a police station steps must be taken to transfer the child to another place as soon as reasonably practicable: see s.189.   C.444.3

Investigation and determination by Principal Reporter

Investigation and determination by Principal Reporter

66.—(1) This section applies where—   C.445
    (a) the Principal Reporter receives in relation to a child—
        (i) notice under section 43 of the making of a child protection order,
        (ii) information from a local authority under section 60,
        (iii) information or a report from a constable under section 61,
        (iv) a section 62 statement,
        (v) evidence under section 63,
        (vi) information from a person under section 64,
        (vii) information from a constable under section 43(5) of the Criminal Procedure (Scotland) Act 1995 (c.46), or
[1]   (viii) a reference from a court under section 48(1) of the Criminal Procedure (Scotland) Act 1995 (c.46)
    (b) it appears to the Principal Reporter that a child might be in need of protection, guidance, treatment or control.
(2) The Principal Reporter must determine—
    (a) whether the Principal Reporter considers that a section 67 ground applies in relation to the child, and
    (b) if so, whether the Principal Reporter considers that it is necessary for a compulsory supervision order to be made in respect of the child.
[1] (2A) In a case where a certificate is supplied under section 48(1) of the Criminal Procedure (Scotland) Act 1995, the Principal Reporter is deemed to have determined under subsection (2)(a) that the Principal Reporter considers that a section 67 ground applies in relation to the child.

(3) The Principal Reporter may make any further investigations relating to the child that the Principal Reporter considers necessary.

(4) The Principal Reporter may require a local authority to give the Principal Reporter a report on—
   (a) the child generally,
   (b) any particular matter relating to the child specified by the Principal Reporter.

(5) A local authority may include in a report given to the Principal Reporter under subsection (4) information given to the local authority by another person.

(6) The report may contain information in addition to any information given to the Principal Reporter under section 60.

NOTE

C.445.1 1. Inserted by the Children's Hearings (Scotland) Act 2011 (Modification of Primary Legislation) Order 2013 (SSI 2013/211) Sch.1 para.20(7) (effective 24 June 2013).

DEFINITIONS

C.445.2 "child": s.199.
"child protection order": ss.202(1) and 37.
"constable": Police and Fire Reform (Scotland) Act 2012 s.99 and the Railway and Transport Safety Act 2003 s.24, discussed above at para.C.435.3.
"compulsory supervision order": ss.202(10) and 83.
"local authority": Local Government (Scotland) Act 1994 s.2.
"Principal Reporter": s.14 and Sch.3 paras 8–10.

GENERAL NOTE

C.445.3 This section, along with ss.68 and 69 lays out, in the fashion characteristic of this Act, in greater detail and with some modifications, what was, in the Children (Scotland) Act 1995, compressed into one section, namely s.56.

It should be noted that while this section refers to the powers and duties of the Principal Reporter, in practice these duties are delegated (Sch.3 para.10) to employees of the Scottish Children's Reporter Administration known as "Reporters". This section applies where the Reporter has received information regarding a child from any of a number of sources. It includes the possible sources of information from various parts of the Act. The section does not apply where the Reporter is required by a sheriff to arrange a hearing either under the Antisocial Behaviour etc. (Scotland) Act 2004 or where a criminal court has remitted a child who has pleaded guilty to, or has been found guilty of, an offence to a hearing for disposal which is dealt with by s.71. It also specifies the powers and duties of the Reporter on receiving a referral and undertaking an investigation. It provides the test to be applied by the Reporter upon receipt of initial information about a child, and the test to be applied in making a final decision. The actions to be taken by the Reporter once the final decision has been made are found in ss.68 and 69.

Subs.(1)

C.445.4 *This section applies where ... a child ....* This section "applies" where a referral is made to the Reporter under para.(a) or the Reporter has decided to undertake an investigation on his or her own initiative under para.(b). This section has to be read in conjunction with s.199 ("Meaning of 'child'"), which repairs a lacuna in the Children (Scotland) Act 1995 which prevented a Reporter from arranging a hearing if the child who was the subject of the referral turned 16 before the hearing could take place: see discussion under s.199(3) to (5). The reader is referred to the discussion in s.67(2)(o) with regard to a child who, despite being 16, remains "of school age" and is being referred on non-attendance grounds.

Subs.(1)(a) and (b)

C.445.5 This subsection lists the possible sources from which a Reporter may receive information about a child, commonly known as a "referral". It draws together the differing sections concerning those who have a duty to provide information, and those who may do so but do not have a duty. While para.(b) ostensibly gives the Reporter a general authorisation to proceed where a referral has not been made, it does not give the Reporter a "roving commission" to seek out children who may be in need of protection, guidance treatment or control. The most common application of this section is the instance where only one child in a household is the

Meaning of "section 67 ground"

subject of a referral; para.(b) would allow the Reporter to treat the other children as having been referred.

Subs.(2A)
   Section 43(5) of the Criminal Procedure (Scotland) Act 1995, as amended, deals with (a) offences under s.21 of the Children and Young People (Scotland) Act 2014, (b) Sch.1 offences and (c) an offence in respect of a person aged 17 or over which constitutes incest. It provides that where a person is convicted of one of these offences the convicting court may: in the case of offences under (a) or (b) refer the child victim to the Reporter; and, in the case of offences under (b) or (c) refer to the Reporter any child who is, or is likely to become, a member of the same household as the perpetrator or victim of such offences. The section (as amended so as to take account of the current legislation) further, and importantly, provides that the sentencing court may certify that the offence shall be a "ground established" for the purposes of the present Act.

C.445.6

Meaning of "section 67 ground"

67.—(1) In this Act "section 67 ground", in relation to a child, means any of the grounds mentioned in subsection (2).

C.446

(2) The grounds are that—
(a) the child is likely to suffer unnecessarily, or the health or development of the child is likely to be seriously impaired, due to a lack of parental care,
(b) a schedule 1 offence has been committed in respect of the child,
(c) the child has, or is likely to have, a close connection with a person who has committed a schedule 1 offence,
(d) the child is, or is likely to become, a member of the same household as a child in respect of whom a schedule 1 offence has been committed,
(e) the child is being, or is likely to be, exposed to persons whose conduct is (or has been) such that it is likely that—
   (i) the child will be abused or harmed, or
   (ii) the child's health, safety or development will be seriously adversely affected,
(f) the child has, or is likely to have, a close connection with a person who has carried out domestic abuse,
(g) the child has, or is likely to have, a close connection with a person who has committed an offence under Part 1, 4 or 5 of the Sexual Offences (Scotland) Act 2009 (asp 9),
(h) the child is being provided with accommodation by a local authority under section 25 of the 1995 Act and special measures are needed to support the child,
(i) a permanence order is in force in respect of the child and special measures are needed to support the child,
(j) the child has committed an offence,
(k) the child has misused alcohol,
(l) the child has misused a drug (whether or not a controlled drug),
(m) the child's conduct has had, or is likely to have, a serious adverse effect on the health, safety or development of the child or another person,
(n) the child is beyond the control of a relevant person,
(o) the child has failed without reasonable excuse to attend regularly at school,
(p) the child—
   [1,3] (i) has been, is being, or is likely to be, subjected to physical, emotional or other pressure to enter into a [...] civil partnership, or
   (ii) is, or is likely to become, a member of the same household as such a child,
[2] (q) the child—
   (i) has been, is being or is likely to be forced into a marriage (that

expression being construed in accordance with section 1 of the Forced Marriage etc. (Protection and Jurisdiction) (Scotland) Act 2011 (asp 15)) or,

(ii) is, or is likely to become, a member of the same household as such a child.

(3) For the purposes of paragraphs (c), (f) and (g) of subsection (2), a child is to be taken to have a close connection with a person if—
(a) the child is a member of the same household as the person, or
(b) the child is not a member of the same household as the person but the child has significant contact with the person.

(4) The Scottish Ministers may by order—
(a) amend subsection (2) by—
 (i) adding a ground,
 (ii) removing a ground for the time being mentioned in it, or
 (iii) amending a ground for the time being mentioned in it, and
(b) make such other amendments of this section as appear to the Scottish Ministers to be necessary or expedient in consequence of provision made under paragraph (a).

(5) An order under subsection (4) is subject to the affirmative procedure.

(6) In this section—
"controlled drug" means a controlled drug as defined in section 2(1)(a) of the Misuse of Drugs Act 1971 (c.38),
"permanence order" has the meaning given by section 80(2) of the Adoption and Children (Scotland) Act 2007 (asp 4),
"schedule 1 offence" means an offence mentioned in Schedule 1 to the Criminal Procedure (Scotland) Act 1995 (c.46) (offences against children under 17 years of age to which special provisions apply).

NOTES

C.446.1
1. Words repealed by the Forced Marriage etc. (Protection and Jurisdiction) (Scotland) Act 2011 (asp 15) Pt 1 s.13(3) (effective 28 November 2011).
2. Inserted by the Forced Marriage etc. (Protection and Jurisdiction) (Scotland) Act 2011 (asp 15) Pt 1 s.13(3) (effective 28 November 2011).
3. As amended by the Children's Hearings (Scotland) Act 2011 (Modification of Primary Legislation) Order 2013 (SSI 2013/211) Sch.1 para.20(8) (effective 24 June 2013).

DEFINITIONS

"affirmative procedure: s.197.
"child": s.199.
"local authority": Local Government (Scotland) Act 1994, s.2.
"permanence order": s.202.1 and Adoption and Children (Scotland) Act 2007, s.80(2).
"relevant person": s.200.

GENERAL NOTE

C.446.2 This section sets out the reasons why a child may be referred to a children's hearing, known as the grounds for referral. The list of grounds is not radically different from s.52 of the 1995 Act. Some grounds are virtually unchanged but note the new grounds that reflect changes in society. It is provided that where the Reporter has come to the considered view that one or more of the grounds in s.67 applies, that the child might be in need of protection, guidance, treatment or control and it is necessary for a compulsory supervision order (CSO) to be made in respect of the child (see s.66(1) and (2)) then the Reporter must refer the child to a children's hearing. However, the Reporter may take the decision that none of the s.67 grounds apply and, consequently, that a CSO is not necessary in respect of the child. Where a child is referred to a children's hearing, this, in itself, is not conclusive proof that a CSO is necessary for the child and the hearing; that is for the hearing to decide.

Subs.(2)

C.446.3 This lists the grounds for referral. Paragraphs (a) to (i) relate to the conduct of persons involved in the child's life; paras (j) to (o) relate to the conduct of the child; and paras (p) and (q) are completely new grounds that relate to a child who is or is likely to be forced into a civil

Meaning of "section 67 ground"

partnership or a marriage or to a child who is, or is likely to become, a member of the same household as such a child.

It is for the Reporter to determine which ground or grounds he or she will apply to the child's situation and which of the applicable grounds to use to bring the child to the hearing (ss.66(2)(a) and 89(3)(a)). The Reporter also specifies the supporting facts on which he or she alleges that the grounds are based (s.89(3)(b)).

Para.(a)—the child is likely to suffer unnecessarily, or the health or development of the child is likely to be seriously impaired, due to a lack of parental care

Parental care relates to the duty of the relevant person or the person who has care and control of the child to safeguard and promote the child's health, development and welfare (see s.1(1) of 1995 Act). It is not necessary for parental care to be delivered by a parent. The reason(s) why there may have been a lack of parental care is not relevant. The main issue is that, for whatever reason, the child is likely to suffer unnecessarily or that his or her health or development is likely to be seriously impaired as a result of lack of parental care, in other words, it is the effect that the failure of care has upon the child that gives rise to the ground. For example, if the relevant person has substance abuse problems, it is not the problems themselves that justify the ground, but the resulting *effect* on the individual child.

C.446.4

"development": this can be taken to mean the physical, emotional, psychological and intellectual development of the child—see *R v Grant*, 2000 S.L.T. 372; 2000 Fam. L.R. 2, Extra Div.

"likely": means not "probably" or "more likely than not", but presenting "a significant or substantial risk"—see *M v McClafferty* [2007] CSIH 88; 2008 Fam. L.R. 22. There is no requirement for actual harm of any sort to have taken place, but there must be evidence that lack of care is likely to cause unnecessary suffering, etc—see *H v Lees, D v Orr*, 1993 J.C. 238; 1994 S.L.T. 908; 1993 S.C.C.R. 900 and *M v Normand*, 1995 S.L.T. 1284; 1995 S.C.C.R. 380. One incident, if sufficiently grave, may be enough—see *Kennedy v S*, 1986 S.C. 43 at 49; 1986 S.L.T. 679. This ground enables action to be taken where information suggests that the child's development is likely to be adversely affected by the actions of those persons who have care and control of the child.

"seriously impaired": a child's health and development will be "seriously impaired" if there is significant failure by the person or persons who have care and control of the child to meet the child's physical and/or psychological needs—see *Re MA (Children) (Care Threshold)* [2009] EWCA Civ 853; 2010 F.L.R. 431; [2010] F.C.R. 456; 2009 Fam. Law 1026. (For further discussion on this term, see: "The National Guidance for Child Protection in Scotland 2010" on the Scottish Government website: *http://www.gov.scot/Resource/Doc/334290/0109279.pdf* [Accessed 5 October 2015]).

"parental care": this is the care given by persons with parental responsibilities and parental rights (ss.1 and 2 of the Children (Scotland) Act 1995); relevant persons (s.200 of this Act) and those who have care and control of a child. This can include care given during an informal arrangement or contact order under s.11 of the 1995 Act. It should be noted that it would be failure by the person concerned to prevent the risk to the child that would give rise to the referral to the children's hearing.

"unnecessarily": many children suffer during their childhoods as a result of illness, conditions or other factors. The suffering referred to in this ground is not that related to such illness or condition but suffering, etc. that is inflicted by those with parental care of the child, which, with the exercise of proper care, could have been avoided.

Lack of parental care occurs when the level of care falls below the objective standard—see *M v McGregor*, 1982 S.L.T. 41. Lack of parental care is not measured in success or lack of success or that the child may be marginally better off living in the care of others—see *H v Harkness*, 1998 S.C. 287; 1998 S.L.T. 1431, but failure to provide necessary medical treatment, even by loving parents acting from sincerely held beliefs, may be enough to justify this ground—see *Finlayson, Applicant*, 1989 S.C.L.R. 601.

Another example would be the criminal offence of female genital mutilation (see Prohibition of Female Genital Mutilation (Scotland) Act 2005) which would remain a stateable ground even where it has been, or is likely to be, performed at the instigation of a parent who has a sincerely held belief that this is an appropriate procedure. As mentioned below under para.(b), any offence under the Prohibition of Female Genital Mutilation (Scotland) Act 2005 where the person mutilated or, as the case may be, proposed to be mutilated, is a child under the age of 17 years, constitutes a ground for referral *qua* Sch.1 offence. The authors would suggest that it would be advantageous if this matter could be more sharply focussed by enacting a specific ground for referral of "causing or permitting female genital mutilation".

Children's Hearings (Scotland) Act 2011

Para.(b)—a schedule 1 offence has been committed in respect of the child

C.446.5 A "schedule 1 offence" is an offence listed in Sch.1 to the Criminal Procedure (Scotland) Act 1995, as amended under the heading "Offences against children under the age of 17 to which special provisions apply". Schedule 1 then goes on to list all the offences that are included under this umbrella. They are:

- any offence under Part 1 of the Criminal Law (Consolidation) (Scotland) Act 1995;
- any offence under s.18 (rape of a young child) or s.28 (having intercourse with an older child) of the Sexual Offences (Scotland) Act 2009;
- any offence under ss.19 (sexual assault on a young child by penetration) or 29 (engaging in penetrative sexual activity with or towards an older child) of the 2009 Act;
- any offence under ss.20 (sexual assault on a young child) or 30 (engaging in sexual activity with or towards an older child) of the 2009 Act;
- any offence under s.42 (sexual abuse of trust towards a child under the age of 17 years but only if the condition set out in s.43(6) of that Act is fulfilled) (2009 Act);
- any offence under ss.12, 15, 22 or 33 of the Children and Young Persons (Scotland) Act 1937;
- any offence under the Prohibition of Female Genital Mutilation (Scotland) Act 2005 where the person mutilated or, as the case may be, proposed to be mutilated, is a child under the age of 17 years;
- any offence under ss.52 or 52A of the Civic Government (Scotland) Act 1982 in relation to an indecent photograph or pseudophotograph of a child under the age of 17 years;
- any offence under ss.1, 9, 10, 11 or 12 of the Protection of Children and Prevention of Sexual Offences (Scotland) Act 2005 in respect of a child under the age of 17 years;
- any other offence involving bodily injury to a child under the age of 17 years;
- any offence involving the use of lewd, indecent or libidinous practice or behaviour towards a child under the age of 17 years;
- any offence under ss.5 (coercing a person into being present during a sexual activity), 6 (coercing a person into looking at a sexual image), 7 (communicating indecently etc.), 8 (sexual exposure) or 9 (voyeurism) of the 2009 Act towards a child under the age of 17 years; and
- any offence under any of ss.21 to 26 or 31 to 37 of the 2009 Act (certain sexual offences relating to children).

For discussion of the key concepts involved in Sch.1 offences, see Kenneth McK. Norrie, *Children's Hearings in Scotland*, 3rd edn (Edinburgh: W. Green, 2013), para.3.07; Brian Kearney, *Children's Hearings and the Sheriff Court*, 2nd edn (Butterworths, 2000) and *Butterworths Scottish Family Law Service*, Ch.12. The offences created by the Sexual Offences (Scotland) Act 2009 are highly complex and the reader is referred to Dr Alastair N. Brown's commentary *Sexual Offences (Scotland) Act 2009* (Edinburgh: W. Green, 2015) and Professor James Chalmers', *New Law on Sexual Offences in Scotland*, being Supplement 1 to Volume 2 of *Gordon's Criminal Law* (Edinburgh: W. Green, 2010).

The Sexual Offences (Scotland) Act 2009 refers to a child who is not yet 13 as a "young child", and a child who has had his or her 13th birthday but is not yet 16 as an "older child". It should be noted that, although the 2009 Act refers to "a child under the age of 17 years", it is generally not possible to bring a person aged 16 years or over to a hearing even if he or she is a victim of one of these offences. As already mentioned, a child aged 16 or over who is already subject to a CSO may be brought to a hearing on this ground as a new ground for referral (this is a consequence of that part of the definition of "child" in s.199(6) and (7)). Where a person aged 16 or over is the victim of one of these offences, he or she cannot (unless subject to a CSO) be brought to a hearing. A child who is, or is likely to become, a member of the same household as that person could be, if considered to be at risk (see below in discussion of ground (d)).

Where ground (b) is relied upon, it is not necessary to identify the offender. This is because the Reporter will frequently state the name of the offender in the grounds. This is because it is important for the children's hearing to be aware of the identity of the offender when considering disposal. The naming of the offender will also be important in relation to the possibility of framing a ground for some other child or children under grounds (c) or (d), discussed below. An offence may qualify under a ground (b) provision even if committed outside Scotland—see *S v Kennedy*, 1996 S.L.T. 1087.

Para.(c)—the child has, or is likely to have, a close connection with a person who has committed a schedule 1 offence

C.446.6 This paragraph is similar to ground (f) under the 1995 Act. The change in wording from "member of the same household" to "has, or is likely to have, a close connection with" reflects the changing nature of modern life. This scope of relationship between the child and the person who has committed a schedule1 offence is not limited to a person who is a member of the same

Meaning of "section 67 ground"

household. This paragraph should be read in conjunction with the definition in subs.(3) below in that being a member of the same household is included within the concept of "having a close connection with".

Whether a child is a member of the same household as the person is a question of fact and there must be evidence of this, but, even where this cannot be shown, it is enough to establish that the child and the person have a close connection.

"likely": there must be a substantial and real, but not remote, chance that the child might have a close connection with a person who has committed a Sch.1 offence. (For more discussion of this, see *H v Lees, D v Orr*, 1993 J.C. 238; 1994 S.L.T. 908; 1993 S.C.C.R. 900 and *M v Normand*, 1995 S.L.T. 1284; 1995 S.C.C.R. 380.)

"member of the same household": the concept of membership of the same household has been the subject of much discussion in case law. "Household" for these purposes means a family unit—a group that generally lives together even if some members come and go. (See *McGregor v H*, 1983 S.L.T. 626; *A v Kennedy*, 1993 S.L.T. 1188; 1993 S.C.L.R. 107; *Kennedy v R's Curator ad litem*, 1992 S.C. 300; 1993 S.L.T. 295; 1992 S.C.L.R. 546; cf. *Cunningham v M*, 2005 S.L.T. (Sh. Ct) 73.

"close connection": subsection (3)(b) states that "close connection" includes "[having] significant contact with". In *JT v Stirling Council* [2007] CSIH 52; 2007 S.C. 783, the word "significant" was discussed in relation to the level of additional support to be provided to the child under the Additional Support for Learning (Scotland) Act 2004 and it was stated:

> "It is a word which has shades of meaning, depending on the context ... at one end of the scale it can mean no more than 'not insignificant' and, at the other, 'important' or 'notable'".

There is no presumption that a child is a member of the same household as his or her parent—see *Ferguson v S*, 1992 S.C.L.R. 866. In *Templeton v E*, 1998 S.C.L.R. 672 at 678E, Sheriff Principal Risk QC emphasised that membership of the same household was a matter of fact and degree. Even where a residence or contact order was made in favour of a separated parent, this may not, of itself, constitute that parent as a member of the same household as the child.

Para.(d)—the child is, or is likely to become, a member of the same household as a child in respect of whom a schedule 1 offence has been committed

This ground requires the child to be, or to be likely to be, a member of the same household, and not merely have a close connection. (See above for a discussion of "household".) This ground provides the Reporter with a valuable opportunity to address a potential child protection issue. It addresses the increased risk to other children who are already in, or may be brought into a household where a child has been the victim of a schedule 1 offence.

C.446.7

It is, of course, not the child who has been the victim who is considered to present the risk but the schedule 1 offender. It should be noted that it is irrelevant that that victim is now an adult—see *K v Gault (No.1)* Paisley Sheriff Court 13 December 2000, Sheriff Principal Kerr QC. It is the *current* risk that is the consideration—see *Kennedy v R's Curator ad litem*, 1992 S.C. 300.

Para.(e)—the child is being, or is likely to be, exposed to persons whose conduct is (or has been) such that it is likely that—
  (i) the child will be abused or harmed, or
  (ii) the child's health, safety or development will be seriously adversely affected

C.446.8

This is a new ground and replaces ground (b) of the 1995 Act (bad associations or moral danger). It provides protection in cases where the child has contact with a person or persons whose behaviour either currently gives or recently has given rise to a reasonable belief that the child is at risk as a result of their contact with that person or persons. There is no requirement that it should always be the same person or that there is a close connection. For example, a parent or carer may have a circle of acquaintance with gang members or drug dealers/users who frequent the house.

It will be necessary to demonstrate a link between the behaviour of the person(s) and risk to the child. This will require very careful evidence gathering.

"persons": one or more individuals not limited to those who are members of the household or who have a close connection. These persons may come into the child's life through adults or through the child's own peer group. The exposure need not be in the child's home.

"exposed": there is no requirement that the child is or is likely to be a member of the same household as the person or persons, nor that they have a close connection. It will require that there be contact that is more than sporadic and that that contact poses a risk to the health, safety or development of the child.

"development": it is clear throughout the Act that development includes physical, emotional, psychological and intellectual—see *R v Grant*, 2000 S.L.T. 372.

Children's Hearings (Scotland) Act 2011

"behaviour": there is no need for the behaviour to be criminal or to have resulted in a conviction for a criminal offence, although it may have done so. It may be sufficient that the person might have behaved in such a way. It is the likely effect on the child that will give rise to the applicability of the ground.

Para.(f)—the child has, or is likely to have, a close connection with a person who has carried out domestic abuse.

C.446.9 This is a new and welcome ground and fills a notable gap in the s.52 grounds of the 1995 Act. There is growing recognition of the detrimental effects that exposure to domestic abuse can have on a child, whether the victim of actual domestic abuse or where the child is affected by abusive situations. For discussion of "close connection" and "likely" see ground for referral (c) above.

"domestic abuse": this is not defined in this Act but "abuse that amounts to domestic abuse" is defined in s.8A of the Protection from Harassment Act 1997; "abuse" is also defined in s.7 of the Protection from Abuse (Scotland) Act 2001. Notably, "domestic abuse" is not defined in the Domestic Abuse (Scotland) Act 2011. The authors concur with Professor Kenneth McK. Norrie's view that abuse ought to be given the widest possible definition (*Children's Hearings in Scotland*, 3rd edn (Edinburgh: W. Green, 2013), para.3–16). Abuse, therefore, can be directed to any person of any generation by someone with whom the child has a close connection. This would include abusive relationships between the child and another child.

"carried out": there is no requirement that the abuse is current. It is sufficient that the individual has a history of domestic abuse as the abuser. A single incident of domestic abuse may be enough—cf. *Kennedy v S*, 1986 S.C. 43 at 49; 1986 S.L.T. 679, but where there is evidence of a course of conduct, this should be founded upon. Evidence may include a criminal conviction, or interdict or an order under the Protection of Harassment Act 1997, or even previous (f) grounds for children associated with the individual. However, the absence of conviction or protective orders will not preclude the use of this ground as long as other evidence is available.

Para.(g)—the child has, or is likely to have, a close connection with a person who has committed an offence under part 1, 4, or 5 of the Sexual Offences (Scotland) Act 2009

C.446.10 The purpose of this ground is to extend the protection given to the child under para.(c) above (" ... is, or is likely to have a close connection with a person who is a schedule 1 offender", i.e. protection from a person who has committed an offence against children under the age of 17). This ground protects children from sex offenders whose victims are not children. It will generally be advantageous to be able to prove the identity of the offender and, since the offence concerned is not an offence by the child, the standard of proof will be the civil standard—on the balance of probabilities. For definition of "likely" and "close connection", see ground (c), above. The complex provisions of the Sexual Offences (Scotland) Act 2009 are discussed in Dr Alastair N. Brown's commentary *Sexual Offences (Scotland) Act 2009* (Edinburgh: W. Green, 2015) and Professor James Chalmers', *New Law on Sexual Offences in Scotland*, being Supplement 1 to Vol.2 of *Gordon's Criminal Law* (Edinburgh: W. Green, 2010).

Para.(h)—the child is being provided with accommodation under s.25 of the 1995 Act and special measures are needed to support the child.

C.446.11 This ground replaces the ground in s.52(2)(l) of the 1995 Act, which applied to children who had been received into care under s.25 of that Act and children who were the subject of a parental responsibilities order under s.86 of that Act (now repealed by the Adoption and Children (Scotland) Act 2007 Sch.3 para.1). The care provided under s.25 of the 1995 Act is commonly known as "voluntary" care since the powers under this section cannot be used to impose compulsory measures as these require the consent of the person with parental responsibilities and rights for the child to be taken into care. Section 25 requires a local authority to provide accommodation for a child within its area whom they consider requires such provision. This may be because the child has no-one who has parental responsibilities and rights for him or her; because he or she has been abandoned or lost; or because the person who is caring for the child is, for whatever reason, unable to do so. In a high percentage of s.25 accommodation cases, the child is accommodated at the request or agreement of the parent.

The wording has changed from the 1995 Act and now merely states that the child requires special measures. Special measures should simply be regarded as measures above and beyond the current provision for the child and which should also require some measure of urgency for the protection, guidance, treatment or control of the child, not merely as a means of trying to secure further resources. The parallel provision in s.52(2)(l) of the Children (Scotland) Act 1995 was rarely used, but Sheriff Kearney at para.[C2031] of *Butterworths Scottish Family Law*

Meaning of "section 67 ground"

Service mentions a case wherein it was employed in respect of a very vulnerable 15-year-old child who was subject to a parental responsibilities order, who was drifting into the company of persons known to the police and was proposing to take up a tenancy on becoming 16 and a supervision requirement with a residence condition was thought to be appropriate.

Para.(i)—a permanence order is in force in respect of the child and special measures are needed to support the child

This ground is similar in scope to (h) ground above and applies where a permanence order is in place under s.80 of the Adoption and Children (Scotland) Act 2007, but where the current measures are not working or are not considered appropriate and further measures are required for the protection, guidance, treatment or control of the child. It will require careful judgment on the part of the Reporter in deciding whether it is appropriate for such a child to be dealt with through the children's hearings system, or whether it would be more appropriate for the local authority to return to court for variation of the permanence order. The Reporter will also have to consider whether other grounds for referral are more appropriate, particularly if the problem has arisen due to the behaviour of the child.

C.446.12

Para.(j)—the child has committed an offence

This remains unchanged from the 1995 Act. This ground applies to all children aged 8 and over. (See s.41A(1) of the Criminal Procedure (Scotland) Act 1995 which increases the age of criminal *prosecution* from age 8 to age 12.) At the time of writing, it is conclusively presumed that no child under the age of eight years can be guilty of any offence. On 5 September 2017 the First Minister intimated that it was the intention of the Government to introduce in the coming session legislation raising the age of criminal responsibility to 12. The allegation by the Children's Reporter that a child is liable to the jurisdiction of a children's hearing by virtue of having committed an offence does not amount to the child being "charged with a criminal offence" in terms of art.6 of ECHR (*S v Miller (No.1)*, 2001 S.L.T. 531, per Lord President Rodger at 54G, H).

C.446.13

In considering whether to bring to a hearing a child accused of committing a criminal offence, the Reporter does not merely require to consider whether there is sufficient evidence. It is necessary to consider whether the offence is sufficiently serious, or that there are sufficient concerns in other areas of the child's life that satisfy the requirement of s.66(2)(b) above. The Reporter must not employ other grounds to avoid bringing the child on criminal offences and thus enable the ground to be proved on the civil standard of proof. (See *Constanda v M*, 1997 S.C. 217; 1997 S.C.L.R. 510 at 512E; 1997 S.L.T. 1396 at 1398C). In this case Lord President Rodger held that, where the content of the grounds of referral were exclusively alleged offences by the child, the criminal standard of proof must be employed:

"To hold otherwise would be to deprive the child of the safeguard which Parliament provided in section 42(6) [of the Social Work (S) Act 1968]. That cannot be allowed, even although the reporter may have acted with the best of intentions and may consider that in seeking to avoid the difficulties posed by section 42(6), she is trying to help the child".

More serious offences at sheriff court level are normally jointly reported to the procurator fiscal service and the Reporter. Discussions are held between the two as to which is the more appropriate forum. The Lord Advocate's Guidelines, which are up-dated from time to time, and a copy of the current version of which is reproduced as the Appendix, provide clear indication as to which cases are likely to be dealt with in the sheriff court. Cases dealt with in either the sheriff court or the High Court may, in certain circumstances (see Criminal Procedure (Scotland) Act 1995 s.49), be remitted to a children's hearing for disposal. Section 102(3) of this Act (discussed below in our commentary on that section) provides that where an application has to be made to the sheriff for determination of a ground for referral, the application is to be made to the sheriff who would have jurisdiction if the child were being prosecuted for the offence. This, however, does not mean that cases involving offences which it would not be within the jurisdiction of the sheriff to hear may not be referred to a children's hearing—see *Walker v SC*, 2003 S.C. 570, sub. nom. *Walker v C*, 2003 S.L.T. 293 (a case of an allegation of rape by the child).

See below in our discussion of s.187 of this Act in relation to provisions as to the rehabilitation of offenders.

Para.(k)—the child has misused alcohol

This ground refers to "misuse" rather than "use of alcohol". Notwithstanding that children are permitted moderate amounts of alcohol under the supervision of a parent or carer, this ground applies where the child him or herself misuses alcohol to the extent that it is considered that it is posing a risk to the child's health, safety or development. This provision reflects art.33

C.446.14

of the United Nations Convention on the Rights of the Child, which requires states parties to take all appropriate measures to protect children from the misuse of drugs. Section 105(1) of the Licensing (Scotland) Act 2005 makes it an offence for a child (i.e. in that Act, a person under 16) to buy or attempt to buy alcohol, and evidence of such an offence would be a useful element in establishing this ground.

Para.(l)—the child has misused a drug (whether or not a controlled drug)

C.446.15 This ground also reflects art.33 of the UNCRC (protection of children from drug abuse). The definition of "drug" is not limited to the drugs listed in Parts 1, 2 and 3 of Sch.2 to the Misuse of Drugs Act 1971. It will include all medicinal drugs that are being used by the child for non-medicinal purposes and psychotropic substances that give what were called "legal highs". Note that glue and other similar substances are not classed as "drugs" and are better dealt with using ground (m), below.

Para.(m)—the child's conduct has, or is likely to have, a serious adverse effect on the health, safety or development of the child or another person

C.446.16 For discussion of "likely", see (c) above. For discussion of "serious", see (a) above.

This is a new ground. The emphasis here is that the child's conduct must have a serious effect on the child him or herself or another person.

Examples of the types of conduct that may give rise to this ground would be:
bullying behaviour;
serious risk taking including sexual behaviour;
behaviour by a child under the age of 8 towards another child or person which could be a criminal offence had the child been aged 8 or over;
self-harming;
involvement with gangs;
active involvement in the drugs trade (cf. para.87 of the Explanatory Notes for this Act which may be referred to as an aid to interpretation of statute—see *AXA General Insurance Ltd v Lord Advocate* [2011] CSIH 31; 2011 S.C. 662; 2011 S.L.T. 439, at [11], [12] and [29]).

The authors would direct the reader to the annotation for ground (j) in that this ground should not be used as an alternative to bringing the child to a hearing on the ground that he or she had committed an offence.

The interface with the criteria for authorisation for secure accommodation should be kept in mind. See s.83(6) of this Act.

Para.(n)—the child is beyond the control of a relevant person

C.446.17 When considering if this ground applies, the test or standard is whether that control is reasonable given the age and maturity of the child. In *Re W (an infant)* [1971] A.C. 682 at 699 and 700; [1971] 2 All E.R. 49, HL, "unreasonableness" was described as including "bigotry, wild prejudice, caprice, fatuousness or excessive lack of commonsense". For this ground to apply, there must be an element of risk to the child. This, therefore, includes the child who has severe autism, acquired brain injury, a psychological condition, etc. The ground does not require a failure of parental care. The reasons are irrelevant, the focus is on the effect on the child. When considering the degree of control that the reasonable relevant person exercises, regard must be had to the parental responsibilities and rights enacted in ss.1 and 2 of the 1995 Act.

There may well be more than one relevant person in relation to a child and the child may be beyond the control of one relevant person but not one or more of the rest. It would appear that being beyond the control of one relevant person would be enough. The authors agree with Professor Norrie (*Children's Hearings in Scotland*, 3rd edn (Edinburgh: W. Green, 2013), para.3–24, fn.93) where he states that: "Reporters are unlikely to refer the child to a hearing solely on the basis that one of several relevant persons cannot control the child although others can and do." Section 81(4), which lists the statutory provisions in relation to which a deemed relevant person is to be treated as a relevant person, does not include Pt 6 of the Act, within which this present section appears. Read literally, his would mean that being beyond the control of a deemed relevant person would not constitute a ground for referral under this paragraph. Professor Norrie, in *Children's Hearings in Scotland*, 3rd edn, para.3.24, fn.92, submits that where a child's welfare is involved an expansive interpretation would be appropriate.

Para.(o)—the child has failed, without reasonable excuse, to attend regularly at school

C.446.18 This ground applies to children of "school age" only (see s.199(2)). Section 31of the Education (Scotland) Act 1980 states that "a person is of school age if he has attained the age of

Meaning of "section 67 ground"

five years and has not attained the age of sixteen years". However, the young person, who has attained the age of sixteen, remains of "school age" until the official "school leaving date" as stated in s.33 of the 1980 Act. An example of this would be where a child turns 16 on or after the 1st March, then he or she will remain of "school age" until the "summer leaving date" (the last day in May (s.33(1) of 1980 Act)). Similarly, where a child turns 16 on or after 1st October, he or she will remain of "school age" until the "winter leaving date" (the date when the school breaks up for Christmas).

What this means is that during the months between March and May or between October and December, a 16-year-old can be referred to a children's hearing on the ground that he or she "has failed without reasonable excuse to attend school regularly". The obvious question here would be to question the effect of such a referral given that, by the time a hearing is convened the young person may be beyond "school age" after which no referral on this ground can be made.

It is the authors' view that, where a young person is referred to a hearing (on this ground only) in the period between him or her turning sixteen and the "school leaving date", the reason may lie in the wider concerns that may come to light during the investigative process. In the case of *O v Rae*, 1993 S.L.T. 570; 1992 S.C.L.R. 208, where the father maintained that information considered by the hearing "must be information which was relevant to the grounds for the referral", Lord President Hope stated that

"the children's hearing have wide powers of investigation ... they are entitled to ask for and to consider information across a wide range and to obtain the views of various people, including social workers or any safeguarder, as to what would be in the best interest of the child".

So, this can be taken to mean that, even though the ground for referral is "failure to attend school regularly", should other facts emerge in the course of investigations, these other facts—which may not be specifically relevant to the grounds for referral—can, and should, feature in the investigative process. However, it is recognised as good practice for the Reporter to found on the ground for referral which is most relevant to the child's needs and not the easiest ground to prove, such as failure to attend school regularly, as an avenue into other grounds–see Brian Kearney, *Children's Hearings and the Sheriff Court*, 2nd edn (Butterworths, 2000), para.16.07.

Absence from school may be established by an attendance certificate which stands unless successfully challenged—Education (Scotland) Act 1980 s.86. It has come to be accepted, following the criminal case of *Kennedy v Clark*, 1970 J.C. 55; 1970 S.L.T. 260 (see also *Kiely v Lunn*, 1983 S.L.T. 207 and *McIntyre v Annan*, 1991 S.C.C.R. 465), that the onus of proof as to "reasonable cause" lies with the child or relevant person. However, as noted by Professor Norrie in his *Children's Hearings in Scotland*, 3rd edn (Edinburgh: W. Green, 2013), para.3–25, it has been questioned by a sheriff, in *O'Hagan v Rae*, 2001 S.L.T. 30 at [36] and [37], whether this is ECHR art.6 compliant. In practice, such matters are rarely decided on the basis of onus and both Reporters and those advising children and/or relevant persons should be ready, where appropriate, to lead such evidence as may be available in relation to reasonable cause.

Para.(p)—the child—(i) has been, or is likely to be, subject to physical, emotional or other pressure to enter into a civil partnership, or (ii) is, or is likely to become, a member of the same household as such a child

"household": see ground (c) above. **C.446.19**
"child": see ground (d) above.

Under-16s cannot lawfully enter into a civil partnership in Scotland. A child may, while under 16, be put under physical, emotional or other pressure to enter into a civil partnership when he or she turns 16 and this ground will apply then. Once the civil partnership has taken place the young person will have reached 16 and will not be under the jurisdiction of the children's hearing system (unless already subject to a CSO—see s.199 of this Act (meaning of "child")). Being forced into a civil partnership may seem a remote possibility, but this provision is necessary to completeness. The provision in s.67(2)(p)(ii) is important in that it enables the Reporter to refer a child who is, or is likely to become, a member of a household containing a person to whom s.67(2)(p)(i) would apply. See below for discussion of this issue in the context of forced marriage.

Para.(q)—the child—(i) has been, or is being or is likely to be forced into a marriage (that expression being construed in accordance with section 1 of the Forced Marriage etc. (Protection and Jurisdiction) (Scotland) Act 2011 (asp 15)) or, (ii) is, or is likely to become, a member of the same household as such a child

"force". This is defined in s.1(6) of the Forced Marriage etc. (Protection and Jurisdiction) **C.446.20**
(Scotland) Act 2011 which provides:

"'force' includes (a) coercion by physical, verbal or psychological means, threatening conduct, harassment or other means, and

(b) knowingly taking advantage of a person's incapacity to consent to marriage or to understand the nature of marriage."

"*household*": see ground (c) above.

"*child*": see ground (d) above.

The possibility of a child being forced into marriage is not a remote one and this provision is of great importance. Of course, as with civil partnerships, under 16s cannot lawfully enter into a marriage in Scotland, but, as we have noted above in relation to the civil partnership provisions, a child may, while under 16, be put under physical, emotional or other pressure to enter into (in this case) a marriage when he or she becomes of lawful age. It must be noted that this ground will also apply where a child of any age travels, or is forced to travel, abroad for preparations for a forced marriage. The Reporter should be careful to differentiate between a forced marriage and an arranged marriage, the difference being the element of free consent. It is also to be noted that marriages may be forced on male as well as female children. (See Forced Marriage etc. (Protection and Jurisdiction) (Scotland) Act 2011 s.1(1) which, in the definition of "protected person", does not differentiate between male and female.)

Note also that, where a child is referred on the basis of ground (q)(ii), i.e. because he or she "is, or is likely to become, a member of the same household as such a child", "such a child" may now be 16 or over, but he or she must have been a child at the time of his or her forced marriage.

It should also be noted here that it is not only children who are forced into marriage, but also, older adult siblings or even a parent.

This may be a very emotive subject and may lead to the break-up of the family. Families may regard intervention by the authorities on such a matter as very unwelcome and possibly shameful, leading to reluctance of family members or the child to appeal for help or to cooperate. Much responsibility will be placed on schools to identify children—whatever their gender—who are at risk. In *City of Edinburgh Council v MS & NS*, Sheriff Court of Lothian and Borders at Edinburgh, 3 March 2015, sub nom. *City of Edinburgh Council v S*, 2015 S.L.T. (Sh. Ct) 69; 2015 G.W.D. 11–19, Sheriff W.A. Sheehan decided that the evidence did not justify the making of a Forced Marriage Protection Order under s.1(1) of the Forced Marriage etc. (Protection and Jurisdiction) (Scotland) Act 2011. This case, discussed by Sheriff B. Kearney in 2015 Fam. L.B. 135–5, illustrates the necessity of leading detailed and persuasive evidence. It also narrates the procedures adopted by Edinburgh City Council in identifying cases which may justify making application for a Forced Marriage Protection Order.

Determination under section 66: no referral to children's hearing

C.447 **68.**—(1) This section applies where, having made a determination under section 66(2) in relation to a child, the Principal Reporter considers that—

(a) none of the section 67 grounds applies in relation to the child, or

(b) it is not necessary for a compulsory supervision order to be made in respect of the child.

(2) If the child is being kept in a place of safety under section 65(2)(b) the Principal Reporter must direct that the child be released from the place of safety.

(3) The Principal Reporter—

(a) must inform the persons mentioned in subsection (4) of the determination and the fact that the question of whether a compulsory supervision order should be made in respect of the child will not be referred to a children's hearing, and

(b) may, if the Principal Reporter considers it appropriate, inform any other person of the determination and that fact.

(4) Those persons are—

(a) the child,

(b) each relevant person in relation to the child,

(c) the relevant local authority for the child,

(d) any person specified in a child protection order in force in relation to the child under section 37(2)(a),

(e) any person who has given the Principal Reporter—

(i) notice under section 43 of a child protection order,

(ii) information under section 60, 61, 64 or 66,

Determination under section 66: no referral to children's hearing

(iii) a report under section 61 or 66,
(iv) a section 62 statement,
(v) evidence under section 63, or
(vi) information under section 43(5) of the Criminal Procedure (Scotland) Act 1995 (c.46).

(5) The Principal Reporter may refer the child to—
(a) the relevant local authority for the child with a view to the authority providing (or making arrangements for the provision by another person or body of) advice, guidance and assistance to the child and the child's family in accordance with Chapter 1 of Part 2 of the 1995 Act (support for children and their families),
(b) such other person or body as may be specified by the Scottish Ministers by order for the purposes of this subsection, with a view to that person or body providing advice, guidance and assistance to the child and the child's family.

(6) After complying with the requirements imposed by subsection (3)(a), the Principal Reporter must not refer the question of whether a compulsory supervision order should be made in respect of the child to a children's hearing unless the Principal Reporter receives new information about the child.

DEFINITIONS
"child": s.199.
"child protection order": ss.202(1) and 37.
"children's hearing": s. 5.
"compulsory supervision order": s.83.
"compulsory supervision order": s.202(1).
"place of safety": ss.202(1) and 189.
"Principal Reporter": s.14 and Sch. 3 paras 8–10.
"relevant local authority": s.201.
"relevant person": s.200.

C.447.1

GENERAL NOTE
This sets out the duties and powers of the Reporter when a decision has been made under s.66(4). It replaces s.56(2) and (5) of the Children (Scotland) Act 1995 and applies where the Reporter has made the determination under s.66 that the child is not to be brought to a hearing.

This section, based on the provisions in s.56(4) and (5) of the 1995 Act, amplifies these provisions by providing much more detailed specification, and also effects some modifications.

C.447.2

Subs. (1)
The two paragraphs within this subsection make clear that the Reporter may not proceed where he or she is satisfied both that neither a s.67 ground exists nor that a compulsory supervision order (CSO) is necessary for the child. If, for example, the Reporter is satisfied that a s.67 ground exists but is not satisfied that a CSO is necessary, then the child should not be referred to a children's hearing and the termination procedures within this section must be engaged. The same conclusion follows where the Reporter believes that a CSO would serve the needs of the child but is not satisfied that a s.67 ground can be made out. The Reporter's decision as to the existence or not of a s.67 ground is a legal judgement on the basis of the available facts, whereas the decision as to the necessity or not of a CSO is of the nature of a value judgement and, consequently, the Reporter, although not technically bound by any of the "overarching principles" must have regard to the proportionality principle imported by the European Convention. If the Reporter thinks that further information on any matter is required he or she may instigate further inquiries under s.66(3) and/or (4) as noted above in our commentary on these provisions.

C.447.3

Subs.(2)
Where a child is being kept in a place of safety under s.43(5) of the Criminal Procedure (Scotland) Act 1995, the Reporter is required to order the release of the child if the decision is that the child is not to be brought to a hearing. That section of the Criminal Procedure (Scotland) Act 1995 permits a police officer to detain a child who has been apprehended.

C.447.4

Subss.(3) and (4)

C.447.5 These subsections replace s.56(4)(a) of the Children (Scotland) Act 1995. Once the Reporter has made the decision not to refer the child to a hearing, he or she is required to notify a number of persons of that decision. The Reporter is obliged to notify the child, relevant persons, the relevant local authority, any person specified in a child protection order, and the person who provided the information (commonly called the referral). While subs.(4) contains the list of those who must be notified, subs.(3)(b) gives the Reporter discretion to inform any other person if he or she considers it appropriate.

This entitlement in subs.(3)(b) is valuable; an example of such a person would be the procurator fiscal, in the event that he or she had an interest to be informed and was not covered by any of the categories set out in subs.(4).

Subss.(5)(a) and (b)

C.447.6 If the Reporter decides not to bring the child to a hearing, and the child is not already subject to a CSO, the Reporter has the discretion to refer the child to their local authority for advice, guidance and assistance. The expectation is that the local authority will comply and offer the needed support. From the point of view of the child and family, support is entirely voluntary and there is no compulsion. If that voluntary support is refused, the Reporter does not have the power to change his or her decision and bring the child to a hearing. This is specifically provided for in subs.(6) below. Paragraph (b) allows Scottish Ministers to add other persons or bodies to the list of those to whom a Reporter may refer the child for such advice, guidance and assistance.

Subs.(6)

C.447.7 This means that the decision not to refer the child to a children's hearing cannot, once that decision has been notified in terms of subs.(3)(a), be retracted unless new circumstances, which are additional to those discovered in the course of the investigation to determine whether to arrange a hearing, comes to the attention of the Reporter. These new circumstances might indicate a quite different ground for referral or they may concern the same ground—for example, when the decision not to arrange a children's hearing was made on the basis of a lack of evidence and fresh evidence has come to light.

Determination under section 66: referral to children's hearing

C.448 **69.**—(1) This section applies where, having made a determination under section 66(2) in relation to a child, the Principal Reporter considers that it is necessary for a compulsory supervision order to be made in respect of the child.

(2) The Principal Reporter must arrange a children's hearing for the purpose of deciding whether a compulsory supervision order should be made in respect of the child.

(3) If the child is being kept in a place of safety under subsection (4) of section 43 of the Criminal Procedure (Scotland) Act 1995 (c.46) at the time the determination is made, the children's hearing must be arranged to take place no later than the third day after the Principal Reporter receives the information under subsection (5) of that section.

(4) If the Principal Reporter has required a local authority to give the Principal Reporter a report under section 66(4), the Principal Reporter may request additional information from the local authority.

(5) If the Principal Reporter has not required a local authority to give the Principal Reporter a report under section 66(4), the Principal Reporter must require a local authority to give the Principal Reporter a report under that section.

DEFINITIONS

C.448.1 "child": s.199.
"children's hearing": s.5.
"compulsory supervision order": s.83.
"place of safety": ss.202(1) and 189.
"local authority": Local Government (Scotland) Act 1994 s.2.
"Principal Reporter": s.14 and Sch.3 paras 8–10.

Requirement under Antisocial Behaviour etc. (Scotland) Act 2004

GENERAL NOTE
The provisions of this section constitute the final step in the route to a hearing which started with the supply of information from the local authority, constable, court or other person under ss.60(3), 61(2), 62(2) and 64(2) and continued through s.66(2).

C.448.2

Subs.(1)
As already mentioned, the Reporter must be satisfied both as to the existence of a s.67 ground and of the child's need for a compulsory supervision order (CSO) before he or she can proceed.

C.448.3

Subs.(2)
Note here the mandatory duty on the Reporter to arrange a children's hearing if the test has been met.

C.448.4

Subs.(3)
In this subsection, note that the hearing must be arranged to take place within three calendar days and not three working days.

C.448.5

Subss.(4) and (5)
These provisions have the effect that a children's hearing which has to dispose of the child's case will have a Social Background Report from a local authority. The effect of subs.(4) is to enable the Reporter to obtain a supplementary, up-to-date report to cover the period of time between the original report and the hearing.

C.448.6

Requirement under Antisocial Behaviour etc. (Scotland) Act 2004

70.—(1) This section applies where—

(a) under section 12(1A) of the Antisocial Behaviour etc. (Scotland) Act 2004 (asp 8) the sheriff requires the Principal Reporter to arrange a children's hearing in respect of a child, and

(b) a compulsory supervision order is not in force in relation to the child.

(2) This Act applies as if—

(a) the requirement of the sheriff were a determination of the sheriff under section 108 that the section 67 ground specified in the statement given to the Principal Reporter under section 12 of the Antisocial Behaviour etc. (Scotland) Act 2004 was established in relation to the child, and

(b) the sheriff had directed the Principal Reporter under section 108(2) to arrange a children's hearing.

C.449

DEFINITIONS
"child": s.199.
"children's hearing": s.5.
"compulsory supervision order": s.83.
"Principal Reporter": s.14 and Sch.3 paras 8–10.

C.449.1

GENERAL NOTE
The amended s.12 of the Antisocial Behaviour etc. (Scotland) Act 2004 is inserted into that Act by Sch.5 para.3 of this present Act; its effect is to empower the sheriff should he or she decide to make an interim or final antisocial behaviour order, to require the Reporter to arrange a hearing. If the sheriff does so decide then the provisions of this present section apply except where the child is already subject to a compulsory supervision order (CSO). Note that this provision in the Antisocial Behaviour etc. (Scotland) Act 2004 applies only to children below the age of 16 years.

C.449.2

Subs.(1)
The decision of the sheriff as to the granting or not of an antisocial behaviour order (ASBO), being a decision under the Antisocial Behaviour etc. (Scotland) Act 2004, and not a decision by virtue of the present Act, is not subject to the overarching principles enacted in ss.25, 27 and 29 of this Act, although the sheriff, as a public authority, will have to observe the proportionality principle of the European Convention. However, before deciding on whether to grant an ASBO the sheriff must require the Reporter to arrange an advice hearing on whether an ASBO is

C.449.3

necessary for the purpose of protecting the persons relevant to the order from further antisocial behaviour by the child; and the sheriff must "have regard" to the advice given. It may be assumed that the sheriff will have received a social background report on the child and this report will have been made available to the children's hearing in terms of r.26(2) of the Children's Hearings (Scotland) Act 2011 (Rules of Procedure in Children's Hearings) Rules 2013 (SSI 2013/194) and that such a report will have covered the issue of whether or not the child is already subject to a compulsory supervision order. The hearing, in deciding what advice to give, will be bound by the paramountcy of welfare principle and, it is thought, the views of the child principle (cf. Children's Hearings (Scotland) Act 2011 (Rules of Procedure in Children's Hearings) Rules 2013 (SSI 2013/194) r.6(1)(b)); it will not, technically, be bound by the minimum intervention principle, but it will be deciding on "necessity" and this amounts to the same thing—it will also be bound by the proportionality principle in the European Convention.

Subs.(2)(a)

C.449.4   *The section 67 ground specified in the statement ....* Section 12 of the Antisocial Behaviour etc. (Scotland) Act 2004, as now worded, requires the sheriff, where he or she elects to require the Reporter to arrange a children's hearing, to give the Reporter a "section 12 statement" specifying which of the s.67 grounds the sheriff considers applies to the child. This will not be the "offence by the child" ground under s.67(2)(j) since, under s.12(1)(b) of the 2004 Act, this ground may not be a ground relied on by the sheriff to require the Reporter to fix a hearing. This may be in deference to the principle, recognised by the First Division in *Constanda v M*, 1997 S.C. 217 and discussed in relation to s.67(2)(m) of the this Act, that a child should not be held as guilty of an offence unless the offence was proved to the criminal standard by corroborated evidence since, in the words of Lord Rodger, Parliament

"must have judged that the protection of the child's right to be treated in this respect like anyone else who is alleged to have committed an offence".

Section 143(1) of the Antisocial Behaviour etc. (Scotland) Act 2004 defines antisocial behaviour as occurring where a person, "A",

"(a)   acts in a manner that causes or is likely to cause alarm or distress or
(b)   pursues a course of conduct that causes or is likely to cause alarm or distress, to at least one person who is not of the same household as A; ..." and s.143(2) enacts "'conduct' includes speech; and a course of conduct must involve conduct on at least two occasions".

The foregoing definitions are wide enough to include a wide range of activities. Acting "in a manner that causes or is likely to cause alarm or distress" is almost the classic definition of breach of the peace, and therefore, although such conduct on the part of the child would entitle a sheriff, on the basis of the civil standard of proof which applies under the Antisocial Behaviour etc. (Scotland) Act 2004, to grant an ASBO, such conduct presumably could not, given the exclusion of the s.67(2)(j) ground from the sheriff's section 12 statement, form the basis of a requirement on the Reporter to arrange a hearing. However, conduct under other s.67 grounds which might include conduct amounting to offences by the child, might found the granting of an ASBO—for example, misuse of a controlled drug under the s.67(2)(i) ground, or many types of "bullying" or "gang behaviour" (which are the examples given in para.87 of the Explanatory Notes), which might include the offences of breach of the peace or assault, might come within ground 67(2)(m) and therefore be able to be included by the sheriff in a section 12 statement and therefore become equivalent to, in the words of this paragraph "a determination of the sheriff under section 108 [i.e. after proof or admission] that the s 67 ground specified ... was established in relation to the child."

The consequence of the foregoing is that the child could be held to have committed an offence without, in the words of Lord Rodger,

"the protection of the child's right to be treated in this respect like anyone else who is alleged to have committed an offence".

This would come about without the interposition of any decision of a hearing which could be the subject of an appeal. It is a question whether this could constitute a breach of art.6 of the European Convention (civil rights and criminal charges to be determined by a fair and impartial tribunal) since the initial decision of the sheriff must surely be regarded as such a tribunal. Moreover, *S v Miller*, 2001 S.C. 977; 2001 S.L.T. 531 decided that a determination by a children's hearing that a child required compulsory measures of supervision did not amount to a determination of a criminal charge under art.6. However, in *S v Miller* Lord Penrose, at [33], adopted Lord Rodger's view, quoted above. It remains a paradox that, whilst the Act finds it right specifically to exclude a s.67(2)(j) "offence by the child" ground from the grounds by virtue of which the sheriff may require the Reporter to arrange a hearing, it should apparently

Case remitted under section 49 of Criminal Procedure (Scotland) Act 1995

allow the possibility of an offence by the child under the guise of grounds 67(2)(l) and (m) to be founded on by the sheriff to justify requiring the Reporter to arrange a hearing.

It may be that, on the basis of the foregoing, those representing the child in the proceedings before the sheriff under the Antisocial Behaviour etc. (Scotland) Act 2004, may feel able to argue that the scheme of the Act is against permitting an offence by the child ground being used as a vehicle to take a child to a hearing in this way and that therefore the sheriff, having regard to the rights of the child in this respect, should refrain from requiring the Reporter to fix a hearing where the *only* ground in the case concerns an offence by the child within another ground, such as ground 67(2)(l) or (m).

In *Wotherspoon v Procurator Fiscal, Glasgow* [2017] HCJAC 17, the Justiciary Appeal Court, after reviewing the authorities, emphasised that for breach of the peace to be established the conduct concerned must be "genuinely alarming and disturbing".

Case remitted under section 49 of Criminal Procedure (Scotland) Act 1995

71.—(1) This section applies where under section 49 of the Criminal Procedure (Scotland) Act 1995 (c.46)—   C.450

(a) a court remits a case to the Principal Reporter to arrange for the disposal of the case by a children's hearing, and

(b) a compulsory supervision order is not in force in relation to the child or person whose case is remitted.

(2) A certificate signed by the clerk of the court stating that the child or person whose case is remitted has pled guilty to, or been found guilty of, the offence to which the case relates is conclusive evidence for the purposes of the children's hearing that the offence was committed by the child or person.

(3) This Act applies as if—

(a) the plea of guilty, or the finding of guilt, were a determination of the sheriff under section 108 that the ground in section 67(2)(j) was established in relation to the child, and

(b) the sheriff had directed the Principal Reporter under section 108(2) to arrange a children's hearing.

DEFINITIONS   C.450.1
"child": s.199.
"children's hearing": s.5.
"compulsory supervision order" ss.202(1) and 83.
"Principal Reporter": s.14 and Sch.3, paras 8–10.

GENERAL NOTE

Section 49 of the Criminal Procedure (Scotland) Act 1995 ("the 1995 Act") as amended, deals with three situations wherein a criminal court may remit to the Reporter to arrange for an advice hearing on the question of disposal, viz.:   C.450.2

(I) where a child or person who **is not** subject to a compulsory supervision order (CSO) or interim compulsory supervision order (ICSO) pleads guilty to, or is found guilty of, an offence (1995 Act s.49(1));

(II) where a child who **is** subject to a CSO or ICSO pleads guilty to, or is found guilty of, an offence (1995 Act, s.49(3)); and

(III) where a person who is not subject to a CSO or an ICSO, who is over 16 but not yet 17½, pleads guilty to or is found guilty of and offence in a summary court (1995 Act, s.49(6)).

The present section deals only with the first and third of these situations and enacts the procedural mechanism whereby the certificate signed by the clerk of the remitting (criminal) court is conclusive evidence that the offence was committed by the child or person concerned. The identical provision in respect of the situation where the child is subject to a CSO is contained within s.130(3) of the Act. The obligations and powers of the remitting criminal court are set out in s.49(2)–(7) of the 1995 Act as amended, and include the provisions that that section does not apply where the sentence for the offence concerned is fixed by law (s.49(5)), or to contraventions of s.51A of the Firearms Act 1968 or s.29 of the Violent Crime Reduction Act 2006, which the criminal court must deal with itself (s.59(3)). The procedure to be followed by the receiving hearing is enacted in r.75 of the Children's Hearings (Scotland) Act 2011 (Rules of Procedure in Children's Hearings) Rules 2013 (SSI 2013/194).

Children's Hearings (Scotland) Act 2011

Subs.(1)(b)
C.450.3 *Compulsory supervision order.* As noted above in the GENERAL NOTE, s.49 of the Criminal Procedure (Scotland) Act 1995, as amended, deals with the situation wherein (to quote the words of s.49(1) of that Act, as amended by Children's Hearings (Scotland) Act 2011 (Modification of Primary Legislation) Order 2013 (SSI 2013/211) Sch.1 para.10(5)) "a child who is not subject to a compulsory supervision order *or an interim compulsory supervision order* [our emphasis]". This present subsection does not include a reference to an interim compulsory supervision order, but we think it should be construed as if a child not subject to an interim compulsory supervision order were included—cf. the observations of Lord President Emslie in *McGregor v H*, referred to below.

Subs.(2)
C.450.4 This is an obviously sensible provision. It does not innovate on the existing law: under s.10 of the Law Reform (Miscellaneous Provisions) (Scotland) Act 1968 it is provided that for the purpose of proving in any civil proceedings that a person has been convicted of an offence an extract conviction shall establish commission of the offence unless the contrary is proved. The application of this provision in the context of the children's hearing system is discussed by Lord President Emslie in *McGregor v H*, 1983 S.L.T. 626 at 629.

Subs.(3)(a)
C.450.5 This provision, by equating the conviction to a determination by the sheriff after a proof hearing, would appear to lay to rest any concern, in a case wherein the child had pleaded guilty in the criminal court, that any difficulty would arise out of the decision in *M v Constanda*, 1999 S.C. 348, 1999 S.L.T. 494 wherein it was held that an admission of grounds at an earlier referral was not to be equated with the situation wherein evidence had been heard. In *McGregor v H*, Lord President Emslie, in the passage referred to above, strongly supports a purposive interpretation of the parallel provisions of the Children (Scotland) Act 1995 and points out that such an interpretation leads to the avoidance of unnecessary procedures.As the grounds are held as established, there is no need for a proof hearing. There is no place for the child or relevant persons to be asked if they accept or do not accept the grounds for referral.

Child in place of safety: Principal Reporter's powers

C.451 **72.**—(1) Subsection (2) applies where—
(a) the Principal Reporter is required by section 69(2) to arrange a children's hearing in relation to a child, and
(b) the child is being kept in a place of safety under section 65(2)(b).
(2) The Principal Reporter may direct—
(a) that the child be released from the place of safety, or
(b) that the child continue to be kept in the place of safety until the children's hearing.

DEFINITIONS
C.451.1 "child": s.199.
"children's hearing": s.5.
"place of safety": s.202(1).
"Principal Reporter": s.14 and Sch.3 paras 8–10.

GENERAL NOTE
C.451.2 This section replaces s.63 (1), (2) and (4) of the Children (Scotland) Act 1995. The duties of the Reporter with regard to timescales and reports from the local authority are contained in s.69. See s.189 below ("Places of safety: restrictions on use of police stations"). It is generally accepted that while a police station may be the only option in some circumstances, it is not an ideal environment for a child, even one whose behaviour has led to arrest and/or charge. Thus, given the importance of the paramountcy principle, the transfer of the child away from the police station to a more suitable location should be undertaken as a matter of urgency.

Subs.(1)
C.451.3 This subsection sets out the circumstances in which the Reporter may use his or her power contained in subs.(2) and applies when a child has been apprehended by the police, is being kept in a place of safety, the police have decided not to proceed with any charges against the child (see s.65(1)), and the Reporter has decided to bring the child to a hearing (see s.66(2)).

Child's duty to attend children's hearing

Subs.(2)

The Reporter has the power to direct either that the child must be released (s.72(2)(a)), or continue to be held in the place of safety (s.72(2)(b)). This is entirely the decision of the Reporter. The section provides no guidance as to the criteria that the Reporter should apply, but the paramountcy principle (s.25) will apply and consequently the Reporter will need to keep the welfare of the child in mind. In addition, as deprivation of liberty where there are no criminal charges is a serious matter, the Reporter would have to have good cause to believe that the release of the child would pose a serious risk to the child or others. In cases where the child's behaviour may pose a serious risk to him or herself or others, the Reporter may well be justified in deciding that the child should remain in the place of safety following the principle contained in s.26 of this Act. It should be noted that the Reporter does not have the power to decide on an alternative place of safety, but may only decide that the child be kept in his or her current location. Should a hearing not take place by the third day after the Reporter receives notification that the child is being held in a place of safety, there is no authority for the continued detention of the child and he or she must be released.

C.451.4

PART 7

ATTENDANCE AT CHILDREN'S HEARING

INTRODUCTION AND PRELIMINARY NOTE

Rather than dealing with duties and rights of attendance together as in ss.43 and 45 of the Children (Scotland) Act 1995, Pt 7 deals with them separately. It should be noted that there has been a change in language from the 1995 Act in that "duty" is used rather than "obligation". There is greater emphasis on the duty of the child and relevant persons to attend, and the list of those persons who have a right to attend children's hearings is more extensive than in the 1995 Act. There is separate provision for the excusing of a child from that part of a grounds hearing where the grounds are being explained in compliance with s.90(1). It is part and parcel of the emphasis in this Act on the importance of the attendance and participation of the child that the child may be excused but not excluded, and their representative may also not be excluded. It continues to be the case that a child who has been excused from attending all or part of a children's hearing may still exercise his or her right to attend. Clarification is given as to criteria to be applied by the hearing when considering whether to excuse a child or a relevant person from attendance at a hearing, or whether to exclude a person who has a right to attend (other than the child and his or her representative). When a person is excluded from all or part of a children's hearing, this section makes provision for the chairing member to provide that person with information as to what happened during his or her absence. This is always subject to the power of the hearing not to disclose information about the child or the child's case (see s.178). It should be noted that in any decision relating to excusing attendance or exclusion, "hearing" means a decision by all of the members of the hearing, not merely the chairing member. It should also be noted that the meaning of "hearing" in Pt 7 varies. Some sections apply to both children's hearings and pre-hearing panels, but others to children's hearings only. Relevant person in Pt 7 includes deemed relevant persons.

C.451.5

It is the Reporter's duty to notify the child and relevant persons of the hearing or pre-hearing panel. Detailed provisions are contained in the Children's Hearings (Scotland) Act 2011 (Rules of Procedure in Children's Hearings) Rules (SSI 2013/194), particularly in Pts 6–11.

Documents which must be provided as part of the notification include the grounds for referral, copies of reports, and all the paperwork which has been provided to the hearing or pre-hearing panel. In the opinion of the authors that, in order to comply with the UNCRC documents should be provided to the child and relevant persons in accessible format. This includes not only formats suitable for the disabled, but translations of documents for children and relevant persons where required. Failure to provide translated materials may give grounds for an appeal.

Child's duty to attend children's hearing

73.—(1) This section applies where by virtue of this Act a children's hearing is, or is to be, arranged in relation to a child.

(2) The child must attend the children's hearing unless the child is excused under subsection (3) or rules under section 177.

(3) A children's hearing may excuse the child from attending all or part of the children's hearing if the children's hearing is satisfied that—

  (a) the hearing relates to the ground mentioned in section 67(2)(b), (c),

C.452

(d) or (g) and the attendance of the child at the hearing, or that part of the hearing, is not necessary for a fair hearing,

(b) the attendance of the child at the hearing, or that part of the hearing, would place the child's physical, mental or moral welfare at risk, or

(c) taking account of the child's age and maturity, the child would not be capable of understanding what happens at the hearing or that part of the hearing.

(4) Where the children's hearing is a grounds hearing, the children's hearing may excuse the child from attending during an explanation given in compliance with section 90(1) only if it is satisfied that, taking account of the child's age and maturity, the child would not be capable of understanding the explanation.

DEFINITIONS

C.452.1 "child": s.199.
"children's hearing": s.5.
"ground": s.67.
"grounds hearing": s.90.

GENERAL NOTE
See Introduction and Preliminary Note, above.

Subs.(1)
C.452.2 It should be noted that the duty to attend, unless excused, does not apply to pre-hearing panels. There is no duty to attend a pre-hearing panel (PHP) and no power to issue a warrant to secure attendance at a PHP. Should the child fail to attend a grounds hearing the hearing, unless it wishes to discharge the referral, should ask the Reporter to arrange another grounds hearing and consider if an interim compulsory supervision order (s.86) should be granted as a matter of urgency or whether, in the event of an application by the Reporter for a warrant to secure attendance (ss.85 and 123), to grant such a warrant. In deciding on the appropriate action to take the hearing will be bound to apply the overarching principles and the European Convention principle of proportionality: it may be, for example, that there is an explanation for the child's non-attendance which indicates that neither of these courses is necessary and that all that is required is for a further grounds hearing to be arranged. For discussion of this see the *Practice and Procedure Manual*, published by Children's Hearings Scotland, at para.4.1.

Subs.(2)
C.452.3 The attendance of the child at a children's hearing is compulsory unless excused under subs.(3) or s.177(2). Whether or not to excuse the child from all or part of the hearing is wholly at the discretion of the hearing. Even if the hearing considers that one or more of the criteria in subs.(3) are met, it is not obliged to excuse the child from attending. However, this subsection does not apply to that portion of a grounds hearing where the explanation of the grounds is provided by the chairing member under s.90(1). This is dealt with in subs.(4) below.

The prerequisite for attendance by a relevant person is notification (see s.74(2)). This wording is absent from this subsection. However, where a child is capable of understanding a notification of a hearing it will be a prerequisite for his or her attendance. (See r.23 of the Children's Hearings (Scotland) Act 2011 (Rules of Procedure in Children's Hearings) Rules 2013 (SSI 2013/194) —"Other information to be given with notification of a children's hearing to the child and each relevant person".) A children's hearing will have to exercise great care in deciding on which option to take, in the event of non-attendance by the child (see annotations to s.88). Procedure at the hearing when the child has failed to attend is governed by r.64 of the Children's Hearings (Scotland) Act 2011 (Rules of Procedure in Children's Hearings) Rules 2013 (SSI 2013/194). The reader is directed to the discussion of the excusing of children by a pre-hearing panel at s.79.

Subs.(3)
C.452.4 This section makes provision for the child's attendance to be excused from all or part of the hearing, if the hearing is satisfied that one or more of three circumstances applies. Although this section does not specifically exclude a grounds hearing from its provision, given the wording of subs.(4), the criteria in (a) and (b) cannot apply to that portion of a grounds hearing in which the grounds are explained in compliance with s.90(1). A relevant person has no right to appeal the decision to excuse a child. The child may still attend even though excused. It should be noted

Child's duty to attend children's hearing

that while r.19 of the Children's Hearings (Scotland) Act 2011 (Rules of Procedure in Children's Hearings) Rules 2013 (SSI 2013/194) ("the Procedural Rules") requires the SCRA to take all reasonable steps to facilitate remote attendance, there is no obligation to do so unless the Reporter is satisfied that the child has a good reason for not attending in person. This appears to be an odd provision, as before the child may request remote attendance by electronic means, he or she must first have been excused from attending and therefore a PHP or children's hearing will already have considered the question of the attendance of the child. Therefore, the Reporter would have to consider very carefully the implications of such a refusal. It should be noted that there is no requirement to provide the child who has been excused from a portion of a hearing with an explanation of what has taken place during their absence as there is for a relevant person who has been excluded (s.76(3)). However, in order to ensure that the child may participate fully in the hearing, the chairing member must use his or her judgement as to what information would be appropriate to give to the child about what happened during his or her absence. Rule 63(3) of the Procedural Rules requires the chairing member, in situations where ground(s) for referral are not accepted or not understood, (i) to confirm and explain the decision, (ii) state the reason for the decision and (iii) to inform the child, each relevant person and any safeguarder of the right to appeal any decision to discharge the referral, make an interim compulsory supervision order or warrant to secure attendance, but the provision in (iii) this is subject to ss.73, 74, 75 and 79.

Subs.(3)(a)

Where the ground of referral relates to offences included in Sch.1 to the Criminal Procedure (Scotland) Act 1995, or those relating to rape, offences against children, and offences by those in a position of trust *and* the hearing considers that the attendance of the child is not necessary for a fair hearing, the child may be excused. This parallels the provisions in s.45(2)(a) of the Children (Scotland) Act 1995. This is clearly designed to protect the child from unnecessary distress.

C.452.5

Subs.(3)(b)

If the children's hearing relates to grounds other than those mentioned in s.67(2)(b), (c) or (g) *and* the hearing considers that the physical, mental or moral welfare of the child is at risk, they may excuse the child from attendance. This replaces the provision in s.45(2)(a) of the Children (Scotland) Act 1995 which allowed the hearing to excuse a child if it would be detrimental to the interests of the child for the child to be present. The current wording is rather stronger than that of the 1995 Act, and is a criterion which should be used with care if the result would be to excuse the child from the entire hearing. Scottish Children's Reporter Administration staff have considerable expertise and experience in managing very difficult circumstances to protect the child and others. Much can be managed to ensure that the child may participate during part or all of the hearing. In addition, the provisions in r.19(2) of the Children's Hearings (Scotland) Act 2011 (Rules of Procedure in Children's Hearings) Rules 2013 (SSI 2013/194) which allow a child to attend by telephone or other electronic means give greater flexibility and protection for the child. We direct the reader to the discussion at subs.(4) below of the implications for grounds hearings.

C.452.6

Subs.(3)(c)

Great care must be exercised by any hearing in deciding to excuse a child from the whole of a hearing solely on the ground that the child would not be capable of understanding what happens. This reason for excusing a child was not part of the Children (Scotland) Act 1995 but its inclusion here reflects what has become a common practice. Simply because a child may not understand all or part of what happens at the hearing may not be sufficient to excuse him or her. If the child is capable of forming a view about an aspect of their life, such as contact, then excusing him or her from attendance at the whole of a hearing may prevent that child from exercising his or her right under s.27(3). Where the views of the child have been presented to the hearing in a report, excusing the child from the whole of the hearing would have the effect of preventing that child from confirming or denying the accuracy of that part of the report under s.121.

C.452.7

Subs.(4)

The explanatory notes to this part of the Act make clear the intention was to ensure that a child who is capable of understanding the explanation of the grounds is present at the hearing to respond to the grounds. This may be entirely appropriate, but the terms of this subsection do not sit well with subs.(3) and with r.19 of the Children's Hearings (Scotland) Act 2011 (Rules of Procedure in Children's Hearings) Rules 2013 (SSI 2013/194). "Attendance" is not defined in

C.452.8

this Act, and the wording of s.73 does not appear to require attendance to be in person. However, r.19 makes for provision for attendance by electronic means *only* where the child has first been excused from attendance by a PHP or a children's hearing. The *only* reason a child may be excused from this part of the hearing is that they are not capable of understanding the explanation of the grounds. The unfortunate result is that a child who is capable of understanding the explanation of the grounds by the chairing member under s.90 cannot be excused from attending that portion of the grounds even if excused from the rest of the hearing because the hearing is satisfied that attendance would put the child's physical, mental or moral welfare at risk. This is in contradiction to subs.(3)(b). The Children (Scotland) Act 1995 did not differentiate between grounds hearings and other hearings and thus this difficulty did not arise. This subsection provides in effect that, notwithstanding the provisions in subs.(3), no child, other than a child who is too young or too immature to understand the explanation of grounds, may be excused from that portion of a grounds hearing under this section.

Relevant person's duty to attend children's hearing

C.453 74.—(1) This section applies where by virtue of this Act a children's hearing is, or is to be, arranged in relation to a child.

(2) Each relevant person in relation to the child who is notified of the children's hearing by virtue of rules under section 177 must attend the children's hearing unless the relevant person is—
  (a) excused under subsection (3) or rules under section 177, or
  (b) excluded from the children's hearing under section 76(2).

(3) A children's hearing may excuse a relevant person from attending all or part of the children's hearing if the children's hearing is satisfied that—
  (a) it would be unreasonable to require the relevant person's attendance at the hearing or that part of the hearing, or
  (b) the attendance of the relevant person at the hearing, or that part of the hearing, is unnecessary for the proper consideration of the matter before the hearing.

(4) A relevant person who is required to attend a children's hearing under subsection (2) and fails to do so commits an offence and is liable on summary conviction to a fine not exceeding level 3 on the standard scale.

DEFINITIONS
C.453.1 "child": s.199.
"children's hearing": s.5.
"excused": s.177.
"exclusion": ss.76, 77.
"relevant person": s.200.

GENERAL NOTE

Subs.(1)
C.453.2 The duty to attend, unless excused, does not apply to pre-hearing panels.

Subs.(2)
C.453.3 Unlike the child's duty to attend, it is made clear that the relevant person only has a duty to attend a hearing *if* he or she has received notification from the Reporter. The reason for this is likely to be the potential for an offence and fine contained in subs.(4) below. A relevant person may be excused attendance (subs.(3) below), or excluded from all or part of a hearing (s.76(2)). Where a relevant person has been excused attendance, r.19 of the Children's Hearings (Scotland) Act 2011 (Rules of Procedure in Children's Hearings) Rules 2013 (SSI 2013/194) allows them to request attendance by remote means. It should be noted that while r.19 of the Rules of Procedure requires the Scottish Children's Reporter Administration to take all reasonable steps to facilitate remote attendance, there is no obligation to do so unless the Reporter is satisfied that the individual has a good reason for not attending in person. This appears to be an odd inclusion, as before the individual may request remote access by electronic means, he or she must first have been excused from attending and therefore a pre-hearing panel (PHP) or children's hearing will already have considered the question of the attendance of the individual. Therefore, the Reporter would have to consider very carefully the implications of such a refusal.

Power to exclude relevant person from children's hearing

Subs.(3)
This replaces s.45(8)(b) of the Children (Scotland) Act 1995 and is in much the same language. Unlike children, the effect on the relevant person of attending a hearing does not form part of the considerations of a hearing with regard to excusing that person from all or part of a hearing. The hearing needs only be satisfied that it would be unreasonable to expect attendance or that their attendance is not necessary for proper consideration. The emphasis is on the need to make decisions about a child without unnecessary delays, rather than on the right of a parent to be present.   C.453.4

Subs.(4)
The Children (Scotland) Act 1995 s.45(9) made it a criminal offence for a relevant person to fail to attend a hearing unless excused. This subsection is identical in its provisions. It is worth reminding the reader that a prerequisite for attendance by a relevant person is that he or she has received notification of the hearing (see s.74(2) above). An example of a hearing being split so as to avoid the child being confronted by persons with whom she had difficulties is found in *CF v MF & GF and Scottish Reporter* [2017] CSIH 44, discussed below under s.81(3) and in the General Note to s.90.   C.453.5

Power to proceed in absence of relevant person

75.—(1) This section applies where a relevant person in relation to a child is required by section 74(2) to attend a children's hearing and fails to do so.   C.454

(2) The children's hearing may, if it considers it appropriate to do so, proceed with the children's hearing in the relevant person's absence.

DEFINITIONS
"child": s.199.
"children's hearing": s.5.
"relevant person": s.200.   C.454.1

GENERAL NOTE
While, as mentioned above in the General Note to s.74, the attendance of relevant person(s) is important because of their close relationship with the child and consequent potential contribution to the hearing's deliberations, this section recognises that the absence of the relevant person should not necessarily frustrate the hearing from proceeding.   C.454.2

Subs.(1)
The duty to attend does not apply to pre-hearing panels.   C.454.3

Subs.(2)
In the event that a relevant person fails to attend a children's hearing, the hearing may continue without him or her if it considers it appropriate to do so. The decision must be made by all members of the hearing, not merely the chairing member. Consideration should include matters such as: whether the hearing is considering a matter that is time-sensitive; the impact of continuing or of delay upon the welfare of the child; the likelihood that the relevant person would attend a subsequent hearing if the case was continued. As with the Children (Scotland) Act 1995, there is no need for a hearing to "start all over again" should a relevant person arrive late (see Professor Kenneth McK. Norrie, *Children (Scotland) Act 1995*, revised edn (Edinburgh: W. Green, 1998), annotation to s.45). The chairing member will need to provide the person with a summary of what happened prior to his or her arrival to ensure that he or she understands what has taken place and is able to participate during the rest of the hearing.   C.454.4

Power to exclude relevant person from children's hearing

76.—(1) This section applies where a children's hearing is satisfied that the presence at the hearing of a relevant person in relation to the child—   C.455
  (a) is preventing the hearing from obtaining the views of the child, or
  (b) is causing, or is likely to cause, significant distress to the child.
(2) The children's hearing may exclude the relevant person from the children's hearing for as long as is necessary.
(3) After the exclusion has ended, the chairing member of the children's

hearing must explain to the relevant person what has taken place in the relevant person's absence.

DEFINITIONS
C.455.1   "child": s.199.
"children's hearing": s.5.
"relevant person": s.200.

GENERAL NOTE
C.455.2   While, as mentioned above in the General Note to s.74, the attendance of relevant person(s) is important because of their close relationship with the child and consequent potential contribution to the hearing's deliberations, this section recognises that in certain specified circumstances the presence of a relevant person may inhibit the child's contribution to the hearing's deliberations.

This section replaces s.46(1) and (2) of the Children (Scotland) Act 1995 and since, unlike s.78, it does not contain a provision extending it to pre-hearing panels, does not apply to them. Professor Kenneth McK. Norrie's general note to s.46 (see Professor McK Norrie, *Children (Scotland) Act 1995*, revised edn (Edinburgh: W. Green, 1998) cannot be improved upon and is as applicable to this Act as to the 1995 Act. We are grateful for his permission to quote it here.

"Given that Art.6 ECHR guarantees that both the child and the relevant person have a right of participation in any civil process in which their rights and interests might be affected (*W v United Kingdom* (1988) 10 E.H.R.R 29; *Venema v The Netherlands* [2003] F.L.R. 552; *TP & KM v United Kingdom* (2002) 34 E.H.RR. 2) the power to exclude a relevant person from a children's hearing must be exercised with extreme caution, and only when absolutely necessary for the purposes stated in this section. It is possible for a single hearing to achieve these purposes by having the child and the relevant person attend separately rather than denying the right to attend and, as always, alternatives which do not infringe, or which interfere with to a lesser extent, the child's and relevant person's Art. 6 rights out always to be considered and preferred over those that do, or do to a greater extent."

The decision to exclude can be made at any time during the hearing, should the hearing feel it necessary.

Subs.(1)
C.455.3   "Relevant person" here includes a deemed relevant person (s.81(4)).

The reasons for exclusion relate exclusively to the child, not to other persons present, therefore the child should be given the opportunity to tell the hearing if he or she feels the need to speak outwith the presence of a relevant person.

The wording of this subsection differs significantly from s.46(1) of the 1995 Act. It does not require the hearing to be "considering" the case, which, as Professor Norrie points out in his annotation to that section (see Norrie, *Children (Scotland) Act 1995* (1998)), would not include that portion of a grounds hearing when the grounds were being put to the child and relevant persons. There is no requirement that the grounds be put to the child and relevant persons at the same time, so they may be kept separate to protect the child. An example of a hearing being split so as to avoid the child being confronted by persons with whom she had difficulties is found in *CF v MF & GF and Scottish Reporter* [2017] CSIH 44, discussed below under s.81(3) and in the General Note to s.90. However, it would be a serious art.6 breach should a relevant person be excluded from a grounds hearing prior to or during the putting of the grounds, thereby preventing him or her from responding to the grounds. However, in the event that the behaviour of a relevant person is such that the hearing feels that there is no alternative but to exclude him or her prior to the grounds being read, then it will be necessary to hold him or her as having not accepted the grounds.

Preventing the hearing from obtaining the views of the child. It is not uncommon for the presence of a relevant person to inhibit a child from exercising his or her right to express a view to the hearing. It does not require that the behaviour be actively preventing the child from expressing a view, such as a relevant person persistently interrupting, contradicting or speaking over the child. It is equally applicable where the child is likely to be inhibited by the mere presence of the relevant person.

Significant distress. The hearing must consider that the effect upon the child is likely to cause distress of a level that is not acceptable. The hearing may consider factors such as: the relationship between the child and the relevant person such that it is actively emotionally damaging to the child; the child may not wish to hurt the feelings of the relevant person by speaking openly; the child may have been abused by the relevant person and is frightened, or it

Power to exclude relevant person's representative from children's hearing

may be that the relevant person uses the opportunity presented by the hearing to undermine the child and his or her current placement. It is not enough that the child has merely expressed the wish to speak to the hearing alone: *G and J Appellants* [2016] SC GLA 45, sub nom. *G v Children's Reporter*, 2016 S.L.T. 293 (a case concerning the exclusion of a relevant person's representative, but the principle is the same).

Subs.(2)
The decision whether to exclude the relevant person is entirely at the discretion of the hearing. Even if the hearing is satisfied that the conditions permitting the exclusion of a relevant person are met, they are not obliged to do so. The decision may be made at any time during the hearing if it is considered necessary. C.455.4

Subs.(3)
The exclusion of the relevant person being a potential art.6 breach, this provision repeats that of the Children (Scotland) Act 1995 s.46(2) by requiring the chairing member to provide the relevant person with the substance of what was said in his or her absence. Where under the 1995 Act provision the chairing member could not withhold any information, this section should be read in conjunction with s.178. This would allow the chairing member to withhold from the relevant person any part of the discussion if to disclose it would be likely to cause significant harm to the child. Withholding such information should not be done lightly. The test is "significant" harm and the hearing will be required to balance the potential harm to the child with the art.6 rights of the relevant person (see *Re D (Minors) (Adoption Reports: Confidentiality)* [1996] A.C. 593, per Lord Mustill at 615 and *Re A (A Child) (Disclosure of Third Party Information)* [2012] UKSC 60; [2012] 3 W.L.R. 1484, per Lady Hale at [21]). The child should be made fully aware before speaking to the children's hearing outwith the presence of the relevant person that the substance of the discussion will likely be given to the relevant person upon their return to the hearing. Any decision to withhold information should be made prior to the return of the relevant person, and the chairing member should take care to ensure that the reasoning of the hearing in making that decision is made clear in the record of proceedings. In practice "redacted" reasons (i.e. excluding confidential matter) for the decision of the children's hearing may in appropriate circumstances be notified to a relevant person—see our discussion of this difficult matter in our commentary on s.178, below, including the official advice on redacting quoted in the paragraph headed "*Official advice as to the practical effect of the foregoing for the conduct of a children's hearing*". C.455.5

Power to exclude relevant person's representative from children's hearing

77.—(1) This section applies where a children's hearing is satisfied that the presence at the hearing of a representative of a relevant person in relation to the child— C.456
    (a) is preventing the hearing from obtaining the views of the child, or
    (b) is causing, or is likely to cause, significant distress to the child.
(2) The children's hearing may exclude the representative from the children's hearing for as long as is necessary.
(3) After the exclusion has ended, the chairing member of the children's hearing must explain to the representative what has taken place in the representative's absence.

DEFINITIONS
    "child": s.199.
    "children's hearing": s.5.
    "chairing member": Sch.7.
    "relevant person": s.200.
    "representative" s.78.

C.456.1

GENERAL NOTE
This section recognises that in certain circumstances the presence of the representative of a relevant person may inhibit the child's participation in the hearing and makes provision for this.

Subs.(1)
This section replaces the provision in s.46(1) of the Children (Scotland) Act 1995 and since, unlike s.78, it does not contain a provision extending it to pre-hearing panels, does not apply to C.456.2

them. The term "representative of the relevant person" includes a lay supporter or advocate as well as a legally qualified representative. The power to exclude a representative is needed as s.78 gives such persons a right to attend. The test is identical to that for exclusion of a relevant person in s.76 above and is purely based on the impact on the child. The considerations we have mentioned above in relation to s.76(3) apply equally here. It is worth noting that the hearing is not required to consider the impact on the relevant person of the exclusion of the representative. The reader is directed to the note by Sheriff Reid (see *G and J Children's Hearing* [2016] S.C. GLA 45) with a caveat that there is no power to exclude the reporter.

Significant distress. Much of what is discussed at a children's hearing is distressing for the child. The hearing will need to be satisfied that the level of distress is likely to be such that it outweighs the need for the child to participate. The test will be simply what the impact on the particular child is likely to be and it is the welfare principle that should guide the hearing in making its decision. It is, of course, the right of the child to refuse to be excused and to remain. Where it is the case that there is information that it is believed should be withheld from the child who is refusing to be excused, then the correct procedure is for a formal request for non-disclosure to be made (see s.178).

Subs.(2)

C.456.3   While exclusion of a relevant person's representative would not cause an art.6 breach in respect of the representative, it could potentially be a breach of the relevant person's rights under that article as the exclusion of the representative may adversely affect the relevant person's ability to participate in the hearing. Thus it is essential that any exclusion be considered carefully, and the representative provided with sufficient information on his or her return to the hearing to allow for him or her to provide effective support to the relevant person. It is not enough that the child has merely expressed the wish to speak to the hearing alone: *G and J Appellants* [2016] SC GLA 45, sub nom. *G v Children's Reporter*, 2016 S.L.T. 293.

Subs.(3)

C.456.4   In the event that a relevant person's representative is excluded from all or part of a hearing, the chairing member has the same obligation to explain to them what has happened during his or her absence. The children's hearing also has the power under s.178 to withhold information from the representative. See our discussion on s.76(3), above, for mention of the recommended practice of notifying "redacted" reasons to a relevant person—the same considerations, mutatis mutandis, apply here. It is worth restating that in contrast with this section, there is no power to exclude the representative of the child (see s.78 below).

Rights of certain persons to attend children's hearing

C.457   **78.**—(1) The following persons have a right to attend a children's hearing—
(a) the child (whether or not the child has been excused from attending),
(b) a person representing the child,
(c) a relevant person in relation to the child (unless that person is excluded under section 76(2)),
(d) a person representing a relevant person in relation to the child (unless that person is excluded under section 77(2)),
(e) the Principal Reporter,
(f) if a safeguarder is appointed under this Act in relation to the child, the safeguarder,
(g) [*Repealed by the Public Bodies (Abolition of Administrative Justice and Tribunals Council) Order 2013 (SI 2013/2042) Sch.1 para.42 (effective 19 August 2013).*]
(h) a member of an area support team (acting in that person's capacity as such),
(i) subject to subsection (5), a representative of a newspaper or news agency.

(2) No other person may attend a children's hearing unless—
(a) the person's attendance at the hearing is considered by the chairing member of the children's hearing to be necessary for the proper consideration of the matter before the children's hearing,

Rights of certain persons to attend children's hearing

(b) the person is otherwise granted permission to attend by the chairing member of the children's hearing, or

(c) the person is authorised or required to attend by virtue of rules under section 177.

(3) The chairing member may not grant permission to a person under subsection (2)(b) if the child or a relevant person in relation to the child objects to the person attending the children's hearing.

(4) The chairing member must take all reasonable steps to ensure that the number of persons present at a children's hearing at the same time is kept to a minimum.

(5) The children's hearing may exclude a representative of a newspaper or news agency from any part of the hearing where it is satisfied that—

(a) it is necessary to do so to obtain the views of the child, or

(b) the presence of that person is causing, or is likely to cause, significant distress to the child.

(6) Where a person is excluded under subsection (5), after the exclusion has ended, the chairing member may explain to the person, where appropriate to do so, the substance of what has taken place in the person's absence.

[1] (7) In this section "children's hearing" includes a pre-hearing panel.

NOTE
1. As amended by the Children's Hearings (Scotland) Act 2011 (Modification of Primary Legislation) Order 2013 (SSI 2013/211) Sch.1 para.20(9) (effective 24 June 2013).

DEFINITIONS
"area support team": Sch.1 para.12(1).
"child": s.199.
"children's hearings": s.5.
"chairing member": s.6(4) and Sch.3 para.7.
"Principal Reporter": s.14 and Sch.3 paras 8–10.
"pre-hearing panel": s.79(2).
"relevant person": s.201.
"safeguarder": s.202.

GENERAL NOTE
The list of those who have a right to attend is more extensive than that in the Children (Scotland) Act 1995, and it should be noted that while these persons have been given a right to attend, the only persons on the list who may be excluded are: the relevant person (s.76(2)) (including here a deemed relevant person (s.81(4)), the relevant person's representative (s.77(2)) and the press (subs.(5), below). Rule 19 of the Children's Hearings (Scotland) Act 2011 (Rules of Procedure in Children's Hearings) Rules 2013 (SSI 2013/194) (hereinafter referred to as 'the Procedural Rules' or the 'Rules') allows for attendance by electronic means for the child or relevant person who has been excused from attendance and the reader is directed to the annotations at ss.73(3)(b) and 74(2). An individual seeking to be deemed as a relevant person (cf. s.79(2)(a)(i)) can request remote attendance under r.19 of the Procedural Rules. It will be at the discretion of the Reporter to decide whether he or she is satisfied that the individual has a reasonable excuse for not attending in person. If so, then the Reporter must take all reasonable steps to facilitate such attendance. For the purposes of this section, a children's hearing includes a pre-hearing panel (PHP) although it must be remembered that there is no duty of attendance by the child or relevant person at a PHP. Any right of a would-be relevant person to attend would be limited to attending that portion of the hearing where relevant person status was being considered.

Subs.(1)
(a) While s.73 deals at some length with the child's duty to attend, the right of the child to attend, which is of even greater importance, is dealt with in only 12 words. There is no provision for the exclusion of the child and thus the child's right to attend is absolute, and cannot be over-ridden if his or her attendance has been excused by a PHP or children's hearing. Unfortunately this is not sufficiently widely adhered to, and children have been prevented from attending. It is essential that when a pre-hearing panel is

asked to excuse a child who is capable of having a view about his or her attendance, that the child's preference about attendance be provided to the PHP. The child should also be given information about remote attendance. The reader is directed to the annotation at s.73(4) above for a discussion of attendance.

(b) The child has the right to have a representative. The representative may be legally qualified, be a lay advocate (including a person from an advocacy service under s.122 of this Act (not yet in force as at time of writing)) or a person of the child's choice such as a relative or other person (see s.104 below). The child who is legally represented may also have the assistance of another person as representative (the Procedural Rules r.11(2)). There is no requirement that the representative be an adult. This subsection gives that representative a right to attend. This is in no way dependent upon the attendance of the child. Rule 11(1) makes clear that the representative may assist the child to express a view, but does not limit their role to that assistance. Where a child is unable to attend a hearing for whatever reason, or has been excused, the presence of a representative can ensure that the child's view is available to the panel, and can ensure that the child has a clear understanding of what happened at the hearing.

(c) The relevant person has a right to attend a hearing or pre-hearing panel held in respect of the child. Exclusion of relevant persons is dealt with in s.76, and the power to proceed with the hearing in the absence of a relevant person in s.75. "Relevant person" includes a person who has been deemed to be a relevant person.

(d) A relevant person is entitled to take a representative to the hearing. As with the child's representative, they may be legally qualified, a lay advocate or a person of the adult's choice, and where legally represented, may also have a lay representative (see r.11). As with the child's representative, the right to attend is not dependent on the presence of the relevant person. The power to exclude the relevant person's representative is contained in s.77 above.

(e) The Principal Reporter's right of attendance will include any employee of SCRA to whom the Principal Reporter has delegated the task (Sch.3 para.10).

(f) The safeguarder's right to attend lasts only for the duration of his or her appointment.

(g) Subsection (g) (which allowed the attendance of a member of the Administrative and Justice Tribunals Council or the Scottish Committee of that Council) has been repealed by the Public Bodies (Abolition of Administrative Justice and Tribunals Council) Order 2013.

(h) This provision allows for the overseeing of hearing members.

(i) There is a balance to be struck between guaranteeing the privacy of the child in the proceedings, and ensuring that proceedings are transparent. Representatives of the press media have always been permitted but they may be excluded from all or part of the hearing if the needs of the child require it. The provisions for excluding the representatives of the press are found in subs.(5).

Subs.(2)

C.457.5   Attendance at children's hearings is to be kept to a minimum (see subs.4), therefore unless a person has a right to attend, or is either authorised or required to attend under s.177, permission must be granted by the chairing member. The chairing member's discretion is subject to subs.(3). The result of the section is a presumption that no one other than those with a right to attend should be there unless one of the criteria at (2)(a) or (b) is met, or unless the person is authorised or required to attend under (2)(c) which refers to the rules under s.177. Apart from those who have a right to attend or are authorised or required to attend, it is for the chairing member to decide on attendance by others for all or part of the hearing or PHP. Where there is no right of attendance, there is no need to exclude such persons and they can be asked to leave all or part of the hearing or PHP. The chairing member has no obligation to provide those persons with information about what happened during their absence, and can use his or her judgement in deciding what information should be provided when the exclusion ends.

(a) It is this paragraph that allows the professionals working with the child and/or the family to attend. It would also allow those caring for or involved with the child's life who are not relevant persons, but who may have a useful contribution to make to attend.

(b) This paragraph allows for the presence of the police, who, not infrequently, are asked by the Reporter to attend because there is an apprehension that the child or a family member may behave in a way that will disturb the hearing or place any of those attending at risk. It also allows for an observer to be present at what is, otherwise, closed proceedings.

(c) Rule 20 of the Procedural Rules specifically authorises constables, prison officers or a person who has in their custody a person who has in his or her custody a person who

Referral of certain matters for pre-hearing determination

has a duty to attend a hearing or PHP. This includes secure unit staff, young person's institution staff and medical staff should the person be held under a medical treatment order. Authorisation to attend allows these persons to be present at the hearing without the consent of the hearing or any other person. There is no provision for their exclusion. It should be noted that the presence of such persons is usually to ensure that the person in their custody cannot abscond or place other persons at any risk. There is no implication that these persons will participate in any way in the hearing.

Subs.(3)

The chairing member may not allow attendance of a person such as an observer under subs.(2)(b) if either the child or a relevant person objects. This right of objection does not apply if the chairing member considers a person's attendance to be necessary to the proper consideration of the case. **C.457.6**

Subs.(4)

This applies only to those persons who do not have a right of attendance. The participation of the child, and indeed a relevant person is at the heart of the hearing. The greater the number of people present, the harder it can be for the child to participate. In addition, hearings must be conducted in compliance with the ECHR and art.8 requires respect for private and family life which would require the restricting of attendance to those whose presence is necessary for the proper consideration of the case (with exceptions for subs.(2)(b)). **C.457.7**

Subs.(5)

This power to exclude, as with the other powers of exclusion, is given to the hearing not merely the chairing member. The criteria mirror those for the exclusion of a relevant person (s.76) or a relevant person's representative (s.77). Judgement as to what amounts to "significant distress" is left to the hearing, but the word "significant" indicates that the distress will not be merely embarrassment. The test will be simply what the impact on the particular child is likely to be and it is the welfare principle that should guide the hearing in making their decision. It will be necessary for the chairing member to ensure that the child understands that no press reporting can identify him or her (see s.182). It should be noted that there is no such provision to exclude a representative of the press if it is the relevant person who finds their presence distressing or inhibiting. "Any part of the hearing" should be taken to mean all or part of the hearing or pre-hearing panel. **C.457.8**

Subs.(6)

Where a representative of a newspaper or news agency has been excluded from part or all of a hearing, the chairing member, unlike in the case of relevant persons or their representatives, is not required to provide him or her with the substance of what happened during that exclusion. It is entirely at the discretion of the chairing member what information, if any, is provided. There is no reason why the chairing member could not deem it appropriate to provide information where the representative has been excluded from the entirety of the hearing. It would not be "appropriate" for the chairing person to explain the substance of what had taken place in the person's absence if doing so would risk significant harm to the child. See discussion under ss.178, 179 and 180. **C.457.9**

PART 8

PRE-HEARING PANEL

Referral of certain matters for pre-hearing determination

79.—[1] (1) Subsections (2) to (5) apply where a children's hearing is to be held in relation to a child by virtue of section 69(2) or Part 9 to 11 or 13. **C.458**

[2] (1A) Subsection (5A) applies (in addition to subsections (2) to (5)) where the children's hearing is—
(a) a subsequent children's hearing under Part 11, or
(b) held for the purposes of reviewing a compulsory supervision order.
(2) The Principal Reporter—
(a) must refer the matter of whether a particular individual should be deemed to be a relevant person in relation to the child for determination by three members of the Children's Panel selected by

the National Convener (a "pre-hearing panel") if requested to do so by—
  (i) the individual in question,
  (ii) the child, or
  (iii) a relevant person in relation to the child,
(b) may refer that matter for determination by a pre-hearing panel on the Principal Reporter's own initiative,
(c) may refer a matter of a type mentioned in subsection (3) for determination by a pre-hearing panel—
  (i) on the Principal Reporter's own initiative, or
  (ii) following a request to the Principal Reporter from the child, a relevant person in relation to the child, or if a safeguarder has been appointed for the child, the safeguarder.
(3) Those matters are—
(a) whether the child should be excused from attending the children's hearing,
(b) whether a relevant person in relation to the child should be excused from attending the children's hearing,
(c) whether it is likely that the children's hearing will consider making a compulsory supervision order including a secure accommodation authorisation in relation to the child,
(d) a matter specified in rules under section 177(2)(a).
(4) For the purposes of subsection (3)(a), the pre-hearing panel may excuse the child from attending the children's hearing only if—
(a) the pre-hearing panel is satisfied that any of paragraphs (a) to (c) of section 73(3) applies, or
(b) the child may be excused under rules under section 177.
(5) For the purposes of subsection (3)(b), the pre-hearing panel may excuse a relevant person in relation to the child from attending the children's hearing only if—
(a) the pre-hearing panel is satisfied that section 74(3)(a) or (b) applies, or
(b) the relevant person may be excused under rules under section 177.
[2] (5A) The Principal Reporter—
(a) must refer the matter of whether an individual deemed to be a relevant person by virtue of section 81 should continue to be deemed to be a relevant person in relation to the child for determination by a pre-hearing panel if requested to do so by—
  (i) the individual so deemed,
  (ii) the child, or
  (iii) a relevant person in relation to the child,
(b) may refer that matter for determination by a pre-hearing panel on the Principal Reporter's own initiative.
(6) A member of the Children's Panel selected for a pre-hearing panel may (but need not) be a member of the children's hearing.

NOTES

C.458.1 1. As amended by the Children and Young People (Scotland) Act 2014 (asp 8) Pt 16 s.84(2) (effective 26 January 2015).
2. Inserted by the Children and Young People (Scotland) Act 2014 (asp 8) Pt 16 s.84(2) (effective 26 January 2015).

DEFINITIONS
"child": s.199.
"children's hearing": s.5.
"children's panel": s.4.
"compulsory supervision order": ss.202(1) and 83.
"National Convener": s.1.
"pre-hearing panel": ss.202(1) and 79(2)(a).

Referral of certain matters for pre-hearing determination

"Principal Reporter" s.14 and Sch.3 paras 8–10.
"relevant person": s.200.
"secure accommodation authorisation": ss.202(1) and 85.

GENERAL NOTE

This section identifies the matters that require determination by a "pre-hearing panel" ("PHP") and sets out the persons who may request that a matter be determined by such a panel. A pre-hearing panel is made up of three members of the Children's Panel selected by the National Convener (in practice by the Area Support Teams (AST)—see *Area Support Teams: Functions, Roles and Responsibilities* (CHS, 2012), para.5.1 found at *http://www.chscotland.gov. uk/our-publications/practice/2012/06/area-support-teams-functions,-roles-and-responsibilities/* [Accessed October 2017]). Subsection (6) provides that a member of a pre-hearing panel may serve on the substantive children's hearing, but does not require this. The make-up of a pre-hearing panel is the same as that of a children's hearing, i.e. it must contain male and female panel members (for discussion of the implications of this, see above in our discussion of s.6(3)(a)) and, so far as practicable, be composed of panel members from the relevant local authority area (s.6(5) of the Act, as added by the Children's Hearings (Scotland) Act 2011 (Modification of Primary Legislation) Order 2013 (SSI 2013/211) Sch.1 para.20(2)). The matters to be determined by a pre-hearing panel have been split between subs.(2)—the matter of a "deemed relevant person" and subs.(3)—the remaining matters. The reason for this split is to allow for the procedures described in subs.(5A) and s.81A below to effect the "un-deeming" of a deemed relevant person where that person, through a change of circumstances, has ceased to be qualified as a deemed relevant person and it is no longer appropriate for that individual to have the rights of a relevant person. The definition of relevant person contained in s.200 is limited to persons who have or who have acquired parental responsibilities and rights in relation to a child by virtue of statutory intervention—see s.200 below—thus further narrowing the scope of the definition that was found in s.93(2)(b)(c) of the 1995 Act. This was despite the decision of the Supreme Court in *Principal Reporter v K* [2010] UKSC 56; 2011 S.C. (U.K.S.C.) 91; 2011 S.L.T. 271 which stated that, for an unmarried father to be considered a relevant person, the wording "or who appears to have established family life with the child with which the decision of a children's hearing may interfere" required to be added to the definition contained in s.93(2)(b)(c) of the 1995 Act. This wording was not incorporated into the definition of relevant person under s.200. However, under s.200(g), the Children's Hearings (Scotland) Act 2011 (Review of Contact Directions and Definition of Relevant Person) Order 2013 (SSI 2013/193) has been brought into force. Article 3(2)(a)(i) of this Order widens the definition of relevant person to include any parent other than a person who has parental responsibilities and rights under Part 1 of the 1995 Act or parental responsibility under Part 1 of the Children Act 1989. Therefore, all biological parents, *except* those who have had parental responsibilities and rights (or, in England, parental responsibility) removed by virtue of an order of court, are relevant persons. It is important to note that fathers should *not* be required to request deemed relevant person status as they are already relevant persons under s.200 (see commentary, below, and see *DH v Scottish Children's Reporter*, 2014 Fam. L.B. 130–6). Where it is accepted that a person is the parent of a child, it is not appropriate for a pre-hearing panel to be called to consider that person's relevant person status. The authors would suggest that such a procedure by a pre-hearing panel or hearing could be incompetent (see *W v C*, 2013 Fam. L.R. 73 at [7]: discussed below in the Preliminary General Note to s.169). The Reporter has no discretion and must treat as a relevant person an individual whom he or she has been told is the parent of the child. If the individual is not notified of the hearing then he would be entitled to attend the hearing and assert that he is a relevant person, and to attend any subsequent court referral. Only where there is a dispute over the paternity of the child, should the father be called upon to produce proof of paternity. It is possible to envisage a situation where two individuals may qualify as relevant persons, e.g. the husband and presumptive father (under s.5 of the Law Reform (Parent and Child) (Scotland) Act 1986) and the mother's partner whose name has been registered on the child's birth certificate. Each individual must be given the status of relevant person. The authors consider that DNA evidence from a "reputable" testing agency is sufficient proof of paternity. The procedural rules in relation to pre-hearing panels are contained in Part 12 of the Children's Hearings (Scotland) Act 2011 (Rules of Procedure in Children's Hearings) Rules 2013 (SSI 2013/194) (as amended in relation to subs. (5A): see below).

C.458.2

Subs.(1)

This sets out the situations under which a pre-hearing panel may be convened, these being when the Reporter has arranged a hearing, whether a grounds hearing, a review hearing or a subsequent hearing.

C.458.3

Subs.(2)(a) and (b)

C.458.4 This relates to the question of whether an individual should be deemed to be a relevant person in relation to the child. A request to the Reporter to arrange a pre-hearing panel (see above for definition) to consider whether or not an individual should be deemed to be a relevant person can be made by the individual, the child or a relevant person. In *V v Locality Reporter Manager, Stirling*, 2013 Fam. L.R. 69 which fell under the Children (Scotland) Act 1995, (discussed below in relation to s.81(3)), the 13-year-old sibling of the referred child had not been invited to attend the children's hearing. It was held that the sibling had established family life with the child and, consequently, was a relevant person who was entitled to be invited to the children's hearing. There was nothing in the report of the case to suggest that the Reporter was aware before the children's hearing that the sibling wished to attend the hearing. It should be noted, therefore, that, under the present legislation, a sibling who considered that he or she was entitled to be a relevant person, could request a pre-hearing panel and the Reporter would be bound to arrange one and notify the sibling under r.45(2)(c) of the Children's Hearings (Scotland) Act 2011 (Rules of Procedure in Children's Hearings) Rules 2013 (SSI 2013/194). (Of course, strictly speaking, as was pointed out in *W v C*, cited above, such a sibling would be a relevant person as a matter of law and therefore not requiring or entitled to be "deemed": see our discussion in General Note, above—but it may be that, were the matter to arise, a broad and pragmatic approach might be adopted.) The effect of deeming an individual to be a relevant person is discussed below under s.81(4). On receiving a request under this subsection, the Reporter has no discretion and *must* convene a pre-hearing panel to consider the request. The Reporter *may*, also, on his or her own initiative, arrange a pre-hearing panel to consider relevant person status.

Note, also, that a safeguarder does not have the power to request that a pre-hearing panel determines the deemed relevant person status of an individual. Nor can a safeguarder appeal a decision of a pre-hearing panel with regard to deemed relevant person status.

The effect of being deemed to be a relevant person is that the individual will have the same rights and duties as a relevant person under s.200 of this Act. Under subs.(5A) below, the Reporter *must* refer to a pre-hearing panel the question of whether a deemed relevant person should continue to be a deemed relevant person.

Subs.(2)(c) and subss.(3), (4) and (5)

C.458.5 The Reporter is not bound to, but *may* on his or her own initiative or by request from the child, a relevant person or the safeguarder, refer to a pre-hearing panel one of the matters listed in subs.(3). These matters are: (a) that the child should be excused from attending the children's hearing; (b) that a relevant person should be excused from attending a children's hearing; (c) whether there is a likelihood that the children's hearing will make a compulsory supervision order that includes a secure accommodation authorisation in relation to the child; or (d) a matter specified by the procedural rules under s.177(2)(a). At the time of writing, no such provisions have been made.

Where a pre-hearing panel makes a determination that a child or relevant person should be excused from attending the children's hearing, this is binding on the children's hearing in so far as it removes the child's or relevant person's duty to attend imposed by ss.73(2) and 74(2). Consequently, the children's hearing could not, by reason of non-attendance only, grant a warrant to secure attendance of the child, and the relevant person could not, by not attending, commit an offence under s.74(4). However, a decision by a pre-hearing panel to excuse a child or relevant person *cannot* prevent the children's hearing, which wanted the child or relevant person to attend, from deferring for this purpose under s.119(2). Where such a step is taken the obligations of the child or relevant person under ss.73(2) and 74(2) respectively would revive. The decision of a pre-hearing panel not to excuse a child or relevant person would not operate to prevent the subsequent children's hearing from using its powers of excusal of the child or relevant person under s.73(3) or s.74(3) respectively.

Where a pre-hearing panel is arranged for any purpose and notification sent to the attendees, the child and/or relevant person who is unable, for whatever reason, to attend in person, may request that the Reporter makes arrangements under r.45(3)(b)(iv) of the Children's Hearings (Scotland) Act 2011 (Rules of Procedure in Children's Hearings) Rules 2013 (SSI 2013/194) (the "Procedural Rules") to arrange for attendance to be via telephone, video link or some other method of communication. (For arrangements to attend children's hearings remotely see commentary above on s.78 and see r.19(2) of the Procedural Rules.) It should be noted that, even where a child has been excused by a pre-hearing panel from his or her duty to attend a children's hearing, the child continues to have a right to attend the hearing under s.78. Similarly, a relevant person who has been excused from the duty to attend by a pre-hearing panel has the right to attend the hearing, except where he or she has been excluded under s.76(2).

Determination of matter referred under section 79

Two important points should be noted. First, excusing a child from attendance at a hearing should not amount to excluding the child from taking part in the hearing and expressing his or her views. Secondly, the child's or relevant person's representative can attend the children's hearing, even where the child or relevant person has been excused attendance.

Subss.(1A) and (5A)
Before the enactment of these provisions the removal of relevant person status was governed by s.142 of the Act, which provided that a children's hearing held to review a compulsory supervision order by varying or continuing it, required to consider whether an individual, who had been deemed to be a relevant person should continue as such. The authors submit, in the discussion of s.81(3), that an individual acquire the status at a relevant person by virtue of having established family life with the child. For consideration of the interrelationship between "relevant person" and "deemed relevant person", see sub-para. headed *The relevant person and the deemed relevant person* at the beginning of para.C.460.5. For cases on deemed relevant person, see commentary on s.81(3), below.

The amendments made by the 2014 Act now enable the deemed relevant person, the child or a relevant person to request that the Reporter convenes a pre-hearing panel with the specific remit of reviewing the status of a deemed relevant person. The Reporter *must* convene such a pre-hearing panel where requested. The Rules for procedures under subs.(5A) are contained in rr.45, 46A, 49A, 50, 52 and 54 of the Procedural Rules, as amended by the Children's Hearings (Scotland) Act 2011 (Rules of Procedure in Children's Hearings) Amendment Rules (SSI 2015/21).

C.458.6

Subs.(6)
The Reporter *may* request a pre-hearing panel to review the status of a deemed relevant person on his or her own initiative.

C.458.7

Determination of matter referred under section 79

80.—[1] (1) This section applies where the Principal Reporter refers a matter to a pre-hearing panel under section 79(2) or (5A).

(2) The Principal Reporter must arrange a meeting of the pre-hearing panel for a date before the date fixed for the children's hearing.

(3) If it is not practicable for the Principal Reporter to comply with subsection (2), the children's hearing must determine the matter referred at the beginning of the children's hearing.

C.459

NOTE
1. As amended by the Children and Young People (Scotland) Act 2014 (asp 8) Sch.5 para.12(2) (effective 26 January 2015).

C.459.1

DEFINITIONS
"children's hearing": s.5.
"pre-hearing panel": s.79.
"Principal Reporter": ss.12 and 14 and Sch.3 paras 8–10.

C.459.2

GENERAL NOTE
Subsection (2) of this section provides that the Reporter must arrange a pre-hearing panel for a date "before" the children's hearing concerned. Rule 45(1) of the Children's Hearings (Scotland) Act 2011 (Rules of Procedure in Children's Hearings) Rules 2013 (SSI 2013/194) (the "Procedural Rules") provides that, where practicable, the Reporter is to give parties notice of the date of a pre-hearing panel no less than five days (note that this is five calendar days not five working days) before the intended pre-hearing panel. This section deals with the situation where it is not practicable to arrange a pre-hearing panel "before" the children's hearing. The five-day timescale in r.45(1), being subject to practicability, is not mandatory and in practice a Reporter may be able to convene parties to a pre-hearing panel on shorter notice, although the child and relevant persons may, justifiably (depending on circumstances), claim that they have had insufficient time to prepare or be able to attend. However, it is thought that where the five-day timescale is not practicable, the Reporter would be entitled to rely on the provisions of s.80(3). Rule 52 of the Procedural Rules provides, inter alia, that the Reporter *must* advise specified persons of which s.79 matter is to be considered by the children's hearing.

C.459.3

Children's Hearings (Scotland) Act 2011

Subs.(3)

C.459.4 The reason for this requirement is obvious—the determination of who is to be a relevant person must be taken at the beginning of the hearing to allow any or all relevant persons to participate in the hearing's deliberations: see General Note, above. The criteria for, and consequences of, a deeming by a children's hearing are the same as those for a pre-hearing panel, discussed below under s.81(3) and (4).

Determination of claim that person be deemed a relevant person

C.460 **81.**—(1) This section applies where a matter mentioned in section 79(2)(a) (a "relevant person claim") is referred to a meeting of a pre-hearing panel.

¹ (2) Where the relevant person claim is referred along with any other matter, the pre-hearing panel must, unless that other matter is a matter mentioned in section 79(5A)(a), determine the relevant person claim before determining the other matter.

(3) The pre-hearing panel must deem the individual to be a relevant person if it considers that the individual has (or has recently had) a significant involvement in the upbringing of the child.

(4) Where the pre-hearing panel deems the individual to be a relevant person, the individual is to be treated as a relevant person for the purposes of Parts 7 to 15, 17 and 18 in so far as they relate to—
  (a) the children's hearing,
  (b) any subsequent children's hearing under Part 11,
  (c) any pre-hearing panel held in connection with a children's hearing mentioned in paragraph (a), (b) or (e),
  (d) any compulsory supervision order, interim compulsory supervision order, medical examination order, or warrant to secure attendance made by—
    (i) a hearing mentioned in paragraph (a) or (b),
    (ii) the sheriff in any court proceedings falling within paragraph (f),
  (e) any children's hearing held for the purposes of reviewing a compulsory supervision order falling within paragraph (d),
  (f) any court proceedings held in connection with a hearing mentioned in paragraph (a), (b) or (e),
  (g) any court proceedings held in connection with an order or warrant falling within paragraph (d),
  (h) the implementation of an order or warrant falling within paragraph (d).

(5) The Scottish Ministers may by order—
  (a) amend subsection (3),
  (b) in consequence of provision made under paragraph (a), make such other amendments as appear to the Scottish Ministers to be necessary or expedient to—
    (i) section 43,
    (ii) section 48,
    (iii) section 51,
    (iv) this section,
  ² (iva) section 81A,
    (v) section 142.

(6) An order under subsection (5) is subject to the affirmative procedure.

(7) Where, by virtue of section 80(3), the children's hearing is to determine the relevant person claim, references in subsections (2) to (4) (other than paragraph (c) of subsection (4)) to the pre-hearing panel are to be read as references to the children's hearing.

NOTES

C.460.1 1. As amended by the Children and Young People (Scotland) Act 2014 (asp 8) Sch.5 para.12(3)(a) (effective 26 January 2015).

Determination of claim that person be deemed a relevant person

2. Inserted by the Children and Young People (Scotland) Act 2014 (asp 8) Sch.5 para.12(3)(b) (effective 26 January 2015).

DEFINITIONS
"affirmative procedure": s.197.
"compulsory supervision order": ss.202(1) and 83.
"interim compulsory supervision order": ss.202(1) and 86.
"medical examination order": ss.202(1) and 87.
"pre-hearing panel": ss.202(1) and 79(2)(a).
"relevant person": s.200.
"warrant to secure attendance": ss.202(1) and 88.

C.460.2

GENERAL NOTE
The core of this section is the test for determining whether a person should be deemed to be a relevant person (subs.(3)) and the prescribing, in subs.(4), of the consequences of deeming. "Undeeming" is dealt with in s.81A, below.

C.460.3

Subs.(2)
As in s.80(3), the reason for this requirement is obvious—the decision will govern who may participate in the hearing's deliberations.

C.460.4

Subs.(3)

The relevant person and the deemed relevant person
As mentioned in the General Note to s.79, the Supreme Court, in the context of the parallel provision (s.93(2)(b)(c) of the 1995 Act), interpreted that provision as including "or who appears to have established family life with the child with which the decision of a children's hearing may interfere". The definition of "relevant person" in s.200 of this Act does not include the formulation devised by the Supreme Court. It may be thought that the "deeming" provisions of this present section may be regarded as filling this gap. However, the test enacted here "that the individual has (or has recently had) a significant involvement in the upbringing of the child" does not mirror the Supreme Court's formulation. These are two different concepts. Of course many persons who have established family life with the child will also have, or recently have had, significant involvement with the upbringing of the child, but there will be some persons who do not. Moreover it has to be remembered that the Supreme Court was defining the persons entitled to the status of relevant persons as a matter of law, and not persons entitled to be deemed as relevant persons.

C.460.5

Whether the formulation by the Supreme Court applies in the context of the present Act
The question may arise as to whether the test formulated by the Supreme Court under the 1995 Act carries over into the 2011 Act. An example of a person who appears to have established family life with the child with which the decision of a children's hearing may interfere was the appellant in *V v Locality Reporter Manager, Stirling*, 2013 Fam. L.R. 69 (a pre-2011 Act case). In this case, V was the sister, aged 13, of the referred child, aged 7. A children's hearing made decisions regarding contact between the child and V, but V had not been invited to that hearing and the hearing had not considered whether she was entitled to participate in the proceedings. On appeal by V, the Reporter conceded that V had established family life with the child with which the decision of the children's hearing had interfered but contended that a restrictive approach ought to be adopted in decisions affecting the numbers attending a children's hearing and that a high standard had to be met where someone other than the genetic father (such as the respondent in *Principal Reporter v K* [2010] UKSC 56; 2011 S.C. (U.K.S.C.) 91; 2011 S.L.T. 271) was concerned. Sheriff A. Wyllie Robertson, rejecting these submissions, allowed the appeal, observing: "The extended definition handed down by the Supreme Court in *Principal Reporter v K* widens the definition of who may be considered a relevant person for proceedings before the children's hearing. It is a stand alone category not restricted in any way by the enacted part of s 93(2)(b)(c)". The sheriff went on to found upon the words of Lady Hale in para.69 of *Principal Reporter v K*:

> "The aim of the hearing is to enlist the family in trying to find solutions to the problems facing the child. This is simply widening the range of such people who have an established relationship with the child and thus has something important to contribute to the hearing."

Sheriff Robertson's phrase "a stand alone category" may carry the implication that the "family life" test should be carried over to the provisions of the 2011 Act.

In an address to the conference convened by the Scottish Child Law Centre on 22 February 2013, Janys M. Scott QC discussed the definition of "relevant person" in s.200 of the Act and the deemed relevant person provisions of the present section of the Act. Our main consideration of the relevant person provisions will appear below in our commentary on s.200, but it is convenient to deal with deemed relevant persons here. In her presentation, Mrs Scott submitted that a reading of the definition of "relevant person" which did not give persons with contact orders an opportunity of a fair hearing at a children's hearing would probably be a violation of such persons' right to respect for family life under the European Convention and that, therefore, if the Act could not be made to work in a way which was compliant with the Convention it could (as subordinate legislation under s.21(1) of the Human Rights Act 1998) be held to be "not law". Addressing the interpretation of the deeming provisions, Mrs Scott concluded:

"The test for 'deeming' a person to be relevant must be interpreted in a way that includes all those with article 6 and article 8 rights if this is necessary to allow them the opportunity to participate in the hearing's decision making".

(See also the decision of Mrs Scott, sitting as a sheriff, in *W v C*, 2013 Fam. L.R. 73 at [7], mentioned below in the Preliminary General Note to s.160 and the General Note to s.200.) The authors consider that, in order to interpret the deeming provisions in this way, it would be necessary to read this subsection thus:

"The pre-hearing panel must deem the individual to be a relevant person if it considers that the individual has (or has recently had) a significant involvement in the upbringing of the child or who appears to have established family life with the child with which the decision of a children's hearing may interfere".

Principles affecting interpretation of statute

As pointed out in *Principal Reporter v K* at [61], there is an important distinction between interpretation and amendment, as explained by Lord Rodger of Earlsferry in *Ghaidan v Godin-Mendoza* [2004] UKHL 30; [2004] 2 A.C. 557 at [121]:

"If the court implies words that are consistent with the scheme of the legislation but necessary to make it compatible with Convention rights, it is simply performing the duty which Parliament has imposed on it and on others. It is reading the legislation in a way that draws out the full implications of its terms and of the Convention rights. And, by its very nature, an implication will go with the grain of the legislation. By contrast, using a Convention right to read in words that are inconsistent with the scheme of the legislation or with its essential principles as disclosed by its provisions does not involve any form of interpretation, by implication or otherwise. It falls on the wrong side of the boundary between interpretation and amendment of the statute".

As explained by Lady Hale in *Principal Reporter v K*, the aim of the hearing is to enlist the family in trying to find solutions to the problems facing the child. In the authors' view the "reading down" of this subsection as proposed above is consistent with this aim and therefore in accordance with the grain of the legislation. It is our view that, if the situation in *V v Locality Authority Manager, Stirling* were to recur, the reasoning of Sheriff Wyllie Robertson, clearly sound under the 1995 Act's provisions, would also be correct under the current legislation. It would further follow that where the Rules governing the duties of the Reporter in convening pre-hearing panels and children's hearings require the Reporter to notify "any individual other than a relevant person who appears to the Reporter to have or recently have had significant involvement in the upbringing of the child" (Children's Hearings (Scotland) Act 2011 (Rules of Procedure in Children's Hearings) Rules 2013 (SSI 2013/194) r.22(2)(c)) then, following Sheriff Wyllie Robertson's decision, this rule would require to be read as if the words "or who appears to have established family life with the child with which the decision of a children's hearing may interfere" were added. Moreover, as noted above in our discussion of s.79(2), if any individual—including a sibling such as in the *V* case—were to request under s.79(2)(a)(i) that the Reporter arrange a pre-hearing panel to determine if he or she should be deemed to be a relevant person then the Reporter would, by virtue of r.45(2)(c) of the said Rules, be bound to notify that individual of the pre-hearing panel. (As to whether a person such as "V" would be entitled to apply to a pre-hearing panel, see our discussion under s.79(2)(a) and (b).)

Cases on deeming of persons as relevant persons

"*Must deem*". Where the pre-hearing panel or the children's hearing determines that an individual satisfies the test for acquiring relevant person status, then, whatever view may be taken of the merits of the individual, the pre-hearing panel or children's hearing "must" deem that individual to be a relevant person. Where such a determination has been made the pre-hearing panel has no further judgment to make or discretion to exercise. Accordingly, for the reasons advanced above in our discussion of s.25, the overarching principle that the welfare of

Determination of claim that person be deemed a relevant person

the child is paramount can have no application. Whether the welfare principle should influence a decision about a deemed relevant person caused some controversy—see Sheriff A. G. McCulloch in *M Appellant*, 2014 Fam. L.B. 127–7 and *X Appellants*, 2013 S.L.T. (Sh. Ct) 125. For discussion of these cases see the contrasting approaches in the articles by Professor Kenneth Norrie ("Children's Hearings, Relevant Persons and the Welfare of the Child", 2014 Fam. L.B. 128–4) and Sheriff Brian Kearney ("Children's hearings, relevant persons and the welfare of the child—Some thoughts on Professor Norrie's comments", 2014 Fam. L.B. 129–2). In *DH v Scottish Children's Reporter*, 2014 Fam. L.B. 130–6 (Haddington sheriff court, April 25, 2014), Sheriff P. Braid recorded that parties were agreed that the relevant person issue "was a question of fact and there was no element of discretion". In *Principal Reporter v K*, above, the Supreme Court, at [69], opined that in a borderline case it would be safer for the children's hearing to include rather than exclude a would-be relevant person and in *W v Children's Reporter*, 2013 S.L.T. (Sh. Ct) 99 (a case under the 1995 Act) at [28], Sheriff Mungo Bovey QC invoked this opinion in relation to the claim by a grandmother.

This issue was resolved by the Court of Session in *MT & AG v Anne Gerry (Locality Reporter)* [2014] CSIH 108; 2015 S.C. 359; 2015 Fam. L.R. 2; Extra Division, 12 December 2014, in which the decision of Sheriff A.G. McCulloch in *X Appellants* was considered and reversed. The court, approving the reasoning of Professor Norrie, referred to above, stated at [13]:

"While, of course, the overall exercise upon which a children's hearing is embarked is concerned with the welfare of the child, the particular decision which a pre-hearing panel requires to reach under section 81(3) is not related to the welfare of the child as such. It is concerned in the proceedings and whether the individual concerned should be made a party to the proceedings with the obligations and rights which flow from conferral of that *locus standi*."

"Has (or has recently had) a significant involvement"
The case of *MF and GF, Appellants* (sometimes referred to as *F & F, Appellants*) 2014 Fam. L. R. 57 (sub nom *F v Principal Reporter*, 2014 Fam. L.B. 29-6), concerned children who had been received into care on 9 July 2012. On 17 February 2014 a pre-hearing panel was faced with the situation wherein grandparents of children, whose contact with the children was, under a compulsory supervision order, to be at the discretion of the social work department, had had no contact with the children since October 2012 with the exception of two chance meeting at children's hearings. On 12 August 2013, a pre-hearing panel, according to Sheriff Reid "had already concluded that the appellants [the grandparents] had (or had recently had) significant involvement in the upbringing of the child prior to them being received into care and, indeed, as late as at 12 August 2013". There had been three review hearings (in September 2013, December 2013 and January 2014) but social work reports were not available. In February 2914 social work reports were available which the hearing considered. The hearing also noted that there had been a dispute between the grandparents and a head teacher as to the degree of the grandparents' involvement with the upbringing of the children prior to their being accommodated in July 20122 and preferred the view of the head teacher on this matter. In the event the hearing continued the CSO and provided that there should be no contact with the grandparents. It also decided that the grandparents should no longer be deemed as relevant persons since they did not have (and had not decently had) significant involvement in the upbringing of the children. The grandparents appealed to the sheriff and the case was heard by Sheriff Stuart Reid. On appeal the sheriff noted that the test for deeming relevant person status was, per s.81(3), whether the individual has (or recently has had) significant involvement in the upbringing of the child. On appeal Sheriff Stuart Reid decided, first, that the children's hearing had erred by going behind the decision of the pre-hearing panel of 12 August 2013 by taking its own view of evidence relating to events before that date and, also by not giving sufficient weight to the consideration that subsequent lapse of time had been caused by state intervention by way of the existing compulsory supervision order and the repeated failure of the social work department timeously to provided reports. On the latter issue the sheriff, while accepting that the passage of time could impair entitlement to relevant person status said, at para [55]: "However in my judgment a children's hearing should be slow to reach such a conclusion in circumstances where the direct, proximate and dominant cause of the diminishing recent involvement with the child is the ongoing intervention of the State itself. There would be an inherent unfairness in the State both restricting a relevant person's involvement with a child and then founding upon that enforced restricted involvement to deny the person further participation in the decision-making process concerning the child." The sheriff accordingly quashed the direction of the hearing that the grandparents were no longer to be deemed relevant persons. (The authors are grateful to Messrs Butterworths for permission to reproduce the

foregoing paragraph from Sheriff Kearney's contribution to *Butterworths Scottish Family Law Service*.)

Sheriff Reid's above decision overruled
Some three years after the decision by Sheriff Reid in *MF and GF, Appellants*, 2014 Fam. L.R. 57 that decision came for consideration by an Extra Division in *CF v MF & GF and Scottish Reporter* [2017] CSIH 44, which involved the same family. The background to this was that in October 2015 a children's hearing decided that the grandparents, MF and GF, no longer met the test to be deemed relevant persons. The grandparents appealed to the sheriff, who, on 29 October 2015 upheld their appeal and deemed the grandparents to be relevant persons. Meantime, on 26 October 2015, at the request of CF, one of the grandchildren, the CSO in respect of CF had been varied to the effect that CF should have no contact with her mother or grandparents. Then, in July 2016, CF, instructed her own solicitor, who on her behalf requested a review hearing and a pre-hearing panel, the latter to consider whether to "undeem" the grandparents as relevant the grandparents as relevant persons. On 1 September 2016 the pre-hearing panel decided that the grandparents should no longer be deemed relevant persons. The grandparents appealed to the sheriff. The appeal was heard by Sheriff Reid (who had been the same sheriff who had heard the first appeal), who upheld their appeal, quashed the order of the pre-hearing panel and deemed the grandparents to be relevant persons, all in terms of s.160(4).The pre-hearing panel had given detailed reasons for its decision, narrating that CF had told it that she no longer wanted to have the grandparents as relevant persons and as such receiving papers and taking part in decisions. She had not seen her grandparents for a year and a half. She did not like it when she saw them and did not want to see them again. There was no bond between them and "previously when she saw them she did not like the way she behaved afterwards". The CSO prevented contact but even without the order she did not want her grandparents to exercise significant involvement in her life anymore. The pre-hearing panel also mentioned that it had considered Sheriff Reid's original judgment and that it had decided that whilst previously the grandparents were relevant the time had now arisen when they no longer met the legal test of significant involvement in her life any more. In the passages in Sheriff Reid's judgment to which the pre-hearing panel referred the sheriff had said that, while accepting that an individual might lose relevant person status because of the passage of time one should be slow to reach such a conclusion where the main cause of the diminishing involvement was the intervention of the state itself (i.e. by the CSO of 1 September 2016 referred to above). In the appeal to the Court of Session the Court identified three issues as central to Sheriff Reid's current decision (reversing the decision of the pre-hearing panel), as focussed in the stated case, viz: (1) that the panel took into account an irrelevant factor, namely the evidence about the relationship between the grandparents and CF prior to 29 October 2015 when the sheriff had deemed them to be relevant persons; (2) that the panel had taken account of another irrelevant factor, namely the child's stated preference that the grandparents should not be relevant persons; and (3) that the panel had given undue weight to the passage of time and failed to give sufficient weight to the effect of state intervention upon the involvement of the grandparents in the upbringing of the child. The Extra Division prefaced its discussion of these issues by recalling and approving of the opinion of Sheriff Principal Gordon Nicholson QC in *W v Schaffer*, 2001 S.L.T. 86 at 87/88 as to the scope of an appeal to the sheriff, to the effect that the only concern of the sheriff is to see if there has been a procedural irregularity, to see if the hearing has failed to give proper consideration to a relevant factor and generally to consider if the hearing's decision is one which could not reasonably be regarded as justified in all the circumstances of the case and that an appeal to the Court of Session may only be made on a point of law or a procedural irregularity (CHSA 2011, s.164(5)). Then, as to point (1), the Court noted that what the sheriff had done on 29 October 2015 did not involve any consideration of the merits of the grandparents' status as relevant persons but had simply ruled that the panel had erroneously looked behind and questioned the initial decision to grant such status. Accordingly, when, in September 2016 the pre-hearing panel had to assess whether the statutory test continued to be met, it was not tied to any assumption that as at October 2015 the test was satisfied. As to whether a pre-hearing panel should be bound by a decision of a previous pre-hearing panel the Court of Session commented at para.[53] that it supported the proposition that an earlier decision should be regarded as "a material fact of real importance" but not regard it as an absolute bar to consideration of information concerning the period before the decision; the court concluded: "There is no rigid system of *res judicata*". As to point (2), the Court of Session accepted that regarding as irrelevant the child's view on the issue of whether there was or recently had been significant involvement in the upbringing of the child might "in a narrow sense" be understandable. However, in the circumstances of the present case, where the child had lived since 2012 without input from or contact with the grandparents, it was "difficult to categorise the panel's reference to the views of the child as a wholly irrelevant factor in the

Determination of claim that person be deemed a relevant person

overall assessment of whether the grandparents still met the test laid down in section 81A(3)." As to point (3), the Court recalled the words of Sheriff Reid at para.[55] of his original judgment, "a children's hearing should be slow to reach such a conclusion in circumstances where the direct proximate and dominant cause of the diminishing recent involvement with the child is the ongoing intervention of the state itself". The Court held that this approach constituted an innovation or gloss on the statutory test which was a purely factual one, and noted the importance, under reference to *MT v Gerry*, 2015 S.C. 359 (discussed below under s.156(1), especially in the paragraph headed *Principles governing sheriff's decision on a legal issue*), where this was the case, of confining consideration to the factual issue concerned. The pre-hearing panel was entitled in the circumstances to take the view that there had been no recent significant involvement in the upbringing of the child. Different people might come to a different view but it was a reasonable and tenable one with which an appellate court, having regard to the principles enunciated in *W v Schaffer*, should not interfere.

Three days contact with a new-born baby held to amount to significant involvement in the upbringing of the child

Some three weeks after Sheriff Reid's original decision in *MF and GF, Appellants*, 2014 Fam. L.R. 57, above, the mother in that case gave birth to a further child. On the third day of the child's life the local authority obtained a child protection order in respect of the child, who was then removed from the mother's care. In the meantime the maternal grandparents (the appellants in Sheriff Reid's case) had visited the mother and child in hospital, held the child, brought presents for the child, and arranged for mother and child to reside with them for a time after leaving hospital. A children's hearing held some three weeks after the birth held, by a majority, that the grandparents were not relevant persons and they appealed to the sheriff. Sheriff S. F. Murphy QC, upheld the appeal (*F and F v Principal Reporter*, 2014 Fam. L.B. 131–5) and held that the visiting by the grandparents, their having held the child and given presents, and the arrangements which had been made for them to accommodate the mother and child, amounted in the circumstances to their having, or recently having had, significant involvement in the upbringing of the child and deemed them to be relevant persons. The appellants' agents had submitted that the ruling in *Principal Reporter v K* to the effect that a person's having established family life with the child with which the decision of a children's hearing might interfere should apply. Sheriff Murphy did not find it necessary to decide this but opined obiter that he would be prepared to read down the provisions of the 2011 Act along the lines advanced in that case in order to ensure compatibility with art.8 of the European Convention. The sheriff also stated that he was satisfied that his decision was in the best interests of the child.

"Recent" held to vary according to circumstances

In *DH v Scottish Children's Reporter*, noted in 2014 Fam. L.B. 130-6. Sheriff P. Braid had to consider the mother's appeal against a majority decision of a pre-hearing panel to deem the child's father as a relevant person. The father attended to the physical needs of his baby from the age of two weeks from June to September 2013. Following an (unproved at the time) allegation that he had threatened to slit the throats of the child and mother, the mother had "agreed to the child's being voluntarily accommodated" failing which a child protection order would be sought. As a result five months had elapsed without contact. The sheriff, observing that "recent" would vary according to circumstances, noting that the father had been described by the mother as a "hands-on father" and considering that his contact with the child had only been removed as a result of state intervention, held that the majority decision had been justified and refused the appeal. (Note: In accordance with the terms of art.3 of the Children's Hearings (Scotland) Act 2011 (Review of Contact Directions and Definition of Relevant Person) Order 2013 (SSI 2013/193) a father, subject to the exceptions specified in art.3(2)(a), is a relevant person *as a matter of right* and has, accordingly, no need to apply to be deemed as such. This provision came into force on June 24, 2013. There is nothing in the sheriff's judgment to indicate that this provision would not have applied to this case.)

...

Biological parents of a child who has been adopted

A biological parent of a child who has been adopted can never be a "relevant person" because, as noted below in our discussion of s.200, the legislation on adoption (Adoption and Children (Scotland) Act 2007 and Adoption and Children Act 2002) makes it clear that an adoption order conveys parental responsibilities and rights to the adoptive parents who, and no-one else, are to be treated as the parents of the child. However, it is easy to envisage a situation wherein the biological parent of a child who has been adopted has recently had "significant involvement in the upbringing of the child".

Further provisions

C.460.6　This subsection lists the provisions in relation to which a deemed relevant person is to be treated as a relevant person. These provisions give the deemed relevant person the right to participate in the various procedures specified. These provisions are echoed in the Children's Hearings (Scotland) Act 2011 (Rules of Procedure in Children's Hearings) Rules 2013 (SSI 2013/194) (hereinafter the "Procedural Rules"). For example, where a warrant to secure attendance is at issue, the provisions that a relevant person's views are to be sought and that a relevant person is to receive a copy of the warrant (the 2013 Rules r.78(2) and (3)) apply equally to a deemed relevant person.

As noted by Professor Norrie in his *Children's Hearings in Scotland*, 3rd edn (Edinburgh: W. Green, 2013), para.3.24, fn.92, the list in s.81(4) does not include s.67, which enacts the grounds for referral, with the consequence that ground (n) ("the child is beyond the control of a relevant person") may not be taken as referring to a deemed relevant person. Professor Norrie suggests that where a child's welfare is at issue the legislation should be interpreted expansively and that the protection, guidance, treatment or control afforded by a compulsory supervision order should not be denied to any child merely because the person who had the duty to control the child traces his or her relevant person status to s.81 rather than s.200.

This may be true where the deeming has been effected on the basis of the individual having significant involvement in the upbringing of the child (which is the only basis recognised by Professor Norrie in *Children's Hearings in Scotland* (2013), para.5.12) but would not always be appropriate where the basis contended for above (having established family life) is involved. The answer may be that the "expansive" interpretation should only be adopted where the deeming has been based on significant involvement in the upbringing of the child: for example it would not be appropriate to treat the older sibling, V, in *V v Locality Reporter Manager, Stirling*, as a relevant person for the purposes of s.67(2)(n). We refer to our discussion above under s.67(2)(n) in relation to the consideration that there might be more than one relevant person for the child, and we agree with Professor Norrie (*Children's Hearings in Scotland* (2013), para.3.24, fn.93) where he states:

"Reporters are unlikely to refer the child to a hearing solely on the basis that one of several relevant persons cannot control the child although others can and do".

In relation to a person deemed to be a relevant person by virtue of having established family life with the child the authors would go further and suggest that it may not be lawful to treat such a person as a relevant person for the purposes of s.67(2)(n) unless that person had also had significant involvement in the upbringing of the child.

Subs.(5)

C.460.7　Scottish Ministers have not so far used the powers of amendment here conferred, but have amended this Part by Part 16 of the Children and Young People (Scotland) Act 2014 by adding s.81A, discussed below.

Determination that deeming of person as relevant person to end

C.460.8　[1] **81A.**—(1) This section applies where a matter mentioned in section 79(5A)(a) is referred to a meeting of a pre-hearing panel.

(2) Where the matter is referred along with any other matter, the pre-hearing panel must determine it before determining the other matter.

(3) The pre-hearing panel must determine that the individual is no longer to be deemed to be a relevant person if it considers that the individual does not have (and has not recently had) a significant involvement in the upbringing of the child.

(4) Where the pre-hearing panel makes a determination as described in subsection (3), section 81(4) ceases to apply in relation to the individual.

(5) Where, by virtue of section 80(3), the children's hearing is to determine a matter mentioned in section 79(5A)(a), references in subsections (2) to (4) to the pre-hearing panel are to be read as references to the children's hearing.

NOTE

C.460.9　1. Inserted by the Children and Young People (Scotland) Act 2014 (asp 8) Pt 16 s.84(3) (effective 26 January 2015).

Appointment of safeguarder

DEFINITIONS
"children's hearing": s.5.
"pre-hearing panel": s.202(1) and s.79(2)(a).
"relevant person": s.200.

GENERAL NOTE
The Act, as originally framed, did not allow for the removal of deemed relevant person status other than by a children's hearing at a review under s.143 and this section addresses this issue.

Subs.(2)
This provision ensures that the pre-hearing panel's determination of whether a person should be a relevant person must take place at the beginning of the hearing so that the person may (or may not) be involved in the subsequent deliberations of the pre-hearing panel.

Subs.(3)
Must determine. In our commentary on s.81(3) above we discuss the test for establishing deemed relevant person status. The same considerations apply here.
No longer to be deemed ... does not have (and has not recently had). In *MF and GF, Appellants*, 2014 Fam. L.R. 57 (sub nom. *F v Principal Reporter*, 2014 Fam. L.B. 129–6, Glasgow sheriff court, March 20, 2014), discussed above in relation to s.80(3), Sheriff Stuart Reid had to consider, in the context of the powers of a children's hearing to review whether an individual should continue to be deemed to be a relevant person, whether that children's hearing had power under s.142(1)(c) to consider events before the original deeming decision and decided that it did not have this power. However, in *CF v MF & GF and Scottish Reporter* [2017] CSIH 44, also discussed above under s.81(3) (in the paragraph beginning "Some three years after the decision ...") the Court of Session held that the original deeming did not involve any consideration of the merits of the grandparents' status as relevant persons but had simply ruled that the panel had erroneously looked behind and questioned the initial decision to grant such status and that therefore when the later pre-hearing panel had to assess whether the statutory test continued to be met, it was not tied to any assumption that as at October 2015 the test was satisfied. In *MF and GF, Appellants*, above, a sheriff had held that a previous pre-hearing panel's decision prevented a later panel from re-considering the information on which the earlier panel had relied. In *CF v MF & GF and Scottish Reporter*, above, the Court of Session disapproved this and commented at para.[53] of its opinion that it supported the proposition that an earlier decision should be regarded as "a material fact of real importance" but not regarded as an absolute bar to consideration of information concerning the period before the decision; the court concluded: "There is no rigid system of *res judicata.*"

Appointment of safeguarder

82.—(1) A pre-hearing panel may appoint a safeguarder for the child to whom the children's hearing relates.

(2) A pre-hearing panel must record an appointment made under subsection (1).

(3) If a pre-hearing panel appoints a safeguarder, it must give reasons for the decision.

(4) Subsection (1) does not apply where a safeguarder has already been appointed.

(5) A safeguarder appointed under this section is to be treated for the purposes of this Act (other than this section) as being appointed by a children's hearing by virtue of section 30.

DEFINITIONS
"child": s.199.
"children's hearing": s.5.
"pre-hearing panel": s.79(2).
"safeguarder": s.202.

GENERAL NOTE
A pre-hearing panel is empowered to appoint a safeguarder if none has been already appointed. As no criteria for the appointment of a safeguarder are provided, it is at the discretion of the panel. There is no requirement that they consider whether a safeguarder is

necessary. If a safeguarder is appointed the panel must give its reasons for so doing. There is no difference in function between a safeguarder appointed by a pre-hearing panel and one appointed by a hearing.

A safeguarder is not bound to consider him or herself as limited to considering the reasons which gave rise to the appointment.

PART 9

CHILDREN'S HEARING

Key definitions

Meaning of "compulsory supervision order"

C.462   83.—(1) In this Act, "compulsory supervision order", in relation to a child, means an order—
   (a) including any of the measures mentioned in subsection (2),
   (b) specifying a local authority which is to be responsible for giving effect to the measures included in the order (the "implementation authority"), and
   (c) having effect for the relevant period.
(2) The measures are—
   (a) a requirement that the child reside at a specified place,
   (b) a direction authorising the person who is in charge of a place specified under paragraph (a) to restrict the child's liberty to the extent that the person considers appropriate having regard to the measures included in the order,
   (c) a prohibition on the disclosure (whether directly or indirectly) of a place specified under paragraph (a),
   (d) a movement restriction condition,
   (e) a secure accommodation authorisation,
   (f) subject to section 186, a requirement that the implementation authority arrange—
      (i) a specified medical or other examination of the child, or
      (ii) specified medical or other treatment for the child,
   (g) a direction regulating contact between the child and a specified person or class of person,
   (h) a requirement that the child comply with any other specified condition,
   (i) a requirement that the implementation authority carry out specified duties in relation to the child.
(3) [*Repealed by the Children's Hearings (Scotland) Act 2011 (Modification of Primary Legislation) Order 2013 (SSI 2013/211) Sch.2 (effective 24 June 2013).*]
(4) A compulsory supervision order may include a movement restriction condition only if—
   (a) one or more of the conditions mentioned in subsection (6) applies, and
   (b) the children's hearing or, as the case may be, the sheriff is satisfied that it is necessary to include a movement restriction condition in the order.
(5) A compulsory supervision order may include a secure accommodation authorisation only if—
   (a) the order contains a requirement of the type mentioned in subsection (2)(a) which requires the child to reside at—
      (i) a residential establishment which contains both secure accommodation and accommodation which is not secure accommodation, or

Meaning of "compulsory supervision order"

   (ii) two or more residential establishments, one of which contains accommodation which is not secure accommodation,
 (b) one or more of the conditions mentioned in subsection (6) applies, and
 (c) having considered the other options available (including a movement restriction condition) the children's hearing or, as the case may be, the sheriff is satisfied that it is necessary to include a secure accommodation authorisation in the order.
(6) The conditions are—
(a) that the child has previously absconded and is likely to abscond again and, if the child were to abscond, it is likely that the child's physical, mental or moral welfare would be at risk,
(b) that the child is likely to engage in self-harming conduct,
(c) that the child is likely to cause injury to another person.
(7) In subsection (1), "relevant period" means the period beginning with the making of the order and ending with—
 (a) where the order has not been continued, whichever of the following first occurs—
   (i) the day one year after the day on which the order is made,
   (ii) the day on which the child attains the age of 18 years,
 (b) where the order has been continued, whichever of the following first occurs—
   (i) the end of the period for which the order was last continued,
   (ii) the day on which the child attains the age of 18 years.
(8) In subsection (2)—
   "medical" includes psychological,
   "specified" means specified in the order.

DEFINITIONS

"child": s.199. C.462.1
"compulsory supervision order": ss.202(1) and 83.
"implementation authority": ss.202(1) and 83(1)(b).
"local authority": Local Government (Scotland) Act 1994 s.2.
"movement restriction condition": ss.202(1) and 84.
"residential establishment": s.202(1).
"secure accommodation": s.202(1).
"secure accommodation authorisation": ss.202(1) and 83(5).

GENERAL NOTE

The compulsory supervision order (CSO) is the substantive disposal of a children's hearing in relation to a child. This section defines the meaning of the CSO and lists the measures which it may contain. Where a grounds hearing is satisfied, having regard to the overarching principles and considered all the relevant information which has been put before it, that it is necessary to do so for the protection, guidance or control of the child it must, under s.91(3)(a), unless deferring under s.93(2), make a CSO. C.462.2

Subs.(1)(a)

The CSO replaces the supervision requirement of s.70 of the Children (Scotland) Act 1995 (the 1995 Act). There has been a change in terminology, but in practice there is little difference. The CSO may have measures attached to it and these are specified in subs.(2). C.462.3

Subs.(1)(b)

The CSO must specify which local authority is responsible for giving effect to any measures (the implementation authority (IA)). The result is that where there is a dispute as to which local authority has responsibility for implementation of the CSO, the IA will continue to have responsibility for giving effect to the order until the dispute is settled, thus avoiding delay in giving effect to the CSO and any measures contained therein. The meaning of "implementation authority" is considered in the Sheriff Appeal Court case *East Renfrewshire Council, Appellant* [2016] SAC (Civ) 14, overruling *East Renfrewshire Council, Applicants*, 2015 G.W.D. 35–564, discussed below in the General Note to s.201. The implementation authority has a duty to give C.462.4

Children's Hearings (Scotland) Act 2011

effect to a CSO (or Interim Compulsory Supervision Order (ICSO)) together with any measures or directions contained therein (see ss.144, 146, 147, 148 and r.67 of the Children's Hearings (Scotland) Act 2011 (Rules of Procedure in Children's Hearings) Rules 2013 (SSI 2013/194) (the "Procedural Rules")). Where the children's hearing considers that the local authority is in breach of the duty under s.144 it may direct the National Convener to take enforcement steps (see commentary to s.146). A local authority named as the IA may apply to the sheriff for a review of the decision (see commentary to ss.166 and 201). Relevant period, meaning the lifespan of the CSO, is defined in subs.(7) below.

Subs.(2)

C.462.5 Where s.70(2) of the 1995 Act referred to "conditions" which could be "imposed", this Act uses the term "measures which may be included". The effect is no different. This list is, at first reading, more extensive. However, in reality it does not extend the powers of the hearing, but "unpacks" the more concentrated language of the 1995 Act. Subsection (7) defines "medical" and "specified".

Subs.(2)(a)

C.462.6 The regulation of the child's residence is not with a specified *person*, but at a specified *place*. This is the same as the provision in s.70(3)(a) of the 1995 Act. This reflects the parental right in s.2(a) of the 1995 Act to regulate the residence of the child. This subsection does not remove that parental right, but, in effect, "suspends" it for a person who has that parental right, and who, due to a decision by a children's hearing, does not have the child residing with them. It also has the effect of requiring a review of the CSO by a hearing if the person or person with whom the child resides under the CSO moves to a new place of residence. The reader is directed to s.145 with regard to the duties of the local authority where the child is directed to reside at a particular place. Regulations re temporary accommodation and the taking of a child to a place or person are contained in regs 6 to 9 of the Children's Hearings (Scotland) Act 2011 (Compulsory Supervision Orders etc.: Further Provision) Regulations 2013 (SSI 2013/149). It should be noted that an interim order need not specify a place, but may merely specify a "place of safety" (see s.86(2)). This section is also applicable to movement restriction conditions which must specify where the child is to reside (s.84), and secure accommodation authorisations (s.85).

Subs.(2)(b)

C.462.7 This provision empowers the person who is either the individual caring for the child or the head of a residential establishment in which the child is placed, to carry out any of the measures included in the CSO, including a movement restriction condition (see subs.(4)) which has the effect of restricting the child's liberty.

This allows the individual to use their own judgement in restricting the liberty of the child if they believe that, given the measures included in the CSO, it is appropriate. Care will have to be taken where a child's liberty is restricted, but it allows carers and establishments to react to circumstances as they arise.

Subs.(2)(c)

C.462.8 Section 178(1) allows for information about the child or the child's case to be withheld from a specified person or persons by a hearing if it is considered that disclosure would be likely to cause significant harm to the child (rr.84 to 87 of the Procedural Rules). The sheriff may also make an information non-disclosure order (s.40). The relevant duties imposed on the Reporter are contained in r.15.

Subs.(2)(d)

C.462.9 See subs.(4) below, ss.84 and 150 of the Act and the Children's Hearings (Scotland) Act 2011 (Movement Restriction Conditions) Regulations 2013 (SSI 2013/210).

Subs.(2)(e)

C.462.10 Authorisation for secure accommodation may be attached to a CSO (and also an interim variation (IVCSO) or an interim compulsory supervision order (ICSO)). The criteria are contained in subs.(6) below. (See also the Procedural Rules rr.94, 95, 96, and ss.135, 136, 151 to 153.)

Subs.(2)(f)

C.462.11 It should be noted that the hearing is allowed to attach a requirement that any "specified" treatment or examination be arranged by the local authority. This means that there must be a

Meaning of "compulsory supervision order"

clear indication of what the medical needs of the child are, rather than being used to authorise a general exploration of the child's health. Any condition regarding medical procedure or treatment is subject to the consent or refusal to consent of a child who has sufficient capacity (see s.186).

Subs.(2)(g)
When considering contact between the child and an individual, it is not just parents or those with parental rights and responsibilities (PRRs) who should be considered. There may be other individuals important to the child, including siblings, other relatives and friends. It should be noted that when the Act was passed, s.83 contained a subs.(3) which required a hearing or a sheriff to consider whether to include a direction regarding contact between the child and an individual when making a CSO. This was removed on amendment but the duty to consider contact is now contained in s.29A. Hearings held to review contact are governed by s.126 and the Procedural Rules r.81.

C.462.12

Subs.(2)(h)
This provision allows the hearing to make a condition concerning any other matter that is considered to be in the interests of the child. It allows for flexibility to adapt the CSO to the needs and circumstances of the individual child. This provision is very wide in its scope and it is of particular importance that the overarching principles in ss.25, 27 and 28 are kept in mind.

C.462.13

Subs.(2)(i)
This is normally used to require the provision of a specified service or the obtaining of an assessment and has the result of requiring the local authority to comply. The reader is directed to subs.(1)(b) above for a discussion of failure by the IA to comply with the CSO.

C.462.14

Subs.(3)
There is now no subs.(3). As noted above this subsection was repealed by the Children's Hearings (Scotland) Act 2011 (Modification of Primary Legislation) Order 2013 (SSI 2013/211) Sch.2, which in effect transferred its provisions to s.29A(1): see above.

C.462.15

Subs.(4)
A movement restriction condition may be attached to a compulsory supervision order or an interim order (CSO or ICSO) by a sheriff or a hearing if it is considered necessary, and only if the conditions in subs.(6) have been satisfied. These conditions are the same as for authorisation for secure accommodation. See the commentary to s.84 for a full discussion.

C.462.16

Subs.(5)(a)
A secure accommodation authorisation must specify which establishment the child will reside in should the authorisation be implemented. These may only be of the types specified in (i) and (ii). It should be noted that a hearing may only include authorisation for secure accommodation where the order has specified the place where the child must live:
> "...the children's hearing is obliged, in all cases in which it may include a secure accommodation authorisation, also to decide where the child is to reside in the event that secure accommodation is not made available to the child. In this way the children's hearing retains control of where the child is to be, even when its first choice has not proved possible" (Professor Kenneth McK. Norrie, *Children's Hearings in Scotland*, 3rd edn (Edinburgh: W. Green, 2013), pp.11–13).

This does not apply to warrants or interim compulsory supervision orders. The reader is directed to s.135 for the requirement to review a compulsory supervision order which contains authorisation for secure accommodation before the end of three months.

C.462.17

Subs.(5)(c)
The deprivation of liberty that is the result of secure accommodation is such that it must be necessary and proportionate. Thus a sheriff or a hearing must be satisfied that none of the alternatives available will be effective. In practice it will require the local authority to provide the hearing with an assessment as to why other options including a movement restriction condition will not suffice. As with movement restriction conditions, the welfare principle will be paramount when a hearing is considering whether to authorise that the child be kept in secure accommodation (s.25(2)), but where it is considered that there is a serious risk of physical or other harm to "members of the public" s.26 allows for the child's welfare to be only a "primary consideration" rather than the paramount consideration. "Members of the public" includes

C.462.18

Children's Hearings (Scotland) Act 2011

members of the child's household, or those with whom he or she has a close connection. Where there is no such risk, the welfare of the child will remain the paramount consideration.

Subs.(6)(a)
C.462.19   It is not sufficient that the child be absconding, but must be placing him or herself at serious risk by so doing. For discussion of "abscond", see below under s.169(1)(b).

Subs.(6)(b)
C.462.20   This is a new provision. To justify the deprivation of liberty, the level of self-harming conduct that has taken place must be recent, and sufficiently serious to place the child at risk of serious harm. Self-harm is not defined in the Act, but is commonly accepted as including not only deliberate physical damage, but also eating disorders and deliberate over-exercising.

Subs.(6)(c)
C.462.21   It should be noted that the wording is that the child is "likely to cause injury". This should be read with s.26 which uses the words "serious harm (whether physical or not)". The risk of harm posed is to the person, not to property.

Meaning of "movement restriction condition"

C.463   **84.** In this Act, "movement restriction condition", in relation to a child, means—
   (a) a restriction on the child's movements in a way specified in the movement restriction condition, and
   (b) a requirement that the child comply with arrangements specified in the movement restriction condition for monitoring compliance with the restriction.

DEFINITIONS
C.463.1   "child": s.199.

GENERAL NOTE
C.463.2   Although movement restriction conditions place often considerable restrictions on the liberty of the child, the advantage in a comparison with secure accommodation is that the child is not living in a locked environment and may even remain at home. A movement restriction condition (MRC) may be included in compulsory supervision order (CSO) including an interim compulsory supervision order (ICSO) or an interim variation of a compulsory supervision order (IVCSO) under s.139(3) and by either a children's hearing (s.83(2)) or a sheriff (see reg.4(1) of the Children's Hearings (Scotland) Act 2011 (Movement Restriction Conditions) Regulations 2013 (SSI 2013/210) the "MR" Regulations).

The criteria for imposing an MRC are contained in s.83(6) and are identical to those for authorisation for secure accommodation. These are discussed in the annotation to s.83(6) above. In addition to compliance with the criteria, the MRC must be "necessary".

The provisions of the MRC that *must* be specified are contained in reg.6(1) of the MR Regulations. These are:
   (a) the place at which the child is required to reside;
   (b) the days of the week during which the child is required to remain at that place, and the period or periods when the child is required to remain there, which period or periods must not exceed 12 hours in any one day; and
   (c) the period for which the movement restriction condition is to have effect, which period must not exceed six months.

It should be noted that, while the maximum duration of an individual MRC is six months any number of further six-month MRCs may be attached to a CSO provided that the conditions still apply and it is considered still to be necessary.

The provisions of the MRC that *may* be specified are contained in reg.6(2) of the MR Regulations. These are:
   (a) any address, location or place which the child is required not to enter;
   (b) any requirements relative to the arrangements for monitoring compliance with the measures contained in the compulsory supervision order or the interim compulsory supervision order and in particular relative to the discharge of functions by any person designated by reg.4(1);

Meaning of "secure accommodation authorisation"

(c) any requirements relative to the child's participation in, or cooperation with, the child's plan;
(d) any contingency arrangements relative to—
  (i) subparagraph (a); or
  (ii) paragraphs (1)(a) and (b),
which the children's hearing or sheriff considers necessary when imposing a movement restriction condition; and
(e) any planned respite care arrangements for the child which the children's hearing or sheriff considers necessary when imposing a movement restriction condition (reg.6(2)).

Regulation 3 of the MR Regulations contains detailed provisions for the incorporation of the MRC into the child's plan.

While the welfare principle is applicable when a hearing is considering whether to impose an MRC (s.25(2)), s.26 does permit the imposition of an MRC where it is inconsistent with the welfare principle, but necessary to protect members of the public from serious harm. "Members of the public" includes members of the child's household, or those with whom he or she has a close connection. It should be noted that the protection is from serious harm "whether physical or not". In such a case the welfare of the child throughout his or her childhood will be a primary consideration rather than the paramount consideration (s.26(2)).

Under the Children (Scotland) Act 1995 it was common practice for a child facing a movement restriction condition to be automatically provided with a legal representative. Movement restriction conditions are not listed in s.191 in those proceedings for which legal aid is automatically available.

The child's compliance with the MRC must be monitored. Regulation 4(1) of the MR Regulations requires that any CSO (which will include a IVCSO or ICSO) which contains an MRC must designate either a responsible local authority officer or any person employed or otherwise instructed by the implementation authority to carry out the functions of monitoring compliance. If services are to be secured by contract or otherwise, the person providing such services must also be designated. Note that that person will include legal personalities such as registered companies. The child may be required to wear a specified device, commonly known as an electronic tag (regs 7 and 8). It should be noted that reg.4(2)(a) requires that monitoring the child's compliance with all of the measures in the CSO (including IVCSO or ICSO) will include their "participation, progress and cooperation in relation to the child's plan". These reviews may not be any more frequent than weekly. More frequent monitoring may be seen as an intrusion into the child's private and family life that is sufficient to be considered as a breach of art.8 of the ECHR.

Procedure at the hearing is provided for in r.95 of the Children's Hearings (Scotland) Act 2011 (Rules of Procedure in Children's Hearings) Rules 2013 (SSI 2013/194). Rule 96 governs the notification of the decision of the review hearing. Section 150(1)(a) and (b) allows Scottish Ministers to make regulations to prescribe the restrictions and monitoring arrangements which may be imposed. These are contained in the MR Regulations, cited above.

Meaning of "secure accommodation authorisation"

85. In this Act, "secure accommodation authorisation", in relation to a child, means an authorisation enabling the child to be placed and kept in secure accommodation within a residential establishment. C.464

Definitions
  "child": s.199.
  "secure accommodation": s.202(1).
  "residential establishment": s.202(1).

C.464.1

General Note
It should be noted that in including authorisation for secure accommodation neither the sheriff nor the children's hearing are making an order that the child must be held in secure accommodation. Unlike other measures, the implementation authority (IA) is not under a duty to implement the authorisation (see further s.144). That decision is taken by the chief social work officer of the IA, but still requires the consent of the person in charge of the residential establishment (the "head of unit") specified in the compulsory supervision order (CSO) (which includes an interim variation of a compulsory supervision order (IVCSO) or interim compulsory supervision order (ICSO)). See regs 4 and 6 of the Children's Hearings (Scotland) Act 2011 (Implementation of Secure Accommodation Authorisation) (Scotland) Regulations 2013 (SSI 2013/212).

C.464.2

In deciding to implement the secure accommodation authorisation it is not sufficient that the hearing or sheriff has considered that it is necessary. The chief social work officer must consult and take the views of each relevant person, the head of the unit, and the child (taking account of the child's age and maturity) and whether placement will be in the best interests of the child. The reader is directed to the discussion of the application of the welfare principle to secure accommodation authorisation at s.83(6)(c). In deciding whether to consent to the accommodation of the child in the unit, the head of the unit must consider two things: whether the placement would be appropriate to the child's needs; and whether the presence of the child would be detrimental to other children in the unit. Where the head of the unit decides not to consent to the placement, reg.8(3) of the Children's Hearings (Scotland) Act 2011 (Implementation of Secure Accommodation Authorisation) (Scotland) Regulations 2013 (SSI 2013/212) requires the chief social worker to require a review of the relevant order by giving notice to the Reporter, and the review must take place no later than three working days after the notice (reg.9).

The deprivation of liberty, which accommodation in secure accommodation represents, means, in the words of Professor Kenneth McK. Norrie,

"that the procedures which lead to a child's detention in secure accommodation must not only satisfy art.6 (due process) and art.8 (private and family life) but must also be justified in terms of art. 5" [right to take proceedings to challenge the lawfulness of the detention] (*Children's Hearings in Scotland*, 3rd edn (Edinburgh: W. Green, 2013), pp.11–10).

Where the chief social work officer has decided not to implement a secure accommodation authorisation the child and each relevant person may request a review of that decision (see reg.7 of the Children's Hearings (Scotland) Act 2011 (Implementation of Secure Accommodation Authorisation) (Scotland) Regulations 2013 (SSI 2013/212)). This Act has extended the right of appeal to not only the decision to impose a secure accommodation authorisation (regs 11, 12 and 13), but also to the decision to implement (reg.12) or not to implement the authorisation (reg.13). For further information, see s.132 (Review of CSO where authorisation for secure accommodation is included); s.162 (Decision by the chief social worker to remove a child from secure accommodation); and the Children's Hearings (Scotland) Act 2011 (Rules of Procedure in Children's Hearings) Rules 2013 (SSI 2013/194) Pt 21).

Meaning of "interim compulsory supervision order"

C.465   **86.**—(1) In this Act "interim compulsory supervision order", in relation to a child, means an order—

(a) including any of the measures mentioned in section 83(2),
(b) specifying a local authority which is to be responsible for giving effect to the measures included in the order ("the implementation authority"), and
(c) having effect for the relevant period.

(2) An interim compulsory supervision order may, instead of specifying a place or places at which the child is to reside under section 83(2)(a), specify that the child is to reside at any place of safety away from the place where the child predominantly resides.

(3) In subsection (1), "relevant period" means the period beginning with the making of the order and ending with whichever of the following first occurs—

(a) the next children's hearing arranged in relation to the child,
(b) the disposal by the sheriff of an application made by virtue of section 93(2)(a) or 94(2)(a) in relation to the child,
(c) a day specified in the order,
(d) where the order has not been extended under section 98 or 99, the expiry of the period of 22 days beginning on the day on which the order is made,
(e) where the order has been extended (or extended and varied) under section 98 or 99, the expiry of the period of 22 days beginning on the day on which the order is extended.

(4) Subsections (3) to (6) (except subsection (5)(a)) of section 83 apply to an interim compulsory supervision order as they apply to a compulsory supervision order.

Meaning of "interim compulsory supervision order"

DEFINITIONS
"child": s.199.
"children's hearing": s.5.
"compulsory supervision order": ss. 202(1) and 83.
"implementation authority": s.86(1)(b).
"local authority": Local Government (Scotland) Act 1994 s.2.
"measures": s.83.
"place of safety": ss.202(1) and 189.
"relevant period": s.83(7).

C.465.1

GENERAL NOTE

The interim compulsory supervision order (ICSO) repairs one of the deficiencies of the Children (Scotland) Act 1995 (the 1995 Act) under which no immediate measures could be taken in the event that grounds were not accepted or not understood, were referred to court, there had been no child protection order and a place of safety warrant was not justified. While an ICSO can regulate the residence of the child, there is no requirement that the child be removed from his or her home. It is much more flexible than s.66 of the 1995 Act (place of safety warrant) which it replaces. Sections 92(2) and 93(5) below make clear that before an ICSO can be made, the hearing must consider that it is required as a matter of urgency. While there are similar timescales and reviews it should be understood that the ICSO is not a warrant, but is a temporary compulsory supervision requirement in which any of the measures in s.83 (2) may be included (see s.94(6)). The ICSO exists to address immediate and urgent needs, not long term needs, and therefore the measures included should be for the short term. An ICSO may include a movement restriction condition or authorisation for secure accommodation. There are minor differences in the imposing of authorisation for secure accommodation (see commentary to s.85) in an ICSO as opposed to a Compulsory Supervision Order. It should be noted that there is no power under an ICSO to find and bring the child before a hearing, which requires a warrant under s.88.

C.465.2

Subs.(1)

An ICSO may contain any of the measures which may be included in a compulsory supervision requirement (cf. s.83(2)) and must specify the local authority which is to be responsible for giving effect to the conditions (the implementation authority). The duration of the order (the relevant period) is specified in subs.(2) below. It should be noted that it cannot act as a warrant to bring the child to a hearing. That would require a warrant under s.123. A child who is subject to an ICSO is a looked after child for the duration of the ICSO (s.17 of Children (Scotland) Act 1995, as amended by Sch.5 to the Children's Hearings (Scotland) Act 2011 s.2(4)(a)).

C.465.3

Subs.(2)

The ICSO differs markedly from the place of safety warrant (1995 Act ss.66, 67) in that there is no requirement that the child be removed from their usual place of residence, although that is possible. It is also within the power of the hearing to specify or not where the child is to reside for the duration of the order, rather than merely specifying a place of safety to be decided by the chief social work officer. This gives the hearing a greater measure of control over the arrangements for the child. It will also permit the child to appeal that part of the decision (see s.154(3)(d) and (e)).

C.465.4

Subs.(3)

The ICSO is intended to have as short a duration as possible. It will end when the earliest of three events occurs: the next children's hearing; a sheriff has found grounds established (s.93(2)(a) or s.94(2)(a)); or a day specified in the order. It has a maximum duration of 22 days, commencing with the day on which the order was made. Note that these are calendar days rather than working days. The hearing also has the power to specify a duration of less than 22 days when making the order as long as the total number of days does not exceed 66. A hearing or a sheriff may extend, or extend and vary, the ICSO for a maximum of a further 22 days beginning on the day on which it is extended or varied and extended. The test is contained in s.96(3), viz, that the hearing or the sheriff must be satisfied that the order is still necessary for the protection, guidance, treatment or control of the child.

C.465.5

Meaning of "medical examination order"

87.—(1) In this Act "medical examination order", in relation to a child, means an order authorising for the relevant period any of the measures mentioned in subsection (2).

(2) The measures are—
(a) a requirement that the child attend or reside at a specified clinic, hospital or other establishment,
(b) subject to section 186, a requirement that a specified local authority arrange a specified medical examination of the child,
(c) a prohibition on the disclosure (whether directly or indirectly) of a place specified under paragraph (a),
(d) a secure accommodation authorisation,
(e) a direction regulating contact between the child and a specified person or class of person,
(f) any other specified condition appearing to the children's hearing to be appropriate for the purposes of ensuring that the child complies with the order.

(3) A medical examination order may include a secure accommodation authorisation only if—
(a) the order authorises the keeping of the child in a residential establishment,
(b) one of the conditions mentioned in subsection (4) applies, and
(c) having considered the other options available the children's hearing is satisfied that it is necessary to do so.

(4) The conditions are—
(a) that the child has previously absconded and is likely to abscond again and, if the child were to abscond, it is likely that the child's physical, mental or moral welfare would be at risk,
(b) that the child is likely to engage in self-harming conduct,
(c) that the child is likely to cause injury to another person.

(5) In this section—
"medical" includes psychological,
"relevant period", in relation to a medical examination order, means the period beginning with the making of the order and ending with whichever of the following first occurs—
(a) the beginning of the next children's hearing arranged in relation to the child,
(b) a day specified in the order,
(c) the expiry of the period of 22 days beginning on the day on which the order is made,
"specified" means specified in the order.

DEFINITIONS
"child": s.199.
"children's hearing": s.5.
"local authority": Local Government (Scotland) Act 1994 s.2.
"residential establishment": s.202(1).
"secure accommodation authorisation": ss.202(1) and 83(5).

GENERAL NOTE
A medical examination order (MEO) is a stand-alone order which has very limited application and duration, and is very specific in purpose. An MEO may only be made by a grounds hearing where the ground or grounds of referral have been either accepted by the child and relevant persons or found established by a court (s.92(3) below) and the hearing has deferred making a decision. The MEO may only be made if the hearing considers that it is necessary for the purpose of obtaining any further information, or carrying out any further investigation needed. It authorises medical examination, which includes psychological (subs.(5)), for a relevant period, with a maximum of 22 days starting on the day that the

order is made. It cannot be continued or extended. Measures may be attached to the MEO: an order regulating contact; a non-disclosure direction; authorisation for the child to be held in secure accommodation and any condition necessary for ensuring the child's compliance, although any medical examination is subject to the child's capacity to consent (s.186 and the Age of Legal Capacity (Scotland) Act 1991 s.2(4)). It would not be competent for a hearing to make both an interim compulsory supervision requirement (ICSO) and a MEO as the range of measures which may be made in the ICSO include medical examination or treatment (s.83(2)(g)) and make an MEO unnecessary. In considering whether to make an MEO, the overarching principles apply.

Subs.(2)

Measures may be attached to an MEO specifying the nature of the examination, whether it is to be arranged by the local authority, and where it is to take place. As in s.83(2)(f), this requires that there be an understanding of the child's medical needs so that the nature of the treatment or examination be specified. The examination of the child may require the child to be resident at the clinic, hospital or other establishment. Authorisation for secure accommodation is also possible, subject to the test in subs.(3). The order may regulate contact between the child and a specified person or class of persons. The hearing may also authorise any other specified condition that they consider to be necessary for ensuring that the child complies with the order, although the hearing may not override a competent child's capacity to consent or refuse to the examination or treatment (s.186 and the Age of Legal Capacity (Scotland) Act 1991 s.2(4)). **C.466.3**

Subs.(3)

The requirements in this subsection are similar to those in s.83(5) but the type of residential establishment is not specified. **C.466.4**

Subs.(4)

The criteria for authorisation for secure accommodation are identical to those in s.83(6). **C.466.5**

Abscond. This concept is not defined in the Act. The reader is directed to our discussion of this concept in our commentary below on s.169(1)(b).

Subs.(5)

This subsection contains the definition of relevant period for the purposes of a medical examination order. It is similar to that for an interim compulsory supervision requirement, but there is no provision for extension or renewal. **C.466.6**

Meaning of "warrant to secure attendance"

88.—(1) In this Act, "warrant to secure attendance", in relation to a child, means a warrant effective for the relevant period— **C.467**
  (a) authorising an officer of law—
    (i) to search for and apprehend the child,
    (ii) to take the child to, and detain the child in, a place of safety,
    (iii) to bring the child before the relevant proceedings, and
    (iv) so far as is necessary for the execution of the warrant, to break open shut and lockfast places,
  (b) prohibiting disclosure (whether directly or indirectly) to any person specified in the warrant of the place of safety.

(2) A warrant to secure attendance may include a secure accommodation authorisation but only if—
  (a) the warrant authorises the keeping of the child in a residential establishment,
  (b) one or more of the conditions mentioned in subsection (3) applies, and
  (c) having considered the other options available the children's hearing or sheriff is satisfied that it is necessary to do so.

(3) The conditions are—
  (a) that the child has previously absconded and is likely to abscond again and, if the child were to abscond, it is likely that the child's physical, mental or moral welfare would be at risk,
  (b) that the child is likely to engage in self-harming conduct,

(c) that the child is likely to cause injury to another person.
(4) In this section—
"relevant period", in relation to a warrant to secure attendance, means—
  (a) where the warrant is granted by a children's hearing, the period beginning with the granting of the warrant and ending with the earlier of—
    (i) the beginning of the relevant proceedings, or
    (ii) the expiry of the period of 7 days beginning with the day on which the child is first detained in pursuance of the warrant,
  (b) where the warrant is granted by the sheriff under section 103(7), the period beginning with the granting of the warrant and ending with the earlier of—
    (i) the beginning of the continued hearing, or
    (ii) the expiry of the period of 14 days beginning with the day on which the child is first detained in pursuance of the warrant,
  (c) where the warrant is granted by the sheriff under any other provision in respect of attendance at proceedings under Part 10, the period beginning with the granting of the warrant and ending with the earlier of—
    (i) the beginning of the relevant proceedings, or
    (ii) the expiry of the period of 14 days beginning with the day on which the child is first detained in pursuance of the warrant,
  (d) where the warrant is granted by the sheriff in respect of attendance at a children's hearing arranged by virtue of section 108, 115, 117(2)(b) or 156(3)(a), the period beginning with the granting of the warrant and ending with the earlier of—
    (i) the beginning of the relevant proceedings, or
    (ii) the expiry of the period of 7 days beginning with the day on which the child is first detained in pursuance of the warrant,
"relevant proceedings", in relation to a warrant to secure attendance, means the children's hearing or, as the case may be, proceedings before the sheriff in respect of which it is granted.

DEFINITIONS

C.467.1 "child": s.199.
"children's hearing": s.5.
"officer of law": s.202(1) and the Criminal Procedure (Scotland) Act 1995.
"place of safety": ss.202(1) and 189.
"residential establishment": s.202(1).
"secure accommodation authorisation": ss.202(1) and 83(5).

GENERAL NOTE

C.467.2 Whereas there was a multiplicity of warrants under the Children (Scotland) Act 1995, this is the only warrant contained in this Act. It is intended for a single purpose—to ensure the attendance of the child at either a children's hearing or a hearing before the sheriff. The reason for the non-attendance is immaterial, it may be that the child has refused to attend, but it could equally be that the child has been withheld from the hearing by an adult or that his or her current whereabouts are unknown. A warrant may only be issued by a children's hearing where the Reporter has applied to the hearing for it to be granted. The hearing has no power to consider one *ex proprio motu* (Children's Hearings (Scotland) Act 2011 (Rules of Procedure in Children's Hearings) Rules 2013 (SSI 2013/194) (the "Procedural Rules") r.78(1)). (For warrants granted by a sheriff see s.103(5), (6) and (7)). A warrant is a strong measure and should only be used where it is considered that there is no realistic alternative. The issuing of a warrant must be proportionate. The welfare of the child remains paramount and a hearing or a sheriff must consider the impact upon the child of the execution of the warrant and its terms with the caveat that the best interests of the child may be over-ridden if the safety of others requires that the child be kept in secure accommodation (s.26). Before granting a warrant to

Meaning of "warrant to secure attendance"

secure attendance the hearing "must seek the views of the child, each relevant person, and any appointed safeguarder, if present at the hearing" (Procedural Rules r.78(2)). It should be remembered that, in the event that the child fails to attend a grounds hearing and has not been excused, s.95(2) allows the hearing to require the Reporter to arrange a further grounds hearing rather than issuing a warrant. The lifespan of a warrant is short, being a maximum of seven days if the child is to be brought to a children's hearing and fourteen days if the child is to be brought to a sheriff court hearing. The child, any relevant person and the safeguarder all have a right to appeal the decision to grant a warrant to secure attendance (s.154(3)(g)) and the right to appeal the decision to implement or not a secure accommodation authorisation included in a warrant (s.162). Apart from the latter right to appeal the decision re implementation, the wording of s.154 would not seem to allow an appeal against the keeping of the child in a place of safety, or the decision not to disclose the whereabouts of the child. The case of *J, Appellant*, 2013 S.L.T. (Sh. Ct) 18; 2013 Fam. L.R. 12 concerned an appeal against only the condition of contact contained in the place of safety warrant under ss.51 and 69(7) and (9). The wording lacked any provision for an appeal against only a condition contained in the warrant. It was held that the appellant's art.8 (right to private and family life) and art.6 (right to a fair hearing) rights were engaged and for the section to be compatible with those rights the provision had to be read as allowing the sheriff on appeal to recall or vary only the contact condition attached to the warrant without having to recall the warrant as a whole. It would follow that there is a parallel with child protection orders in that an appeal may not be against the imposition of the warrant but against any of the measures contained in the warrant (see Procedural Rules r.17— Duties of the Reporter, where a child is detained under a warrant to secure the attendance of the child).

Subs.(1)(a) and (b)

The warrant issued by a sheriff or hearing gives the police considerable powers, not only to bring the child to a hearing, but to search for him or her, and if necessary to break into locked premises. The child may also be taken to and kept at a place of safety. Section 189 places restrictions on the use of police stations as places of safety. The Reporter must provide the child, each relevant person and any safeguarder with a copy of the warrant together with details of those persons' right to appeal the grant of the warrant (Procedural Rules r.78(3)).

C.467.3

In normal circumstances the police are required to notify a parent or carer of the whereabouts of the child. This subsection allows for that notification to be withheld. The hearing or sheriff will require to consider such withholding in the same way that they would consider imposing the withholding of the whereabouts of the child as a condition of a compulsory supervision order (CSO) or interim order or child protection order (CPO).

Subs.(2)

Authorisation for secure accommodation may be included in the warrant and the requirements are identical to those which may be included in a medical treatment order (s.87(3)), and differ only from the authorisation which may be included in a compulsory supervision order (including an interim compulsory supervision order), in that there is no need to specify the type of residential establishment and accordingly the requirements in s.83(5)(a) to the effect that the place must contain both secure and non-secure accommodation, or that there must be two places, one with secure accommodation and the other without it, does not apply.

C.467.4

Subs.(3)

The conditions which must be met before authorisation for secure accommodation may be included in a warrant to secure attendance are identical to those for compulsory supervision orders, interim compulsory supervision orders (s.83(6)) and medical examination orders (s.87(4)).

C.467.5

Subs.(4)

The lifespan of a warrant is brief and ends at the earlier of: the start of the relevant proceedings; the expiry of seven days when it is issued by a children's hearing or a sheriff to bring a child to a children's hearing; or the expiry of fourteen days when issued by a sheriff to bring a child to court hearing. Rule 17(2) requires that where a warrant has been issued by a children's hearing, and the child has been detained in a place of safety, the Reporter must, wherever practicable, arrange a children's hearing to take place on the first working day after the child was first detained. A warrant may be used when a child has refused to attend, or where a child has been prevented from attending.

C.467.6

Children's Hearings (Scotland) Act 2011

Statement of grounds

Principal Reporter's duty to prepare statement of grounds

C.468 **89.**—(1) This section applies where the Principal Reporter is required by virtue of section 69(2) to arrange a children's hearing in relation to a child.
(2) The Principal Reporter must prepare the statement of grounds.
(3) In this Act "statement of grounds", in relation to a child, means a statement setting out—
(a) which of the section 67 grounds the Principal Reporter believes applies in relation to the child, and
(b) the facts on which that belief is based.

DEFINITIONS
C.468.1   "child": s.199.
"children's hearing": s.199.
"Principal Reporter": s.14 and Sch.3 paras 8–10.

GENERAL NOTE
C.468.2   Where the Reporter decides to arrange a children's hearing in respect of a child (s.69(2)) it is his or her responsibility to decide which of the grounds of referral in s.67 are applicable (s.66(2)). The Reporter draws up the document known as the statement of grounds in a form which is specified by r.14 of the Children's Hearings (Scotland) Act 2011 (Rules of Procedure in Children's Hearings) Rules 2013 (SSI 2013/194) (the "Procedural Rules"). That document must contain not only the ground that the Reporter believes is applicable, but the facts that give rise to that belief. These are commonly referred to as the "supporting statements". It should be noted that r.14 requires that where the ground for referral is that the child has committed an offence (s.67(2)(j)) the ground must have the same degree of specification as would be required for an adult facing criminal proceedings and the statement of grounds must also specify the nature of the offence in question (Criminal Procedure (Scotland) Act 1995 s.138(4) and Sch.3). There are detailed rules contained in Pts 6 to 11 of the Procedural Rules concerning the Reporter's duty to provide notification of hearings together with the relevant documentation. Given the importance of the statement of grounds it is essential that it is provided to children and relevant persons in accessible format where needed.

Grounds hearing

Grounds to be put to child and relevant person

C.469 **90.**—(1) At the opening of a children's hearing arranged by virtue of section 69(2) or 95(2) (the "grounds hearing") the chairing member must—
[1] (a) explain to the child and each relevant person in relation to the child—
(i) each section 67 ground specified in the statement of grounds, and
(ii) the supporting facts in relation to that ground,
(b) ask them whether they accept that each ground applies in relation to the child.
[2] (1A) In relation to each ground that a person accepts applies in relation to the child, the chairing member must ask the person whether the person accepts each of the supporting facts.
[2] (1B) Where under subsection (1A) any person does not accept all of the supporting facts in relation to a ground, the ground is taken for the purposes of this Act to be accepted at the grounds hearing only if the grounds hearing considers that—
(a) the person has accepted sufficient of the supporting facts to support the conclusion that the ground applies in relation to the child, and
(b) it is appropriate to proceed in relation to the ground on the basis of only those supporting facts which are accepted by the child and each relevant person.
[2] (1C) Where a ground is taken to be accepted for the purposes of this Act by virtue of subsection (1B), the grounds hearing must amend the statement

Grounds to be put to child and relevant person

of grounds to delete any supporting facts in relation to the ground which are not accepted by the child and each relevant person.

[2] (1D) In this section, "supporting facts", in relation to a section 67 ground, means facts set out in relation to the ground by virtue of section 89(3)(b).

(2) This section is subject to section 94.

NOTES
1. Substituted by the Children and Young People (Scotland) Act 2014 (asp 8) Pt 16 s.85 (effective 26 January 2015).
2. Inserted by the Children and Young People (Scotland) Act 2014 (asp 8) Pt 16 s.85 (effective 26 January 2015).

C.469.1

DEFINITIONS
"chairing member": Sch.1 para.7.
"child": s.199.
"children's hearing": s.5.
"grounds hearing": ss.202(1) and 90.
"relevant person": s.201.
"safeguarder": s.202(1).
"statement of grounds": ss.202(1) and 89(3).

C.469.2

GENERAL NOTE
As the ground(s) for referral are the legal basis for bringing a child before a children's hearing, it is of the essence that the statement of grounds must be put to the child and to each relevant person at the start of the grounds hearing so that they may declare whether or not they accept them. It is the applicable stated grounds that are accepted or not rather than the supporting statements, although in practice the statements of fact are also put to the child and relevant person. It is important that the child and relevant persons understand they are being asked whether they agree that the "facts" averred are applicable to the child. It is entirely possible for the child and/or relevant persons to agree that the supporting facts in the statement of grounds are correct, but not agree that the grounds themselves are applicable. It is therefore essential that the child and relevant person(s) understand the s.67(2) grounds in the statement of grounds. It is the chairing member who has a duty to provide an explanation of the relevant ground or grounds (Children's Hearings (Scotland) Act 2011 (Rules of Procedure in Children's Hearings) Rules 2013 (SSI 2013/194) r.59), as amended by r.5 of the Children's Hearings (Scotland) Act 2011 (Rules of Procedure in Children's Hearings) Amendment Rules 2015 (SSI 2015/21) (the "Procedural Rules"). The chairing member must take particular care in providing an explanation to ensure that it remains true to the meaning of the ground(s) as the child or relevant person may rely on that explanation. Much will depend on the skill of the chairing member to provide an explanation suitable for the individual child and each relevant person. It is the ability of the child to understand this explanation that is the basis of the decision of a prehearing panel or hearing to excuse a child from attendance at that portion of a grounds hearing (s.73(4)).

C.469.3

It should be noted that there is no need for the child and each relevant person to have the grounds put to them while both are present together. It may be difficult for a child to respond to the ground(s) for referral or a supporting fact in the presence of the relevant person(s). Rule 59(1) of the Procedural Rules allows for a relevant person to be excluded if their presence is preventing the child from accepting or denying the ground or grounds for referral. This is a different criterion from those in s.76—it is much wider and the chairing member need only consider that the presence of the relevant person will prevent the child from accepting or not the ground for referral. Interestingly it is the decision of the chairing member, not the hearing, as to whether to exclude a relevant person during the putting of the ground for referral to the child. While that rule only concerns the exclusion of a relevant person, a hearing would be able to exclude a representative of a relevant person under s.77. On the return of the excluded relevant person(s) to the hearing, r.59(2) requires that the chairing member must provide him or her with an explanation of what occurred during the period of exclusion. In practice this means that the chairing member must explain to all present whether the child accepted or did not accept the ground(s). The chairing member need not, however, disclose any information that would be likely to cause significant harm to the child (see s.178(1) and r.6(2) of the Procedural Rules). It follows that an information non-disclosure request regarding the child's acceptance or non-acceptance of the ground(s) for referral would be inappropriate. An example of a hearing being split so as to avoid the child being confronted by persons with whom she had difficulties is found in *CF v MF & GF and Scottish Reporter* [2017] CSIH 44, discussed above under s.81(3) in the sub-paragraph beginning "Some three years after the decision by Sheriff Reid". This was a case wherein a pre-hearing panel had to ascertain the views of the child as to whether grandparents, whom she did not wish to have contact with, should continue to be deemed as relevant person. Lord Malcolm, at para.[18] of the court's judgment, narrates that the pre-hearing consisted of two parts, the first involving the child, with her solicitor and foster carer, the solicitor for the grandparent and the Reporter, and the second part taking place in another room with everyone present except the child and with the Reporter informing those present of what had happened at the first part of the hearing.

Neither the Act nor the Procedural Rules say much about the role of the Reporter. We think the reader will appreciate being directed to the terms of the guidance regarding this in the *The Practice and Procedure Manual* (published by Children's Hearings Scotland in June 2013), under the heading "The role of the Children's Reporter at a children's hearing":

"2.8 The Children's Reporter has a right to attend a children's hearing. There are four parts to the role of the Children's Reporter at the hearing:
1. Fulfilling legal obligations. This is mainly in relation to the record of proceedings.
2. Supporting fair process. This can include offering a view to the hearing about a legal or procedural issue in the same way as any other hearing participant. This view can be offered in response to a question or on the Children's Reporter's initiative."

Subss.(1A) to (1D)

C.469.4 Subsection (1A) makes clear that the chairing member must ask whether the child and relevant person accept the "supporting facts". Subsections (1B) to (1D) provide for the situation where there is partial acceptance of supporting facts. In this event the grounds hearing must decide (per subs.(1B), (a)) if the accepted facts "add up" to the ground for referral and (per subs.(1B)), if it is appropriate to proceed on the basis of the admitted grounds. If these decisions are in the affirmative, then the grounds hearing must, (per subs.(1C)), amend the statement of grounds appropriately.

Subs.(2)

C.469.5 This makes clear that before a ground for referral can be "accepted", it must have been understood. Where the hearing is satisfied that the child or relevant person is not capable of understanding the ground, or has not understood the explanation of it which has been given, then the hearing should proceed under s.94.

Grounds accepted: powers of grounds hearing

C.470 91.—(1) This section applies where—
(a) each ground specified in the statement of grounds is accepted, or
(b) at least one of the grounds specified in the statement of grounds is accepted and the grounds hearing considers that it is appropriate to make a decision on whether to make a compulsory supervision order on the basis of the ground or grounds that have been accepted.

(2) If the grounds hearing considers that it is appropriate to do so, the grounds hearing may defer making a decision on whether to make a compulsory supervision order until a subsequent children's hearing.

(3) If the grounds hearing does not exercise the power conferred by subsection (2) the grounds hearing must—
(a) if satisfied that it is necessary to do so for the protection, guidance, treatment or control of the child, make a compulsory supervision order, or
(b) if not so satisfied, discharge the referral.

(4) In subsection (1), "accepted" means accepted by the child and (subject to sections 74 and 75) each relevant person in relation to the child.

DEFINITIONS

C.470.1 "child": s.199.
"children's hearing": s.5.
"compulsory supervision order": ss.202(1) and 83.
"grounds hearing": s.90.
"relevant person": s.201.
"statement of grounds": ss.202(1) and 89(3).

Powers of grounds hearing on deferral

GENERAL NOTE

This section deals with the situation where the child and relevant person accept ground(s) for referral, including making provision for the situation where there is partial acceptance of ground(s) for referral.

Subs.(1)

A hearing may only proceed to considering a compulsory supervision order (CSO) if the child and each relevant person has accepted that the s.67(2) ground in the statement of grounds apply. Where there is more than one ground for referral the hearing may proceed if the child or relevant person accepts at least one of the ground(s).

Subs.(2)

In the event that, for whatever reason, the hearing feels that it cannot make a substantive decision, it has the power to defer the decision to a further hearing. The hearing may: appoint a safeguarder if none has been appointed; require the Reporter to obtain a report or reports; set a date for the subsequent hearing; or determine that for either the child or a relevant person to participate effectively he or she requires to be represented by a solicitor or counsel and that it is unlikely that the individual will arrange for such representation and therefore require the Reporter to notify the Scottish Legal Aid Board of that determination, and the reasons therefor and the name and address of the individual (Children's Hearings (Scotland) Act 2011 (Rules of Procedure in Children's Hearings) Rules 2013 (SSI 2013/194) r.61(1)). For the hearing's powers on deferral see s.92 (powers of grounds hearing on deferral); s.93 (grounds not accepted: application to sheriff or to discharge); s.94 (child or relevant person unable to understand grounds); s.95 (child fails to attend grounds hearing).

Subs.(3)

If the hearing decides to proceed to a substantive decision, the test that must be applied is whether a CSO is necessary for the protection, guidance, treatment or control of the child. This is a change in language from the Children (Scotland) Act 1995 which merely required the hearing to consider that "compulsory measures of supervision are necessary" (s.70(1) of 1995 Act). The overarching principles and the European Convention principle of proportionality also apply. If the hearing is not satisfied that a CSO is necessary the grounds of referral must be discharged. Once discharged, the facts which had been averred in the discharged referral cannot be used in a subsequent referral unless there are fresh facts which, along with the facts of the discharged referral, amount to a new ground for referral. There is no explicit authority for this, but the approach of the court in *Kennedy v S*, 1986 S.L.T. 679 at 681, where the court supported the use, in a subsequent referral, of material in respect of which the Reporter had previously intimated no proceedings, where there were fresh facts averred, supports his view. A decision by the hearing to discharge a ground for referral or to make a CSO is appealable by the child and relevant persons (see Pt 15).

"*protection, guidance, treatment or control*". None of "protection, guidance, treatment or control" is defined and therefore the ordinary meanings of the words apply.

Powers of grounds hearing on deferral

92.—(1) This section applies where under section 91(2) the grounds hearing defers making a decision in relation to a child until a subsequent children's hearing.

(2) If the grounds hearing considers that the nature of the child's circumstances is such that for the protection, guidance, treatment or control of the child it is necessary as a matter of urgency that an interim compulsory supervision order be made, the grounds hearing may make an interim compulsory supervision order in relation to the child.

(3) If the grounds hearing considers that it is necessary to do so for the purpose of obtaining any further information, or carrying out any further investigation, that is needed before the subsequent children's hearing, the hearing may make a medical examination order.

DEFINITIONS
"child": s.199.
"children's hearing": s.5.
"interim compulsory supervision order": ss.202(1) and 86.

"grounds hearing": ss.202(1) and 90.
"medical examination order": ss.202(1) and 89.

GENERAL NOTE

This section prescribes the powers of a grounds hearing where that hearing decides to defer making a substantive decision. As pointed out Kenneth McK. Norrie, *Children's Hearings in Scotland*, 3rd edn (Edinburgh: 2013), a "decision" means a majority decision. Professor Norrie expresses the view that in the event of no agreed majority view it would be necessary to defer and we agree with this.

Subss.(1) and (2)

C.471.2 These subsections apply where the grounds hearing has been unable to proceed to making a substantive decision either because the grounds of referral have not been accepted or understood, or where further information is required. The interim compulsory supervision order (ICSO) is discussed more fully at s.86. This section, together with s.93, contains the circumstances in which an ICSO may be used. Although it replaces the s.66 warrant of the Children (Scotland) Act 1995 (the 1995 Act) and has a similar lifespan, the ICSO is not a warrant, but a short term compulsory supervision order. It may only be used where there is urgency.

This section prescribes the powers of a grounds hearing where that hearing decides to defer making a substantive decision. As pointed out Kenneth McK. Norrie, *Children's Hearings in Scotland*, 3rd edn (Edinburgh: 2013), a "decision" means a majority decision. Professor Norrie expresses the view that in the event of no agreed majority view it would be necessary to defer and we agree with this.

Subs.(2)(a)

C.471.3 *Make an application to the sheriff.* Rule 3.45(1) of the Act of Sederunt (Child Care and Maintenance Rules) 1997 (SI 1997/291) as amended by Act of Sederunt (Children's Hearings (Scotland) Act 2011) (Miscellaneous Amendments) 2013 (SSI 2013/172) (the "1997 Rules") provides that the Application, in Form 60, is to be made within seven days of the direction to the Reporter and lodged with the sheriff clerk of the district in which the child is habitually resident. The term "habitually resident" is not defined but we think that many people would regard treating the child's home as the child's "habitual residence" as reflecting ordinary English usage. We believe that an analysis of the relevant statutory provisions confirms that this is the appropriate interpretation. Under s.17 of the Act, children's hearings are generally to be held within the relevant local authority for the child and s.201 enacts that the "relevant local authority" is that within which the child predominantly resides and provides that periods of residence in a residential establishment are not to be taken into account when assessing where the child predominantly resides: we consider that these provisions indicate that the legislature intended that a child's "habitual" residence is his or her usual home (usually, but not invariably with parent(s)). Under r. 3.45(1B) the sheriff may, on cause shown, remit an application to another sheriff court. The sheriff, where considering whether to direct the application to be remitted to another court, will have regard to the convenience of parties and witnesses. This is a procedural decision to which the overarching principles do not apply (see *MT and AG v Anne Gerry (Locality Reporter)* [2014] CSIH 108, sub nom. *MT v Gerry*, 2015 S.C. 359, sub nom. *T v Locality Reporter*, 2015 Fam. L. R. 2), but the desirability, where the child's actual residence is far from his or her habitual residence, e.g. in a distant residential establishment, of avoiding requiring the child having to be escorted a long way across Scotland to attend a proof hearing, will weigh with the sheriff in deciding on whether to remit to another court. Similarly, where an offence is alleged to have been committed by the child away from his or her habitual residence, with the consequence that, under s.102(2), the application must be lodged within the jurisdiction of the offence, the application could, having regard to the convenience of all concerned, be remitted to the child's home court.

Discharge the referral. Even where the grounds for referral are accepted, it may be that the hearing is satisfied that it is justified in discharging the referral as they do not consider that it is necessary for the protection, guidance, treatment or control of the child that a compulsory supervision order is made. If the referral is discharged, the circumstances leading to that referral may not be relied upon as the only foundation for a future referral: see observations above under s.91(3).

Subs.(3)

C.471.4 This section introduces the use of the medical examination order (MEO). For the full annotation to the MEO see s.87 above. It replaces that part of the s.66 warrant (s.66(4)(a)) of

Grounds not accepted: application to sheriff or discharge

the 1995 Act. The medical examination order is a stand-alone order, and does not form part of an ICSO. It may only be made by a hearing where grounds of referral have either been accepted by the child and each relevant person or have been found established by the court and the grounds hearing has deferred making a decision. (See s.120(6) for the making of a medical examination order by a review hearing.) It has a maximum duration of 22 days beginning on the day that the order is made and cannot be continued. Any medical examination is subject to the child's capacity to consent to medical treatment, therefore no child with the capacity to make a decision regarding medical treatment or procedure under s.2(4) of the Age of Legal Capacity (Scotland) Act 1991 can be forced to undergo examination (s.186).

While a child is resident at a clinic, hospital, or other establishment, or accommodated for the duration of the MEO, the implementation authority will have the same duties towards that child as if he or she was a looked after child (s.17(c) of the 1995 Act).

For the purpose of. The test for the making of an MEO is that it is necessary to obtain further information or to carry out any further investigation in order for the subsequent hearing to make a decision. See General Note to s.87. The overarching principles and the European Convention principle of proportionality also apply.

Grounds not accepted: application to sheriff or discharge

93.—(1) This section applies where—
(a) at least one of the grounds specified in the statement of grounds is accepted but the grounds hearing does not consider that it is appropriate to make a decision on whether to make a compulsory supervision order on the basis of the ground or grounds that have been accepted, or
(b) none of the grounds specified in the statement of grounds is accepted.
(2) The grounds hearing must—
(a) direct the Principal Reporter to make an application to the sheriff for a determination on whether each ground that is not accepted by the child and (subject to sections 74 and 75) each relevant person in relation to the child is established, or
(b) discharge the referral.
(3) Subsections (4) and (5) apply if the grounds hearing gives a direction under subsection (2)(a).
(4) The chairing member must—
(a) explain the purpose of the application to the child and (subject to sections 74 and 75) each relevant person in relation to the child, and
(b) inform the child that the child is obliged to attend the hearing before the sheriff unless excused by the sheriff.
(5) If the grounds hearing considers that the nature of the child's circumstances is such that for the protection, guidance, treatment or control of the child it is necessary as a matter of urgency that an interim compulsory supervision order be made, the grounds hearing may make an interim compulsory supervision order in relation to the child.
(6) An interim compulsory supervision order made under subsection (5) may not include a measure of the kind mentioned in section 83(2)(f)(i).
(7) In subsection (1), "accepted" means accepted by the child and (subject to sections 74 and 75) each relevant person in relation to the child.

C.472

DEFINITIONS
"chairing member": Sch.1 para.7.
"child": s.199.
"compulsory supervision order": ss.202(1) and 83.
"grounds hearing": ss.202(1) and 90.
"interim compulsory supervision order": ss.202(1) and 86.
"Principal Reporter": s.14 and Sch.3 paras 8–10.
"relevant person": s.201.
"statement of grounds": ss.202(1) and 89(3).

C.472.1

Children's Hearings (Scotland) Act 2011

GENERAL NOTE

C.472.2 This section deals with the situation where the child and relevant person do not accept ground(s) for referral, including making provision for the situation where more than one ground for referral has been put to the child and relevant person and not all have been accepted—in the latter event the hearing may only make a decision on whether or not to make a compulsory supervision order if it is satisfied that it is appropriate to proceed on the basis of the ground(s) which have been accepted. The hearing of course also has the option of discharging the referral or the ground(s) for referral which have not been accepted.

Subss.(1) and (2)

C.472.3 Where the child and relevant person(s) have understood the explanation of the grounds for referral and those ground(s) have not been accepted by a child or a relevant person the hearing has two options. Either the referral may be discharged, or the Reporter may be directed to make an application to the sheriff. The Reporter, where so directed, has no discretion as to whether to make the application to the court. Consideration of evidence does not form part of the power of the children's hearings and therefore it is the sheriff who must decide on the basis of evidence led whether the ground(s) for referral are established. It should also be noted that even where the grounds for referral have been accepted by the child and relevant person(s), the hearing may still make the decision to refer the case to the sheriff for proof. The most common reason for this is that while the ground(s) for referral has been accepted, the supporting facts have been disputed, and the hearing considers that if it were to use the power to amend the ground (Children's Hearings (Scotland) Act 2011 (Rules of Procedure in Children's Hearings) Rules 2013 (SSI 2013/194) r.59(4)), the supporting statements as amended would be insufficient to establish the ground(s) for referral.

Subs.(2)(a)

Make an application to the sheriff. Rule 3.45(1) of the Act of Sederunt (Child Care and Maintenance Rules) 1997 (SI 1997/291) as amended by Act of Sederunt (Children's Hearings (Scotland) Act 2011) (Miscellaneous Amendments) 2013 (SSI 2013/172) (the "1997 Rules") provides that the Application, in Form 60, is to be made within seven days of the direction to the Reporter and lodged with the sheriff clerk of the district in which the child is habitually resident. The term "habitually resident" is not defined but we think that many people would regard treating the child's home as the child's "habitual residence" as reflecting ordinary English usage. We believe that an analysis of the relevant statutory provisions confirms that this is the appropriate interpretation. Under s.17 of the Act, children's hearings are generally to be held within the relevant local authority for the child and s.201 enacts that the "relevant local authority" is that within which the child predominantly resides and provides that periods of residence in a residential establishment are not to be taken into account when assessing where the child predominantly resides: we consider that these provisions indicate that the legislature intended that a child's "habitual" residence is his or her usual home (usually, but not invariably with parent(s)). Under r. 3.45(1B) the sheriff may, on cause shown, remit an application to another sheriff court. The sheriff, where considering whether to direct the application to be remitted to another court, will have regard to the convenience of parties and witnesses. This is a procedural decision to which the overarching principles do not apply (see *MT and AG v Anne Gerry (Locality Reporter)* [2014] CSIH 108, sub nom. *MT v Gerry*, 2015 S.C. 359, sub nom. *T v Locality Reporter*, 2015 Fam. L.R. 2), but the desirability, where the child's actual residence is far from his or her habitual residence, e.g. in a distant residential establishment, of avoiding requiring the child having to be escorted a long way across Scotland to attend a proof hearing, will weigh with the sheriff in deciding on whether to remit to another court. Similarly, where an offence is alleged to have been committed by the child away from his or her habitual residence, with the consequence that, under s.102(2), the application must be lodged within the jurisdiction of the offence, the application could, having regard to the convenience of all concerned, be remitted to the child's home court.

Discharge the referral. Even where the grounds for referral are accepted, it may be that the hearing is satisfied that it is justified in discharging the referral as they do not consider that it is necessary for the protection, guidance, treatment or control of the child that a compulsory supervision order is made. If the referral is discharged, the circumstances leading to that referral may not be relied upon as the only foundation for a future referral: see observations above under s.91(3).

Subs.(4)

C.472.4 Where the hearing has decided to direct the Reporter to make an application to the sheriff, it becomes the responsibility of the chairing member to provide the child with an explanation of

Child or relevant person unable to understand grounds

what that means. Where the child is capable of understanding the explanation of the grounds for referral, the child must also be told that they will be obliged to attend the court hearing.

Subss.(5) and (6)
If the children's hearing has made the decision to require the Reporter to make an application to the court, the hearing may impose an interim compulsory supervision order (ICSO). The test is contained in subs.(5): that it is necessary for the protection, guidance, treatment or control of the child. The overarching principles and the European Convention principle of proportionality also apply. Any of the measures contained in s.83(2) may be included in the ICSO except a requirement that the local authority arrange a specified medical examination or treatment for the child.

Subs.(7)
This section is subject to the provisions in s.74 which gives the hearing the power to excuse a relevant person from attendance at a hearing. Unlike the child who may not be excused from that portion of the hearing where the grounds of referral are to be explained to him or her, there is no such provision for a relevant person. Where the presence of a relevant person may inhibit the child from accepting or denying the grounds of referral, s.76 permits the hearing to exclude the relevant person from attendance at that part of the hearing. The hearing does not require confirmation from the child that this is the case, it may use its judgement. The chairing member is required to provide the relevant person with an explanation of what happened during his or her absence (but this is subject to the provision in s.178 that a children's hearing need not disclose any information about the referred child where this would cause significant harm to the child: see our discussion under s.178). Any relevant person's representative may also be excluded from the hearing where the explanation of the grounds of referral is made to the child (s.77). An information non-disclosure request regarding the child's response to the ground(s) of referral would be impracticable.

Child or relevant person unable to understand grounds

94.—(1) Subsection (2) applies where the grounds hearing is satisfied that the child or a relevant person in relation to the child—
  (a) would not be capable of understanding an explanation given in compliance with section 90(1) in relation to a ground, or
  (b) has not understood the explanation given in compliance with section 90(1) in relation to a ground.
(2) The grounds hearing must—
  (a) direct the Principal Reporter to make an application to the sheriff to determine whether the ground is established, or
  (b) discharge the referral in relation to the ground.
[1] (3) In the case mentioned in subsection (1)(a), the chairing member need not comply with section 90(1) in relation to that ground as respects the person who would not be capable of understanding an explanation given in compliance with section 90(1) in relation to the ground.
(4) If the grounds hearing gives a direction under subsection (2)(a), the chairing member must—
  (a) in so far as is reasonably practicable comply with the requirement in paragraph (a) of section 93(4), and
  (b) comply with the requirement in paragraph (b) of that section.
(5) If the grounds hearing gives a direction under subsection (2)(a), section 93(5) applies.

NOTE
1. As amended by the Children and Young People (Scotland) Act 2014 (asp 8) Sch.5 para.12(4) (effective 26 January 2015).

DEFINITIONS
  "chairing member": Sch.1 para.7.
  "child": s.199.
  "grounds hearing": ss.202(1) and 90.
  "Principal Reporter": s.14 and Sch.3 paras 8–10.
  "relevant person": s.201.

GENERAL NOTE

C.473.3   It is the chairing member who has the responsibility of providing the child and the relevant person(s) with the explanation of the ground(s) for referral (s.90(1)(a)), but it is the decision of the hearing as to whether or not that explanation has been understood. Where the hearing is satisfied that the child or relevant person would not be capable of understanding the chairing member's explanation of the grounds for referral, or has not understood that explanation, the hearing has the choice of either dismissing the ground(s) for referral or requiring the Reporter to make an application to the court. Where there has been more than one ground for referral, but only one has been accepted by the child and relevant persons the hearing may either dismiss the remaining ground(s), or may direct the Reporter to make an application to the court with regard to the denied ground(s)—see our discussion in the General Note to s.90. Where the hearing has decided to require the Reporter to make an application to the sheriff court for consideration as to whether or not the ground(s) of referral should be established it is the responsibility of the chairing member to provide the child and relevant person(s) with an explanation of what that means, and to ensure that the child understands that he or she must attend the court hearing unless excused by the sheriff. The children's hearing does not have the power to excuse the child from attendance at the court hearing. Where the chairing member considers that the child or relevant person(s) would also be unable to understand his or her explanation of the application to the court, he or she is not required to provide such an explanation. Subsection (5) provides that where the hearing has directed the Reporter to apply to the sheriff for a proof hearing then s.93(5) applies—i.e. if it considers that the child's circumstances are such that, for the protection, guidance, treatment or control of the child, an interim compulsory supervision order is necessary as a matter of urgency, then the hearing may make such an order.

Subs.(2)(a)

C.473.4   *Make an application to the sheriff.* See above under subs.93(2)(a). The same considerations apply here.

Child fails to attend grounds hearing

C.474   **95.**—(1) This section applies where—
(a) a child fails to attend a grounds hearing arranged by virtue of section 69(2) or subsection (2), and
(b) the child was not excused from attending the grounds hearing.
(2) The grounds hearing may require the Principal Reporter to arrange another grounds hearing.
[1] (3) Subsection (4) applies where under subsection (2) the grounds hearing requires the Principal Reporter to arrange another grounds hearing.
[1] (4) If the grounds hearing considers that the nature of the child's circumstances is such that for the protection, guidance, treatment or control of the child it is necessary as a matter of urgency that an interim compulsory supervision order be made, the grounds hearing may make an interim compulsory supervision order in relation to the child.
[1] (5) An interim compulsory supervision order made under subsection (4) may not include a measure of the kind mentioned in section 83(2)(f)(i).

NOTE

C.474.1   1. Inserted by the Children and Young People (Scotland) Act 2014 (asp 8) Pt 16 s.86 (effective 26 January 2015).

DEFINITIONS

C.474.2   "child": s.199.
"grounds hearing": ss.202(1) and 90.
"interim compulsory supervision order": ss.202(1) and 86.
"measure": s.83.
"Principal Reporter": s.14 and Sch.3 paras 8–10.

GENERAL NOTE

C.474.3   This section must be read with the provisions of s.73(4) in mind, viz:
"(4) Where the children's hearing is a grounds hearing, the children's hearing may excuse the child from attending during an explanation given in compliance with section 90(1)

Children's hearing to consider need for further interim compulsory supervision order

only [our emphasis] if it is satisfied that, taking account of the child's age and maturity, the child would not be capable of understanding the explanation."

These provisions signal that it is imperative for the child, except where young age or lack of maturity prevent the understanding of the explanation of the ground(s) for referral, to be personally present in order to accept or not the ground(s) for referral. Accordingly where a child of sufficient age and maturity and who has been duly notified of the hearing does not attend at the hearing the hearing does not have the option, as with the relevant person(s), of proceeding in absence (s.75(2)), or of treating the grounds as having been denied by the child. This section allows the hearing to require the Reporter to arrange another grounds hearing to allow the child to attend. This provision is consistent with the emphasis throughout this Act on the importance of the participation of the child, in particular with regard to responding to the ground for referral. The hearing may consider the making of an interim compulsory supervision order (s.92) and the reader is directed to s.86 for the meaning of interim compulsory supervision order. While circumstances may justify the issuing of a warrant for attendance (s.123), a hearing does not have the power to issue one *ex proprio motu*, but only on application by the Reporter. The detailed procedures to be followed in relation to this section are set out in r.64 of the Procedural Rules, as amended by r.6 of the Children's Hearings (Scotland) Act 2011 (Rules of Procedure in Children's Hearings) Amendment Rules 2015 (SSI 2015/21).

Subs.(5)

Section 83(2)(f)(ii) contains a requirement that the implementation authority arrange specified medical or other treatment for the child. To have included such a power in an interim compulsory supervision order under this section could be regarded as making a substantive disposal at a stage before the children's hearing, by virtue of the ground(s) having been accepted or proved, was entitled to do so.

Children's hearing to consider need for further interim order

Children's hearing to consider need for further interim compulsory supervision order

96.—(1) This section applies where—
   (a) under section 93(5) a grounds hearing makes an interim compulsory supervision order in relation to a child, and
   (b) the order will cease to have effect before the disposal of the application to the sheriff to which it relates.

(2) The Principal Reporter may arrange a children's hearing for the purpose of considering whether a further interim compulsory supervision order should be made in relation to the child.

(3) If the children's hearing is satisfied that the nature of the child's circumstances is such that for the protection, guidance, treatment or control of the child it is necessary that a further interim compulsory supervision order be made, the children's hearing may make a further interim compulsory supervision order in relation to the child.

[1] (4) The children's hearing may not make a further interim compulsory supervision order in relation to the child if it would be the third such order made under subsection (3) in consequence of the same interim compulsory supervision order made under section 93(5).

NOTE
1. As amended by the Children and Young People (Scotland) Act 2014 (asp 8) Pt 16 s.87 (effective 26 January 2015).

DEFINITIONS
"child": s.199.
"children's hearing": s.5.
"interim compulsory supervision order": ss.202(1) and 86.
"Principal Reporter": s.14 and Sch.3 paras 8–10.

GENERAL NOTE
This section applies where a hearing has made an interim compulsory supervision order (ICSO) under s.93(5) and the relevant period of 22 days will expire before the case will come

before the sheriff for determination. A children's hearing may twice extend the ICSO each for a maximum of a further 22 days, but the combined duration of the ICSO and any extension cannot exceed 66 days. The hearing is in no position to know whether the application will be heard within the 22 days. It is the Reporter who will have the necessary information about the date of the court hearing and will know whether a hearing will be needed to consider an extension. The Reporter does not have the discretion not to arrange a hearing for such consideration and thus to allow the ICSO to fall. In considering whether an ICSO requires to be extended, the hearing continues to apply the test whether, as a matter of urgency, the order is needed for the protection, guidance, treatment or control of the child (cf. definition at s.86 above). The hearing will also have to consider whether any measures attached to the ICSO need to be varied, added, removed or changed. The overarching principles and the European Convention principle of proportionality apply to the hearing's consideration of this. This section does not apply to pre-hearing panels. The child, each relevant person and any appointed safeguarder may appeal the decision to extend the ICSO (s.154) and, once the appeal has been lodged, may seek a suspension of the children's hearing decision (see s.158).

Application of Part where compulsory supervision order in force

Application of Part where compulsory supervision order in force

C.476 **97.**—(1) This Part has effect in relation to a child mentioned in subsection (2) with the modifications set out in subsections (3) to (6).

(2) The child is a child in relation to whom a compulsory supervision order is in force.

(3) References to a decision on whether to make a compulsory supervision order are to be read as references to a decision on whether to review the compulsory supervision order.

(4) Section 91 applies as if for subsections (2) and (3) there were substituted—

"(2) The grounds hearing is to be treated as if it were a hearing to review the compulsory supervision order (and sections 138, 139 and 142 apply accordingly).".

(5) References to an interim compulsory supervision order are to be read as references to an interim variation of the compulsory supervision order.

(6) Section 96(4) does not apply.

DEFINITIONS
C.476.1 "child": s.199.
"compulsory supervision order": ss.202(1) and 83.
"grounds hearing": ss.202(1) and 90.
"interim compulsory supervision order": ss.202(1) and 86.

GENERAL NOTE
C.476.2 This section repairs a deficiency in the Children (Scotland) Act 1995 which made no provision for interim changes to a compulsory supervision order (CSO) where a hearing deferred a substantive decision. Where a child is already subject to a CSO and a hearing decides to defer a substantive decision, it may vary the compulsory supervision order. The provisions of s.96(1), (2), and (3) apply to the imposition of the variation of the CSO. The hearing must be satisfied that there is an urgent need for the variation and that it is necessary for the protection, guidance, treatment or control of the child. The variation of the CSO is an interim order thus the variations must be needed immediately and not be answering long term needs. The order is varied on a temporary basis for a maximum of 22 days. Unlike the interim supervision order there is no specified limit to the total duration of the variation, although the CSO that is varied must be continued before the limit of the relevant period (s.83(7)). The overarching principles and the European Convention principle of proportionality apply to the hearing's consideration of this. The child, each relevant person and any appointed safeguarder may appeal the decision to vary the CSO (s.154) and, once the appeal has been lodged, may seek a suspension of the children's hearing decision (see s.158).

Subs.(6)
C.476.3 Section 93(5) comprises the provision that a further ICSO may not be made if this were the third such order.

Application for extension or variation of interim compulsory supervision order

Part 10

Proceedings before sheriff

Application for extension or variation of interim compulsory supervision order

98.—(1) This section applies where—
(a) a child is subject to an interim compulsory supervision order ("the current order"), and
[1] (b) (i) the current order is made under section 93(5) and by virtue of section 96(4) a children's hearing would be unable to make a further interim compulsory supervision order, or
(ii) the current order is made under section 100(2).
(2) The Principal Reporter may, before the expiry of the current order, apply to the sheriff for an extension of the order.
(3) The Principal Reporter may, at the same time as applying for an extension of the current order, apply to the sheriff for the order to be varied.
(4) The current order may be extended, or extended and varied, only if the sheriff is satisfied that the nature of the child's circumstances is such that for the protection, guidance, treatment or control of the child it is necessary that the current order be extended or extended and varied.

Note
1. As amended by the Children's Hearings (Scotland) Act 2011 (Modification of Primary Legislation) Order 2013 (SSI 2013/211) Sch.1 para.20(10) (effective 24 June 2013).

Definitions
"children's hearing: s.5.
"interim compulsory supervision order": ss.202(1) and 86.
"Principal Reporter: s.14 and Sch.3 paras 8–10.

General Note
See ss.91 and 92 (above) and the discussions thereof as to the circumstances in which it will be lawful and appropriate for a children's hearing to grant an interim compulsory supervision order (ICSO). The provisions of the present section could be invoked (a) where the hearing has still to receive information which it considers necessary for the proper disposal of the child's case; and (b) where the hearing has directed an application to the sheriff for proof in terms of ss.93(2) or 94(2) and it appears that the diet before the sheriff will not be fixed before the expiry of 66 days from the day that ICSO is made. As a result of the amendment of subs.(1), referred to below, the provisions of this section, and the following section, now apply where a child is not subject to an ICSO but the sheriff considers that an ICSO is necessary. See commentary on s.100(2). Unlike an ICSO made by a children's hearing, a sheriff is not restricted to any time limit, but must specify an end date (see Form 65A of the Act of Sederunt (Care and Maintenance) Rules 1997 (SI 1997/291)).

Subs.(1)(a)
It will be recalled that a child may become subject to an ICSO under ss.92(2), 93(5) and 96(3) of the Act.

Subs.(1)(b)
This subsection has been amended by the Children's Hearings (Scotland) Act 2011 (Modification of Primary Legislation) Order 2013 (SSI 2013/211) Sch.1 para.20(10). As noted in the General Note to s.86(3) above, under reference to s.86(3), the present Act, echoing the provisions in respect of warrants in s.66(3)(a) of the 1995 Act, includes a provision that an ICSO has a duration of up to 22 days, with provision for extension, with or without variation, by subsequent hearing(s). This provision refers to s.96(4) of this Act which, echoing the provisions in relation to warrants in s.66(8) of the 1995 Act, prohibits the extension of an ICSO by a children's hearing beyond a continuous period of 66 days.

A children's hearing would not be able to make a further ICSO because it would take the length of the ICSO beyond the total time limit of 66 days.

Subs.(2)

C.477.5 *Before the expiry of the current order.* The duration of the "current order" is governed by s.86(1) and (3) of the Act, when read with ss.93(5) and 96. See our discussion under these provisions. It will be recalled that the effect of these sections is, first, that an ICSO may last: (i) until any date specified in the order up to a maximum of 22 days, (ii) until the disposal of the case by a sheriff at a proof hearing, or (iii) until the date of the children's hearing arranged for the child; secondly, that a grounds hearing may, if it thinks necessary, make an ICSO; and thirdly, that where a grounds hearing has made an ICSO it may, if satisfied that this is necessary for the protection, guidance, treatment or control of the child, make further interim compulsory supervision orders provided that the maximum duration of these orders does not exceed 66 days (see s.96(4)). The practical effect of this is that a grounds hearing may make an initial interim compulsory supervision order of 22 days, a second interim compulsory supervision order of 22 days and a third ICSO of 22 days. The reference here to the "current order" will generally be to the third order, by the end of which the 66 days will be due to expire and it is now to the sheriff that the Reporter makes an application if further time is required. As to the provisions in relation to the duration of the sheriff's order, see below in the discussion of subs.(4).

May ... apply to the sheriff for the order to be varied. This constitutes a small, but important, innovation of the provision for renewal of warrants in s.66(1) of the 1995 Act. The "measures" which may be ordered under an ICSO, are substantially the same as those competent in a final compulsory supervision order (CSO) and are listed as paras (a) to (i) of s.83(2). However an ICSO, under s.86(2), may, where making provision for where the child is to reside, simply order that the child "is to reside at any place of safety away from the place where the child predominantly resides" whereas a CSO under s.83(2)(a) must specify the particular place. Accordingly, a sheriff who is satisfied that a child is not well settled in the place of safety where he or she has been placed under the ICSO will have the power to vary the ICSO by specifying another place as the place where the child is required to reside. Other examples of the possible exercise by the sheriff of the power to vary would be where an ICSO contained a movement restriction condition (s.83(2)(d)), a secure accommodation authorisation (s.83(2)(e)) or a contact direction (s.83(2)(g)) where the sheriff considered that such condition, authorisation or direction should be cancelled or varied. The decision to vary or not to vary an ICSO in these or other competent respects, could be made by the sheriff on the motion of a party or on the sheriff's own motion.

Subs.(4)

C.477.6 In considering these matters, the sheriff will require to have regard to all of the three overarching principles and also the principle of proportionality imported by the European Convention. This subsection serves to emphasise the paramountcy of the welfare of the child principle. Of course, the minimum intervention principle and the views of the child principle also apply. In considering whether or not, and if so to what extent, to vary the conditions of an ICSO the sheriff may have access to reports and information which were not available before and these may be enough to satisfy him or her that the ICSO should be varied. In the event that the ICSO is to be recalled, as mentioned above in the General Note to s.28, the minimum intervention principle refers to intervention in the child's life and not minimum interference with orders already granted. Accordingly, this principle should not deter the sheriff from making an ICSO or varying an ICSO where appropriate. However, sheriffs will also be aware of the importance of stability for a child and may, therefore, in a marginal case, be cautious of ordering a change where it is not completely clear that the change will benefit the child.

Termination of an ICSO can be effected by the occurrence of any of the further procedural steps found in s.86(3)(a)–(e). This is reflected in Form 65A of the Act of Sederunt (Care and Maintenance) Rules 1997 (SI 1997/291) as amended by Act of Sederunt (Children's Hearings (Scotland) Act 2011) (Miscellaneous Amendments) 2013 (SSI 2013/172) which prescribes the form for recording the making of an ICSO. Form 65B provides that the applicant for an extension or variation is to "insert details of the extension or extension and variation sought"— the clear implication being that a term of any extension sought will be stated.

It is essential to understand that the legislature cannot have intended an extension to be without limitation of time—this is made clear by s.99(2) which refers to the necessity of any application for a further variation or extension to be made "before the expiry of the order". Consequently, the court's order should specify the expiry date. This is not new. Section 67(2)(a) of the 1995 Act (dealing with warrants) required an expiry limit to be stated without specifying what it should be. However, it is important to remember, having regard to the minimum intervention principle and the principle of proportionality, that an ICSO should not be allowed to persist for an unnecessarily long period. As pointed out in Kenneth McK. Norrie, *Children (Scotland) Act 1995*, 2nd edn (Edinburgh: W. Green, 2004), p.144:

"The longer the child is kept away from home before a dispositive decision is made the

Sheriff's power to make interim compulsory supervision order

more likely a challenge can be made to the whole process under both Art.8 (right to respect for private and family life) and Art.6 (right to a fair hearing within a reasonable time) of the ECHR".

The court must keep the period of the ICSO as short as possible and consistent with the needs of the child. Should a further extension be desired, it can be requested under s.99.

Further extension or variation of interim compulsory supervision order

99.—(1) This section applies where an interim compulsory supervision order is— C.478
 (a) extended, or extended and varied, under section 98(4), or
 (b) further extended, or further extended and varied, under subsection (4).

(2) The Principal Reporter may, before the expiry of the order, apply to the sheriff for a further extension of the order.

(3) The Principal Reporter may, at the same time as applying for a further extension of the order, apply to the sheriff for the order to be varied.

(4) The sheriff may further extend, or further extend and vary, the order if the sheriff is satisfied that the nature of the child's circumstances is such that for the protection, guidance, treatment or control of the child it is necessary that the order be further extended or, as the case may be, further extended and varied.

DEFINITIONS
 "interim compulsory supervision order": ss.202(1) and 86.
 "Principal Reporter: s.14 and Sch.3 paras 8–10.

GENERAL NOTE
 There is no limit specified in the Act as to the number of times a sheriff may further extend an C.478.1
ICSO. This, in effect, accords with the provision in s.67(1) of the 1995 Act allowing repeated applications for renewal of warrants. However, the comments above on s.98(4) in relation to the undesirability of unduly prolonged intervention apply here and the court will require to be fully convinced that any requested further application is justified.

Power to make interim compulsory supervision order

Sheriff's power to make interim compulsory supervision order

100.—(1) This section applies where— C.479
 (a) a child is not subject to an interim compulsory supervision order, and
 (b) an application to the sheriff by virtue of section 93(2)(a) or 94(2)(a) in relation to the child has been made but not determined.

(2) If the sheriff is satisfied that the nature of the child's circumstances is such that for the protection, guidance, treatment or control of the child it is necessary as a matter of urgency that an interim compulsory supervision order be made, the sheriff may make an interim compulsory supervision order in relation to the child.

DEFINITIONS
 "child": s.199.
 "interim compulsory supervision order": ss.202(1) and 86.

GENERAL NOTE
 This section empowers the sheriff to make an interim compulsory supervision order (ICSO) C.479.1
when a referral comes to the court in order that a proof hearing may be fixed.

Subs.(1)(b)
 Applications hearings (commonly referred to as "Proof Hearings") under ss.93(2)(a) and C.479.2
94(2)(a) are made where, respectively, grounds are not accepted or not understood and a children's hearing has directed the Reporter to apply to the sheriff for a proof hearing. The power vested in the sheriff to make an interim compulsory supervision order (ICSO) takes effect on the lodging of the application. There is no provision in the Act of Sederunt (Care and

Maintenance) Rules 1997 (SI 1997/291) as amended, providing procedure for the sheriff to consider whether to grant an ICSO at this stage and Form 60 of these Rules (the application to the sheriff under s.93(2)(a) or s.94(2)(a) does not contain any reference to the possible granting of an ICSO at this stage. It is thought that where the Reporter wishes the sheriff to grant such an order, a request for this should be included in the initial application. The sheriff would fix a hearing on the matter at which all parties to whom the application had been notified, including the child cited by the notice, would have the right to attend and have their stances considered. The sheriff's decision would be subject to the overarching principles and the EC principle of proportionality.

Subs.(2)

C.479.3   While there was power vested in a sheriff under s.68(6) of the 1995 Act to grant an order to find and keep a child who did not turn up at an Application Hearing (a similar power is conferred on the sheriff under s.103(5) and (7) of the present Act) there was no power vested in the sheriff under the 1995 Act to grant a warrant in relation to a child who was not already being kept under a warrant.

The present provision is a valuable innovation—nowadays proof hearings can last for many days and it may become clear to the sheriff that the needs of the child who is not already in a place of safety may demand that he or she should be transferred to a place of safety pending the proof hearing. As noted above there is no rule prescribing the procedure to be followed by the sheriff when considering an ICSO at this stage. In the event that a child who has been duly cited does not appear at the hearing before the sheriff to consider this matter, then the sheriff (a) may grant a warrant to secure the attendance of the child (see s.103(7)); and/or (b) after making appropriate enquiries, make an ICSO under s.100(2). All three of the overarching principles and the proportionality principle of the European Convention apply where the sheriff is considering these matters.

Section 118(3), discussed below, enacts that where a child is already subject to a compulsory supervision order (i.e. as a result of an earlier referral) this is to be read as empowering the sheriff to make an interim variation of that order.

Application to establish grounds

Hearing of application

C.480   **101.**—(1) This section applies where an application is made to the sheriff by virtue of section 93(2)(a) or 94(2)(a).

(2) The application must be heard not later than 28 days after the day on which the application is lodged.

(3) The application must not be heard in open court.

DEFINITION

C.480.1   "application": ss.93(2)(a) and 94(2)(a).

GENERAL NOTE

C.480.2   This section, and the following sections up to and including s.109, deal with the procedure to be followed where application has been made to the sheriff for proof of grounds for referral (often referred to simply as a "proof hearing"). These sections substantially follow the general approach of the Act of separating out individual provisions into sections what were subsections in a single section (s.68) of the 1995 Act. The procedural rules governing these matters are contained in Part VII (rr.3.44 to 3.52) of the Act of Sederunt (Care and Maintenance) Rules 1997, as amended by the Act of Sederunt (Child Care and Maintenance Rules) (Amendment) (Children's Hearings (Scotland) Act 2011) 2013 (SSI 2013/172) (the "1997 Rules"). The proof hearing before the sheriff is a pivotal stage in the procedure, since on it depends the survival or not of the referral. The substantial function of the sheriff is to assess the evidence presented by the Reporter and other parties and decide whether or not the ground(s) for referral are established in accordance with law. The sheriff is here considering sufficiency and quality of evidence and is not subject to the "overarching principles" enacted in ss.25 and following. For example, as noted above in our commentary on s.25(1), the provision that the court is to regard the need to safeguard and promote the welfare of the child as the paramount consideration is not to be taken literally and has no direct application to the deliberations of the sheriff. The decision of the sheriff will establish whether or not the "threshold" has been passed so that the stage may be reached where consideration by a children's hearing can be considered and ruled upon. The function of the sheriff is lucidly described by the words of Lady Hale in *Re S-B*

Hearing of application

(Children) (Care Proceeding: Standard of Proof) [2010] 1 A.C. 678 at 687/688, paras [18]–[19], which were specifically approved in the Scottish context in *West Lothian Council v B* [2017] UKSC 15; 2017 S.L.T. 319 at para.21. Her Ladyship stated:

"Social workers are the detectives. They amass a great deal of information about a child and his family. They put the evidence they have assembled before a court and ask for an order ... The court subjects the evidence of the local authority to critical scrutiny, finds what the facts are ... The standard of proof may be different, but the roles of the social workers and prosecutors are similar. They bring to the court those cases where there is a good case to answer. It is for the court to decide whether a case has been made out."

The 1997 Rules include, in r.3.46A, prescriptions for the expeditious determination of Applications including empowering the sheriff to order parties to take steps towards (a) instructing a single expert, (b) using affidavits, (c) restricting the issues for proof, (d) restricting witnesses and (e) applying for evidence to be taken by live link in accordance with r.3.22. In Glasgow Sheriff Court these are reflected in Practice Note No.1 of 2015, referred to below under subs.(1) of this section, subs.(1) of s.105 and the General Note to s.155. In *P v LD, SW and JD*, Glasgow Sheriff Court, 20 July 2016; 2016 G.W.D. 27-490, an opposed adoption petition, Sheriff Anwar rejected an objection that evidence from social workers amounted to expert evidence which they were not qualified to give, and commented at para.[59] of her judgment that making assessments and forming opinions was "a central function of their role".

Subs.(1)
An application is made.   C.480.3
Computation of time for lodging of application. Rule 3.45 of the Act of Sederunt (Child Care and Maintenance Rules) 1997 (SI 1997/291), as amended, (the "1997 Rules") provides that the Reporter must lodge an application with the sheriff clerk within seven days of being directed to do so by a children's hearing. While under the 1995 Act an argument could be mounted saying that the seven days runs from the day after the direction by the hearing (see B. Kearney, *Children's Hearings and the Sheriff Court*, 2nd edn (Butterworths, 2000), para.30.07), the wording of sections of this Act (e.g. s.157(2)) run counter to this argument, and consequently the day of the direction by the hearing should be regarded as "day one", with the consequence, for example, that, for a direction made on Friday 12 December 2014, the last day for lodging the application with the sheriff clerk would be Thursday 18 December 2014.

Court procedure on lodgement of application. Rule 3.7(1)(a) of the 1997 Rules provides that, where a safeguarder has not already been appointed for the child, the sheriff is to consider the appointment of a safeguarder "as soon as reasonably practicable after the lodging of the application". It is good practice for the sheriff clerk to present the application to the sheriff on the day of the lodgement of the application and the sheriff should consider the appointment of a safeguarder at that time. The Reporter may on occasion attach a note to the application suggesting the appointment of a safeguarder. The sheriff may, in the exercise of power at common law, appoint a curator *ad litem*.

Procedural hearing after lodging of application. Rule 3.45(4) of the 1997 Rules introduces the "procedural hearing". This may be fixed by the sheriff in order to ascertain whether grounds which were, at the children's hearing, not accepted by a relevant person are now to be accepted by that person—see ss.105 and 106 and the discussion below. Under r.3.45(5) any procedural hearing must be fixed "before the expiry of the period of 7 days beginning with the day on which the application is lodged". This is to be taken as meaning that the day on which the application is lodged is to be treated as "day one" (see above for discussion of "Computation of time for lodging of application"). There is no provision within r.3.45 for using this procedural hearing to enable the sheriff to ascertain from parties the likely length of any proof hearing and to set a provisional timetable. In operating the provisions of s.68 of the 1995 Act and r.3.45 of the 1997 Rules some sheriffs developed the practice of fixing pre-proof hearings at which such matters could be considered. (See B. Kearney, *The Scottish Children's Hearings System in Action* (Tottel, 2007), p.232, fn.91.) This practice was non-statutory but obviously defensible because it facilitated expeditious procedure. In Glasgow, Sheriff Principal C.A.L. Scott QC has issued, as Practice Note No.1 (2015), *Children's Referrals under the Children's Hearings (Scotland) Act 2011*, which includes: a requirement for the Reporter, when lodging the application, to lodge a provisional list of witnesses and a note of the likelihood of a long or complex proof (paras 3.1 and 3.2); a requirement on parties to try to agree matters (para.3.3); provision (in para.3.4) for a "first hearing" to deal with procedural matters such as the appointment of a safeguarder, whether the Reporter has disclosed relevant information, whether the child's attendance should be dispensed with under s.103(3) of the Act, whether, in a case under s.94(2)(a), to dispense with the hearing of evidence and whether the case should be treated as a "complex" case in terms of Part 4 of the Practice Note, thus engaging special rules, including the fixing of a "case management hearing" (para.4.3).

Subs.(2)

C.480.4 *Must be heard.* Even where a procedural hearing has taken place an application must be "heard" at a diet under this provision. "Heard" here means started. In practice proof hearings are frequently adjourned or continued after this diet. The diet must however be a properly convened diet (*H v Mearns*, 1974 S.C. 152; 1974 S.L.T. 184). If this diet is not held in time the application falls, but the Reporter can found on the same grounds to make a fresh referral (*McGregor v L*, 1983 S.L.T. (Sh. Ct) 7).

Not later than 28 days after the day on which the application is lodged. See discussion above under subs.(1), "Computation of time for lodging of application". This present subsection substantially replicates s.68(2) of the 1995 Act, but with a change of wording in that this subsection says "not later than 28 days after" as opposed to the 1995 Act's wording "within twenty-eight days of". The wording of this subsection may support the view that "day one" in this instance is to be taken as the day after the day of the application, but the safe course will always be to count the day of the application as "day one".

Subs.(3)

C.480.5 The parallel provision in the 1995 Act is s.93(5), which provides that all children's hearing related procedures in the sheriff court are to be heard by the sheriff "in chambers". In practice such proceedings have often—sometimes because of the number of persons involved—had to be held in a closed court room (i.e. with the public excluded). Sheriffs have long regarded it as within their powers to deem such room in the court as they thought right to be "chambers". The wording of this subsection makes it clear that proofs in closed courts are in order.

Jurisdiction and standard of proof: offence ground

C.481 **102.**—(1) This section applies where an application is to be made to the sheriff to determine whether the ground mentioned in section 67(2)(j) is established in relation to a child.

(2) The application must be made to the sheriff who would have jurisdiction if the child were being prosecuted for the offence or offences.

(3) The standard of proof in relation to the ground is that which applies in criminal proceedings.

(4) It is immaterial whether the application also relates to other section 67 grounds.

DEFINITIONS

C.481.1 "child": s.199.

GENERAL NOTE

C.481.2 While it is fundamental to the children's hearings system that children should be treated according to their needs, irrespective of whether these needs have been demonstrated by the committing of an offence or by any of the "care or protection" grounds, it has always been recognised that proof of the offence ground must be achieved by evidence which meets the criminal standard—*beyond reasonable doubt*. The main thrust of this section re-affirms this principle. It will be recalled that the age of criminal responsibility in Scotland is eight years old and the age of criminal prosecution in Scotland is 12 years old. (See ss.41 and 42, respectively, of the Criminal Procedure (Scotland) Act 1995: as amended.) On 5 September 2017 the First Minister intimated that it was the intention of the government to introduce in the coming session legislation raising the age of criminal responsibility to 12.

Subs.(2)

C.481.3 This replicates s.68(3)(a) of the 1995 Act. Cases in which the ground for referral is that the child has committed a criminal offence are treated rather differently in a number of respects from all other cases. This subsection provides a special jurisdictional rule for such cases to the effect that the sheriff to whom the application for proof is made must be a sheriff within whose territorial jurisdiction the case could be tried if there were to be a criminal prosecution. There is, however, no implication that a ground for referral cannot competently comprise an offence which a sheriff could not try, such as rape—see *Walker v C (No.2)*, 2003 S.L.T. 293. The requirement for application to be made to the sheriff who would have criminal jurisdiction has the consequence that where, for example, the offence was said to have been committed by a child resident in, say, Glasgow, and was therefore dealt with at a children's hearing there then, if the offence was said to have been committed in another area, say Dumfries and Galloway, the

Child's duty to attend hearing unless excused

application to the sheriff for proof hearing required to be made in Dumfries and Galloway. This is reflected in the Act of Sederunt (Child Care and Maintenance Rules) 1997 (SI 1997/291), as amended by the Act of Sederunt (Children's Hearings (Scotland) Act 2011) (Miscellaneous Amendments) 2013 (SSI 2013/172) r.3.45(1). However, r.3.45(1B) of these Rules allows the sheriff, on cause shown, to remit the case to another sheriff court. This is a valuable provision, leaving it open to the sheriff to allow the proof to take place in the most convenient forum.

Subs.(3)

This replicates s.68(3)(b) of the 1995 Act. The ground based on an alleged offence by the referred child is the only ground which requires to be proved to the criminal standard, i.e. beyond reasonable doubt and (at the time of writing) by corroborated evidence. All other grounds, including those where an offence by a person other than the referred child is averred, may be proved on the balance of probability—cf. *McGregor v D*, 1977 S.C. 330; 1977 S.L.T. 182 and *Harris v F*, 1991 S.L.T. 242; 1991 S.C.L.R 124. The Reporter may not avoid the higher standard of proof applicable where the child is averred to have committed offences by seeking to show that such commission amounts to another ground for referral—*Constanda v M*, 1997 S.L.T. 1396; 1997 S.C.L.R 510. This consideration may be material in relation to the new ground for referral enacted in s.67(2)(m)—conduct of the child has or is likely to have a serious adverse effect on the child or another: see discussion above of s.67(2)(j).

Subs.(4)

Where there are other grounds in addition to the ground based on an alleged offence by the child, the standard of proof for these other grounds is the civil standard, i.e. on the balance of probabilities.

Child's duty to attend hearing unless excused

103.—(1) This section applies where an application is made to the sheriff by virtue of section 93(2)(a) or 94(2)(a).

(2) The child to whom the application relates must attend the hearing of the application unless the child is excused from doing so under subsection (3).

(3) The sheriff may excuse the child from attending all or part of the hearing of the application where—
  (a) the hearing relates to the ground mentioned in section 67(2)(b), (c), (d) or (g) and the attendance of the child at the hearing, or that part of the hearing, is not necessary for a fair hearing,
  (b) the attendance of the child at the hearing, or that part of the hearing, would place the child's physical, mental or moral welfare at risk, or
  (c) taking account of the child's age and maturity, the child would not be capable of understanding what happens at the hearing or that part of the hearing.

(4) The child may attend the hearing of the application even if the child is excused from doing so under subsection (3).

(5) If the child is not excused from attending the hearing but the child does not attend the sheriff may grant a warrant to secure attendance in relation to the child.

(6) Subsection (7) applies if—
  (a) the hearing of the application is to be continued to another day, and
  (b) the sheriff is satisfied that there is reason to believe that the child will not attend on that day.

(7) The sheriff may grant a warrant to secure attendance in relation to the child.

DEFINITIONS
  "child": s.199.
  "warrant to secure attendance": s.88.

GENERAL NOTE

The provisions in this section, for the most part, mirror s.73 of this Act ("Child's duty to attend children's hearing"). This section also replicates with some modifications and

Children's Hearings (Scotland) Act 2011

refinement, the provisions in s.68(4), (5) and (6) of the 1995 Act. Rules 3.1 to 3.24 of the Act of Sederunt (Child Care and Maintenance Rules) 1997 (SI 1997/291), as amended (the "1997 Rules") include provisions governing the relative procedure before the sheriff.

Subs.(2)

C.482.3 This replicates s.68(4)(b) of the 1995 Act. The provisions in relation to service on the child are contained in r.3.4 of the 1997 Rules. Under r.3.3 of these Rules the sheriff may dispense with service on the child where he or she is satisfied "so far as practicable and taking account of the age and maturity of the child" that service on the child would be inappropriate.

Subs.(3)

C482.4 Where the sheriff excuses a child under this provision, then the child's representative, and any safeguarder, curator *ad litem*, and relevant person shall be permitted to remain (1997 Rules, r.3.47(5)).

Subs.(3)(a)

C.482.4 *A fair hearing*. The word "fair" replaces the word "just" in the 1995 Act, perhaps with the intention of more exactly reflecting art.6(1) of the European Convention.

Subs.(3)(b)

C.482.5 This expands upon "detrimental to the interests of the child" in the 1995 Act.

Subs.(3)(c)

C.482.6 In practice under the 1995 Act, babies and toddlers were frequently not brought to sheriff court proceedings, but sometimes Reporters, out of caution, would arrange for them to attend. This provision very usefully makes explicit provision for this situation.

Subs.(4)

C.482.7 Even if formally excused from attending, the child's right to attend is secured here. This subsection mirrors the child's right to attend a children's hearing under s.78(1)(a).

Subss.(5) to (7)

C.482.8 These subsections have to be read with s.88 ("Meaning of 'warrant to secure attendance'"), which inter alia expands on and refines provisions in s.68(6) and (7) of the 1995 Act. Subsection (5) allows for the possibility of the child being apprehended and brought to court on the day of the proceedings by an officer of law under s.88(1)(a), while subss.(6) and (7) deal with the situation where the proof has to be continued. The provision that before granting a warrant the sheriff must be satisfied that there is reason to "believe" that the child will not attend at the continued diet, is an innovation and reflects the consideration that the minimum intervention principle and the European Convention principle of proportionality require that the order should be made only when no less extreme measure will achieve the aim of ensuring the child's presence. The decision of the sheriff will also be governed by the paramountcy of welfare principle. It follows that the sheriff must have reliable information on which to found a reasonable belief that the child will not attend. Such belief might be founded on credible information, for example, that the child has failed to attend hearings in the past, that he or she has stated that he or she has no intention of coming or that a person having care of the child is likely to obstruct attendance. A warrant to secure attendance may contain a secure accommodation authorisation only where the conditions set out in s.88(2) are met (i.e. that the child has previously absconded, and is likely to abscond again, putting his or her welfare at risk, or that the child is likely to harm him or herself or others). A warrant to secure attendance lasts for 14 days from the date of the child's being first detained in pursuance of the warrant or until the beginning of the continued hearing before the sheriff, whichever is earlier (s.88(4)(b)).

Child and relevant person: representation at hearing

C.483 **104.**—(1) This section applies where an application is made to the sheriff by virtue of section 93(2)(a) or 94(2)(a).

(2) The child may be represented at the hearing of the application by another person.

(3) A relevant person in relation to the child may be represented at the hearing of the application by another person.

Child and relevant person: representation at hearing

(4) A person representing the child or relevant person at the hearing need not be a solicitor or advocate.

DEFINITIONS
"child": s.199.
"relevant person": s.200.

C.483.1

GENERAL NOTE
This section replicates the provisions in s.68(4) of the 1995 Act which dealt with the representation of the child and relevant person. Where the child's representative is to be a solicitor or counsel the child will almost always require to have recourse to the Legal Aid provisions in ss.28B to 28S of the Legal Aid (Scotland) Act 1986 (interpolated by s.191 of the 2011 Act, discussed below in our commentary on that section) and in Pts 3 and 4 of the Children's Legal Assistance (Scotland) Regulations 2013 (SSI 2013/200).

C.483.2

Subs.(1)
This provides that the provisions of this section relate only to application proceedings arising out of situations where the ground(s) for referral have not been accepted or where the explanation of the ground(s) for referral has not been capable of being understood or has not been understood. However, as we shall see, this Act, unlike the 1995 Act, extends some similar provisions to the proceedings before the sheriff in relation to review of a grounds determination—see below for discussion of ss.110 to 117.

C.483.3

Subss.(2)–(4)
The child and any relevant person may of course be represented by a solicitor or an advocate (meaning here a member of the Faculty of Advocates), but subs.(4) provides that a person who is not a solicitor or an advocate may represent the child and any relevant person. In *McKenzie v McKenzie* [1971] P. 33; [1970] 3 W.L.R. 472; [1970] 3 All E.R. 1034 the English Court of Appeal re-affirmed it as the recognised practice that a litigant in person could have an individual sitting beside him at the bar of the court in order to give quiet advice including the suggesting of possible lines of questioning, but not asking questions him or herself. This individual became known as a "McKenzie friend". Subsection (4) makes clear that the non-lawyer may (differing in this from the McKenzie friend) perform all the functions, including examination and cross-examination of witnesses, which would be open to the child or relevant person—see the Act of Sederunt (Child Care and Maintenance Rules) 1997 (SI 1997/291), as amended (the 1997 Rules) r.3.21(3) or by an advocate or solicitor. The lay representative must throughout the proceedings satisfy the sheriff that he or she is a suitable person to represent the child or relevant person and is authorised to do so (r.3.21(2) of the 1997 Rules). In the event of the sheriff considering that a proposed lay representative was not suitable, or not duly authorised, the sheriff should consider an adjournment in order for an alternative individual to be found.

C.483.4

Possible conflict of interest; confidentiality. Where the representative is a solicitor or advocate (necessarily instructed by a solicitor) then care will require to be taken as to him or her acting for more than one party in case of possible conflict of interest. Rule B2.1.2 of the *Law Society of Scotland Practice Rules 2011* provides "You shall not act for two or more parties whose interests conflict". The associated *Guidance Related to Rule B2.1: Conflict of Interest Generally* provides:

"**A. Conflict of Interest Generally**
It is a well established principle that solicitors should not act for clients where there is a conflict of interest between them. This is codified in rule B2.1.2 which states that 'You shall not act for two or more parties whose interests conflict.' That statement in entirely unqualified and is the guiding principle which governs the rest of rule B2.1. Conflict of interest is amplified in rule B1.7 which states that:
'1.7.1 You must not act for two or more clients in matters where there is a conflict of interest between the clients or for any client where there is a conflict between the interest of the client and your interest or that of your practice unit.
'1.7.2 Even where there is only a potential conflict of interest you must exercise caution. Where the potential for conflict is significant, you must not act for both parties without full knowledge and express consent of the clients.'
The rules do not contain a definition of conflict of interest. It has been said that it is hard to define but you know it when you see it. Unfortunately some only seem to see it long after it has appeared and when it is too late. There are three elements that need to be considered. First, if you would give different advice to different clients about the same matter there is a conflict of interest between them. It does not matter that the clients may

be agreed about what they wish to do. Second, if your actings on behalf of one client would have an adverse impact on a matter you are dealing with for another client, there is a conflict, even if on the face of it the matters are unrelated. Third, if you are unable to disclose relevant information to one client because of a duty of confidentiality to another client there is a conflict of interest. This also means that if you cannot act for one of them you cannot breach confidentiality by telling them about that.

> Conflict of interest is not a matter for the judgment of the client—it is a matter for your judgment."

It is not difficult in cases where lack of parental care is alleged, to envisage a conflict of interest situation which would rule out joint representation of the child and relevant person or more than one relevant person. However, potential conflict of interest can arise in other situations, as where a person, possibly now in a relationship with a parent, is accused of a Schedule 1 offence against the child. In such a case the "caution" enjoined by r.1.7.2 must be observed, against the background of the obvious difficulty of obtaining "full knowledge and express consent" of a child in such a stressful situation.

The provision that a person who is not a solicitor or an advocate may represent a child or relevant person is reflected in the provision in s.122(2) of the Act requiring the chairing member of a hearing to inform the child of the availability of advocacy services. As at time of writing, the provision of advocacy services is very uneven throughout Scotland and s.122 has not yet been brought into force. As mentioned above, r.3.21(2) of the 1997 Rules provides that a person who is not a solicitor or an advocate must satisfy the sheriff that he or she is a suitable person to represent the party and that he or she is authorised to do so. One of the factors which will influence the sheriff in deciding on suitability will be the possibility of conflict of interest. The provision for non-legal representation does not extend to a safeguarder who, if he or she wishes to be represented, must employ a solicitor or an advocate instructed by a solicitor.

Position of curator ad litem

C.483.5 As noted in B. Kearney, *Children's Hearings and the Sheriff Court*, 2nd edn (Butterworths, 2000), para.34.03 the sheriff may, exercising common law powers, appoint a curator *ad litem* to a child. The Age of Legal Capacity (Scotland) Act 1991 s.3 provides that nothing in that Act is to affect

> "any rule or practice whereby the court may, in any civil proceedings, appoint a curator *ad litem* to a person under the age of 16 years".

Clause 34(3) of the draft Bill which preceded the present Act provided that the sheriff "must not appoint a curator *ad litem* for the child", but this provision was seriously criticised and does not appear in the Act, which, like the 1995 Act, does not mention the term "curator *ad litem*". The term "curator *ad litem*" does, however, appear in r.3.5(2)(ca) and r.3.5A of the 1997 Rules and, as more fully narrated below in the General Note to s.101, in r.3.5A of these Rules, which provides that papers lodged in the process must be made available to, and kept confidentially by, any safeguarder or curator *ad litem*. It follows that the court's inherent power to appoint a curator *ad litem* (discussed in *Macphail on Sheriff Court Practice*, edited by Sheriff T. Welsh, 3rd edn (Edinburgh: W. Green, 2006), paras 4.23 to 4.28) still exists. In *NJDB v JEG* [2012] UKSC 21, sub nom. *B v G*, 2012 S.C. (UKSC) 293; 2012 S.L.T. 840; 2012 Fam. L.R. 56, a child contact case originating in the sheriff court wherein the sheriff had appointed a solicitor as curator *ad litem* to the child, the Supreme Court discussed the status and functions of the curator *ad litem* at paras [35] and [36]. The court commented that there had been lack of clarity as to the role of the curator *ad litem* in the circumstances of the case. The ostensible purpose of appointing him appeared to have been to obtain a report, but the sheriff had recognised him as a party to the case and the curator had, acting as a party litigant, cross-examined witnesses and ultimately given evidence himself as to matters with which he had become involved. The court, under reference to the Act of Sederunt (Sheriff Court Ordinary Cause Rules) (SI 1993/1956), as amended, observed that a curator *ad litem* was not in the position of an agent for a client, but was an officer of the court charged with the duty of safeguarding the interests of the child—the curator *ad litem* was the *dominus litis* (i.e. the person effectively in charge of the case of the ward, in this case the child) and that, as such, the proper course would be for him, if necessary, to instruct a solicitor to represent him and not find himself in the position of giving evidence in a case where he was also acting as a solicitor. The court noted that issues surrounding the safeguarding of the interests of the child, including the function of the curator *ad litem*, had been considered by the Scottish Civil Courts Review, under the chairmanship of Lord Gill. These matters are dealt with in paras 100 to 112 of the *Report of the Scottish Civil Courts Review*. At time of writing the Scottish Parliament is considering legislation arising out of the recommendations in this Report. In the meantime curators *ad litem* will require to have regard to the observations of the Supreme Court in *NJDB*.

Application by virtue of section 93: ground accepted before determination

Ground accepted before application determined

Application by virtue of section 93: ground accepted before determination

105.—(1) This section applies where—
(a) an application is made to the sheriff by virtue of section 93(2)(a) in relation to a ground, and
(b) before the application is determined, the ground is accepted by the child and each relevant person in relation to the child who is present at the hearing before the sheriff.

[1] (1A) The reference in subsection (1)(b) to the ground being accepted is, in relation to a ground which was not accepted by virtue of section 90(1B), a reference to all of the supporting facts in relation to the ground being accepted.

(2) Unless the sheriff is satisfied in all the circumstances that evidence in relation to the ground should be heard, the sheriff must—
(a) dispense with hearing such evidence, and
(b) determine that the ground is established.

NOTE
1. Inserted by the Children and Young People (Scotland) Act 2014 (asp 8) Sch.5 para.12(5) (effective 26 January 2015).

DEFINITION
"child": s.199.
"relevant person": s.200.

GENERAL NOTE
This section provides for the circumstances where (i) at the children's hearing either the child or any relevant person has not accepted the ground(s) for referral concerned, and the hearing has directed that an application be made to the sheriff, and (ii) after the application has been lodged with the sheriff court, the ground is now accepted by the child and the relevant person or persons. When this happens the sheriff, unless satisfied that evidence should be heard, must dispense with hearing evidence and determine that the ground concerned is established. The authors consider that where the sheriff is convinced that the ground has been fully understood and full-heartedly accepted by the child and the relevant person(s) the sheriff is bound to regard this as a matter of fact and "must"(subject to the radical right to insist on the hearing of evidence enacted in subs.(2), discussed below) dispense with the hearing of evidence and determine that the ground involved is established and that any consideration of whether this would promote the welfare of the child would be relevant.

Subs.(1)
Before the application is determined. In practice, examples of occasions when the dispensing with evidence may be considered are:
  (i) At the initial hearing fixed by the court under s.101(2) of the Act. Rule 3.45(1)(c) of the Act of Sederunt (Child Care and Maintenance Rules) 1997 (SI 1997/291) still refers to this hearing as "a hearing on evidence as required under s 102(2) of the 2011 Act", but it is nowadays rare for a hearing on evidence to be held at this time and it is trite procedural law that, provided a properly convened hearing is held, the proceedings under s.101(2) may be adjourned to allow a proof hearing, see *H v Mearns*, 1974 S.C. 152; 1974 S.L.T. 184; this is reflected, for example, by *Sheriffdom of Glasgow and Strathkelvin, Practice Note No 1 of 2015* (referred to above in the General Note to s.101), paras 3.4 to 3.6;
  (ii) At any pre-proof or case management hearing fixed by the court in the exercise of its powers at common law (cf. *Sheriffdom of Glasgow and Strathkelvin, Practice Note No 1 of 2015*, paras 4.3 and 4.4, under the heading *Case Management Hearings*);
  (iii) At the beginning of the proof hearing. On these occasions the sheriff should take such steps as seem necessary to ascertain what the stance of parties is as to acceptance or not of the ground(s); and
  (iv) While it will usually be at one of these times that the sheriff will consider the issue of dispensing with evidence, it is clear from the wording of this subsection that the issue may be addressed at any time before the final determination by the sheriff. This is

reflected in r.3.47(A1) of the Act of Sederunt (Child Care and Maintenance Rules) 1997 (SI 1997/291), as amended, which provides that if at a hearing on evidence, or any adjournment or continuation thereof, the ground(s) (as amended if amendment has been allowed) "are no longer in dispute" the sheriff "may" determine the application without hearing evidence—once again the radical right of the sheriff to insist on hearing evidence is preserved.

The child and each relevant person in relation to the child who is present at the hearing before the sheriff. Here the "hearing before the sheriff" must mean one of the hearings listed above as (i) to (iv). Accordingly, the sheriff must ascertain the stances of: the child, *if present*, and each relevant person *who is present*. What is the position if the child, and one or more relevant person, who has not accepted the ground at the hearing stage, is not present or represented at the hearing before the sheriff? A number of possibilities may arise. These may include the following scenarios:

1. *Position where child is not present or represented*

In a case where the ground for referral is based on character or conduct of the child (i.e. under s.67(h) to (m)) there must be a fair trial of the issues under art.6(1) of the European Convention and therefore it would not be right for any material decision to be taken in the absence of the child or his or her representative. Consequently, any argument that the child's not appearing to contest the ground for referral amounted to acceptance would fall to be rejected. In the case where the ground for referral is an offence by the child there is the additional consideration that such a child has all the rights of an accused person (cf. per Lord Rodger of Earlsferry in *Constanda v M*, 1997 S.C.C.R. 510 at 511F). It may be that rarely, if ever, will the sheriff in such circumstances be asked to dispense with evidence in the absence of the child. It is thought that, if so moved, the sheriff should be "satisfied in all the circumstances that evidence in relation to the ground should be heard" and refuse the motion.

2. *Position where the blamed relevant person is present and admits the ground*

At a hearing where the ground for referral is an offence against or conduct likely to be detrimental to, the child (i.e. under s.67(2)(a) to (g) or (p) and (q)) the court, where the "offender" is a relevant person who is present and admits the ground, may be justified in giving consideration to dispensing with evidence and determining the ground as established.

3. *Position where blamed person is not present*

However, where the person said to be involved in the actings alleged to have caused the ground, e.g. a third party or a relevant person who is not present, then different considerations will apply. In such a situation the court may justifiably be cautious of holding, without hearing any evidence, that such a person has been guilty of an offence or involved in conduct detrimental to the child and may decide against dispensing with evidence and request the Reporter to adduce evidence, perhaps including the testimony of the accused person, thus tending to avoid the risk of infringing that person's right to a fair trial of the issues under art.6(1) of the European Convention. In a case wherein the ground for referral is an offence against or conduct detrimental to the child (i.e. under s.67(2)(a), (b) or (p)) there is the additional consideration, identified by the Supreme Court in *Principal Reporter v K* [2010] UKSC 56; 2011 S.L.T. 271; [2011] 1 W.L.R. 18 at [44]:

"No child should be brought up to believe that she has been abused if in fact she has not, any more than any child should be persuaded by the adult world that she has not been abused when in fact she has."

4. *Position where a child who has not accepted the ground for referral at the children's hearing is not present or represented*

Where the child is not present or represented it is submitted that the sheriff should not dispense with evidence. In the event of a s.105 motion being made at a proof hearing, it will be unlikely that the child will not be present or represented, but should this occur then it would not be appropriate for the hearing of evidence to be dispensed with and the sheriff would have two alternatives, namely, to allow the proof to proceed and hear the available evidence or to adjourn the proof to a later date and consider granting a warrant to secure the child's attendance under s.103(5) of the Act.

5. *Position where relevant person (who has not been 'blamed') is not present when s.105 motion is being considered*

The position in relation to a relevant person who is identified as having been responsible for the ground for referral and who is present at the s.105 proceedings has been considered above at 2. In the case of a relevant person who has not been blamed, the position may be different: now the focus is on whether the ground should be held as established when the relevant person, as carer of the child, is not there to accept or not accept the ground for referral. Where such a relevant person who has not accepted the ground for referral at the children's hearing stage is not present at a s.105 motion hearing then the meaning of the words "each relevant person who is present at the hearing before the sheriff" requires to be addressed. It may be submitted to the

Application by virtue of section 94: ground accepted by relevant person

sheriff that the decision of the relevant person not to attend the hearing indicates that the relevant person is not contesting the ground for referral and information, possibly in written form, may be laid before the sheriff that the relevant person has so stated. The child may be admitting the ground. The authors are aware that under the 1995 Act some sheriffs have refused to dispense with the hearing of evidence where a relevant person has not been present on the view that since s.68(8) of that Act states "where ... the child and the relevant person accept any of the grounds" this must mean that the relevant person has to be personally present to state his or her acceptance.

On the other hand some sheriffs have taken the view that where there is information that the relevant person now agrees the ground then this is enough. In the authors' view, it is desirable for the relevant person to be present at the hearing before the sheriff. However, as in contrast with the position in relation to the child, there is no power to issue a warrant in these circumstances, and the sheriff may, depending on the weight of the information that the absent relevant person agrees the ground, be prepared to accept this and dispense with hearing evidence. See below in the discussion of subs.(2) for consideration of the practicalities.

Subs.(2)

Unless the sheriff is satisfied ... the sheriff must ... dispense with such evidence ... . Where the legal requisites set out in subs.(1) are met, the sheriff is obliged to dispense with the hearing of evidence and to determine that the ground in question is established. The way in which this is worded might suggest that once the decision that this section applies then the onus, as it were, passes to the sheriff to satisfy himself or herself that evidence should be led. However, the sheriff's decision as to whether he or she is satisfied is discretionary and therefore subject to the overarching principle of the welfare of the child being paramount, and s.3(1) of the Human Rights Act 1998 requires any statute to be read and given effect to, where possible, in a way that is Convention compliant. This principle should, having regard to art.6(1) of the Convention, incline the sheriff to give careful consideration as to dispensing with evidence where there is some doubt if it is safe to do so. Moreover, in a marginal case the interests of the child may demand that matters be explored rather than dealt with by admission. Any doubt as to whether dispensing with evidence is competent should generally be resolved in favour of requiring the evidence to be heard and thus preventing the possibility that evidence dispensed with at this stage may require to be led in an application for review of grounds determination under s.110. The purpose of enabling the sheriff to dispense with evidence is to expedite the proceedings. This will be frustrated if it has been too readily assumed that the sheriff will dispense with the evidence. Accordingly, Reporters should be very cautious before deciding not to have witnesses and any other evidence available.

C.484.5

Application by virtue of section 94: ground accepted by relevant person before determination

106.—(1) This section applies where—

(a) an application to the sheriff is made by virtue of section 94(2)(a) in relation to a ground on the basis that the child would not understand, or has not understood, an explanation given in compliance with section 90(1)(a), and

(b) before the application is determined the ground is accepted by each relevant person in relation to the child who is present at the hearing before the sheriff.

[1] (1A) The reference in subsection (1)(b) to the ground being accepted is, in relation to a ground which was not accepted by virtue of section 90(1B), a reference to all of the supporting facts in relation to the ground being accepted.

(2) The sheriff may determine the application without a hearing unless—

(a) a person mentioned in subsection (3) requests that a hearing be held, or

(b) the sheriff considers that it would not be appropriate to determine the application without a hearing.

(3) The persons are—

(a) the child,

(b) a relevant person in relation to the child,

(c) if a safeguarder has been appointed, the safeguarder,

C.485

(d) the Principal Reporter.

(4) If the sheriff determines the application without a hearing, the sheriff must do so before the expiry of the period of 7 days beginning with the day on which the application is made.

NOTE
C.485.1   1. Inserted by the Children and Young People (Scotland) Act 2014 (asp 8) Sch.5 para.12(6) (effective 26 January 2015).

DEFINITION
C.485.2   "child": s.199.
"relevant person": s.200.
"safeguarder": ss.202(1) and 30(1).

GENERAL NOTE
C.485.3   This section addresses the situation where, at the children's hearing stage, the child has not been able to understand the explanation of, or has not understood, the ground(s) for referral and an application has been made to the sheriff to determine if the ground is established. The main thrust of this section, when read with r.3.45(3) to (9) of the Act of Sederunt (Child Care and Maintenance Rules) 1997 (SI 1997/291), as amended, is to provide procedure for an early check on whether the grounds are now accepted by the relevant person and to provide that, if the grounds are accepted by the relevant person, the sheriff, unless he or she considers it is necessary to hear evidence, may dispense with the hearing of evidence and hold the ground as established. There is no clear trigger for the sheriff to invoke this provision. In view of this and with regard to the very tight time limit imposed by subs.(4), it may be that these provisions will not often be used. Where the words "the hearing before the sheriff" are used in subs.(1)(b) this would appear to be a reference to the procedural hearing provided for by r.3.46(4) of the said Rules.

Subs.(1)(b)
C.485.4   *Who is present at the hearing before the sheriff.* As mentioned in the General Note, above, this would appear to be a reference to a procedural hearing under r.3.46(4) of the Act of Sederunt (Child Care and Maintenance Rules) 1997 (SI 1997/291), as amended.

Fixing a procedural hearing under r.3.45. This rule empowers the sheriff to fix a "procedural hearing" in the cases covered by this section (but not for the cases covered by s.105). By virtue of para.(5) of this rule this procedural hearing must take place "before the expiry of 7 days beginning with the day on which the application is lodged". By para.(6) of this rule this hearing is to be intimated to parties "as the sheriff thinks fit"—a flexible provision no doubt driven by the tight timescale. Paragraph (7) provides that at this procedural hearing the sheriff may discharge the hearing on evidence and determine the application, but only subject to the provisions of para.(9), which provides:

"Where—
(a) a relevant person does not accept the section 67 grounds in the statement of grounds at the procedural hearing;
(b) section 106(2)(a) or (b) of the 2011 Act applies; or
(c) the sheriff has not fixed a procedural hearing;
a hearing on evidence must take place in accordance with rule 3.47".

The substantial meaning of this rule is that (against the background of the child not being able to understand or not understanding the explanation of the ground for referral which was given at the grounds hearing) where the relevant person(s) appear at a procedural hearing under r.3.45(4) and accepts the ground for referral then the sheriff "may" discharge the hearing on evidence and hold the ground for referral concerned as established. In any other situation, i.e. where the child, any relevant person, any safeguarder or the Reporter wishes an evidential hearing (this is the effect of s.106(2)(a)) or the sheriff him or herself wishes an evidential hearing, then an evidential hearing must take place (this is the effect of s.106(2)(b)). The provision in para.(7)(c) that an evidential hearing must take place if the sheriff has not fixed a r.3.45(4) procedural hearing would seem to rule out the possibility of the sheriff's dispensing with hearing evidence, etc. in the event of it emerging at any pre-proof hearing that the relevant person now understood and accepted the disputed ground. This seems odd and may not have been the intention of the legislature. However, the competence of dispensing with evidence at a hearing on evidence is preserved by r.3.47(A1) of these Rules, which allows the sheriff to determine the application without hearing evidence where the ground(s) are no longer in dispute.

Withdrawal of application: termination of orders etc. by Principal Reporter

Subs.(1)(b)
Each relevant person who is present at the hearing before the sheriff. See above in the discussion of s.105(1) at (II), (III) and (V) for discussion of the various situations concerning the presence of the relevant person. All the considerations mentioned there apply, allowing for appropriate differences, here. Moreover the whole tone of s.106 seems to tend against dispensing with proof too readily, perhaps owing to the consideration that here the child's stance will not generally be ascertainable.

C.485.5

Subs.(2)
The sheriff may. Here, in contrast with s.105(2), the exercise by the sheriff of his or her independent judgment as to the appropriateness of dispensing with proof is emphasised by the use of the word "may".

C.485.6

Withdrawal of application: termination of orders etc.

Withdrawal of application: termination of orders etc. by Principal Reporter

107.—(1) This section applies where—
(a) an application is made to the sheriff by virtue of section 93(2)(a) or 94(2)(a), and
(b) before the application is determined, due to a change of circumstances or information becoming available to the Principal Reporter, the Principal Reporter no longer considers that any ground to which the application relates applies in relation to the child.
(2) The Principal Reporter must withdraw the application.
(3) If one or more grounds were accepted at the grounds hearing which directed the Principal Reporter to make the application, the Principal Reporter must arrange a children's hearing to decide whether to make a compulsory supervision order in relation to the child.
(4) If none of the grounds was accepted at the grounds hearing, any interim compulsory supervision order or warrant to secure attendance which is in force in relation to the child ceases to have effect on the withdrawal of the application.

C.486

DEFINITIONS
"child": s.199.
"compulsory supervision order": s.83.
"interim compulsory supervision order": s.86.
"Principal Reporter": s.14 and Sch.3.
"relevant person": s.200.
"safeguarder": ss.202(1) and 30(1).
"warrant to secure attendance": s.88.

C.486.1

GENERAL NOTE
This section deals with the procedures in relation to "withdrawal" ("abandonment" in the former legislation) by the Reporter of applications to the sheriff. The section does not differentiate between applications in relation to ss.93(2)(a) (non-acceptance of grounds) and 94(2)(a) (non-understanding of grounds).

C.486.2

Subs.(1)(b)
Rule 3.46(1) of the Act of Sederunt (Child Care and Maintenance Rules) 1997 (SI 1997/291) (the "1997 Rules") simply conferred on the Reporter an (unqualified) power to "abandon" the application, in whole or in part, at any time before determination. This subsection specifies further information or change of circumstances as pre-requisites of withdrawal. Simple change of mind on the part of the Reporter is not mentioned. Rule 3.46(1) of the 1997 Rules provides that the Reporter may withdraw the application at any time, but this could not take away from the provisions of the primary legislation. However if, for any reason, a Reporter came to the view that the evidence would not support a ground for referral it would be wrong for him or her to allow the application to go ahead and a decision to withdraw on this basis would be unlikely to be challenged.
Any. Means "any one of".

C.486.3

Subss.(2) and (3)
C.486.4 In the event of an application in respect of which the Reporter wishes to withdraw all the grounds for referral, either in whole or in part, then he or she may lodge a Minute of Withdrawal or make a motion at the hearing (the 1997 Rules r.3.46(1)). No specific style for this is enacted. In practice withdrawal by verbal motion is often employed. The withdrawal must, under r.3.46(2), be intimated and thereafter, where the withdrawal covers the whole application, the sheriff will dismiss the application and discharge the referral and any proof hearing which has been fixed will fall. (In general a referral, once made, is in the hands of the children's hearing: the foregoing provision constitutes an exception to this.) In the case of an application containing more than one ground, one or more of which has been withdrawn, but where one or more has already been accepted, the sheriff will dismiss the referral only in respect of the withdrawn ground(s) and the Reporter will, under subs.(3), arrange a children's hearing to consider disposal and, unless there is one or more unaccepted ground outstanding, any proof hearing which has been fixed will fall. The situation wherein, in a multiple ground referral, one or more of the grounds is withdrawn but one or more is still not accepted (and is therefore still outstanding) is not specifically dealt with in this section, but clearly the case will continue in the usual way and any proof hearing will stand in order to allow evidence to be led in relation to the non-admitted ground(s).

Subs.(4)
C.486.5 Where no ground for referral was originally accepted and withdrawal in respect of all grounds has been effected, then any compulsory supervision order, interim compulsory supervision order or warrant to secure attendance lapses automatically.

Determination of application

Determination: ground established

C.487 **108.**—(1) This section applies where the sheriff determines an application made by virtue of section 93(2)(a) or 94(2)(a).

(2) If subsection (4) applies, the sheriff must direct the Principal Reporter to arrange a children's hearing to decide whether to make a compulsory supervision order in relation to the child.

(3) In any other case, the sheriff must—
  (a) dismiss the application, and
  (b) discharge the referral to the children's hearing.
(4) This subsection applies if—
  (a) the sheriff determines that one or more grounds to which the application relates are established, or
  (b) one or more other grounds were accepted at the grounds hearing which directed the Principal Reporter to make the application.
(5) In subsection (4)(b), "accepted" means accepted by the child and (subject to sections 74 and 75) each relevant person in relation to the child.

DEFINITIONS
C.487.1 "child": s.199.
  "children's hearing": s.5.
  "Principal Reporter": s.14 and Sch.3.
  "relevant person": s.200.

GENERAL NOTE
C.487.2 This section deals with the outcome of a proof hearing before the sheriff. It does not differentiate between applications which were made by virtue of ss.93(2)(a) (non-acceptance of grounds) and 94(2)(a) (non-understanding of grounds). It also deals with the position where one ground or more has been accepted at the grounds hearing, and the application has been made to the sheriff for proof in relation to the non-admitted ground(s).

Subss.(2) and (4)
C.487.3 These provide for the situation where grounds are admitted or proved. Subsection (4)(a) refers to the situation where the sheriff comes to the legal conclusion that the evidence which has been led before him or her is sufficient in law and also sufficiently credible, reliable and

Determination: ground established

convincing to lead to the conclusion that the disputed ground(s) for referral have been proved to the appropriate standard (the criminal standard for any s.67(2)(j) ground, and the civil standard for all the others). This is a legal decision in relation to which, as noted above in the discussion of s.25, the overarching principle of the welfare of the child has no application—nor do either of the other overarching principles. Once this determination by the sheriff has been made the jurisdiction of the sheriff terminates (apart from the power to make an interim order, see s.109 below) and the disposal of the child's case reverts to the children's hearing. The sheriff may wish to explain this to those present when announcing his or her decision. It is not proper for the sheriff to make any suggestion as to how the hearing might deal with the case (cf. *M v McGregor*, 1982 S.L.T. 41 at 44 and *Kennedy v A*, 1986 S.L.T. 358).

Subs.(3)

This subsection does not provide for automatic cancellation of orders and warrants which are in force. This may be taken as implied since the referral is being "dismissed". However, it is suggested that it may be good practice for the sheriff in discharging a referral to include words to the effect "and accordingly recalls and cancels all outstanding warrants and orders", and agents should make the appropriate motion(s).

C.487.4

Subs.(4)

This subsection deals with the situation where one or more of the original grounds for referral has been accepted by the child and relevant person(s) at the stage of the grounds hearing. This may occur where the sheriff has held the disputed ground as established—in which case the sheriff must direct the Reporter to arrange a children's hearing in respect of all these grounds. This may also occur where the sheriff has held that the disputed ground, or grounds, has not been established, in which case the sheriff, although dismissing the application in respect of these grounds, must direct the Reporter to arrange a children's hearing in respect of the grounds which were admitted by the child and relevant person at the grounds hearing.

C.487.5

Subs.(5)

And, subject to sections 74 and 75, each relevant person in relation to the child. A relevant person has the right, unless excluded under s.76(2), to attend a children's hearing—see s.78(1)(c). Section 74(2) provides that where a relevant person has been appropriately notified of a children's hearing he or she must, unless excused or excluded, attend the children's hearing. Excusal may be granted at a pre-hearing panel (see s.79(3)(b)) or by the hearing itself (s.74(3)). See s.74(3) for the possible reasons for excusal. See s.76(1) for the competent reasons for exclusion. Exclusion of a relevant person and/or his or her representative may, under ss.76(2) and 77(2), be "for as long as necessary". The chairing member of the hearing must, however, (except where the non-disclosure provisions of s.178, which we discuss under that section, apply) explain to the excluded relevant person what has taken place in his or her absence, thus giving that person such background information as may be necessary to enable him or her to accept or not the ground for referral. Failure to allow this would risk contravening the human rights of the relevant person and indeed of the child—see *Principal Reporter v K*, 2011 S.C. (U.K.S.C.) 91; 2011 S.L.T. 271 at [41] to [44]. Provided this has been done and the relevant person has accepted the ground concerned at the hearing which directed the application, then the sheriff can safely and indeed must direct the Reporter to arrange a hearing for disposal of the child's case.

C.487.6

The present section is also stated to be subject to s.75 of the Act, subs.(2) of which empowers a hearing to proceed in the absence of the relevant person if it considers it appropriate to do so. It is submitted that, where the children's hearing has proceeded in the absence of the relevant person, it will not be possible to say that the relevant person has accepted the ground concerned at the grounds hearing and that therefore it will not be competent for the sheriff to direct the Reporter to arrange a hearing by virtue of the provision in subs.(4)(b) of this section and that accordingly the sheriff should hear evidence—cf. discussion above of s.105(2). Of course, if the relevant person has appeared at the proof hearing and accepted a ground for referral then the sheriff will be entitled to have regard to this acceptance in determining whether the ground has been established.

It is further submitted that where the relevant person (i) has not been present at the hearing and admitted a ground for referral which infers criminality or civil fault on him or her, and (ii) is not present at the proof hearing, then the sheriff, in view of, inter alia, the observations of the Supreme Court in *Principal Reporter v K* at the passages cited above and elsewhere, must exercise care that the rights of such persons are protected. The sheriff may wish to check whether the relevant person has been lawfully cited and/or made aware of the diet and on whatever information may be available to explain his or her non-attendance. The court will of course be reluctant to allow any unnecessary delay in proceeding with the child's case but where a situation arises where serious allegations are being made against a relevant person in relation to conduct involving the child which for one reason or another the relevant person has not had the opportunity of disputing, then, in the interests of justice for the relevant person (and indeed, as pointed out in *Principal Reporter v K*, possibly for the child also), it may be necessary for the court to consider an adjournment in order to allow the relevant person an opportunity to attend.

Determination: power to make interim compulsory supervision order etc.

C.488   109.—(1) This section applies where the sheriff directs the Principal Reporter to arrange a children's hearing to decide whether to make a compulsory supervision order in relation to the child.

(2) Subsection (3) applies if immediately before the hearing at which the sheriff determined the application made by virtue of section 93(2)(a) or 94(2)(a) an interim compulsory supervision order was not in force in relation to the child.

(3) If the sheriff is satisfied that the nature of the child's circumstances is such that for the protection, guidance, treatment or control of the child it is necessary as a matter of urgency that an interim compulsory supervision order be made, the sheriff may make an interim compulsory supervision order in relation to the child.

(4) Subsection (5) applies if immediately before the hearing at which the sheriff determined the application made by virtue of section 93(2)(a) or 94(2)(a) an interim compulsory supervision order was in force in relation to the child.

(5) If the sheriff is satisfied that the nature of the child's circumstances is such that for the protection, guidance, treatment or control of the child it is necessary that a further interim compulsory supervision order be made, the sheriff may make a further interim compulsory supervision order in relation to the child.

(6) If the sheriff is satisfied that there is reason to believe that the child would not otherwise attend the children's hearing, the sheriff may grant a warrant to secure attendance.

(7) If the sheriff makes an interim compulsory supervision order under subsection (3) or (5) specifying that the child is to reside at a place of safety, the children's hearing must be arranged to take place no later than the third day after the day on which the child begins to reside at the place of safety.

DEFINITIONS
C.488.1   "child": s.199.
"children's hearing": s.5.
"compulsory supervision order": s.83.
"interim compulsory supervision order": s.86.
"place of safety": ss.202(1) and 189.
"Principal Reporter": s.14 and Sch.3 paras 8–10.
"relevant person": s.200.
"warrant to secure attendance": s.88.

GENERAL NOTE
C.488.2   See the commentaries on ss.98, 99 and 100, above, for discussion of the principles applicable when the making of an interim compulsory supervision order is being considered. These principles apply here.

Subs.(1)
C.488.3   As noted above in the discussion of s.100, the sheriff has the power to make an interim compulsory supervision order from the time the application is lodged. This subsection confirms that this power may be exercised at the time when the sheriff announces his or her final determination of the case. Part VI of the Act of Sederunt (Child Care and Maintenance Rules) 1997 (SI 1997/291) (headed "Warrant for Further Detention of Child") has been revoked by the

Determination: power to make interim compulsory supervision order etc.

Act of Sederunt (Children's Hearings (Scotland) Act 2011) (Miscellaneous Amendments) 2013 (SSI 2013/172) art.3(29) and no Form of Application or rules in relation to the making of an interim compulsory supervision order under this section has been enacted. However, when operating this section the sheriff must observe the general principles of equity and fairness. The three overarching principles and the European Convention principle of proportionality also apply.

Subss.(2) to (5)

"Interim compulsory supervision order" (ICSO) is defined in s.86 of the Act: it may contain the measures listed in s.83(2). These measures include a requirement that the child reside in a specified place, but while such a requirement will frequently be imposed in an ICSO it is not mandatory. Section 86(1)(b) also requires that the ICSO name the local authority which is to be responsible for implementing such measures as it contains (the "implementation authority"). Subsections (2) and (4) separate out the situations of the child in respect of whom an ICSO was not in force at the beginning of the proof hearing and the child in respect of whom an ICSO was then in place. The principles governing the granting or not of an ICSO are the same in each case. These principles are discussed in the commentaries to ss.98, 99 and 100. As noted above in the discussion of subs.(1), there are no procedural rules governing the operation of this section. However, the procedure where the sheriff is attaching a requirement that the child is to reside in a specified place of safety is covered by subs.(7), discussed below; but in any event, both where such a requirement is being considered and where this is not being considered, it is submitted that the sheriff, in order to achieve fairness and take account of the needs of the child should take appropriate steps, perhaps along the following lines. Different considerations will apply depending on whether the child is or is not present and represented. Where the child is present and represented it is suggested that the sheriff should intimate:

(i) that he or she is considering making an ICSO;
(ii) which of the measures within s.83(2) are in contemplation;
(iii) which local authority is to be the implementation authority; and
(iv) the duration of the interim compulsory supervision order in terms of s.86(3) of the Act.

The sheriff should then invite submissions from all who are present, including the child and/or the child's representative. In cases where the child is not present, it is suggested that the sheriff should intimate as in points (i) to (iv) above and invite submissions from those present. The issue for the sheriff, in cases where an ICSO order is not in place at the outset (subs.(2) and (3)) will be whether an ICSO is "necessary as a matter of urgency" and, in cases where an ICSO *is* in force at the outset (subs.(4) and (5)), whether a further ICSO is "necessary". As already mentioned, the three overarching principles and the European Convention principle of proportionality apply and sheriffs may feel uneasy about, e.g. attaching a residence condition (under s.83(2)(a)) or other condition under s.83(2) which tends to abridge the liberty of the child, particularly where the child has not been present or represented and therefore has not had a say in the matter. It is important to note that the paramount consideration is the welfare of the child and, while always required to examine closely whether the circumstances are such as to render such an order necessary and beneficial, the sheriff may conclude that it is necessary and beneficial and proceed to make it.

C.488.4

Subs.(6)

This corresponds approximately with s.68(10)(b)(ii) of the 1995 Act, which provided for the granting of a warrant where the sheriff was satisfied that a warrant was necessary in the child's interests or that the child was likely to run away. The omission in the present provision of any reference to the child's interests (contrasting with s.63(10)(b)(ii) of the 1995 Act) does not greatly signify since the sheriff is bound to apply the paramountcy of welfare and the minimum intervention principles.

C.488.5

Subs.(7)

A "warrant to secure attendance" is defined in s.88, which includes, at s.88(4)(c), the provision that such a warrant is effective from the granting of the warrant until the "beginning of the relevant proceedings" or the expiry of 14 days from the day on which the child is detained under the warrant, whichever is the earlier. The effect of this subsection is that the "relevant proceedings" will take the form of a children's hearing which must be held on a date within the period of three calendar days (not "working days") starting with the day after the child arrived at the place of safety. Accordingly, where a child was received into a place of safety under these provisions on 22 December 2014 a children's hearing would have to be held on or before 25 December 2014, and if it was not held within this period the authority to retain the child in the place of safety would cease to have effect.

C.488.6

Children's Hearings (Scotland) Act 2011
Review of sheriff's determination

INTRODUCTORY AND GENERAL NOTE

C.488.7 These sections replace, with important modifications, the provisions of s.85 of the 1995 Act. Before 1995 there was no enacted procedure for dealing with the situation wherein, after a grounds determination by the sheriff, fresh evidence had emerged potentially casting doubt on the sheriff's determination. A party who wished to maintain that this had occurred required to have recourse to the specialised and difficult process of application to the *nobile officium* of the Court of Session. There were two examples of this, viz. the case of *R v Kennedy*, 1993 S.L.T. 910 and the "Ayrshire Child Abuse Case", reported in *L, Petitioners (No.1)*, 1993 S.L.T. 130 and *L, Petitioners (No.2)*, 1993 S.L.T. 342 in which apparently irreconcilable decisions were reached in the Court of Session. Section 85 of the 1995 Act provided a statutory basis for such situations.

While the procedures provided for in these present sections are recognisably similar to those of the earlier legislation, the opportunity has been taken to introduce important refinements and clarifications. In common with many other provisions in this Act, that which was in the 1995 Act dealt with in a single section is here separated out and spread over several sections.

When may an application for review be made under these sections?
Section 110 applications are competent at any time after the sheriff has made a determination under s.108. Accordingly, it is competent for such an application to be made immediately after the sheriff's announcement of his or her decision, although it seems likely that the typical application will not emerge until substantially later, that is, after the matter has been disposed of by a hearing and possibly even after the child has reached adulthood.

Position of the child pending a s.110 application, where compulsory supervision order has been imposed pursuant upon original order
In a case wherein, after a proof hearing at which the sheriff has held a ground or grounds as established and the subsequent children's hearing has made a compulsory supervision order (CSO), the question arises as to the status of that CSO where a s.110 application has been made and is still in process. There is an analogy with a criminal appeal based on new evidence, where the conviction stands until and unless quashed by the Appeal Court. Moreover, in *Stirling v M*, 1995 S.C.L.R. 460 it was held that a supervision requirement continued to subsist pending an appeal, and Lord Murray observed:

"If a child at risk is subject to a supervision requirement for its own protection, it does not seem to us to be in keeping with the purposes of the Act that, pending appeal against discharge of that requirement, there should be no supervision for the protection of the child".

Moreover, a s.110 application for review of a grounds determination is not an appeal. It is submitted that consequently any CSO already imposed subsists in the ordinary way as provided in s.83 unless and until, as a result of a s.110 application, the grounds determination has been recalled under s.114(3)(a).

Position where a s.110 application is made before a hearing has had opportunity to consider making a compulsory supervision order
This situation could arise where the s.110 application is made before the reporter has arranged a children's hearing following the proof hearing, where the reporter has arranged a hearing which has not yet taken place, or where a hearing has taken place but deferred its decision for some reason. Such situations are rare and so far as the authors are aware there has not so far been an application for such a review in this situation. The authors are inclined to the view that the reasoning of Lord Murray in *Stirling v M*, 1995 S.C.L.R. 460, in relation to the position in appeals, would have equal application pending a review of grounds application and that therefore the procedures pursuant upon the ground or grounds already established should be allowed to continue until and unless these grounds are displaced on review. In the event of new evidence emerging which plausibly called into question the original grounds determination the Reporter would require to consider his or her position in relation to the original referral and the court would require to ensure that the review of grounds determination was proceeded with as expeditiously as possible.

Position of the child in the event of an appeal under these sections
A determination by the sheriff in respect of an application under s.110(2) is appealable to the Sheriff Appeal Court and/or the Court of Session under s.163(1)(ii). For discussion of the position of the child in the event of such an appeal see below in the commentary on s.116.

Application for review of grounds determination

110.—(1) This section applies where the sheriff makes a determination under section 108 that a section 67 ground (other than the ground mentioned in section 67(2)(j) if the case was remitted to the Principal Reporter under section 49 of the Criminal Procedure (Scotland) Act 1995) is established in relation to a child (a "grounds determination").

(2) A person mentioned in subsection (3) may apply to the sheriff for a review of the grounds determination.

(3) The persons are—
(a) the person who is the subject of the grounds determination (even if that person is no longer a child),
(b) a person who is, or was at the time the grounds determination was made, a relevant person in relation to the child.

DEFINITIONS
"child": s.199.
"grounds determination": ss.202(1) and 110(1).
"Principal Reporter": s.14 and Sch.3 paras 8–10.
"relevant person": s.200.

GENERAL NOTE
For discussion of the background see Introductory and General Note, above. Where at a grounds hearing one or more ground has not been accepted, or not been understood, and a proof hearing before the sheriff has taken place at which one or more grounds has been established by the sheriff, then this section provides a possible means of reviewing the sheriff's determination.

Subs.(1)
The sheriff makes a determination under section 108. It is a pre-requisite that the sheriff shall have made a determination under s.108. This repeats the substance of the wording of s.85(2) the Children (Scotland) Act 1995 and consequently maintains the position that an application under this section cannot be made where there has been no "determination" by the sheriff, e.g. where ground(s) were accepted by the child or relevant person at the grounds hearing and the child or relevant person wishes to retract the acceptance. However, it is possible to figure a situation where a child or relevant person might wish to contend in particular circumstances that what had been said to the sheriff and recorded as an acceptance had not been a true acceptance and that, therefore, the treating it as such amounted to a determination by the sheriff, thus permitting a possible argument that this section should have application.

Other than the ground mentioned in s.67(2)(j) if the case was remitted to the Reporter under s.49 of the Criminal Procedure (Scotland) Act 1995. Where a case is remitted under s.49 the sheriff has no "determining" function and this provision might therefore be regarded as unnecessary: it does, however, make clear that there can be no review of a grounds determination in such cases. This should be defensible against any challenge under art.6(1) of the European Convention on Human Rights on the basis that (assuming of course that the proceedings before the court at the criminal trial have been lawfully carried through) the child had, in the criminal trial, all the safeguards provided to an accused person under our criminal procedure.

Subs.(2)
May apply to the sheriff. No form of application is prescribed in the Act or in the Rules, but r.3.62 of the Act of Sederunt (Child Care and Maintenance Rules) 1997 (SI 1997/291), as amended, lists the matters which such an application should specify, including:
"(b) the name and address (if known) of the person who is the subject of the grounds determination (even if that person is no longer a child), if not the applicant;
(c) the name and address of the safeguarder (if any);
(d) the name and address of the curator *ad litem* (if any);
(e) the name and address of any person who is, or was at the time the grounds determination was made, a relevant person in relation to the child, if not the applicant".

It is the clear implication that these persons (where not the applicant) should be served with the application.

Subs.(3)

C.489.5 This subsection makes clear (as the 1995 Act did not) that title vests in the child after the "child" has ceased to be a child, and that title vests in a person who was a relevant person at the time of the original determination. As noted by Professor Norrie in his *Children's Hearings in Scotland*, 3rd edn (Edinburgh: W. Green, 2013), para.8–39, these provisions may be available to a relevant person who considers that new evidence has emerged which would enable him or her to clear his or her name of an unjust imputation in the original determination. There is still no provision enabling a person who was not a relevant person to open up a sheriff's determination that he or she had been involved in the mistreatment of a child.

Sheriff: review or dismissal of application

C.490 **111.**—(1) This section applies where an application is made under section 110.

(2) If subsection (3) applies the sheriff must review the grounds determination.

(3) This subsection applies if—
   (a) there is evidence in relation to the ground that was not considered by the sheriff when making the grounds determination,
   (b) the evidence would have been admissible,
   (c) there is a reasonable explanation for the failure to lead that evidence before the grounds determination was made, and
   (d) the evidence is significant and relevant to the question of whether the grounds determination should have been made.

(4) If subsection (3) does not apply, the sheriff must dismiss the application.

DEFINITION

C.490.1 "grounds determination": ss.202(1) and 110(1).

GENERAL NOTE

C.490.2 This section substantially reflects the provisions in s.85(3) and (5) of the 1995 Act. Like these provisions this section does not specify in detail the procedure to be adopted. This is covered in the Act of Sederunt (Child Care and Maintenance Rules) 1997 (SI 1997/291), as amended, rr.3.62 to 3.63. However, this section, when read with s.114, appears to allow a "two stage" procedure, with the first stage comprising an examination of the application, with the option of dismissal if the conditions set out in s.111(3) do not appear to be satisfied, and the second stage (assuming the applicant has avoided dismissal at the first stage) comprising the sheriff's substantial "review" of the issues specified in s.111(3). There is no requirement for the sheriff to hear evidence, but since the purpose of these provisions is to enable changed circumstances to be addressed, there will generally have to be new evidence, either in the form of oral testimony or Joint Minute of Admissions, and it is unlikely, given that the s.110 application will *ex hypothesi* have survived the "first stage", that the applicant would not wish to adduce evidence. However, it is possible that a review of grounds determination may be based on a changed understanding of the meaning of the ground for referral concerned, perhaps following a later court decision. It is thought that a review of grounds determination based on the argument that, in the absence of a later court decision, the original grounds determination had been based on an error of law, would not be competent, since such a matter could have been challenged on appeal. After hearing such evidence and/or argument the sheriff, depending on his or her view of the evidence and submissions, may either "refuse" the application or "recall" the grounds determination and take whatever other steps may appear appropriate—see below in discussion of s.114. The foregoing was substantially the procedure adopted by the court under the former legislation—see Brian Kearney, *Children's Hearings and the Sheriff Court*, 2nd edn (Butterworths, 2000), Ch.57 and Kenneth McK. Norrie, *Children's Hearings in Scotland*, 2nd edn (Edinburgh: W. Green, 2005), Ch.12 and Kenneth McK. Norrie, *Children's Hearings in Scotland*, 3rd edn (Edinburgh: W. Green, 2013), para.8–44. The layout of these sections fortifies the appropriateness of this approach for the present legislation.

Subs.(2)

C.490.3 See discussion of the "two stage" procedure in the General Note, above.

Child's duty to attend review hearing unless excused

Subs.(3)(a)
Evidence... that was not considered. This might include evidence that scientific opinion which had been adduced at the proof hearing was now recognised as being flawed (see, for example, *R. v Cannings* [2004] EWCA Crim 1; [2004] 1 All E.R. 725) or even that an expert witness who gave evidence has been discredited (cf. *Meadow v General Medical Council* [2006] EWCA Civ 1390; [2007] Q.B. 462; [2007] 1 All E.R. 1). This might also include evidence which the sheriff did not hear because he or she had dispensed with the hearing of evidence under ss.105 or 106 above. This illustrates the difference between the admission of grounds admitted at the stage of the hearing, which cannot be re-opened, and the admission of grounds at the proof hearing before the sheriff, which can be re-opened. The procedural explanation of this lies in the consideration that the latter involves a "determination" by the sheriff and the former does not. However, the substantial justification for this difference is less easy to detect. Why should, for example, a relevant person who has accepted a ground before the sheriff, perhaps after some evidence has been led, be entitled, where on fresh (exculpatory from his or her point of view) evidence having emerged, be entitled to ask for a review when a relevant person who has accepted the ground at the children's hearing, and fresh evidence has later emerged, not be so entitled? Experience would suggest that the admission before or during a proof hearing would be more likely to be an informed decision than at the earlier stage.

C.490.4

Subs.(3)(b)
This reflects s.85(b)(ii) of the 1995 Act, but note that the provision in s.85(b)(i) of the 1995 Act—"[such evidence] is likely to be credible and reliable"—is omitted here. This is welcome since assessing the trustworthiness of evidence is essentially a matter for proof and the concept of judging the likelihood of credibility and reliability on the basis of written averment is not a happy one.

C.490.5

Subs.(3)(c)
This reflects s.85(3)(c) of the 1995 Act. This is a less demanding test than that which the Court of Session applied in the application under the *nobile officium* in *L, Petitioners (No 2)* 1993 S.L.T. 1342 at 1343E, where it was held that evidence could be heard only if the circumstances were "exceptional and unforeseen". A reasonable explanation might include the non-availability of the evidence for whatever reason (so long as not directly attributable to the applicant), or because of new understandings which have developed since the original finding (see General Note, above).

C.490.6

Subs.(3)(d)
The first part of s.85(3)(a) of the 1995 Act referred to "evidence the existence or significance of which might materially have affected the determination of the original application". The present wording is more objective in tone, but conveys substantially the same meaning.

C.490.7

Subs.(4)
The possibility of dismissal will fall to be decided at the "first stage", referred to above. In *Y v Principal Reporter* (Unreported 24 April 1998, Wick Sheriff Court, Sheriff I.A. Cameron, referred to in Brian Kearney, *Children's Hearings and the Sheriff Court*, 2nd edn (Butterworths, 2000), para.57.07) the sheriff, after hearing submissions on the application and answers (lodged for the Reporter), dismissed the application. In ordinary civil procedure "dismissal" on grounds of lack of relevancy of pleadings leaves open the possibility of raising a further action with different (it is to be hoped improved) pleadings. For discussion of the circumstances in which a further s.110 application may be competent after a previous application has been unsuccessful, see below in the discussion of s.114.

C.490.8

Child's duty to attend review hearing unless excused

112.—(1) This section applies where—
(a) a hearing is to be held by virtue of section 111(2) for the purpose of reviewing a grounds determination, and
(b) the person who is the subject of the grounds determination is still a child.

(2) The child must attend the hearing unless the child is excused by the sheriff on a ground mentioned in section 103(3).

(3) The child may attend the hearing even if the child is excused under subsection (2).

C.491

(4) If the sheriff is satisfied that there is reason to believe that the child would not otherwise attend the hearing, the sheriff may grant a warrant to secure attendance.

DEFINITIONS
C.491.1
"child": s.199.
"grounds determination": ss.202(1) and 110(1).
"warrant to secure attendance": ss.202(1) and 88.

GENERAL NOTE
C.491.2 These are new provisions. Their effect is to place the child who is the subject of a s.110 application *and who is still a child at the time of the review of grounds determination proceedings* in the same position, in relation to rights and duties to attend the proceedings, as the child at the stage of a proof hearing under s.101. This is consistent with the aim of trying at all stages to ensure effective participation by the child. This is important standing the re-enactment, in ss.115 and 117, of the provisions in s.87(5)(b) of the 1995 Act, to the effect that the sheriff may, in appropriate circumstances, hold as established a ground or grounds for referral other than those founded upon in the original application. See discussion below of ss.115 and 117. Where the child concerned is no longer a child then that individual, whom we shall call the "former child", has no obligation to attend. The rights of the former child are not prescribed in the Act or in the Rules, but it cannot have been the intention of the legislature to prevent the former child from attending. The procedural rules are contained in the Act of Sederunt (Child Care and Maintenance Rules) 1997 (SI 1997/291), as amended. Rule 3.62(1)(b) of these Rules require that the application for review of grounds determination shall contain "the name and address (if known) of the person [i.e. the child] who is the subject of the grounds determination (even if that person is no longer a child), if not the applicant", and r.3.63(2) provides for notification to the persons named in the application for review.

This requirement to serve on the former child supports the view that the former child has the right to attend the hearing of the application.

Subs.(3)
C.491.3 As with the position in relation to a proof hearing, the right of the child to attend even where the child's attendance has been excused, is preserved. This provision does not of course bear upon the position of the former child who, having no obligation to attend, cannot be the subject of excusal procedure.

Subs.(4)
C.491.4 All three of the overarching principles, and the proportionality principle of the European Convention, apply when a warrant to secure attendance is being considered. In effect a warrant to secure attendance should only be granted where the child's presence is essential for a just disposal of the case and there is no other practicable way of securing his or her attendance.

Child and relevant person: representation at review hearing

C.492   113.—(1) This section applies where a hearing is to be held by virtue of section 111(2) for the purpose of reviewing a grounds determination.

(2) The person who is the subject of the grounds determination ("P") may be represented at the hearing by another person.

(3) A relevant person in relation to P (or, where P is no longer a child, a person who was a relevant person in relation to P at the time the grounds determination was made) may be represented at the hearing by another person.

(4) A person representing P or the relevant person (or person who was a relevant person) at the hearing need not be a solicitor or advocate.

DEFINITIONS
C.492.1
"child": s.199.
"grounds determination": ss.202(1) and 110(1).
"relevant person": s.200.

Sheriff's powers on review of grounds determination

GENERAL NOTE
These are new provisions, but they reflect the practice of the court in relation to the (very few) applications under s.85 of the 1995 Act.

Subs.(4)
The right to be represented by a person who is not a solicitor or an advocate is conferred only on the child and relevant person. The Reporter will be present at s.110 hearings (cf. Act of Sederunt (Child Care and Maintenance Rules) 1997 (SI 1997/291), as amended, rr.3.62(b) and 3.63(1)) and may appear if qualified under the Children's Hearings (Scotland) Act 2011 (Rights of Audience of the Principal Reporter) Regulations 2012 (SSI 2012/335) or be represented by a solicitor or advocate. The provision that the child and relevant person may be represented by a non-lawyer should not be taken as implying that the issues liable to be involved in s.110 hearings are likely to be non-legal or straightforward. On the contrary, the matters specified in s.111(3)—such as admissibility of evidence, relevancy of evidence and reasonable explanation for failure to lead evidence originally—are notoriously liable to raise difficult legal issues. It may be that, having regard to the necessity of securing effective participation and equality of arms, sheriffs will be amenable to motions for adjournments in order to try to secure legal representation and that the Scottish Legal Aid Board will appreciate the need for such representation in order to secure that the proceedings are European Convention compliant.

Sheriff's powers on review of grounds determination

114.—(1) This section applies where the sheriff reviews a grounds determination by virtue of section 111(2).

(2) If the sheriff is satisfied that the section 67 ground to which the application relates is established, the sheriff must refuse the application.

(3) If the sheriff determines that the ground to which the application relates is not established, the sheriff must—
   (a) recall the grounds determination, and
   (b) make an order discharging (wholly or to the extent that it relates to the ground) the referral of the child to the children's hearing.

DEFINITIONS
"child": s.199.
"grounds determination": ss.202(1) and 110(1).

GENERAL NOTE
This section deals with the powers of the sheriff after he or she, not having dismissed the application under s.111(4), has proceeded to consider the application on its merits in the light of such evidence as has been led. In so far as this section deals with the situation wherein the sheriff sustains the applicant's submission that the ground concerned cannot be sustained, it is based on the provisions in s.85(6)(a) of the 1995 Act. The provision in subs.(2) empowering the sheriff to "refuse" the application is a terminological innovation, the possible effect of which is discussed below.

Where a sheriff is considering an application under these provisions he or she is in effect revisiting the decision of the sheriff in the original proof hearing after the application under s.92(4)(a) or 93(4)(a). As noted above in the discussion of s.108(2) and (4), such a decision is a legal decision in relation to which, as noted above in the discussion of s.25, the overarching principle of the welfare of the child has no application—nor do either of the other overarching principles.

Subs.(1)
See General Note, above.

Subs.(2)
Section 85 of the 1995 Act contained no provision empowering the sheriff to "refuse" the application but instead provided, in s.85(6)(b), that where any ground in the original application was established the sheriff was empowered to proceed in accordance with s.68(10) of that Act—i.e. remit to the Reporter to fix a disposal hearing (as would be done after a proof hearing which found a ground for referral to have been established). The significance of these somewhat complex (and now superseded) provisions is discussed in Kenneth McK. Norrie, *Children's Hearings (Scotland) Act 1995*, 2nd edn (Edinburgh: W. Green, 2004), p.185. The

present provision requiring the sheriff to "refuse" the application where he or she is satisfied that the ground for referral concerned is established is clearer. The effect of such refusal will depend on the position of the child at the time of refusal—see above: *Position of the child pending an application under these sections* in the Introductory Note to ss.110 to 118.

Competency of a further s.110 application?

C.493.5   As mentioned above in the discussion of s.111(4), "dismissal" under ordinary civil procedure admits of a possible further action on the basis of improved pleadings. However, after proof a further action on the same grounds and between the same parties may be incompetent on the principle of res judicata—for discussion of this principle and the associated concepts of *res noviter veniens ad notitiam* ("a new matter coming to the attention of the court") and "competent but omitted" see *Macphail on Sheriff Court Practice*, 3rd edn (Edinburgh: W. Green, 2006), paras 2.104 to 2.113. In the event of a further application *by the same person* after refusal of that person's application by virtue of s.114(2) it is thought that new and relevant alleged fact or facts (*res noviter*) would have to be averred in order to make the fresh application competent. On the other hand, where the earlier application had been dismissed under s.114, it may be possible that, on the analogy with ordinary civil procedure, an application based on the same factual averments but differently formulated application may be competent. It is a condition of res judicata ("the matter having already been decided may not be re-opened") that the earlier proceeding was at the instance of the same party, accordingly where a further application is lodged by a different person (e.g. by the child where an earlier application by a relevant person has been considered and dismissed or refused) then such further application may be competent. In other words, if the action has been dismissed it can be raised again differently formulated, but if the action has been refused, it can only be raised again if there are new facts or where another person is raising it.

So far as the authors are aware, there has been no example of an attempt to make a further application either under s.85 of the 1995 Act or the provisions of the 2011 Act where an earlier application has been unsuccessful.

Since the above paragraph was written the decision in *CF v MF & GF and Scottish Reporter* [2017] CSIH 44, discussed above under s.81(3) has been decided, in which Lord Malcolm observed that "there is no rigid system of *res judicata*". This was said in relation to decisions of pre-hearing panels and it remains to be seen if the courts would take the same view in proceedings in the sheriff court.

Recall: power to refer other grounds

C.494   **115.**—(1) This section applies where—
  (a) the sheriff makes an order under section 114(3), but
  (b) another section 67 ground specified in the same statement of grounds that gave rise to the grounds determination is accepted or established.

(2) If the person to whom the grounds determination relates is still a child, the sheriff must direct the Principal Reporter to arrange a children's hearing for the purpose of considering whether a compulsory supervision order should be made in relation to the child.

(3) If the sheriff is satisfied that the nature of the child's circumstances is such that for the protection, guidance, treatment or control of the child it is necessary as a matter of urgency that an interim compulsory supervision order be made, the sheriff may make an interim compulsory supervision order in relation to the child.

(4) If the sheriff is satisfied that there is reason to believe that the child would not otherwise attend the children's hearing, the sheriff may grant a warrant to secure attendance.

[1] (5) If the sheriff makes an interim compulsory supervision order under subsection (3) specifying that the child is to reside at a place of safety, the children's hearing must be arranged to take place no later than the third day after the day on which the child begins to reside at the place of safety.

NOTE

C.494.1   1. Inserted by the Children's Hearings (Scotland) Act 2011 (Modification of Primary Legislation) Order 2013 (SSI 2013/211) Sch.1 para.20(11) (effective June 24 2013).

Recall: powers where no grounds accepted or established

DEFINITIONS
"child": s.199.
"compulsory supervision order": ss.202(1) and 83.
"grounds determination": ss.202(1) and 110(1).
"interim compulsory supervision order": ss.202(1) and 86.
"place of safety": ss.202(1) and 189.
"Principal Reporter": s.14 and Sch.3 paras 8–10.
"warrant to secure attendance": ss.202(1) and 88.

C.494.2

GENERAL NOTE

Subsection 5 was added by the Children's Hearings (Scotland) Act 2011 (Modification of Primary Legislation) Order 2013 (SSI 2013/211) para.20(11). "Day" here means calendar day, with the day after the child was received into the place of safety counting as "day one".

These provisions reflect, with important modification, the provisions of s.85(6)(b) of the 1995 Act.

C.494.3

Subs.(1)

This situation will arise where, at the proof hearing in relation to a case where more than one ground for referral was held as established, the sheriff has in consequence directed the Reporter to arrange a disposal hearing. As submitted above in *Position of the child pending an application under these sections* in the Introductory and General Note to ss.110 to 118, the launching of a s.110 application does not of itself interrupt the progress through the system of a child during his or her childhood. The sustaining by the sheriff of the challenge to one of these grounds and its consequent recall under s.114(3)(a) will have changed the child's position and therefore rendered any disposal by the arranged hearing potentially inappropriate and a hearing to consider the remaining grounds is clearly necessary.

C.494.4

Subs.(2)

Section 85(6)(b) of the 1995 Act provides that the sheriff "may" proceed in accordance with s.68(10) of that Act (i.e. direct the Reporter to arrange a hearing to consider the ground(s) for referral which the sheriff has held as established). However, commentators, including Professor Norrie in his *Children (Scotland) Act 1995*, 2nd edn (Edinburgh: W. Green, 2004), p.185 and Sheriff Brian Kearney, *Children's Hearings and the Sheriff Court*, 2nd edn (Butterworths, 2000), para.57.16, agree that this in effect must be read as "shall". The present wording "must" recognises this. Professor Norrie comments at pp.179 and 180 of his *Children's Hearings in Scotland*, 2nd edn (Edinburgh: W. Green, 2005) that where a hearing has not been arranged it would

C.494.5

> "normally be pointless for the sheriff to remit to the reporter if the reporter is already in the process of arranging a children's hearing. The sheriff ought therefore to inquire of the reporter during the rehearing as to the situation in this respect before making his decision whether to remit the case to the reporter".

We agree that this might be done, but even if it is not done the sheriff must direct the Reporter to arrange a hearing: if the Reporter has already set in motion arrangements for a hearing (as could happen where the s.110 application is lodged soon after the grounds determination which is the subject of the application) then these arrangements can stand provided the Reporter is able to ensure that the papers relative to the sheriff's determination under s.114(3) are made available to all timeously, in terms of the Children's Hearings (Scotland) Act 2011 (Rules of Procedure in Children's Hearings) Rules 2013 (SSI 2013/194) r.34(6). If this cannot be done then the already arranged hearing will require to be adjourned till the date of the s.115 hearing. Since the sheriff's remitting under this section is, in the specified circumstances, mandatory, the sheriff is not here subject to any of the overarching principles.

Subss.(3) and (4)

All three of the overarching principles, and the European Convention principle of proportionality, apply to each of these two subsections, e.g. before granting a warrant to secure attendance, the sheriff must consider if there is any other, less invasive, way of securing the child's attendance. See commentary on s.88, above.

Satisfied that there is reason to believe. See discussion of "reasonable grounds to believe" in commentary on s.39, above: the wording here means the same thing.

C.494.6

Recall: powers where no grounds accepted or established

116.—(1) This section applies where—
(a) the sheriff makes an order under section 114(3), and

C.495

(b) none of the other section 67 grounds specified in the statement of grounds that gave rise to the grounds determination is accepted or established.

(2) If a compulsory supervision order that is in force in relation to the person who is the subject of the grounds determination was in force at the time of the grounds determination, the sheriff must require a review of the compulsory supervision order.

(3) In any other case, the sheriff must—
   (a) terminate any compulsory supervision order that is in force in relation to the person who is the subject of the grounds determination, and
   (b) if that person is still a child, consider whether the child will require supervision or guidance.

(4) Where that person is still a child and the sheriff considers that the child will require supervision or guidance, the sheriff must order the relevant local authority for the child to provide it.

(5) Where the sheriff makes such an order, the relevant local authority for the child must give such supervision or guidance as the child will accept.

DEFINITIONS

C.495.1   "child": s.199.
"compulsory supervision order": ss.202(1) and 83.
"relevant local authority": s.201.

GENERAL NOTE

C.495.2   This section deals with the situation where the sheriff has, in a review of a grounds determination, recalled the original grounds determination and recalled the referral in relation to the recalled ground. The section prescribes what is to happen
   (i) where, at the time when the original grounds determination was made, a compulsory supervision order (CSO) in relation to a separate ground for referral was in force and
   (ii) where, at the time of the original grounds determination, a CSO was in force in relation to the ground for referral which has been recalled.
The wording of subs.(3)(a) is not clearly focussed, and requires a purposive interpretation—see discussion below. We are indebted to Professor Kenneth McK Norrie for sharing with us his thoughts on the interpretation of this section.

Subs.(2)

C.495.3   The CSO referred to must be one based on a ground separate and different from the ground that has been recalled. The effect of this subsection is to ensure the continuance of this CSO subject to such variation, if any, as the sheriff, reviewing it in the light of the information now available, may consider necessary and appropriate. The reader is directed to subs.(3) below for examples.

Subs.(3)

C.495.4   *In any other case* .... Other than what? On the face of it this refers to a situation other than the situation envisaged in subs.(2), thus meaning "where no CSO was in force at the time of the making of the original, now recalled, grounds determination". But this does not sit well with the provision in subs.(3)(a) that the sheriff must "terminate any compulsory supervision order that is in force in relation to the person who is the subject of the grounds determination". Moreover, taken literally, subs.(3)(a) would require the sheriff to terminate a CSO based on, for example, a ground for referral based on sexual abuse of the child simply because the sheriff had recalled, say, a determination that the child had committed an offence. This would be absurd and cannot have been what the legislature intended. It is submitted that the purpose of this provision is to require the sheriff to terminate any existing CSO *based on the same ground for referral which the sheriff has recalled*, and that therefore "In any other case" should be read down as "In any case wherein the child was not subject to a compulsory supervision order when the grounds determination was made, but was made subject to such an order subsequently on the on the basis of the ground successfully challenged." To read down a statute by inserting some forty words may seem adventurous, but for a lucid justification of such an approach when it goes with "the grain" of the legislation see the speech of Lord Rodger of Earlsferry in *Ghaidan v Godin-Mendoza* [2004] UKHL 30; [2004] 2 A.C. 557; [2004] 3 W.L.R. 113, especially at [50] and,

New section 67 ground established: sheriff to refer to children's hearing

for the application of this approach in Scotland, see the judgment of Lord Hope and Lady Hale in *Principal Reporter v K* [2010] UKSC 56; 2011 S.C. (U.K.S.C.) 91; 2011 S.L.T. 271; [2011] 1 W.L.R. 18 at para.[61].

Subs.(3)(b) and subss.(4) and (5)
These provisions apply where the subject of the original grounds determination is still a child. "Child" here means a child as defined in s.199 and therefore includes a person over 16 but under 18 who is still subject to a CSO which was imposed independently of the grounds determination concerned and has not been terminated. The decision of the sheriff under subs.(3)(b) is one to which the paramountcy of the welfare of the child principle applies, but is not listed in s.27 (views of the child principle) or s.29 (minimum intervention principle). However the European Convention principle of proportionality will apply.

New section 67 ground established: sheriff to refer to children's hearing

117.—(1) This section applies where—
(a) by virtue of section 110 the sheriff is reviewing a grounds determination, and
(b) the sheriff is satisfied that there is sufficient evidence to establish a section 67 ground that is not specified in the statement of grounds that gave rise to the grounds determination.
(2) The sheriff must—
(a) determine that the ground is established, and
(b) if the person to whom the grounds determination relates is still a child, direct the Principal Reporter to arrange a children's hearing for the purpose of considering whether a compulsory supervision order should be made in relation to the child.
(3) If the sheriff is satisfied that the nature of the child's circumstances is such that for the protection, guidance, treatment or control of the child it is necessary as a matter of urgency that an interim compulsory supervision order be made, the sheriff may make an interim compulsory supervision order in relation to the child.
(4) If the sheriff is satisfied that there is reason to believe that the child would not otherwise attend the children's hearing, the sheriff may grant a warrant to secure attendance.
[1] (5) If the sheriff makes an interim compulsory supervision order under subsection (3) specifying that the child is to reside at a place of safety, the children's hearing must be arranged to take place no later than the third day after the day on which the child begins to reside at the place of safety.

NOTE
1. Inserted by the Children's Hearings (Scotland) Act 2011 (Modification of Primary Legislation) Order 2013 (SSI 2013/211) Sch.1 para.20(12) (effective June 24 2013).

DEFINITIONS
"child": s.199.
"children's hearing": s.5.
"compulsory supervision order": ss.202(1) and 83.
"grounds determination": ss.202(1) and 110(1).
"interim compulsory supervision order": ss.202(1) and 86.
"place of safety": s.202(1).
"Principal Reporter": s.14 and Sch.3 paras 8–10.
"statement of grounds": s.89(3).
"warrant to secure attendance": s.88.

GENERAL NOTE
The main thrust of this section is to prescribe the procedure where the sheriff has, when considering a review of a grounds determination, concluded that a fresh ground for referral exists. As recognised in Kenneth McK Norrie, *Children's Hearings in Scotland*, 3rd edn (2013), para.8–49 and in Brian Kearney, *Children's Hearings and the Sheriff Court*, 2nd edn (Bloomsbury Professional, 2000), para.57.11 the sheriff, if minded to find that a fresh ground

for referral is established, should indicate his or her intention of doing so and allow parties the opportunity of rebuttal. Not to do this would risk non-compliance with art.6(1) of the European Convention on Human Rights, particularly in the event of any finding inferring misconduct on the part of a person who was not party to the proceedings. In *Principal Reporter v K* [2010] UKSC 56; 2011 S.C. (U.K.S.C.) 91; 2011 S.L.T. 271; [2011] 1 W.L.R. 18 at [14] Lord Hope and Lady Hale said: "Yet K was given no opportunity to be heard so that he could refute the allegations. This strikes us as quite contrary to one of the rules of natural justice, the right to be heard". On such a situation arising it is suggested that the sheriff might employ the inherent jurisdiction of the court to order intimation on such a person with a view to admitting him or her to the proceedings—see *Macphail on Sheriff Court Practice*, 3rd edn (2006) at 2.09:

> "Under the inherent jurisdiction of the court to preserve the administration of justice the sheriff is empowered to take notice of certain matters whether or not they have been urged upon him by any of the parties to the action. It is thought that such matters include any aspect of the litigation which may cause prejudice to a specific public interest in the regular conduct of litigation, or the interests of third parties not called in the action ... ".

Subs.(3)

C.496.4 The sheriff here would be subject to the paramountcy of the welfare of the child principle, but not to the views of the child principle or the minimum intervention principle, since this decision is not listed in s.27 or s.29 of the Act. The sheriff would, however, be subject to the European Convention principle of proportionality.

Subs.(4)

C.496.5 The sheriff here will be subject to all three of the overarching principles and to the European Convention principle of proportionality. The latter, and the minimum intervention principle, will require the sheriff to take account of any information as to whether or not some method other than granting a warrant to secure attendance would be likely to bring about the attendance of the child.

Reason to believe.

C.496.6 The sheriff must be clear in his or her mind that there is reason to "believe" and not merely "suspect" that the child will not attend unless a warrant is granted. See above for our discussion of these concepts under s.38(2)(a).

Subs.(5)

C.496.7 This provision reflects the primacy of the Children's hearing in dealing with a child's case.

Third day.

C.496.8 The reference here is to "day" i.e. calendar day, not "working day", thus reflecting the importance which the Act attaches to a speedy examination of the necessity of holding the child in a place of safety. Accordingly where, by virtue of this section, a child began to reside in a place of safety on a Thursday, the children's hearing would require to be held on or before the following Sunday. This exactly reflects the time limitation of a child protection order—see s.38(2)(a) above.

Application of Part where compulsory supervision order in force

Application of Part where compulsory supervision order in force

C.497 **118.**—(1) This Part has effect in relation to a child mentioned in subsection (2) with the modifications set out in subsections (3) to (5).

(2) The child is a child in relation to whom a compulsory supervision order is in force.

(3) References to an interim compulsory supervision order are to be read as references to an interim variation of the compulsory supervision order.

(4) References to the sheriff directing the Principal Reporter to arrange a children's hearing to decide whether to make a compulsory supervision order in relation to the child are to be read as references to the sheriff requiring a review of the compulsory supervision order.

(5) Sections 98 and 99 do not apply.

DEFINITIONS
C.497.1 "child": s.199.

Application of Part where compulsory supervision order in force

"compulsory supervision order": ss.202(1) and 83.
"interim compulsory supervision order": ss.202(1) and 86.
"Principal Reporter": s.14 and Sch.3 paras 8–10.
"children's hearing": s.5.

GENERAL NOTE
This section provides for the situations where the child with whom the sheriff is dealing is already subject to a compulsory supervision order (CSO). C.497.2

Subs.(3)
This provision will apply where, in the progress through the system of a child already subject to a CSO, the question of how to deal with the child *ad interim* arises. This may occur where the application for a proof hearing has been made but not determined (s.100(1)(b)) and the case has come before the sheriff and, for whatever reason, the proof has not been concluded. This provision deals with the situation where a CSO is already in place; this contrasts with the situation of a child who was not already in the system and the sheriff would be considering making an interim compulsory supervision order (ICSO) under s.100(2). However, making an ICSO would not sit well where the child is already subject to a full compulsory supervision order (CSO) and accordingly this subsection empowers the sheriff, if he or she considers that the existing compulsory supervision order does not meet the requirements of the child, to vary the existing CSO in whatever way appears right in terms of s.100(2)—for example, the circumstances of the new referral may indicate to the sheriff that a direction in relation to contact with a particular person (which was not included in the existing CSO) should be imposed by virtue of s.83(2)(g). It should be noted that the sheriff does not need to consider that there is an element of urgency when granting an interim variation of a compulsory supervision order (IVCSO). This contrasts with the granting of an ICSO which must be required as a matter of urgency (see s.100(2)). In the event that the sheriff is satisfied that the terms of the existing CSO remain appropriate, then the sheriff need take no action under this head. It is suggested, however, that it would be helpful to social workers and others connected with the child's case for the sheriff, if taking no action, to include in the interlocutor words to the effect that the terms of the existing CSO have been noted and that no variation is being ordered. In deciding on whether any variation is required the sheriff must have regard to the overarching principles and the European Convention principle of proportionality. C.497.3

Subs.(4)
Similar considerations underlie this provision as those referred to in the foregoing. Where a CSO is already in force it will be appropriate for a hearing to review the terms of the existing order. The powers of a children's hearing on review of a CSO are contained in s.138 of the Act. The procedure at such hearings is prescribed in r.62 of the Children's Hearings (Scotland) Act 2011 (Rules of Procedure in Children's Hearings) Rules 2013 (SSI 2013/194). C.497.4

Subs.(5)
Sections 98 and 99 contain provisions regulating the situations wherein an ICSO is to be extended and providing for applications for such extensions. This subsection appears to mean that where the expression "interim compulsory supervision order" appears in these sections it is not to be read as reference to an interim variation of a compulsory supervision order. It should be noted that the time limit of 22 days does not apply to an IVCSO granted under this section. C.497.5

PART 11

SUBSEQUENT CHILDREN'S HEARINGS

INTRODUCTORY NOTE TO PART 11
Sections 119 and 120 together provide the options available to a children's hearing which is held subsequent to a hearing where a decision has been deferred because one of the following applies: grounds were accepted at the grounds hearing but a decision was deferred (s.91(2)); where grounds which were not accepted or not understood were found established by the sheriff (s.108); where a ground for referral has been held by the sheriff not to be established and has been discharged, but some other ground(s) for referral has been accepted or held established (s.115(2)); the sheriff has found grounds not established, but has found another s.67 ground established (s.117(2)(b)). Further, the hearing may use its discretion to continue to a subsequent

Children's Hearings (Scotland) Act 2011

hearing if it considered appropriate. This builds in flexibility to what would otherwise be an exhaustive list.

Children's hearing following deferral or proceedings under Part 10

C.498   **119.**—(1) This section applies where a children's hearing is arranged by the Principal Reporter by virtue of section 91(2), 107(3), 108, 115(2) or 117(2)(b) or subsection (2).

(2) If the children's hearing considers that it is appropriate to do so, the children's hearing may defer making a decision on whether to make a compulsory supervision order until a subsequent children's hearing.

(3) If the children's hearing does not exercise the power conferred by subsection (2) the children's hearing must—
  (a) if satisfied that it is necessary to do so for the protection, guidance, treatment or control of the child, make a compulsory supervision order, or
  (b) if not so satisfied, discharge the referral.

(4) Subsection (5) applies where—
  (a) the child is excused by virtue of section 73(3) or 79(3)(a) or rules under section 177, or
  (b) a relevant person in relation to the child is excused by virtue of section 74(3) or 79(3)(b) or rules under section 177.

(5) The children's hearing may, despite the excusal, defer its decision to a subsequent children's hearing under this section without further excusing the person.

GENERAL NOTE
See Introductory Note to Pt 11, above.

DEFINITIONS
C.498.1   "child": s.199.
"children's hearing": s.5.
"compulsory supervision order": ss.202(1) and 83.
"Principal Reporter": s.14 and Sch.3 paras 8–10.
"relevant person": s.201.

Subs.(1)
C.498.2   This section applies to a hearing which is held because either the previous grounds hearing or a review hearing deferred making a decision, or sheriff court proceedings have taken place under Pt 10 of the Act and the case has been referred to the children's hearing. See also Introductory Note above.

Subs.(2)
C.498.3   The hearing is not required to make a substantive decision but may further defer the decision where the hearing considers it appropriate to do so. The paramountcy of the welfare of the child principle will apply and the hearing will require to make timely decisions and to avoid unnecessary delays. The hearing may consider making an interim compulsory supervision order or a further interim compulsory supervision order if it is considered necessary as a matter of urgency (see s.120(3) and (5)).

Subs.(3)
C.498.4   This section reiterates the criteria for making a compulsory supervision order (CSO) (see annotation for s.91(3) above for discussion).

Subss.(4) and (5)
C.498.5   Where a hearing or pre-hearing panel has excused a child or relevant person the subsequent hearing is not bound by that decision, but may decide that his or her presence is necessary and may defer the decision until a further hearing to allow the person to attend. In *F & F Appellants* (sometimes cited as *F v Principal Reporter*), 2014 Fam. L. R. 57 a sheriff, when considering the powers of a pre-hearing panel in deciding if individuals were still to be deemed as relevant persons, took the view that when assessing whether they had or recently had had significant

involvement in the upbringing of the child, the panel should not go behind the decision of an earlier pre-hearing panel by taking its own view of events before the earlier decision. This decision may favour the argument that a hearing, when considering to defer under this section, should not look at the circumstances preceding the earlier decision. However the decision as to whether or not to defer may be one in relation to which the whole circumstances, including those in existence before the previous decision would be regarded as relevant. The case of *F & F* was considered by the Court of Session in *CF v MF & GF and Scottish Reporter* [2017] CSIH 44. Both *F & F* and *CF v MF & GF* are discussed above under s.81(3).

If the hearing has reasonable cause to believe that the child will not attend the subsequent hearing a warrant may be issued if it is necessary and proportionate (see ss.88 and 123).

Powers of children's hearing on deferral under section 119

120.—(1) This section applies where under subsection (2) of section 119 a children's hearing defers making a decision in relation to a child until a subsequent children's hearing under that section.

(2) Subsection (3) applies if immediately before the children's hearing which takes place under section 119 an interim compulsory supervision order was not in force in relation to the child.

(3) If the children's hearing considers that the nature of the child's circumstances is such that for the protection, guidance, treatment or control of the child it is necessary as a matter of urgency to make an interim compulsory supervision order, the children's hearing may make an interim compulsory supervision order in relation to the child.

(4) Subsection (5) applies if immediately before the children's hearing which takes place under section 119 an interim compulsory supervision order was in force in relation to the child.

(5) If the children's hearing is satisfied that the nature of the child's circumstances is such that for the protection, guidance, treatment or control of the child it is necessary that a further interim compulsory supervision order be made, the children's hearing may make a further interim compulsory supervision order in relation to the child.

(6) If the children's hearing considers that it is necessary to do so for the purpose of obtaining any further information, or carrying out any further investigation, that is needed before the subsequent children's hearing, the hearing may make a medical examination order.

C.499

DEFINITIONS
"child": s.199.
"Children's hearing": s.5.
"compulsory supervision order": ss.202(1) and 83.
"interim compulsory supervision order": ss.202(1) and 86.
"medical examination order": ss.202 (1) and 89.
"Principal Reporter": s.14 and Sch.3 paras 8–10.

C.499.1

GENERAL NOTE
See Introductory Note to Part 11, above. Where a hearing held under s.119 has deferred a decision, the hearing may make, continue or vary an interim compulsory supervision order (ICSO) or make a medical examination order. For details and discussion of these orders the reader is directed to the annotations for ss.86 and 89 above.

C.499.2

Subss.(2) to (5)
Where an ICSO is not already in place the hearing may, where there is urgency, make such an order. Where an ICSO is already in place, the hearing may, where there is urgency, make a further ICSO in such terms as it thinks will address the needs of the child.

C.499.3

Subs.(6)
The test of urgency contained in subss.(3) and (5) is not provided for here.

C.499.4

PART 12

CHILDREN'S HEARINGS: GENERAL

Views of child

Confirmation that child given opportunity to express views before hearing

C.500　　**121.**—(1) This section applies where a children's hearing is held in relation to a child by virtue of this Act.

(2) The chairing member of the children's hearing must ask the child whether the documents provided to the child by virtue of rules made under section 177 accurately reflect any views expressed by the child.

(3) The chairing member need not comply with subsection (2) if, taking account of the age and maturity of the child, the chairing member considers that it would not be appropriate to do so.

DEFINITIONS
C.500.1　　"chairing member": Sch.1 para.7.
　　　　　　"child": s.199.
　　　　　　"children's hearing": s.5.

GENERAL NOTE
C.500.2　　Rule 8 of the Children's Hearings (Scotland) Act 2011 (Rules of Procedure in Children's Hearings) Rules 2013 (SSI 2013/194) (the "Procedural Rules") requires the writer of any document given to the members of a pre-hearing panel (PHP) or children's hearing to include any views expressed to him or her by the child. This was not a requirement under the Children (Scotland) Act 1995 (the 1995 Act) although it was considered to be best practice. The present provision is consistent with the increased emphasis in this Act on the participation of the child. The Procedural Rules require that the child, unless not capable of understanding the material (see r.18), be given all of the documents which have been provided to the Children's hearing or PHP, subject to any non-disclosure request (see rr.84 and 15). It is the Reporter who decides whether or not the child is capable of understanding the material. Under the 1995 Act the practice was to provide reports only to children aged 12 years of age or over. We understand that current practice is for the Reporter to presume that no child under 12 would be capable of understanding the hearing papers but that Reporters should consider the matter on a case by case basis. A child under the age of 12 may well have the capacity to understand some or all of the material and the decision as to whether the child is capable of understanding the material should not be decided by age alone. The chairing member is required to ask the child whether his or her reported views are accurate, and if the response is that they are not, to clarify the child's views. This should not be limited to a child who has received the materials. Where a child is capable of understanding the explanation of his or her reported views, he or she should be given the opportunity to say whether those views were reported accurately. Where the reported views are contained in a document which has been provided after the notification by the Reporter, the chairing member will require to be satisfied that the child has had sufficient opportunity to consider the material before being asked whether the views reported are accurate. It should be noted that the decisions are those of the chairing member alone. In *M v Local Reporter Manager*, 2014 Fam. L.R. 102, an Extra Division had to consider the situation wherein a child had expressed views orally to an earlier hearing but these views had not been incorporated into the reasons for the decision of that hearing. At para.28 of its judgment the Court narrated the terms of this present section and considered whether the decision of the hearing constituted a document provided to the child by virtue of r.34(6)(b) of the Procedural Rules. The Court decided that the reasons for the decision of the hearing did not fall into this category and therefore there had been no procedural irregularity.

Children's advocacy services

Children's advocacy services

C.501　　[1] **122.**—(1) This section applies where a children's hearing is held in relation to a child by virtue of this Act.

General power to grant warrant to secure attendance

(2) The chairing member of the children's hearing must inform the child of the availability of children's advocacy services.

(3) The chairing member need not comply with subsection (2) if, taking account of the age and maturity of the child, the chairing member considers that it would not be appropriate to do so.

(4) The Scottish Ministers may by regulations make provision for or in connection with—
 (a) the provision of children's advocacy services,
 (b) qualifications to be held by persons providing children's advocacy services,
 (c) the training of persons providing children's advocacy services,
 (d) the payment of expenses, fees and allowances by the Scottish Ministers to persons providing children's advocacy services.

(5) The Scottish Ministers may enter into arrangements (contractual or otherwise) with any person other than a local authority, CHS or SCRA for the provision of children's advocacy services.

(6) Regulations under this section are subject to the affirmative procedure.

(7) In this section, "children's advocacy services" means services of support and representation provided for the purposes of assisting a child in relation to the child's involvement in a children's hearing.

NOTE
1. Not yet in force. C.501.1

DEFINITIONS
"affirmative procedure": ss.197 and 202(1). C.501.2
"chairing member": Sch.1 para.7.
"child": s.199.
"children's hearing": s.5.
"Children's Hearings Scotland": ss.202(1) and 2.
"Scottish Children's Reporter Administration": s.15.

GENERAL NOTE
It should be noted that at the time of writing this section is not in force. The child is entitled C.501.3 to a representative at a children's hearing or pre-hearing panel (see annotation to s.78) and this representative may be a member of a children's advocacy service. Subsection (1) requires the chairing member to inform a child of "the availability of children's advocacy services". This does not mean that the chairing member must provide full details of any services in the area, but to let the child know that advocacy is something that he or she may consider. Although the section does not require the hearing to be continued for the child who indicates that he or she would wish to obtain advocacy support, it is implicit that the hearing should consider it otherwise there would be little point in the chairing member advising the child about advocacy services. Subsections (4), (5) and (6) allow Scottish Ministers to make regulations concerning the standards, training and any payment for advocacy services. The fact that the section is not yet in force means that chairing members do not, at present, need to provide such information to the child, but it does not remove the child's right to the use of an advocacy service worker as representative.

Warrants to secure attendance

General power to grant warrant to secure attendance

123.—(1) This section applies where in relation to a child— C.502
 (a) a children's hearing has been or is to be arranged, or
 (b) a hearing is to take place under Part 10.

(2) On the application of the Principal Reporter, any children's hearing may on cause shown grant a warrant to secure the attendance of the child at the children's hearing or, as the case may be, the hearing under Part 10.

Children's Hearings (Scotland) Act 2011

C.502.1 DEFINITIONS
"child": s.199.
"children's hearing": s.5.
"Principal Reporter": s.14 and Sch.3 paras 8–10.
"warrant to secure attendance": s.88.

C.502.2 GENERAL NOTE
Subsection (1)(a) of this section is applicable only to children's hearings as there is no duty of attendance at pre-hearing panels (s.88). It should be noted that a hearing may not grant a warrant to secure attendance *ex proprio motu*, but only on application by the Reporter (subs.(2)). The warrant can be issued either because the child is refusing to attend or because the child is being withheld from the hearing by an adult. The warrant may be granted in order to secure the child's attendance at a children's hearing or at the first calling at the sheriff court where a hearing is to take place under Pt 10 of this Act. In the latter case, the hearing may only issue the warrant to secure attendance at the first calling of the case before the sheriff; any subsequent warrants for attendance at court may only be issued by the sheriff (s.103(5)). The hearing is not obliged to grant a warrant, but must be satisfied that it is necessary and proportionate to do so. The reader is directed to the annotations concerning warrants to secure attendance at ss.88 and 103(5). Rule 78 of the Children's Hearings (Scotland) Act 2011 (Rules of Procedure in Children's Hearings) Rules 2013 (SSI 2013/194) (the Procedural Rules) governs procedure where a hearing is considering granting a warrant and the duties of the Reporter where a warrant is granted by a hearing. The procedure where a warrant is being considered by a hearing is governed by r.78 of the Procedural Rules.

Child's age

Requirement to establish child's age

C.503 **124.**—(1) This section applies where a children's hearing is held by virtue of this Act.
(2) The chairing member of the children's hearing must ask the person in respect of whom the hearing has been arranged to declare the person's age.
(3) The person may make another declaration as to the person's age at any time.
(4) The chairing member need not comply with the requirement in subsection (2) if the chairing member considers that the person would not be capable of understanding the question.
(5) Any children's hearing may make a determination of the age of a person who is the subject of the hearing.
(6) A person is taken for the purposes of this Act to be of the age—
   (a) worked out on the basis of the person's most recent declaration, or
   (b) if a determination of age by a children's hearing is in effect, worked out in accordance with that determination.
(7) Nothing done by a children's hearing in relation to a person is invalidated if it is subsequently proved that the age of the person is not that worked out under subsection (6).

C.503.1 DEFINITIONS
"chairing member": Sch.1 para.7.
"children's hearing": s.5.

C.503.2 GENERAL NOTE
It should be noted that this section refers to "person" not "child". A child may be referred to the hearing by the Reporter up to the age of 16, or older if the referral was received by the Reporter before the person turned 16. It should be noted that the definition of a child under s.199 of this Act includes a person who is of school age where the ground for referral is under s.67(2)(o) (non-attendance at school without reasonable cause). A person aged over 16 years and under 17 years and 6 months may be referred by a court where that person has either pled guilty to a criminal offence or been found guilty of a criminal offence (see s.49(6)(c) of the Criminal Procedure (Scotland) Act 1995). Once the person is subject to a compulsory supervision order (CSO) by the hearing he or she is a "child" for the purposes of the hearing until the order is terminated or the person reaches 18 years of age (see s.199(7)). A CSO includes

Review of contact direction

an interim compulsory supervision order. The decisions of a Children's hearing are not invalidated if the child's age is wrong (Kenneth McK. Norrie, *Children's Hearings in Scotland*, 3rd edn (Edinburgh: W. Green, 2013), para.2-11) unless the person is over the age of 16 years when referred to the Reporter or over the age of 17 years and 6 months when referred by the court where he or she has been found guilty or has pleaded guilty to a criminal offence in the adult court. In either case any order made by a hearing is invalid. Where the person is unable to provide an age due to non-age or any other reason the hearing will decide the age of the child on the basis of information provided informally at the hearing. In the event of any doubt as to the age of the person, it may be necessary for the hearing to obtain an expert opinion. It should be noted that while the question concerning the age of the person is put by the chairing member, any decision regarding the age of the person is made by the hearing (r.124 of the Children's Hearings (Scotland) Act 2011 (Rules of Procedure in Children's Hearings) Rules 2013 (SSI 2013/194) (the Procedural Rules)). Note that this section is particularly applicable to children with inadequate documentation such as asylum-seeking or trafficked children. Such a case is *AU v Glasgow City Council and the Advocate General* [2017] CSIH 12 which concerned a young refugee whose age had been assessed by Glasgow City Council who disputed the assessment by raising an action of declarator. Rejecting a submission that declarator was incompetent, Lord Woolman held that declarator was competent, but that judicial review was the preferable procedure. His Lordship reviewed the Scottish and English authorities and referred to *Age Assessment Practice An Age Assessment Practice Pathway for Social Workers in Scotland*, published by Glasgow City Council and the Scottish Refugee Council in 2012.

Compulsory supervision orders: review

Compulsory supervision order: requirement to review

125.—(1) This section applies where a children's hearing is making, varying or continuing a compulsory supervision order. C.504

(2) Where the order being made contains a movement restriction condition (or the order is being varied so as to include such a condition), the children's hearing must require the order to be reviewed by a children's hearing on a day or within a period specified in the order.

(3) In any other case, the children's hearing may require the order to be so reviewed.

DEFINITIONS
"children's hearing": s.5. C.504.1
"compulsory supervision order": ss.83 and 202(1).
"movement restriction condition": ss.84 and 202(1).

GENERAL NOTE
This section provides for flexibility in the reviewing of a "movement restriction condition". C.504.2
For further discussion, see the annotation to s.84 above.

Contact orders and permanence orders

Review of contact direction

126.—(1) This section applies where, in relation to a child— C.505
  (a) a children's hearing—
    (i) makes a compulsory supervision order,
    (ii) makes an interim compulsory supervision order, an interim variation of a compulsory supervision order or a medical examination order which is to have effect for more than 5 working days, or
    (iii) continues or varies a compulsory supervision order under section 138, and
  (b) the order contains (or is varied so as to contain) a measure of the type mentioned in section 83(2)(g) or 87(2)(e) ("a contact direction").

(2) The Principal Reporter must arrange a children's hearing for the purposes of reviewing the contact direction—

Children's Hearings (Scotland) Act 2011

(a) if an order mentioned in subsection (3) is in force, or
(b) if requested to do so by an individual who claims that the conditions specified for the purposes of this paragraph in an order made by the Scottish Ministers are satisfied in relation to the individual.

(3) The orders are—
(a) a contact order regulating contact between an individual (other than a relevant person in relation to the child) and the child, or
(b) a permanence order which specifies arrangements for contact between such an individual and the child.

(4) The children's hearing is to take place no later than 5 working days after the children's hearing mentioned in subsection (1)(a).

(5) If a children's hearing arranged by virtue of paragraph (b) of subsection (2) considers that the conditions specified for the purposes of that paragraph are not satisfied in relation to the individual, the children's hearing must take no further action.

(6) In any other case, the children's hearing may—
(a) confirm the decision of the children's hearing mentioned in subsection (1)(a), or
(b) vary the compulsory supervision order, interim compulsory supervision order or medical examination order (but only by varying or removing the contact direction).

(7) Sections 73 and 74 do not apply in relation to a children's hearing arranged by virtue of subsection (2).

DEFINITIONS
C.505.1 "chairing member": Sch.1 para.7.
"child": s.199.
"children's hearing": s.5.
"compulsory supervision order": ss.202(1) and 83.
"contact direction": s.41(3).
"contact order": s.202(1) and the Children (Scotland) Act 1995 s.11(2)(d).
"interim variation": ss.202(1) and 140.
"medical examination order": ss.202(1) and 89.
"permanence order": ss.202(1) and the Adoption and Children (Scotland) Act 2007 s.80(2).

GENERAL NOTE
C.505.2 In limited circumstances an individual who is not the child or a relevant person can require the Reporter to arrange a hearing to review a contact direction. The circumstances are that a children's hearing has made a compulsory supervision order (CSO), an interim compulsory supervision order (ICSO), an interim variation of a compulsory supervision order (IVCSO) or a medical examination order (MEO) which will last for more than five days which includes a measure regulating contact *and* either:
(a) There is in force an order for contact between the child and the individual under s.11 of the Children (Scotland) Act 1995 (the 1995 Act) or contact between the child and the individual has been regulated in a permanence order under s.80 of the Adoption and Children (Scotland) Act 2007; or
(b) the individual has or has recently had significant involvement in the upbringing of the child but has not been deemed a relevant person under s.81(3), s.80(3), s.160(4)(b) or s.164 and is not a relevant person under (Children's Hearings (Scotland) Act 2011 (Review of Contact Directions and Definition of Relevant Person) Order 2013 (SSI 2013/193) art.2.

These individuals have no right of attendance at the hearing and no right to appeal a decision of the hearing, thus this section protects the rights of those who have an order from a court regulating their contact with the child. Those who have or have had significant involvement in the upbringing of the child but are not relevant persons are likely to be persons who have not yet had their deemed relevant person status considered by a hearing or pre-hearing panel or those who have chosen not to seek deemed relevant person status. It should be remembered that in *Principal Reporter v K* [2010] UKSC 56, 2011 S.C. (U.K.S.C.) 91, 2011 S.L.T. 271, 2011 1 W.L.R. 18 a person who has established family life with the child is automatically a relevant person and need not rely on this section.

While this goes some way to rectifying the position of persons who have contact with the child but who do not have rights with regard to children's hearings, it does not fully address the problems of those who have an established family life with the child. A person whose contact with the child was regulated in an order by the hearing has no right of appeal and no right to ask for that contact to be regulated unless he or she meets the criteria in subs.(3). In particular siblings or children of the family who are under the age of 16 and whose contact with the child is regulated by a decision of the hearing have no right to request a review of or appeal against such a decision. These children are unlikely to satisfy the conditions in subss.2(b) and (3). A sibling under the age of 16 is unlikely to have an order for contact under s.11 of the 1995 Act, as these are orders relating to parental rights and parental responsibilities and have been held to have been incompetent for those under the age of 16 (*D v H*, 2004 S.L.T. (Sh Ct) 73; 2004 Fam. L.R. 41). It is unusual for a permanence order to contain provision regarding contact given the long-term nature of the order. Notwithstanding the decision in *V v Locality Reporter Manager*, 2012 Fam. L.R. 69 (Stirling Sheriff Court) it is unlikely that a hearing will consider that a child under the age of 16 meets the criteria in subs.2(b). Given the judgment in *Principal Reporter v K* [2010] UKSC 56; 2011 S.C. (U.K.S.C.) 91; 2011 S.L.T. 271, 2011 1 W.L.R. 18 it is submitted that this provision could be open to challenge by a person who has an established family life with the child.

It is surprising that there is no requirement in the Children's Hearings (Scotland) Act 2011 (Rules of Procedure in Children's Hearings) Rules 2013 (SSI 2013/194) (the Procedural Rules) for notification of a contact measure to be given to the individual concerned, but it would be a likely ECHR breach for the Reporter to fail to provide such a notification of the measure, its details, and the individual's right to request a review under this section. The individual would have no right to any other information concerning the child or the other decisions of the hearing. Rule 42 of the Procedural Rules provides for notification of the decision of the s.126 review hearing. Section 144 requires the implementation authority ("IA") (ss.83(1)(b) and 86(1)(b)) to give effect to a compulsory supervision order (which includes an interim order). This means that the IA will be under a duty to ensure that any contact direction is complied with where the child is accommodated. Thus the onus will be on the relevant person where the child resides at home or the local authority, (where the child has been accommodated), to contact the individual to make arrangements for the contact to take place and to make the child available for the ordered contact.

The timescale for a review is very tight. A review may only take place within five working days after the day on which the children's hearing which made the order took place. It should be clearly understood that the review is only of the direction which regulates contact, not of the CSO, ICSO, or IVCSO or any measures included therein. The purpose of the hearing is to review an existing direction and thus cannot be used by an individual, who wishes to have contact with the child, to obtain an order. Procedure at a hearing to review a contact direction is governed by r.74 of the Procedural Rules. The first step is for the hearing to be satisfied that the individual who has requested the review satisfies the conditions in subs.(2)(b) above where an order mention in subs.(3) is not in force. Where the hearing must consider whether the individual has or has recently had substantial involvement in the upbringing of the child, the test must be applied in the same way as when a hearing or pre-hearing panel considers an application for deemed relevant person status; it is a factual test and the welfare of the child should not form any part of the hearing's considerations. Once satisfied that the individual satisfies the conditions in subs.(2)(b) or (3), the hearing must seek the views of the child, any relevant person, any appointed safeguarder, and any individual who satisfies those conditions. Only then may the hearing proceed to making a decision to confirm the decision of the hearing which made, varied or continued the contact direction. The hearing may not make any decision which does not relate to the contact direction but may only: (a) confirm the decision of the hearing which made or continued the contact direction; (b) vary the CSO, ICSO or MEO (but only by varying or removing the contact direction), varied or removed the contact direction. There is no right of appeal. This has been described as

"an inherently suspicious position since the individual who claims to have significant involvement in the upbringing of the child will, if that claim is rejected, have no means of influencing the terms of an order that might ... impinge upon his or her civil rights" (Kenneth McK. Norrie, *Children's Hearings in Scotland*, 3rd edn (Edinburgh: W. Green, 2013), para.13-42)."

Rule 42 of the Procedural Rules governs the arranging by the Reporter of a hearing under this section.

Referral where failure to provide education for excluded pupil

Referral where failure to provide education for excluded pupil

127.—(1) This section applies where it appears to a children's hearing that—
(a) an education authority has a duty under section 14(3) of the Education (Scotland) Act 1980 (c.44) (education authority's duty to provide education for child excluded from school) in relation to the child to whom the children's hearing relates, and
(b) the authority is failing to comply with the duty.

(2) The children's hearing may require the National Convener to refer the matter to the Scottish Ministers.

(3) If a requirement is made under subsection (2), the National Convener must—
(a) make a referral to the Scottish Ministers, and
(b) give a copy of it to the education authority to which it relates and the Principal Reporter.

DEFINITIONS

"child": s.199.
"education authority": Education (Scotland) Act 1980 s.135(1).
"National Convener": s.1.
"Principal Reporter": s.14 and Sch.3 paras 8–10.

GENERAL NOTE

This section applies where a child of school age (whether attending a "school" (as defined in s.135(1) of the Education (Scotland) Act 1980 (the "1980 Act")), or a "special school" (as defined in s.29(1) of the Education (Additional Support for Learning) (Scotland) Act 2004) has been excluded from attendance at school *and* where the education authority responsible for the provision of education for that child has not implemented its duty under s.14(3) of the 1980 Act, namely, to provide alternative education for the child. Where this situation exists, the children's hearing may require the National Convener to make a referral to Scottish Ministers *and* to give a copy of the referral to the education authority responsible for the education of the child.

Several matters should be noted:
(1) Section 1(1) of the 1980 Act imposes a duty on every education authority to provide adequate and efficient provision of school education for their area.
(2) There are only two lawful reasons why a school pupil may be excluded from school and these are set out in reg.4 of the Schools General (Scotland) Regulations 1975 (SI 1975/1135). The reasons are that:
"(a) [the education authority] are of the opinion that the parent of the pupil refuses or fails to comply, or to allow the pupil to comply, with the rules, regulations, or disciplinary requirements of the school; or
(b) [the education authority] consider that in all the circumstances to allow the pupil to continue his attendance at the school would be likely to be seriously detrimental to order and discipline in the school or the educational well-being of the pupils there."
(3) The duty on an education authority to provide education continues even where the child has been excluded from school (see para.61 of *included, engaged and involved part 2: a positive approach to managing school exclusions*, found at http://www.gov.scot/Publications/2011/03/17095258/0 [Accessed 13 February 2017]).
(4) A child who is looked after by a local authority within the meaning of s.17(6) of the Children (Scotland) Act 1995 is deemed to have additional support needs (as defined in s.1 of the Education (Additional Support for Learning) (Scotland) Act 2004), but only if the education authority responsible for that child forms the view that the child or young person is, or is likely to be, unable without the provision of additional support, to benefit from the school education provided.
(5) Over 90 per cent of all school exclusions are for less than one week and the average length of an exclusion is three days (see *Statistical Bulletin: Summary Statistics for Schools in Scotland, No.1 2010 Edition: 1st December, 2010* found at http://www.gov.scot/Publications/2011/03/04154230/0 [Accessed 13 February 2017]). Conse-

Duty to consider applying for parenting order

quently, reference to the provisions of this section is likely to be made in extreme circumstances only.

Subs.(1)
Where it appears to the children's hearing. The authors consider that it would be good practice for the children's hearing to routinely enquire about the education of the child.

C.506.3

Subs.(1)(a) and (b)
There is no ground under s.67(2) of this Act that relates specifically to a child who has been excluded from school and for whom the education authority is failing to comply with its duty under s.14(3) of the 1980 Act. This is because, where a child has been excluded from school in line with the criteria set out in the 1975 Regulations, that absence is considered to be an "authorised absence" (see para.3.1 of *included, engaged and involved part 1: attendance in scottish schools*, found at http://www.gov.scot/Publications/2007/12/05100056/0 [Accessed 13 February 2017]) and, as such, would not be covered by s.67(2)(o)—the child has failed without reasonable excuse to attend regularly at school.

(However, this appears to be inconsistent with s.35(2) of the 1980 Act which states that "a child who has been required to discontinue for any period his attendance at a school on account of his parent's refusal or failure to comply with the rules, regulations or disciplinary requirements of the school, shall, unless the court otherwise determines, be deemed to have failed without reasonable excuse to attend regularly at the school.")

It must be assumed, therefore, that the excluded child has been brought to a children's hearing on one or more s.67(2) grounds for referral and that it has come to the attention of the children's hearing (by whatever means) that the child, at the time of the children's hearing, is excluded from school *and* the education authority responsible for that child is failing to comply with its duty under s.14(3) of the 1980 Act, which states:

"(3) If a pupil withdraws, excluded by the education authority (or with the consent of the authority in circumstances where he would have been so excluded but for his withdrawal), from a public school in their area they shall, without undue delay—
"(a) provide school education for him in a school managed by them;
(b) make arrangements for him to receive such education in any other school the managers of which are willing to receive him; or
(c) make such special arrangements as are mentioned in subsection (1) above."

The duty to provide continuing education to an excluded child is enforceable in law. Consequently, the meaning of "without undue delay" becomes a crucial definition as this will be the trigger for a children's hearing to request that the National Convener refers the matter to the Scottish Ministers under subs.(3). Paragraph 63 (as at time of writing) of *included, engaged and involved part 2* (2011) states:
"It is reasonable to expect alternative education provision after 3 days."

C.506.4

Subs.(2)
This subsection gives the children's hearing discretion as to whether or not to require the National Convener to refer the matter to Scottish Ministers. The decision to follow the requirement will depend on the length of the exclusion and whether or not any alternative education (or plans for alternative education) has been put in place at the time of the hearing.

C.506.5

Subs.(3)(b)
The purpose of giving to the relevant education authority a copy of the referral to Scottish Ministers will serve the purpose of ensuring that the education authority fulfils its duty under s.14 of the 1980 Act.

C.506.6

Parenting order

Duty to consider applying for parenting order

128.—(1) This section applies where a children's hearing constituted for any purpose in respect of a child is satisfied that it might be appropriate for a parenting order to be made in respect of a parent of the child under section 102 of the Antisocial Behaviour etc. (Scotland) Act 2004 (asp 8) (the "2004 Act").

(2) The children's hearing may require the Principal Reporter to consider whether to apply under section 102(3) of the 2004 Act for such an order.

C.507

(3) The children's hearing must specify in the requirement—
(a) the parent in respect of whom it might be appropriate for the order to be made, and
(b) by reference to section 102(4) to (6) of the 2004 Act, the condition in respect of which the application might be made.
(4) In this section, "parent" and "child" have the meanings given by section 117 of the 2004 Act.

DEFINITIONS

C.507.1 "children's hearing": s.5.
"parenting order": Antisocial Behaviour etc. (Scotland) Act 2004 s.103.
"Principal Reporter": s.14 and Sch.3 paras 8–10.

GENERAL NOTE

C.507.2 Parenting orders were introduced with antisocial behaviour orders in the Antisocial Behaviour etc. (Scotland) Act 2004 (the 2004 Act). A parenting order places an obligation on the "parent" to comply with any requirements specified within the order. The circumstances in which an order may be applied for are specified in s.102(3)–(7) of the 2004 Act. When a children's hearing "constituted for whatever reason" is held and the hearing considers that it might be appropriate that a parenting order is made in respect of a parent of the child, the hearing has a duty to require the Principal Reporter to consider making an application under s.102(3) of the 2004 Act. The Principal Reporter is not obliged to make the application. This Act contains no criteria for deciding that a parenting order is appropriate, but as a parenting order is "a matter relating to the child" both the welfare principle and the views of the child principle apply to the decision by the hearing and a court in the case of an appeal and, de facto, to the consideration by the Reporter. It should be noted that the definition of "parent" in s.117 of the 2004 Act is wider than that of relevant person in this Act and includes not only persons with parental rights and parental responsibilities (whether under the Children (Scotland) Act 1995, a permanence order, or adoption) but also an individual who has charge or control over the child (other than by reason only of the individual's employment) which includes kinship carers. A "child", under s.117 of the 2004 Act is defined as a person under 16 years of age. A parenting order could be an alternative to a compulsory supervision order, or could co-exist. Professor Kenneth McK. Norrie points out (*Children's Hearings in Scotland*, 3rd edn (Edinburgh: W. Green, 2013), para.6–20) that a parenting order could be used to ensure the attendance of a relevant person at a hearing as warrants for attendance are only competent with regard to the attendance of the child. Parenting orders are rare. (For rules governing the making of such orders, see r.83 of the Children's Hearings (Scotland) Act 2011 (Rules of Procedure in Children's Hearings) Rules 2013 (SSI 2013/194) (the "Procedural Rules").)

PART 13

REVIEW OF COMPULSORY SUPERVISION ORDER

Requirement for review

Requirement under Antisocial Behaviour etc. (Scotland) Act 2004

C.508 **129.**—(1) Subsection (2) applies where—
(a) under section 12(1A) of the Antisocial Behaviour etc. (Scotland) Act 2004 (asp 8) the sheriff requires the Principal Reporter to arrange a children's hearing in respect of a child, and
(b) a compulsory supervision order is in force in relation to the child.
(2) The Principal Reporter must initiate a review of the compulsory supervision order.

DEFINITIONS

C.508.1 "child": s.199.
"children's hearing": s.5.
"compulsory supervision order": s.83.
"Principal Reporter": s.14 and Sch.3 paras 8–10.

Duty of implementation authority to require review

GENERAL NOTE

Where a sheriff has made an antisocial behaviour order or interim order in respect of a child who is subject to a compulsory supervision order (CSO), the sheriff has the option of making a referral to the Reporter if he or she considers that a s.67(2) ground (other than ground (j)—the child has committed an offence) applies in relation to the child. The Reporter must then initiate a review of the CSO.

It should be noted that, where a CSO is not in force in relation to the child, the sheriff may make a referral to the Reporter on any s.67(2) ground except ground (j), and the Reporter will deal with it in the usual manner.

Case remitted under section 49 of Criminal Procedure (Scotland) Act 1995

130.—(1) This section applies where, in relation to a child—
  (a) a court remits a case under section 49 of the Criminal Procedure (Scotland) Act 1995 to the Principal Reporter to arrange for the disposal of the case by a children's hearing, and
  (b) a compulsory supervision order is in force in relation to the child.

(2) The Principal Reporter must initiate a review of the compulsory supervision order.

(3) A certificate signed by the clerk of the court stating that the child has pled guilty to, or been found guilty of, the offence to which the case relates is conclusive evidence for the purposes of the children's hearing held for the purposes of reviewing the order that the offence was committed by the child.

(4) This Act applies as if the plea of guilty, or the finding of guilt, were a determination of the sheriff under section 108 that the ground in section 67(2)(j) was established in relation to the child.

DEFINITIONS
"child": s.199.
  "children's hearing": s.5.
  "compulsory supervision order" ss.202(1) and 83.
  "Principal Reporter": s.14 and Sch.3 paras 8–10.

GENERAL NOTE

This section deals with the procedure to be followed where a criminal court refers a child who is subject to a compulsory supervision order (CSO) to a children's hearing under s.49 of the Criminal Procedure (Scotland) Act 1995. We have set out the substantial provisions of said s.49 in the General Note to s.71, which deals with such a remit where the child is not subject to a CSO. The reader is referred to our whole discussion of s.71, which applies, mutatis mutandis, here. The particularities are noted below.

Subs.(3)

Since this section deals with a child who is subject to a CSO the Reporter must arrange a review hearing in relation to that order. This will enable the review hearing to make such changes, if any, which may be necessary and appropriate in the light of the criminal conviction.

Subs.(4)

Since the plea of guilty in the criminal court (certified by the clerk of that court under subs.(3)) is by this subsection made equivalent to a ground under s.67(2)(j) having been established by the sheriff, there is no need for the review hearing to put the ground to the child or relevant person(s).

Duty of implementation authority to require review

131.—(1) The implementation authority must, by notice to the Principal Reporter, require a review of a compulsory supervision order in relation to a child where the authority is satisfied that one or more of the circumstances set out in subsection (2) exist.

(2) Those circumstances are—
  (a) the compulsory supervision order ought to be terminated or varied,
  (b) the compulsory supervision order is not being complied with,

(c) the best interests of the child would be served by the authority making one of the following applications, and the authority intends to make such an application—
  (i) an application under section 80 of the Adoption and Children (Scotland) Act 2007 (asp 4) (the "2007 Act") for a permanence order,
  (ii) an application under section 92 of the 2007 Act for variation of such an order,
  (iii) an application under section 93 of the 2007 Act for amendment of such an order,
  (iv) an application under section 98 of the 2007 Act for revocation of such an order,
(d) the best interests of the child would be served by the authority placing the child for adoption and the authority intends to place the child for adoption,
(e) the authority is aware that an application has been made and is pending, or is about to be made, under section 29 or 30 of the 2007 Act for an adoption order in respect of the child.
[1] (f) the authority becomes aware that the child is subject to a compulsory supervision order by virtue of regulations made under section 190 of this Act.

(3) The Scottish Ministers may by regulations specify the period within which a requirement under subsection (1) must be made where the implementation authority is satisfied as to the existence of the circumstances mentioned in subsection (2)(a) to (d).

(4) Different periods may be specified for different circumstances, or classes of circumstances.

(5) Where an implementation authority is under a duty to require a review under subsection (1) by virtue of being satisfied as to the existence of the circumstances mentioned in subsection (2)(e), the authority must do so as soon as practicable after the authority becomes aware of the application.

NOTE

C.510.1 1. Inserted by the Children's Hearings (Scotland) Act 2011 (Transfer of Children to Scotland—Effect of Orders made in England and Wales or Northern Ireland) Regulations 2013 (SSI 2013/99) reg.7(3) (effective 24 June 2013).

DEFINITIONS

C.510.2 "child": s.199.
"compulsory supervision order": ss.202(1) and 83.
"implementation authority": ss.83(1)(b) and 86(1)(b).
"Principal Reporter": s.14 and Sch.3 paras 8–10.

GENERAL NOTE

C.510.3 This section provides for those circumstances under which an Implementation Authority (IA) is obliged to require the Principal Reporter to arrange a hearing to review a compulsory supervision order (CSO). The mechanism is simple—a notice is given to the Reporter who is obliged to arrange a review hearing. Upon receiving notice from the IA that a review is required, the Principal Reporter has a duty to arrange a children's hearing (s.37(1)(a)(ii)) for the purpose of reviewing the CSO (subs.(1) and s.137(a)). The reader is directed to s.137 for provisions relating to the duties of the Reporter in arranging the hearing.

Subs.(2)(a)

C.510.4 The over-arching principles include the minimum intervention principle (s.28(2)), thus a child who does not require protection, guidance, treatment or control should not be subject to a CSO. In addition, a CSO is an interference in the ECHR art.8 rights of the child and his or her family and as such should not continue where not necessary and proportionate. As the IA is under a duty to give effect to a compulsory supervision order (s.144(1)) the IA cannot merely ignore a CSO if it thinks this is no longer needed. While it is a matter of judgment for the IA whether it is likely that the CSO is not required, it is obliged to require a review hearing so that the hearing

Duty of implementation authority to require review

members may make the formal decision as to whether or not the CSO should be terminated. The duty of the IA to give effect to a CSO includes any measures attached to it (s.144(2)). Again it is a matter of professional judgement by the IA as to whether any current measures are no longer needed, or whether other measures may be required for the protection, guidance, treatment or control of the child, but what changes, if any, should be made is the decision of the hearing.

Subs.(2)(b)

This provision applies to those circumstances where the CSO is not being complied with, not through any failure by the IA, but because compliance is not possible for reasons outwith the control of the IA. It may be that compliance is not possible because a required service is not available, however, it is most likely to be that the child, relevant person(s) or other person is not complying with the CSO or any measure attached because compliance is not possible for another reason. Most commonly this concerns measures regulating contact between the child and another person. It may be that the individual has failed to attend for contact, the child is refusing contact, or the behaviour of the individual at contact is such that contact is not in the interests of the child. Where a child remains at home under the CSO and the relevant person(s) with the care of the child refuses or fails to comply with the CSO, the IA will be unable to give effect to it and will consequently require to seek a review hearing as a matter of urgency. As failure by the IA to give effect to the CSO can result in enforcement (s.146), it is necessary to return to the hearing so that it and/or the measure(s) may be reconsidered.

C.510.5

Subs.(2)(c)(i)

Where the IA is satisfied that the interests of the child are best served by applying for a permanence order it must require the Principal Reporter to arrange a review hearing. This hearing serves two purposes. First, to review the CSO to ensure that it reflects the current needs of the child, and secondly to prepare a report giving its advice for the IA and any court that may consider the application. This should not be confused with the advice hearing held under s.95. Professor Kenneth McK. Norrie has provided a clear description of the procedure and the nature of the report (*Children's Hearings in Scotland*, 3rd edn (Edinburgh: W. Green, 2013), paras 12–16 to 12–23). Where the IA is to apply for a variation or amendment of a permanence order or for its revocation, if the child is still subject to a CSO, the hearing will be required to consider the CSO and to provide a report to the IA and court—see s.141(2). It should be noted that s.96 of the Adoption and Children (Scotland) Act 2007 allows a hearing only to vary a CSO on an interim basis while the application is before the court. Note also that s.89(b) and (c) of the Adoption and Children (Scotland) Act 2007 requires the sheriff to make an order ending a CSO on granting a permanence order only if satisfied that it is no longer necessary. Where the CSO arises from concerns regarding the treatment of the child it is normally the case that it is no longer considered necessary. Where the CSO arises from the behaviour of the child it may well be considered that the child is still in need of the protection, guidance, treatment or control provided by the CSO.

C.510.6

Subs.(2)(d) and (e)

Where the IA intends to place a child for adoption, where the child is subject to a CSO, it must require the Principal Reporter to arrange a review hearing. It should be noted that this duty also applies to a registered adoption service which intends to place the child for adoption (s.106 of the Adoption and Children (Scotland) Act 2007). Where the IA becomes aware that an application for adoption is to be made to the court under s.29 (adoption by certain couples) or s.30 (adoption by one person) of the Adoption and Children Scotland Act 2007, the IA must require the Principal Reporter to arrange a review hearing. Subsection 5 below requires that the IA do so as soon as practicable after becoming aware of the application. The hearing to review the CSO must also provide a report in the same way as that for the permanence order in (a), (b) and (c) above.

C.510.7

Subs.(2)(f)

Where the IA becomes aware (through the receipt of a formal notice from the designated authority (England and Wales) or the authority or the education and library board (Northern Ireland) that a child who is subject to an order made in England and Wales or in Northern Ireland (under s.190) is to be transferred into its area, it must require the Principal Reporter to arrange a hearing for the purposes of reviewing the order. The particular provisions are contained in the Children's Hearings (Scotland) Act 2011 (Transfer of Children to Scotland—Effect of Orders made in England and Wales or Northern Ireland) Regulations 2013 (SSI 2013/99). The qualifying orders in England and Wales are all contained in the Children Act 1989

C.510.8

being: a care order made under s.31(1)(a), a supervision order made under s.31(1)(b) or an education supervision order made under s.36(1) (regs 2, 3 and 4). The qualifying orders in Northern Ireland are contained in the Children (Northern Ireland) Order 1995 (SI 1995/775), being a care order made under art.50(1)(a), a supervision order made under art.50(1)(b) or an education supervision order made under art.55(1) (regs 2, 5 and 6). Regulation 7 provides that the orders are to be given effect to in Scotland as if they were CSOs and that the hearing must take place no later than 20 working days after the notice is received by the Principal Reporter (s.137(3A) of this Act). In *In Re X (A Child) and Re Y (A Child)* [2016] EWHC 2271 (Fam.) it was noted that s.25 of the (English) Children Act 1989 did not permit the placement of a child in secure accommodation in Scotland and this led to an application to the *nobile officium* of the Court of Session, reported as *Cumbria County Council, Petitioner* [2016] CSIH 92; 2017 S.L.T. 34. See under s.190(2) for discussion of these cases.

Subs.(3)

C.510.9   This subsection allows the Scottish Government to impose timescales by means of regulations. As at time of writing the authors are not aware of any such regulations beyond those contained in s.137, the Children's Hearings (Scotland) Act 2011 (Transfer of Children to Scotland—Effect of Orders made in England and Wales or Northern Ireland) Regulations 2013 (SSI 2013/194), and in the Children's Hearings (Scotland) Act 2011 (Rules of Procedure in Children's Hearings) Rules 2013 (SSI 2013/99).

Subs.(4)

C.510.10   This section allows for different timescales to be imposed to reflect different circumstances. The authors are not aware of any timescales beyond those contained in s.137, the Children's Hearings (Scotland) Act 2011 (Transfer of Children to Scotland—Effect of Orders made in England and Wales or Northern Ireland) Regulations 2013, and in the Children's Hearings (Scotland) Act 2011 (Rules of Procedure in Children's Hearings) Rules 2013. As the IA cannot be sure at what stage it will become aware of an application under ss.29 or 30 of the Adoption and Children (Scotland) Act 2007 (adoption by certain couples or an individual) it would not be practicable to require a particular time scale. It is sufficient to expect that the IA will require a review hearing as quickly as possible after becoming aware of the application. For further discussion relevant to the Children's Hearings (Scotland) Act 2011 (Transfer of Children to Scotland—Effect of Orders made in England and Wales or Northern Ireland) Regulations 2013 (SSI 2013/194), see under s.190(2).

Right of child or relevant person to require review

C.511   **132.**—(1) This section applies where a compulsory supervision order is in force in relation to a child.

(2) The child may by giving notice to the Principal Reporter require a review of the order.

(3) A relevant person in relation to the child may by giving notice to the Principal Reporter require a review of the order.

(4) The order may not be reviewed—
   (a) during the period of 3 months beginning with the day on which the order is made,
   (b) if the order is continued or varied, during the period of 3 months beginning with the day on which it is continued or varied.

(5) The Scottish Ministers may by regulations provide that, despite subsection (4), where the order includes a secure accommodation authorisation, the order may be reviewed during a period specified in the regulations.

DEFINITIONS

C.511.1   "child": s.199.
"compulsory supervision order": ss.202(1) and 83.
"Principal Reporter": s.14 and Sch.3 paras 8–10.
"relevant person": s.201.
"secure accommodation authorisation": ss.202(1) and 83(5).

GENERAL NOTE

C.511.2   The child and any relevant person (including a deemed relevant person) may require the Reporter to arrange a hearing to review a compulsory supervision order (CSO) and any measures included therein once three calendar months have passed since the hearing that made the order. It will be remembered that while under s.138(3)(c) the Children's hearing may "continue" a CSO, this amounts to making a new CSO—see the judgment of Sheriff J. K. McGowan in *D, Appellant*, 2014 Fam. L.R. 66 at para.[52], discussed below under s.138(3). The Reporter has no discretion, but must arrange a hearing. The day on which the order is made (or continued) is the day at which the "clock starts ticking". Notice that the individual requires that a review hearing is held must be given to the Reporter in writing. Writing includes electronic means assuming, of course, that the Reporter is satisfied that the notice is genuine and provided it is capable of being reproduced in legible form (s.193(2) and (3)(b)) and, if electronic form is used, the communication is to taken to be received on the day it is sent (s.193(4)). As subs.(4) uses the phrasing that "the order may not be reviewed", there is no reason why notice may not be given prior to that date, although the review hearing may not take place until after that date. Thus, if the requirement of a review relates to a hearing which took place on 23 July, the review cannot take place before 22 October. Thus, unless any of ss.133, 134 or 136, apply, new ground(s) of referral are referred to a hearing, or the implementation authority requests a review, a children's hearing cannot take place more often than once every three months. For reviews of contact directions the reader is directed to s.126.

Subs.(5)

Neither the Secure Accommodation (Scotland) Regulations 2013 (SSI 2013/205) ("SA Regs") nor the Children's Hearings (Scotland) Act 2011 (Implementation of Secure Accommodation Authorisation) (Scotland) Regulations 2013 (SSI 2013/212) ("Impl Regs") contains, in the recitals at the beginning of the Regulations, any explicit reference to this subsection, but as they deal with, inter alia, the time limits for fixing reviews, it may be helpful to readers to mention these provisions here. The provisions of these Regulations are complex and highly prescriptive. When issues arise in practice they will require to be scrutinised with care. We will only provide some pointers.

C.511.3

- *Child placed in secure accommodation under CSO containing no secure accommodation authorisation.*
  The chief social work officer must immediately advise the Reporter who must arrange a review within 72 hours of placement (SA Regs, reg.7(4)(b) and (5)).
- *Child placed in secure accommodation where the relevant order [meaning an interim compulsory supervision order (ICSO) or a medical examination order (MEO)] contains no secure accommodation authorisation.*
  The chief social work officer must immediately advise the Reporter who must arrange a review within 72 hours of placement. (SA Regs, reg.8(5)(b) and (6)(a), (b), (e) and (f)). Where an ICSO by a children's hearing and the children's hearing is not permitted to make a further ICSO, the Reporter must apply for an extension or variation thereof (SA Regs, reg.8(6)(c). Where an ICSO has been made by the sheriff the Reporter must apply for an extension thereof within 72 hours of placement in secure accommodation. (SA Regs, reg.8(6)(d)).
- *Looked after child placed in secure accommodation*
  Where a looked after child has been placed in secure accommodation the chief social work officer must immediately inform, inter alios, the Reporter who must, if he considers a CSO is necessary, arrange a children's hearing within 72 (or at most 96) hours of placement. (SA Regs, regs 9(5)(a)(iv) and 10(5) and (6).
- *Child detained under s.44 or 5(1)(a)(ii) of the Criminal Procedure (Scotland) Act 1995*
  A child being held in secure accommodation by virtue of these provisions is entitled to the protections enacted in the SA Regs, regs 11 and 12, which include the provision that the chief social work officer considers that the placement is in the child's best interests (reg.11(2)(b)(i)) and the requirement that the chief social work officer and head of unit review the case within seven days of placement and thereafter (reg.13(1)(a)–(c)).
- *Where the chief social work officer has decided not to implement, or has not implemented, a secure accommodation authorisation*
  Where this occurs the child and/or relevant person may require the chief social work officer to review this decision and the chief social work officer must review this decision within 72 hours (Impl Regs, reg.7(3)) and advise, inter alios, the Reporter of his or her decision (Impl Regs, reg.7(4)(d)).
- *Where the chief social work officer has decided to implement a secure accommodation authorisation but head of unit has not consented*
  Where this occurs the chief social work officer must advise the Reporter, who must arrange a review of the order concerned to take place no more than three working days of receiving this notification, and the hearing may vary the order concerned, but only to the

extent of varying or removing the secure accommodation authorisation. (Impl Regs, regs 8(3) and 9.)
- Where a child is in secure accommodation
Where a child is in secure accommodation by virtue of a decision of the chief social work officer, a review under Impl Regs, reg.7 or a decision of the sheriff under regs 13(3)(a) or 14(3)(a) of Impl Regs, the chief social work officer must keep the matter under review, including holding an initial review within seven days of the placement, and monthly thereafter and when required by the child or a relevant person (Impl Regs, reg.10(1)–(3)).
- Appeals
There are provisions for appeals against decisions of the chief social work officer in relation to secure accommodation (Act, s.162 and Impl Regs, regs (11)–(14)).

Principal Reporter's duty to initiate review

C.512   **133.** The Principal Reporter must initiate a review of a compulsory supervision order in relation to a child if—
(a) the order will expire within 3 months, and
(b) the order would not otherwise be reviewed before it expires.

DEFINITIONS
C.512.1   "child": s.199
"compulsory supervision order": ss.202(1) and 83
"Principal Reporter": s.14 and Sch.3 paras 8 to 10

GENERAL NOTE
C.512.2   A compulsory supervision order (CSO) lasts for no more than 365 days from the day on which it was made or continued (s.83(7)). No CSO can continue after the individual's 18th birthday (s.83(7)). If the order has not been continued before that date, it ceases to have effect. When a CSO has ceased to have effect then, provided the age requirements are met, the person could only be brought to a hearing if new circumstances arose to which grounds of referral were applicable and which indicated a need for a CSO. This section requires the Reporter to ensure that he or she starts the process of arranging an "annual" review prior to the date when the CSO is within three months of expiration unless the order is to be otherwise reviewed.

Duty to initiate review if child to be taken out of Scotland

C.513   **134.**—(1) This section applies where—
(a) a child is subject to a compulsory supervision order,
(b) a relevant person in relation to the child proposes to take the child to live outwith Scotland, and
(c) the proposal is not in accordance with the order or an order under section 11 of the 1995 Act.

(2) The relevant person must give notice of the proposal to the Principal Reporter and the implementation authority at least 28 days before the day on which the relevant person proposes to take the child to live outwith Scotland.

(3) If the Principal Reporter receives notice under subsection (2), the Principal Reporter must initiate a review of the compulsory supervision order.

DEFINITIONS
C.513.1   "child": s.199
"compulsory supervision order": ss.202(1) and 83
"implementation authority": ss.83(1)(b) and 86(1)(b)
"Principal Reporter": s.14 and Sch.3 paras 8–10
"relevant person": s.201

GENERAL NOTE
C.513.2   Where a child is subject to a compulsory supervision order (CSO), and a relevant person wishes to take the child to live outwith Scotland (not merely for a holiday or brief visit) unless it is in accordance with the CSO or an order under s.11 of the Children (Scotland) Act 1995, he or she may not do so until a review hearing has been held and a children's hearing agrees with the move. Subsection (2) imposes a duty on the relevant person who proposes to take the child

Duty to initiate review: secure accommodation authorisation

outwith Scotland to give both the Reporter and the implementation authority (IA) a minimum of 28 days' notice of his or her intention to do so. Notice should be in writing, but may be accepted by electronic means if the Reporter and IA are satisfied that that notice is genuine and is capable of being reproduced in legible form (s.193(2) and (3)(b) and, if electronic form is use, the communication is taken to be received on the day it is sent (s.193(4)). The Reporter has no discretion as to whether to arrange a review hearing. If notice is not given by the relevant person and the IA becomes aware of the plan to take the child from Scotland, the authority should require a review under subs.2 above. The jurisdiction of the children's hearing is limited to Scotland. A child may remain subject to a CSO while accommodated elsewhere in the United Kingdom, as for the purposes of the CSO his or her "habitual residence" will remain that of the IA, but when the child is resident with a relevant person (outwith Scotland) it may result in a change of "habitual residence" and thus removal from the jurisdiction of the children's hearing, and thus lead to a frustration of the CSO.

This Act imposes no sanction on a person who removes a child without complying with the provisions of this section but see suggestion that this may constitute "wrongful removal" under the Hague Convention in Kenneth McK. Norrie *Children's Hearings in Scotland*, 3rd edn (Edinburgh: W. Green, 2013) at para.13–18, p.228, fn.72.

Duty to initiate review: secure accommodation authorisation

135.—(1) Subsection (2) applies where a compulsory supervision order includes a secure accommodation authorisation (which has not ceased to have effect by virtue of section 151(5)). C.514

(2) The Principal Reporter must initiate a review of the order—
   (a) before the end of the period of 3 months beginning with the day on which the order is made, and
   (b) if the order is varied or continued, before the end of the period of 3 months beginning with the day on which it is varied or continued.

DEFINITIONS
"child": s.199 C.514.1
"compulsory supervision order": ss.202(1) and 83
"Principal Reporter": s.14 and Sch.3 paras 8–10
"secure accommodation authorisation": ss.202(1) and 83(5)

GENERAL NOTE
Where a compulsory supervision order (CSO) includes authorisation for secure accommodation, the authorisation has been implemented (s.151) and the child has not been removed from secure accommodation (s.151(4)), the CSO must be reviewed before the end of three calendar months. The relevant period starts with the day on which the order is made, varied or continued, which is aimed at preserving the rights of the child. The deprivation of liberty which results from the keeping of a child in secure accommodation is such that it is appropriate that it be kept under regular review to ensure that it is still necessary. When considering placement of the child in secure accommodation the chief social work officer must, inter alia, take into account the views of: the child (subject to age and maturity); each relevant person; and the head of unit; and assess whether placement in secure accommodation would be in the child's best interests: Children's Hearings (Scotland) Act 2011 (Implementation of Secure Accommodation Authorisation) (Scotland) Regulations 2013 (SSI 2013/212) reg.4(3)(a) and (b)(ii). While the child is in secure accommodation, the managers, in consultation with the head of the unit, must ensure that the welfare of the child so placed and kept is safeguarded and promoted: Secure Accommodation (Scotland) Regulations 2013 (SSI 2013/205) reg.4. C.514.2

It will be remembered that the chief social worker has a duty under s.151(4) to remove the child from secure accommodation if he or she considers that it is no longer necessary for the child to be kept there. A review should be requested under s.131(2)(a). Where a CSO contains authorisation for secure accommodation, the right of the child and relevant persons to require a review under s.132 becomes unnecessary, as a review hearing will take place. It does not affect the right of review of a contact direction under s.126.

Duty to initiate review where child transferred

C.515 **136.**—The Principal Reporter must initiate a review of a compulsory supervision order in relation to a child where the child is transferred under section 143(2).

DEFINITIONS
C.515.1 "child": s.199
"Principal Reporter": s.14 and Sch.3 paras 8–10

GENERAL NOTE
C.515.2 Where the child is transferred in cases of urgent necessity (s.143(2)) the Reporter must arrange a review hearing. This places a duty on the Implementation Authority (IA) to notify the Reporter urgently as the timescale is very tight, being three working days beginning with the day that the child is transferred (s.137(3)). It must be remembered that a compulsory supervision order (or interim compulsory supervision order or interim variation of a compulsory supervision order) may include a measure regulating the residence of the child (s.83(2)(a)) and that measure will specify the address at which the child is to reside. The IA is under a duty to comply with an order made by a hearing (s.144) thus, where the welfare of the child urgently requires that he or she be moved, it is necessary that a children's hearing consider whether the move is in the interests of the child, and to make a decision regarding his or her residence. This section does not apply where the order does not specify the residence of the child as in the case of a child protection order or an interim order which does not specify the place of safety. Rule 36 of the Rules of Procedure governs the provision of information for a review hearing under this section.

Functions of Principal Reporter and children's hearing

Duty to arrange children's hearing

C.516 **137.**—(1) This section applies where a compulsory supervision order is in force in relation to a child and—
  (a) a review of the order is required or initiated by virtue of any of—
    (i) sections 107, 108, 115 and 117 (all as modified by section 118),
    (ii) sections 116, 125, 129 to 136 and 146, or
  (b) the child's case is referred to the Principal Reporter under section 96(3) or 106 of the Adoption and Children (Scotland) Act 2007 (asp 4).

(2) The Principal Reporter must arrange a children's hearing to review the compulsory supervision order.

(3) If the review is initiated under section 136, the children's hearing must be arranged to take place before the expiry of the period of 3 working days beginning with the day on which the child is transferred.

¹ (3A) If the review is initiated under section 131(2)(f) the children's hearing must be arranged to take place no later than 20 working days after notice is given to the Principal Reporter under s.131(1).

(4) The Principal Reporter must require the implementation authority to give the Principal Reporter any reports that the authority has prepared in relation to the child and any other information which the authority may wish to give to assist the children's hearing.

(5) The Principal Reporter may require the implementation authority to give the Principal Reporter a report on—
  (a) the child generally,
  (b) any particular matter relating to the child specified by the Principal Reporter.

(6) The implementation authority may include in a report given to the Principal Reporter under subsection (4) or (5) information given to the authority by another person.

Powers of children's hearing on review

NOTE
Inserted by the Children's Hearings (Scotland) Act 2011 (Transfer of Children to Scotland—Effect of Orders made in England and Wales or Northern Ireland) Regulations 2013 (SSI 2013/99) reg. 7(4) (effective 24 June 2013).

DEFINITIONS
"child": s.199
"chief social work officer: s.202(1)
"children's hearing": s.5
"compulsory supervision order": s.202(1) and s.83
"implementation authority": s.83(1)(b) and s.86(1)(b)
"Principal Reporter": s.14 and Sch.3 paras 8–10

C.516.1

GENERAL NOTE
This section lists the circumstances in which the Reporter is required to arrange a hearing to review a compulsory supervision order (CSO) other than under ss.129 to 136. Timescales are only provided for in two instances: subs.(3) where the child is transferred in cases of urgent necessity (s.136); and where an order made outwith Scotland has been given effect to as if it was a CSO (s.190). The former is very tight, being only three working days beginning on the day that the child is transferred, and the latter being 20 working days beginning with the day on which the Reporter has received notice under s.190. Rule 35 of the Children's Hearings (Scotland) Act 2011 (Rules of Procedure in Children's Hearings) Rules 2013 (SSI 2013/194) (the "Procedural Rules") governs the information to be given to the members of the hearing by the Reporter.

The hearing must be provided with any reports that the implementation authority ("IA") has prepared regarding the child. The Reporter has no discretion as to whether to ask for the reports, and the IA has no discretion as to whether or not to provide them (subs.4). The Reporter may also decide whether to ask for other information from the IA and may specify what information is required. The IA must comply. The IA may also provide any other information that is considered by it to be of assistance to the hearing and it is interesting to note that the IA is particularly empowered to provide information received from a third party (subs.6).

It should also be noted that regs 7 to 9 of the Secure Accommodation (Scotland) Regulations 2013 (SSI 2013/205) (the "SA Regs") empower the placement of a child in secure accommodation who is: subject to a CSO; interim compulsory supervision order; or medical examination order which does not contain authorisation for secure accommodation; accommodated by the local authority under s.25 of the Children (Scotland) Act 1995; or subject to a permanence order (see s.80 of Adoption and Children (Scotland) Act 2007). The child may only be accommodated in secure accommodation if both the chief social work officer and the head of the unit are satisfied that one of the conditions in reg.4 applies (these are identical to the conditions in s.83(6) of this Act) and that placement there is in the best interests of the child. Within 24 hours of the placement the child's case must be referred to the Reporter. The Principal Reporter must review the case in accordance with reg.7(5) of the SA Regs within 72 hours. If he or she decides that no hearing is necessary the child must be removed from secure accommodation. In the event of a referral and information that a looked after child, or a child subject to a permanence order, having been placed in secure accommodation being notified to the Reporter under reg.9(5)(b) of the SA Regs, and the Reporter determines (under SA Regs, reg.10(5)) that a CSO is necessary then the hearing should be held within 72 hours of the child's placement under reg.9, unless it is not reasonable, in which case a further 24 hours is permitted (reg.10(6)). Rule 34 of the procedural rules governs the information to be given to the child and relevant person(s) for a hearing arranged under this section. Rule 35 governs the information to be given to the hearing under this section.

C.516.2

Powers of children's hearing on review

138.—(1) This section applies where a children's hearing is carrying out a review of a compulsory supervision order in relation to a child.

(2) If the children's hearing considers that it is appropriate to do so, the children's hearing may defer making a decision about the compulsory supervision order until a subsequent children's hearing under this section.

(3) Otherwise, the children's hearing may—
   (a) terminate the compulsory supervision order,
   (b) vary the compulsory supervision order,

C.517

(c) continue the compulsory supervision order for a period not exceeding one year.

(4) The children's hearing may vary or continue a compulsory supervision order only if the children's hearing is satisfied that it is necessary to do so for the protection, guidance, treatment or control of the child.

(5) [*Repealed by the Children's Hearings (Scotland) Act 2011 (Modification of Primary Legislation) Order 2013 (SSI 2013/211) Sch.2 (effective June 24 2013).*]

(6) If the children's hearing terminates the compulsory supervision order, the children's hearing must—
  (a) consider whether supervision or guidance is needed by the child, and
  (b) if so, make a statement to that effect.

(7) If the children's hearing states that supervision or guidance is needed by the child, it is the duty of the relevant local authority for the child to give such supervision or guidance as the child will accept.

(8) Subsection (9) applies where—
  (a) a child or relevant person in relation to the child is excused under section 73(2), 74(2) or 79 from attending the children's hearing, and
  (b) the hearing defers its decision until a subsequent children's hearing.

(9) The children's hearing need not excuse the child or relevant person in relation to the child from attending the subsequent children's hearing.

DEFINITIONS

C.517.1 "child": s.199
"children's hearing": s.5
"compulsory supervision order": s.202(1) and s.83
"local authority": Local Government (Scotland) Act 1994 s.2
"relevant local authority": s.201
"relevant person": s.201

GENERAL NOTE

C.517.2 It is an essential feature of the children's hearings system to provide for a continuing overview of the child's progress and consequently the powers given to a review hearing entitle that hearing fully to consider the child's current position and to obtain such up-to-date information as it thinks may be necessary.

Subs.(1)
C.517.3 The procedure is governed by r.60 of the Children's Hearings (Scotland) Act 2011 (Rules of Procedure in Children's Hearings) Rules 2013 (SSI 2013/194) (the "Procedural Rules").

Subs.(2)
C.517.4 This allows a hearing to continue the making of a substantive decision to another date where it is considered appropriate. It allows the hearing to obtain further information, which is considered necessary to enable a substantive decision to be made. The ethos of the children's hearing system is one of avoiding delay in making a decision, hence the requirement that deferral must be appropriate.

Subs.(3)
C.517.5 In reviewing a compulsory supervision order (CSO), if the hearing has not deferred the decision it may terminate, vary or continue the CSO. Although the language of the section is "continue", in effect the hearing is issuing a new CSO albeit that it may contain identical measures. Thus the test, contained in subs.(4) is the same as that in s.91(3)(a). The relevant period remains one year beginning on the day *after* the day on which the order is made, *or* the day on which the child attains 18 years of age (s.83(7)(a)).

Subs.(4)(a) and (b)
C.517.6 The test that the hearing must apply in making a decision about whether to continue, vary or terminate a CSO is the same as that in ss.91(3) and 119(3), and the overarching principles will apply. In the case of *D, Appellant*, 2014 Fam. L.R. 66; 2014 G.W.D. 21-405 Sheriff McGowan states that

Powers of children's hearing on deferral under section 138

"it would appear unlikely that the necessary preconditions for the continuing of a supervision requirement would be less stringent than the preconditions necessary for the making of a supervision requirement in the first place. After all, on one view, in *continuing* a supervision requirement the Panel is still *making* a supervision requirement." [Emphasis is the Sheriff's.]

That appeal concerned an order made under the Children (Scotland) Act 1995 (hence the language) but it is equally applicable to this Act. In continuing the CSO, as has been said, the hearing is making a new CSO and therefore should give consideration as to whether any measures contained are still justified in current circumstances, and whether the needs of the child require variation.

[*Subs(5) repealed on amendment*]

Subs.(6)

If the hearing decides that the CSO is no longer necessary and should not be continued, it must then consider whether the child needs supervision or guidance and if so, make a statement to that effect. In practical terms this means that there is a duty on a hearing on terminating a CSO to consider whether the child requires further help. As this imposes a duty on the relevant local authority to provide that support, the hearing should include the statement in its written reasons with details of the sort of supervision or guidance considered necessary. It should be understood that the statement is not a "decision" since there is no further involvement of the hearing system in the child's life. There is no requirement that the child accept the supervision or guidance (see subs.7 below). There is no appeal re the contents of the statement.

C.517.7

Subs.(7)

Where the hearing has decided to terminate the CSO and has stated that the child is in need of supervision and guidance, the local authority relevant to the child has a duty to provide it. There is no duty on the child or relevant persons to accept that support. It should be noted that the relevant local authority for the child post-CSO may not be the same as the local authority which was responsible for implementing the CSO (the implementation authority). In any case the local authority for the child has duties to the child as a former "looked after" child (cf. Support and Assistance of Young People Leaving Care (Scotland) Regulations 2003 (SSI 2003/608)).

C.517.8

Subs.(8) and (9)

Where a hearing is reviewing a CSO and the child or a relevant person has been excused from attending that review hearing, and it is the decision of that review hearing to defer its decision, the original excusal applies to the deferred hearing and there is no need to excuse the child or relevant person from the subsequent hearing. The hearing can however require the child or relevant person to attend the subsequent hearing and is not bound by the previous decision to excuse. It should be remembered that even if a child has been excused from a hearing, he or she still has a right to attend, and may attend by telephone or electronic means (r.19 of the Procedural Rules).

C.517.9

Powers of children's hearing on deferral under section 138

139.—(1) This section applies where under subsection (2) of section 138 a children's hearing defers making a decision about the compulsory supervision order in relation to a child until a subsequent children's hearing under that section.

C.518

(2) The children's hearing may continue the compulsory supervision order until the subsequent children's hearing.

(3) If the children's hearing considers that the nature of the child's circumstances is such that for the protection, guidance, treatment or control of the child it is necessary as a matter of urgency that the compulsory supervision order be varied, the children's hearing may make an interim variation of the compulsory supervision order.

DEFINITIONS
"child": s.199
"children's hearing": s.5
"compulsory supervision order": ss.202(1) and 83
"interim variation of a compulsory supervision order": ss.202 (1) and 140

C.518.1

GENERAL NOTE
C.518.2   This section applies where a child is already subject to a compulsory supervision order (CSO) and the hearing arranged to review the CSO has deferred making a decision. The section provides the hearing with two choices. The first is to continue the CSO. On the face of it this may seem unnecessary as the child is already subject to a CSO that will subsist if not continued until the subsequent hearing; however, where deferring the hearing could result in the CSO terminating due to the relevant period passing, continuing the CSO will avoid the problem. The second choice is to vary the CSO on an interim basis: making an interim variation of a compulsory supervision order (IVCSO). The test for making an IVCSO is largely the same as that for making, continuing or varying a CSO: that the child is in need of protection, guidance, treatment or control and that making the order is necessary. However in addition there is a requirement that variation is required as a matter of urgency for the protection, guidance, treatment or control of the child. If it is not an urgent need, then any variation should be deferred until the subsequent hearing. The duration of the IVCSO is specified in s.140(4).

Interim variation of compulsory supervision order

C.519   **140.**—(1) In this Act, "interim variation", in relation to a compulsory supervision order made in relation to a child, means a variation of the order having effect for the relevant period.

(2) An interim variation may vary the order so that, instead of specifying a place or places at which the child is to reside under section 83(2)(a), the order specifies that the child is to reside at any place of safety away from the place where the child predominantly resides.

(3) Section 83(5)(a) does not apply to the varied order.

(4) In subsection (1), the "relevant period" means the period beginning with the variation of the order and ending with whichever of the following first occurs—

(a) the next children's hearing arranged in relation to the child,
(b) the disposal by the sheriff of an application made by virtue of section 93(2)(a) or 94(2)(a) relating to the child,
(c) a day specified in the variation,
(d) the expiry of the period of 22 days beginning with the day on which the order is varied.

NOTE
C.519.1   1. As amended by the Children's Hearings (Scotland) Act 2011 (Modification of Primary Legislation) Order 2013 (SSI 2013/211) Sch.1 para.20(13) (effective June 24 2013).

DEFINITIONS
C.519.2   "child": s.199
"children's hearing": s.5
"compulsory supervision order": ss.202(1) and 83
"place of safety": ss.202(1) and 189

GENERAL NOTE
C.519.3   Under the Children (Scotland) Act 1995, where a hearing was reviewing a supervision requirement, and deferred a decision, then, unless a place of safety warrant was justified, no interim changes could be made. The interim variation of a compulsory supervision order (IVCSO) replaces the place of safety warrant of the Children (Scotland) Act 1995 s.69.

Subs.(1)
C.519.4   The term "interim variation" has the specific meaning of a variation of a compulsory supervision order that has effect for a relevant period. The definition of relevant period is contained in subs.(4).

Subs.(2)
C.519.5   Where a compulsory supervision order (CSO), which contains a measure regulating the residence of the child, it must specify the place at which the child must live, the IVCSO, which is designed to deal with an urgent need, need not specify the place of safety. In this respect the IVCSO replaces the place of safety warrant under s.69 of the Children (Scotland) Act 1995.

Preparation of report in circumstances relating to permanence order

Where necessary in the circumstances the order may simply require the child to reside at "a place of safety". A place of safety must not include the place at which the child is ordinarily resident. The reader is directed to s.202(1), when read with s.189, for the definition of a place of safety.

Subs.(3)

An interim variation of a CSO may include authorisation for secure accommodation but this subsection provides that the limitations contained in s.83(5)(a) do not apply. Where authorisation for secure accommodation is to be considered, the child should be provided with legal representation.

Subs.(4)

It is clear that an IVCSO is intended to last for as short a term as is possible. The "relevant period" is the shortest of the options which are: until the start of the next children's hearing; the disposal of an appeal to the sheriff under Pt 10 of this Act; a day specified in the order; the end of a period of 22 days which starts on the day that the IVCSO is made. No more than three such orders may be made (s.87 of the Children and Young People (Scotland) Act 2014). It should be noted that the sheriff is not limited in the number of orders that can be made (ss.98 and 99 of this Act).

Preparation of report in circumstances relating to permanence order or adoption

141.—(1) This section applies where a review of a compulsory supervision order in relation to a child is required under subsection (1) of section 131 in the circumstances mentioned in subsection (2)(c), (d) or (e) of that section.

(2) On determining the review under section 138(3), the children's hearing must prepare a report providing advice about the circumstances to which the review relates for—

(a) the implementation authority, and

(b) any court that requires (or may subsequently require) to come to a decision about an application of the type mentioned in section 131(2)(c) or (e).

(3) The report must be in such form as the Scottish Ministers may determine.

(4) If an application of the type mentioned in section 131(2)(c) or (e) is (or has been) made, the court must have regard to the report when coming to its decision about the application.

DEFINITIONS
"child": s.199
"children's hearing": s.5
"compulsory supervision order": ss.83 and 202(1)
"implementation authority": s.83(1)(b) and s.86(1)(b)
"permanence order": s.202(1) and Adoption and Children (Scotland) Act 2007 s.80(2)

GENERAL NOTE

This section applies where the local authority: is intending to apply to the court for the granting, varying or amending of a permanence order (s.131(c)); intends to place the child for adoption (s.131(d)); or is aware that an application is pending or about to be made under ss.29 or 30 of the Adoption and Children (Scotland) Act 2007 (asp 4) (s.131(e)). The Reporter is required to arrange a review of the CSO (s.137). The hearing must, on determining that review, provide advice to the implementation authority and the court. The advice contained in that report must be given regard to by the court in determining the application, but is not binding upon it. The required content of the report is contained in reg.3 of the Adoption and Children (Scotland) Act 2007 (Compulsory Supervision Order Reports in Applications for Permanence Orders) Regulations 2014 (SSI 2014/113).

Review of relevant person determination

Review of determination that person be deemed a relevant person

C.521 **142.**—(1) This section applies where, in relation to a child—
(a) a children's hearing determines a review of a compulsory supervision order by varying or continuing the order,
(b) an individual is deemed to be a relevant person by virtue of section 81, and
(c) it appears to the children's hearing that the individual may no longer have (nor recently have had) a significant involvement in the upbringing of the child.

[1] (1A) But this section does not apply where the matter of whether the individual should continue to be deemed to be a relevant person in relation to the child—
(a) has been determined by a meeting of a pre-hearing panel held in relation to the children's hearing, or
(b) is, by virtue of section 80(3), to be determined by the children's hearing.

(2) The children's hearing must review whether the individual should continue to be deemed to be a relevant person in relation to the child.

(3) If the children's hearing considers that it is appropriate to do so, the children's hearing may defer determining the review under subsection (2) until a subsequent children's hearing under this section.

(4) Otherwise, if the children's hearing determines that the individual does not have (and has not recently had) a significant involvement in the upbringing of the child then—
(a) the children's hearing must direct that the individual is no longer to be deemed to be a relevant person, and
(b) section 81(4) ceases to apply in relation to the individual (except in relation to any appeal arising from the determination mentioned in subsection (1)(a)).

NOTE

C.521.1 1. Inserted by the Children and Young People (Scotland) Act 2014 (asp 8) Sch.5 para.12(7) (effective 26 January 2015).

DEFINITIONS

C.521.2 "child": s.199
"children's hearing": s.5
"compulsory supervision order": ss.83 and 202(1)
"relevant person": s.201
"pre-hearing panel": ss.79(2) and 202(1)

GENERAL NOTE

C.521.3 The provisions of this section reflect a concern that an individual should only be deemed to be a relevant person while he or she continues to meet the criterion of having or having recently had substantial involvement in the upbringing of the child. This section does not, of course, apply to persons who are automatically considered to be relevant persons (s.200 as amended). It is important to understand that this section only applies where an individual has already been deemed to be a relevant person by a previous hearing or a pre-hearing panel with the exception of a pre-hearing panel held in relation to the current hearing. The child, relevant person(s), and the individual concerned each has a right to appeal a decision made under this section to the sheriff (s.160). The cases of *MF and GF, Appellants* (sometimes referred to as *F & F, Appellants*), 2014 Fam. L. R. 57 (sub nom. *F v Principal Reporter*, 2014 Fam. L.B. 29-6) and *CF v MF & GF and Scottish Reporter* [2017] CSIH 44, discussed above under s.81(3), are relevant here.

Subs.(1) and (1A)

C.521.4 The section does not apply where a pre-hearing panel has already considered the question—

Review of determination that person be deemed a relevant person

which means prior to the hearing, not in the past. Thus where the individual's deemed relevant person status has been considered by a pre-hearing panel held prior to the hearing, the hearing may not revisit that decision. It also does not apply where the matter has been referred to the hearing under s.80(3). This section permits the hearing to consider *ex proprio motu* whether an individual should continue to be deemed to be a relevant person without the question having being referred to them by the Reporter (s.79(2)(b)), at the request of the child (s.79(2)(a)(ii)), a relevant person (s.79(2)(a)(i), the individual (s.79(2)(a)(iii)) or the safeguarder (s.79(3)). The practical result is that where s.80(3) requires the hearing to consider the matter of deemed relevant person status at the start of the hearing, this section allows it to be considered during the hearing if the question arises where a referral has not been made. If the question does arise, the hearing should consider it immediately.

Subs.(2)

Where it appears to the hearing that the individual no longer fits the criterion (s.1(c)), which is identical to that in s.81(3), they must review that person's deemed relevant person status. In *MF and GF, Appellants*, above, a sheriff had held that s previous pre-hearing panel's decision prevented a later panel from re-considering the information on which the earlier panel had relied. In *CF v MF & GF and Scottish Reporter*, above, the Court of Session disapproved this and commented at para [53] of its opinion that it supported the proposition that an earlier decision should be regarded as "a material fact of real importance" but not regarded as an absolute bar to consideration of information concerning the period before the decision; the Court concluded: "There is no rigid system of *res judicata*".

In reviewing an individual's relevant person status, the hearing must apply the same test to the same standard. Where the individual is no longer deemed to be a relevant person he or she will lose all of the rights attached to that status and s.81(4) will no longer apply. The individual has the right to appeal the decision to the sheriff court, as does the child and relevant person(s) (s.160). The reader is referred back to the annotation for s.81A for the pre-hearing panel's power to end deemed relevant person's status.

C.521.5

Subs.(3)

The hearing does have the power to defer the decision to a subsequent hearing. Where the individual concerned is not present, it would be obviously unjust to consider the question of his or her relevant person status and the hearing should defer the decision. It may also be necessary to defer where the individual concerned feels that he or she has had insufficient notice and requires time to prepare or where other persons such as the child or other relevant person(s) are not present and who have a right to a view on the question. In the case of *F & F, Appellants*, above, the grandfather of the children was not present at the hearing which considered and removed his deemed relevant person status, nor were the children who were old enough to express a view on the matter. Sheriff Reid at paras 63–64 observed that

"the hearing should not have proceeded to determine the section 142(2) review ... instead the hearing should have exercised its power under s.142(3) ... to defer a decision...".

Where the decision has been deferred, it would not be necessary for a pre-hearing panel to be convened to consider the question. The rights of the individual as a deemed relevant person will subsist until the question is considered at the subsequent hearing. The matter would be considered at a subsequent hearing rather than a pre-hearing panel prior to the subsequent hearing thus avoiding unnecessary procedures.

C.521.6

Subs.(4)

Where the hearing has applied the test and decides that the individual no longer meets the criterion they must end the deemed relevant person status. From that point the individual loses all rights under s.81(4). As with the original decision this is a purely factual test and the welfare principle does not apply. Where the hearing considers that the individual does continue to meet the criterion there is no need to make a decision to continue the status. Thus the decision is purely one as to whether to end deemed relevant person status. It should be noted that a hearing under this section may only consider removing *deemed* relevant person status. There is no power under this section to interfere with relevant person status which arises as a matter for law: see discussions in Preliminary General Note to s.160 and General Note to s.200.

C.521.7

Part 14

Implementation of Orders

Power to transfer child in cases of urgent necessity

Transfers in cases of urgent necessity

C.522   **143.**—(1) Subsection (2) applies where a child is residing at a particular place by virtue of a compulsory supervision order or interim compulsory supervision order containing a measure of the type mentioned in section 83(2)(a).

(2) If it is in the interests of the child or another child in the place that the child be moved out of the place as a matter of urgent necessity then, despite the order, the chief social work officer may transfer the child to another place.

Definitions

C.522.1   "chief social work officer": s.202(1).
"child": s.199.
"compulsory supervision order": ss.202(1) and 83.
"interim compulsory supervision order": ss.202 (1) and 86.
"measures": s.83.

General Note

C.522.2   An implementation authority (IA) (see ss.83(1)(b) and 86(1)(b)) is obliged to comply with an order by a children's hearing (see s.144) and thus may only remove a child from a place specified by a measure included in a compulsory supervision order (including an interim variation of a compulsory supervision order) or an interim compulsory supervision order if there is an urgent need to do so. Situations which may lead to this include:
   (a) sudden breakdown of the placement;
   (b) damage to the premises which render them unsuitable for the child; or
   (c) death or serious illness of a carer.

Should an urgent situation arise the IA may move the child but must require the Reporter to arrange a review hearing under s.131(2). It should be noted that the urgency may relate to another child at the placement who may be another accommodated child or a child of the household.

Implementation of compulsory supervision order

Implementation of compulsory supervision order: general duties of implementation authority

C.523   **144.**—(1) The implementation authority must give effect to a compulsory supervision order.

(2) The implementation authority must in particular comply with any requirements imposed on it in relation to the child by the compulsory supervision order.

(3) The duties which an implementation authority may be required to carry out under a compulsory supervision order include securing or facilitating the provision for the child of services of a kind which the implementation authority does not provide.

Definitions

C.523.1   "child": s.199.
"compulsory supervision order": s. 202(1) and s.83.
"implementation authority": ss.202(1), 83(1)(b) and 86(1)(b).

General Note

C.523.2   The implementation authority (IA) is the local authority which has been specified in a compulsory supervision order (including an interim variation of compulsory supervision order) or an interim compulsory supervision order as being responsible for implementing the order.

Breach of duties imposed by sections 144 and 145

The order includes any measures included therein (see s.83). Subsection (3) includes a responsibility to obtain or facilitate services which the IA does not provide and therefore may have to be obtained elsewhere. This could include specialist educational provision. Section 146 deals with breaches of this duty. The resources of the IA should not dictate the services available to the child. The paramount consideration remains the welfare of the child (s.25).

Duty where order requires child to reside in certain place

145.—(1) Subsection (2) applies where, under a compulsory supervision order, a child is required to reside—
  (a) in accommodation provided by the parents or relatives of the child, or by any person associated with them or the child, or
  (b) in any other accommodation not provided by a local authority.
(2) The implementation authority must from time to time—
  (a) investigate whether, while the child is resident in that accommodation, any conditions imposed under the compulsory supervision order are being complied with, and
  (b) if the authority considers that conditions are not being complied with, take such steps as the authority considers reasonable.

DEFINITIONS
  "child": s.199.
  "compulsory supervision order": s.202(1) and s.83.
  "implementation authority: ss.202(1), 83(1)(b) and 86(1)(b).
  "local authority": Local Government (Scotland) Act 1994, s.2.

GENERAL NOTE
  Where a child's place of residence is regulated by a compulsory supervision order (CSO) and is not accommodation which is provided by a local authority (which may be in an area outwith the implementation authority (IA), the IA has a duty to ensure that any conditions imposed by the CSO are being complied with. It will be remembered that the measure attached to the CSO regulating the residence of the child will specify a place of residence rather than residence with a particular person or persons. These conditions may be that specified persons are not resident within the premises, or that that particular equipment is provided. Subsection (4) allows the IA to take such steps as are reasonable to fulfil the condition(s). The local authority will need, also, to be satisfied that the child is actually resident in the place specified. This may include installing specialist equipment to meet the needs of the child. This section will apply to the family home, kinship care, and non-local authority foster care.

Breach of duties imposed by sections 144 and 145

146.—(1) This section applies where, on determining the review of a compulsory supervision order under section 138(3), it appears to the children's hearing that the implementation authority is in breach of a duty in relation to the child imposed on the authority under section 144 or 145.
(2) The children's hearing may direct the National Convener to give the authority notice in accordance with subsection (3) of an intended application by the National Convener to enforce the authority's duty.
(3) The notice must—
  (a) set out the respects in which the authority is in breach of its duty in relation to the child, and
  (b) state that if the authority does not perform that duty before the expiry of the period of 21 days beginning with the day on which the notice is given, the National Convener, on the direction of the children's hearing, is to make an application to enforce the authority's duty.
(4) The National Convener must, at the same time as giving the notice, send a copy of the notice to—
  (a) the child,
  (b) each relevant person in relation to the child.
(5) If a children's hearing gives a direction under subsection (2), the

Children's Hearings (Scotland) Act 2011

children's hearing must require that a further review of the compulsory supervision order take place on or as soon as is reasonably practicable after the expiry of the period of 28 days beginning on the day on which the notice is given.

(6) If, on that further review, it appears to the children's hearing carrying out the further review that the authority continues to be in breach of its duty, the children's hearing may direct the National Convener to make an application under section 147.

(7) In determining whether to direct the National Convener to make an application under section 147 to enforce the authority's duty, the children's hearing must not take into account any factor relating to the adequacy of the means available to the authority to enable it to comply with the duty.

DEFINITIONS

C.525.1 "children's hearing": s.5.
"compulsory supervision order": ss.202(1) and 83.
"implementation authority": ss.202(1) , 83(1)(b) and 86(1)(b).
"National Convener": s.1.

GENERAL NOTE

C.525.2 This section, with the following two sections, provides procedure whereby a children's hearing, if it considers in the course of a review that an implementation authority (IA) is not carrying out its duties under the compulsory supervision order (CSO) concerned, may initiate procedures aimed at enforcing compliance. These procedures are not often resorted to, but their existence provides for an additional incentive to the local authority involved to attend to its responsibilities and reflects the central role of the children's hearing in the working of the system.

Subs.(1)

C.525.3 *In breach of duty.* Where a children's hearing has concerns about what the IA has been doing it will have to consider whether the actions, or non-actions, which it is considering are such as to constitute a breach of duty: if it appeared, for example, that the requirements of a CSO had not been complied, e.g. a measure for contact not being facilitated due to a lack of staff or resources.

Subs.(2)

C.525.4 *The children's hearing may direct ...* The children's hearing is not obliged to direct the National Convener to give the IA notice. The matter is for the children's hearing to decide, and its decision will be subject to the paramountcy of the welfare of the child principle and the views of the child principle. It is unlikely, although it would be competent, to take no action where the breach of duty was in any way material, but the hearing has the option, under s.138(4), of deferring making a compulsory supervision order (CSO) until a subsequent hearing, and may take this course where, for example, the social worker appearing before it may suggest that the matter could be rectified soon. If, at the date of the subsequent hearing, this had not been accomplished, then that hearing would still have the power to direct the National Convener to take action. When such a direction is given the chairing member **must** include in the record of the decision details of how the IA is failing in its duty and **may** prepare a report for the National Convener providing such additional information as the hearing thinks appropriate (Children's Hearings (Scotland) Act 2011 (Rules of Procedure in Children's Hearings) Rules 2013 (SSI 2013/194) (the "Procedural Rules")) r.67(1). Where the children's hearing, at the time or at a subsequent hearing, decides to direct the National Convener, it must at the same time require the Reporter to arrange a further review of the CSO—see discussion below of subs.(5).

The National Convener. Any direction given by the children's hearing under this subsection will be addressed simply to the National Convener. As to how the National Convener may deal with any such direction, see discussion below of subs.(3).

Subs.(3)

C.525.5 This subsection provides that the notice which the National Convener may send out is to set out the way in which (in the hearing's view) the IA is in breach of duty and state that if the IA does not comply within 21 days the National Convener, on the direction of the children's hearing (see discussion of subs.(6) below), is to set in motion the enforcement procedures enacted in s.147. As noted above in our discussion of subs.(2) the chairing member must put in

Application for order

the record of the decision details of the alleged breach of duty and may provide a report for the National Convener. Rule 67(2) of the Procedural Rules requires the Reporter to give the National Convener a copy of the record of decision and any report—thus providing the National Convener with the information which he or she will require when preparing the notice.

Subs.(5)

After the children's hearing has given a direction under subs.(2) the Reporter will require to keep the matter under scrutiny and liaise with the IA as to its progress in implementing the CSO. The 28 days specified here allows for the IA to comply with the 21-day time provision in subs.3(b).

As soon as reasonably practicable. While the use of the term "reasonably" practicable may seem to give more flexibility than simply "practicable", there would seem to be no reason why more than a day or two beyond the 28 should be allowed to elapse. The reasonable practicability here is from the point of view of the Reporter, not the IA.

Subss.(6) and (7)

It is to be hoped that in most cases the IA will, by the time of the further review, have taken steps which will satisfy the review hearing that its duties are now being complied with. In the event that the review hearing decides that the IA is still in breach of duty, the hearing "may" direct the National Convener to proceed with the enforcement provisions i.e. by making an application to the sheriff principal under s.147. The matter is for the children's hearing to decide, and its decision will be subject to the paramountcy of the welfare of the child principle and the views of the child principle. It may be difficult to envisage circumstances in which, matters having reached this stage, the children's hearing would not make the direction to the National Convener, but it is conceivable that events may have overtaken the situation that gave rise to that part of the CSO that has not been implemented. By virtue of subs.(7) the children's hearing, in deciding whether or not to direct the National Convener to proceed, may not take into account any factor relating to the adequacy of the resources of the IA. This limitation does not apply to the sheriff principal in considering the matter—see below in our discussion of s.147.

In the event that the IA maintained to the review hearing that it was not in breach of duty, this should be explained by the social worker to the hearing, which would require to consider its view of this explanation and take it into account as far as it thought appropriate. In the event of the IA not accepting that it was in breach, and the review hearing still directing the National Convener to proceed, then this would have to be examined by the sheriff principal—see below in our discussion of s.147.

Application for order

147.—(1) The National Convener must, if directed to do so under section 146(6), apply to the relevant sheriff principal for an order to enforce an implementation authority's duty in relation to a child.

(2) The relevant sheriff principal is the sheriff principal of the sheriffdom in which the principal office of the implementation authority is situated.

(3) The National Convener may not make such an application, despite the direction given under section 146(6), unless—
  (a) the National Convener has given the authority notice in relation to the duty in compliance with a direction given under section 146(2), and
  (b) the authority has failed to carry out the duty within the period specified in the notice.

(4) The application is to be made by summary application.

DEFINITIONS
  "implementation authority": ss.202(1), 83(1)(b) and 86(1)(b).
  "National Convener": s.1.

GENERAL NOTE

This section enacts the procedural machinery for the National Convener where a review children's hearing, which considers that an implementation authority is in breach of duty, has given a direction to the National Convener under s.146(2), discussed above. It is to be noted, as more fully discussed below, that the National Convener is not to proceed to take action unless he or she has given to the implementation authority notice in terms of s.146(2).

Subss.(1) and (2)
C.526.3 The application which the National Convener may make is to the sheriff principal of the sheriffdom wherein the principal office of the implementation authority is situated. This is an "application", not an appeal, and accordingly, since s.109 of the Courts Reform (Scotland) Act 2014 transfers only the **appellate** jurisdiction of the sheriff principal to the Sheriff Appeal Court, that court is not involved here.

Subss.(1) and (3)
C.526.4 Subs.(3), in spite of the mandatory nature of the "must" in subs.(1), enacts two pre-conditions which have to be complied with before the National Convener may make application to the sheriff principal. First, the National Convener must have given to the IA the formal notice under s.146(2). Since, under this provision, the National Convener will have been "directed" by the children's hearing to give the implementation authority the appropriate notice, it would seem that this pre-condition, barring accidental oversight, will normally be satisfied. Secondly, the IA must have failed to carry out the duty concerned within the 21 days specified in the notice by virtue of s.146(3)(b). The matter has only come to the National Convener by virtue of the review children's hearing having, under s.146(6) "directed" the National Convener to make application to the sheriff principal. However, by enacting in subs.(3) that the National Convener may not make the application: "despite the direction given in s.146(6) "unless" (b) the authority has failed to carry out the duty within the period specified in the notice", it would seem clear that the National Convener is to satisfy him or herself that this is the case, even where this means disagreeing with the children's hearing. This is the view expressed by Professor Norrie in Kenneth McK. Norrie, *Children's Hearings in Scotland*, 3rd edn (Edinburgh: W. Green, 2013) at 13.34, and we agree with him.

Subs.(4)
C.526.5 The form of procedure before the sheriff principal is "summary application", the rules for which are in the Act of Sederunt (Summary Applications and Appeals etc.) Rules 1999 (SI 1999/929). In the course of this procedure the implementation authority, if so minded, may advance any defence it may have to the claim that it is in breach of duty. For further discussion of this see below under s.148(1).

Order for enforcement

C.527 **148.**—(1) The sheriff principal may, on an application by the National Convener under section 147, make an order requiring the implementation authority that is in breach of a duty imposed by virtue of a compulsory supervision order to carry out that duty.
(2) Such an order is final.

DEFINITIONS
C.527.1 "compulsory supervision order: ss.202(1) and 83.
"implementation authority": ss.202(1) , 83(1)(b) and 86(1)(b).
"National Convener": s.1.

GENERAL NOTE
C.527.2 This section deals with the powers of the sheriff principal in an application by the National Convener to enforce compliance with duty by an implementation authority.

Subs.(1)
C.527.3 "*The sheriff principal may* ...". The issue is for the judgment of the sheriff principal. If the sheriff principal considers that the implementation authority is not in breach of duty he or she will refuse the application. If the sheriff principal decides that the implementation authority is in breach of duty he or she may grant the application and make an order requiring compliance within a specified time. However this is not mandatory for the sheriff principal, who may take the view that a change of circumstances has made an order inappropriate. The sheriff principal is not, as the children's hearing is by virtue of s.146(7), bound to disregard "any factor relating to the adequacy of the means available to the authority to enable it to comply with the duty". Accordingly the sheriff principal may be entitled to refuse to make an order if enforcing the

Movement restriction conditions: regulations etc.

order would be unduly burdensome on the implementation authority—this is the view expressed by Professor Norrie in Kenneth McK. Norrie *Children's Hearings in Scotland*, 3rd edn (Edinburgh: W. Green, 2013) at 13.36. No sanction for failing to comply with the sheriff principal's order is enacted. Presumably, therefore, the remedy is proceedings for contempt of court. For discussion of contempt of court proceedings *see Macphail on Sheriff Court Practice*, 3rd edn (2006), paras 2.18–2.25 and *AB and CD, Petitioners* [2015] CSIH 25, 2015 S.L.T. 269.

Compulsory supervision orders etc.: further provision

Compulsory supervision orders etc.: further provision

149.—(1) The Scottish Ministers may by regulations make provision about—   C.528
- (a) the transmission of information relating to a child who is the subject of an order or warrant mentioned in subsection (2) to any person who, by virtue of the order or warrant, has or is to have control over the child,
- (b) the provision of temporary accommodation for the child,
- (c) the taking of the child to any place in which the child is required to reside under the order or warrant,
- (d) the taking of the child to—
  - (i) a place of safety under section 169 or 170,
  - (ii) a place to which the child falls to be taken to under section 169(2), or
  - (iii) a person to whom the child falls to be taken to under section 170(2).

(2) The orders and warrants are—
- (a) a compulsory supervision order,
- (b) an interim compulsory supervision order,
- (c) a medical examination order,
- (d) a warrant to secure attendance.

DEFINITIONS
"child": s.199.   C.528.1
"compulsory supervision order": ss.202(1) and 83.
"interim compulsory supervision order": ss.202(1) and 86.
"medical examination order": ss.202(1) and 87.
"place of safety": ss.202(1) and 189.
"warrant to secure attendance": ss.202(1) and 88.

SUBORDINATE LEGISLATION UNDER THIS SECTION
Children's Hearings (Scotland) Act 2011 (Compulsory Supervision Orders etc.: Further Provision) Regulations 2013 (SSI 2013/149)

GENERAL NOTE
This is an empowering section. The above-mentioned Regulations contain important provisions authorising the sharing of information in relation to children who are subject to various orders and the provision of temporary accommodation for such children. The provisions in relation to the sharing of information are of particular importance since where information is not shared this may put the child at risk.   C.528.2

Movement restriction conditions: regulations etc.

Movement restriction conditions: regulations etc.

150.—(1) The Scottish Ministers may by regulations prescribe—   C.529
- (a) restrictions, or
- (b) monitoring arrangements,

that may be imposed as part of a movement restriction condition.

(2) Regulations under subsection (1) may in particular—

(a) prescribe the maximum period for which a restriction may have effect,
(b) prescribe methods of monitoring compliance with a movement restriction condition,
(c) specify devices that may be used for the purpose of that monitoring,
(d) prescribe the person or class of person who may be designated to carry out the monitoring, and
(e) require that the condition be varied to designate another person if the person designated ceases to be prescribed, or fall within a class of person, prescribed under paragraph (d).

(3) Regulations under subsection (1) are subject to the affirmative procedure.

(4) The Scottish Ministers may—
(a) make arrangements (contractual or otherwise) to secure the services of such persons as they think fit to carry out monitoring, and
(b) make those arrangements in a way that provides differently for different areas or different forms of monitoring.

(5) Nothing in any enactment or rule of law prevents the disclosure to a person providing a service under an arrangement made under subsection (4) of information relating to a child where the disclosure is made for the purposes only of the full and proper provision of monitoring.

DEFINITIONS
"affirmative procedure": s.197.
"child": s.199.
"movement restriction condition": ss.202(1) and 84.

SUBORDINATE LEGISLATION UNDER THIS SECTION
Children's Hearings (Scotland) Act 2011 (Movement Restriction Conditions) Regulations 2013 (SSI 2013/210).

GENERAL NOTE
This is an empowering section. At the time of writing, the relevant subordinate legislation enacted under this section is as noted above.

Secure accommodation

Implementation of secure accommodation authorisation

151.—(1) Subsections (3) and (4) apply where a relevant order or warrant made in relation to a child includes a secure accommodation authorisation.

(2) A relevant order or warrant is—
(a) a compulsory supervision order,
(b) an interim compulsory supervision order,
(c) a medical examination order,
(d) a warrant to secure attendance.

(3) The chief social work officer may implement the authorisation only with the consent of the person in charge of the residential establishment containing the secure accommodation in which the child is to be placed (the "head of unit").

(4) The chief social work officer must remove the child from secure accommodation if—
(a) the chief social work officer considers it unnecessary for the child to be kept there, or
(b) the chief social work officer is required to do so by virtue of regulations made under subsection (6).

(5) A secure accommodation authorisation ceases to have effect once the child is removed from secure accommodation under subsection (4).

Implementation of secure accommodation authorisation

(6) The Scottish Ministers may by regulations make provision in relation to decisions—
  (a) by the chief social work officer—
    (i) whether to implement a secure accommodation authorisation,
    (ii) whether to remove a child from secure accommodation,
  (b) by the head of unit whether to consent under subsection (3).
(7) Regulations under subsection (6) may in particular—
  (a) specify—
    (i) the time within which a decision must be made,
    (ii) the procedure to be followed,
    (iii) the criteria to be applied,
    (iv) matters to be taken into account or disregarded,
    (v) persons who must be consulted,
    (vi) persons who must consent before a decision has effect,
  (b) make provision about—
    (i) notification of decisions,
    (ii) the giving of reasons for decisions,
    (iii) reviews of decisions,
    (iv) the review of the order or warrant containing the secure accommodation authorisation where the head of unit does not consent.
(8) Regulations under subsection (6) are subject to the affirmative procedure.

DEFINITIONS

"affirmative procedure": ss.202(1) and 197.
"child": s.199.
"chief social work officer": s.202(1).
"compulsory supervision order": ss.202(1) and 83.
"interim compulsory supervision order": ss.202 (1) and 86.
"medical examination order": ss.202 (1) 89.
"movement restriction condition": ss.202(1) and 84.
"residential establishment": ss.202 (1).
"secure accommodation": s.202(1).
"secure accommodation authorisation": ss.202(1) and 83(5).
"warrant to secure attendance": s.88.

C.530.1

SUBORDINATE LEGISLATION UNDER THIS SECTION

Children's Hearings (Scotland) Act 2011 (Consequential Transitional Provisions and Savings Order 2013 (SI 2013/1465)
Children's Hearings (Scotland) Act 2011 (Implementation of Secure Accommodation Authorisation) (Scotland) Regulations 2013 (SSI 2013/205).

GENERAL NOTE

It will be remembered that a children's hearing does not make an order requiring the child to be held in secure accommodation, rather the decision authorises the local authority to place the child in a "secure unit". The reader is directed to the annotation to s.85 for a discussion of authorisation for secure accommodation. The regulations are contained in the Children's Hearings (Scotland) Act 2011 (Implementation of Secure Accommodation Authorisation) (Scotland) Regulations 2013 (SSI 2013/212) (the "Implementation Regulations") The child and relevant persons have the right to appeal the decision of the chief social worker to the sheriff court, whether that decision is to implement or not implement the authorisation, or to remove the child from the secure accommodation (regs 11, 12, 13 and 14).

C.530.2

Subs.(1) and (2)

The list of relevant orders or warrants does not include authorisation for secure accommodation under a child protection order (CPO), but interim variations of compulsory supervision orders will be included as these are compulsory supervision orders.

C.530.3

Children's Hearings (Scotland) Act 2011

Subs.(2)

C.530.4   Implementation of authorisation for secure accommodation is the decision of the chief social work officer for the implementation authority, but it also requires the consent of the person in charge of the particular establishment. Regulation 6 contains the considerations that must be addressed by the head of the unit. (See annotation to s.85 for a discussion of the decision whether to implement authorisation for secure accommodation.) It should be noted that the list of relevant orders does not include a CPO which includes authorisation for secure accommodation. This is the case whether it is a CPO made by a sheriff or continued by a hearing at the second working day hearing. This is likely to be due to the very short duration and urgent nature of the CPO.

Subss.(3), (6) and (7)

C.530.5   Article 16(4)(c) of the Children's Hearings (Scotland) Act 2011 (Consequential Transitional Provisions and Savings Order 2013 (SI 2013/1465) provides that where the head of unit is consulted he or she must "(a): assess whether placement in secure accommodation within the residential establishment managed by the head of unit would—(i) be appropriate to the child's needs having regard to that establishment's statements of purpose; and (ii) not, in the opinion of the head of unit, be detrimental to the other children residing in that unit." Under Art 16(4)(b) and (c) the head of unit must record this decision and send it to the chief social work officer within 48 hours.

Subs.(4)

C.530.6   The placement of a child in secure accommodation results in a serious deprivation of his or her liberty. The definition of child (s.199) includes a young person. It is an interference with the child's right to a family life, and a profound intrusion into most aspects of the life and privacy of the child. It is therefore of the utmost importance that no one is kept in secure accommodation for longer than is necessary and proportionate. Regulation 10 of the Implementation Regulations imposes a duty on the chief social work officer for the implementation authority to review the placement. The reviews are frequent—the first after seven days and thereafter a review each month of the previous review (reg.10(2)). Regulation 10(3) allows the child and relevant person(s) to request a review. The reviews must consider whether the conditions in ss.83(6), 87(4) or 88(3) still apply, what the child's needs are and whether they are being met, and the views of the child, each relevant person and the head of the unit in which the child is placed. The decision is that of the chief social work officer. This subsection both requires and allows the chief social worker to remove the child when he or she considers it unnecessary for the child to remain there, or where regulations so require. The decision and the reasons therefor must be provided to the Principal Reporter, the child, each relevant person and the head of the unit. The decision may be appealed (reg.14 of the Implementation Regulations). The removal of the child may trigger the implementation authority's duty under s.131(2)(a) require a review hearing to vary the order of a children's hearing which included the authorisation for secure accommodation, whether a compulsory supervision order (including an interim variation of compulsory supervision order) or an interim compulsory supervision order. A compulsory supervision order (which includes an interim variation of a compulsory supervision order) made by a children's hearing which contains authorisation for secure accommodation must specify either a residential establishment which contains both secure accommodation and accommodation which is not secure (s.83(5)(a)(i)) or two or more residential establishments, one of which contains secure accommodation (s.83(5)(a)(ii). It should be noted that this does not apply to an interim compulsory supervision order which may simply specify that the child is to reside at any place of safety away from the place where the child predominantly resides (see s.86(2)). This ensures that if the child is removed from the secure accommodation (and covers the situation where secure accommodation authorisation has not been implemented) by the chief social work officer, he or she is then placed in accommodation which has been approved by a children's hearing as suitable for the child. If a child is removed from secure accommodation under this section, the local authority is no longer empowered to place the child in a secure unit and would have to seek authorisation from a children's hearing to do so.

Subs.(7)

C.530.7   The timescales are contained in reg.10 of the Implementation Regulations. The reader is directed to the commentary to subs.(4) above for details.

Secure accommodation: placement in other circumstances

152.—(1) The Scottish Ministers may by regulations make provision specifying circumstances in which a child falling within subsection (3) may be placed in secure accommodation.

(2) Regulations under subsection (1) may in particular include provision for and in connection with—
  (a) the procedure to be followed in deciding whether to place a child in secure accommodation,
  (b) the notification of decisions,
  (c) the giving of reasons for decisions,
  (d) the review of decisions,
  (e) the review of placements by a children's hearing.

(3) A child falls within this subsection if—
  (a) a relevant order or warrant is in force in relation to the child, and
  (b) the relevant order or warrant does not include a secure accommodation authorisation.

(4) A relevant order or warrant is—
  (a) a compulsory supervision order,
  (b) an interim compulsory supervision order,
  (c) a medical examination order,
  (d) a warrant to secure attendance.

(5) Regulations under subsection (1) are subject to the affirmative procedure.

C.531

DEFINITIONS
"affirmative procedure": ss.202(1) and 197.
"child": s.199.
"compulsory supervision order": ss.202(1) and 83.
"interim compulsory supervision order": ss.202 (1) and 86.
"medical examination order": ss.202(1) and 87.
"secure accommodation": s.202(1).
"secure accommodation authorisation": ss.202(1) and 83(5).
"warrant to secure attendance": s.88.

C.531.1

SUBORDINATE LEGISLATION UNDER THIS SECTION
Secure Accommodation (Scotland) Regulations 2013 (SSI 2013/205).
Secure Accommodation (Scotland) Amendment Regulations 2015 (SSI 2015/20).

GENERAL NOTE
There may be circumstances which warrant placing a child in a secure unit where the child is subject to a relevant order made by a children's hearing but that order does not contain authorisation for secure accommodation. The regulations are contained in the Secure Accommodation (Scotland) Regulations 2013 (SSI 2013/205) as amended, above.

The decision is that of the chief social work officer and the head of the unit (regs 7 and 8), and the criteria for such a placement are the same as those in s.83 6) (reg.7(2), (3)). Placement must be considered by the head of the unit and the chief social work officer to be in the best interests of the child (reg.7(2)). The maximum time that a child may be accommodated in a secure unit in these circumstances is 72 hours within any period of 28 days.The time may be consecutive or cumulative (reg.5). Thus the provision is one that allows the chief social work officer to react to an urgent situation. The Reporter must be notified in writing immediately, as must each relevant person (reg.7(4)) and no later than 24 hours after the child has been placed. The requirement remains even if the child has been released within that 24-hour period. The Reporter is obliged to arrange a children's hearing to take place within 72 hours of the child being placed in the secure accommodation (reg.8). Where an ICSO was made by a children's hearing under s.95(4) the Reporter must arrange for the children's hearing which the grounds hearing has required to be arranged under s.95(2) to take place before the expiry of 72 hours of the placement in secure accommodation (reg.8(6)(ba)). Where the child is subject to an interim compulsory supervision order (ICSO) and the hearing would be unable to extend it as the maximum 66 days would expire (s.96) it will be necessary for the Reporter to make application to the sheriff for a further extension of the ICSO. Where the ICSO had been made by a sheriff

C.531.2

under ss.98, 99 or 100 of this Act the Reporter will need to make application to the sheriff for a further extension.
The decision is appealable and appeals are detailed in reg.11A.

Secure accommodation: regulations

C.532 **153.**—(1) The Scottish Ministers may by regulations make provision about children placed in secure accommodation by virtue of this Act.
(2) Regulations under subsection (1) may in particular include provision—
(a) imposing requirements on the Principal Reporter,
(b) imposing requirements on the implementation authority in relation to a compulsory supervision order or an interim compulsory supervision order,
(c) imposing requirements on the relevant local authority for a child in relation to a medical examination order or a warrant to secure attendance,
(d) in connection with the protection of the welfare of the children.
(3) Regulations under subsection (1) are subject to the affirmative procedure.

DEFINITIONS
C.532.1 "affirmative procedure": ss.202(1) and 197.
"child": s.199.
"compulsory supervision order": ss.202(1) and 83.
"implementation authority": ss.83(1)(b) and 86(1)(b).
"interim compulsory supervision order": ss.202 (1) and 86.
"medical examination order": ss.202(1) and 87.
"movement restriction condition": ss.202(1) and 84.
"Principal Reporter": s.14 and Sch.3 paras 8–10.
"secure accommodation": s.202(1).
"secure accommodation authorisation": ss.202(1) and 83(5).
"warrant to secure attendance": s.88.

SUBORDINATE LEGISLATION UNDER THIS SECTION
Secure Accommodation (Scotland) Regulations 2013 (SSI 2013/205).
Children's Hearings (Scotland) Act 2011 (Implementation of Secure Accommodation Authorisation (Scotland) Regulations 2013 (SSI 2013/205).

GENERAL NOTE
C.532.2 This is an empowering section.

PART 15

APPEALS

Appeal against decision of children's hearing

Appeal to sheriff against decision of children's hearing

C.533 **154.**—(1) A person mentioned in subsection (2) may appeal to the sheriff against a relevant decision of a children's hearing in relation to a child.
(2) The persons are—
(a) the child,
(b) a relevant person in relation to the child,
(c) a safeguarder appointed in relation to the child by virtue of section 30.
(3) A relevant decision is—
(a) a decision to make, vary or continue a compulsory supervision order,
(b) a decision to discharge a referral by the Principal Reporter,

Appeal to sheriff against decision of children's hearing

(c) a decision to terminate a compulsory supervision order,
(d) a decision to make an interim compulsory supervision order,
(e) a decision to make an interim variation of a compulsory supervision order,
(f) a decision to make a medical examination order, or
(g) a decision to grant a warrant to secure attendance.

(4) An appeal under subsection (1) may be made jointly by two or more persons mentioned in subsection (2).

(5) An appeal under subsection (1) must be made before the expiry of the period of 21 days beginning with the day on which the decision is made.

DEFINITIONS
"child": s.199.
"compulsory supervision order": ss.202(1) and 83.
"habitually resident": see commentary on subs.(1) below.
"interim compulsory supervision order": ss.202(1) and 86.
"medical examination order": ss.202(1) and 87.
"relevant person": s.200.
"safeguarder": ss.202(1) and 30(1).
"warrant to secure attendance": ss.202(1) and 88.

C.533.1

GENERAL NOTE
Consistently with the pattern of the Act this section lists decisions of children's hearings which are appealable. Section 161, discussed below, deals separately with appeals from decisions of children's hearings affecting contact orders and permanence orders. A consequence of adopting the approach of listing the competent appeals is, of course, that a decision not specified is not appealable. Section 51(1)(a) of the Children (Scotland) Act 1995 provided that "any decision" of a children's hearing could be appealed and it was left to case law (e.g. *H v McGregor*, 1973 S.C. 95; 1973 S.L.T. 110 and *Sloan v B*, 1991 S.L.T. 530 at 545L) to rule that procedural decisions were not to be appealable. This has now been recognised here by the omission of such procedural decisions from the list—see discussion below of subs.(3). Decisions of pre-hearing panels, other than relevant person decisions which are specially dealt with in s.160(2), are not listed as appealable.

C.533.2

The list of appealable decisions does not include an appeal which seeks to displace a ground for referral which has been admitted at a grounds hearing or established by the sheriff at a proof hearing. However, as noted by Professor Norrie in his commentary *Children's Hearings (Scotland) Act 1995*, 2nd edn (Edinburgh: W. Green, 2004), p.94, "facts" (not included in the ground for referral) can be presented to hearings; in consequence of this an appellant may adduce evidence at an appeal aimed at establishing that the hearing was mistaken in its assessment of facts. In general, the courts are reluctant to displace fact-based decisions of children's hearings. In *M v Locality Reporter Manager* [2014] CSIH 62; 2014 Fam. L.R. 102; 2014 G.W.D. 24-453 (which we shall discuss further in our commentary on ss.156, 163 and 177) a mother appealed against the decision of a sheriff upholding the decision of a children's hearing as to the amount of contact between herself and her daughters. The appellant had led no evidence before the sheriff and, in her appeal to the sheriff, had

"concentrated on what were submitted to be the legal deficiencies of the children's hearing's decision not to vary the contact direction, rather than concentrating on the substantive merits, from the perspective of the welfare of the children, of making the variation which the appellant wished."

An Extra Division, refusing the mother's appeal, commented at [39] that, given the procedure, mentioned above, which had been adopted before the sheriff, the courts could not resolve the contact issue because they did not "have access to all the facts bearing on what is an entirely fact-sensitive question". As we shall see when considering s.156(1), the test to be applied by the appellate court is whether that court is "satisfied" that the decision appealed against is "justified". In Brian Kearney, *Children's Hearings and the Sheriff Court*, 2nd edn (Butterworths, 2000), para.49.15, it is suggested that it would be open to an appellant to argue "that the grounds for referral were not properly accepted at a children's hearing". The test under s.51(5) of the 1995 Act was "satisfied *in all the circumstances of the case* [emphasis added]", and it may be that the omission of the emphasised words from s.156(1) may be regarded as limiting the scope of appeals and therefore as taking something away from this argument.

Forms for appeals are contained in Forms 61 ff. in Sch.1 of the Act of Sederunt (Child Care and Maintenance Rules) 1997 (SI 1997/291), as amended (the "1997 Rules").

For consideration of the provisions for appeal against the decision of the sheriff see below in the discussions of ss.163 to 165.

Subs.(1)

C.533.3　*May appeal to the sheriff.* Under r.3.53(1A) and (1B) of the 1997 Rules an appeal should be in Form 61 of the 1997 Rules, which includes:

"4. The decision is not justified because [*state briefly the reasons why the decision is being appealed against*]."

The appeal must be accompanied by a copy of the decision appealed against and any relevant document that was before the children's hearing and must be lodged with the sheriff clerk of the sheriff court district in which the child is habitually resident or, on cause shown, such other court as the sheriff may direct: see the 1997 Rules r.3.53(1A)(c). See above in our commentary on s.93(2)(a) for discussion of "habitual residence" and the circumstances in which it may be appropriate to remit to another court. The same considerations apply, *mutatis mutandis*, here. An appeal may be signed by the appellant or his or her representative (1997 Rules r.3.53(2)). An appeal by a child may be signed on the child's behalf by a safeguarder (1997 Rules r.3.53(3)): this repeats the provision in the 1995 legislation, but we find it difficult, given that the appeal is the child's appeal, to envisage a situation in which it would be appropriate for the safeguarder to sign an appeal on the child's behalf because:

(1) if the child has capacity under s.2(4A) and (4B) of the Age of Legal Capacity (Scotland) Act 1991, then he or she would sign the appeal or instruct a solicitor;
(2) the safeguarder can bring an appeal in his or her own right; and
(3) there should be no appeal in the name of a child who does not have capacity.

In certain appeals those who have been served with the notice of appeal may lodge answers (r.3.55 of the 1997 Rules).

A children's hearing. This section deals with appeals against decisions of children's hearings, not decisions of pre-hearing panels. Appeals from "relevant person" determinations of a pre-hearing panel are provided for by s.160. There is no appeal from decisions (under s.79(3), read with s.79(2)(c)) of a pre-hearing panel in relation to: the appointment or non-appointment of a safeguarder; the excusal or non-excusal of a child or relevant person from attending a children's hearing; where a secure accommodation authorisation by a children's hearing is likely; or under rules enacted under s.177(2)(a). Appeals against decisions of the chief social work officer in relation to the implementation or otherwise of secure accommodation authorisations are dealt with in s.162, discussed below.

Subs.(2)(a)

C.533.4　*The child.* A person under 16, if of sufficient understanding of what is involved, may act on his or her own behalf or instruct legal representation—Age of Legal Capacity (Scotland) Act 1991 s.2(4A) and (4B). A parent may, but only where practicable and "in the interests of the child", act as the child's legal representative—Children (Scotland) Act 1995 s.1(1)(d). It will not be in the child's interests to be so represented where, as may well occur in "care or protection" cases, the parent is alleged to have neglected or mistreated the child. A safeguarder may appeal on behalf of the child—see discussion below.

Subs.(2)(b)

C.533.5　*Relevant person.* This includes a person deemed to be a relevant person by a pre-hearing panel or a children's hearing—see s.81(4)(f) and (7).

Subs.(3)

C.533.6　As mentioned in the General Note, only decisions mentioned in this list or in s.161 are appealable and consequently procedural decisions are not appealable. Some examples of such procedural decisions are: a decision to defer to a subsequent hearing, under ss.91(2) or 138(2); a decision, under s.93(2)(a), to direct the Reporter to apply to the sheriff for a proof hearing where the ground for referral has not been admitted (cf. *H v McGregor*, 1973 S.C. 95; 1973 S.L.T. 110); and the decision of a children's hearing to appoint or not appoint a safeguarder under s.30 of the Act. Professor Norrie, in his commentary *Children's Hearings in Scotland*, 2nd edn (Edinburgh: W. Green, 2005), pp.212, 213 discusses further procedural decisions not appealable under the 1995 Act and his discussion applies here mutatis mutandis. As in the 1995 Act the Reporter is not empowered to appeal a decision of a children's hearing.

Appeal to sheriff against decision of children's hearing

Subs.(3)(b)
A decision to discharge a referral by the Principal Reporter. This refers to any referral which has been made by the Principal Reporter. Under the 1995 Act, appeals against discharge of a referral were rare.

C.533.7

Subs.(3)(c)
It was competent under s.73(9)(b) of the 1995 Act for a children's hearing to terminate a supervision requirement and this was appealable by virtue of the generalised provision of s.51(1) of that Act when read with s.51(5)(a). This paragraph makes explicit provision for this. Professor Norrie in his *Children's Hearings in Scotland*, 3rd edn (Edinburgh: W. Green, 2013), para.14–02, fn.5, comments that such an appeal would be "rare in the extreme" and refers to *Thomson, Petitioner*, 1998 S.C. 848; 1998 S.L.T. 1066; 1998 S.C.L.R. 898, which was an unusual case wherein a supervision requirement for a 17-year-old had been terminated because he was being dealt with under the criminal justice system: he did not appeal at the time and this was an (unsuccessful) attempt by him to persuade the Court of Session to exercise the *nobile officium* to permit a late appeal against the termination of the supervision requirement so that he could attempt to recover "child" status.

C.533.8

Subs.(3)(d) and (e)
An appeal against the making of an interim compulsory supervision order (ICSO) is competent in respect of the ICSO as a whole or against one or more of the measures included in it—cf. *J, Appellant*, 2013 S.L.T. (Sh. Ct) 18. The appeal may be made under para.(d) against the order as originally granted, or under para.(e) where a variation of the order has been made. Where an appeal against an ICSO containing a secure accommodation authorisation is being considered it may be appropriate, where this authorisation has been implemented by the Chief Social Work Officer (cf. s.162(4)(a)), to consider an appeal under s.162(3) against the Chief Social Work Officer's decision. For discussion of appeals against the Chief Social Work Officer's decision to implement or not to implement, see our discussion of s.162.

C.533.9

Subs.(3)(f)
An appeal against the making of a medical examination order (MEO) is competent in respect of the MEO as a whole or against one or more of the measures included in it. As with an appeal against the making of an ICSO, where a MEO includes a secure accommodation authorisation it may be appropriate, where this authorisation has been implemented by the Chief Social Work Officer (cf. s.162(4)(a)), to consider an appeal under s.162(3) against the Chief Social Work Officer's decision.

C.533.10

Subs.(3)(g)
Once again, where a secure accommodation authorisation has been made and implemented, it may be appropriate for consideration to be given to appealing under s.162(3) against the Chief Social Work Officer's decision to implement.

C.533.11

Subs.(4)
As mentioned above in the discussion of s.104(2)–(4), a legal representative will be cautious of acting for more than one party in case of possible conflict of interest. For fuller consideration of the issues of conflict of interest and confidentiality which may arise, see the discussion above of s.104(2)–(4) under the heading "*Possible conflict of interest – confidentiality*".

C.533.12

Subs.(5)
The wording prescribing the time limit for an appeal is the same as in s.51(1)(a) of the 1995 Act. The argument has been advanced in the context of the provisions of the 1995 Act that "day one" is the day after the children's hearing concerned—see Kearney, *Children's Hearings and the Sheriff Court* (2000), para.50.09. However, in view of the wording of this provision, when considered along with the wording in s.157(2), that the time limit for certain appeals is to be "before the expiry of three days after the day on which the appeal is made", it now seems clear, for the purposes of this present subsection, that the day of the decision is to be regarded as "day one". The sheriff court has no power to extend this limit, since the provision in the Act of Sederunt (Statutory Appeals) 1981 (SI 1981/1591) giving the sheriff a discretion to do so has been repealed by the Act of Sederunt (Sheriff Court Summary Application Rules) (SI 1993/3240). In *Thomson, Petitioner*, 1998 S.C. 848; 1998 S.L.T. 1066; 1998 S.C.L.R. 898, discussed above under subs.(3)(c), the Inner House decided, in the particular circumstances of that case, not to employ the *nobile officium* of the Court of Session to extend the limit.

C.533.13

Children's Hearings (Scotland) Act 2011

Procedure

C.534 **155.**—(1) This section applies where an appeal under section 154 is made.

(2) The Principal Reporter must lodge with the sheriff clerk a copy of—

(a) the decision, and the reasons for the decision, of the children's hearing,

(b) all information provided by virtue of rules under section 177 to the children's hearing, and

(c) the report of the children's hearing.

(3) The appeal must not be heard in open court.

(4) The sheriff may (but need not) hear evidence before determining the appeal.

(5) The sheriff may hear evidence from—

(a) the child,

(b) a relevant person in relation to the child,

(c) an author or compiler of a report or statement provided to the children's hearing that made the decision,

(d) the Principal Reporter,

(e) where the appeal is against a decision to make, grant, vary or continue an order or warrant including a secure accommodation authorisation in respect of the child—

(i) the person in charge of the secure accommodation specified in the secure accommodation authorisation, and

(ii) the chief social work officer, and

(f) any other person who the sheriff considers may give material additional evidence.

(6) The sheriff may require any person to give a report to the sheriff for the purpose of assisting the sheriff in determining the appeal.

[1] (7) Subsection (6) applies in relation to a safeguarder only if regulations under section 34 so provide.

NOTE

C.534.1 1. As amended by the Children's Hearings (Scotland) Act 2011 (Modification of Primary Legislation) Order 2013 (SSI 2013/211) Sch.1 para.20(14) (effective June 24 2013).

DEFINITIONS

C.534.2 "chief social work officer": s.202(1).
"child": s.199.
"Principal Reporter": s.14 and Sch.3 paras 8–10.
"relevant person": s.200.
"safeguarder": ss.202(1) and 30(1).
"secure accommodation authorisation": ss.202(1) and 85.

GENERAL NOTE

C.534.3 This section, when read with Pt VIII (rr.3.53 to 3.58) of the Act of Sederunt (Child Care and Maintenance) Rules 1997 (SI 1997/291), as amended, (the 1997 Rules) covers the procedural steps in an appeal to the sheriff against a decision of a children's hearing. They do not cover the (limited) appeals against decisions of a pre-hearing panel, which are included in s.160, discussed below. The provisions here replicate, with some considerable refinements, the provisions of s.51(2) and (3) of the Children (Scotland) Act 1995 and some of the provisions in Part VIII of the 1997 Rules. The detailed provisions are discussed below, but the general position is:

(a) it is likely that many appeals will continue to be conducted by argument on all sides on the basis of existing reports;

(b) a good number of appeals will be conducted by parties calling existing witnesses, mainly report writers, and asking questions aimed at clarifying or qualifying opinions in existing reports;

(c) in some cases a party or parties will invite the sheriff to call for additional reports from existing sources;

(d) in some few cases parties may invite the sheriff to call for report(s) from new sources and parties may then call such persons to give evidence;

(e) on rare occasions the sheriff will on his or her own motion call for additional report(s)

Procedure

from existing sources and cause arrangements to be made for the respective witnesses to attend the appeal hearing; and

(f) exceptionally, the sheriff may commission a report from a new source and cause arrangements to be made for the report writer to attend the appeal hearing.

The rules of good practice in relation to proof hearings, discussed above in commentary on s.101(1) in the paragraph headed "Procedural hearings after lodging of application", apply, mutatis mutandis, to appeals. Paragraph 1.3 of the Glasgow Practice Note No.1 of 2015 provides for this explicitly.

Subs.(1)

As noted above these provisions apply only to the decisions of children's hearings (as opposed to pre-hearing panels) listed in s.154(3). **C.534.4**

Subs.(2)(b)

There are numerous provisions within the Children's Hearings (Scotland) Act 2011 (Rules of Procedure in Children's Hearings) Rules 2013 (SSI 2013/194) (made by virtue of the provisions in ss.177 and 195 of the Act) in relation to the furnishing of information to hearing members, including the provisions in rr.26, 28, 29, 30, 32, 33, 35, 36, 38, 39, 40, 41, 42, 43, 44, 52, 53, 70, 72, 73, 75, 80 and 94. The amount of paperwork placed before the sheriff in relation to an appeal varies enormously. Sometimes there will only be a handful of reports, on other occasions there will be a very substantial bundle. We shall submit, on our discussion below of subss.(4) and (5), that the sheriff should examine these papers in order to consider whether it will be appropriate to hear evidence from any person he or she considers may give additional evidence. Where there is a large number of papers for the sheriff's consideration those responsible for managing the court business should expect the sheriff to require to take time to read the documents and possibly to require arrangements to be made for the attendance of any person whose evidence the sheriff may require. **C.534.5**

Subs.(3)

This echoes the provision in s.93(5) of the 1995 Act which enacted that children's hearings' proceedings before the sheriff were to be held "in chambers". The present provision effects no practical change since sheriffs have long assumed the power to declare any part of the court building as "chambers". In Glasgow Sheriff Court these cases are generally dealt with in the special suite set aside for this purpose. In other courts, and in Glasgow when the children's suite is occupied, a court is used for these cases and the general public is excluded. **C.534.6**

Subss.(4) and (5)

These subsections contain key provisions and have to be read along with the provisions of s.156. See below for our discussion of s.156 wherein the apparent intention of the legislature to create a wide scope for appeal is discussed. Subsection (4) makes clear that the sheriff may, but is not obliged to, hear "evidence". In practice many appeals are disposed of on the basis of submissions made by parties and/or representatives of parties. However, as provided in s.156(1) and (2), the decision of the appeal depends on whether or not the sheriff is "satisfied" that the decision of the children's hearing which is being challenged is "justified". It will be recalled that s.25 of the Act, replicating s.16(1) of the Children (Scotland) Act 1995 (and reflecting the tone of the provisions for children's hearings in the Social Work (Scotland) Act 1968), obliges the court to have regard to the need to safeguard and promote the welfare of the child as the paramount consideration. As mentioned in our discussion of s.25, above, this provision does not mean that the court's decisions on matters of fact or law are to be governed by reference to the interests of the child. The paramountcy of the welfare of the child principle is, however, relevant to decisions as to how a case is to be proceeded with (cf. *G v Scanlon*, 2000 S.C.L.R. 1 wherein, in refusing an adjournment of a proof hearing regarding a child "K", an Extra Division, at 5C, noted with approval that "the sheriff saw it as in K's interests to proceed that day, and put that interest above any interest there might be in deferment"). The provision in subs.(5)(f) empowering the sheriff to hear evidence from any other person the sheriff considers may give material evidence goes further than the provision in s.51(3)(c) of the 1995 Act empowering the sheriff to call for any report he or she considers may assist him or her in deciding the appeal and, it is submitted, endows the sheriff with a more proactive role than he or she possesses in ordinary civil procedure. As noted above in our discussion of subs.(2)(b), the sheriff, before the hearing of an appeal, will be provided with information which may sometimes be voluminous and the sheriff will require to take the time to examine it and decide on the possibility of calling for fresh evidence. In considering this the sheriff will require to balance the interest of the child, referred to in *G v Scanlon*, above, in achieving a speedy disposal and, on the **C.534.7** other hand, the potential importance of the fresh evidence which will be in the interest of the child to obtain a just decision.

Subs.(5)

C.534.8 *May hear evidence from.* The appellant should move the appeal, address the court in support of the reasons advanced in Form 61, and, if so advised, lead evidence; and it will be for the respondent(s) to do likewise. The sheriff may hear evidence from any of the persons listed in subs.(5). By using the word "from" without the words "or on behalf of" this provision appears not to authorise parties to adduce evidence of others, but the wide discretion vested in the sheriff by para.(f) empowers the sheriff to hear evidence from any person and sheriffs will be ready to hear argument from a party that a particular witness should be heard. As noted above in our discussion of s.154, the sheriff may also use this power to call witnesses *ex proprio motu*. However, sheriffs must have regard to the observations of the Supreme Court in relation to the conduct of cases involving children in *NJDB v JEG* sub nom. *B v G* [2012] UKSC 21; 2012 S.C. (U.K.S.C.) 293; 2012 S.L.T. 840; 2012 S.C.L.R. 428 at [34]:

"In the meantime there are measures which the courts can take in order to set their house in order. One obvious step is for sheriffs to exercise their existing powers to ensure that proceedings are conducted with reasonable expedition".

Subs.(5)(a)

C.534.9 *Child.* There is no lower age limit in relation to a child giving evidence. The classic early work, W.G. Dickson, *A Treatise on the Law of Evidence in Scotland*, edited by P.J. Hamilton Grierson (Edinburgh: T. & T. Clark, 1887), reports at para.1544 that children as young as four years have been admitted as witnesses in criminal cases. The former rule known as the competency test, viz., that a potential child witness had to be "examined" by the court as to whether he or she would be likely to give trustworthy evidence has been abolished by s.24 of the Vulnerable Witnesses (Scotland) Act 2004. However, in proceedings dedicated to promoting the welfare of children, practitioners and sheriffs are careful to try to avoid causing unnecessary distress to children called as witnesses.

Subs.(5)(b)

C.534.10 *Relevant person.* This includes a person who has been deemed to be a relevant person by a pre-hearing panel—see s.81(4)(f) and (7).

Subss.(5)(c) and (7)

C.534.11 *An author or compiler of a report or statement provided to the children's hearing that made the decision.* In *M v Locality Reporter Manager*, 2014 Fam. L.R. 102; 2014 G.W.D. 24-453 the children had expressed views to a children's hearing but no record had been made of this. On appeal to the sheriff, and from the sheriff's decision to the Court of Session, it was contended that the failure to record these expressed views amounted to a procedural irregularity. The Court of Session, at [28], examined the terms of r.62(2) (each hearing member to state their decision) and r.62(3) (chairing member to confirm and explain reasons for decision) of the Children's Hearings (Scotland) Act 2011 (Rules of Procedure in Children's Hearings) Rules 2013 (SSI 2013/194) (the "Procedural Rules") and noted that the chairing member had to ensure that a record is made of the decision and reasons and sign this. The court then noted that, under r.88 of the Procedural Rules, the Reporter must notify these to the child, each relevant person and any safeguarder. Against this background the court concluded:

"The decisions and reasons, as recorded in writing, then become part of what are referred to in the Rules as 'all decisions and reasons', copies of which, in terms of rule 34(3)(b), must be provided by the Reporter to the child, each relevant person and the safeguarder prior to the hearing and, in terms of rule 35(1)(b), be provided to the members of the hearing. They are to be contrasted with 'any report or other information' which must be provided to the child, each relevant person and the safeguarder in terms of rule 34(6)(b); and, 'any report or other document' which must be provided to members in terms of rule 35(1)(j)."

Applying this reasoning to the present provision it would appear that the chairing member (or for that matter any other member) of a children's hearing is not to be regarded as the "author or compiler of a report or statement provided to the children's hearing" with the consequence that this provision does not by itself authorise the sheriff to hear evidence from any panel member. It would, however, presumably be open to the sheriff to hear from a panel member by virtue of subs.(7). Sheriff Brian Kearney in his *Children's Hearings and the Sheriff Court*, 2nd edn (Butterworths, 2000), paras 52.12 and 52.13, discusses the issue of hearing members as witnesses and, on the basis that if Parliament had intended to introduce the unusual

Determination of appeal

procedure of having members of a tribunal of first instance giving evidence justifying their decision it would have said this in clear terms, concludes that it would not be appropriate for the sheriff to examine a hearing member as to the merits of the hearings' decision. We agree with this view and think it has application to the present provisions. Professor Norrie also agrees with this (see his *Children's Hearings in Scotland*, 3rd edn (Edinburgh: W. Green, 2013), para.14.11, fnn.26 and 27). It is submitted that if a hearing member is cited to an appeal hearing then that member must of course attend but should seek the direction of the court as to what questions, if any, he or she is to answer (and, of course, comply with any directions the sheriff may make as to what questions must be answered).

Subs.(5)(d)
The Principal Reporter. Here, as elsewhere in the Act, "Principal Reporter", by virtue of para.10(1) of Sch.3, includes any person to whom the Principal Reporter has lawfully delegated his or her functions. In practice this will mean the Reporter who was present at the hearing concerned, or possibly a Reporter from that Reporter's office who is fully versed in the case.

C.534.12

Subs.(5)(e)
These are new explicit provisions, but reflect existing practice. The "chief social work officer" is defined in s.202(1) by reference to s.3 of the Social Work (Scotland) Act 1968 and means, where a compulsory supervision order or interim compulsory supervision order is involved, the officer appointed by the implementation authority, and, where a medical examination order or warrant to secure attendance is involved, the relevant local authority for the child concerned. In practice where evidence is required from social work the allocated social worker, or possibly his or her manager, will generally be called. Where evidence is required in relation to the secure accommodation then it will generally be appropriate for this to be given personally by the person in charge.

C.534.13

Subss.(5)(f) and (6)
See discussion of subss.(4) and (5) above, and see below the General Note on s.156 and the discussion of s.156(1), particularly in relation to the concept of the sheriff being "satisfied". Subsection (5)(f), read with subs.(4), seems to reflect the provisions of, and practice under, s.51(3) of the 1995 Act which empowered the sheriff to "call for a further report which he considers may assist him in deciding the appeal". Subsection (6) goes beyond this and enacts that the sheriff may "require any person" whom he or she considers may help in determining the appeal to give evidence. It is thought that this can only refer to a person who has had some dealings with the child's case and that it cannot mean that the sheriff should have the power to identify, say, a particular psychiatrist or social worker, unconnected with the case, and compel him or her to come to court and give evidence.

C.534.14

Subs.(7)
Regulation 6 of the Children's Hearings (Scotland) Act 2011 (Safeguarders Further Provisions) Regulations 2012 (SSI 2012/336) provides that the sheriff may require a safeguarder appointed in relation to the child to give a report for the purposes of assisting the sheriff in determining an appeal under s.154.

C.534.15

Determination of appeal

156.—(1) If satisfied that the decision to which an appeal under section 154 relates is justified, the sheriff—

(a) must confirm the decision, and
(b) may take one or more of the steps mentioned in subsection (3) if satisfied that the circumstances of the child in relation to whom the decision was made have changed since the decision was made.

(2) In any other case, the sheriff—
(a) must—
  (i) where the decision is a decision to grant a warrant to secure attendance, recall the warrant,
  (ii) where the decision is a decision to make an interim compulsory supervision order or a medical examination order, terminate the order,
(b) may take one or more of the steps mentioned in subsection (3).
(3) Those steps are—

C.535

(a) require the Principal Reporter to arrange a children's hearing for any purpose for which a hearing can be arranged under this Act,
(b) continue, vary or terminate any order, interim variation or warrant which is in effect,
(c) discharge the child from any further hearing or other proceedings in relation to the grounds that gave rise to the decision,
(d) make an interim compulsory supervision order or interim variation of a compulsory supervision order, or
(e) grant a warrant to secure attendance.

[1] (3A) If the sheriff continues or varies a compulsory supervision order under subsection (3)(b), the sheriff—
(a) must, if the order contains a movement restriction condition (or is being varied so as to include such a condition), require the order to be reviewed by a children's hearing on a day or within a period specified in the order,
(b) may, in any other case, require the order to be so reviewed.

(4) If the sheriff discharges a child under subsection (3)(c), the sheriff must also terminate any order or warrant which is in effect in relation to the child.

(5) The fact that a sheriff makes, continues or varies an order, or grants a warrant, under subsection (1)(b) or (2)(b) does not prevent a children's hearing from continuing, varying or terminating the order or warrant.

NOTE

C.535.1   1. Inserted by the Children's Hearings (Scotland) Act 2011 (Modification of Primary Legislation) Order 2013 (SSI 2013/211) Sch.1 para.20(15) (effective June 24 2013).

DEFINITIONS
C.535.2   "child": s.199.
"children's hearing": s.5.
"interim compulsory supervision order": ss.202(1) and 86.
"Principal Reporter": s.14 and Sch.3 paras 8–10.
"warrant to secure attendance": ss.202(1) and 88.
"interim compulsory supervision order": ss.202(1) and 86.

GENERAL NOTE
C.535.3   This section reflects s.51(4) to (6) of the Children (Scotland) Act 1995, with some important modifications, including the new provision that in the case of an unsuccessful appeal the sheriff may, while confirming the decision of the hearing, nevertheless, where the child's circumstances have changed, take any of the steps, set out in subs.(3), which are competent where an appeal has been successful. The courts have generally adopted a conservative stance in relation to the scope of appeals. Whether this may have to be reconsidered is discussed below in our discussion of subs.(1). Where the sheriff decides to confirm the decision of the children's hearing *simpliciter*, i.e. without taking any of the steps referred to in subs.(2) or (3) he or she may, but is not obliged to, issue a note of reasons, but, where making any other disposal, the sheriff must issue a note of reasons (Act of Sederunt (Child Care and Maintenance Rules) 1997 (SI 1997/291), as amended (the 1997 Rules) r.3.58(2)).

Subs.(1)
C.535.4   *If satisfied that the decision to which an appeal under section 154 relates is justified* ... Section 51 of the 1995 Act put matters rather differently:

"(4) Where the sheriff decides that an appeal under this section has failed he shall confirm the decision of the children's hearing.

(5) Where the sheriff is satisfied that the decision of the children's hearing is not justified in all the circumstances of the case he shall allow the appeal".

In *W v Schaffer*, 2001 S.L.T. (Sh. Ct) 86 at 87J, Sheriff Principal C.G.B. Nicholson QC observed that the Act

"[s]omewhat curiously does not explicitly set out grounds for appeal, but provides, in subsection (5) that where the sheriff 'is satisfied that the decision of the children's hearing is not justified in all the circumstances of the case', he is to allow the appeal and allow the case to proceed in certain specified ways. Consequently, what the subsection appears to be saying, albeit somewhat obliquely, is that the ground of an appeal to a sheriff is to be that

Determination of appeal

the decision of the children's hearing was not justified in all the circumstances of the case."

Sheriff Principal Nicholson then refers to the words of Professor Norrie in his *Children (Scotland) Act 1995*, revised edn (Edinburgh: W. Green, 1998), p.87 to the effect that these words do not allow the sheriff to allow the appeal merely because he has a difference of opinion with the hearing as to the correct disposal of the case and pointing out that it is "perfectly conceivable that two different, even opposing, disposals are justifiable as to the correct disposal of the case". Sheriff Principal Nicholson goes on to conclude, at 87L, that

"the task facing a sheriff to whom an appeal has been taken is not to reconsider the evidence which was placed before the hearing with a view to making his own decision on that evidence. Instead the sheriff's task is to see if there has been some procedural irregularity in the conduct of the case; to see whether the hearing has failed to give proper, or any, consideration to a relevant factor in the case; in general to consider whether the decision reached by the hearing can be characterised as one which could not, upon any reasonable view, be regarded as justified in all the circumstances of the case."

As mentioned above in the General Note to s.154, the omission of the words "in all the circumstances of the case" from the present provision may tend to suggest a limitation of the scope of appeals. However, the case of *M v Locality Reporter Manager* [2014] CSIH 62; 2014 Fam. L.R. 102; 2014 G.W.D. 24–453 has to be considered. As mentioned above in the General Note to s.154, this was an appeal by a mother from a sheriff's decision to uphold the decision of a children's hearing to maintain quite limited contact between the mother and her daughters. In the course of her submissions the mother's counsel (see para.[41] of the court's opinion) said that those acting for the appellant did not ask the sheriff to hear evidence, and submitted that the sheriff, under the 2011 Act, had power to undertake a wide review of the children's hearing's decision, but

"had felt constrained by the interpretation of the extent of the sheriff's jurisdiction provided by Sheriff Principal Nicholson in *W v Schaffer* 2001 S.L.T. (Sh Ct) 86 at 87K to 88A, a statement of the law which is endorsed by Norrie, *Children's Hearings in Scotland* (3rd edit) at para 13–14".

The court did not find it necessary to further discuss this but commented, at [42]: "The question of whether what was said in *W v Schaffer* was both correct and comprehensive is for another day". (In *CF v MF & CF and Scottish Reporter* [2017] CSIH 44, discussed above under s.81(3), an Extra Division, at para.[37], agreed with Sheriff Principal Nicholson's approach, no argument having been addressed to it on the correctness of the decision in *W v Schaffer*.)

Commentators have differed in emphasis in their interpretations of the provisions for appeals against determinations of children's hearings. Professor Norrie, in the passage quoted above by Sheriff Principal Nicholson, supports what might be described as the "restrictive" approach. This reflects the decision by Sheriff (as he then was) J.S. Mowat, who, in relation to s.49(2) of the Social Work (Scotland) Act 1968, stated in *D v Sinclair*, 1973 S.L.T. (Sh. Ct) 47 at 48:

"In approaching this case I had the firm view that the appropriate procedure for appeals against determinations of a children's hearing made it clear that a sheriff should not interfere with the determination simply because he felt that another form of treatment might be preferable. . . . Accordingly, I consider that a sheriff should not allow an appeal unless there was some flaw in the procedure adopted by the hearing or he was satisfied that the hearing had not given proper consideration to some factor in the case."

Sheriff Kearney, in his *Children's Hearings and the Sheriff Court*, 2nd edn (Butterworths, 2000), para.47.05, raises the possibility that the power to substitute the sheriff's own disposal conveyed by s.51(5)(c)(iii) of the 1995 Act might lead to a change of attitude on the part of sheriffs as to their powers on appeal, but comes to the conclusion that sheriffs "may" continue to follow Sheriff Mowat's approach. The Scottish Government issued a "Policy Memorandum" in relation to the Bill which preceded this Act and we should therefore consider the implications of this.

Statutory interpretation—Parliamentary papers

It is now recognised that certain parliamentary papers issued in relation to legislation may be referred to by the courts when interpreting such legislation. In *R (Westminster City Council) v NASS* [2002] UKHL 38; [2002] 1 W.L.R. 2956; 2002 4 All E.R. 654, Lord Steyn, after recalling the practice introduced by the UK Parliament in 1999 of issuing explanatory notes along with the publication of a Bill, made observations on this. His Lordship's remarks are summarised in *Bennion on Statutory Interpretation*, edited by Oliver Jones, 6th edn (Lexis Nexis, 2013), p.592 in a quotation from the judgment of Brooke LJ in *Flora (Tarlochan Singh) v Wakom (Heathrow) Ltd* [2006] EWCA Civ. 1103; [2006] All E.R. 982; [2007] 1 W.L.R. 402 at [15]–[17], thus:

"The text of the Act does not have to be ambiguous before a court may be permitted to take into account an Explanatory Note to understand the contextual scene in which the Act is set (*NASS* para [5]). In so far as this material casts light on the objective setting or contextual scene of the statute, and the mischief to which it is aimed, it is always an admissible aid to construction. Lord Steyn, however, ended his exposition of the value of Explanatory Notes as an aid to construction by saying at para [6]:

'What is impermissible is to treat the wishes and desires of the Government about the scope of the statutory language as reflecting the will of Parliament. The aims of the Government in respect of the meaning of clauses as revealed in Explanatory Notes cannot be attributed to Parliament. The object is to see what is the intention expressed by the words enacted.'"

Since then there have been frequent references to such material in the Scottish courts, e.g. in *AXA General Insurance Ltd v Lord Advocate*, 2011 S.C. 662; [2011] CSIH 31 at [21].

When the Children's Hearings (Scotland) Bill was published in February 2010, a Policy Memorandum was published in order to comply with r.9.3.3(c) of the Parliament's Standing Orders. This Memorandum, so far as concerns appeals, includes:

"*Policy objective*

380. To continue the ability to appeal a decision of a children's hearing. The Bill makes provision for an appeal of a hearing's decision to be made to the sheriff. There is no policy change in continuing this right. However, the Bill does clarify the scope of appeal and review that is available to the sheriff in considering any appeal, and makes it clear that the sheriff has available to him the power to conduct a wide review of the issues that a hearing considered. We anticipate that the sheriff would use the full range of these powers infrequently.

Key information

382. Current legislation provides that appeals to the sheriff can be wide in scope (such as that it can be effectively a re-hearing of the matter, if the sheriff considers this appropriate). The scope of appeal was deliberately broadened by the 1995 Act as compared with the appeal process outlined in the Social Work (Scotland) Act 1968. This is clear from a number of statements made at Westminster by Government Ministers during the parliamentary passage of the 1995 Act. A wide scope of appeal (albeit to be used infrequently) was the deliberate legislative intention of the 1995 Act.

383. Providing the sheriff with a wide potential scope of appeal is in line with the stated intention of Kilbrandon that there was a significant role for the sheriff in the Children's Hearings system, such as deciding upon the grounds for referral if they are not accepted by the child or relevant person.

384. Under section 51 of the 1995 Act the sheriff has various options as to disposal of a section 51 appeal and these include the power to substitute his own decision for that of the children's hearing. The sheriff is not limited to remitting back to the hearing for a decision, and this suggests that the sheriff can address the merits.

385. In all appeals the sheriff will have a copy of all reports etc. and may ask for further reports or cite witnesses. Most appeals however consist of the solicitor for the appellant making his case, which is then answered by the Reporter who was present at the children's hearing (in around 70% of appeals it is the same Reporter who appears). In most cases the sheriff then makes a finding without having heard evidence. However, it is for the sheriff to decide this.

386. Therefore the intention of the 1995 Act was to widen the scope of the appeal to the sheriff, as compared with the 1968 Act and in legislative terms this widening was achieved. Some case law has not however reflected this widening.

387. An Inner House judgement in the *SK v Paterson* case in October 2009 [sub nom *K v Paterson* [2009] CSIH; 2009 S.L.T. 1019 (at para.62)] gives some support to there currently being a wide potential scope of appeal and a relevant extract from the opinion is below:

"The provisions of section 51 require that the Sheriff have placed before him all the reports and statements that were before the children's hearing, together with all reports of the children's hearing itself and the reasons for its decision. The Sheriff is also entitled to hear evidence from, or on behalf of, the appellant and the respondent and to examine the authors or compilers of any reports or statements and call for any further reports he deems to be necessary. The Sheriff's power under section 51 entitles him to investigate the issue...".

388. The Bill therefore reflects the appeal provisions in the 1995 Act and also clarifies that a wide potential scope of appeal is available to the sheriff should they consider this necessary in the circumstances of the case before the court. The Bill seeks to remedy the ambiguity of current powers and allow for consistent application of the power for a wide review, if the sheriff considers it justifiable in all the circumstances."

Determination of appeal

Principles governing the sheriff's decision—general

In *M v Locality Reporter Manager* [2014] CSIH 62; 2014 Fam. L.R. 102; 2014 G.W.D. 24–453, the court said that the question of the correctness of *W v Schaffer*, 2001 S.L.T. (Sh. Ct) 86, was "for another day". Should that day come it may be, having regard to the terms of the Policy Memorandum quoted above, that sheriffs will be entitled to adopt, in an appropriate case, a more interventional approach than that adopted by Sheriff Mowat in *D v Sinclair*, 1973 S.L.T. (Sh. Ct) 47 and by Sheriff Principal Nicholson in *W v Schaffer*. (In *CF v MF & CF and Scottish Reporter* [2017] CSIH 44, discussed above under s.81(3), an Extra Division, at para [37], agreed with Sheriff Principal Nicholson's approach, no argument having been addressed to it on the correctness of the decision in *W v Schaffer*.)

Principles governing sheriff's decision on a legal issue

In deciding any purely legal issue in the appeal the sheriff will generally require to decide the matter on its merits since the paramountcy of welfare principle, for the reasons set out in the discussion above of s.25, does not have direct application. However, in *M, Appellant*, 2014 Fam. L.B. 127–7 and *X, Appellants*, 2013 S.L.T. (Sh. Ct) 125, cases about the decisions of pre-hearing panels as to whether a person had the characteristics of a relevant person, Sheriff A.G. McCulloch relied on the paramountcy of the welfare of the child principle—saying, e.g. at [6] of the former, that his decision "must have at its heart the 'best interests of the child' principle." (In *W v Children's Reporter*, 2013 S.L.T. (Sh. Ct) 99 (a case under the 1995 Act) at [28], Sheriff Mungo Bovey QC invoked this decision in relation to the claim by a grandmother.) Commentators have differed on this issue. Professor Kenneth McK. Norrie, in his article in 2014 Fam. L.B. 128–4, examines these decisions of Sheriff A.G. McCulloch. Professor Norrie concludes:

"Section 25 does not, in other words, apply to the evaluative determination of whether a person meets the test in s.81(3), just as it does not apply to the evaluation of the facts that found a s.67 ground."

Replying to this at 2014 Fam. L.B. 130–6, Sheriff Kearney argues that the decision on relevant person matters, being in this context a procedural issue, is appropriately governed by the paramountcy of the welfare of the child principle.

Sheriff McCulloch's decision in *X, Appellants*, 2013 S.L.T. (Sh. Ct) 125, was appealed to the Court of Session which, in *MT & AG v Anne Gerry (Locality Reporter)* [2014] CSIH 108, expressly approving Professor Norrie's stance, reversed the sheriff's decision and held, at [12], that the test for assessing relevant person status was "a factual one" and "not a decision which, reflecting the terms of section 25(1) of the 2011 Act, was 'a matter relating to the child.'"

Scope of appeal on legal issue

In his article Professor Norrie further expresses the opinion that Sheriff McCulloch's reliance on the paramountcy of the welfare of the child principle here is unjustifiable because "it is well-known that sheriffs cannot overrule decisions of children's hearings just because they disagree with them". Sheriff Kearney observes that this opinion is based on Professor Norrie's view of the line of authority from *D v Sinclair* to *W v Schaffer*, both cited above, and comments:

"The sheriff here, a qualified lawyer, was considering the submission that the lay tribunal appealed from had misdirected itself on a matter of mixed fact and law. It would surely be paradoxical if the appellate tribunal, on concluding that there had been such a misdirection, were not empowered to correct it."

The Court of Session in *MT & AG v Anne Gerry (Locality Reporter)* [2014] CSIH 108, did not deal with this issue and, standing the observation of the Court of Session in *M v Locality Reporter Manager* [2014] CSIH 62, that the question of the correctness of *W v Schaffer* was "for another day", the issue would appear to be open. However, as mentioned above, in *CF v MF & CF and Scottish Reporter* [2017] CSIH 44, discussed above under s.81(3), an Extra Division, at para.[37], agreed with Sheriff Principal Nicholson's approach, no argument having been addressed to it on the correctness of the decision in *W v Schaffer*.

Subs.(1)(b)

May take one or more of the steps mentioned in subsection (3). These are the same steps as are competent where the sheriff is not "confirming" the decision of the children's hearing. In effect the statute is according to the sheriff, where the circumstances of the child have changed, the same powers as are accorded to the sheriff when not confirming the decision of the children's hearing. This is a new provision but is not as novel as may appear. In the case of *D v Sinclair*, 1973 S.L.T. (Sh. Ct) 47, Sheriff Mowat, on 10 November 1972, held that the children's hearing had not acted in any improper way but, owing to the considerations that, since the date of the decision appealed against, 5 September 1972, the child's truancy seemed to have ceased and the

C.535.5

Children's Hearings (Scotland) Act 2011

family were waking up to their responsibilities, he decided to allow the appeal and ordered that the matter should be referred back to a hearing so that these matters may be further investigated and considered. This approach had been commended by the Second Division in *Kennedy v B*, 1972 S.C. 128; 1973 S.L.T. 38 and has been recognised to some extent by Professor Norrie in the first edition of his *Children's Hearings in Scotland* (Edinburgh: W. Green, 1997), p.185 (middle paragraph) and by Sheriff Kearney in his *Children's Hearings and the Sheriff Court*, 2nd edn (Butterworths, 2000), para.49.14. Accordingly, this provision may be regarded as an example of the present statute recognising formally what had become the practice.

The circumstances of the child ... have changed. What may constitute a change of circumstances will be a matter of fact for the decision of the sheriff in whatever of the infinite variety of situations may be presented in the appeal concerned. The change, however, must be of some substance, because *de minimis non curat lex* ("the law does not care about very little things" – *Sharrat v Central London Bus Co Ltd (The Accident Group Test Cases)* [2003] 4 All E.R. 590 at [226]). However, in this as in other matters concerning children, the courts and others must always try to envisage circumstances from the child's point of view and what may seem a "very little thing" to an adult may mean a lot to a child. In a particular case a change of mind by the child may or may not be a change of circumstances of sufficient materiality to have a decisive effect.

Subs.(2)

C.535.6 *In any other case.* That is where the sheriff does other than confirm the decision of the children's hearing.

Subs.(2)(a) and (b)

C.535.7 This deals with two orders affecting the liberty of the child and provides in effect that where the sheriff is in favour of sustaining an appeal against either of these orders the sheriff, in addition to having the wide range of choice of disposals provided for in subs.(3), must recall the order concerned. The making of an interim variation of a compulsory supervision order—which is enacted as an appealable matter under s.154(3)(e)—is not included here.

Subs.(3)(a)

C.535.8 This is the approximate equivalent of s.51(5)(c)(i) of the Children (Scotland) Act 1995, but uses the wording "for any purpose for which a hearing can be arranged under this Act" instead of "for reconsideration of their decision", but in practice this is the provision empowering a sheriff who wishes to sustain an appeal but only to the extent of remitting the child's case back to a hearing for disposal. Until the 1995 Act, this was the only disposal by which a sheriff could sustain an appeal while keeping the child within the system since, under s.49(5)(b) of the Social Work (Scotland) Act 1968, it was provided that where the sheriff allowed an appeal against a disposal by a hearing the sheriff's powers were to

"remit the case with reasons for his decision to the children's hearing for reconsideration of their decision or discharge the child from any other hearing or other proceedings in relation to the grounds for the referral of the case".

Between the 1968 Act and the 1995 Act, the case of *Kennedy v A*, 1986 S.L.T. 358 (IH) authoritatively decided that the sheriff, in remitting back, was not entitled to give directions or make observations as to the disposal of the case. In this case Lord Justice Clerk Ross, referring to the terms of s.49(5) of the 1968 Act requiring the sheriff to give "reasons", stated that

"it is one thing for the sheriff to give reasons for his decision and quite another thing to make observations or give directions".

Sheriff Kearney in *Children's Hearings and the Sheriff Court* (2000), para.53.06, suggested that the power given to the sheriff by s.51(5)(c)(iii) to substitute his or her own disposal might raise the question as to whether the *ratio* of *Kennedy v A* remained in force, but in practice the courts continued to follow this case. In Professor Norrie's, *Children's Hearings in Scotland*, 2nd edn (Edinburgh: W. Green, 2005), p.219 (when read with fn.15) it is said that the concept of the children's hearing being the appropriate forum for the disposing of children's cases under the system "is the very foundation of the whole children's hearing system". This is of course true, but it is possible to figure a situation wherein a sheriff who is minded to allow an appeal may, recognising the primacy of the children's hearing in matters of disposal, prefer not to impose his or her own disposal, but also wish, in the note of reasons, to focus the attention of the hearing on a particular possible mode of disposal for its acceptance or rejection. The terms of the Policy Memorandum, referred to above, may be regarded as fortifying the legitimacy of such a procedure.

Subs.(3)(b)–(e)

C.535.9 These provisions are the approximate equivalent of s.51(5)(c)(iii) of the Children (Scotland) Act 1995 which in effect conferred on the sheriff the power to substitute his or her own disposal,

Determination of appeal

being the same powers (set out in s.70 of that Act) as would be open to a children's hearing. The layout of the present provisions is, however, different in that s.70 of the 1995 Act specifies, in subss.(3) to (6), the features of a "supervision requirement", whereas this subsection, by referring to "order" and "warrant" sends us back to the "Key definitions" comprising ss.83 to 88 of this Act. "Orders" are: a compulsory supervision order (CSO) (s.83); an interim compulsory supervision order (ICSO) (s.86); and a medical examination order (MEO) (s.87). A "warrant" is a "warrant to secure attendance" (s.88).

It will be recalled that subss.(1) and (2) confer these powers on the sheriff both when "confirming" the children's hearing's decision (but where the child's circumstances have changed) and "in any other case" (i.e. where the sheriff decides that he or she is not "satisfied" that the hearing's decision is justified—in effect sustaining the appeal). The effect of these provisions is to place the case wherein the appeal against the decision has failed (but the child's circumstances have changed) on the same basis, in respect of the sheriff's powers of disposal when ruling on the appeal, as the case wherein the appeal has succeeded. This means that the sheriff must select from the list comprising paras (b) to (e) in this subsection the order or orders which are to be made in his or her interlocutor at the conclusion of the appeal. Where the sheriff disposes of the appeal by continuing or varying a CSO by virtue of (b), the sheriff must, under subs.(3A), require the CSO to be reviewed and, where the CSO contains, or is being varied so as to contain, a movement restriction condition, this review must take place on a day or within a period specified in the CSO.

Types of appeal
There are two kinds of appeal, viz appeals based on an alleged irregularity or point of law, and appeals challenging factual conclusions. We shall look at these in turn.

Appeals on basis of an irregularity or point of law
These are not mentioned specifically as grounds of appeal, but have been recognised as such from the beginning—see the quotation from Sheriff Mowat in the case of *D v Sinclair*, 1973 S.L.T. (Sh. Ct) 47, and the observation in *CM and BM v Kennedy*, 1995 S.C.L.R. 15 at 19E:

"Nothing is said in section 49(1) [of the Social Work (Scotland) Act 1968] about the grounds on which an appeal may lie to the sheriff under that subsection. But in our opinion it is clear that an appeal may be taken at that stage on the ground of an irregularity in the conduct of the case by a children's hearing".

Such an appeal would be competent against any of the decisions listed in s.154(3) of the 2011 Act. Appeals on this basis include decisions ultra vires (i.e. beyond the powers of the children's hearing), in contravention of a statutory provision or in breach of the relevant rules. See Kearney, *Children's Hearings and the Sheriff Court* (2000), paras 49.07 to 49.12 and Kenneth McK. Norrie, *Children's Hearings in Scotland*, 3rd edn (Edinburgh: W. Green, 2013), para.14–14 for fuller discussion. It was said in *M v Locality Reporter Manager* [2014] CSIH 62 at [27], that

"a failure to have regard to a relevant factor whether by a children's hearing or any other decision-maker is not of itself a procedural irregularity; an error of law perhaps but not a procedural irregularity".

An irregularity must be material before an appeal can succeed—e.g. the founding in the ground for referral on a current statutory provision but citing a former (repealed) statute (as in *McGregor v A*, 1982 S.L.T. 45) would not be material and, if that were the only successful ground of appeal and the sheriff was otherwise "satisfied" in terms of s.156(1), then the appeal would fail. At the other end of the spectrum, where in the course of an appeal it emerged that a radical defect which could not be rectified existed, in that the "hearing" decision appealed from had been made by an improperly constituted hearing (cf. *H v Mearns*, above) then the sheriff would have no option but to sustain the appeal, terminate, under s.156(3)(b), whatever order had been made and discharge the child from the system under s.156(c). The sheriff would require to do this even if he or she thought that the child required protection, guidance, treatment or control—cf. the observations by Lord Rodger of Earlsferry on due process in *Constanda v M*, 1997 S.L.T. 1396; 1997 S.C.L.R. 510, quoted above in our discussion of s.67(2)(m). However, not every procedural irregularity will lead to a successful appeal: unless the irregularity is fundamental and irreparable (as in *H v Mearns*, 1974 S.C. 152; 1974 S.L.T. 184) it is "necessary for it to be shown that the occurrence concerned was damaging to the justice of the proceedings" (*C v Miller*, 2003 S.L.T. 1379; 2004 S.C.L.R. 55 at [71]).

Between these two extremes are irregularities or procedural or legal errors which, while not leading to fundamental nullity, are significant but reparable, such as an apparent failure to give a mature child the opportunity to indicate if she or he wished to give views or a failure to consider a disposal which had been strongly recommended. In such situations the sheriff may allow the appeal and must then decide whether to proceed by remitting back to the hearing to

Children's Hearings (Scotland) Act 2011

consider the omitted matter or take the matter over and deal with it him or herself, using the powers conferred by s.156(3)(b)(c) or (d). In his *Children's Hearings in Scotland*, 3rd edn (2013), para.14.18, Professor Norrie states:

"Nevertheless, in the generality of cases, if a range of justifiable measures are available it is all the more important that the child and relevant person are able fully to participate in the choice of which measure to include in the order, and in most cases this will be best assured by returning the case to the children's hearing for disposal".

We would not disagree with this, but would recall that the powers of the sheriff to obtain evidence from those mentioned in s.155(5) and (6) and to dispose of the case as provided in paras (b) to (e) of this present subsection and in subs.(3A) of this section may incline the sheriff, in the light of the observations in the Policy Document, mentioned above, to dispose of the case him or herself, where it seems expedient to do so. It will be recalled that the powers of the sheriff include making an interim order (interim compulsory supervision order or interim variation of a compulsory supervision order). In coming to his or her decision, the sheriff would require to apply the paramountcy of the welfare of the child, the minimum intervention and the views of the child principles, and the EC proportionality principle.

Appeals other than appeals on ground of irregularity or legal or procedural error—appeals raising issues of fact

The privileged position of the court or tribunal which has heard the evidence is well established. In the leading case of *Thomas v Thomas*, 1948 S.C. (HL) 45 at 55; 1948 S.L.T. 2 at 6, Lord Thankerton quoted with approval the words of Lord Shaw of Dunfermline in *Clarke v Edinburgh and District Tramways Co*, 1919 S.C. (HL) 35 at 37:

"In my opinion the duty of an appellate Court in those circumstances is for the Judge of it to put to himself, as I do now in this case the question: Am I—who sit here without those advantages, sometimes broad and sometimes subtle, which are the privilege of the Judge who heard and tried the case—in a position, not having these privileges, to come to a conclusion that the Judge who had them was plainly wrong? If I cannot be satisfied in my own mind that the Judge with those privileges was plainly wrong, then it appears to me to be my duty to defer to his judgment."

Thus, even in a case such as *Thomas*, where a printed transcript of the evidence was available, the decision of the court of first instance as to matters of fact was held to be preferred.

It is submitted that the position of the sheriff in an appeal against a decision of a children's hearing is different from that of the appellate court in ordinary civil jurisdiction. Children's hearings' decisions as to disposal are made substantially on the basis of reports, which are of course available to the sheriff. The sheriff can request and indeed "require" further reports, which *ex hypothesi* were not available to the hearing and the sheriff, unlike a civil appeal court, can hear evidence from all who gave information to the hearing. The totality of these considerations appear to equate with the words of para.380 of the Policy Memorandum in that they

"clarify the scope of appeal and review that is available to the sheriff in considering any appeal, and make it clear that the sheriff has available to him the power to conduct a wide review of the issues that a hearing considered";

all of this, in the words of para.384, "suggests that the sheriff can address the merits".

We think that sheriffs, mindful of the ruling of the House of Lords in *Thomas*, will continue to be reticent about displacing decisions of fact made by children's hearings, but the power to do so in a particular case is valuable.

For a comprehensive survey of the scope for displacing the judgment of fact by the tribunal of first instance, see Kenneth McK. Norrie, "Appellate Deference in Scottish Child Protections Cases", Edin.L.R. 2016, 20(2), 149–177.

Principles to be observed

Professor Norrie, in his *Children's Hearings in Scotland*, 3rd edn (2013), para.14–18 states, in relation to the sheriff's decision to allow or not the appeal and whether to take any of the steps available under s.156(2) or (3):

"The sheriff's decision in this regard is determined only by whether he is satisfied that the decision being appealed against was justified or not, and is not dependent on the application of the principles in ss.25, 26, 27 and 29. (Footnote): 'Paramountcy or primacy of welfare, children's views and minimum intervention.' And, as we have already seen, the decision is not to be made according to whether the sheriff agrees with the hearing's decision ... ".

This expression of opinion is of course predicated on Professor Norrie's adherence to what we have called the "restrictive" interpretation of the sheriff's powers on appeal (and is not universally true even on that interpretation since, as Professor Norrie himself recognises later in the same paragraph, the sheriff should use his powers to impose his own disposal "only when it achieves the only possible good outcome, or an order has to be changed as a matter of urgency"). However, if the wider interpretation of the sheriff's powers on appeal, outlined above, were to be accepted then the sheriff, who would in effect be putting him or herself in the position of the children's hearing, would be bound by paramountcy of welfare, the child's views and the minimum intervention principles. Like Professor Norrie we would, at least, "expect" that sheriffs would be reticent of employing these wider powers. In the event of the sheriff considering whether to grant a warrant to secure attendance under subs.(3)(e) the sheriff, whatever view is taken of the sheriff's powers on appeal, would be bound by all three of the overarching principles and the European Convention principle of proportionality and would therefore have to consider inter alia if some method other than a warrant would be likely to secure the child's attendance.

Subs.(3A)
These provisions reflect the centrality of the children's hearing in relation to disposal, and para.(a) emphasises this by ensuring that the children's hearing has its say where, when owing to a movement restriction order being involved, the liberty of the child is in issue. The provision in para.(b) empowering (but not requiring) the sheriff, where no movement restriction order is involved, to require a review puts the sheriff in the same position as a children's hearing under s.125(3); consequently the sheriff, in making his or her decision as to whether to require a review, should have regard to the same considerations as would such a children's hearing—see above in our discussion of s.125(3).

C.535.10

Subs.(4)
It might be thought that the discharge of the child from any hearing etc. would, automatically, terminate any related order or warrant, and indeed that was the assumption made in s.51(5)(c)(ii) of the 1995 Act, which did not make this explicit requirement. It will now be proper practice for the sheriff, when thus discharging a child, to include in his or her interlocutor words to the effect "and discharges the child AB from all orders and warrants in force in relation to this referral".

C.535.11

Subs.(5)
This can only apply where the determination of the sheriff has been other than to discharge the child under subs.(3)(c) above, that is, it applies only where the sheriff's determination results in the child remaining within the system and, therefore, a further children's hearing will take place. The effect of this subsection is to confirm that such a children's hearing is empowered to dispose of the child's case in the usual way. We have submitted above that the sheriff may, on the view of the sheriff's appellate powers which we have advanced, in an appropriate case remit back to the children's hearing with a suggestion as to disposal. The consequence is that the children's hearing would require to consider any such suggestion in the light of the latest information, but would not be bound to follow it.

C.535.12

Time limit for disposal of appeal against certain decisions

157.—(1) This section applies where an appeal under section 154 relates to a decision of a children's hearing to—
  (a) make a compulsory supervision order including a secure accommodation authorisation or movement restriction condition,
  (b) make an interim compulsory supervision order,
  (c) make an interim variation of a compulsory supervision order,
  (d) make a medical examination order, or
  (e) grant a warrant to secure attendance.
(2) The appeal must be heard and disposed of before the expiry of the period of 3 days beginning the day after the day on which the appeal is made.
(3) If the appeal is not disposed of within that period, the authorisation, condition, order, variation or, as the case may be, warrant ceases to have effect.

C.536

DEFINITIONS
  "compulsory supervision order": ss.202(1) and 83.
  "interim compulsory supervision order": ss.202(1) and 86.
  "medical examination order": ss.202(1) and 87.

C.536.1

"movement restriction condition": ss.202(1) and 84.
"secure accommodation authorisation": ss.202(1) and 85.
"warrant to secure attendance": ss.202(1) and 88.

General Note

C.536.2 The requirements listed in subs.(1) have many of the characteristics of the warrant under the Children (Scotland) Act 1995. Accordingly, like such a warrant, the appeal provisions are subject to a short timescale. The inclusion of the compulsory supervision order containing a secure accommodation authorisation is new and satisfactory. This, along with the provisions in s.162 introducing the right to appeal against decisions of the Chief Social Work Officer in relation to the implementation of secure accommodation authorisations, reflects the legislature's concern that decisions seriously affecting the liberty and welfare of the child should be subject to appropriate and prompt judicial oversight.

Period of notice
In general, in proceedings before the sheriff citations or notices must be made not later than 48 hours, or in the case of postal citation, 72 hours before the diet concerned (see r.3.13 of the Act of Sederunt (Child Care and Maintenance Rules) 1997 (SI 1997/291) as amended by Act of Sederunt (Children's Hearings (Scotland) Act 2011) (Miscellaneous Amendments) 2013 (SSI 2013/172) (the "1997 Rules") but in the case of appeals under this section and ss. 160(1), 161(1) and 162(3) the period of notice is as directed by the sheriff (the 1997 Rules, r.3.13(2)(a)).

Position of child pending appeal against an order under this section
The general rule is that the lodging of an appeal means that the order appealed against need not be complied with until the appeal is disposed of: *Macleay v Macdonald*, 1928 S.C. 776; 1928 S.L.T. 463. However, the provision in s.158, below, in relation to suspension of a compulsory supervision order pending appeal, entails that, once made, the order has to be implemented and remains in force pending the disposal of the appeal unless successful application is made to suspend it (cf. *Stirling v D*, 1995 S.C. 358; 1995 S.L.T. 1089; 1995 S.C.L.R. 460).

Subss.(2) and (3)
C.536.3 Beginning *the day after the day on which the appeal is made*. The clear intention of the legislature here is that the day *after* the appeal is lodged is to be "day one" when calculating the time limit for disposal of the appeal. "Day" here means calendar day, not working day. It follows that an appeal lodged on Wednesday 30 December 2015 must be heard *and disposed of* on or before Saturday 2 January 2016 (even at cost of some inconvenience to all concerned), and that unless this is accomplished the order etc appealed against will fall. Rule 3.55 of the Act of Sederunt (Child Care and Maintenance) Rules 1997 (SI 1997/291), as amended, allows for the tight timescale by excluding from appeals under this section the usual rule that any answers must be lodged not later than seven days before the appeal diet—in effect, answers may be lodged at any time before, or at, the appeal diet.

Compulsory supervision order: suspension pending appeal

Compulsory supervision order: suspension pending appeal

C.537 **158.**—(1) This section applies where—
(a) an appeal is made under section 154 against a decision to make, vary, continue or terminate a compulsory supervision order, and
(b) the person making the appeal requests the Principal Reporter to arrange a children's hearing to consider whether the decision should be suspended pending the determination of the appeal.

(2) As soon as practicable after the request is made, the Principal Reporter must arrange a children's hearing to consider whether the decision should be suspended pending the determination of the appeal.

Definitions
C.537.1 "children's hearing": s.5.
"compulsory supervision order": ss.202(1) and 83.
"Principal Reporter": s.14 and Sch.3 paras 8–10.

Compulsory supervision order: suspension pending appeal

GENERAL NOTE

This section reflects s.51(9) of the Children (Scotland) Act 1995, but with a significant difference: this section permits suspension of the "decision" of the children's hearing to make a compulsory supervision order (CSO), whereas s.51(9) of the 1995 Act permitted suspension of the CSO itself. This had the consequence, decided upon in *S v Proudfoot*, 2002 S.L.T. 743; 2002 Fam. L.R. 92 OH, that an appeal against a condition of a supervision requirement and not against the supervision requirement itself, was not competent. Professor Norrie, in his *Children's Hearings in Scotland*, 3rd edn (Edinburgh: W. Green, 2013), paras 10–20 and 14–32, expresses the view that the present wording makes competent an appeal against a decision to attach a particular measure to a CSO and we agree with this. *NB:* It is notable that the power to suspend pending appeal is restricted to "decisions to make, vary or continue a compulsory supervision order" only. For example, there is no provision for suspension pending appeal in relation to appeals against: a decision to make an interim compulsory supervision order; a decision to make an interim variation of a CSO; a decision to make a medical examination order; a decision to grant a warrant to secure attendance; a relevant person determination (s.160); a decision affecting a contact or permanence order (s.161); or a decision by the Chief Social Work Officer to implement or not, a secure accommodation authorisation, or to remove a child from secure accommodation (s.162). The decision of a children's hearing under this section is *not* appealable as it does not appear in the list of appealable decisions in s.154(3) discussed above.

A request to the Reporter to arrange a hearing can only be made after an appeal has been lodged with the sheriff.

Professor Norrie, in his *Children's Hearings in Scotland*, 3rd edn (Edinburgh: W. Green, 2013), para.14–34 states that a decision of a children's hearing to suspend or not to suspend pending appeal of a measure would seem not to be open to judicial review and cites *S v Proudfoot*, 2002 S.L.T. 743; 2002 Fam. L.R. 92 OH. In this case a mother petitioned for judicial review seeking declarator that a children's hearing held on 13 August 2001 had erred in refusing to suspend a condition of a supervision requirement to the effect that the child was to reside in Quarriers Village at weekends. As mentioned above, the court held that the hearing had been correct in deciding that it had no power to suspend a condition of a supervision requirement while leaving the supervision requirement itself in force. However, the first reason of the presiding judge, Lord Menzies, for refusing the petition was that it was incompetent because at the time the petition was raised, 7 February 2002, over three months had expired since the decision of the children's hearing and therefore the mother had, under s.73(6) of the Children (Scotland) Act 1995, the alternative remedy of seeking a review of the hearing's decision to impose a supervision requirement. It was against this background that Lord Menzies held, at 745B, that

"by the time the petition was raised the petitioner had an alternative statutory remedy available to her. In these circumstances there is no supervisory jurisdiction vested in the court, and the petition is incompetent."

However, a decision of a children's hearing not to suspend a measure of a CSO is not exactly parallel to a decision of a children's hearing to make a CSO, which was the equivalent context of *S v Proudfoot*. The right to require a review of a CSO is enacted in s.132 of the Act, but no right to review the decision to refuse to suspend a condition of a CSO is enacted in s.132 or anywhere else in the Act. Accordingly a person aggrieved by a decision of a children's hearing not to suspend a measure of a CSO would appear to have no "alternative remedy" under the Act and therefore the possible remedy of judicial review may remain open. The scope of the application of the concept of "alternative remedy" is examined in Right Hon. Lord Clyde and Denis Edwards, *Judicial Review* (Edinburgh: W. Green/SULI, 2000), Ch.12.

Subs.(1)(a)

To make, vary, continue or terminate. Section 51(9) of the 1995 Act conferred appeal rights "against a decision of a children's hearing in relation to a supervision requirement" and entitled the appellant to apply to a children's hearing "for suspension of the requirement appealed against".

When read with s.73(9) of the 1995 Act, it would appear that a right to appeal was being conferred not only where a supervision requirement was imposed in the first instance, but also where it was continued or varied in terms of s.73(9)—this is the interpretation adopted by Professor Norrie in his *Children's Hearings in Scotland*, 2nd edn (Edinburgh: W. Green, 2005), p.220. This subsection makes this explicit by echoing the terms of s.138(3) of this Act.

Subs.(2)

A children's hearing, in considering an application to suspend a CSO, will have to apply the paramountcy of welfare and the views of the child principles. Section 28(1), which enacts the minimum intervention principle, does not expressly mention the suspension of a CSO, but it does mention the continuing of a CSO and since a hearing considering a request for suspension will in effect be considering the continuing of a measure attached to a CSO, the applicability of the minimum intervention principle is implied. The hearing will also have to have regard to the European Convention principle of proportionality.

Frivolous and vexatious appeals

Frivolous and vexatious appeals

159.—(1) This section applies where the sheriff—
[1] (a) determines an appeal under section 154 or 161 by confirming a decision of a children's hearing to vary or continue a compulsory supervision order, and
 (b) is satisfied that the appeal was frivolous or vexatious.
[1] (2) The sheriff may order that, during the period of 12 months beginning on the day of the order, the person who appealed must obtain leave from the sheriff before making another appeal under section 154 or 161 against a decision of a children's hearing in relation to the compulsory supervision order.

NOTE
1. As amended by the Children's Hearings (Scotland) Act 2011 (Modification of Primary Legislation) Order 2013 (SSI 2013/211) Sch.1 para.20(16) (effective 24 June 2013).

DEFINITION
"children's hearing": s.5.
"compulsory supervision order": ss.202(1) and 83.

GENERAL NOTE
This section reflects s.51(7), read with s.73(8) of the 1995 Act, but makes two significant, and welcome, changes, namely the limitation of the application of this section to appeals by the same person and the empowering of the sheriff to grant leave to appeal where a "frivolous or vexatious" order has been made.

Subs.(1)(a)
An appeal under section 154 or 161. The provisions of this section only apply to appeals under ss.154 and 161. Accordingly they do not apply to appeals against a relevant person determination (s.160), a decision affecting a contact or permanence order (s.161) or a decision of the Chief Social Work Officer to implement or not to implement a secure accommodation authorisation or to remove a child from secure accommodation (s.162).
Confirming a decision. Only in an appeal which has resulted in the decision of the children's hearing being sustained, i.e. been unsuccessful, does this section apply: this recognises that an appeal which has been successful could not reasonably be categorised as frivolous or vexatious.
To vary or continue a compulsory supervision order. This means that the frivolous/vexatious appeals provisions are not available to the sheriff in relation to an appeal against the initial imposition of a compulsory supervision order. This accords with the 1995 Act.
The person who appealed. Section 51(7) of the 1995 Act applied to "any subsequent appeal", thus disenfranchising any party who had not been involved in the appeal held to be frivolous. As submitted by Professor Norrie his commentary, *Children's Hearings (Scotland) Act 1995*, 2nd edn (Edinburgh: W. Green, 2004), p.96, this ran the risk of infringing the rights of such a party under the fair trial provisions in art.6 of the European Convention. The present provisions remedy this.

Subs.(1)(b)
This adds "vexatious" to the 1995 Act's provision. Neither concept is defined, and both are perhaps more readily recognised than described. The concept of vexatious litigants is discussed in *Macphail on Sheriff Court Practice*, 3rd edn by Sheriff T. Welsh (Edinburgh: W. Green, 2006), paras 4.122 and 4.123. The use of these provisions will only be occasional, but experience has shown that when necessary they are very valuable in limiting the disruption to children's lives caused by the launching of untenable and sometimes spiteful appeals, with the appellant secure in the knowledge that there is no provision in these cases for an award of expenses

Appeal to sheriff against relevant person determination

against an unsuccessful litigant. An example is found in *MB v Douglas Hill, Locality Reporter Manager* [2017] SAC (Civ) 10, wherein a children's hearing, inter alia, refused a mother contact with one of her children until a parenting assessment became available but the mother had refused to countenance such an assessment. The mother appealed to the sheriff but made no allegation that the sheriff had erred in law or that there had been a procedural irregularity. The sheriff held that the appeal was without merit and also made an order under s.159(2) on the ground that the appeal had been frivolous. The mother appealed to the SAC and argued that her rights under Art 8 of the European Convention on Human Rights had been infringed. The SAC refused the appeal, holding that the sheriff had been justified in his substantive decision and in the s.59(2) order. The court commented that the latter was justified by the consideration that unnecessary appeals were distressing to the children and that any meritorious appeal was saved by the provision in s.159(2) entitling an appeal with leave of the sheriff.

In *Geraldine McWilliams v Russell* [2017] SC GLA 64 it is narrated that the defender was a vexatious litigant, that he had lodged a counter-claim in the substantive action, and that the Court of Session had ruled that he could only proceed with the counter-claim after the conclusion of the substantive action, and then only with leave of the Court of Session.

The sheriff's decision as to whether an appeal is "frivolous or vexatious" may be thought to be a decision of mixed fact and law and thus, following the logic of *MT & AG v Anne Gerry (Locality Reporter)* [2014] CSIH 108, 2015 S.C. 359, sub nom. *T v Locality Reporter*, 2015 Fam. L.R. 2 discussed above in our commentary on s.156(1), not to be subject to the paramountcy of welfare or the views of the child principles.

Subs.(2)
Must obtain leave from the sheriff. This provision also innovates on the provisions of the 1995 Act and further enhances compliance with the European Convention by recognising that circumstances may arise in a particular case whereby an appeal may be permissible even although an earlier appeal (even by the same appellant) has been held to have been frivolous or vexatious. An order requiring a vexatious litigant to obtain leave of the court does not infringe rights under art.6 of the European Convention—*HM Advocate v Bell*, 2002 S.L.T. 527. The decision of the sheriff as to whether or not to grant leave will be affected by the sheriff's view of whether or not the proposed appeal has any reasonable prospect of success. This is a legal issue and as such not prima facie subject to the paramountcy of the welfare of the child principle—see above for our discussion of s.25. See also the discussion of the scope of the application of this principle in *MT & AG v Anne Gerry (Locality Reporter)* [2014] CSIH 108, 2015 S.C. 359, sub nom. *T v Locality Reporter*, 2015 Fam. L.R. 2. However, it is thought that the paramountcy of the welfare of the child principle might indirectly apply in that it would be difficult for a sheriff not to grant leave to appeal if the sheriff considered that it would be in the child's interests for the appeal to proceed.

C.538.6

Other appeals

Appeal to sheriff against relevant person determination

160.—(1) A person mentioned in subsection (2) may appeal to the sheriff against—
- (a) a determination of a pre-hearing panel or a children's hearing that an individual—
  - (i) is or is not to be deemed a relevant person in relation to a child,
  - (ii) is to continue to be deemed, or is no longer to be deemed, a relevant person in relation to a child,
- (b) a determination of a review under section 142(2) that an individual is to continue to be deemed, or no longer to be deemed, a relevant person in relation to a child.

(2) The persons are—
(a) the individual in question,
(b) the child,
(c) a relevant person in relation to the child,
(d) two or more persons mentioned in paragraphs (a) to (c) acting jointly.

(3) If satisfied that the determination to which the appeal relates is justified, the sheriff must confirm the determination.

(4) If not satisfied, the sheriff must—
(a) quash the determination, and

C.539

(b) where the determination is a determination of a pre-hearing panel or children's hearing under section 81 that the individual should not be deemed a relevant person in relation to the child, make an order deeming the individual to be a relevant person in relation to the child.

(5) Where the sheriff makes an order under subsection (4)(b), section 81(4) applies to the individual as if a pre-hearing panel had deemed the individual to be a relevant person.

(6) An appeal under this section must be—
(a) made before the expiry of the period of 7 days beginning with the day on which the determination is made,
(b) heard and disposed of before the expiry of the period of 3 days beginning with the day on which the appeal is made.

NOTE

C.539.1   1. Substituted by the Children and Young People (Scotland) Act 2014 (asp 8) Sch.5 para.12(8) (effective 26 January 2015).

DEFINITIONS

C.539.2   "child": s.199.
"children's hearing": s.5.
"pre-hearing panel" s.79(2).
"relevant person": s.200.

PRELIMINARY GENERAL NOTE

C.539.3   This section deals with the decision of a pre-hearing panel (or, as the case may be, a children's hearing) that an individual is or is not to be, or is or is not to continue to be, a deemed relevant person. When discussing such issues it is necessary to keep in mind:
(1) that in the scheme of this Act there are persons who are, as a matter of law, "automatically" relevant persons (as distinct from "deemed relevant persons", i.e. the persons listed in s.200(1) of the Act and the reader is directed to the General Note to s.200 and the Preliminary General Note to s.160);
(2) that by judicial decision, *Principal Reporter v K* [2010] UKSC 56; 2011 S.C. (U.K.S.C.) 91; 2011 S.L.T. 271; 2011 Fam. L.R. 2; 2011 1 W.L.R. 18 at [69], a person having family life with the child with which the decision of a children's hearing may interfere must, owing to the effect of art.8 of the European Convention on Human Rights, be treated as a relevant person (not as a deemed relevant person)—see the discussion of this issue in the decision of Sheriff J.M. Scott QC in *W v C*, 2013 Fam. L.R. 73 at [7];
(3) that, consequently, the provisions in this section, which deal with deemed relevant person status, have no direct relevance to automatic relevant person status, which is conferred either, on the one hand, by s.200 of the Act, or, on the other hand, in the words of Sheriff Scott in *W v C*, 2013 Fam. L.R. 73 at [14], "involvement in the decision-making at the children's hearing is a matter of right for persons with art.8 rights."

GENERAL NOTE

C.539.4   A pre-hearing panel may deem an individual to be a relevant person or determine that that status should end under, respectively, ss.81(3) and 81A and a full children's hearing may do so under s.80(3) where it is impracticable for a pre-hearing panel to be arranged prior to a children's hearing or where the matter has arisen without notice (see r.55 of the Children's Hearings (Scotland) Act 2011 (Rules of Procedure in Children's Hearings) Rules 2013 (SSI 2013/194) (the "Procedural Rules"). Where a person has been deemed to be a relevant person in relation to a child and a compulsory supervision order (CSO) ordered for that child and the CSO becomes the subject of a review by a children's hearing under Pt 13 of the Act, then, by virtue of s.142(2), the deeming decision also comes under review. The provisions of the present section provide for appeals against such deeming and deeming-related decisions. These provisions may give rise to consequential problems in relation to the children's hearings concerned—see below in the discussion of subs.(6).

The decision of the sheriff in an appeal under this section is a decision on a matter of law and as such is not subject to the overarching principles: see *MT v Gerry* [2014] CSIH 108, 2015 S.C. 359, sub nom. *T v Locality Reporter*, 2015 Fam. L.R. 2.

Appeal to sheriff against relevant person determination

Subs.(1)(b)
A review hearing may wish to review a relevant person determination in circumstances, including: (i) removing the deemed relevant person status from a person who is present at the review hearing; and (ii) removing the deemed relevant person status from a person who is not present at the review hearing. Section 142(3) empowers this review hearing to defer determining the review hearing until a subsequent hearing. It is submitted that it may be appropriate for such a review hearing to consider exercising this power where it is considering terminating relevant person status in either of these cases. Where the deemed relevant person is present he or she may wish time to consider his or her position (for example to consider whether to seek legal representation). Where the deemed relevant person is not present it may be particularly important to defer the decision, since coming to such a decision in the absence of the relevant person could amount to an appealable irregularity. The matter will of course be for the hearing to consider in the light of the information before it. In *MF and GF, Appellants* (sometimes referred to as *F & F, Appellants*), 2014 Fam. L.R. 57 (sub nom. *F v Principal Reporter*, 2014 Fam. L.B. 29-6), discussed above under s.81(3), a children's hearing had made a CSO and deemed the appellants (grandparents of the children) to be relevant persons. After a considerable lapse of time, during which Social Enquiry Reports on the suitability of the appellants' having contact were repeatedly not produced and during which time the appellants only saw the children incidentally at children's hearings, the ultimate review hearing took place. At this review hearing, at which one of the appellants was not present, the hearing, on the basis that the appellants did not now fall into the category of having, or recently having had, significant involvement in the upbringing of the child, directed that the appellants were no longer to be deemed as relevant persons. On appeal the sheriff quashed this decision on the ground, inter alia, that the review hearing had given insufficient attention to the fact that the lack of contact with the appellants had been a consequence of the failure by the state, per the social work department of the local authority, to provide a Social Enquiry Report and that it should have deferred its decision so that the absent appellant could be present and the views of the children obtained. As noted above under s.81(3) the ratio of the sheriff's decision was disapproved in *CF v MF & GF and Scottish Reporter* [2017] CSIH 44, but the sheriff's view that the review hearing should have deferred its decision was not an issue which was before the court.

C.539.5

One of the decisions which may be appealed against is a decision at a review hearing, or any deferment thereof, held under s.142(2) that an individual is or is not to continue to be deemed as a relevant person. Accordingly the issue for the sheriff who is considering such an appeal is whether, if the condition of being a deemed relevant person enacted in s.81(3), "has (or recently has had) significant involvement in the upbringing of the child".

There is no power in a review hearing under subs.(1)(b) as such to deem any individual to be a relevant person. There is, however, nothing to prevent a hearing considering the question of whether another individual should be deemed to be a relevant person under s.80(3) and the Children's Hearings (Scotland) Act 2011 (Rules of Procedure in Children's Hearings) Rules 2013 (SSI 2013/194) r.55(1).

Subs.(2)(a)
The individual in question. Thus a person whose request under s.79(2)(a)(i) to be deemed a relevant person and whose request has been considered applying the criteria set out in s.81(3) but turned down, is entitled to appeal. Technically an individual whose request has been granted would also have a right of appeal, but this contingency is remote.

C.539.6

Subs.(2)(b)
The child. For consideration of the capacity of the child in this context see above in discussion of s.154(2)(a).

C.539.7

Subs.(2)(c)
Relevant person. This means a person who qualifies as a relevant person in terms of the definition enacted in s.200 of the Act and any individual who has been deemed to be a relevant person, see s.81(4) of the Act. In practice this will mean a person who has been convened to the children's hearing by the Reporter by a provision such as r.21(2)(b) of the Procedural Rules. This provision provides such a person with the right to appeal against a decision deeming (or not deeming) another person as a relevant person.

C.539.8

Subs.(2)(d)
For consideration of the position of a legal representative in relation to a joint appeal, see discussion above of s.154(4).

C.539.9

Subs.(3)
C.539.10 *Satisfied.* For consideration of this concept see discussion above of s.156(1). The same factors apply, mutatis mutandis, here.

Subs.(4)
C.539.11 In short, the sheriff is empowered to substitute his or her own decision for that of the hearing.

Subs.(5)
C.539.12 See above for discussion of s.81(4), which lists the legal consequences of a deeming decision.

Subs.(6)
C.539.13 *Appeal against a relevant person determination of a pre-hearing panel.* The timing of a relevant person determination by a pre-hearing panel ideally will have regard to the need to allow for the appeal days (seven days to appeal and three days for disposal of appeal) to expire and the need properly to convene a deemed relevant person to the children's hearing concerned. In practice, the reality of scheduling hearings may not make it practicable. It has to be noted that (a) under r.22 of the Procedural Rules, the Reporter must, no later than seven days before the intended hearing, notify each relevant person (which by virtue of s.81(4) of this Act includes a deemed relevant person) of the intended date of the children's hearing; and (b) under r.22(2)(c) the Reporter must also notify the date of the intended hearing to any person who appears to the Reporter to have, or recently has had, recent significant involvement in the upbringing of the child—with the consequence that such persons, who may well in course be deemed to be relevant persons, may already have received notification of the intended children's hearing before being so deemed.

Appeal to sheriff against decision affecting contact or permanence order

C.540 **161.**—(1) A person mentioned in subsection (2) may appeal to the sheriff against a relevant decision of a children's hearing in relation to a child.

(2) The person is an individual (other than a relevant person in relation to the child) in relation to whom—
   (a) a contact order is in force regulating contact between the individual and the child,
   (b) a permanence order is in force which specifies arrangements for contact between the individual and the child, or
   (c) the conditions specified for the purposes of section 126(2)(b) are satisfied.

(3) A relevant decision is a decision under section 126(6) relating to a compulsory supervision order.

(4) If the sheriff is satisfied that the relevant decision is justified, the sheriff must confirm the decision.

(5) If not satisfied, the sheriff must vary the compulsory supervision order by varying or removing the measure contained in the order under section 83(2)(g).

(6) An appeal under this section must be—
   (a) made before the expiry of the period of 21 days beginning with the day on which the relevant decision is made,
   (b) heard and disposed of before the expiry of the period of 3 days beginning with the day on which the appeal is made.

DEFINITIONS
C.540.1 "child": s.199.
"children's hearing": s.5.
"compulsory supervision order": ss.202(1) and 83.
"contact order": s.202(1) of the 2011 Act and s.11(2)(d) of the Children (Scotland) Act 1995.
"permanence order": s.202(1) of the 2011 Act and s.80(2) of the Adoption and Children (Scotland) Act 2007.
"relevant person": s.200.

GENERAL NOTE
C.540.2 This section requires to be read along with s.126, which deals with certain decisions of children's hearings to make: a compulsory supervision order (CSO), an interim compulsory

Appeal to sheriff against decision affecting contact or permanence order

supervision order (ICSO), an interim variation of a compulsory supervision order (IVCSO) or a medical examination order (MEO), which is to have effect for more than five working days. This is a new provision that applies to the limited class of individuals who have contact with the child as provided under subs.(2). Under the 1995 Act, these individuals' contact with the child could be varied or reduced without them having any redress. This section should also be read in conjunction with ss.126 (above) and 165 (below). The substantive provision of s.126 is that the Reporter must arrange a review hearing in respect of such a contact direction in any of three situations viz:

(I) where a contact order (meaning an order of court under s.11(2)(d) of the Children (Scotland) Act 1995) is in force;

(II) where a permanence order under s.82(2) of the Adoption and Children (Scotland) Act 2007 is in force; and

(III) where requested by an individual claiming that he or she complies with conditions specified by Scottish Ministers in a statutory order—this means, at present, in terms of art.2 of the Children's Hearings (Scotland) Act 2011 (Review of Contact Directions and Definition of Relevant Person) Order 2013 (SSI 2013/193) (the 2013 Order), an individual, not being a relevant person or a deemed relevant person, who has or recently has had significant involvement in the upbringing of the child.

The overall purpose of s.126 is to bring about that the arrangements for contact with a child which have been made by a children's hearing can, where there are contact arrangements in force by virtue of statutory orders under the Children (Scotland) Act 1995 or the Adoption and Children (Scotland) Act 2007, be revisited by a children's hearing in the light of the statutory order concerned and, in so far as concerns the contact arrangements, confirmed or varied. Also, the right of a person who is not a relevant person or a deemed relevant person, but may claim relevant person status by having, or recently having had, significant involvement in the upbringing of the child, is secured. Note, however, that the right of a person who has established family life with the child with which a decision of a children's hearing might interfere (see *Principal Reporter v K* [2010] UKSC 56; 2011 S.C. (U.K.S.C.) 91; 2011 S.L.T. 271; [2011] 1 W.L.R. 18; 2011 H.R.L.R. 8 at [69]) is not secured, unless an expansive "reading down" of art.2(2) of the 2013 Order is adopted. The provisions of ss.73 and 74 of the Act in relation to the obligations of the child and relevant person to attend children's hearings do not apply to these review hearings (s.126(7)). The decision of a review hearing under s.126(2) is subject to all three overarching principles and the European Convention principle of proportionality.

This present section enacts special appellate procedure for appeals against such decisions and, reflecting the importance of a speedy resolution of such matters, allows for an early appeal against such decisions.

Although there is no express provision in this section (as distinct from s.162(6)) that the proceedings are not to be held in open court, in practice it is accepted that these proceedings are in camera.

Period of notice

The period of notice in appeals under this section is "as directed by the sheriff": see discussion above in the General Note to s.157.

Subs.(2)

Other than a relevant person. Under s.126(3)(a) contact orders regulating contact between a relevant person and a child are excluded from the categories of cases subject to these review hearings' procedures, and consequently, relevant persons are similarly excluded from the appeals procedures. **C.540.3**

Subs.(2)(c)

This refers back to s.126(2)(b), which refers to the conditions now set out in art.2 of the 2013 Order: see General Note, above. **C.540.4**

Subs.(4)

Satisfied. As to the scope of the appeal to the sheriff on appeal (in relation to whether the sheriff should take the "restrictive/conservative" approach or regard him or herself as entitled to sustain the appeal merely because he or she concludes that the decision appealed from is wrong), see discussion above under s.156(1). The same considerations apply, mutatis mutandis, here. **C.540.5**

Subs.(5)

Whatever view the sheriff takes as to the scope of the appeal (see above under subs.(4)), the sheriff's function is limited to considering the issue of contact, and it is not open to the sheriff to take any of the other measures listed in s.83(2). **C.540.6**

Subs.(6)(a) and (b)

C.540.7 *Beginning with the day on which.* For the reasons advanced above in the discussion of s.154(5), it is submitted that "day one" in relation to each of these provisions is the day on which the relevant decision/appeal is made. "Day" here means calendar day, not working day as defined in s.202(1).

Appeal to sheriff against decision to implement secure accommodation authorisation

C.541 **162.**—(1) This section applies where a relevant order or warrant made in relation to a child includes a secure accommodation authorisation.

(2) A relevant order or warrant is—
(a) a compulsory supervision order,
(b) an interim compulsory supervision order,
(c) a medical examination order,
(d) a warrant to secure attendance.

(3) The child or a relevant person in relation to the child may appeal to the sheriff against a relevant decision in relation to the authorisation.

(4) A relevant decision is a decision by the chief social work officer—
(a) to implement the authorisation,
(b) not to implement the authorisation,
(c) to remove the child from secure accommodation.

(5) An appeal under subsection (3) may be made jointly by—
(a) the child and one or more relevant persons in relation to the child, or
(b) two or more relevant persons in relation to the child.

(6) An appeal must not be held in open court.

(7) The Scottish Ministers may by regulations make further provision about appeals under subsection (3).

(8) Regulations under subsection (7) may in particular—
(a) specify the period within which an appeal may be made,
(b) make provision about the hearing of evidence during an appeal,
(c) make provision about the powers of the sheriff on determining an appeal,
[1] (d) provide for appeals to the Sheriff Appeal Court and Court of Session against the determination of an appeal.

(9) Regulations under subsection (7) are subject to the affirmative procedure.

NOTE
C.541.1 1. As amended by the Courts Reform (Scotland) Act 2014 (Consequential and Supplemental Provisions) Order 2015 (SSI 2015/402) Sch.1(1) para.7(3) (effective 1 January 2016).

DEFINITIONS
C.541.2 "'affirmative procedure": s.197.
"chief social work officer": s.202(1).
"child": s.199.
"compulsory supervision order": ss.202(1) and 83.
"interim compulsory supervision order": ss.202(1) and 86.
"medical examination order": ss.202(1) and 87.
"relevant person": s.200.
"secure accommodation authorisation": ss.202(1) and 85.
"warrant to secure attendance": ss.202(1) and 88.

GENERAL NOTE
C.541.3 Under the Children (Scotland) Act 1995 appeals against orders containing a secure accommodation authorisation were appealable to the sheriff under the general provisions in s.51(1) of that Act. Such appeals are of course still competent under this Act by virtue of the provisions in s.154. The provisions in relation to implementation of such an authorisation are contained in ss.151 to 153, discussed above. As with s.70(9) of the 1995 Act (read with s.71(1) of that Act), the responsibility of implementing or not a secure accommodation authorisation

Appeal to sheriff against decision to implement secure accommodation

rests, by virtue of s.151(3) of this Act, with the Chief Social Work Officer of the local authority (with the consent of the "head of unit"). The notification requirements on the chief social work officer who has decided to implement, or not to implement, a secure accommodation authorisation are contained in the Children's Hearings (Implementation of Secure Accommodation Authorisation) (Scotland) Regulations 2013 (SSI 2013/212) (the Implementation Regulations) reg.5 of which provides, inter alia: that the child and relevant person must be advised of their right to appeal; that where the decision is not to implement, they may require the decision to be reviewed (by the Chief Social Work Officer); and that where intimation is not duly made the Chief Social Work Officer will be deemed not to have implemented the secure accommodation authorisation. The procedures for the Chief Social Work Officer in carrying out such a review are set out in reg.7 of the Implementation Regulations. As already mentioned, the Chief Social Work Officer may only implement a secure accommodation authorisation with the consent of the person in charge of the residential establishment (the "head of unit") (see s.151(3)). The obligations of the head of unit in relation to considering whether to consent to implement a secure accommodation authorisation are set out in regs 6 and 8 of the Implementation Regulations, including the duty, where the decision is not to consent to the secure accommodation authorisation (except where an interim compulsory supervision order or medical examination order would expire within 48 hours), of requiring a review of this decision by notifying the Reporter. On receiving such notification, the Reporter must arrange a review hearing within three working days and such review may vary the interim compulsory supervision order or medical examination order but only by varying or removing the secure accommodation authorisation (see Implementation Regulations reg.9). Where a child is in secure accommodation the Chief Social Work Officer must keep the child's case under review as set out in the Implementation Regulations reg.10.

This present section provides for an appeal against a decision of the Chief Social Work Officer to implement or otherwise a secure accommodation authorisation. No such provision appeared in the 1995 Act. The inclusion of this provision in the present Act is an example of the legislature's intention to promote and protect the rights and interests of the child and is welcome. Scottish Ministers have made the above noted procedural regulations by virtue of their powers under subss.(7) and (8). Accordingly, the procedures for these appeals, discussed below under subs.(8), is governed by these Regulations and not by the provisions for "ordinary" appeals enacted in ss.154 to 157.

As to the scope of the appeal to the sheriff (in relation to whether the sheriff should take the "restrictive/conservative" approach or regard him or herself as entitled to sustain the appeal merely because he or she concludes that the decision appealed from is wrong), see discussion above under s.156(1). The same considerations apply, mutatis mutandis, here.

A decision of the Chief Social Work Officer under s.151(3) of the Act, not being a decision of a court or a children's hearing, is not per se subject to the overarching principles, but where taking a decision on considering implementation the chief social work officer must take into account (subject to s.26), inter alia: the views of the child, depending on age and maturity (see the Implementation Regulations reg.4(3)(a)(i)); the child's best interests (the Implementation Regulations reg.4(3)(b)(ii)); and the European Convention principle of proportionality. It follows that the overarching principles, including the minimum intervention principle, apply in all but name to the decision of the Chief Social Work Officer. Accordingly, failure to apply these principles may found an appeal.

Period of notice

The period of notice in appeals under this section is "as directed by the sheriff": see discussion above in the General Note to s.157.

Subs.(2)

The enactments in relation to these orders are found in: **C.541.4**
- ss.91(3)(a), 107(3), 118(4) and 119(1) and (3) (making or review of compulsory supervision order);
- ss.92(2), 93(5), 96(3), 97(5), and 120(5) (making, varying or granting a further, interim compulsory supervision order);
- ss.92(3) and 120(6) (making a medical examination order); and
- s.123 (granting a warrant to secure attendance).

Subs.(3)

As noted already, a safeguarder now generally has an independent right of appeal. That being **C.541.5** so it is surprising that a safeguarder appointed in relation to the child is not included as having a right to appeal here.

Subs.(5)
C.541.6 As mentioned above in our discussion of s.154(4), a legal representative will be cautious of acting for more than one party in case of possible conflict of interest. For fuller consideration of the issues of conflict of interest and confidentiality which may arise, see the discussion of s.104(2)–(4) under the heading *"Possible conflict of interest—Confidentiality"*.

Subs.(7)
C.541.7 The Secure Accommodation (Scotland) Regulations 2013 (SSI 2013/205) (the Secure Accommodation Regulations) have been enacted.

Subs.(8)
C.541.8 Some of the provisions of the Implementation Regulations have been discussed above in the General Note. The procedures for appeals against decisions of the Chief Social Work Officer are contained in regs 11 to 14 of the Implementation Regulations. Any appeal must be made within 21 calendar days of the decision by the Chief Social Work Officer, counting the day of that decision as "day one". There is no prescribed form for the appeal. The appeal must be heard and disposed of by the sheriff before the expiry of the period of three days beginning with the day after the appeal has been lodged. The sheriff may, but is not obliged to, hear evidence before determining the appeal. By virtue of reg.11(4) the sheriff may hear evidence from: (a) the child; (b) each relevant person in respect of the child; (c) the Chief Social Work Officer; (d) the head of unit (i.e. the person in charge of the residential establishment concerned); (e) the Reporter; and (f) any other person whom the sheriff considers may give additional material evidence. By virtue of reg.11(5) the sheriff "may require any person to give a report to the sheriff for the purpose of assisting the sheriff in determining the appeal". As mentioned above in the discussion of s.155(5)(f) and (6), these provisions may not mean that the sheriff should have the power to identify, say, a particular psychiatrist or social worker, unconnected with the case, and compel him or her to come to court and give evidence, but would seem only to refer to a person who has had some dealings with the child's case. The tight timescale applicable in these appeals may make it difficult, but should not make it impossible, for the sheriff to secure the evidence of such a person where the sheriff considers it necessary for a proper disposal of the appeal. Where the sheriff is satisfied that a decision to implement a secure accommodation authorisation is justified the sheriff must confirm the decision and in any other case the sheriff may take either or both of these steps, viz:

    (a) make an order directing the chief social work officer to remove the child from the secure accommodation;

    (b) make an order requiring the Reporter to arrange a children's hearing for any purpose competent under the Act (see reg.12).

Where the sheriff is satisfied that a decision not to implement a secure accommodation authorisation is justified the sheriff *must* confirm that decision and *may* make an order requiring the Reporter to arrange a children's hearing for any purpose competent under the Act (see reg.13(1) and (2)); in any other case the sheriff may take either or both of these steps, viz:

    (a) make an order directing the Chief Social Work Officer to place the child in secure accommodation;

    (b) make an order requiring the Reporter to arrange a children's hearing for any purpose competent under the Act (see reg.13(3)).

Where the sheriff is satisfied that a decision to remove a child from secure accommodation is justified the sheriff *must* confirm the decision and *may* make an order requiring the Reporter to arrange a children's hearing for any purpose competent under the Act (see reg.14(1) and (2)); in any other case the sheriff may take either or both of these steps, viz:

    (a) direct the Chief Social Work Officer to place the child in secure accommodation and vary the order or warrant which is in effect to include a secure accommodation authorisation; and

    (b) require the Reporter to arrange a children's hearing for any purpose competent under the Act (see reg.14(3)).

An appeal under this section is not an appeal against a judicial decision, but against a decision of an official of a local authority and accordingly it may prima facie appear that the scope of the appeal would be governed by the principles (the "Wednesbury principles") enunciated in *Associated Provincial Picture Houses Ltd v Wednesbury Corp* [1948] 1 K.B. 223 at 229; [1947] 2 All E.R. 680 and that consequently the sheriff's function on appeal would be confined to considering whether the Chief Social Work Officer had not had regard to the appropriate law, had taken into account an irrelevant matter, had not taken into account a relevant matter or had done "something so absurd that no sensible person could ever dream that it lay within the powers of the authority". It is submitted, however, that this would not be the proper approach in the context of a system aimed at safeguarding and promoting the

Appeals to sheriff principal and Court of Session: children's hearings etc.

welfare of the child and that the sheriff, where he or she concluded, on the whole available evidence, that the Chief Social Work Officer had made the wrong decision, would be obliged to reverse or vary that decision and substitute the sheriff's own decision. A decision by a sheriff sustaining, reversing or varying the Chief Social Work Officer's decision to implement or not a secure accommodation authorisation is clearly "a decision about a matter relating to the child" (see s.25(1)) and accordingly the paramount consideration for the sheriff will be to assess, on the basis of all the available evidence, including any evidence laid before the sheriff at the appeal by virtue of reg.11(3)–(5) of the Implementation Regulations, whether placement in secure accommodation is "necessary to safeguard and promote the welfare of the child throughout the child's childhood."

Appeals to sheriff principal and Court of Session

Appeals to sheriff principal and Court of Session: children's hearings etc.

163.—(1) A person mentioned in subsection (3) may appeal by stated case to the sheriff principal or the Court of Session against—
(a) a determination by the sheriff of—
 (i) an application to determine whether a section 67 ground (other than the ground mentioned in section 67(2)(j) if the case was remitted to the Principal Reporter under section 49 of the Criminal Procedure (Scotland) Act 1995) is established,
 (ii) an application under section 110(2) for review of a finding that a section 67 ground is established,
 (iii) an appeal against a decision of a children's hearing,
 (iv) an application under section 98 for an extension of an interim compulsory supervision order,
 (v) an application under section 99 for a further extension of an interim compulsory supervision order,
(b) a decision of the sheriff under section 100 to—
 (i) make an interim compulsory supervision order,
 (ii) make an interim variation of a compulsory supervision order.

(2) A person mentioned in subsection (3) may, with leave of the sheriff principal, appeal by stated case to the Court of Session against the sheriff principal's decision in an appeal under subsection (1).

(3) The persons are—
(a) the child,
(b) a relevant person in relation to the child,
(c) a safeguarder appointed in relation to the child by virtue of section 30,
(d) two or more persons mentioned in paragraphs (a) to (c) acting jointly, and
(e) the Principal Reporter.

(4) Despite subsections (1) and (2), a safeguarder may not—
(a) appeal against a determination by the sheriff of a type mentioned in subsection (1)(a)(i) or (ii), or a decision of the sheriff of a type mentioned in subsection (1)(b),
(b) appeal to the Court of Session against the sheriff principal's decision in such an appeal.

(5) Despite subsection (1), the Principal Reporter may not appeal against a determination by the sheriff confirming a decision of a children's hearing.

(6) Subsection (7) applies in relation to—
(a) an appeal against a determination by the sheriff of an application under section 110(2) for review of a finding that a section 67 ground is established,
(b) an appeal to the Court of Session against the sheriff principal's decision in such an appeal.

(7) In subsection (3)(a) and (b)—
(a) the references to the child are to the person in relation to whom the

section 67 ground was established (even if that person is no longer a child),

(b) the reference to a relevant person in relation to the child includes a person who was, at the time the section 67 ground was established, a relevant person in relation to the child.

(8) An appeal under this section must be made before the expiry of the period of 28 days beginning with the day on which the determination or decision appealed against was made.

(9) An appeal under this section may be made—
(a) on a point of law, or
(b) in respect of any procedural irregularity.

(10) On deciding an appeal under subsection (1), the sheriff principal or the Court of Session must remit the case to the sheriff for disposal in accordance with such directions as the court may give.

(11) A decision in an appeal under subsection (1) or (2) by the Court of Session is final.

(12) In subsection (1)(a)(ii), the reference to a determination by the sheriff of an application under section 110(2) for review of a finding that a section 67 ground is established includes a reference to a determination under section 117(2)(a) that a ground is established.

DEFINITIONS

C.542.1 "child": s.199.
"interim compulsory supervision order": ss.202(1) and 86.
"Principal Reporter": s.14 and Sch.3 paras 8–10.
"relevant person": s.200.
"safeguarder": ss.202(1) and 30(1).

GENERAL NOTE

Important preliminary Note

C.542.2 With effect from 1 January 2016 the appellate functions (but not the administrative functions) of the sheriff principal in relation to civil business were transferred to the Sheriff Appeal Court. This was effected, not by an amendment of the Children's Hearings (Scotland) Act 2011, but by s.109 of the Courts Reform (Scotland) Act 2014, which provides:

109.— Abolition of appeal from the sheriff to the sheriff principal

(1) No appeal may be taken to the sheriff principal against any decision of a sheriff in civil proceedings.

(2) Subsection (3) applies to any provision of pre-commencement enactment that—
(a) provides for an appeal to the sheriff principal from any decision of a sheriff in civil proceedings, or
(b) restricts or excludes such an appeal.

(3)The provision has effect as if for the reference to the sheriff principal there were substituted a reference to the Sheriff Appeal Court.

(4) In subsection (2), "pre-commencement enactment" means an enactment passed or made before this section comes into force.

Section 136(1) of the Courts Reform (Scotland) Act 2014 defines "civil proceedings" as including proceedings under the Children's Hearings (Scotland) Act 2011. The reference in s.109(4) of that Act to "an enactment passed or made" makes clear that the section applies to statutory instruments as well as statutes. The use of the term "appeal" in s.109(1) and (2)(a) of that Act would seem to mean that applications to the sheriff principal to exercise an administrative/judicial function would not be affected by s.109 and that therefore an application under s.147(1) of the Children's Hearings (Scotland) Act 2011 for an order to enforce an implementation authority's duty in relation to a child would still have to be made to the sheriff principal. It would also appear that power in the sheriff principal under r.3.59(11) of the Act of Sederunt (Care and Maintenance) Rules 1997 (SI 1997/291), as amended, to extend the time limits in stated case procedure, not being an appellate matter, would still vest in the sheriff principal, although this would be anomalous, since one would expect matters concerning the management of an appeal to be dealt with by the appellate tribunal. In short, wherever there is a provision relating to the sheriff principal in his or her appellate capacity, this is to be taken as a reference to the Sheriff Appeal Court. The Rules for the Sheriff Appeal court are found principally in the Act of Sederunt (Sheriff Appeal Court Rules) 2015 (SSI 2015/356) ("the 2015

Appeals to sheriff principal and Court of Session: children's hearings etc.

Rules"), and there are some additional provisions in the Act of Sederunt (Rules of Court of Session, Sheriff Appeal Court Rules Amendment) (Sheriff Appeal Court) 2015 (SSI 2015/419). Rule 1.3 of the 2015 Rules provides that when any period of time specified in the Rules expires on a Saturday, Sunday or public or court holiday, the period is extended to expire on the next day that the office of the Clerk to the Sheriff Appeal Court is open for civil business. Rule 2.1 of the 2015 Rules provides that the Sheriff Appeal Court may relieve a party from the consequences of a failure to comply with a provision in the Rules which has been caused by a mistake, oversight or any other excusable cause, with the Court having the power to impose conditions before granting such relief.

This section substantially replicates the much more compact provisions in s.51(11) to (14) of the Children (Scotland) Act 1995. It includes, as appealable, a sheriff's decision to make, vary or extend the newly enacted interim compulsory supervision order. The exclusion in s.51(15)(a) of the 1995 Act of any right of appeal against the decision of the sheriff in relation to an application for a child protection order remains in force, but does not require explicit provision here—this exclusion is simply conveyed by the non-inclusion of such a decision in the list of appealable decisions in subs.(a) of this section.

By virtue of Act of Sederunt (Rules of Court of Session 1994) (SI 1994/1443, Sch.2 (41) Appeals under Statute. V, Pt 15 of Children's Hearings (Scotland) Act 2011; 41.39, "Hearing in Private", the Court of Session may (and in practice routinely does) order the proceedings before it to the held in private. Proceedings in the Sheriff Appeal Court are also held in private.

Subs.(1)

Stated case. The procedural rules, including prescribed forms and timescales, are contained in rr.3.59 to 3.61A of the Act of Sederunt (Child Care and Maintenance) Rules 1997 (SI 1997/291), as amended (the 1997 Rules). No Form for an application to the sheriff to state a case has been enacted. The appellant is, per r.3.59(1), to "specify the point of law upon which the appeal is to proceed or the procedural irregularity, as the case may be". The application must then be intimated by the appellant to the persons listed in r.3.59(2) of the 1997 Rules and, within 21 calendar days of the lodgement of the application, the sheriff, under r.3.59(3) of these Rules, must issue a draft stated case containing findings in fact or in law, or a narrative of the proceedings, the appropriate questions of law or details of the procedural irregularity concerned and a note of the reasons for his or her decision(s). Parties have seven days to propose adjustments to the draft stated case and the sheriff may, and if he or she proposes to reject any adjustment, must, allow a hearing for appropriate procedure (see 1997 Rules r.3.59(4) and (5)). Then, after the time for lodging adjustments has expired or, as the case may be, after the hearing on adjustments, the sheriff has 14 days to state and sign the case (see 1997 Rules r.3.59(6)). The case stated by the sheriff should include:

"(a) Questions of law, framed by him, arising from the points of law stated by the parties and such other questions of law as he may consider appropriate; (b) any adjustments, proposed under paragraph (4), which are rejected by him; (c) a note of the procedural irregularity averred by the parties and any questions of law or other issue which he may consider arises therefrom, as the case may be" (see 1997 Rules r.3.59(7)).

Some useful discussion of the formulation of a stated case is included in *JM v Eileen Taylor, Locality Reporter Manager* [2014] CSIH 62; 2014 Fam. L.R. 102; 2014 G.W.D. 24–453, mentioned above in our discussion of s.156(1). In this case the sheriff had refused an appeal against a decision of a children's hearing to allow a mother very limited supervised contact with her daughters. The questions stated by the sheriff included "(2) Was I justified in reaching the decision I did?" The Court of Session criticised the form of this question and commented at [24]:

"... in posing a question for the opinion of the court, when the sheriff's determination in its turn is subject to appeal, the question is whether the sheriff erred on a point of law or there has been a procedural irregularity. Accordingly, in the framing of a stated case 'it is essential that specific and relevant questions must be posed in the case in order to focus the error or errors of law which it is contended have been made by the sheriff': *C v Miller* 2003 S.L.T. 1379 at para 80. This question does not do that".

The case also illustrates the importance of framing questions so as fully to address the issue involved. The appellant wished to argue that her rights under art.8 of the European Convention had been interfered with. It will be recalled that art.8 provides:

"*Right to respect for private and family life*
1. Everyone has the right to respect for his private and family life, his home and his correspondence.
2. There shall be no interference by a public authority with the exercise of this right except such as is in accordance with the law and is necessary in a democratic society in the interests of national security, public safety or the economic well-being of the

C.542.3

country, for the prevention of disorder or crime, for the protection of health or morals, or for the protection of the rights and freedoms of others."

The question formally posed was "(4) Did I err in being satisfied that article 8 in respect of the appellant had not been interfered with?". At [30] the court narrated that parties were agreed that this question had to be answered in the affirmative because

"the making of a supervision requirement with a direction as to contact, albeit in accordance with law, was an interference by the state in both the appellant's and the children's right to respect for their family life ...".

However, the court observed that the "apposite" question in this case was whether this admitted interference was justified as necessary "for the protection of health and morals, or for the protection of the rights and freedoms of others [here the children]." The sheriff had not addressed this issue by assessing whether the direction as to contact was proportionate to meet the risks which presented and accordingly, although the literal answer to the question posed was "Yes", it did not follow that the appeal should succeed since the apposite question had not been asked. The court noted:

"The sheriff had been applied to with a view to her adjusting her question to one which better reflected what was in issue between the parties, but she had declined to do so, for reasons which were not clear."

We do not know the detail of the submissions which were made to the sheriff but in any event at least two messages may be drawn from this facet of this case: a party should attempt to persuade the sheriff to state questions which focus precisely on the issue in respect of which they consider the sheriff has erred; and it is good practice for the sheriff, when narrating under r.3.59(7)(b) any proposed adjustments which have been rejected, to state clearly the reasons for rejection.

The sheriff principal or the Court of Session. Leave to appeal is not required for an appeal to the sheriff principal (i.e. now the Sheriff Appeal Court) or for an appeal direct to the Court of Session. Subsection (2) requires leave to be obtained from the sheriff principal (i.e. now the Sheriff Appeal Court) for a further appeal to the Court of Session—for discussion of the principles affecting the consideration of leave to appeal see below under subs.(2).

Subs.(1)(a)(i)

C.542.4 *(Other than the grounds mentioned in s.67(2)(j) if the case was remitted to the Principal Reporter under s.49 of the Criminal Procedure (Scotland) Act 1995).* The determination of a sheriff under a s.67(2)(j) ground (an alleged offence by the child) is of course generally appealable, as is a determination in relation to any other ground. However, where a case has been remitted by a criminal court under s.49(1)(a) of the Criminal Procedure (Scotland) Act 1995 following a plea of guilty by a child to the offence concerned or a finding of guilt by the court, there is no room for an application to the sheriff for a proof hearing, and therefore there can be no determination by the sheriff which would be susceptible to any appeal. This does not contravene the child's right to due process, whether under art.6(1) of the European Convention or otherwise, since the child had, in the criminal trial, all the safeguards provided to an accused person under our criminal procedure. Practitioners will of course be aware, when representing a child in a criminal court, that, if aggrieved by the decision of that court, an appeal to the High Court of Justiciary should be considered.

Subs.(1)(a)(ii)

C.542.5 This subparagraph provides that a decision by the sheriff in relation to the review of a grounds determination under s.110(2) is appealable. This provision reflects s.51(11)(a)(iii) of the 1995 Act.

Subs.(1)(a)(iv) and (v) and (b)

C.542.6 As mentioned in the General Note above, these provisions are precipitated by the introduction by the Act of the interim compulsory supervision order.

Subs.(2)

C.542.7 A would-be appellant must decide on whether to appeal to the Sheriff Appeal Court or directly to the Court of Session. "Leave" (i.e. consent) of the sheriff whose decision is being appealed against is not required. If an appellant chooses to appeal to Sheriff Appeal Court then either side may take a further appeal to the Court of Session, but only with leave of the sheriff Appeal Court. In considering which forum to appeal to the appellant should be aware of both legal and practical considerations. In the event that a significant point of law is involved, and/or where there are differing decisions amongst former sheriffs principal, then a direct appeal to the Court of Session may be attractive. On the practical side, appeals to the Sheriff Appeal Court

Appeals to sheriff principal and Court of Session: children's hearings etc.

tend to be disposed of more quickly than appeals to the Court of Session—always an important factor from the time perspective of the child.

With leave of the sheriff principal. A person wishing the Sheriff Appeal Court to grant leave to appeal must, within seven days of the decision appealed against, do so by lodging with the Clerk of the Sheriff Appeal Court an application in Form 30.5 of the Act of Sederunt (Sheriff Appeal Court Rules) 2015 (SSI 2015/356) ("the 2015 Rules"), stating the point of law or procedural irregularity founded upon, and the Clerk of the Sheriff Appeal Court must fix a hearing on the matter before the procedural Appeal Sheriff within 14 days of receiving the application and intimate the date, time and place of that hearing to the parties—see r.30.5 of the 2015 Rules. No guidance is given to sheriffs principal as to the circumstances in which leave should be granted, but, as pointed out in Kenneth McK. Norrie, *Children's Hearings (Scotland) Act 1995*, 2nd edn (Edinburgh: W. Green, 2004), p.97, the aim of the parallel provision in the 1995 Act was to try to discourage the use of the appeal to the sheriff principal as a delaying tactic—see *Hansard*, HL Vol.565, col.1152 (1995). Leave was granted *ex proprio motu* in *K and F, Applicants*, 2002 S.L.T. (Sh. Ct) 38 because the sheriff principal considered that the appeal before him had ranged over "uncharted territory" and because his decision appeared to differ from that of the Outer House judge in *C, Petitioner*, 2002 Fam. L.R. 42. The provisions as to fixing a hearing on leave to appeal, referred to above, are new, and the Sheriff Appeal Court may consider that it should allow parties to decide on whether to ask for leave rather than granting leave *ex proprio motu*: at least, when contemplating granting leave, the Sheriff Appeal Court should ventilate this at the appeal hearing so that the matter may be argued by both sides.

The principles relevant for the court where considering leave to appeal are discussed in Brian Kearney, *Children's Hearings and the Sheriff Court*, 2nd edn (Butterworths, 2000), para.54.31 and, in the general context of civil procedure, in *Macphail on Sheriff Court Practice*, 3rd edn by Sheriff T. Welsh (Edinburgh: W. Green, 2006), Ch.18, notably at para.18.50.

The sheriff's decision on whether or not to grant leave to appeal is a legal issue and as such not prima facie subject to the paramountcy of the welfare of the child principle—see above for our discussion of s.25. See also the discussion of the scope of the application of this principle in *MT & AG v Anne Gerry (Locality Reporter Manager)* [2014] CSIH 2018, sub nom. *MT v Gerry*, 2015 S.C. 359; sub nom. *T v Locality Reporter*, 2015 Fam. L.R. 2, IH, Extra Division in our discussion above of s.159(1)(b). However, as noted in our said discussion, it is thought that the paramountcy of the welfare of the child principle might indirectly apply: assessments of the likely success or failure of an appeal are sometimes matters of fine judgment and, in such a case, the principles of according paramountcy to the safeguarding and promotion of the welfare of the child and of taking account of the views of the child may perhaps legitimately weigh with the Sheriff Appeal Court when considering whether or not to grant leave to appeal.

Subs.(3)

Giving an independent right of appeal to the safeguarder is new, but otherwise these provisions reflect those in s.51(12)(a) of the 1995 Act. Subsection (4), discussed below, sets limits on the type of decisions which a safeguarder may appeal against. The powers of a curator ad litem are considered below at the end of the discussion of subs.(4). **C.542.8**

Subs.(3)(b)

Relevant person. This includes a person deemed to be a relevant person by a pre-hearing panel or children's hearing—see s.81(4)(f) and (7). It should also be noted that there is no provision here for an appeal by a person who claims to be a relevant person but has not so far been recognised as such or deemed to be a relevant person. See above for discussion of s.160(2)(c) in relation to the position of such a person in the context of the "deeming" procedures, including consideration of the case *V v Locality Reporter Manager*, 2013 Fam. L.R. 69, in which a would-be relevant person who had not been invited the children's hearing succeeded in being recognised as entitled to participate in the appeal to the sheriff. **C.542.9**

Subs.(3)(d)

As mentioned above in our discussions of ss.154(4) and 162(5), a legal representative will be cautious of acting for more than one party in case of possible conflict of interest. For fuller consideration of the issues of conflict of interest and confidentiality which may arise see the discussion of s.104(2)–(4) under the heading "*Possible conflict of interest—confidentiality*". **C.542.10**

Subss.(3)(e) and (5)

Under this Act, as in the 1995 Act, the Reporter, although not accorded any right to appeal against decisions of children's hearings, has certain rights of appeal against decisions of sheriffs. However, despite this, the Reporter has no right of appeal against a sheriff's decision to confirm **C.542.11** the decision of a children's hearing. This was not expressly enacted in the 1995 Act but, as pointed out in Norrie, *Children's Hearings (Scotland) Act 1995* (2004), p.97, the wording in s.51(12)(b) of that Act, "the Principal Reporter on behalf of the children's hearing" made it clear that the Reporter could only have an interest to appeal where the sheriff's decision had gone against the hearing's decision and consequently the Reporter could have no right of appeal where the sheriff upheld the hearing's decision. Presumably the reference to the Principal Reporter acting "on behalf of the children's hearing" has been excised here in order reflect the separation of the Reporter's function from that of the children's hearing.

Subs.(4)

C.542.12 These provisions enact that a safeguarder has no right of appeal against the decision of the sheriff (or as the case may be the Sheriff Appeal Court) in the following situations:

(a) after proof in relation to a s.67 ground or in relation to a determination by the sheriff in an application for review of a s.67 ground determination; and

(b) in relation to the making or varying of an interim compulsory supervision order. In terms of s.30(1), the task of a safeguarder is "to safeguard the interests of the child to whom the children's hearing relates", and this is implied in s.31 which deals with the appointment of a safeguarder by the sheriff. That being so, the rationale of denying to the safeguarder any right of appeal in these circumstances is not easy to discern, since on the face of it a situation could well arise where a safeguarder might take the view that the decision of a sheriff to hold established (or not to hold established) a ground for referral was erroneous and that to leave it standing would not best promote the interests of the child. In a case in 2000 (*Cunninghame v J and S*, 2000 Fam. L.B. 46–5), potentially pre-adoptive foster carers, who were not at the time qualified as relevant persons and who therefore had no standing in the referral proceedings, were alleged to have seriously assaulted the child, a baby. The children's hearing, and later the sheriff, appointed a safeguarder who, in what she perceived to be the child's interests, embraced the stance of the pre-adoptive foster carers and, when the case came to the sheriff court, acted as a contradictor to the Reporter and the relevant person (who aligned herself with the Reporter). After proof the sheriff sustained the stance of the safeguarder and discharged referral. In the event that the sheriff had come to the opposite decision the interests of justice would seem to demand that the safeguarder should have a right of appeal. Of course in many cases the child may be able to appeal and perhaps obtain legal representation. However, this will not be open where, as in the *Cunninghame* case, the child is a baby, and at the present time the securing of legal representation may be difficult.

Position of curator ad litem

The continuing power of the sheriff to appoint a curator *ad litem* is covered in the discussion above of s.104(2)–(4), to which the reader is referred. As mentioned there, the Supreme Court has recognised that a curator *ad litem* is *dominus litis*. In *Macphail on Sheriff Court Practice* (2006) it is said at para.4.12:

"A *dominus litis* is a person standing behind a nominal party to the action, who has an interest in the subject matter of the action which is so direct and dominant that he is in control of that party's conduct of the proceedings in the action".

That being so it would appear that the right of appeal conferred on the child by subs.(3)(a) of this section will be exercisable by any curator *ad litem*. Thus it would seem that a curator *ad litem* would have the right to appeal against those decisions mentioned in subs.(4) which a safeguarder, by virtue of that subsection, is debarred from appealing against. This is consistent with the opinion expressed in Kearney, *Children's Hearings and the Sheriff Court* (2000), para.34.21. This view (as expressed in the first edition of Sheriff Kearney's book at p.351) is referred to, apparently with approval, by Sheriff Kelbie in his commentary on *Ross v Kennedy*, 1995 S.C.C.R. 1160 at 1162C.

Subss.(6) and (7)

C.542.13 These provisions simply make clear that the right (conferred by subs.(3)(a) and (b)) to appeal to the Sheriff Appeal Court and/or the Court of Session against a sheriff's ruling in an application for review of a sheriff's earlier s.67 determination is vested in the child, even after the child has ceased to be a child, and the person who was the relevant person at the time when the s.67 determination was made. See above for discussion of the position of any curator *ad litem*. It is submitted that the right to appeal would also extend to the curator *ad litem*, as *dominus litis* in relation to the child, where that curator *ad litem* was in office at the time when the s.67 determination was made.

Appeals to sheriff principal and Court of Session: children's hearings etc.

Subs.(8)
Beginning with the day on which. For the reasons advanced above in the discussion of s.154(5), it is submitted that "day one" in relation to this provision is the day on which the relevant determination/decision was made.

C.542.14

Subs.(9)
This echoes the substance of s.51(11) of the 1995 Act. For discussion of possible grounds of appeal see discussion above under s.156(3)(b)–(e).

C.542.15

Subs.(10)
The sheriff, in appeals against decisions of children's hearings, is not empowered to give directions to the children's hearing when remitting a child's case back—see above for the discussion of s.156(3)(a) (including the submission that under the present legislation the sheriff may be entitled to make suggestions to the children's hearing for its consideration). However, this subsection makes it plain that the Sheriff Appeal Court or as the case may be the Court of Session "must" on deciding an appeal, remit the case to the sheriff with such directions as to disposal of the case by the sheriff as the court may give. This replicates the substance of s.51(14) of the 1995 Act, which is discussed in Kearney, *Children's Hearings and the Sheriff Court* (2000), para.54.29, where it is submitted that such directions may in an appropriate case include directions as to the disposal of the case. This interpretation was adopted by Professor Norrie, in his commentary *Children's Hearings (Scotland) Act 1995* (2004), p.98 and in his *Children's Hearings in Scotland*, 3rd edn (Edinburgh: W. Green, 2013), para.14–48. This view is substantially based on the decision of the Second Division in *Kennedy v A*, 1986 S.L.T. 358. In this case the sheriff, in dealing with an appeal from a decision of a children's hearing had to decide whether a children's hearing was entitled to impose a condition relating to "access" (in the terminology then current) in a supervision requirement under the Social Work (Scotland) Act 1968. The sheriff, in addition to holding that the children's hearing was entitled to impose a condition affecting access, had made observations including a direction that the children's hearing must now proceed to make long term decisions about the child's future. In holding that the sheriff was not entitled to make such observations and directions the court stated, at 342 H–I:

C.542.16

"This was an appeal under s. 49 of the Act of 1968, and if the sheriff is satisfied that the decision of the children's hearing is not justified in all the circumstances of the case, he may then, as he thinks fit, remit the case with the reasons for his decision to the children's hearing for reconsideration of their decision. It is thus clear that the sheriff is required to give reasons for his decision, but it is one thing to give reasons for his decision and quite another thing to make observations or give directions. In our opinion, the sheriff clearly exceeded his powers in making these observations and making these directions. He is not in the same position as this court which is expressly empowered under s. 50(3) of the Act of 1968 to remit the case back to the sheriff for disposal 'in accordance with such directions as the court may give.'"

The issue of the powers of the Court of Session on appeal re-emerged in the much more recent case of *M v Locality Reporter Manager* [2014] CSIH 62; 2014 Fam. L.R. 102; 2014 G.W.D. 24–453, mentioned and discussed above in the General Note to s.154 and under s.156(1). In this case, the sheriff had sustained a decision of a children's hearing to allow very limited contact with the mother of three girls and to require that that contact be supervised. Various detailed criticisms of the reasons stated by the children's hearing had been made at the appeal to the sheriff and all had been rejected by the sheriff. An Extra Division agreed with the substantial decision of the sheriff, and, noting that the Reporter was about to arrange a review hearing on 16 July 2014, being a date four days after the date of the court's own decision, remitted to the sheriff

"with a view to her continuing the supervision orders with the consequence that that they will be subject to review by the children's hearing on 16 July 2014."

The court preceded this decision by commenting, at [35]:

"In terms of section 163(10) of the 2011 Act, on deciding an appeal such as this, the court must remit the case to the sheriff for disposal in accordance with such directions as the court may give. That is consistent with the role of this court being limited to answering such disputed questions of law as may be necessary for the sheriff to exercise his wider jurisdiction under section 156 of the 2011 Act."

On the face of it this observation runs counter to the view of the Second Division in *Kennedy v A*, 1986 S.L.T. 358, quoted above. That case was not discussed in *M v Locality Reporter Manager*, and was not perhaps necessary for the court's decision, which should not necessarily be regarded as the final word on the Court of Session's appellate powers. As mentioned in our discussion above of s.156(1), the court in *M v Locality Reporter Manager* also commented, at

[42], that what we have called the "restrictive" interpretation of the appellate court's powers embodied in *W v Schaffer*, 2011 S.L.T. (Sh. Ct) 86 at 87K to 88A is a matter "for another day" and until that day comes it may be, as we have submitted in our discussion of s.156(1) under the heading "*Principles governing the sheriff's decision—general*" that, having regard to the issues there discussed, sheriffs will be entitled to adopt, in an appropriate case, a more interventional approach than that adopted by Sheriff Principal Nicholson in *W v Schaffer*. In *CF v MF & CF and Scottish Reporter* [2017] CSIH 44, discussed above under s.81(3), an Extra Division, at para.[37], agreed with Sheriff Principal Nicholson's approach, no argument having been addressed to it on the correctness of the decision in *W v Schaffer*.

Subs.(11)

C.542.17 As in the 1995 Act there is no provision within the children's hearing system for any appeal to the Supreme Court (formerly the House of Lords). However, in the event of a judicial review being sought (e.g. *S v Proudfoot*, 2002 S.L.T. 743) there would be the possibility of such an appeal. Also a decision by a sheriff, in the course of an action for parental responsibilities and rights under s.11(2)(b) of the 1995 Act, to grant a motion by an unmarried father to be accorded the status of a relevant person, reached the Supreme Court by way of an action of suspension raised by the Principal Reporter—see *Principal Reporter v K* [2010] UKSC 56; 2011 S.L.T. 271; [2011] 1 W.L.R. 18; 2011 H.R.L.R. 8.

Subs.(12)

C.542.18 This subsection simply makes clear that a decision by a sheriff, in disposing of a review of a grounds determination under s.110, that a new ground for referral has been established is covered by the appeal provisions in subs.(1) of this section.

Appeals to sheriff principal and Court of Session: relevant persons

C.543 **164.**—(1) A person mentioned in subsection (3) may appeal by stated case to the sheriff principal or the Court of Session against a decision of the sheriff in an appeal against a determination of a pre-hearing panel or children's hearing that an individual is or is not to be deemed a relevant person in relation to the child.

(2) A person mentioned in subsection (3) may, with leave of the sheriff principal, appeal by stated case to the Court of Session against the sheriff principal's decision in an appeal under subsection (1).

(3) The persons are—
 (a) the individual in question,
 (b) the child,
 (c) a relevant person in relation to the child,
 (d) two or more persons mentioned in paragraphs (a) to (c) acting jointly.

(4) An appeal under this section must be made before the expiry of the period of 28 days beginning with the day on which the decision appealed against is made.

(5) An appeal under this section may be made—
 (a) on a point of law, or
 (b) in respect of any procedural irregularity.

(6) On deciding an appeal under subsection (1), the sheriff principal or the Court of Session must remit the case to the sheriff for disposal in accordance with such directions as the court may give.

(7) A decision in an appeal under subsection (1) or (2) by the Court of Session is final.

DEFINITIONS

C.543.1 "child": s.199.
 "children's hearing": s.5.
 "pre-hearing panel": ss.202(1) and 79(2)(a).
 "relevant person": s.200.

GENERAL NOTE

C.543.2 The appellate jurisdiction of the sheriff principal has now been transferred to the Sheriff Appeal Court: see discussion above of s.163. For discussion of the appeal to the sheriff in

Appeals to sheriff principal and Court of Session: relevant persons

relation to decisions of pre-hearing panels (PHPs) and children's hearings as to relevant person issues, see above under s.160. This present section provides that the decision of the sheriff on these matters is appealable in the usual way. As illustrated by the decision of the Supreme Court in *Principal Reporter v* K [2010] UKSC 56; 2011 S.C. (U.K.S.C.) 91; 2011 S.L.T. 271; [2011] 1 W.L.R. 18; 2011 H.R.L.R. 8, the issue of who may or may not be a relevant person is of crucial importance in the working of the children's hearings system. It is therefore unsurprising that determinations of sheriffs in appeals from PHPs or children's hearings on this matter are themselves susceptible to possible appeal. As noted below in the discussion of subs.(3)(b) it is surprising that a safeguarder is not empowered to take such an appeal.

Subs.(1)
   Stated case. See discussion under s.163(1). C.543.3

Subss.(1) and (2)
   For consideration of the issues surrounding appealing to the sheriff principal (now the Sheriff C.543.4 Appeal Court) or the Court of Session and the factors in relation to leave to appeal, see the discussion of s.163(1) and (2), above. For discussion of the procedures for seeking leave to appeal from the Sheriff Appeal Court to the Court of Session, see above under s.163(2).

Subs.(3)
   Position of any curator ad litem appointed in relation to the child. See above in the discussion of C.543.5 s.163(4) where it is submitted in relation to appeals under that section that a curator *ad litem* should have a right of appeal. It may be possible to mount a similar argument here, but in this section, in contrast with s.163(3)(c), no specific power is accorded to any safeguarder to appeal. The rationale of this is not apparent, since a safeguarder's responsibility to safeguard the interests of the child might well be thought to include challenging a decision of a sheriff that a particular individual should or should not be accorded the status of a relevant person. However, that is the clear effect of this subsection. That being so, the argument in favour of a curator *ad litem*'s having a right of appeal here might be countered by a submission that since the legislature had not extended this right to a safeguarder (who has the powers and duties of a curator *ad litem*) it could not have been the intention of the legislature to extend this right to a curator *ad litem*.

Subs.(3)(a)
   The individual in question. This in effect refers back to the use of this phrase in s.79(2)(a)(i) C.543.6 which attaches this description to the would-be relevant person who may request the Principal Reporter to arrange a PHP to consider his or her application. Where that individual is aggrieved by the decision of the PHP (or, as the case may be, a children's hearing under s.80(3)) then he or she may appeal under this section. It follows that an individual who has not requested the Principal Reporter to arrange such a hearing—e.g. someone who has only heard of the proceedings after the time for so requesting has expired and now wishes to be declared to be a relevant person—will have no right of appeal under this section. A formal procedure available to such an individual would appear to be an application to the *nobile officium* of the Court of Session, but in practice he or she might wish to await the next review hearing of the child's case and, before that hearing, request a PHP under said s.79(2)(a)(i).

Subs.(3)(c)
   "Relevant person" here includes a "deemed relevant person". See s.81(4). C.543.7

Subs.(4)
   See the discussion of s.163(8), above. The same considerations apply here. C.543.8

Subs.(5)
   See the discussion of s.163(9), above. The same considerations apply here. C.543.9

Subs.(6)
   See the discussion of s.163(10), above. The same considerations apply here. C.543.10

Subs.(7)
   See the discussion of s.163(11), above. The same considerations apply here. C.543.11

Appeals to sheriff principal and Court of Session: contact and permanence orders

C.544 **165.**—(1) A person mentioned in subsection (3) may appeal by stated case to the sheriff principal or the Court of Session against a decision of the sheriff in an appeal under section 161.

(2) A person mentioned in subsection (3) may, with leave of the sheriff principal, appeal by stated case to the Court of Session against the sheriff principal's decision in an appeal under subsection (1).

(3) The person is an individual (other than a relevant person in relation to the child) in relation to whom—
  (a) a contact order is in force regulating contact between the individual and the child,
  (b) a permanence order is in force which specifies arrangements for contact between the individual and the child, or
  (c) the conditions specified for the purposes of section 126(2)(b) are satisfied.

(4) An appeal under this section must be made before the expiry of the period of 28 days beginning with the day on which the decision appealed against was made.

(5) An appeal under this section may be made—
  (a) on a point of law,
  (b) in respect of any procedural irregularity.

(6) On deciding an appeal under subsection (1), the sheriff principal or the Court of Session must remit the case to the sheriff for disposal in accordance with such directions as the court may give.

(7) A decision in an appeal under subsection (1) or (2) by the Court of Session is final.

DEFINITIONS
C.544.1 "child": s.199.
"contact order": s.202(1) and s.11(2)(d) of the Children (Scotland) Act 1995.
"permanence order": s.202(1) and s.80(2) of the Adoption and Children (Scotland) Act 2007.
"relevant person": s.200.

GENERAL NOTE
C.544.2 The appellate jurisdiction of the sheriff principal has now been transferred to the Sheriff Appeal Court: see discussion above of s.163. For discussion of the appeal to the sheriff in relation to decisions of children's hearings as to contact and permanence orders, see above under s.161. This present section provides that the decision of the sheriff on these matters is appealable in the usual way. This is a new provision that applies to the limited class of individuals who have contact with the child as provided under subs.(3) below. Under the Children (Scotland) Act 1995 these individuals' contact with the child could be varied or reduced without them having any redress. This section should also be read in conjunction with ss.126 and 161, above. For discussion of the procedures for seeking leave to appeal from the Sheriff Appeal Court to the Court of Session, see above under s.163(2).

Subs.(1)
C.544.3 *Stated case.* See discussion under s.163(1).

Subss.(1) and (2)
C.544.4 For consideration of the issues surrounding appeals to the Sheriff Appeal Court or the Court of Session and the issues in relation to leave to appeal, see above the discussion of s.163(1) and (2).

Subs.(3)
C.544.5 *Other than a relevant person.* Under s.126(3)(a) contact orders regulating contact between a relevant person and a child are excluded from the categories of cases subject to the appeal provisions in s.126(2), and consequently relevant persons are similarly excluded from the appeals procedures both at the children's hearing's stage (s.161(2)) and here.

Review of requirement imposed on local authority

Subs.(3)(c)
This refers back to s.126(2)(b), which refers to the conditions set out in art.2(2) of the Children's Hearings (Scotland) Act 2011 (Review of Contact Directions and Definition of Relevant Person) Order 2013 (SSI 2013/193) which describes the person entitled to require the Reporter to arrange a children's hearing for the purpose of reviewing a contact direction as "the individual, who is not a relevant person in relation to the child, has or recently has had significant involvement in the upbringing of the child".

Note that, as mentioned in our discussion in the General Note to s.161 of the persons entitled to appeal to the sheriff against decisions affecting contact or permanence orders, that the right of a person who has established family life with the child with which a decision of a children's hearing might interfere (see *Principal Reporter v K* [2010] UKSC 56; 2011 S.C. (U.K.S.C.) 91; 2011 S.L.T. 271; [2011] 1 W.L.R. 18; 2011 H.R.L.R. 8 at [69]) is not secured, unless an expansive "reading down" of art.2(2) of the 2013 Order is adopted.

C.544.6

Subs.(4)
See the discussion of s.163(8), above. The same considerations apply here.

C.544.7

Subs.(5)
See the discussion of s.163(9), above, which refers back to discussion of s.156(3)(b)–(e). The same considerations apply here.

C.544.8

Subs.(6)
See the discussion of s.163(10), above. The same considerations apply here.

C.544.9

Subs.(7)
See above the discussion of s.163(11), above. The same considerations may apply here.

C.544.10

Requirement imposed on local authority: review and appeal

Review of requirement imposed on local authority

166.—(1) This section applies where a duty is imposed on a local authority by virtue of—
 (a) a compulsory supervision order,
 (b) an interim compulsory supervision order, or
 (c) a medical examination order.
(2) If the local authority is satisfied that it is not the relevant local authority for the child in respect of whom the duty is imposed, the local authority may apply to the sheriff for a review of the decision or determination to impose the duty on it.
(3) The sheriff may review the decision or determination to impose the duty with or without hearing evidence.
(4) The sheriff may hear evidence from—
 (a) any local authority,
 (b) the National Convener,
 (c) the child in respect of whom the duty is imposed,
 (d) a person representing that child,
 (e) a relevant person in relation to that child,
 (f) a person representing that person.
(5) Where the duty is imposed on the local authority by a children's hearing, the sheriff may require the Principal Reporter to lodge with the sheriff clerk a copy of the decision (and reasons) of the children's hearing.
(6) The sheriff must determine which local authority is the relevant local authority for the child.
(7) Where the local authority that made the application under subsection (2) is the relevant local authority for the child, the sheriff must confirm the decision of the children's hearing or the determination of the sheriff.
(8) Where another local authority is the relevant local authority for the child, the sheriff—

C.545

(a) must vary the order which imposed the duty so that the duty falls on that local authority, and
(b) may make an order for that local authority to reimburse such sums as the sheriff may determine to the local authority which made the application under subsection (2) for any costs incurred in relation to the duty.

DEFINITIONS

C.545.1 "child": s.199.
"children's hearing": s.5.
"compulsory supervision order": ss.202(1) and 83.
"interim compulsory supervision order": ss.202(1) and 86.
"medical examination order": ss.202(1) and 87.
"National Convener": s.1 and Sch.1 paras 8 to 10.
"relevant local authority": s.201.
"relevant person": s.200.

GENERAL NOTE

C.545.2 A compulsory supervision order (CSO) or an interim compulsory supervision order (ICSO) made by a children's hearing must specify a local authority (the "implementation authority") which is to be responsible for carrying out the measures concerned (see ss.83(1)(b) and 86(1)(b)). So must an ICSO made by a sheriff under ss.100, 115(3) or 156(3)(d). A children's hearing, where making a medical examination order (MEO), is entitled to specify a local authority which is required to arrange the medical examination of the child (s.87(2)(b)). Sections 144 to 148 provide for procedures which may be adopted to enforce the duties placed on the "implementation authority" under a CSO (but not under an ICSO). The present section provides procedures whereby a local authority, which has been specified as the "relevant local authority" in relation to a child, considers that it is not the "relevant local authority" may apply to the sheriff to "review" the decision to identify it as such. "Relevant local authority" is defined substantially as the local authority within whose area the child predominantly resides, or, where the child does not predominantly reside in the area of a particular local authority, the local authority with whose area the child has the closest connection (for discussion of "close connection" see s.67(2)(c)) but leaving out of account any period of residence in a residential establishment (see discussion below of *East Renfrewshire Council, Applicants* 17 October 2014, Inverness Sheriff Court, Sheriff D.O. Sutherland—unreported, but noted and discussed by Sheriff B Kearney in 2015 Fam. L.B. 138–1 and 2016 Fam. L.B. 139–1). The specifying by a children's hearing of a particular local authority as the "implementation authority" may have onerous implications for the local authority concerned, as witness the case of *Principal Reporter v Glasgow City Council*, 2011 Fam. L.R. 118. This was a case in which Glasgow City Council had been specified as the relevant local authority in relation to a supervision requirement made by a children's hearing in another local authority area. Glasgow City Council argued that it was not the "relevant local authority" as defined in the Act, as amended, in that the supervision requirement had been imposed by another local authority from whose area the child had been transferred. The sheriff principal observed that in a case such as this common sense dictated that where there was a transfer of a case to a children's hearing in a different local authority area then the local authority of that different area should be the authority charged with looking after the child. In the event the sheriff principal was able to hold that Glasgow City Council, in the circumstances surrounding the taking over of the requirement, could properly be regarded as being the imposing authority and were accordingly the relevant local authority. The case highlighted the important consequences for local authorities which are identified as being responsible for the implementation of orders of children's hearings. The present section introduces a remedy for a local authority which considers it has been wrongly so identified. In *East Renfrewshire Council, Applicants*, above, a children's hearing in Inverness had determined that the applicants were the implementation authority in relation to a CSO. The background was that the child, whose age is not mentioned in the sheriff's judgment but who seems, as at 2014, to have been mature enough to express views, was born in the Highland Region and lived in that region with his mother until a date in 2012 when the child was moved to a residential establishment in England, where the child was still accommodated, by virtue of a CSO. In April 2013 the mother, and a brother of the child, moved to an address in East Renfrewshire in order to facilitate contact with the child, the mother having advised East Renfrewshire Council of the child's being accommodated in England. East Renfrewshire Council argued that it was not the relevant local authority, and therefore should not have been specified as the implementation authority. The arguments of the parties were based on the premise that the relevant provisions were s.201(1) and (2)(a) of the Act, which provide:

"(1) In this Act, 'relevant local authority' in relation to a child means—
  (a) the local authority in whose area the child predominantly resides, or
  (b) where the child does not predominantly reside in the area of a particular local authority, the local authority within whose area the child has the closest connection.
(2) For the purposes of subsection (1)(a), no account shall be taken of—
  (a) any period of residence in a residential establishment.
  ...
(3) For the purposes of subsection (1)(b), no account is to be taken of—
  (a) any connection with an area that relates to a period of residence in a residential establishment."

The East Renfrewshire Council, in its application to the sheriff for review, submitted that the effect of these provisions was that the period during which the child had been resident in England did not count and that therefore the only relevant period was the period during which the child had been resident in Highland Region. The council further submitted that the principle of the paramountcy of the welfare of the child had no application. The sheriff held that by leaving out of account any period of residence in a residential establishment the Act meant only that the child is not to be considered to be resident in an area simply because he was living in a residential home in that area, and that the substantial test was which local authority the child had the closest connection with. Applying this test the sheriff, refusing the application for review, noted that there was social work evidence before him to the effect that it was hoped that after a substantial period of time the child would be returned to his mother, and held that the child's closest connection was with East Renfrewshire, where his mother and a sibling resided. The sheriff further observed that the paramountcy of the welfare of the child principle was applicable, but this did not appear to be central to his decision. The East Renfrewshire Council appealed to the sheriff principal against the decision of the sheriff. Sheriff Principal Derek C W Pyle allowed the appeal (see *East Renfrewshire Council, Appellants*, Inverness Sheriff Court, 14 September 2015, unreported, but noted by Sheriff B. Kearney in 2015 Fam. L.B. 138–1 and 2016 Fam. L.B. 139–1), and held that what has been called the "stop the clock" approach should be applied. This approach, which is discussed in *Re BC (A Minor)* [1995] 3 F.C.R. 598 and *Northamptonshire CC v Islington LBC*, 2001 Fam 364, treats the provision in s.105(6) of the Children Act 1989 to the effect that when considering what is the "ordinary residence" of a child of any period where the child has been living in a school or other institution is to be disregarded, means that "the clock stopped" at the beginning of that period, with the consequence that the local authority within whose area the child resided immediately before this is regarded as the child's ordinary residence—with the consequence, in the *East Renfrewshire* case, that the relevant local authority for the child was Highland Region. Sheriff Principal Pyle also ruled, under reference to *T v Locality Reporter*, 2015 Fam. L.R. 2 (sub nom. *MT v Gerry* [2014] CSIH 108; 2015 S.C. 359, discussed above under s.159(1)(b)), that the sheriff had erred in holding that the paramountcy of the welfare of the child principle enacted in s.25 of the Children's Hearings (Scotland) Act 2011 was applicable when determining the relevant local authority in respect of a child. In a subsequent case, dealing with the same child, Highland Region made application to the sheriff at Paisley for review of a further decision by a children's hearing specifying it as the relevant local authority and the sheriff at Paisley, while agreeing with Sheriff Principal Pyle that the paramountcy of the welfare of the child principle had no application, differed from the reasoning of Sheriff Principal Pyle on the substantive issue, and held East Renfrewshire Council to be the relevant local authority. On this the sheriff at Paisley was sustained by the Sheriff Appeal Court in *East Renfrewshire Council, Appellant* [2016] SAC (Civ) 14; 2016 G.W.D. 38–679: see our discussion below in the General Note to s.201.

It is interesting to note that s.201 states that no account is to be taken of any period of residence "in a residential establishment". On the face of it, a period of residence with foster or kinship carers or a period in a hospital would not seem to be covered.

Subs.(1)

See the first three sentences of the General Note for the references to the legislative provisions for the CSO, ICSO and MEO. C.545.3

Subs.(2)

The Form of Application and the Form for Intimation comprise Forms 64A and 64B of the Act of Sederunt (Child Care and Maintenance) Rules 1997 (SI 1997/291), as amended. C.545.4

Relevant local authority. See discussion above in the General Note.

Subss.(2) and (3)

C.545.5 *Review.* The procedure before the sheriff here is that of review as distinct from appeal. The essential characteristic in civil procedure of "review" as distinct from "appeal" is that in the former it is clear that the reviewing court has to re-examine the merits of the decision or determination of the initial tribunal or court and come to its own view as to the correctness of that decision or determination. As mentioned above under s.156(3)(b)–(e) in our discussion of the restrictive and non-restrictive approach to appeals, sheriffs may be reticent in using possibly wide powers on appeal: however where, as here, the sheriff's function is to review the decision of the children's hearing, no such reticence is appropriate and where the reviewing sheriff, with or without hearing new evidence, comes to be of the opinion that a different conclusion would be the right one, then he or she need have no hesitation in reversing the original decision or determination and substituting an appropriate new one. Rules 3.54A and 3.58B of the Act of Sederunt (Child Care and Maintenance) Rules 1997 (SI 1997/291), as amended, prescribe the procedure. The court's powers include the power to "allow such further procedure as the sheriff thinks fit" (r.3.58B(3)).

Subs.(4)

C.545.6 As with the provisions for who may appeal in "relevant person" appeals (see discussion above under s.164(3)), the reason for omission of a safeguarder from the persons from whom the sheriff may hear evidence is not clear. It may perhaps be regarded as an indication that, consistently with the ruling of Sheriff Principal Pyle in *East Renfrewshire Council, Applicants*, that the paramountcy of the welfare of the child principle has no application here. Moreover the "catch-all" provisions in s.155(5)(f) and (6), allowing the sheriff to hear evidence and obtain a report from any person he or she considers would assist in deciding the appeal, are not present here. However, this subsection lists the persons from whom the sheriff "may" hear evidence, and the list may not therefore be regarded as exhaustive. Moreover Forms 64A and 64B of the Act of Sederunt (Child Care and Maintenance) Rules 1997 (SI 1997/291), as amended, respectively require specification in the application of the name and contact details of any safeguarder and any curator *ad litem* and require the sheriff clerk to intimate to any safeguarder and curator *ad litem* with a view to their lodging answers within seven days if so advised. It is therefore thought that the sheriff may hear evidence from any safeguarder or curator *ad litem*. The power of the court to "allow such further procedure as the sheriff thinks fit" (r.3.58B(3)) would seem to support this view.

Subs.(4)(b)

C.545.7 *The National Convener.* This is one of the functions of the National Convener which he or she is empowered to delegate under Sch.1 para.10(1) to the Act. In practice it will be exceptional for the National Convener to give evidence in person.

Subs.(4)(d) and (f)

C.545.8 *A person representing* .... In ordinary civil procedure it is unusual, and generally undesirable, for a person who is representing a party to give evidence—see the comments of Lord Reed in *NJDB v JEG*, sub nom. *B v G* [2012] UKSC 21; 2012 S.L.T. 840; 2012 S.C.L.R. 428; 2102 Fam. L.R. 56 at [35] and [36] (discussed above in relation to s.104(2)–(4)) in relation to a solicitor's having given evidence of fact in a sheriff court contact case. However, where the issue is, as here, the appropriateness or otherwise of a particular local authority having the duty to implement orders of a children's hearing the evidence of a representative, legal or otherwise, may well be relevant, and these provisions specifically allow for this.

Subs.(4)(e)

C.545.9 *Relevant person.* This includes any deemed relevant person—s.81(4)(h).

Subs.(6)

C.545.10 See discussion above of subss.(2) and (3) for consideration of whether the paramountcy of the welfare of the child principle is applicable when the sheriff is considering this matter.

Subss.(7) and (8)

C.545.11 The sheriff must decide the matter him or herself: there is no scope for remitting to the children's hearing for reconsideration. It may happen that the applicant local authority will have incurred expense, perhaps considerable expense, as a result of having been specified as the relevant local authority and, if successful in having the obligations towards the child transferred to another local authority, the sheriff has the power to order re-imbursement. In *East Renfrewshire Council, Applicants* (17 October 2014), discussed above, it appears that the

Appeals to sheriff principal: section 166

Highland Council apparently made a claim against the East Renfrewshire Council for expenditure incurred while working with the child before his transfer to England. The sheriff refused this claim and commented that there was no evidence before the court as to what had actually been paid during this period. It seems to us that such a claim would in any event be incompetent since this subsection provides only for re-imbursement where the applicant local authority has been successful in having another local authority specified as the relevant local authority. The sheriff's observations are, however, a reminder that an applicant authority which wishes to obtain a re-imbursement order should be ready to present evidence of what has been expended and justifying the decision to incur it. In the event the sheriff principal, sustaining the appeal, made an order ordering that Highland Council reimburse such sums as the sheriff determines to the appellants for the costs incurred in relation to the duty of implementing the compulsory supervision order (CPO). As at the time of writing the parties are not in agreement as to whether this obligation to reimburse applies from the date of the original CPO or from the date when the children's hearing made the variation of the CPO, and the matter is with the sheriff principal for their decision. The reference at the end of subs.(7) to "the determination of the sheriff" must refer to a sheriff who has made an ICSO in terms of s.100.

Appeals to sheriff principal: section 166

167.—(1) A local authority may appeal by stated case to the sheriff principal against—
  (a) the determination by the sheriff under section 166(6) of which local authority is the relevant local authority for a child,
  (b) the making of an order by the sheriff under section 166(8)(b).
(2) A person mentioned in subsection (3) may appeal by stated case to the sheriff principal against the determination by the sheriff under section 166(6) of which local authority is the relevant local authority for a child.
(3) The persons are—
  (a) the child to whom the determination relates,
  (b) a person representing that child,
  (c) a relevant person in relation to that child,
  (d) a person representing that person.
(4) An appeal under this section must be made before the expiry of the period of 28 days beginning with the day on which the determination or, as the case may be, order was made.
(5) An appeal under this section may be made—
  (a) on a point of law, or
  (b) in respect of any procedural irregularity.
(6) On determining an appeal under this section, the sheriff principal must remit the case to the sheriff for disposal in accordance with such directions as the court may give.
(7) A determination of an appeal under this section is final.

C.546

DEFINITIONS
  "child": s.199.
  "relevant local authority": s.201.
  "relevant person": s.200.

C.546.1

GENERAL NOTE
This section allows for appeal against a sheriff's determination under s.166. For an example of an appeal to the sheriff principal against a s.166 determination by a sheriff, see above in General Note to s.166 and commentary on s.166(7) and (8). As noted above in the General Note to s.163, the appeal from the sheriff's determination now lies to the Sheriff Appeal Court.

C.546.2

Subs.(1)
A local authority may appeal against either or both of the elements in the sheriff's determination, thus a local authority which has had relevant local authority status transferred to it may appeal against the decision to specify it as the relevant local authority and/or any decision that it has to reimburse the applicant authority for any costs incurred by the applicant authority during the period when the applicant authority was carrying out duties as the relevant local authority.

C.546.3

Children's Hearings (Scotland) Act 2011

Stated case. See discussion under s.163(1): the same considerations apply here, except that, as provided in subs.(7) hereof, there is no appeal against the sheriff principal's determination, and therefore no provision in relation to leave to appeal.

Subss.(2) and (3)

C.546.4 Here, as in s.164(c), no right of appeal is conferred on a safeguarder. This is surprising, given that, as mentioned above in our discussion of s.166(4), Forms 64A and 64B of the Act of Sederunt (Child Care and Maintenance) Rules 1997 (SI 1997/291), as amended, appear to treat safeguarders and curators *ad litem* as potential parties. The possible competence of an appeal by a curator *ad litem* is considered above in the discussion of s.164(c), and the same considerations apply here.

Subs.(4)

C.546.5 See the discussion of s.163(8), above. The same considerations apply here.

Subs.(5)

C.546.6 See the discussion of s.163(9), above. The same considerations apply here.

Subs.(6)

C.546.7 See the discussion of s.163(10), above. The same considerations apply here.

Subs.(7)

C.546.8 This contrasts with the provisions as to appeals under ss.163, 164 and 165. Until the creation of the Sheriff Appeal Court the finality of the decision of the sheriff principal left open the possibility of conflicting decisions at sheriff principal level without any obvious way of reconciling them, but a decision of the Sheriff Appeal Court will be regarded as binding throughout Scotland, until and unless overruled by a decision throughout Scotland, until and unless overruled by a decision of the Inner House of the Court of Session.

PART 16

ENFORCEMENT OF ORDERS

Enforcement of orders

C.547 168.—(1) Subsection (2) applies where a relevant order authorising the keeping of a child in a particular place (an "authorised place") is in force in relation to a child.
   (2) An officer of law may enforce the order—
   (a) by searching for and apprehending the child,
   (b) by taking the child to the authorised place,
   [1] (c) where—
      (i) it is not reasonably practicable to take the child immediately to the authorised place,
   by taking the child to and detaining the child in a place of safety for as short a period of time as is practicable, and
   (d) so far as is necessary, by breaking open shut and lockfast places.
   (3) In this section, "relevant order" means—
   (a) a child assessment order,
   (b) a child protection order,
   (c) an order under section 55,
   (d) a compulsory supervision order,
   (e) an interim compulsory supervision order,
   (f) a medical examination order.

NOTE

C.547.1 1. As amended by the Children's Hearings (Scotland) Act 2011 (Modification of Primary Legislation) Order 2013 (SSI 2013/211) Sch.1 para.20(17) (effective June 24 2013).

Enforcement of orders

DEFINITIONS
"child": s.199.
"child assessment order": ss.202(1) and 35.
"child protection order": ss.202(1) and 37.
"compulsory supervision order": ss.202(1) and 83.
"interim compulsory supervision order": ss.202(1) and 86.
"medical examination order": ss.202(1) and 87.
"officer of law": ss.202(1) and s.307(1) of Criminal Procedure (Scotland) Act 1995.
"order under section 55": an order by a justice of the peace where a sheriff was not available.
"place of safety": ss.202(1) and 189.

C.547.2

GENERAL NOTE

This section provides for the means whereby the various orders specified may be enforced. Section 58 of the Act provides that the applicant for, and any person specified in, a child assessment order (CAO), a child protection order (CPO) or an order under s.55 "may only take such steps to implement the order as the applicant (or other person) reasonably believes are necessary to safeguard or promote the welfare of the child". For consideration of this see below in our discussions of subss.(2)(c) and (3).

C.547.2

Subs.(1)

A particular place. The six orders listed in subs.(3) employ various formulations in respect of "place". The CAO provision (s.35(3)(b)) refers to "any place". The CPO provisions (subss.37(2)(b) and (2)(c)) refer respectively to "place of safety" and "any place where the child is staying (whether or not the child is resident there)". The compulsory supervision order (CSO) provision (s.83(2)(a)) refers to "a specified place". The interim compulsory supervision order (ICSO) provisions (s.86(1)(a), when read with s.83(2)(a), also refers to "a specified place"; but s.86(2) provides that an ICSO may simply specify "that the child is to reside at any place of safety away from the place where the child predominantly resides". The provisions for an order under s.55 refer (at s.55(1)(b) and (c)) respectively to "a place of safety" and "any place where the child is staying". The medical examination order (MEO) provision (s.87(2)(a)) refers to "a specified clinic, hospital or other establishment". Each of these is embraced here.

C.547.3

Subs.(2)

It follows from the provision in s.58, mentioned above in our GENERAL NOTE, that an officer of law (as "any other person specified" in a CAO, a CPO or a s.55 order) may only take such steps to implement the order as he or she "reasonably believes" are necessary to safeguard or promote the welfare of the child. Taken literally this could mean that if the officer reasonably believed that implementing the order would not safeguard or promote the welfare of the child then he or she should not take any step to implement it. It is thought that taking such a course, which would seem to be theoretically competent would be exceptional and that, if it were taken the officer would require immediately to advise the Reporter and/or the local authority concerned so that the position could be considered. In the case of a CPO the local authority may request the Reporter to apply to the sheriff (or the Reporter apply *ex proprio motu*) to vary or terminate the order under s.48(1)(d) or (f). This allows for flexibility for a material change in circumstances subsequent to the issuing of the order. Before exercising this power, great care and consideration would be required to ensure that the decision is proportionate in all respects. As discussed above in the General Note to s.58, in *B Petitioner* [2015] CSIH 25; 2015 S.C. 545; 2015 S.L.T. 269; 2015 Fam. LR 88 social workers had not implemented a court order in relation to contact and the sheriff had found them to be in contempt of court. In a petition to the nobile officium the Inner House quashed the sheriff's decision. Lord Malcolm, delivering the substantial opinion of the Court, noted at para.[28] that the sheriff had said that there could be

C.547.4

> "an extreme situation where a social worker may believe it unsafe to comply with legal requirements. There may be an occasion when to comply would place a child at material risk of serious harm to life or limb. However, in my opinion, in order to maintain a fair and proportionate system it is necessary to ensure that if there is a proposal to act in conflict with an existing order, it must be scrutinised and reviewed by an appropriate body at the earliest opportunity."

And Lord Malcolm apparently approved this, saying, at para.[31] "The sheriff herself recognises that there may be circumstances when a social worker requires to take immediate and decisive action on her own account."

More generally, we think the effect of s.58 is to direct the officer of law to keep the welfare of the child firmly in mind, for example when deciding whether it is necessary to use the power to break open lockfast places, and also to make every effort to take the child to the authorised place before concluding that it is not reasonably practicable to do so. See also our discussion of subs.(2)(c).

Subs.(2)(c)

C.547.5 *Taking the child to and detaining the child in a place of safety*. A "place of safety" is defined in s.202(1) as:
"(a) a residential or other establishment provided by a local authority,
(b) a community home within the meaning of section 53 of the Children Act 1989 (c.41),
(c) a police station,
(d) a hospital or surgery, the person or body of persons responsible for the management of which is willing temporarily to receive the child,
(e) the dwelling-house of a suitable person who is so willing, or
(f) any other suitable place the occupier of which is so willing".

The effect of s.58, referred to above, will be that the officer of law should, when enforcing a CAO, a CPO or a s.55 order (and, in practice, any of the orders listed in subs.(3) of this section—see discussion below), do his or her best to place the child within the place of safety which will best safeguard or promote the welfare of the child. Section 189, discussed below, provides that placement in a police station should only resorted to where placement elsewhere is impracticable and that where a police station is used the child should be kept there for the minimum possible time.

Subs.(3)

C.547.6 Reverting to the effect of s.58, discussed above: the orders mentioned in this subsection include the CSO, ICSO and the MEO, which do not figure in s.58. However it is thought that the thrust of the Act is that the officer of law, when enforcing these orders should have in mind the need to safeguard and promote the welfare of the child and should, for example, when placing the child in a place of safety under subs.(2)(c) of this section, try to find the place of safety which would best do so.

Child absconding from place

C.548 **169.**—(1) This section applies where—
(a) a child requires to be kept in a particular place by virtue of—
 (i) a child assessment order,
 (ii) a child protection order,
 (iii) an order under section 55,
 (iv) section 56,
 (v) section 65,
 (vi) a compulsory supervision order,
 (vii) an interim compulsory supervision order,
 (viii) a medical examination order,
 (ix) a warrant to secure attendance, or
 (x) section 143, and
(b) the child absconds from that place or, at the end of a period of leave, fails to return to that place.

(2) The child may be arrested without warrant and taken to that place.

(3) If a court is satisfied that there are reasonable grounds for believing that the child is within premises, the court may grant a warrant authorising an officer of law to—
(a) enter premises, and
(b) search for the child.

(4) The court may authorise the officer of law to use reasonable force for those purposes.

(5) Where the child is returned to the place mentioned in subsection (1), but the occupier of that place is unwilling or unable to receive the child—
(a) the officer of law returning the child must immediately notify the Principal Reporter of that fact, and
(b) the child must be kept in a place of safety until the occurrence of the relevant event.

(6) In subsection (5), the relevant event is—

Child absconding from place

(a) in the case mentioned in sub-paragraph (i) of subsection (1)(a), the end of the period specified in the child assessment order,
(b) in the case mentioned in sub-paragraph (ii) of that subsection, whichever of the following first occurs—
  (i) the children's hearing arranged under section 45 or 69,
  (ii) the termination of the child protection order,
(c) in the case mentioned in sub-paragraph (iii) of that subsection, whichever of the following first occurs—
  (i) the order ceasing to have effect under section 55(4) or (5),
  (ii) the determination by the sheriff of an application for a child protection order in respect of the child,
(d) in the case mentioned in sub-paragraph (iv) of that subsection, whichever of the following first occurs—
  (i) the giving of notice under subsection (5) of section 56, or
  (ii) the end of the period mentioned in subsection (3) of that section,
(e) in the case mentioned in sub-paragraph (v) of that subsection, whichever of the following first occurs—
  (i) the giving of a direction by the Principal Reporter under section 68(2) or 72(2)(a), or
  (ii) the children's hearing arranged by virtue of section 69(2),
(f) in the case mentioned in sub-paragraph (vi) of that subsection, the children's hearing arranged by virtue of section 131(2)(b),
(g) in the cases mentioned in sub-paragraphs (vii) and (ix) of that subsection whichever of the following first occurs—
  (i) the next children's hearing that has been arranged in relation to the child,
  (ii) the next hearing before the sheriff relating to the child that is to take place by virtue of this Act,
(h) in the cases mentioned in sub-paragraphs (viii) and (x) of that subsection, the next children's hearing that has been arranged in relation to the child.

NOTE

1. The words "arrested without warrant and" have been removed by the Criminal Justice (Scotland) Act 2016 Sch.2 para.24, but this provision has not yet been brought into force.

C.548.1

DEFINITIONS
"child": s.199.
"child assessment order": ss.202(1) and 35.
"child protection order": ss.202(1) and 37.
"children's hearing": s.5.
"compulsory supervision order": ss.202(1) and 83.
"interim compulsory supervision order": ss.202(1) and 86.
"medical examination order": ss.202(1) and 87.
"officer of law": s.202(1) and Criminal Procedure (Scotland) Act 1995 s.307(1).
"order under section 55": an order by a justice of the peace where a sheriff was not available.
"place of safety": ss.202(1) and 189.
"Principal Reporter": s.14 and Sch.3 paras 8–10.
"section 56": Constable's power to remove child to place of safety.
"section 65": Provision of information by constable: child in a place of safety.
"warrant to secure attendance": ss.202(1) and 88.
"section 143": Transfers in cases of urgent necessity.

C.548.2

GENERAL NOTE

This section provides that a child who absconds, or fails to return from after a period of leave, from a place where he or she is being held by virtue of any of the orders or provisions listed, may be arrested without warrant (until and unless the projected amendment is brought into force) and returned to that place. It also empowers the court to grant warrant to search for the child and for the procedures to be adopted where the occupier of the place is unwilling or unable to receive the child. These provisions can have no application in relation to a child who

C.548.3

is residing at a place other than by virtue of any of the orders or provisions listed, e.g. a child being accommodated by a local authority on a voluntary basis—such a child might of course, depending on circumstances, be eligible for referral to a children's hearing under s.67(2)(n) (child beyond the control of a relevant person).

Subs.(1)(b)

C.548.4 *Absconds.* This concept is nor defined in this Act. In *R v Lilley* [2002] EWCA Crim 3115, an accused who had been granted bail in the course of his trial and failed to turn up at the trial was described as having 'absconded'. In *D v South Tyneside Health Care NHS Trust* [2003] EWCA Civ 878, a mental health patient was described as having on occasions 'absconded' and returned voluntarily, thereby implying that intention not to return is not a necessary element in absconding—in this case the term 'abscond' was being used in a common-sense way, and the issue of a precise definition was not discussed. In *Welsh v Richardson*, 2012 S.L.T. 1153 two individuals were charged with having knowingly harboured or concealed two girls who had absconded from a children's home. There was evidence that the girls had said they intended to go out from the home on the day concerned and visit a particular flat. They were given verbal instructions not to go to that flat but otherwise there was no restriction on them leaving the home. In the event they did leave the home. There was evidence that they did go to the flat in order to obtain cigarettes but, as recorded by the Justiciary Appeal Court judgment delivered at the subsequent appeal, there was "no indication that they did so with the intention of 'running away' from the home and not returning". At the conclusion of the prosecution case the sheriff was moved to hold that there was no evidence capable of establishing that the girls had absconded. The sheriff refused the motion and convicted. On appeal the Court of Session noted that "abscond" was not defined in the Children (Scotland) Act 1995 and noted that the definitions in the Shorter OED and the Collins English Dictionary were respectively "to leave hurriedly and in secret, to escape from justice" and "to run away secretly especially from an open institution or to avoid prosecution or punishment". The court, as mentioned above, found no indication the girls did what they did they did so with the intention of running away from the home and not returning. The court accordingly held that it had not been proved that the girls had absconded and allowed the accused's appeal against conviction.

Subs.(2)

C.548.5 As at time of writing the words "arrested without warrant and" are still in place, but will disappear when and if the provision in Sch. 2 para.24 of the Criminal Justice (Scotland) Act 2016 is brought into force. The effect of the removal of these words will be that the officer of law will not be obliged or entitled to use any words to the effect that the child is being "arrested", which may be thought to contain overtones to the effect that the child is thought to have committed an offence by running away. (It is the person who knowingly assists etc. the child who is running away, who may be committing an offence—see s.171 below.) The officer of law may however, by virtue of this subsection, once amended, compel the child, even without "arresting" the child, to come with him or her to the place.

Subss.(3) and (4)

C.548.6 These provisions do not specify who may or must apply for a warrant. Therefore, this will depend upon the circumstances, thus, it might be an application by the local authority, the police or even the Reporter.

Subs.(5)(b)

C.548.7 *Place of safety.* See discussion above of s.168(2)(c). Section 58 does not apply in terms of acting in compliance with this present section, but the thrust of the Act towards safeguarding and promoting the welfare of the child has the consequence that the place of safety selected should be that which best achieves this. As provided by s.189, the selection of a police station as the place of safety should be regarded as the last resort and the child should be kept there for the minimum possible time. The reader is directed to the definition of "place of safety" in s.202(1) and to s.189(2) and (3).

Subs.(6)(b)(i), (c)(ii), (e)(ii), (f), (g) and (h)

C.548.8 The decisions of the sheriff and of the hearings mentioned will be subject to the overarching principles and the European Convention principle of proportionality.

Child absconding from person

170.—(1) This section applies where—
(a) a person has (or is authorised to have) control of a child by virtue of—
  (i) a child assessment order,
  (ii) a child protection order,
  (iii) an order under section 55,
  (iv) section 56,
  (v) section 65,
  (vi) a compulsory supervision order,
  (vii) an interim compulsory supervision order,
  (viii) a medical examination order,
  (ix) a warrant to secure attendance, or
  (x) section 143, and
(b) the child absconds from that person.
(2) The child may be arrested without warrant and taken to that person.
(3) If a court is satisfied that there are reasonable grounds for believing that the child is within premises, the court may grant a warrant authorising an officer of law to—
(a) enter premises, and
(b) search for the child.
(4) The court may authorise the officer of law to use reasonable force for those purposes.
(5) Where the child is returned to the person mentioned in subsection (1), but the person is unwilling or unable to receive the child—
(a) the officer of law returning the child must immediately notify the Principal Reporter of that fact, and
(b) the child must be kept in a place of safety until the occurrence of the relevant event.
(6) In subsection (5), the relevant event is—
(a) in the case mentioned in sub-paragraph (i) of subsection (1)(a), the end of the period specified in the child assessment order,
(b) in the case mentioned in sub-paragraph (ii) of that subsection, whichever of the following first occurs—
  (i) the children's hearing arranged under section 45 or 69,
  (ii) the termination of the child protection order,
(c) in the case mentioned in sub-paragraph (iii) of that subsection, whichever of the following first occurs—
  (i) the order ceasing to have effect under section 55(4) or (5),
  (ii) the determination by the sheriff of an application for a child protection order in respect of the child,
(d) in the case mentioned in sub-paragraph (iv) of that subsection, whichever of the following first occurs—
  (i) the giving of notice under subsection (5) of section 56, or
  (ii) the end of the period mentioned in subsection (3) of that section,
(e) in the case mentioned in sub-paragraph (v) of that subsection, whichever of the following first occurs—
  (i) the giving of a direction by the Principal Reporter under section 68(2) or 72(2)(a), or
  (ii) the children's hearing arranged by virtue of section 69(2),
(f) in the case mentioned in sub-paragraph (vi) of that subsection, the children's hearing arranged by virtue of section 131(2)(b),
(g) in the cases mentioned in sub-paragraphs (vii) and (ix) of that subsection whichever of the following first occurs—
  (i) the next children's hearing that has been arranged in relation to the child,

(ii) the next hearing before the sheriff relating to the child that is to take place by virtue of this Act,

(h) in the cases mentioned in sub-paragraphs (viii) and (x) of that subsection, the next children's hearing that has been arranged in relation to the child.

NOTE

C.549.1 1. The words "arrested without warrant and" have been removed by the Criminal Justice (Scotland) Act 2016, Sch.2 para.24, but this provision has not yet been brought into force.

DEFINITIONS

C.549.2 "child": s.199.
"child assessment order": ss.202(1) and 35.
"child protection order": ss.202(1) and 37.
"children's hearing": s.5.
"compulsory supervision order": ss.202(1) and 83.
"interim compulsory supervision order": ss.202(1) and 86.
"medical examination order": ss.202(1) and 87.
"officer of law": s.202(1) and Criminal Procedure (Scotland) Act 1995 s.307(1).
"order under section 55": an order by a justice of the peace where a sheriff was not available.
"place of safety": ss.202(1) and 189.
"Principal Reporter": s.14 and Sch.3 paras 8–10.
"section 56": Constable's power to remove child to place of safety.
"section 65": Provision of information by constable: child in a place of safety.
"warrant to secure attendance": ss.202(1) and 88.
"section 143": Transfers in cases of urgent necessity.

GENERAL NOTE

C.549.3 This section substantially replicates, in relation to a "person" the provisions which s.169 enacts in relation to "place". We accordingly refer to our entire discussion above of that section, which applies mutatis mutandis here. "Person" is not defined in the Act, but it seems clear that the reference is to natural persons and not legal persons (limited companies etc.).

Subs.(1)(b)

C.549.4 *Absconds.* For the meaning of this, see under s.169(1)(b).

Subs.(2)

C.549.5 As at time of writing the words "arrested without warrant and" are still in place, but will disappear when and if the provision in Sch.2 para.24 of the Criminal Justice (Scotland) Act 2016 is brought into force. The effect of the removal of these words will be that the officer of law will not be obliged or entitled to use any words to the effect that the child is being "arrested", which may be thought to contain overtones to the effect that the child is thought to have committed an offence by running away. (It is the person who knowingly assists etc. the child who is running away, who may be committing an offence—see s.171 below.) The officer of law may, however, by virtue of this subsection, once amended, compel the child, even without "arresting" the child, to come with him or her to the person.

Offences related to absconding

C.550 **171.**—(1) This section applies where—
(a) a child requires to be kept in a particular place by virtue of—
   (i) a child assessment order,
   (ii) a child protection order,
   (iii) a compulsory supervision order,
   (iv) an interim compulsory supervision order,
   (v) a medical examination order, or
   (vi) a warrant to secure attendance, or
(b) a person has (or is authorised to have) control of a child by virtue of such an order or warrant.
(2) A person commits an offence if the person—

Offences related to absconding

(a) knowingly assists or induces the child to abscond from the place or person,
(b) knowingly harbours or conceals a child who has absconded from the place or person, or
(c) knowingly prevents a child from returning to the place or person.

(3) The person is liable on summary conviction to a fine not exceeding level 5 on the standard scale, to imprisonment for a term not exceeding 6 months or to both.

(4) This section is subject to—
(a) section 38(3) and (4) of the 1995 Act,
(b) section 51(5) and (6) of the Children Act 1989 (c.41), and
(c) Article 70(5) and (6) of the Children (Northern Ireland) Order 1995 (S.I. 1995/755 (N.I. 2)).

DEFINITIONS

"child": s.199.
"child assessment order": ss.202(1) and 35.
"child protection order": ss.202(1) and 37.
"children's hearing": s.5.
"compulsory supervision order": ss.202(1) and 83.
"interim compulsory supervision order": ss.202(1) and 86.
"medical examination order": ss.202(1) and 87.
"warrant to secure attendance": ss.202(1) and 88.

C.550.1

GENERAL NOTE

This section creates offences where a person colludes with a child who has absconded from a place where, or person with whom, the child is being kept under the listed orders or warrant, who harbours or conceals such a child, or prevents such a child from returning to the place or person where he or she was being kept.

C.550.2

Subs.(2)

To abscond ... has absconded. A child only "absconds" where there is an intention to run away. See discussion of the meaning of "abscond" in commentary above on s.169(1)(b) including reference to *Welsh v Richardson* [2012] HCJAC 114, 2012 S.L.T. 1153. It should be noted that there is no reference in this present section, in contrast to s.169(1)(b), to the child having, at the end of a period of leave, failed to return. However in *Welsh* it was said in para.[10] at page 115L:

"Failure to return after a period of leave can, in our judgment, be said to provide prima facie evidence of an intention not to return before the order requiring the child to reside at the relevant place has expired and therefore to amount to a deemed abscondment. This is, in our view, a quite different situation from the present ...".

The present section is offence-making and its terms will require to be interpreted strictly. It remains to be seen what approach a criminal court will take to its interpretation.

Knowingly. This emphasises that there must be full criminal intent ("mens rea") on the part of the offender before the offence can be complete. In a classic case on this subject, *Sweet v Parsley* [1970] A.C. 132, Lord Reid said at 149:

"... for it is firmly established by a host of authorities that mens rea is an essential ingredient of every offence unless some reason can be found for holding that it is not necessary.

It is also firmly established that the fact that other sections of the Act expressly require mens rea, for example where they contain the word 'knowingly' is not in itself sufficient to justify a decision which is silent as to mens rea creates an absolute offence."

It is thought, however, that it would not here be necessary for the alleged offender to know the precise order or warrant listed in subs.(1)(a) under which the child was being kept, and that it would be sufficient to establish that he or she knew that the child had run away from lawful custody.

C.550.3

Subs.(4)(a)

As Professor Norrie notes (at Kenneth McK. Norrie, *Children (Scotland) Act 1995* 2nd edn. (Edinburgh: W. Green, 2004), p.75), local authorities may provide short-term (i.e. for a period not exceeding 7 or, exceptionally, 14 days) refuge for children who appear to be at risk and who request to be provided with this. Sections 38(3) and (4) of the Children (Scotland) Act 1995

C.550.4

provide that the offences of harbouring, etc, runaway children enacted by s.89 of that Act do not apply unless the period to which the harbouring relates has followed within two days of the end of a previous period of such refuge being provided. The rationale of this provision would appear to be to rule out the use of such short-term refuge as a long-term facility by allowing the child to be re-admitted immediately after the expiry of the short-term period.

Subs.(4)(b) and (c)
C.550.5   These provisions provide that no offence of harbouring etc. is committed in England and Wales and Northern Ireland where a child who is subject to a relevant Scottish order is being kept by a person holding an appropriate certificate.

PART 17

PROCEEDINGS UNDER PART 10: EVIDENCE

Use of evidence obtained from prosecutor

C.551   **172.**—(1) This section applies where an application is made to the sheriff—
(a) to determine whether a section 67 ground is established, or
(b) to review a grounds determination.
(2) The Principal Reporter may request a prosecutor to give the Principal Reporter evidence held by the prosecutor in connection with the investigation of a crime or suspected crime if the Principal Reporter considers that the evidence might assist the sheriff in determining the application.
(3) The request may relate only to evidence lawfully obtained in the course of the investigation.
(4) The prosecutor may refuse to comply with the request if the prosecutor reasonably believes that it is necessary to retain the evidence for the purposes of any proceedings in respect of a crime (whether or not the proceedings have already commenced).

DEFINITIONS
C.551.1   "grounds determination": ss.202(1) and 110(1).
"Principal Reporter": s.14 and Sch.3 paras 8–10.

GENERAL NOTE
C.551.2   This section empowers the Reporter to request the Crown to supply evidence lawfully obtained in the course of a criminal investigation but provides that the prosecutor may refuse this request where this is thought to be necessary.

Subs.(2)
C.551.3   The evidence concerned may relate to a crime alleged to have been committed by the child or by a third party. The test is whether the Reporter considers the evidence to be relevant to the ground for referral.

Subs.(3)
C.551.4   *May refuse.* The prosecutor has the right to refuse the Reporter's request, but only if he or she considers it "necessary" to so refuse for the purpose of the criminal proceedings, current or intended. In practice there is constructive co-operation between the Crown and Procurator Fiscal Service ("COPFS") and the Reporters.

Cases involving sexual behaviour: evidence

C.552   **173.**—(1) This section applies where—
(a) an application is made to the sheriff—
  (i) to determine whether a section 67 ground is established, or
  (ii) to review a grounds determination, and
(b) the ground involves sexual behaviour engaged in by any person.
(2) In hearing the application the sheriff must not, unless the sheriff makes

an order under section 175, admit evidence, or allow questioning of a witness designed to elicit evidence, which shows or tends to show one or more of the circumstances mentioned in subsection (3) in relation to a person mentioned in subsection (4).

(3) The circumstances are that the person—
(a) is not of good character (whether in relation to sexual matters or otherwise),
(b) has, at any time, engaged in sexual behaviour not forming part of the subject-matter of the ground,
(c) has, at any time (other than shortly before, at the same time as or shortly after the acts which form part of the subject-matter of the ground), engaged in behaviour (not being sexual behaviour) that might found an inference that the person is not credible or the person's evidence is not reliable,
(d) has, at any time, been subject to any condition or predisposition that might found the inference that the person is not credible or the person's evidence is not reliable.

(4) The persons are—
(a) the child,
(b) a person giving evidence for the purposes of the hearing,
(c) any other person evidence of whose statements is given for the purposes of the hearing.

(5) In subsection (4)(c), "statements" includes any representations, however made or expressed, of fact or opinion.

(6) In this section and section 174, references to sexual behaviour engaged in include references to having undergone or been made subject to any experience of a sexual nature.

DEFINITIONS
"child": s.199.
"grounds determination": ss.202(1) and 110(1).

C.552.1

GENERAL NOTE
This section, along with ss.174 and 175, deals with the conduct of proof hearings before the sheriff after an application has been made to the sheriff under ss.93(2)(a) or 94(2)(a), being applications where the ground for referral have not been admitted, or not understood, and under s.110(2), being hearings before the sheriff for review of a grounds determination. These provisions can be traced back to the ss.274 and 275 of the Criminal Procedure (Scotland) Act 1995. They were applied to children's hearings cases by s.23 of the Vulnerable Witnesses (Scotland) Act 2004, which the 2011 Act repeals (Sch.6). The broad purpose of these provisions is to prohibit the questioning of persons (generally but not exclusively alleged victims of sexual offences) involved in sexual activity as to their character or sexual activity not relating to the ground for referral concerned except where the sheriff, in the interests of justice, allows an application for such questioning to be pursued.

C.552.2

Subss.(1)(b) and (6)
The provisions apply where the ground for referral involves any sexual behaviour initiated by, or experienced by, any person.

C.552.3

Subs.(2)
For discussion of the circumstances in which the sheriff may allow questioning, see below under s.175(3)–(5).

C.552.4

Subs.(3)
As provided in subs.(1) these provisions only apply where the ground for referral involves "sexual behaviour" by a person. However the questions which are prohibited (unless permitted by the sheriff) are not confined to, although they include, questions relating to sexual conduct, for example, a question tending to elicit evidence that the person is not of good character might be a prohibited question.

C.552.5

Children's Hearings (Scotland) Act 2011

Subs.(4)(a) and (c)

C.552.6 By virtue of s.2 of the Civil Evidence (Scotland) Act 1988 hearsay evidence is admissible in civil cases towards proving the content of the hearsay. Paragraph (a) in s.9 of that Act defines civil cases as including proof hearings in children's hearings cases for all grounds for referral except ground s.67(2)(j) (alleged offence by the child). Accordingly where, for example, abuse of, or an offence against, the child forms part of the ground for referral, a statement made by a person can be used towards establishing the ground concerned. This applies where the person does not give evidence and even where the person does give evidence contradicting what was said in the statement. Thus in *F (A Parent) v Kennedy (Reporter to the Children's Panel) (No.2)*, 1993 S.L.T. 1284 the decision of the sheriff to prefer the evidence contained in the prior statement to the evidence given in court by the child was sustained—see per Lord Justice Clerk Ross at 1287. The effect of these present provisions would be to prohibit (except with the express permission of the sheriff under s.175) any question in the categories listed in subs.(3) being directed to the child or the person speaking to the child's statement.

Cases involving sexual behaviour: taking of evidence by commissioner

C.553 **174.**—(1) Subsection (2) applies where—
(a) a commissioner is appointed under section 19 of the Vulnerable Witnesses (Scotland) Act 2004 (asp 3) to take evidence for the purposes of a hearing before the sheriff—
  (i) to determine whether a section 67 ground is established, or
  (ii) to review a grounds determination, and
(b) the ground involves sexual behaviour engaged in by any person.

(2) The commissioner must not, unless the sheriff makes an order under section 175, take evidence which shows or tends to show one or more of the circumstances mentioned in section 173(3) in relation to a person mentioned in section 173(4).

DEFINITION

C.553.1 "grounds determination": s.202(1) and s.110(1).

GENERAL NOTE

C.553.2 Section 19 of the Vulnerable Witnesses (Scotland) Act 2004 provides for evidence to be taken by a commissioner. This section provides, as one would expect, that the same rules as to questioning, discussed above under s.173, as apply to the proceedings before the sheriff, also apply to the proceedings before the commissioner. The High Court of Justiciary issued Practice Note No.3 of 2005 in relation to Commissions ordered by that court. The Practice Note includes the following:

"Conduct of the commission

10. The commissioner has the authority of the court to take evidence from a specified witness or witnesses. He or she has the authority to require the parties to show respect for the proceedings and the power to control the proceedings to allow the commission to be completed effectively. If the conduct of any party to the proceedings prevents the commission being conducted effectively, the commissioner will report this to the court. If the commissioner is a judge of the High Court, he or she has the powers to control the conduct of proceedings that he or she would otherwise have while sitting as a judge.

11. The commissioner will determine any particular matter necessary for the effective conduct of the commission proceedings (for example, whether any adjournments are necessary for the comfort of the witness or to allow the accused to consult with their representatives)."

This Practice Note is not of course binding in proceedings under this section, but it may be regarded as providing some guidance. This Practice Note has now been superseded by Practice Note No.1 0f 2017 which deals extensively with the details of applying for and conducting evidence on commission in the context of a High Court jury trial. Nevertheless the foregoing still affords useful general guidance. It is to be noted that any application to permit questions to be asked which would otherwise be prohibited under s.173(2) is to be made to the sheriff and not to the commissioner. Accordingly, a party wishing to ask "prohibited" questions should make application to the sheriff under s.175.

Sections 173 and 174: application to sheriff for order as to evidence

175.—(1) On the application of a person mentioned in subsection (2), the sheriff may, if satisfied as to the matters mentioned in subsection (3) make an order—
(a) admitting evidence of the kind mentioned in section 173(2),
(b) allowing questioning of the kind mentioned in that section,
(c) enabling evidence of the kind mentioned in section 174(2) to be taken.
(2) Those persons are—
(a) the child,
(b) a relevant person in relation to the child,
(c) the Principal Reporter,
[1] (d) a safeguarder appointed in relation to the child by virtue of section 30.
(3) Those matters are—
(a) the evidence or questioning will relate only to—
  (i) a specific occurrence or specific occurrences of sexual behaviour or other behaviour demonstrating the character of the person,
  (ii) specific facts demonstrating the character of the person,
  (iii) a specific occurrence or specific occurrences of sexual behaviour or other behaviour demonstrating a condition or predisposition to which the person is or has been subject, or
  (iv) specific facts demonstrating a condition or predisposition to which the person is or has been subject,
(b) the occurrence, occurrences or facts are relevant to establishing the ground, and
(c) the probative value of the evidence is significant and is likely to outweigh any risk of prejudice to the proper administration of justice arising from its being admitted or elicited.
(4) References in this section to an occurrence or occurrences of sexual behaviour include references to undergoing or being made subject to any experience of a sexual nature.
(5) In this section "proper administration of justice" includes—
(a) appropriate protection of the person's dignity and privacy, and
(b) ensuring the facts and circumstances of which the sheriff is made aware are relevant to an issue to be put before the sheriff and commensurate with the importance of that issue to the sheriff's decision on the question whether the ground is established.

NOTE
1. As amended by the Children's Hearings (Scotland) Act 2011 (Modification of Primary Legislation) Order 2013 (SSI 2013/211) Sch.1 para.20(18) (effective June 24 2013).

DEFINITIONS
"child": s.199.
"Principal Reporter": s.14 and Sch.3 paras 8–10.
"relevant person": s.200.
"safeguarder": ss.202(1) and 30(1).

GENERAL NOTE
This section contains the pivotal provisions in relation to this group of sections. It prescribes the test which the sheriff is to apply when moved to permit questions which would otherwise be prohibited under s.173(2). The decision of the sheriff on these matters is one of fact and of law, with a heavily factual component and accordingly the paramountcy of the welfare of the child principle enacted in s.25 does not apply in its express terms. However, as discussed below, the paramountcy of the welfare of the child principle will be a background consideration for the sheriff in considering some of the issues. The court (and, in this instance, this would include any commissioner) has always had the power to secure that witnesses are examined with courtesy and without bullying, and the sheriff (or, as the case may be, the commissioner) has the right and duty to intervene if it appears that insulting or merely annoying questions are being

Children's Hearings (Scotland) Act 2011

posed—see *Falconer v Brown* (1893) 1 Adam 96 (cited in *Macphail on Sheriff Court Practice*, 3rd edn (Edinburgh: W. Green, 2006) paras 16.39 and 16.75) and this still applies where permission has been granted under this section to allow questions which would otherwise be prohibited. The Court may also intervene to limit repetitive or unnecessary questioning—cf. per Lord Reed in *NJDB v JEG*, [2012] UKSC 21, 2012 S.C. (U.K.S.C.) 293 (also sub nom *B v G*) at para.[34]. Rule 3.81A of the Act of Sederunt (Child Care and Maintenance Rules) 1997 (SI 1997/291) as amended by Act of Sederunt (Children's Hearings (Scotland) Act 2011) (Miscellaneous Amendments) 2013 (SSI 2013/172) provides

"(1) Where the sheriff makes an order under section 175(1) or (c) [presumably meaning 'section 175(1) (a) or (c)'] of the 2011 Act the appellant shall lodge any relevant recording and documents with the sheriff clerk".

Subs.3(a) and (b)

C.554.4 The proposed questions must refer to specific matters and not simply to general impressions. The applicant for permission will require to identify the matters concerned and explain, so far as necessary, their relevance to the ground concerned. The Form to be used is Form 79, as amended, in Sch.1 of the Act of Sederunt (Child Care and Maintenance Rules) 1997 (SI 1997/291) as amended by Act of Sederunt (Children's Hearings (Scotland) Act 2011) (Miscellaneous Amendments) 2013 (SSI 2013/172).

Subs.(3)(c)

C.554.5 This provision is a key element in the whole section. It is based on the premise (see subs.(5) below) that the "proper administration of justice" includes "appropriate protection of the person's dignity and privacy" and that accordingly **unnecessary** evidence affecting the dignity and privacy of the witness (who may or may not be a child witness) is to be avoided. This provision in effect enjoins the sheriff to assess the importance of the evidence which is said to be likely to affect the decision on the existence or not of the ground for referral concerned, to consider the position if the motion to allow a question or line of questioning was granted and to decide whether the exploration of the potential evidence concerned would be likely to produce evidence of such a degree of importance as would the outweigh the erosion of that aspect of the proper administration of justice which consisted in the appropriate protection of the witness's dignity and privacy. In *Kerseboom (Michel) v HM Advocate* [2016] HCJAC 51; 2017 J.C. 47; 2016 S.C.L. 834, the preliminary trial judge had refused an application under s.275 of the Criminal Procedure (Scotland) Act 1995 (from which, as mentioned above in the General Note to s.173 of this Act, this set of provisions is substantially derived) where evidence (as to the medical/sexual history of the complainer) was sought to be admitted. In sustaining the decision of the judge at the preliminary hearing the Justiciary Appeal Court said at para.[16]:

"... we consider that the procedural hearing judge was correct in deciding in the circumstances it [the evidence concerned] would be of such little evidential value that it could not be said that the probative value of it would outweigh the risk to the administration of justice from its admission".

See also *M v HM Advocate (No.2)* [2013] HCJAC 22; 2013 S.L.T. 380; 2013 S.C.C.R. 215, 2013 G.W.D. 8-170, and the cases therein cited. We think that there is a question as to how far the approach of the Justiciary Appeal Court ought to be followed in cases arising in the children's hearings system. As mentioned above the paramountcy of the welfare of the child principle enacted in s.25 does not apply in its express terms, but it must always be kept in mind that the thrust of the children's hearings legislation is to safeguard and promote the interests and welfare of the child. It will of course always be in the interests of the child that he or she be accorded due administration of justice. In *Principal Reporter v K* [2010] UKSC 56; 2011 S.C. (U.K.S.C.) 91; 2011 S.L.T. 271; 2011 1 W.L.R. 18 it was said at para.44:

"The children's hearing has to have the best and most accurate information that it can in order to make the best decisions about the child. Everyone is deprived of that information if findings of fact are made by agreement without the participation of the very person whose conduct is in question. If decisions are then made on an inaccurate factual basis the child is doubly let down. Not only is the everyday course of her life altered but she may be led to believe bad things about an important person in her life. No child should be brought up to believe that she has been abused if in fact she has not, any more than any child should be persuaded by the adult world that she has not been abused when in fact she has."

Subs.(4)

C.554.6 This makes clear that the content of the questions relating to sexual behaviour mentioned in subs.(3)(i) and (iii) includes both sexual behaviour initiated by the witness and sexual behaviour to which the witness has been subjected or exposed.

Subs.(5)
See discussion above of subs.(3)(c).

Amendment of Vulnerable Witnesses (Scotland) Act 2004

176.—(1) The Vulnerable Witnesses (Scotland) Act 2004 (asp 3) is amended as follows.

(2) In section 11 (interpretation of Part 2 of Act), in subsection (5)—
  (a) after "Part—" insert—
    ""the 2011 Act" means the Children's Hearings (Scotland) Act 2011 (asp 1),",
  (b) in the definition of "civil proceedings", for the words from "any proceedings" to the end substitute "relevant proceedings", and
  (c) after the definition of "court" insert—
    ""relevant proceedings" means proceedings under Part 10 of the 2011 Act (other than section 98 or 99),".

(3) In section 12 (order authorising the use of special measures for vulnerable witnesses), after subsection (7) add—
  "(8) In the case of relevant proceedings, the child witness notice or vulnerable witness application—
    (a) must be lodged or made before the commencement of the hearing at which the child or, as the case may be, vulnerable witness is to give evidence,
    (b) on cause shown, may be lodged or made after the commencement of that hearing.".

(4) After section 16 insert—
  "16A Relevant proceedings: Principal Reporter's power to act for party to proceedings
  (1) Subsection (2) applies where a child witness or other person who is giving or is to give evidence in or for the purposes of relevant proceedings (referred to in this section as "the party") is a party to the proceedings.
  (2) The Principal Reporter may, on the party's behalf—
    (a) lodge a child witness notice under section 12(2),
    (b) make a vulnerable witness application for an order under section 12(6),
    (c) make an application under section 13(1)(a) for review of the current arrangements for taking a witness's evidence.".

(5) After section 22 insert—
  "22A Giving evidence in chief in the form of a prior statement
  (1) This section applies to proceedings in relation to—
    (a) an application made by virtue of section 93 or 94 of the 2011 Act to determine whether the ground mentioned in section 67(2)(j) of that Act is established, or
    (b) an application under section 110 of that Act for review of a finding that the ground mentioned in section 67(2)(j) of that Act is established.
  (2) The special measures which may be authorised by virtue of section 12 or 13 for the purpose of taking the evidence of a vulnerable witness at a hearing to consider such an application include (in addition to those listed in section 18(1)) the giving of evidence in chief in the form of a prior statement in accordance with subsections (3) to (10).
  (3) Where that special measure is to be used, a statement made by the vulnerable witness (a "prior statement") may be lodged in evidence for the purposes of this section by or on behalf of the party citing the vulnerable witness.
  (4) A prior statement is admissible as the witness's evidence in chief, or as part of the witness's evidence in chief, without the witness being required to adopt or otherwise speak to the statement in giving evidence.

Children's Hearings (Scotland) Act 2011

(5) A prior statement is admissible as evidence of any matter stated in it of which direct oral evidence by the vulnerable witness would be admissible if given at the hearing.

(6) A prior statement is admissible under this section only if—
   (a) it is contained in a document, and
   (b) at the time the statement was made, the vulnerable witness would have been a competent witness for the purposes of the hearing.

(7) Subsection (6) does not apply to a prior statement—
   (a) contained in a precognition on oath, or
   (b) made in other proceedings (whether criminal or civil and whether taking place in the United Kingdom or elsewhere).

(8) A prior statement of a type mentioned in subsection (7) is not admissible for the purposes of this section unless it is authenticated in such manner as may be prescribed by regulations made by statutory instrument by the Scottish Ministers.

(9) This section does not affect the admissibility of any statement made by any person which is admissible otherwise than by virtue of this section.

(10) In this section—
   "document" has the meaning given by section 262(3) of the Criminal Procedure (Scotland) Act 1995 (c.46),
   "statement"—
      (a) includes—
         (i) any representation, however made or expressed, of fact or opinion, and
         (ii) any part of a statement, but
      (b) does not include a statement in a precognition other than a precognition on oath.

(11) For the purposes of this section, a statement is contained in a document where the person who makes it—
   (a) makes the statement in the document personally,
   (b) makes a statement which is, with or without the person's knowledge, embodied in a document by whatever means or by any person who has direct personal knowledge of the making of the statement, or
   (c) approves a document as embodying the statement.

(12) A statutory instrument containing regulations under subsection (8) is subject to annulment in pursuance of a resolution of the Scottish Parliament.".

NOTE
C.555.1 1. As amended by the Children's Hearings (Scotland) Act 2011 (Modification of Primary Legislation) Order 2013 (SSI 2013/211) Sch.1 para.20(19) (effective 24 June 2013).

DEFINITIONS
C.555.2 "child": s.199.
"Principal Reporter": s.14 and Sch.3 paras 8–10.

SUBORDINATE LEGISLATION UNDER THIS SECTION
Vulnerable Witnesses (Giving evidence in relation to the determination of Children's Hearing grounds: Authentication of Prior Statements) (Scotland) Regulations 2013 (SSI 2013/215) (made under the powers conferred by s.22A(8) of the Vulnerable Witnesses (Scotland) Act 2004).

GENERAL NOTE
C.555.3 This section:
   (1) amends the Vulnerable Witnesses (Scotland) Act 2004 (the 2004 Act) so as to apply provisions of that Act to the provisions of the present Act, including providing that the

Amendment of Vulnerable Witnesses (Scotland) Act 2004

proceedings to which the 2004 Act applies include the proceedings before the sheriff enacted under the provisions in Pt 10 of the present Act;
(2) amends the 2004 Act so as to enable the Reporter to act for parties in specified procedures under the 2004 Act; and
(3) amends the 2004 Act by making detailed provisions as to the giving of evidence in said proceedings before the sheriff.

In order to place these provisions in context it is necessary to recall some of the provisions of the 2004 Act. Section 11(1) of the 2004 Act, as amended by the Victims and Witnesses (Scotland) Act 2014 s.22, provides, so far as material, that a person is to be categorised as "a vulnerable witness" for the purposes of that Act where—
"(a) that person is under the age of 18 on the date of the commencement of proceedings ..., or
(b) where the person is not a child witness, there is a significant risk that the quality of the evidence to be given by the person will be diminished by reason of—
(i) mental disorder (within the meaning of section 328 of the Mental Health (Care and Treatment) (Scotland) Act 2003 (asp 13), or
(ii) fear or distress in connection with giving evidence in the proceedings."

The 2004 Act provides that a child may only give evidence where the court has made an order under s.12(1) of that Act either authorising "special measure or measures" as to the mode of taking that evidence or ordering that the child witness is to give evidence without any special measure.

In *GM v MB and AS*, 2016 S.L.T. (Sh Ct) 279; 2016 Fam. L.R. 96 (also see 2017 Fam. L.B. 146–7). Sheriff (as he then was) Craig Turnbull had to consider, under the ordinary jurisdiction of the sheriff, a contact case wherein the appropriateness or not of special measures for three children, whose circumstances differed, had to be determined. Sheriff Turnbull examined the issues, including the consideration that the defender (the children's mother) was a party litigant. The sheriff noted that there was, in children's hearings' procedures, no provision parallel to that in s.288F of the Criminal Procedure (Scotland) Act 1995 prohibiting personal conduct of an accused's defence in certain cases involving vulnerable witnesses; the sheriff, however, took into account the undesirability of allowing a party litigant to examine/cross-examine a child witness and for this reason, when assessing what special measure or measures were appropriate, concluded that the only special measure appropriate in such circumstances was the appointment of a commissioner and the use of interrogatories and cross-interrogatories. The reader is referred to the sheriff's comprehensive and penetrating judgment.

Subs.(2)

This is the provision, referred to in the General Note above, wherein the provisions of the 2004 Act are made to apply to the proceedings before the sheriff under Pt 10 of the present Act. C.555.4
   "Relevant proceedings" means proceedings under Pt 10 of the 2011 Act (other than under ss.98 and 99, which empowers the sheriff, on the motion of the Reporter, to extend or vary, or further extend or vary, an interim child protection order (ICPO)). The procedural rules for a motion under this section are contained in r.3.33 of the Act of Sederunt (Child Care and Maintenance Rules) 1997 (SI 1997/291) as amended by Act of Sederunt (Children's Hearings (Scotland) Act 2011) (Miscellaneous Amendments) 2013 (SSI 2013/172) (the "1997 Rules") which, per r.3.33(4) ("The sheriff, after allowing such further procedure as he thinks fit") seems to envisage the possibility of evidence being led.

Subs.(3)

Under s.12(1) of the 2004 Act a child may only give evidence where the court has made an order under s.12(1) of that Act either authorising "special measure or measures" as to how the evidence is to be taken or ordering that the child witness is to give evidence without any special measure. The possible "special measures" are set out in s.18(1) of the 2004 Act and are, following the lettering within that subsection: C.555.5
"(a) taking of evidence by a commissioner in accordance with section 19,
(b) use of a live television link in accordance with section 20,
(c) use of a screen in accordance with section 21,
(d) use of a supporter in accordance with section 22, and
(e) such other measures as the Scottish Ministers may, by order made by statutory instrument, prescribe."
The rules for Applications for evidence by live link are found in r.3.22 of the 1997 Rules, which inter alia prescribes the use of Forms 44A and 44B.
   More than one special measure may be ordered (2004 Act s.12(2)(a), cf. *AMI v Dunn* [2012] HCJAC 108; 2013 J.C. 82, a decision under the parallel provisions of the Criminal Procedure (Scotland) Act 1995 s.271). In addition to the special measures listed above the court may, in the

case of a vulnerable witness in a proof wherein the ground for referral is that specified in s.67(2)(j) (alleged offence by the referred child), allow evidence to be taken by way of a prior statement (see discussion below of subs.(5)).

This present subsection prescribes the procedures to be followed by parties wishing to call a child or vulnerable witness. Whilst this subsection allows, on cause shown, the lodging of a child witness notice after the commencement of the hearing, it is, obviously, good practice for this to be done in advance where practicable, since preparations may be required to put the special measure(s) in place. The sheriff has power to vary the special measures—see 2004 Act s.13(1)(a).

Subs.(4)

C.555.6 The provision introduced by this subsection enables the Reporter to carry out the specified procedures. This will facilitate the work of a party litigant.

Subs.(5)

C.555.7 Since the enactment of s.2 of the Civil Evidence (Scotland) Act 1988 (the 1988 Act) it has been competent to lead hearsay evidence towards proving the truth of its content in civil proceedings, with "civil proceedings" being defined as including proceedings under the children's hearings system, except where the ground for referral was an alleged offence by the referred child—see the 1988 Act s.9, definition of "civil proceedings", subpara.(a). This present subsection permits, where the witness concerned is a vulnerable witness (either by being a child or otherwise qualifying as a vulnerable witness) and where the taking of this evidence has been ordered as a "special measure" under the 2004 Act, evidence by way of prior statement in cases wherein the ground for referral *is* an alleged offence by the referred child (s.67(2)(j)). This subsection provides for how the prior statement is to be presented and prescribes the conditions for its admissibility. Practitioners should be aware, when considering the weight of hearsay evidence, that it may be less persuasive than direct evidence. In *JS v Childrens' Reporter* [2016] CSIH 74, 2017 S.C. 31, sub nom. *S v Children's Reporter*, 2016 S.L.T. 1235; 2016 Fam.L. R. 166, the Inner House, considering hearsay evidence, but not of a vulnerable witness, said at [30]:

"Where that [the possibility of cross-examination] is available it is often described as 'the best evidence'. Implicit in that expression is the assumption that that is the best way of getting at the truth. Where the potential informant is a child we would understand that that is thought no longer to be so. Nevertheless, given the benefits to the fact-finder and any person wishing to challenge the evidence that are seen as arising from the immediacy of direct parole evidence and by its testing by cross-examination, it is generally for the party who proposes to depart from reliance on 'the best evidence' to justify the position that he is adopting."

The following are references to the subsections within s.22A of the 2004 Act, as reproduced above.

Subs.(3) By providing that the prior statement (which must be within a "document" (see paras (6)(a) and (10)) just "may be lodged", this provision seems to countenance its being produced without having been lodged previously, but clearly it is good practice for it to be lodged in advance.

Subs.(4) This contains the central provision, viz, that the witness does not require to be personally present to "adopt or speak to" the statement. The reference to the statement being "part of the witness's evidence in chief" envisages the situation wherein the witness is giving evidence, with the statement being used to supplement the witness's oral testimony. In this situation it would seem that the witness would be able to be cross-examined as to the content of the statement, subject of course to any of the limitations on cross-examination, in cases involving sexual behaviour, enacted in s.173.

Subs.(6) This provides that a "prior statement", if it is to be admitted in evidence by virtue of this section, must be contained in a document and must, at the time when the vulnerable witness made the statement, have been a competent witness.

Subss.(7) and (8) These provide that where the prior statement is contained in a precognition on oath or in other proceedings (civil or criminal, whether in UK or elsewhere) then, to be admissible, it must be authenticated as prescribed by a statutory instrument enacted by the Scottish Ministers. The statutory instrument so enacted is SSI 2013/215, noted above. It contains the "Form of certificate of authentication of a prior statement for the purposes of section 22A(8) of the Vulnerable Witnesses (Scotland) Act 2004". The provision in subs.(7) to the effect that subs.(6) (statement to be in writing and witness must have been a competent witness at the time of making it) does not apply to a duly authenticated statement, would seem merely to reflect that where a precognition on oath or other proceedings have taken place it is presumed that the record must be in writing and that the individual was a competent witness at the time.

Subs.(9) As mentioned above, s.2 of the Civil Evidence (Scotland) Act 1988 allows for the admissibility of hearsay evidence to prove the truth of its content. This paragraph makes clear that the provisions of this section, in making special provision for admitting the evidence of vulnerable witnesses, does not take away any provisions (in s.2 of the 1988 Act or elsewhere) allowing evidence to be admitted.

Subs.(10) Section 262(3) of the Criminal Procedure (Scotland) Act 1995 provides, so far as material:

"'document' includes, in addition to a document in writing—
    (a) any map, plan, graph or drawing;
    (b) any photograph;
    (c) any disc, tape, sound track or other device in which sounds or other data (not being visual images) are recorded so as to be capable (with or without the aid of some other equipment) of being reproduced therefrom; and
    (d) any film, negative, tape, disc or other device in which one or more visual images are recorded so as to be capable (as aforesaid) of being reproduced therefrom;
'film' includes a microfilm;
'made' includes (other than in section 261A) allegedly made."

The provision that "document" does not apply to a statement in a precognition (other than a precognition on oath) reflects a well-entrenched principle of the law of evidence. For discussion of this principle, see *KJC v HM Advocate*, 1994 S.C.C.R. 560, *Young v National Coal Board*, 1960 S.C. 6 and *Kerr v HM Advocate*, 1958 J.C. 14.

Subs.(11) These provisions give a very wide application to the concept of a statement contained in a document.

Subs.(12) As at time of writing the statutory instrument SSI 2013/215, referred to above, has not been annulled and the authors are not aware of any intention on the part of the Scottish Ministers to annul it.

PART 18

MISCELLANEOUS

Children's hearings: procedural rules

Children's hearings: procedural rules

177.—(1) The Scottish Ministers may make rules about the procedure relating to children's hearings.

(2) Rules may in particular make provision for or in connection with—
(a) specifying matters that may be determined by pre-hearing panels,
(b) constituting children's hearings,
(c) arranging children's hearings,
(d) notifying persons about children's hearings,
(e) attendance of persons at children's hearings,
(f) specifying circumstances in which persons may be excused from attending children's hearings,
(g) specifying circumstances in which persons may be excluded from children's hearings,
(h) obtaining the views of the child to whom a children's hearing relates,
    (i) provision of specified documents to—
        (i) members of children's hearings,
        (ii) the child to whom a children's hearing relates,
        (iii) relevant persons in relation to the child to whom a children's hearing relates,
        (iv) any other specified persons,
(j) withholding of specified documents from persons mentioned in paragraph (i),
(k) prescribing the form of the statement of grounds,
(l) the recording and transmission of information,
(m) representation of persons at children's hearings,
(n) payment of expenses,
(o) appeals.

(3) In making rules in pursuance of subsection (2)(i)(i), the Scottish

Ministers must ensure that any views expressed by the child to whom a children's hearing relates are reflected in a specified document.

(4) Rules containing provision of the type mentioned in subsection (2)(a), (e), (f), (g), (j) or (m) are subject to the affirmative procedure.

(5) In this section—
"children's hearing" includes pre-hearing panel,
"specified" means specified in the rules.

DEFINITIONS

C.556.1 "affirmative procedure": ss.202(1) and 197.
"child": s.199.
"children's hearing": s.5.
"pre-hearing panel": ss.202(1) and 79(2)(a).
"relevant person": s.200.
"statement of grounds": ss.202(1) and 89(3).

GENERAL NOTE

C.556.2 This is an empowering section. We shall not here discuss all the individual rules enacted by virtue of this section, but will note, in reference to certain subsections, some significant points.

Subs.(2)(n)

C.556.3 *Payment of expenses.* Rule 3.19 of the Act of Sederunt (Child Care and Maintenance Rules) 1997 (SI 1997/291) provides:

"No expenses shall be awarded in any proceedings to which this Chapter [i.e. Chapter 3] applies".

This was left unamended by the Act of Sederunt (Children's Hearings (Scotland) Act 2011) (Miscellaneous Amendments) 2013 (SSI 2013/172). "Chapter 3" is now headed "CHILDREN'S HEARINGS: APPLICATIONS TO THE SHERIFF" and includes the proceedings before the sheriff arising in the children's hearings system, and the reader is directed to the text of Ch.3, as amended by the Act of Sederunt (Children's Hearings (Scotland) Act 2011) (Miscellaneous Amendments) 2013 (SSI 2013/172) art.3(29) and the Act of Sederunt (Sheriff Appeal Court Rules) (Amendment) Rules (SSI 2016/194) r.4. It is to be noted that the Act of Sederunt (Sheriff Appeal Court Rules) 2015 (SSI 2015/356) r.30.3 provides:

"(1) At the hearing [of an appeal to the Sheriff Appeal Court], a party may only notice questions of law or procedural irregularities of which notice has not been given if the Court permits the party to do so.

(2) Where the Court grants permission, it may do so on such conditions as to expenses or otherwise as the Court thinks fit."

While the said Chapter 3 refers, in r.3.59(1), to sections of the 2011 Act dealing with appeals to the "sheriff principal", it is clear from s.109(2) and (3) of the Courts Reform (Scotland) Act 2014 that this is now to be read as appeals to the Sheriff Appeal Court, and accordingly that the prohibition of awards of expenses contained in said r.3.19 is intended to apply to proceedings in the Sheriff Appeal Court. It is submitted that the legislature may not have intended to depart from the well-established practice of not allowing awards of expenses in children's hearings cases, and that the prohibition of such awards contained in r.3.19 should be preferred.

Subs.(3)

C.556.4 Rule 8 of the Children's Hearings (Scotland) Act 2011 (Rules of Procedure in Children's Hearings) Rules 2013 (SSI 2013/194) (the "Procedural Rules") provides that, where any document which is to be given to a children's hearing or pre-hearing panel, it must contain any views expressed by the child which have been given to the person who has prepared that document. Rules 34(3)(b) and 35(1)(b) of the Procedural Rules provide respectively that "all decisions and reasons" must be provided by the Reporter to parties and to the hearing members. Rules 34(6)(b) and 35(1)(f) provide respectively that "any report or other information" must be provided by the Reporter to parties and to the hearing members. (Section 121 of the Act provides that at a hearing the chairing member must ask the child whether the documents provided accurately express his or her views and r.58(2) of the Procedural Rules provides procedures for the chairing member to clarify matters if the child says his or her views are not accurately reflected.) In *JM v Taylor* [2014] CSIH 62; 2015 S.C. 71, sub nom. *M v Locality Reporter Manager*, 2014 Fam. L.R. 102 (discussed above in relation to the procedure in appeals under ss.156 and 163), it was argued that the children had expressed certain views which had not been recorded and that this amounted to a procedural irregularity

Children's hearing: disclosure of information

since the decision and reasons constituted "any report or other information". Repelling this submission an Extra Division held that the decision and reasons, recorded in writing, were not in the category of "any report or other information" and that consequently r.8 had not been contravened and therefore no procedural irregularity had taken place.

Where the child's views have been the subject of a confidentiality request this will require to be handled with great care: see below in our discussion of s.178.

Disclosure of information

Children's hearing: disclosure of information

178.—(1) A children's hearing need not disclose to a person any information about the child to whom the hearing relates or about the child's case if disclosure of that information to that person would be likely to cause significant harm to the child.

(2) Subsection (1) applies despite any requirement under an enactment (including this Act and subordinate legislation made under it) or rule of law for the children's hearing—
  (a) to give the person an explanation of what has taken place at proceedings before the hearing, or
  (b) to provide the person with—
    (i) information about the child or the child's case, or
    (ii) reasons for a decision made by the hearing.

C.557

DEFINITIONS
"children's hearing": s. 5.
"child": s.199.

C.557.1

GENERAL NOTE

This is an important section. In a system which is aimed at safeguarding and promoting the welfare of the child it is necessary to provide so far as practicable that nothing done or said in the proceedings should put the child at risk. This section aims to minimise such risk by empowering a children's hearing not to disclose information where disclosure would be likely to cause significant harm to the child. This is an innovation in children's hearings' procedures. Such provisions have existed in family proceedings in the sheriff court for some time and can now be found in the Act of Sederunt (Sheriff Court Ordinary Cause Rules) 1993 (SI 1993/1956) r.33.20 which empowers the sheriff to record the child's views in writing and entitles the sheriff to direct that this record should

C.557.2

"(a) be sealed in an envelope marked 'Views of the child – confidential';
(b) be kept in the court process without being recorded in the inventory of productions;
(c) be available to the sheriff only;
(d) not to be opened by any person other than a sheriff; and
(e) not form a borrowable part of the process."

These rules have no application in relation to children's hearings procedure but we note them here since they form the background to the sheriff court decisions in *Dosoo v Dosoo* and *McGrath v McGrath*, cited below in our discussion of the difficulties, jurisprudential and practical, in implementing "confidentiality" provisions of this type.

Subs.(1)

The language of this provision is permissive in that by saying "need not" it leaves open the theoretical possibility that the hearing may decide to disclose information which would be likely to cause significant harm to the child. It is difficult to envisage a situation wherein the hearing would be happy about making such a decision, but that the possibility is left open reflects the delicacy of the issues involved here.

C.557.3

A children's hearing. The provision is aimed at the hearing members, and it will be for them, not just the chairing member, to decide on this issue, although, as noted below, this provision may affect the duties of the chairing member.

A person. This means any person, not just persons participating in the hearing: the generalised power conferred by subs.(2)(b)(ii) to not disclose information in the reasons for the decision has the effect of denying the information to anyone who may see the decision.

265

Children's Hearings (Scotland) Act 2011

Balancing confidentiality and fairness

C.557.4 The power to deny information to persons participating in the hearing is of prime importance. It means, for example, that a relevant person may be denied access to the information which has formed the basis for the hearing's decision. That relevant person may be a person who is being blamed for his or her conduct, as when a carer is being accused by the child of ill-treating the child. Denying to a person who is being found to have committed any misconduct without disclosing to him or her the ground for making that finding is contrary to that principle of natural justice that requires that a person being so blamed should be made aware of the content of the accusation so that he or she may try to rebut it. However, the denial of such disclosure is what this provision authorises, but the courts have emphasised that power to deny accused persons vital information on ground of "confidentiality" is one which must be exercised with great care and to try to balance the principle of fair and open justice with the need to protect the child from risk. In *Re A (a child)* [2012] UKSC 60; [2013] 2 A.C. 66; [2013] 1 All E.R. 761, Lady Hale described this as attempting "to reconcile the irreconcilable". Lady Hale referred with approval to the speech of Lord Mustill in *Re D (minors) (adoption reports: confidentiality)* [1996] A.C. 593 at 615D–H. In this case Lord Mustill states:

"It is a fundamental principle of fairness that a party is entitled to disclosure of all materials which may be taken into account by the court when reaching a decision adverse to that party"

and then put forward the approach which should be adopted for the situation wherein the court had to deal with information received in confidence. We think the essence of his Lordship's comments may be summarised thus:

First, the court should consider whether disclosure of the material "would involve a real possibility of significant harm to the child".

Secondly, if there was a real possibility of significant harm to the child, the court should consider whether the overall interests of the child would benefit from non-disclosure "weighing on the one hand the interest of the child in having the material properly tested, and on the other the magnitude of the risk that harm will occur and the gravity of the harm if it does occur".

Thirdly, "if the interests of the child point towards non-disclosure, the next and final step is for the court to weigh that consideration, and its strength in the circumstances of the case, against the interest of the parent or other party in having the opportunity to see and respond to the material. In the latter regard the court should take into account the importance of the material to the issues in the case".

Lord Mustill concludes, at 615H:

"Non-disclosure should be the exception and not the rule. The court should be rigorous in its examination of the risk of the feared harm to the child, and should order non-disclosure only when the case for doing so is compelling".

The approach of Lord Mustill was followed by Sheriff Daphne Robertson in *Dosoo v Dosoo*, 1999 S.C.L.R. 905 and by Sheriff Principal Edward Bowen in *McGrath v McGrath*, 1999 S.C.L.R. 1121.

What amounts to "significant harm"

C.557.5 In *Re L (A Child) (Care: Threshold Criteria)* [2007] 1 F.L.R. 2050; [2007] Fam. Law 297, Hedley J said that it would be unwise to attempt an all-embracing definition of "significant harm" since this was fact-specific and had to retain the breadth of meaning that human frailty required of it. In *JT v Stirling Council* [2007] CSIH 52; 2007 S.C. 783 an Extra Division expressed the view that the emphasis conveyed by "significant" was best recognised by construing "significant" as importing more than "not insignificant".

A useful description of "significant harm" can be found at paras 40 to 45 of the "National Guidance for Child Protection in Scotland 2014" found at *http://www.gov.scot/Resource/0045/00450733.pdf* [Accessed 25 January 2017], which states that

" 'significant harm' is a complex matter and subject to professional judgement based on a multi-agency assessment of the circumstances of the child and their family".

In *ZM, AM v Locality Reporter* [2016] SAC (Civ) 16 the Sheriff Appeal Court discussed, at [10] to [12], the analogous concept of "significant contact".

Official advice as to the practical effect of the foregoing for the conduct of a children's hearing

C.557.6 The "Practice and Procedure Manual", issued by Children's Hearings Scotland in June 2013 (found at *http://www.chscotland.gov.uk/our-publications/practice/2013/06/practice-and-procedure-manual/* [Accessed 25 January 2017]) and from time to time updated, discusses this issue in Pt 8, paras 8.7–8.9, and includes:

"8.8 The test of significant harm is a high one and the decision to withhold information from a person otherwise entitled to it should not be taken lightly. The spirit of a children's hearing is of openness and participation and therefore withholding information from a party otherwise entitled to it should be *exceptional*.

Finding information upsetting or the preference of a person will *not* be sufficient to meet the test of significant harm. An example of where this provision may be used would be where the child makes a significant disclosure whilst speaking to the panel members without the relevant persons present.

8.9 Before considering the use of this power [i.e. the power not to disclose information about the child to a person] panel members should consider whether it is first appropriate to defer the hearing to another day. If panel members are satisfied that a substantive decision could and should be made, then full reasons for the decision, including the withheld information, must be given to those entitled to it. Reasons, minus the withheld information, must be given to those entitled to it. Reasons, minus the withheld information, must be provided to the person to whom the non-disclosure relates. The Children's Reporter will redact the information in the reasons and decisions before it is sent to the person who is not to receive it."

A practical difficulty—and what to say to a child who wishes information to be treated as "confidential"

In the event of a hearing agreeing to treat information as "confidential" and consequently omitting this information from its reasons, there may be the possibility that the person to whom the "redacted" reasons is supplied will be able, owing to the nature of the hearing's decision, to deduce that something undisclosed has been said by the child, and perhaps even the substance of the omitted information. Accordingly we would suggest that, when receiving a request from the child, in the absence of an excluded person, for information to be treated as confidential, the chairing member should explain that while the information can be kept out of the formal documentation, it cannot be guaranteed that the excluded person may be not be able to make a good guess as to what was said in his or her absence.

C.557.7

Non-disclosure of information—the duties of the Reporter

Where information in a report is withheld the Reporter must ensure its removal from the report sent to the person concerned (r. 15(1) of the Children's Hearings (Scotland) Act 2011 (Rules of Procedure in Children's Hearings) Rules 2013 (SSI 2013/194) the "Procedural Rules") and must "inform the persons to whom the Reporter other document or information has been given under the Act , or these Rules, of the identity of the person from whom the information is being withheld, and what information is being withheld from that person" (r. 15(2) of the Procedural Rules).

Non-disclosure requests in relation to reports under s.93(2) of the Adoption and Children (Scotland) Act 2007

It is now provided by r.77(7) of the Procedural Rules, inserted by r.7 of the Children's Hearings (Scotland) Act 2011 (Rules of Procedure in Children's Hearings) Amendment Rules 2015 (SSI 2015/21) that where the Reporter has, under said r.15, removed information given to the persons concerned must within five days, give to the court requiring the report: (a) the report; (b) the redacted report; and (c) details of the determination of the children's hearing of the non-disclosure request, etc. (see r.8).

Sharing of information: prosecution

179.—(1) This section applies where— C.558
(a) by virtue of this Act, the Principal Reporter, a children's hearing or the sheriff has determined, is determining or is to determine any matter relating to a child,
(b) criminal proceedings have been commenced against an accused,
(c) the proceedings have not yet been concluded, and
(d) the child is connected in any way with the circumstances that gave rise to the proceedings, the accused or any other person connected in any way with those circumstances.

(2) The Principal Reporter must make available to the Crown Office and Procurator Fiscal Service any information held by the Principal Reporter relating to the prosecution which the Service requests for the purpose of—
(a) the prevention or detection of crime, or
(b) the apprehension or prosecution of offenders.

DEFINITIONS
C.558.1   "child": s.199.
"children's hearing": s.5.
"Principal Reporter": s.14 and Sch.3 paras 8–10.

GENERAL NOTE
C.558.2   This section imposes a duty on the Reporter, where criminal proceedings are in progress against any accused person, to supply to the Crown Office and Procurator Fiscal Service (COPFS) any information in the Reporter's possession, relevant to the prosecution of such proceedings, which the COPFS may request. The terms of this section are substantially self-explanatory.

Subs.(1)(a)
C.558.3   This provision makes clear the comprehensive scope of this section: it applies at all stages of the Reporter's dealing with a child's case, from the time when the Reporter receives information under s.66 onwards.

Sharing of information: panel members

C.559   **180.**—(1) A local authority must comply with a request from the National Convener to provide to the National Convener information about the implementation of compulsory supervision orders by the authority.

(2) The National Convener may disclose information provided by a local authority under subsection (1) to members of the Children's Panel.

DEFINITIONS
C.559.1   "children's panel": s.4 and Sch.2.
"compulsory supervision order": ss.202(1) and 83.
"local authority": Local Government etc. (Scotland) Act 1994 s.2.
"National Convener": s.1 and Sch.1 paras 8–10.

GENERAL NOTE
C.559.2   This section requires a local authority to supply the National Convener with any information he or she may request about how the local authority concerned is implementing a compulsory supervision order (CSO), and empowers the National Convener to disclose such information to panel members. It will be recalled that ss.147 and 148 provide for the situation where a children's hearing considers that the implementation authority is in breach of duty under a CSO and include provision for the National Convener to apply to the Sheriff Principal for an order to enforce compliance. Section 148(3) provides that the National Convener may not make such an application unless he or she has given appropriate notice to the local authority and "the authority has failed to carry out the duty within the period specified in the notice". One of the effects of this present section is to give the National Convener the right to investigate the actings of the local authority with a view to considering whether or not this condition is satisfied. The functions of the National Convener referred to in this section are amongst those which, under Sch.1 para.10(1), the National Convener may delegate to a person or class of persons authorised by the National Convener.

Implementation of compulsory supervision orders: annual report

Implementation of compulsory supervision orders: annual report

C.560   **181.**—(1) The National Convener must, as soon as is reasonably practicable after the end of each financial year, prepare and submit to the Scottish Ministers a report about implementation of compulsory supervision orders during the year—
(a) in Scotland as a whole, and
(b) in each local authority area.

(2) The National Convener must give a copy of the report to each member of the Children's Panel.

(3) The Scottish Ministers must lay the report before the Scottish Parliament.

Publishing restrictions

(4) For the purposes of preparing the report, the National Convener may require each local authority to provide to the National Convener for each financial year—
(a) information about—
(i) the number of compulsory supervision orders for which the authority is the implementation authority,
(ii) changes in the circumstances that led to the making of the orders,
(iii) the ways in which the overall wellbeing of children who are subject to the orders has been affected by them, and
(b) such other information relating to the implementation of the orders as the National Convener may require.
(5) Information provided under subsection (4) must not identify (or enable the identification of) a particular child.
(6) In this section, "financial year" has the meaning given by paragraph 24(3) of schedule 1.

DEFINITIONS
"children's panel": s.4 and Sch.2.   C.560.1
"National Convener": s.1 and Sch.1 paras 8–10 and 24.

GENERAL NOTE
This section obliges the National Convener to prepare annually a report on the implementation of compulsory supervision orders. By virtue of Sch.1 para.10(2)(a) this is not a function which the National Convener is allowed to delegate. The provisions of this section are substantially self-explanatory. (Part 3 (ss.7–18) of the Children and Young People (Scotland) Act 2014 enacts provisions as to the preparation of a "children's services plan" which may involve the National Convener: under s.8(1) of that Act the local authority and the local health board are to prepare such a plan and under s.14 the National Convener is to provide the local authority with "information, advice or assistance" in preparing this plan.)   C.560.2

Publishing restrictions

Publishing restrictions

182.—(1) A person must not publish protected information if the publication of the information is intended, or is likely, to identify—   C.561
(a) a child mentioned in the protected information, or
(b) an address or school as being that of such a child.
(2) A person who contravenes subsection (1) commits an offence and is liable on summary conviction to a fine not exceeding level 4 on the standard scale.
(3) It is a defence for a person ("P") charged with a contravention of subsection (1) to show that P did not know or have reason to suspect that the publication of the protected information was likely to identify a child mentioned in the protected information, or, as the case may be, an address or school of such a child.
(4) In relation to proceedings before a children's hearing, the Scottish Ministers may in the interests of justice—
(a) dispense with the prohibition in subsection (1), or
(b) relax it to such extent as they consider appropriate.
(5) In relation to proceedings before the sheriff under Part 10 or 15, the sheriff may in the interests of justice—
(a) dispense with the prohibition in subsection (1), or
(b) relax it to such extent as the sheriff considers appropriate.
(6) In relation to proceedings in an appeal to the Court of Session under this Act, the Court may in the interests of justice—
(a) dispense with the prohibition in subsection (1), or
(b) relax it to such extent as the Court considers appropriate.

Children's Hearings (Scotland) Act 2011

(7) The prohibition in subsection (1) does not apply in relation to the publication by or on behalf of a local authority or an adoption agency of information about a child for the purposes of making arrangements in relation to the child under this Act or the Adoption and Children (Scotland) Act 2007 (asp 4).

(8) In subsection (7), "adoption agency" has the meaning given by the Adoption and Children (Scotland) Act 2007.

(9) In this section—
[1] "children's hearing" includes a pre-hearing panel,
"protected information" means—
  (a) information in relation to—
    (i) a children's hearing,
    (ii) an appeal against a decision of a children's hearing,
    (iii) proceedings before the sheriff under Part 10 or 15, or
    (iv) an appeal from any decision of the sheriff or sheriff principal made under this Act, or
  (b) information given to the Principal Reporter in respect of a child in reliance on, or satisfaction of, a provision of this Act or any other enactment,
"publish" includes in particular—
  (a) to publish matter in a programme service, as defined by section 201 of the Broadcasting Act 1990 (c.42), and
  (b) to cause matter to be published.

NOTE

C.561.1 1. As amended by the Children's Hearings (Scotland) Act 2011 (Modification of Primary Legislation) Order 2013 (SSI 2013/211) Sch.1 para.20(20) (effective 24 June 2013).

DEFINITIONS

C.561.2 "adoption agency": Adoption and Children (Scotland) Act 2007 s.119(1).
"child": s.199.
"children's hearing": s.5.
"pre-hearing panel": s.79(2)(a).
"Principal Reporter": s.14 and Sch.3 paras 8–10.
"programme service": Broadcasting Act 1990 s.201.

GENERAL NOTE

C.561.3 The proceedings in children's hearings are private; members of the public are not entitled to be present. Section 78, discussed above, lists persons having the right to attend. The Act and the various rules are scattered with provisions reflecting the privacy of children's hearings' procedures. For example: s.181(5) provides that the National Convener's annual report on the implementation of compulsory supervision orders must not contain information enabling the identity of the child to be discovered; r.20 of the Children's Hearings (Scotland) Act 2011 (Rules of Procedure in Children's Hearings) Rules 2013 (SSI 2013/194) had to be enacted to make special provision allowing the escorts of persons in custody to attend children's hearings and pre-hearing panels; and ss.101(3) and 155(3) provide respectively that proof hearings and appeals before the sheriff must not be heard in open court. In the Court of Session the rule is that the court is empowered to direct that all or part of the appeal should be heard in private (Act of Sederunt (Rules of Court of Session 1994), Sch.2, Pt 3 (41), Appeals under Statute, V, Part 15 of the Children's Hearings (Scotland) Act 2011, 41.39) and in practice the court routinely directs the proceedings to be held in private. However, the refusal to allow extraneous persons from attending children's hearings' procedures is not absolute. Section 78(2) of the Act empowers the chairing member to allow extraneous persons to be present in certain circumstances and sheriffs have the right to admit to a hearing in chambers such persons as they may think fit: the appropriateness of admitting the press to a proof hearing before the sheriff was discussed in *Sloan v B*, 1991 S.C. 412 at 444. This present section prohibits all persons from publishing information which is intended, or likely to identify, the name, or the address or the school of, any child involved in children's hearings' proceedings, including appeals from pre-hearing panels. The section also allows for a statutory defence, and allows specific exceptions to the prohibition.

Mutual assistance

Subs.(1)
A person. Here this includes a "legal" person (e.g. a limited company) as well as a natural person.

Subs.(3)
Know or have reason to suspect. It is thought that these are not disjunctive alternatives: i.e. successfully to invoke this defence the accused would have to show not only that he or she did not know that the publication was likely to reveal the prohibited matter, but also that he or she did not have reason to suspect this.

Subss.(4)–(6)
In the "James Bulger" case, reported on the substantial sentencing issue as *R. v Secretary for State for the Home Department Ex p. Venables* [1998] A.C. 407; [1997] 3 W.L.R. 23 the trial judge exercised his discretion in favour of revealing the names of the two accused, aged 10½ or thereby. The authors are not aware of any example of a Scottish court dispensing with the prohibition enacted in subs.(1).

Subs.(9)(a)(iv)
Sheriff principal. This now means the Sheriff Appeal Court (s.109 of the Courts Reform (Scotland) Act 2014).

Mutual assistance

Mutual assistance

183.—(1) A person mentioned in subsection (2) must comply with a request by another such person for assistance in the carrying out of functions conferred by virtue of this Act.

(2) The persons are—
(a) CHS,
(b) the National Convener,
(c) SCRA,
(d) the Principal Reporter.

(3) A person mentioned in subsection (4) must comply with a request by a local authority for assistance in the carrying out of the local authority's functions under this Act.

(4) The persons are—
(a) another local authority,
(b) a health board constituted under section 2 of the National Health Service (Scotland) Act 1978 (c.29).

(5) A request under this section must specify the assistance that is required.

(6) Nothing in this section requires a person to comply with a request if—
(a) it would be incompatible with any function (whether conferred by statute or otherwise) of the person to whom it is directed, or
(b) it would unduly prejudice the carrying out by the person to whom the request is directed of the person's functions.

DEFINITIONS
"CHS": s.2.
"local authority": Local Government etc. (Scotland) Act 1994 s.2.
"The National Convener": s.1.
"SCRA": s.15.
"The Principal Reporter": s.14 and Sch.3 paras 8–10.

GENERAL NOTE
The provisions of this section are substantially self-explanatory. They would appear to include situations where, for example, the implementation authority does not provide a specific service or where the child has been placed outwith the implementation authority and requires a specific service. This duty does not preclude the providing authority from recouping the cost of the service.

Subs.(2)
C.562.3   Note that "persons" here refers to "legal" persons as well as to "natural" persons.

Enforcement of obligations on health board under section 183

C.563   **184.**—(1) This section applies where—
   (a) the implementation authority in relation to a compulsory supervision order has made a request for assistance from a health board under section 183(3),
   (b) the request is in connection with the implementation of the compulsory supervision order, and
   (c) the implementation authority is satisfied that the health board has unreasonably failed to comply with the request.

   (2) The implementation authority may refer the matter to the Scottish Ministers.

   (3) On receiving a reference under subsection (2), the Scottish Ministers may, if they are satisfied that the health board has unreasonably failed to comply with the request, direct the health board to comply with the request.

   (4) The health board must comply with a direction under subsection (3).

DEFINITIONS
C.563.1   "compulsory supervision order": ss.202(1) and 83.
   "implementation authority": ss.202(1), 82(1)(b) and 86(1)(b).

GENERAL NOTE
C.563.2   This section is substantially self-explanatory. While this is a less strong form of enforcement imposed by s.146 (above), it is, nevertheless, a valuable indication that it is not only the implementation authority, but also the health board (and education authority (see s.127 above)) that have duties towards a child under a compulsory supervision order.

Proceedings before sheriff under Act

Amendment of section 32 of Sheriff Courts (Scotland) Act 1971

C.564   **185.**—(1) Section 32 of the Sheriff Courts (Scotland) Act 1971 (c.58) (power of Court of Session to regulate civil procedure in sheriff court) is amended as follows.

   (2) In subsection (1)—
   (a) after paragraph (eb) insert—
      "(ec) enabling a witness (including a witness who is outwith Scotland) in proceedings under Part 10 or 15 of the Children's Hearings (Scotland) Act 2011 to give evidence by a means specified in the act of sederunt that does not require the witness to be physically present in court in such circumstances, and subject to such conditions, as may be specified in the act of sederunt,
      (ed) prescribing circumstances in which a party to proceedings under Part 10 or 15 of the Children's Hearings (Scotland) Act 2011 may be prohibited from personally conducting the examination of witnesses,",
   (b) after paragraph (i) insert—
      "(ia) permitting a party to proceedings under the Children's Hearings (Scotland) Act 2011 to be represented (including through the making of oral submissions to the sheriff on the party's behalf), in such circumstances as may be specified in the act of sederunt, by a person who is neither an advocate nor a solicitor,", and
   (c) after paragraph (k) insert—
      "(ka) prescribing functions of safeguarders appointed by the

Amendment of section 32 of Sheriff Courts (Scotland) Act 1971

sheriff in relation to proceedings under Part 10 or 15 of the Children's Hearings (Scotland) Act 2011,

(kb) prescribing rights of safeguarders appointed by the sheriff in relation to proceedings under Part 10 or 15 of the Children's Hearings (Scotland) Act 2011 to information relating to the proceedings,".

(3) After subsection (4) add—

"(5) In subsection (1), "civil proceedings" includes proceedings under the Children's Hearings (Scotland) Act 2011.".

NOTE

Most of the Sheriff Courts (Scotland) Act 1971, including s.32 of that Act, was repealed by the Courts Reform (Scotland) Act 2014 Sch.5 para.6(2), but s.32 of the 1971 Act was saved by art.7 of the Courts Reform (Scotland) Act 2014 (Commencement No.2, Transitional and Saving Provisions) Order 2015 (SSI 2015/77). Consequently, the amendments to the said s.32 contained in this present section are in force.

C.564.1

DEFINITION

"safeguarder": ss.202(1) and 30(1).

C.564.2

GENERAL NOTE

This section amends s.32 of the Sheriff Courts (Scotland) Act 1971 so as to empower the Court of Session to regulate the procedures under the 2011 Act, as listed within the section. These powers have not been used, but we have indicated where provisions relative to, or similar to, the procedures concerned may be found. In December 2016 the Scottish Government and the Scottish Children's Reporter Administration published an open paper, *Personal Examination of Child and Other Vulnerable Witnesses in Children's Hearing Proof and Appeal Proceedings* (available at *http://www.scottishciviljusticecouncil.gov.uk/docs/librariesprovider4/ flc-meeting-files/flc-meeting-papers-12-december-2016/paper-4-1a—sg-and-scra-policy-paper— examination-of-child-and-vulnerable-witnesses-in-children-39-s-hearings.pdf?sfvrsn=2* [Accessed 10 May 2017]). We discuss this below.

C.564.3

Subs.(2)(a)

Rule 19 of the Children's Hearings (Scotland) Act 2011 (Rules of Procedure in Children's Hearings) Rules 2013 (SSI 2013/194) entitles a child, relevant person or individual who wants to be deemed a relevant person to attend a pre-hearing panel or children's hearing by way of telephone, video link or otherwise—see the rule for its detailed provisions. There is no parallel provision in respect of proceedings before the sheriff.

C.564.4

Section 176 of this Act amends the Vulnerable Witnesses (Scotland) Act 2004 by adding to that Act s.22A, which entitles the evidence of a vulnerable witness in a proof hearing where the ground for referral is an alleged offence by the child under s.67(2)(j) to be given by way of a prior statement (thereby possibly avoiding the witness being personally present) where the circumstances specified in said s.22A apply—see above for our discussion in s.176.

Section 173 contains provisions limiting the kinds of questions which may be put to a witness at a proof hearing where the ground for referral involves sexual behaviour by any person (see above for our discussion of s.173), but does not contain any provision prohibiting a party from questioning a witness.

The paper, *Personal Examination of Child and Other Vulnerable Witnesses in Children's Hearing Proof and Appeal Proceedings*, referred to in the General Note above, notes that no procedure has been enacted prescribing circumstances in which a party to proceedings under Pt 10 or Pt 15 of the Act may be prohibited from personally conducting examination of witnesses, quotes an example wherein a child witness had been shocked by being personally cross-examined by both her father and mother concerning alleged physical abuse of her, and strongly recommends the enactment of appropriate rules. The paper refers to the case of *GM v MB and AS*, 2016 S.L.T. (Sh Ct) 279; 2016 Fam. L.R. 96 (commented on in 2017 Fam. L.B. 146), discussed above in our commentary on s.176.

Subs.(2)(b)

Rule 3.21 of the Act of Sederunt (Child Care and Maintenance Rules) 1997 (SI 1997/291) (the 1997 Rules) (unchanged by the Act of Sederunt (Children's Hearings (Scotland) Act 2011) (Miscellaneous Amendments) 2013 (SSI 2013/172)) provides that any party may be represented by an advocate (meaning a member of the Faculty of Advocates) or a solicitor and also allows

C.564.5

Children's Hearings (Scotland) Act 2011

representation by another representative authorised by the party provided the person concerned satisfies the sheriff throughout the proceedings that he or she is suitable. The recital to the 1997 Rules (obviously, having regard to the date of these Rules) does not include a reference to the amendment of the Sheriff Courts (Scotland) Act 1971 effected by this present section.

Subs.(2)(c)

C.564.6   The provisions relating to safeguarders are contained in the Children's Hearings (Scotland) Act 2011 (Safeguarders Panel) Regulations 2012 (SSI 2012/54) and the Children's Hearings (Scotland) Act 2011 (Safeguarders: Further Provision) Regulations 2012 (SSI 2012/336). The recitals to these Regulations do not refer to the amendment of the Sheriff Courts (Scotland) Act 1971 effected by this present section.

Consent of child to medical examination or treatment

Consent of child to medical examination or treatment

C.565   **186.**—(1) Nothing in this Act prejudices any capacity of a child enjoyed by virtue of section 2(4) of the Age of Legal Capacity (Scotland) Act 1991 (c.50) (capacity of child with sufficient understanding to consent to surgical, medical or dental procedure or treatment).

(2) In particular, where—
 (a) under an order mentioned in subsection (3) any examination or treatment is arranged for the child, and
 (b) the child has the capacity mentioned in section 2(4) of the Age of Legal Capacity (Scotland) Act 1991,
the examination or treatment may be carried out only if the child consents to it.

(3) Those orders are—
 (a) a child assessment order,
 (b) a child protection order,
 (c) a compulsory supervision order,
 (d) an interim compulsory supervision order,
 (e) a medical examination order.

DEFINITIONS

C.565.1   "child": s.199.
"child assessment order": ss.202(1) and 35.
"child protection order": ss.202(1) and 37.
"compulsory supervision order": ss.202(1) and 83.
"interim compulsory supervision order": ss.202(1) and 86.
"medical examination order": ss.202(1) and 87.

GENERAL NOTE

C.565.2   Section 2(4) of the Age of Legal Capacity (Scotland) Act 1991 (the 1991 Act) provides:
 "(4) A person under the age of 16 years shall have legal capacity to consent on his own behalf to any surgical, medical or dental procedure or treatment where, in the opinion of a qualified medical practitioner attending him, he is capable of understanding the nature and possible consequences of the procedure or treatment."

This present section makes clear that where an order in the categories listed in subs.(3) has been made, this does not take away the right of a child under the age of 16 to refuse to allow the procedure or treatment concerned provided the medical practitioner attending the child considers that the child is capable of understanding the nature of the proposed procedure or treatment and its possible consequences. It is worth reminding readers that "procedure or treatment" includes assessment, whether physical or psychological. Sections enacting the various orders make the orders subject to this present section: s.35(2), child assessment orders; s.37(2)(d), child protection orders; s.83(2)(f), compulsory supervision orders; s.86(1)(a), when read with s.83(2)(f), interim compulsory supervision orders; and s.87(2)(b), medical examination orders. As discussed by Professor Kenneth McK. Norrie in his *Children's Hearings in Scotland*, 3rd edn (Edinburgh: W. Green, 2013), paras 11–21 and 11–28, a children's hearing may impose, by virtue of s.83(2)(h) ("a requirement that the child comply with any other specified condition") a condition requiring the child to submit to medical treatment. A requirement under s.83(2)(h) is a requirement on the child, as distinct from the requirements/authorisations

in ss.35(2), 37(2)(d), 83(2)(f) and 87(2)(b) which are directed at local authorities, and consequently a child who has been made subject to a requirement under s.83(2)(h) who exercises his or her right to refuse to consent under s.2(4) of the Age of Legal Capacity (Scotland) Act 1991 will be regarded as having breached the condition and therefore will require to be brought back to a hearing for review under s.131(2)(b). Professor Norrie comments:
> "A children's hearing, however, ought to give especially careful consideration to the appropriateness of imposing such a condition when they know that the child is refusing."

We agree with this.

Subs.(2)(b)
The child has the capacity mentioned in section 2(4) of the Age of Legal Capacity (Scotland) Act 1991. Under s.2(4) of the 1991 Act it is for the medical practitioner to make the decision as to the child's capacity. Medical practitioners must be astute to consider the question of whether the child has the capacity to give, and has in fact given, informed consent. The issue of informed consent was considered by the Supreme Court in *Montgomery v Lanarkshire Health Board* [2015] UKSC 11, 2015 S.C. (U.K.S.C.) 63, 2015 S.L.T. 189, [2015] A.C. 1430 which, although not a case concerning a child, enunciates principles applicable in children's cases.

C.565.3

Rehabilitation of offenders

INTRODUCTORY NOTE

The ethos of the children's hearings system with regard to children accused of committing criminal offences is to focus on the needs of the child in the round, how the child came to offend and to look at the whole child without focusing on punishment, commonly referred to as "needs not deeds". Unfortunately, children referred to the hearing on offence grounds have acquired a criminal record for the offences. This is generally accepted to be disproportionate in most instances. This part of the Act seeks to redress the balance by only imposing a criminal record for the more serious offences. The following two sections are not yet in force as the changes require changes to Westminster legislation, both primary and subsidiary. How the following provisions will work out in practice must await this further legislation.

C.565.4

Rehabilitation of Offenders Act 1974: treatment of certain disposals by children's hearings

[1] **187.**—(1) The Rehabilitation of Offenders Act 1974 (c.53) is amended as follows.

(2) In section 8B (protection afforded to spent alternatives to prosecution: Scotland)—

(a) after subsection (1) insert—

> "(1A) For the purposes of this Act, a person has also been given an alternative to prosecution in respect of an offence if (whether before or after the commencement of this section) in proceedings before a children's hearing to which subsection (1B) applies—
> (a) a compulsory supervision order (as defined in section 83 of the 2011 Act) has been made or, as the case may be, varied or continued in relation to the person, or
> (b) the referral to the children's hearing has been discharged (whether wholly or in relation to the ground that the person committed the offence).
>
> (1B) This subsection applies to proceedings if the proceedings were taken in relation to the person on the ground (whether alone or with other grounds) that the person had committed the offence and—
> (a) the ground was accepted for the purposes of the 2011 Act by—
> (i) the person, and
> (ii) any person who was a relevant person as respects those proceedings, or
> (b) the ground was established or treated as established for the purposes of the 2011 Act.

C.566

(1C) In subsections (1A) and (1B)—
"the 2011 Act" means the Children's Hearings (Scotland) Act 2011,
"relevant person"—
(a) has the meaning given by section 200 of the 2011 Act, and
(b) includes a person who was deemed to be a relevant person by virtue of section 81(3), 160(4)(b) or 164(6) of that Act.

(1D) For the purposes of this Act, a person has also been given an alternative to prosecution in respect of an offence if (whether before or after the commencement of this section) in proceedings before a children's hearing to which subsection (1E) applies—
(a) a supervision requirement has been made or, as the case may be, varied or continued under the Children (Scotland) Act 1995 ("the 1995 Act") in relation to the person, or
(b) the referral to the children's hearing has been discharged (whether wholly or in relation to the ground that the person committed the offence).

(1E) This subsection applies to proceedings if the proceedings were taken in relation to the person on the ground (whether alone or with other grounds) that the person had committed the offence and—
(a) the ground was accepted for the purposes of the 1995 Act by the person and, where necessary, the relevant person (as defined in section 93(2) of that Act), or
(b) the ground was established, or deemed to have been established, for the purposes of that Act.", and
(b) in subsection (2), for "subsection (1)" substitute "subsections (1), (1A) and (1D)".

(3) In Schedule 3 (protection for spent alternatives to prosecution: Scotland), after sub-paragraph (1)(a) of paragraph 1 insert—

"(aa) in the case of—
(i) a compulsory supervision order referred to in paragraph (a) of subsection (1A) of that section, the period of 3 months beginning on the day the compulsory supervision order is made or, as the case may be, varied or continued, or
(ii) a discharge referred to in paragraph (b) of subsection (1A) of that section, the period of 3 months beginning on the day of the discharge,

(ab) in the case of—
(i) a supervision requirement referred to in paragraph (a) of subsection (1D) of that section, the period of 3 months beginning on the day the supervision requirement is made or, as the case may be, varied or continued, or
(ii) a discharge referred to in paragraph (b) of subsection (1D) of that section, the period of 3 months beginning on the day of the discharge,".

NOTE

1. Not yet in force—see Introductory Note, above.

Places of safety: restrictions on use of police stations

Criminal record certificates

Criminal record certificates

[1] **188.** In section 113A of the Police Act 1997 (c.50) (criminal record certificates)—
  (a) in subsection (6), in the definition of "relevant matter", after paragraph (b) insert—
    "(ba) an alternative to prosecution of the type mentioned in section 8B(1A) or (1D) of that Act which relates to an offence specified in an order made by the Scottish Ministers by statutory instrument, including any such alternative to prosecution which so relates and which is spent under Schedule 3 to that Act,
    (bb) a supervision requirement made in relation to a person by a children's hearing under section 44 of the Social Work (Scotland) Act 1968 in the circumstances mentioned in subsection (6A) if the supervision requirement relates to an offence specified in an order under paragraph (ba),
    (bc) the discharge under section 43 of the Social Work (Scotland) Act 1968 of the referral of a person to a children's hearing in the circumstances mentioned in subsection (6A) if the discharge relates to an offence specified in an order under paragraph (ba),", and
  (b) after that subsection, insert—
    "(6A) The circumstances are—
      (a) the person was referred to the children's hearing on the ground (whether alone or among other grounds) mentioned in section 32(2)(g) of the Social Work (Scotland) Act 1968 (commission of offence), and
      (b) the ground was accepted by the person and, where necessary, by the person's parent or established to the satisfaction of the sheriff under section 42 of that Act.
    (6B) An order under paragraph (ba) of the definition of "relevant matter" in subsection (6) may specify an offence by reference to a particular degree of seriousness.
    (6C) A statutory instrument containing an order under paragraph (ba) of the definition of "relevant matter" in subsection (6) may not be made unless a draft of the instrument containing the order has been laid before, and approved by resolution of, the Scottish Parliament.".

NOTE
1. Not yet in force—see Introductory Note, above.

Places of safety

Places of safety: restrictions on use of police stations

189.—(1) This section applies where a person is authorised or required under this Act to keep or detain a child in a place of safety.

(2) A child may be kept or detained in a police station only if it is not reasonably practicable to keep or detain the child in a place of safety which is not a police station.

(3) Where a child is being kept or detained in a police station, the person must take steps to identify a place of safety which is not a police station and transfer the child to that place as soon as is reasonably practicable.

DEFINITIONS
C.568.1 "child": s.199.
"place of safety": s.202(1).

GENERAL NOTE
C.568.2 An order may be made to keep a child in a "place of safety" under s.37 (child protection order), s.55 (application to justice of the peace), s.56 (power of constable to remove child to place of safety), s.86(2) (meaning of interim compulsory supervision order), or s.140(2) (interim variation of compulsory supervision order). All of these orders must be required as a matter of urgent necessity and where it is considered that the welfare of the child requires that he or she be removed from his or her current location, the orders may include a requirement that he or she be held in a "place of safety". While this may have been arranged prior to the order being made, some circumstances may not have allowed the luxury of a prepared place for the child. It is particularly likely where a police constable has exercised his or her power under s.56, no preliminary preparation will have been undertaken. Section 202(1) contains the list of those places which may be considered as places of safety. While the list of possible places of safety includes a police station, a police station is not a suitable environment except as a temporary measure while a more suitable place is found. This section allows for a child to be kept at a police station only if no other place has been found and only until a suitable placement is found. The duty to find a place other than a police station is imposed upon the person authorised or required under the Act to keep the child in the place of safety.

Orders made outwith Scotland

Effect of orders made outwith Scotland

C.569 **190.**—(1) The Scottish Ministers may by regulations make provision for a specified non-Scottish order which appears to them to correspond to a compulsory supervision order to have effect as if it were such an order.
(2) Regulations under subsection (1)—
  (a) may provide that a non-Scottish order is to have such effect only—
    (i) in specified circumstances,
    (ii) for specified purposes,
  (b) may modify the following enactments in their application by virtue of the regulations to a non-Scottish order—
    (i) the Social Work (Scotland) Act 1968,
    (ii) this Act,
  (c) are subject to affirmative procedure.
(3) In this section—
  "non-Scottish order" means an order made by a court in England and Wales or in Northern Ireland,
  "specified" means specified in the regulations.

DEFINITIONS
C.569.1 "affirmative procedure": ss.202(1) and 197.
"compulsory supervision order": ss.202(1) and 83.

GENERAL NOTE
C.569.2 This section empowers the Scottish Ministers to make regulations prescribing the extent to which non-Scottish orders may be implemented in Scotland.

Subs.(2)
C.569.3 The Children's Hearings (Scotland) Act 2011 (Transfer of Children to Scotland—Effect of Orders made in England and Wales or Northern Ireland) Regulations 2013 (SSI 2013/99) has been made under this section. These Regulations provide substantially for the situation where a child has been made subject to a specified order in England or Wales or Northern Ireland and it is proposed that the child is to transfer his or her residence to Scotland. In this situation the local authority which obtained the order has to notify the "receiving" local authority in Scotland and then, provided the receiving authority has agreed in writing to take over the care of the child, the English/Welsh or Northern Irish order has effect as if it were a compulsory supervision order. These Regulations (per reg.7(3) and (4)) also amend this Act by adding at the end of s.131(2):

Effect of orders made outwith Scotland

"(f) the authority becomes aware that the child is subject to a compulsory supervision order by virtue of regulations made under section 190 of this Act"
and modifying s.137 by inserting after s.137(3):
"(3A) If the review is initiated under section 131(2)(f) the children's hearing must be arranged to take place no later than 20 working days after notice is given to the Principal Reporter under s.131(1)."

The effect of this is to require the implementation authority (which will be the "receiving authority") to give notice to the Principal Reporter of the transfer to it of the child and require a review within 20 working days of giving such notice.

It is to be noted that the provisions of this present section deal with the child who has been made subject to the non-Scottish order and in respect of whom a change of residence to Scotland is in prospect. The section does not operate so as to allow an English, Welsh or Northern Irish court or local authority to make an order effective in Scotland. A cross-border enforcement matter arose in *In Re X (A Child) and Re Y (A Child)* [2016] EWHC 2271 (Fam.) (12 September 2016). In this case, involving originally two separate cases, the local authorities concerned had applied to the court to authorise placement in secure accommodation and, there being no such accommodation accessible in England, the possibility of authorising placement in Scotland was ventilated. The judges remitted the matter to the Family Division, where the President, Sir James Munby, after noting that s.25 of the Children Act 1989 did not permit placement of a child in secure accommodation in Scotland, held that a Court in England had inherent jurisdiction to authorise such a placement but, as there was no legislative provision enabling such an order to be implemented in Scotland, the local authority should apply to the *nobile officium* of the Court of Session with a view to enabling this. In the course of his extensive and penetrating judgment the President reviewed various aspects of cross-border family issues and noted, for example at [25], that the Children's Hearings (Scotland) Act 2011 (Consequential and Transitional Provisions and Savings) Order 2013 (SI 2013/1465) provides, in art.7(1), that the place specified in s.83(2)(a) of the 2011 Act "may be a place in England or Wales". (It is to be noted that art.7(2) of the same Order provides that, where the place specified in s.83(2)(a) is in England or Wales, the person in charge of that place may "restrict the child's liberty to the extent that the person in charge considers appropriate having regard to the measures included in the order.") The President concluded by commenting, at [74], that there were in this area "serious lacunae in the law" and suggesting that these could perhaps be addressed jointly by the Law Commission of England and Wales and the Law Commission of Scotland. The English local authorities speedily arranged for application to be made to the Court of Session and on 19 October 2016 an Extra Division held that the Court of Session had inherent power to exercise the *nobile officium* as *parens patriae*, and granted the appropriate interim orders—*Cumbria County Council, Petitioner* [2016] CSIH 92, 2017 S.L.T. 34. The court echoed the view of Sir James Munby to the effect that there were several gaps in the legislation affecting cross-border issues and expressed the strong hope that these would be addressed soon.

Part 19

Legal aid and advice

GENERAL NOTE

This section of the Act amends the Legal Aid (Scotland) Act 1986 (the 1986 Act) to make special provision for assistance for children and relevant persons in hearings matters. The provisions are complex and must be read in conjunction with the Children's Legal Assistance (Scotland) Regulations 2013 (SSI 2013/200). Rather confusingly, legal aid for children's hearings matters is now entitled "children's legal aid" although it is available not only to children but also adults (relevant persons and safeguarders). This section defines the meaning of "children's legal aid" as being representation by a solicitor or member of the Faculty of Advocates in specified proceedings. It includes not only active representation but also all the work involved prior to proceedings and incidental to them. The section numbers 28B–M and 33B refer to the sections in the 1986 Act which this section amends and replaces. There are a number of significant changes.

C.569.4

First, the system of legal representatives which was provided by local councils and arranged for by the Reporter has been ended. Children and relevant persons will now be required to arrange for their own legal representation. Where the legal representative was provided in only limited circumstances, under this part of the Act, the availability of legal representation is wider. It must be understood that in civil matters the child must have capacity to instruct legal representation (Age of Legal Capacity (Scotland) Act 1991 s.2(4A)). The child merely requires to have "a general understanding of what it means to do so" and it is the solicitor who assesses whether the child has sufficient understanding. From the point of view of the solicitor, the child must be able to act as the client, instruct the solicitor and have the basis of a stateable case. Note that the provisions in s.2(4A) of the 1991 Act do not apply in criminal matters (see s.2(4C) of 1991 Act). However, children's hearings matters are considered to be civil law including where the ground for referral is under s.67(2)(j)—an alleged criminal offence by the child.

Secondly, with regard to applications by the child:
- In some limited circumstances legal assistance will be automatically available for the child. (See s.28C of the 1986 Act for the four specified hearings.) For these hearings only, the application is not subject to the tests of merit or means.
- Where the child is applying for children's legal aid in relation to proceedings under Pts 10 or 15 there is a new additional test. The Scottish Legal Aid Board must consider that it is in the child's best interest that legal aid is made available (1986 Act s.28D). Why children should have an extra hurdle is not clear, but it would be exceedingly odd for it to be considered not in the interests of a child who wishes representation to receive it if he or she satisfy the normal tests. The authors understand that to date no application for children's legal aid has been refused on the grounds that it would not be in the interests of the child.
- Unlike civil legal aid applications, a child's application (apart from automatic legal aid) is subject only to the child's own means. Parental income is not considered, and thus parents will not be required to make a financial contribution (s.28D(3)(c) of 1986 Act), and the child will not be required to obtain his or her parent(s) financial information.

Thirdly, there is some distinction made between relevant persons and deemed relevant persons in some applications where relevant persons are not subject to the merits test, but deemed relevant persons are.

Fourthly, the Scottish Legal Aid Board is empowered to require solicitors wishing to practise in the Children's Hearing System to register with the Board and to undertake specified training each year. Section 192 also empowers the Board to contract for legal services for children's legal aid.

Changes to the provision of automatic legal assistance may be made by regulation by Scottish Ministers.

The rules and determination of an application by the Scottish Legal Aid Board are complex, can change, and are outwith the scope of these annotations. Readers are advised to make specific enquiries of the Board and are directed for further information to the SLAB website at www.slab.org.uk [Accessed 25 January 2017].

Legal aid and advice

C.570   **191.** After section 28A of the Legal Aid (Scotland) Act 1986 (c.47) insert—

"Part 5A
Children's legal aid

28B Children's legal aid
(1) This Part applies to children's legal aid.
(2) In this Act, "children's legal aid" means representation by a solicitor and, where appropriate, by counsel in proceedings mentioned in subsection (3), on the terms provided for in this Act, and includes all such assistance as is usually given by a solicitor or counsel in the steps preliminary to or incidental to those proceedings.
(3) The proceedings are—
(a) proceedings before the sheriff in relation to an application under section 48 of the 2011 Act (application for variation or termination of child protection order),
(b) proceedings before a children's hearing arranged by virtue of section 45 or 46 of the 2011 Act (children's hearing following making of child protection order),
(c) proceedings before a children's hearing or a pre-hearing panel if the children's hearing or the panel considers that it might be necessary to make a compulsory supervision order including a secure accommodation authorisation in relation to the child to whom the proceedings relate,
(d) proceedings before a children's hearing to which section 69(3)

Legal aid and advice

of the 2011 Act applies (children's hearing following arrest of child and detention in place of safety),
(e) proceedings under Part 10 or 15 of the 2011 Act.
(4) In this Part—
"compulsory supervision order" has the meaning given by section 83 of that Act,
"pre-hearing panel" has the meaning given by section 79 of that Act,
"secure accommodation authorisation" has the meaning given by section 85 of that Act.

28C Circumstances where children's legal aid automatically available
(1) Subsection (2) applies where—
(a) an application is made under section 48 of the 2011 Act for variation or termination of a child protection order,
(b) a children's hearing is arranged in relation to a child by virtue of section 45 or 46 of the 2011 Act,
(c) a children's hearing or a pre-hearing panel considers that it might be necessary to make a compulsory supervision order including a secure accommodation authorisation in relation to a child, or
(d) a children's hearing to which section 69(3) of the 2011 Act applies is arranged in relation to a child.
(2) If assistance by way of representation has not been made available to the child, children's legal aid is available to the child for the purposes of—
(a) proceedings before the sheriff in relation to the application mentioned in paragraph (a) of subsection (1),
(b) the children's hearing mentioned in paragraph (b) or, as the case may be, (c) or (d) of that subsection, and
(c) if that children's hearing is deferred, any subsequent children's hearing held under Part 11 of the 2011 Act.
(3) The Scottish Ministers may by regulations—
(a) modify subsection (1),
(b) modify subsection (2) and section 28B(3) and (4) in consequence of modifications made under paragraph (a).

28D Availability of children's legal aid: child
(1) Subsection (2) applies in relation to proceedings under Part 10 or 15 of the 2011 Act (other than an appeal to the sheriff principal or the Court of Session).
(2) Children's legal aid is available to the child to whom the proceedings relate if, on an application made to the Board, the Board is satisfied that the conditions in subsection (3) are met.
(3) The conditions are—
(a) that it is in the best interests of the child that children's legal aid be made available,
(b) that it is reasonable in the particular circumstances of the case that the child should receive children's legal aid, and
(c) that, after consideration of the disposable income and disposable capital of the child, the expenses of the case cannot be met without undue hardship to the child.
(4) Subsection (5) applies in relation to an appeal to the sheriff principal or the Court of Session under Part 15 of the 2011 Act.
(5) Children's legal aid is available to the child to whom the proceedings relate if, on an application made to the Board, the Board is satisfied that—
(a) the conditions in subsection (3) are met, and

(b) the child has substantial grounds for making or responding to the appeal.

28E Availability of children's legal aid: relevant person
(1) Subsection (2) applies in relation to—
(a) proceedings before the sheriff in relation to an application under section 48 of the 2011 Act (application for variation or termination of child protection order), and
(b) proceedings under Part 10 or 15 of the 2011 Act (other than an appeal to the sheriff principal or the Court of Session).
(2) Children's legal aid is available to a relevant person in relation to the child to whom the proceedings relate if, on an application made to the Board, the Board is satisfied that the conditions in subsection (3) are met.
(3) The conditions are—
(a) that it is reasonable in the particular circumstances of the case that the relevant person should receive children's legal aid, and
(b) that, after consideration of the disposable income and disposable capital of the relevant person, the expenses of the case cannot be met without undue hardship to the relevant person.
(4) Subsection (5) applies in relation to an appeal to the sheriff principal or the Court of Session under Part 15 of the 2011 Act.
(5) Children's legal aid is available to a relevant person in relation to the child to whom the appeal relates if, on an application made to the Board, the Board is satisfied that—
(a) the conditions in subsection (3) are met, and
(b) the relevant person has substantial grounds for making or responding to the appeal.
(6) In this Part, "relevant person"—
(a) has the meaning given by section 200 of the 2011 Act, and
(b) includes a person deemed to be a relevant person by virtue of section 81(3), 160(4)(b) or 164(6) of that Act.

28F Availability of children's legal aid: appeals relating to deemed relevant person
(1) Subsection (2) applies in relation to—
(a) an appeal under section 154 or 163(1)(a)(iii) or (2) of the 2011 Act arising from a determination of a children's hearing mentioned in section 142(1)(a) if by virtue of section 142(4)(b) an individual is no longer to be deemed to be a relevant person,
(b) an appeal to the sheriff under section 160(1)(a) of that Act against a determination of a pre-hearing panel or children's hearing that an individual is not to be deemed a relevant person in relation to a child,
(c) an appeal to the sheriff under section 160(1)(b) of that Act against a direction under section 142(4)(a) that an individual is no longer to be deemed a relevant person in relation to a child,
(d) an appeal to the sheriff principal or the Court of Session under section 164(1) of that Act against a decision of the sheriff in an appeal under section 160(1)—
　(i) confirming a determination that an individual is not to be deemed a relevant person in relation to a child, or
　(ii) quashing a determination that an individual is to be deemed a relevant person in relation to a child, and
(e) an appeal to the Court of Session under section 164(2) of that Act against a determination of the sheriff principal where the effect of the sheriff principal's determination is that an

Legal aid and advice

individual is not to be deemed a relevant person in relation to a child.

(2) Children's legal aid is available to the individual if, on an application made to the Board, the Board is satisfied—
  (a) that it is reasonable in the particular circumstances of the case that the individual should receive children's legal aid,
  (b) that, after consideration of the disposable income and disposable capital of the individual, the expenses of the case cannot be met without undue hardship to the individual, and
  (c) that—
    (i) in relation to an appeal mentioned in paragraph (a) of subsection (1), the individual has substantial grounds for making or, as the case may be, responding to the appeal,
    (ii) in relation to an appeal mentioned in any other paragraph of that subsection, the individual has substantial grounds for making the appeal.

28G Conditions

The Board may make the grant of children's legal aid subject to such conditions as the Board considers expedient; and such conditions may be imposed at any time.

28H Board to establish review procedures

(1) The Board must establish a procedure under which a person whose application for children's legal aid has been refused may apply to the Board for a review of the application.

(2) The Board must establish a procedure under which any person receiving children's legal aid which is subject to conditions by virtue of section 28G may apply to the Board for a review of any such condition.

28J Board's power to require compliance with conditions

The Board may require a person receiving children's legal aid to comply with such conditions as it considers expedient to enable it to satisfy itself from time to time that it is reasonable for the person to continue to receive children's legal aid.

28K Contributions to the Fund

(1) A person in receipt of children's legal aid (the "assisted person") may be required by the Board to contribute to the Fund in respect of any proceedings in connection with which the assisted person is granted children's legal aid.

(2) A contribution under subsection (1) is to be determined by the Board and may include—
  (a) if the assisted person's disposable income exceeds £3,355 a year, a contribution in respect of income which is not to be more than one-third of the excess (or such other proportion of the excess, or such amount, as may be prescribed by regulations made under this section), and
  (b) if the assisted person's disposable capital exceeds £7,504, a contribution in respect of capital which is not to be more than the excess (or such proportion of the excess or such lesser amount as may be prescribed by regulations made under this section).

(3) Regulations under this section may prescribe different proportions or amounts for different amounts of disposable income and for different cases or classes of case.

28L Power of Scottish Ministers to modify circumstances in which children's legal aid to be available

(1) The Scottish Ministers may by regulations modify this Part so as to—
 (a) extend or restrict the types of proceedings before a children's hearing in connection with which children's legal aid is to be available, and
 (b) specify the persons to whom children's legal aid is to be available.

(2) If regulations are made making children's legal aid available to a child, the regulations must include provision—
 (a) requiring the Board to be satisfied that—
  (i) one of the conditions in subsection (3) is met, and
  (ii) the conditions in section 28D(3) are met before children's legal aid is made available, and
 (b) requiring the Board, in determining for the purposes of subsection (3)(b)(ii) whether the child would be able to participate effectively in the proceedings, to take into account in particular the matters mentioned in subsection (4).

(3) The conditions are—
 (a) that it might be necessary for the children's hearing to decide whether a compulsory supervision order or, as the case may be, an interim compulsory supervision order should include or (where a compulsory supervision order is being reviewed) continue to include a secure accommodation authorisation, and
 (b) that—
  (i) the condition in paragraph (a) is not met, and
  (ii) for the purpose of enabling the child to participate effectively in the proceedings before the children's hearing, it is necessary that the child be represented by a solicitor or counsel.

(4) The matters are—
 (a) the nature and complexity of the case (including any points of law),
 (b) the ability of the appropriate person, with the assistance of any accompanying person, to consider and challenge any document or information before the children's hearing,
 (c) the ability of the appropriate person, with the assistance of any accompanying person, to give the appropriate person's views at the children's hearing in an effective manner.

(5) If regulations are made making children's legal aid available to a person other than the child to whom the proceedings relate, the regulations must include provision—
 (a) requiring the Board to be satisfied that the conditions in subsection (6) are met before children's legal aid is made available, and
 (b) requiring the Board, in determining for the purposes of the condition in subsection (6)(a) whether the person would be able to participate effectively in the proceedings, to take into account in particular the matters mentioned in subsection (4).

(6) The conditions are—
 (a) that, for the purpose of enabling the person to participate effectively in the proceedings before the children's hearing, it is necessary that the person be represented by a solicitor or counsel,
 (b) that it is reasonable in the particular circumstances of the case that the person should receive children's legal aid, and

Legal aid and advice

    (c) that, after consideration of the disposable income and disposable capital of the person, the expenses of the case cannot be met without undue hardship to the person or the dependants of the person.

(7) In subsection (4)—

"accompanying person" means a person entitled to accompany the child or other person to the children's hearing by virtue of rules under section 177 of the 2011 Act,

"appropriate person" means—

    (a) for the purposes of subsection (2)(b), the child,

    (b) for the purposes of subsection (5)(b), the other person.

(8) The Scottish Ministers may by regulations modify—

    (a) the matters for the time being set out in subsection (4),

    (b) the definition of "accompanying person" for the time being set out in subsection (7).

Part 5B
Children's legal assistance

28M Register of solicitors and firms eligible to provide children's legal assistance

(1) The Board must establish and maintain a register of—

    (a) solicitors who are eligible to provide children's legal assistance, and

    (b) the firms with which such solicitors are connected.

(2) A sole solicitor who wishes to provide children's legal assistance must be included in the register maintained under this section both as a solicitor and as a firm.

(3) Only those solicitors who are included in the register maintained under this section may provide children's legal assistance.

(4) Subject to subsection (5), a solicitor may provide children's legal assistance only when working in the course of a connection with a firm included in the register maintained under this section.

(5) Where the Board employs a solicitor under sections 26 and 27 to provide children's legal assistance—

    (a) the Board may only employ a solicitor who is included in the register maintained under this section,

    (b) the entry in the register relating to the solicitor's name must include a note that the solicitor is so employed,

    (c) the Board is not to be regarded as a firm for the purposes of this section and is not required to be included in the register.

(6) The Scottish Ministers may by regulations make provision about qualifications to be held by persons who may be included in the register maintained under this section.

(7) Subsections (5) to (15) of section 25A apply in relation to the register maintained under this section as they apply in relation to the Register subject to the modifications mentioned in subsection (8).

(8) Those modifications are—

    (a) subsections (8) and (9) are to be read as if references to the code were references to the code of practice under section 28N for the time being in force, and

    (b) subsection (9) is to be read as if the reference to criminal legal assistance were a reference to children's legal assistance.

28N Code of practice

(1) The Board must prepare a draft code of practice in relation to the carrying out by solicitors of their functions with regard to the provision of children's legal assistance.

(2) Different provision may be made for different cases or classes of case.

(3) Subsections (3) to (8) of section 25B apply in relation to a draft code prepared under subsection (1) above as they apply in relation to a draft code prepared under subsection (1) of that section.

28P Duty to comply with code of practice

(1) Solicitors and firms included in the register maintained under section 28M(1) must comply with the requirements of the code of practice under section 28N for the time being in force.

(2) The Board must monitor the carrying out by those solicitors and firms of their duty under subsection (1).

(3) For the purpose of carrying out its duty under subsection (2) the Board may use the powers conferred on it by sections 35A and 35B.

28Q Non-compliance with code of practice

(1) Section 25D applies in relation to a solicitor or firm included in the register maintained under section 28M(1) and the code of practice under section 28N for the time being in force as it applies in relation to a registered solicitor or registered firm and the code subject to the modifications mentioned in subsection (2).

(2) Those modifications are—
  (a) references to the Register are to be read as if they were references to the register maintained under section 28M(1),
  (b) subsection (6) is to be read as if the references to criminal legal assistance were references to children's legal assistance.

28R Further provision as to removal of name from register

(1) Subsection (2) applies where the Board is satisfied (whether on being informed by the solicitor concerned or otherwise) that a solicitor who is included in the register maintained under section 28M(1)—
  (a) has become connected with a firm whose name is not included in that register, and
  (b) is no longer connected with a firm whose name is included in that register.

(2) The Board must remove the solicitor's name from the register.

(3) Subsections (6) to (9) of section 25D (as applied by section 28Q) apply in relation to a solicitor whose name is removed from the register under subsection (2) above as they apply in relation to a solicitor whose name is removed from the register under subsection (4) of that section (as applied by section 28Q).

28S Publication of register etc.

Section 25F applies in relation to the register maintained under section 28M(1) as it applies in relation to the Register.".

DEFINITIONS
"child": s.199.
"children's hearing": s.5.
"child protection order": ss.202(1) and 37.
"compulsory supervision order": ss.202(1) and 83.
"pre-hearing panel": ss.202(1) and 79(2).
"relevant person": s.201.
"secure accommodation authorisation": ss.202(1) and 83(5).

Power to make regulations about contracts for provision of children's legal aid

Power to make regulations about contracts for provision of children's legal aid

192. After section 33A of the Legal Aid (Scotland) Act 1986 insert—
"Contracts for the provision of children's legal assistance

33B Contracts for the provision of children's legal assistance
(1) The Scottish Ministers may by regulations made under this section empower the Board to enter into contracts with relevant firms for the provision by relevant solicitors connected with those firms of children's legal assistance.
(2) Regulations under this section may prescribe—
  (a) the procedures to be followed by the Board in awarding any such contract, and
  (b) subject to subsection (3), any terms and conditions which are to be included in any such contract.
(3) Regulations under this section must provide that any contract entered into by virtue of this section must include a provision that, in the event of the termination of the contract, or a breach of it by the relevant firm concerned, the Board may—
  (a) withhold payments under the contract, and
  (b) require the firm to secure the transfer to a relevant solicitor of—
    (i) any work currently being undertaken by any solicitor connected with them for any client by way of children's legal assistance, and
    (ii) notwithstanding any lien to which any such solicitor might otherwise be entitled, any documents connected with any such work.
(4) Regulations under this section may provide that where the Board has by virtue of this section entered into contracts with any relevant firms for the provision of children's legal assistance in any area, then, unless it seems to the Board to be inappropriate in a particular case, any person seeking such assistance in that area is to be required to instruct a relevant solicitor connected with one of those firms.
(5) Any money due to a firm under a contract made by virtue of this section is to be paid to the firm—
  (a) firstly, out of any amount payable by the client in accordance with section 11(2),
  (b) secondly, by the Board out of the Fund.
(6) For the purposes of sections 32 and 33, the money paid to a firm, as provided in subsection (5) above, in respect of a contract made by virtue of this section is to be taken to be a payment made in accordance with this Act, and no solicitor connected with such a firm is entitled to any other payment out of the Fund in respect of any work done by the solicitor by virtue of such a contract.
(7) In this section—
  "relevant firm" means a firm included in the register maintained under section 28M(1),
  "relevant solicitor" means a solicitor included in the register maintained under section 28M(1).".

GENERAL NOTE
See General Note under Pt 19 ("Legal Aid and Advice"). At the time of writing, no Regulations have been enacted under this section.

Children's Hearings (Scotland) Act 2011

PART 20

GENERAL

Formal communications

Formal communications

C.572 **193.**—(1) The following are formal communications—
(a) a notice,
(b) a determination,
(c) a direction,
(d) a report,
(e) a statement,
(f) a referral under section 127.
(2) A formal communication must be in writing.
(3) That requirement is satisfied by a formal communication in electronic form which is—
(a) sent by electronic means, and
(b) capable of being reproduced in legible form.
(4) A formal communication sent in accordance with subsection (3) is to be taken to be received on the day it is sent.

GENERAL NOTE

C.572.1 This section, after defining "formal communication", provides that such a communication shall be in writing, and permits such communication to be effected electronically provided it is capable of being reproduced in legible form. The section also makes the significant provision that when electronic form is employed the communication is to be taken as being received on the date of dispatch. The period of notice which applies generally (i.e. where electronic form is not employed), is prescribed by r.3.13 of the Act of Sederunt (Child Care and Maintenance Rules) 1997 (SI 1997/291) as amended by the Act of Sederunt (Children's Hearings (Scotland) Act 2011) (Miscellaneous Amendments) 2013 (SSI 2013/172) which provides:

"3.13—(1) Subject to paragraph (2), citation or notification authorised or required by this Chapter shall be made not later than forty-eight hours, or in the case of postal citation seventy-two hours, before the date of the diet to which the citation or notice relates.

(2) Paragraph (1) shall not apply in relation to citation or notice of the following applications or proceedings:

(a) an appeal referred to in section 157(1), 160(1), 161(1) or 162(3) of the 2011 Act;
(b) a hearing in respect of an exclusion order where an interim order has been granted in terms of rule 3.36;
(c) a hearing on an application to vary or terminate a child protection order;
(d) an application for a child assessment order;

in which cases the period of notice and the method of giving notice shall be as directed by the sheriff."

Forms

Forms

C.573 **194.**—(1) The Scottish Ministers may determine—
(a) the form of documents produced by virtue of this Act, and
(b) the manner in which those documents are to be conveyed.
(2) The Scottish Ministers may in particular determine that documents may be conveyed by electronic means.

GENERAL NOTE

C.573.1 This is an empowering section. We have referred to some of the enacted Forms at the appropriate places. The Forms are found in Sch.1 of the Act of Sederunt (Child Care and Maintenance Rules) 1997 (SI 1997/291) as amended by Act of Sederunt (Children's Hearings (Scotland) Act 2011) (Miscellaneous Amendments) 2013 (SSI 2013/172). The provision in

Subordinate legislation

subs.(2), like the provision in s.193(3), reflects the increasing scope for electronic communication.

Subordinate legislation

Subordinate legislation

195.—(1) Any power of the Scottish Ministers to make subordinate legislation under this Act is exercisable by statutory instrument.
(2) Any such power includes power to make—
(a) such incidental, supplementary, consequential, transitional, transitory or saving provision as the Scottish Ministers think necessary or expedient,
(b) different provision for different purposes.
(3) Except in any case where subordinate legislation under this Act is subject to the affirmative procedure or the super-affirmative procedure, subordinate legislation under this Act is subject to the negative procedure.
(4) Subsections (2) and (3) do not apply to an order under section 206(2).

DEFINITIONS
"affirmative procedure": s.197.
"negative procedure": s.196.
"super-affirmative procedure": s.198.

GENERAL NOTE
This section provides the Scottish Ministers with extensive powers, exercisable by statutory instrument, to make provisions including "such incidental, supplementary, consequential, transitional, transitory or saving provision as the Scottish Ministers think necessary or expedient" and prescribes the procedures which are to be employed when exercising these powers. The power to amend primary legislation by delegated legislation has long caused some concern. In 1932 the *Report of the Committee on Ministers' Powers* (HMSO, 1932), Cmd.4060 it was said, at p.61, that it should be used only where there were compelling grounds. (We are indebted to H.W.R. Wade, *Administrative Law*, 6th edn (Clarendon Press, 1988), p.853, for this reference.) This concern is reflected in the observations of Lord Keith of Kinkell who, in *R v Secretary of State for Social Security ex p. Britnell*, 1991 1 W.L.R. 198, after referring to an earlier case said:
> "The judgments contain passages to the effect that the power to modify [by subordinate legislation] the provisions of a statute should be narrowly and strictly construed, and that view is indeed the correct one."

See also per Henry LJ in *Hyde Park Residence Ltd v Secretary of State for the Environment, Transport and the Regions* (2000) P. and C.R. 419 at 423; [2000] All E.R. (D) 64 at [29]. However, the power to amend statute by delegated legislation has in recent years been resorted to often enough. In the present Act a degree of parliamentary oversight of the use of this power is provided for by the requirement in subs.(3) of this section that all uses of this power are subject to procedures in the Scottish Parliament, viz. where the Act has so specified, the super-affirmative procedure or the affirmative procedure or, where neither of these procedures is specified, by the negative procedure (see ss.196 to 198 below). One justification for conferring these powers on Scottish Ministers could be to enable the introduction of additional grounds of referral, made desirable by changing social conditions, without the necessity, with the accompanying delay, of enacting primary legislation. It is possible to envisage, for example, that as our knowledge of the modes and extent of people trafficking increases, it may be thought appropriate to formulate a specific ground for referral based upon this practice. Also, as suggested by under s.67(2) para.(a), consideration might be given to enacting a specific ground for referral of "causing or permitting female genital mutilation".

Subs.(4)
Section 206(2) of this Act provides:
> "(2) The provisions of this Act, other than sections 193 to 202, 204, 205 and this section, come into force on such day as the Scottish Ministers may by order appoint."

This present subsection means that the provisions identified in s.206(2) may be brought into effect by a statutory instruments which will have effect without going through any of the parliamentary procedures enacted in ss.196–198.

Negative procedure

C.575 **196.**—(1) Subsection (2) applies where subordinate legislation under this Act is subject to the negative procedure.

(2) The statutory instrument containing the subordinate legislation is subject to annulment in pursuance of a resolution of the Scottish Parliament.

GENERAL NOTE
C.575.1 See General Note to s.195 above. This provision is the least demanding of the provisions for parliamentary oversight of statutory instruments made by Scottish Ministers in that the instrument may be made without the MSPs having had its terms laid before them. However, this should not render this parliamentary oversight ineffective since various persons and bodies, including the Family Law sub-Committee of the Law Society of Scotland, Children's Hearings Scotland, the Children and Young Peoples Commissioner, Scotland and the Scottish Children's Reporter Administration, on becoming aware of the terms of the instrument, would be able, if they thought it proper, to seek to arrange for annulment procedures to be initiated. Scottish Ministers will be aware of this when considering the terms of any statutory instrument.

Affirmative procedure

C.576 **197.**—(1) Subsection (2) applies where subordinate legislation under this Act is subject to the affirmative procedure.

(2) The subordinate legislation must not be made unless a draft of the statutory instrument containing the subordinate legislation has been laid before, and approved by resolution of, the Scottish Parliament.

GENERAL NOTE
C.576.1 See General Note to s.195 above. The affirmative procedure is more demanding than the negative procedure (s.196), but less demanding than the super-affirmative procedure (s.198). The statutory instruments attracting the affirmative procedure are those under the following sections: 10(1)(e), 18(1)(e), 81(5), 122(4), 150(1), 151(6), 152(1), 153(1), 162(7), 177(2)(a), (e), (f), (g), (j) and (m), 190(1), 200(1)(g) and 204.

Super-affirmative procedure

C.577 **198.**—(1) Subsections (2) to (6) apply where subordinate legislation under this Act is subject to the super-affirmative procedure.

(2) The subordinate legislation must not be made unless a draft of the statutory instrument containing the subordinate legislation has been laid before, and approved by resolution of, the Scottish Parliament.

(3) Before laying a draft instrument before the Parliament under subsection (2), the Scottish Ministers must consult—
  (a) such persons who are under 21 years of age as they consider appropriate, and
  (b) such other persons as they consider appropriate.

(4) For the purposes of such a consultation, the Scottish Ministers must—
  (a) lay a copy of the proposed draft instrument before the Parliament,
  (b) publish in such a manner as the Scottish Ministers consider appropriate a copy of the proposed draft instrument, and
  (c) have regard to any representations about the proposed draft instrument that are made to them within 60 days of the date on which the copy of the proposed draft instrument is laid before the Parliament.

(5) In calculating any period of 60 days for the purposes of subsection (4)(c), no account is to be taken of any time during which the Parliament is dissolved or is in recess for more than 4 days.

(6) When laying a draft instrument before the Parliament under subsection (2), the Scottish Ministers must also lay before the Parliament an explanatory document giving details of—
  (a) the consultation carried out under subsection (3),

(b) any representations received as a result of the consultation, and
(c) the changes (if any) made to the proposed draft instrument as a result of those representations.

GENERAL NOTE
See General Note to s.195 above. The statutory instruments attracting the super-affirmative procedure are those under the following sections: 10(1)(a)–(d), which deal with varying the functions of the National Convener or transferring these functions to someone else; and 18(1)(a)–(d), which deal with varying the functions of the Principal Reporter or transferring these functions to someone else. Obviously changes such as those specified in these sections would go to the heart of the children's hearings system—hence the requirement for detailed consultation and consideration imposed by the super-affirmative procedure. The requirement to consult with young people imposed by subs.(3)(a) reflects the aim of the legislature to involve young people in the decision making process and thus, it is to be hoped, increasing the likelihood that their needs will be satisfactorily addressed.

Interpretation

Meaning of "child"

199.—(1) In this Act, "child" means a person who is under 16 years of age (but subject to subsections (2) to (9)).

(2) In paragraph (o) of section 67(2) and the other provisions of this Act in their application in relation to that paragraph, "child" means a person who is of school age.

(3) Subsection (4) applies where a person becomes 16 years of age—
(a) after section 66 applies in relation to the person, but
(b) before a relevant event.

(4) For the purposes of the application of this Act to the person, references in this Act to a child include references to the person until a relevant event occurs.

(5) A relevant event is—
(a) the making of a compulsory supervision order in relation to the person,
(b) the notification of the person under section 68(3) that the question of whether a compulsory supervision order should be made in respect of the person will not be referred to a children's hearing, or
(c) the discharge of the referral.

(6) Subsection (7) applies if—
(a) a compulsory supervision order is in force in respect of a person on the person's becoming 16 years of age, or
(b) a compulsory supervision order is made in respect of a person on or after the person becomes 16 years of age.

(7) For the purposes of the application of the provisions of this Act relating to that order, references in this Act to a child include references to the person until whichever of the following first occurs—
(a) the order is terminated, or
(b) the person becomes 18 years of age.

(8) Subsection (9) applies where a case is remitted to the Principal Reporter under section 49(7)(b) of the Criminal Procedure (Scotland) Act 1995.

(9) For the purposes of the application of this Act to the person whose case is remitted, references in this Act to a child include references to the person until whichever of the following first occurs—
(a) a children's hearing or the sheriff discharges the referral,
(b) a compulsory supervision order made in respect of the person is terminated, or
(c) the person becomes 18 years of age.

Definitions

C.578.1 "compulsory supervision order": ss.202(1) and 83.
"Principal Reporter": s.14 and Sch.2 paras 8–10.

General Note

C.578.2 The age at which a child becomes an adult in Scots law has not changed. Parental responsibilities and rights under ss.1 and 2 of the Children (Scotland) Act 1995 cease when the child becomes 16 (save the responsibility under s.1(2)(b) to provide guidance up to the age of 18).

Referral to a children's hearing can be made up to a child's 16th birthday, but subss.(2) to (9) of this section set out the exceptions to that provision.

Subs.(2)

C.578.3 Where ground for referral 67(2)(o) arises—the child "has failed without reasonable excuse to attend regularly at school"—then the definition of "child" is extended to include the child who has already turned 16 but has not yet reached "school leaving age". An example of this would be where a child turns 16 on or after 1 March in any year, then he or she will remain of "school age" until the "summer leaving date" (the last day in May—see s.33(1) of the Education (Scotland) Act 1980). Similarly, where a child turns 16 on or after 1 October in any year, then he or she will remain of "school age" until the "winter leaving date" (the first day of the Christmas holiday period—s.33(3)(a) and (b) of 1980 Act). This means that a young person may be referred under ground 67(2)(o), but under no other ground for referral, during the period that he or she is 16 years old, but remains of school leaving age, i.e. still on the school roll, until the passing of the relevant school leaving date.

It could happen that, by the time a children's hearing is convened to consider a ground under para.(o), the relevant school leaving date has passed and it may be considered that the circumstances of the young person are such that a compulsory supervision order may be appropriate and necessary. The competence of relying on such circumstances would be a consequence of the reasoning in *O v Rae*, 1993 S.L.T. 570; 1992 S.C.L.R. 318, where Lord President Hope, in response to the father's contention that information considered by the hearing "must be information which was relevant to the grounds of referral" stated that

> "the children's hearing have wide powers of investigation ... they are entitled to ask for and to consider information across a wide range and to obtain the views of various people, including social workers or any safeguarder, as to what would be in the best interest of the child".

This could be taken to mean that, even though the ground for referral relates to school attendance, should other facts emerge in the course of investigations, these other facts can, and should, be considered as part of the hearing process.

However, it is the authors' view that it would not be appropriate to bring a child to a hearing under this ground for referral in order to address issues that would be more appropriately dealt with under any other ground. In his commentary on *O v Rae*, 1992 S.C.L.R. 318 at 325–327, Alan Finlayson, a former senior Reporter, referred, at 326E, to the possibility that Reporters

> "could be tempted to include the minimum of allegations required to establish grounds lest a subsequent children's hearing find themselves restricted in the information they were permitted to take into account when reaching their decision as a result of a finding at a proof",

and commented adversely on such an approach, stating, at 327D:

> "Ideally, grounds for referral and reasons for intervention should give as much fair notice as possible to children and parents as to the matter and extent of the problems which are to be addressed."

Subss.(3) to (5)

C.578.4 These subsections address the situation where, at the time the Reporter receives notification or information under s.66(1)(a)(i) to (vii), the child is under the age of 16, but becomes 16 *after* the s.66 application or *before* "a relevant event". They provide that the person concerned remains a child, and therefore potentially subject to the jurisdiction of a children's hearing, until a "relevant event" takes place, with "relevant event" being defined in subs.(5) as: (a) the making of a compulsory supervision order in relation to the person; (b) the notification of the person under s.68(3) that the question of whether a compulsory supervision order should be made in respect of the person will not be referred to a children's hearing; or (c) the discharge of the referral. This is a welcome change from the 1995 Act where, if a hearing was not held prior to the child becoming 16, the authority to do so was lost. Under this new procedure, the remit of the children's hearing continues until the case is discharged finally.

Meaning of "relevant person"

Subss.(6) and (7)
This retains the previous provision to the effect that, where a compulsory supervision order is in place prior to a child becoming 16 and continues after his or her 16th birthday, the (now) young person will continue to be subject to the provisions of the 2011 Act. A child in this situation is sometimes referred to as a "statutory child", but the authors do not favour this inelegant expression.

Subsection (7)(b) confirms that the provisions of the Act will cease when the person becomes 18 years of age.

Subs.(8)
This subsection sets the procedure that will apply where a person has been charged with an offence and pleads guilty to, or has been found guilty of, the offence, *and* where that person is:
 (a) not the subject of a compulsory supervision order;
 (b) over the age of 16; and
 (c) not within six months of attaining the age of 18.

Where these circumstances apply, the court may remit the case to a children's hearing for disposal. Once a referral has taken place, the case will remain with the children's hearing until:
 (a) it is discharged;
 (b) a compulsory supervision order made in respect of the person is terminated; or
 (c) the person becomes 18 years of age.

Meaning of "relevant person"

200.—(1) In this Act, "relevant person", in relation to a child, means—
 (a) a parent or guardian having parental responsibilities or parental rights in relation to the child under Part 1 of the 1995 Act,
 (b) a person in whom parental responsibilities or parental rights are vested by virtue of section 11(2)(b) of the 1995 Act,
 (c) a person having parental responsibilities or parental rights by virtue of section 11(12) of the 1995 Act,
 (d) a parent having parental responsibility for the child under Part 1 of the Children Act 1989 (c.41) ("the 1989 Act"),
 (e) a person having parental responsibility for the child by virtue of—
  (i) section 12(2) of the 1989 Act,
  (ii) section 14C of the 1989 Act, or
  (iii) section 25(3) of the Adoption and Children Act 2002 (c.38),
 (f) a person in whom parental responsibilities or parental rights are vested by virtue of a permanence order (as defined in section 80(2) of the Adoption and Children (Scotland) Act 2007 (asp 4)),
 (g) any other person specified by order made by the Scottish Ministers.
 (2) For the purposes of subsection (1)(a), a parent does not have parental responsibilities or rights merely by virtue of an order under section 11(2)(d) or (e) of the 1995 Act.
 (3) An order made under subsection (1)(g) is subject to the affirmative procedure.

DEFINITIONS
 "child": s.199.
 "parent": Children (Scotland) Act 1995 s.15(1).
 "affirmative procedure": s.197.

GENERAL NOTE
As commented in the General Note to s.79, the definition of relevant person in this present section does not incorporate that part of s.93(2)(b) and (c) of the Children (Scotland) Act 1995, which states that a relevant person includes "any person who appears to be a person who ordinarily (and other than by reason only of his employment) has charge of, or control over, the child". Some of the implications of this in relation to the decision of the Supreme Court in *Principal Reporter v K* [2010] UKSC 56; 2011 S.C. (U.K.S.C.) 91; 2011 S.L.T. 271; [2011] 1 W.L.R. 18; 2011 H.R.L.R. 8 are discussed in the General Note to s.79 and the reader is referred to that discussion, which was in the context of the "deeming" provisions. The concept of entitlement to relevant person status as a matter of law, as distinct from as a consequence of the

deeming provisions is lucidly discussed in the decision of Sheriff J.M. Scott QC in *W v C*, 2013 Fam. L.R. 73 at [7].

However, for the purposes of this commentary on s.200, the definition of relevant person must be considered in the context of who is entitled to enjoy the status of relevant person as a matter of law, and without resort to the deeming provisions. The concept of entitlement to relevant person status as a matter of law, as distinct from as a consequence of the deeming provisions is lucidly discussed in the decision of Sheriff J.M. Scott QC in *W v C* , 2013 Fam. L.R. 73 at [7]. It will be recalled that in *Principal Reporter v K* in the judgment of Lord Hope and Lady Hale at [69], it was said, in the context of the apparent violation of the unmarried father's right under art.8 of the European Convention:

"The potential for violation could therefore be cured by inserting the words 'or who appears to have established family life with the child with which the decision of a children's hearing may interfere'. This goes very much with, rather than against, the grain of the legislation. The aim of the hearing is to enlist the family in trying to find solutions to the problems facing the child. This is simply widening the range of such people who have an established relationship with the child and, therefore, have something important to contribute to the hearing. Mostly, these will be unmarried fathers, but occasionally it might include others".

It is the view of the authors that the Supreme Court must be regarded as laying down a universal criterion for the definition of "relevant person", not indissolubly linked with the terminology of s.93(2)(b) and (c) of the 1995 Act, quoted above. If it should be argued that the present definition of "relevant person" lacked the words "any person who appears to be a person who ordinarily (and other than by reason only of his employment) has charge of, or control over, the child", which were the words which the Supreme Court added in its formulation, and that, therefore, the Supreme Court's reasoning could not be applied here, we would reply that the words of the Supreme Court's formulation could, without violence and "going very much with" the grain of the Act, be added to any of the categories listed in subss.(a) to (f) and indeed must, by virtue of s.3 of the Human Rights Act 1998, be so added in order to comply with s.3(1) of that Act if a violation of art.8 of the Convention is to be avoided.

Subsections (1)(a) and (d) refer to the term "parent". Section 15(1) of the 1995 Act provides that the term "parent" means "someone, of whatever age, who is that person's genetic father or mother". This general provision is, however, made subject to: Part IV of the Adoption (Scotland) Act 1978; ss.27 to 30 of the Human Fertilisation and Embryology Act 1990; Ch.3 of Part 1 of the Adoption and Children (Scotland) Act 2007 (asp 4); and Part 2 of the Human Fertilisation and Embryology Act 2008 and any regulations made under s.55(1) of the 2008 Act. All of these provisions are precise and detailed and will require to be consulted in individual cases. Part IV, s.39 of the Adoption (Scotland) Act 1978 and Part I, s.40 of the Adoption and Children (Scotland) Act 2007 provide substantially that an adopted child is the child of the adopters and of no-one else and s.28(1) of the 2007 Act provides substantially that an adoption order vests parental responsibilities and rights in the adopters. Consequently, as stated by Lady Hale in *Re P (A Child) (Adoption: Unmarried Couples)* [2008] UKHL 38; [2009] 1 A.C. 173; [2008] 3 W.L.R. 76; 2008 H.R.L.R. 37 at [85]: "It [i.e. adoption] severs, irrevocably and for all time, the legal relationship between the child and her family of birth".

It follows that the birth parents of a child who has been adopted can never be relevant persons as a matter of right. For discussion of the position of biological parents whose child has been adopted as possible deemed relevant persons, see above under s.81(3). Sections 27 to 30 of the Human Fertilisation and Embryology Act 1990 provide substantially that the woman in whom sperm has been artificially implanted and the man who is the source of that sperm are, respectively, the mother and father of the child. Part 2 of the Human Fertilisation and Embryology Act 2008 contains very detailed provisions in relation to the child who is born by artificially assisted reproduction, including provisions to the effect that where such a child is adopted that child becomes the child of the adopters.

It is important to recall here that the Children's Hearings (Scotland) Act 2011 (Review of Contact Directions and Definition of Relevant Person) Order 2013 (SSI 2013/193) art.3, provides that a "parent" of any child, except one falling into the categories listed in s.3(2)(a) and (b), is a relevant person for the purposes of subs.(1)(g) of this section. It should be noted that there is a lack of clarity, or at least grammatical infelicity, in the wording of para.(2) of art.3 in that the words "but, by virtue of an order of court, no longer has them", which appear in para.(2)(a)(ii), are clearly intended to qualify the content of para.(2)(a)(i). This has not been achieved grammatically, but is made clear in the Explanatory Note to the Order, and is, in any event, obvious in order to make sense.

Accordingly, each of the following is a "relevant person", unless parental responsibilities and rights have been removed by order of court:

    1. The genetic mother (Children's Hearings (Scotland) Act 2011 (Review of Contact

Meaning of "relevant local authority"

  Directions and Definition of Relevant Person) Order 2013 (SSI 2013/193) art.2(a)(i) (except where the child is adopted (Adoption and Children (Scotland) Act 2007 ss.28, 29 and 35(2)) or the subject of a permanence order (Adoption and Children (Scotland) Act 2007 ss.80(2) and 87);
 2. The genetic father (Children's Hearings (Scotland) Act 2011 (Review of Contact Directions and Definition of Relevant Person) Order 2013 (SSI 2013/193) art.2(a)(i) (except where the child is adopted (Adoption and Children (Scotland) Act 2007 ss.28, 29 and 35(2)) or the subject of a permanence order (Adoption and Children (Scotland) Act 2007 ss.80(2) and 87);
 3. Any person who appears to have established family life with the child with which the decision of a children's hearing may interfere (see discussion above);
 4. Where the child has been adopted, the adoptive mother (Adoption and Children (Scotland) Act 2007 s.80(2));
 5. Where the child has been adopted, the adoptive father (Adoption and Children (Scotland) Act 2007 s.80(2));
 6. Any parent who has been granted a parental responsibilities and rights order by virtue of the Children (Scotland) Act 1995 s.11(2);
 7. The woman in a same-sex partnership who is the partner of a woman who gave birth by artificial insemination unless she did not consent to her partner being artificially inseminated (Human Fertilisation and Embryology Act 2008 s.42, hereinafter referred to as the "Human Fertilisation Act");
 8. In the case of two women in respect of whom no civil partnership is in place and one gives birth by artificial insemination, then the other woman may be a parent, and therefore a relevant person, provided no man is treated as the father and no woman is treated as the mother of the child (under ss.35 or 42 of the Human Fertilisation Act) and provided the "agreed female parenthood conditions" set out in s.44 of that Act are satisfied (Human Fertilisation Act 2008 s.43);
 9. Where the genetic mother of a child and a parent of the child by virtue of s.4 of the 1995 Act (father) or s.4A of the 1995 Act (female parent by virtue of Human Fertilisation Act s.43, discussed above) the father or, as the case may be, the other woman may agree that they shall each have parental responsibilities and rights—thus acquiring relevant person status;
 10. A man who may be presumed to be the father of a child if married to the mother at any time between the child's conception and the child's birth or has been registered as the child's father;
 11. A man married to a woman who has given birth to a child by artificial insemination by another (i.e. by AID) unless the man did not consent to the artificial insemination (Human Fertilisation Act 2008 s.35);
 12. A man not married to a woman who has given birth by AID, provided the "agreed fatherhood conditions" enacted in s.37 of the Human Fertilisation Act were satisfied (Human Fertilisation Act s.36);
 13. Any two persons who have been granted an order under the Human Fertilisation Act s.54(1). (Such an order is only to be granted where the two persons are married, in a civil partnership, or, not being within the forbidden degrees, are living together in an enduring family relationship);
 14. A person qualifying under the English Acts listed in subss.(d) and (e);
 15. A person qualifying under art.12(2) of the Children (Northern Ireland) Order 1995 (SI 1995/755 (N 12)) (Children's Hearings (Scotland) Act 2011 (Review of Contact Directions and Definition of Relevant Person) Order 2013 (SSI 2013/193) art.2(b)(i)).

The writers gratefully acknowledge the assistance they have derived from Kenneth McK. Norrie, *Children's Hearings in Scotland*, 3rd edn (Edinburgh: W. Green, 2013), paras 2–13 to 2–20 in the preparation of this part of their commentary.

Subs.(2)
This provision must be read with the Children's Hearings (Scotland) Act 2011 (Review of Contact Directions and Definition of Relevant Person) Order 2013 (SSI 2013/193) art.2(a)(i), referred to above.

C.579.3

Meaning of "relevant local authority"

201.—(1) In this Act, "relevant local authority", in relation to a child, means—

(a) the local authority in whose area the child predominantly resides, or
(b) where the child does not predominantly reside in the area of a

C.580

particular local authority, the local authority with whose area the child has the closest connection.

(2) For the purposes of subsection (1)(a), no account is to be taken of—
(a) any period of residence in a residential establishment,
(b) any other period of residence, or residence in any other place, prescribed by the Scottish Ministers by regulations.

(3) For the purposes of subsection (1)(b), no account is to be taken of—
(a) any connection with an area that relates to a period of residence in a residential establishment,
(b) any other connection prescribed by the Scottish Ministers by regulations.

DEFINITIONS

C.580.1 "child": s.199.
"local authority": Local Government etc. (Scotland) Act 1994 s.2.
"residential establishment": s.202(1), as amended by the Children's Hearings (Scotland) Act 2011 (Modification of Primary Legislation) Order 2013 (SSI 2013/211) para.20(21)(a)(i).

GENERAL NOTE

C.580.2 The terms of this section define the concept of "relevant local authority". Much of the importance of this definition stems from the provisions in ss.83(1)(b), 86(1)(b) and 87(2)(b) to the effect that a children's hearing, when making respectively a compulsory supervision order (CSO) or an interim compulsory supervision order (ICSO), require to specify the particular local authority (the "implementation authority") which is to be responsible for giving effect to the measures included in the order concerned. These provisions have to be read along with s.166(1) and (2), which provides that where a duty is imposed on a local authority under these provisions and a local authority which is satisfied that it is not the "relevant local authority" for the child may apply to the sheriff for a review of the decision to specify it as the relevant local authority, with the sheriff having the power, under s.166(6), to determine which local authority is the relevant local authority for the child.

The first part of the definition, "the local authority in whose area the child predominantly resides", has not given rise to any issue which has come to the attention of the courts. However, the second part of the definition,

"where the child does not predominantly reside in the area of a particular local authority, the local authority with whose area the child has the closest connection" has, when read in conjunction with the provision in subs.(3) that "For the purposes of subsection (1)(b), no account is to be taken of—
(a) any connection with an area that relates to a period of residence in a residential establishment",

has given rise to the controversy analysed in *East Renfrewshire Council, Applicants*, decided initially by Sheriff D.O. Sutherland in Inverness on 17 October 2014 and, on appeal, by Sheriff Principal Derek C.W. Pyle on 14 September 2015. We have cited and extensively discussed this case above, in relation to s.166, where we noted that Sheriff Principal Pyle, reversing Sheriff Sutherland, held that what had been called the "stop the clock" principle applied in the interpretation of subs.(3)(a) and that consequently the period spent by the child in England fell to be disregarded, leaving Highland Council as the relevant local authority. The reader is referred to our discussion of the background to this case. The issue of which authority was the relevant local authority for the same child who had been the subject of the proceedings in the *East Renfrewshire Council* case arose again when on 1 March 2016 a children's hearing specified Highland Council as the implementation authority (and therefore as the relevant local authority), for the child. Highland Council applied to the sheriff for review under s.166 of the Act. Sheriff Thomas McCartney, who had been referred to the decision of Sheriff Principal Pyle, referred to above, differed from that decision, and stated at [33] of his (unreported) judgment:

"S. 201(3)(a) provides that no account is to be taken of any connection with an area as described therein. The area of which no account is to be taken is the one that relates to the period of residence in a residential establishment",

and, at [34]:

"My assessment is that s.201(3)(a) does not provide that no account is to be taken of a period of time".

Accordingly the sheriff held that East Renfrewshire Council was the implementation

Interpretation

authority. East Renfrewshire Council appealed to the Sheriff Appeal Court—see *East Renfrewshire Council, Appellant* [2016] SAC (Civ) 14; 2016 G.W.D. 38–679.

Refusing the appeal, the Sheriff Appeal Court stated at [21]

"that Sheriff McCartney is correct to find that what requires to be disregarded is not the 3 years period in the residential establishment in Lancashire but rather 'any connection with an area' and the area is one that 'relates to the period of residence in a residential establishment'. In this appeal that area is Lancashire."

This, being a decision of the Sheriff Appeal Court, and not further appealable (see this Act, s.167(7) when read with s.109(3) of the Courts Reform (Scotland) Act 2014), must be regarded as settling the law on this matter.

Both the Sheriff Appeal Court and Sheriff McCartney agreed with Sheriff Principal Pyle that the welfare principle had no application in interpreting this section.

Interpretation

202.—(1) In this Act, unless the context otherwise requires—

"the 1995 Act" means the Children (Scotland) Act 1995 (c.36),

"affirmative procedure" is to be construed in accordance with section 197,

"CHS" means Children's Hearings Scotland,

"chief social work officer" means the officer appointed under section 3 of the Social Work (Scotland) Act 1968 (c.49) by—
  (a) in relation to a compulsory supervision order or an interim compulsory supervision order, the implementation authority,
  (b) in relation to a medical examination order or a warrant to secure attendance, the relevant local authority for the child to whom the order or warrant relates,

"child assessment order" means an order mentioned in section 35,

"child protection order" means an order mentioned in section 37,

"compulsory supervision order" has the meaning given by section 83,

"contact order" has the meaning given by section 11(2)(d) of the 1995 Act,

"crime" has the meaning given in section 307(1) of the Criminal Procedure (Scotland) Act 1995 (c.46),

"functions" includes powers and duties; and "confer", in relation to functions, includes impose,

"grounds determination" has the meaning given by section 110(1),

"grounds hearing" has the meaning given by section 90,

"implementation authority"—
  (a) in relation to a compulsory supervision order, has the meaning given by section 83(1)(b),
  (b) in relation to an interim compulsory supervision order, has the meaning given by section 86(1)(b),

"interim compulsory supervision order" has the meaning given by section 86,

"interim variation", in relation to a compulsory supervision order, has the meaning given by section 140,

"medical examination order" has the meaning given by section 87,

"movement restriction condition" has the meaning given by section 84,

"negative procedure" is to be construed in accordance with section 196,

"officer of law" has the meaning given by section 307(1) of the Criminal Procedure (Scotland) Act 1995 (c.46),

"parental responsibilities" has the meaning given by section 1(3) of the 1995 Act,

"parental rights" has the meaning given by section 2(4) of the 1995 Act,

"permanence order" has the meaning given by section 80(2) of the Adoption and Children (Scotland) Act 2007 (asp 4),

"place of safety", in relation to a child, means—
  (a) a residential or other establishment provided by a local authority,
  (b) a community home within the meaning of section 53 of the Children Act 1989 (c.41),
  (c) a police station,
  (d) a hospital or surgery, the person or body of persons responsible for the management of which is willing temporarily to receive the child,
  (e) the dwelling-house of a suitable person who is so willing, or
  (f) any other suitable place the occupier of which is so willing,
"pre-hearing panel" has the meaning given by section 79(2)(a),
"prosecutor" has the meaning given by section 307(1) of the Criminal Procedure (Scotland) Act 1995 (c.46),
"residential establishment" means—
  (a) an establishment in Scotland (whether managed by a local authority, a voluntary organisation or any other person) which provides residential accommodation for children for the purposes of this Act, the 1995 Act or the Social Work (Scotland) Act 1968 (c.49),
  (b) a home in England or Wales that is—
    (i) a community home within the meaning of section 53 of the Children Act 1989 (c.41),
    (ii) a voluntary home within the meaning of that Act, or
    (iii) a private children's home within the meaning of that Act, or
[1] (c) an establishment in Northern Ireland that is—
    (i) a private children's home within the meaning of the Children (Northern Ireland) Order 1995 (S.I. 1995/755),
    (ii) an authority home provided under Part VII of that Order, or
    (iii) a voluntary home provided under Part VIII of that Order,
"safeguarder" has the meaning given by section 30(1),
"school age" has the meaning given by section 31 of the Education (Scotland) Act 1980 (c.44),
[2] "secure accommodation" means accommodation provided for the purpose of restricting the liberty of children which—
  (a) in Scotland, is provided in a residential establishment approved in accordance with regulations made under section 78(2) of the Public Services Reform (Scotland) Act 2010 (asp 8),
  (b) in England, is provided in a children's home (within the meaning of the Care Standards Act 2000 (c.14) ("the 2000 Act")) in respect of which a person is registered under Part 2 of that Act, except that before the coming into force of section 107(2) of the Health and Social Care (Community Health Standards) Act 2003 (c.43), "secure accommodation" means accommodation in relation to England which—
    (i) is provided in a children's home (within the meaning of the 2000 Act) in respect of which a person is registered under Part 2 of that Act, and
    (ii) is approved by the Secretary of State for the purpose of restricting the liberty of children,
  (c) in Wales, is provided in a children's home (within the meaning of the 2000 Act) in respect of which a person is registered under Part 2 of that Act,
"secure accommodation authorisation" has the meaning given by section 85,
"statement of grounds" has the meaning given by section 89(3),
"subordinate legislation" means—

Transitional provision etc.

 (a) an order,
 (b) regulations, or
 (c) rules,
"super-affirmative procedure" is to be construed in accordance with section 198,
[4] "supporting facts" has the meaning given by section 90(1D),
"warrant to secure attendance" has the meaning given by section 88, and
"working day" means every day except—
 (a) Saturday and Sunday,
 (b) 25 and 26 December,
 (c) 1 and 2 January.
 (2) References in this Act to a decision of a children's hearing are references to a decision of a majority of the members of a children's hearing.
 [3] (2A) References in this Act to a determination of a pre-hearing panel are references to a determination of a majority of the members of a pre-hearing panel.
 (3) References in this Act to varying a compulsory supervision order, an interim compulsory supervision order or a medical examination order include varying the order by adding or removing measures.

NOTES
1. Substituted by the Children's Hearings (Scotland) Act 2011 (Modification of Primary Legislation) Order 2013 (SSI 2013/211) Sch.1 para.20(21)(a)(i) (effective 24 June 2013).
2. As amended by the Children's Hearings (Scotland) Act 2011 (Modification of Primary Legislation) Order 2013 (SSI 2013/211) Sch.1 para.20(20)(a)(ii) (effective 24 June 2013).
3. Inserted by the Children's Hearings (Scotland) Act 2011 (Modification of Primary Legislation) Order 2013 (SSI 2013/211) Sch.1 para.20(20)(b) (effective 24 June 2013).
4. Inserted by the Children and Young People (Scotland) Act 2014 (asp 8) Sch.5 para.12(9) (effective 26 January 2015).

C581.1

General

Consequential amendments and repeals

 203.—(1) Schedule 5 contains minor amendments and amendments consequential on the provisions of this Act.
 (2) The enactments specified in schedule 6, which include enactments that are spent, are repealed to the extent specified.

C.582

Ancillary provision

 204.—(1) The Scottish Ministers may by order make such supplementary, incidental or consequential provision as they consider appropriate for the purposes of, in consequence of, or for giving full effect to, any provision of this Act.
 (2) An order under subsection (1) may modify any enactment (including this Act).
 (3) An order under this section containing provisions which add to, replace or omit any part of the text of an Act is subject to the affirmative procedure.

C.583

Transitional provision etc.

 205.—(1) The Scottish Ministers may by order make such provision as they consider necessary or expedient for transitory, transitional or saving purposes in connection with the coming into force of any provision of this Act.
 (2) An order under subsection (1) may modify any enactment (including this Act).

C.584

Children's Hearings (Scotland) Act 2011

Short title and commencement

206.—(1) This Act may be cited as the Children's Hearings (Scotland) Act 2011.

(2) The provisions of this Act, other than sections 193 to 202, 204, 205 and this section, come into force on such day as the Scottish Ministers may by order appoint.

(3) An order under subsection (2) may contain transitional, transitory or saving provision in connection with the coming into force of this Act.

GENERAL NOTE

Sections 193 to 202, 204, 205 and this present section were brought into force on 7 January 2011. Section 203 was brought partially in force on 31 January 12 and further partially (but still not completely) brought into force on 24 June 2013. All other sections, except ss.122, 187 and 188 (discussed above under these sections) are in force.

SCHEDULE 1

CHILDREN'S HEARINGS SCOTLAND

(introduced by section 3)

Status

1.—(1) CHS—
   (a) is not a servant or agent of the Crown, and
   (b) does not enjoy any status, immunity or privilege of the Crown.
(2) CHS's property is not property of, or property held on behalf of, the Crown.

Membership

2.—(1) The members of CHS are to be appointed by the Scottish Ministers.
(2) There are to be no fewer than five and no more than eight members.
(3) The Scottish Ministers may by order amend sub-paragraph (2) so as to substitute for the numbers of members for the time being specified there different numbers of members.
(4) A member holds and vacates office on terms and conditions determined by the Scottish Ministers.
(5) The Scottish Ministers may appoint a person to be a member only if satisfied that the person has knowledge and experience relevant to the functions of CHS and the National Convener.
(6) The Scottish Ministers may appoint a person to be a member only if satisfied that the person, after appointment, will have no financial or other interest that is likely to prejudicially affect the performance of the person's functions as a member of CHS.
(7) The Scottish Ministers may reappoint as a member a person who has ceased to be a member.

Persons disqualified from membership

3. A person is disqualified from appointment, and from holding office, as a member if the person is or becomes—
   (a) a member of the House of Commons,
   (b) a member of the Scottish Parliament, or
   (c) a member of the European Parliament.

Resignation of members

4. A member of CHS may resign office by giving notice in writing to the Scottish Ministers.

Removal of members

5.—(1) The Scottish Ministers may revoke the appointment of a member of CHS if—
   (a) the member becomes insolvent,
   (b) the member is incapacitated by physical or mental illness,

Schedule 1

    (c) the member has been absent from meetings of CHS for a period longer than 3 months without the permission of CHS,
    (d) the member is otherwise unfit to be a member or unable for any reason to discharge the functions of a member.
 (2) For the purposes of sub-paragraph (1)(a) a member becomes insolvent when—
    (a) a voluntary arrangement proposed by the member is approved,
    (b) the member is adjudged bankrupt,
    (c) the member's estate is sequestrated,
    (d) the member's application for a debt payment programme is approved under section 2 of the Debt Arrangement and Attachment (Scotland) Act 2002 (asp 17), or
    (e) the member grants a trust deed for creditors.

Remuneration, allowances etc.

6.—(1) CHS must pay to its members—
    (a) such remuneration as the Scottish Ministers may determine, and
    (b) such allowances in respect of expenses properly incurred by members in the performance of their functions as may be so determined.
 (2) CHS must—
    (a) pay to or in respect of any person who is or has been a member of CHS such pension, allowances or gratuities as the Scottish Ministers may determine, or
    (b) make such payments as the Scottish Ministers may determine towards provision for the payment of a pension, allowance or gratuity to or in respect of such a person.
 (3) Sub-paragraph (4) applies where—
    (a) a person ceases to be a member otherwise than on the expiry of the person's term of office, and
    (b) it appears to the Scottish Ministers that there are circumstances which make it right for the person to receive compensation.
 (4) CHS must make a payment to the person of such amount as the Scottish Ministers may determine.

Chairing meetings

7.—(1) The Scottish Ministers must appoint one of the members of CHS to chair meetings of CHS (the "chairing member").
 (2) The chairing member holds and vacates that office on terms and conditions determined by the Scottish Ministers.
 (3) If a person is appointed as the chairing member for a period that extends beyond the period of the person's appointment as a member, the person's appointment as a member is taken to have been extended so that it ends on the same day as the period of appointment as chairing member ends.
 (4) The chairing member may resign that office by giving notice in writing to the Scottish Ministers.
 (5) If the chairing member is for any reason unable to chair a meeting of members, a majority of the members present at the meeting may elect one of those members to chair the meeting.

The National Convener

8.—(1) CHS is, with the approval of the Scottish Ministers, to appoint a person as the National Convener (other than the first National Convener).
 (2) CHS may, with the approval of the Scottish Ministers, reappoint a person as the National Convener.
 (3) CHS must take reasonable steps to involve persons who are under 21 years of age in the process for selection of a person for appointment or reappointment under this paragraph.
 (4) The period for which a person is appointed or reappointed under this paragraph is 5 years.
 (5) A person appointed or reappointed under this paragraph holds and vacates office on terms and conditions determined by CHS and approved by the Scottish Ministers.
 (6) The Scottish Ministers may by regulations prescribe qualifications that must be held by the National Convener.
 (7) A person is disqualified from appointment, and from holding office, as the National Convener if the person is or becomes—
    (a) a member of the House of Commons,
    (b) a member of the Scottish Parliament, or
    (c) a member of the European Parliament.
 (8) The National Convener may appeal to the Scottish Ministers against dismissal by CHS.

(9) CHS is the respondent in an appeal under sub-paragraph (8).
(10) The Scottish Ministers may by regulations make provision about—
   (a) the procedure to be followed in appeals under sub-paragraph (8),
   (b) the effect of making such an appeal,
   (c) the powers of the Scottish Ministers for disposing of such appeals (including powers to make directions about liability for expenses),
   (d) the effect of the exercise of those powers.

Supplementary powers of National Convener

9. The National Convener may do anything that the National Convener considers appropriate for the purposes of or in connection with the functions conferred on the National Convener by virtue of this Act or any other enactment.

Delegation of National Convener's functions

10.—(1) The functions of the National Convener conferred by virtue of this Act or any other enactment (other than the functions mentioned in sub-paragraph (2)) may be carried out on the National Convener's behalf by a person who is—
   (a) authorised (whether specially or generally) by the National Convener for the purpose, or
   (b) a person of a class of person authorised (whether specially or generally) by the National Convener for the purpose.
(2) The functions are—
   (a) the function conferred by paragraph 24,
   (b) functions conferred by paragraph 1(2) to (6) of schedule 2.
(3) The National Convener may not under sub-paragraph (1) authorise the Principal Reporter, SCRA or a local authority to carry out a function on behalf of the National Convener.
(4) The National Convener may not under sub-paragraph (1) authorise a person employed by SCRA or a local authority to carry out the function conferred on the National Convener by section 8.
(5) If under sub-paragraph (1) the National Convener delegates the function conferred on the National Convener by section 8, the National Convener may not delegate any other function to the same person under that sub-paragraph.
(6) Nothing in sub-paragraph (1) prevents the National Convener from carrying out any function delegated under that sub-paragraph.
(7) The Scottish Ministers may by regulations prescribe the qualifications to be held by a person to whom a function, or a function of a class, specified in the regulations is delegated.
(8) A person to whom a function is delegated under sub-paragraph (1) must comply with a direction given to the person by the National Convener about the carrying out of the function.
(9) CHS may pay to a person to whom a function is delegated under sub-paragraph (1) such expenses and allowances as the Scottish Ministers may determine.

Staff

11.—(1) CHS may employ any staff necessary to ensure the carrying out of CHS's functions.
(2) Staff are employed on terms and conditions determined by CHS and approved by the Scottish Ministers.
(3) CHS may—
   (a) pay a pension, allowance or gratuity, including by way of compensation for loss of employment, to or in respect of an eligible person,
   (b) make payments towards the provision of a pension, allowance or gratuity, including by way of compensation for loss of employment, to or in respect of an eligible person,
   (c) provide and maintain schemes (whether contributory or not) for the payment of a pension, allowance or gratuity, including by way of compensation for loss of employment, to or in respect of an eligible person.
(4) CHS may, with the approval of the Scottish Ministers, determine—
   (a) who, of the persons who are or have ceased to be employees of CHS, are to be eligible persons, and
   (b) the amount that may be paid or provided for.
(5) Sub-paragraphs (6) and (7) apply where—
   (a) a person employed by CHS becomes a member of CHS, and
   (b) the person was (because the person was an employee of CHS) a participant in a pension scheme established and administered by CHS for the benefit of its employees.

Schedule 1

(6) CHS may determine that the person's service as a member of CHS is to be treated for the purposes of the scheme as service as an employee of CHS whether or not any benefits are to be payable to or in respect of the person under paragraph 6.

(7) Any discretion which the scheme confers on CHS as to the benefits payable to or in respect of the person is to be exercised only with the approval of the Scottish Ministers.

Area support teams: establishment and membership

12.—[1] (1) The National Convener must establish [...] a committee (to be known as an area support team) for each area that the National Convener designates for the purposes of this paragraph.

(2) An area designated under sub-paragraph (1) is to consist of one or more local authority areas.

[2] (3) The National Convener—
  (a) must keep the designation of areas under sub-paragraph (1) under review, and
  (b) may at any time revoke a designation or make a new one.

[2] (3A) In exercising the powers to make and revoke designations, the National Convener must ensure that at all times each local authority area falls within an area designated under sub-paragraph (1).

[2] (3B) Revocation of a designation under sub-paragraph (1) has the effect of dissolving the area support team established in consequence of the designation.

[2] (3C) Before deciding to make or revoke a designation under sub-paragraph (1), the National Convener must consult each affected local authority.

[2] (3D) In sub-paragraph (3C), "affected local authority" means—
  (a) in the case of making a designation, each local authority whose area falls within the area proposed to be designated,
  (b) in the case of revoking a designation, each constituent authority for the area support team established in consequence of the designation.

[2] (3E) On making or revoking a designation under sub-paragraph (1), the National Convener must notify each local authority which was consulted under sub-paragraph (3C) in relation to the decision to make or revoke the designation.

(4) The National Convener must appoint as members of an area support team—
  (a) one person nominated by each constituent authority (if the authority chooses to make a nomination),
  (b) such other persons nominated by constituent authorities as the National Convener considers appropriate,
  (c) a member of the Children's Panel who lives or works in the area of the area support team, and
  (d) sufficient other persons so that the number of members nominated by a local authority is no more than one third of the total number of members.

(5) An area support team may not include the Principal Reporter or a member or employee of SCRA.

(6) An area support team may establish sub-committees consisting of persons who are members of the area support team.

(7) In this paragraph and paragraphs 13 and 14 "constituent authority", in relation to an area support team (or a proposed area support team), means a local authority whose area falls within the area of the area support team.

NOTE
1. As amended by the Children and Young People (Scotland) Act 2014 (asp 8) Pt 16 s.88(2) (effective January 26, 2015).
2. Substituted by the Children and Young People (Scotland) Act 2014 (asp 8) Pt 16 s.88(2) (effective January 26, 2015).

Transfer of members from CPACs

13.—[1] (1) This paragraph applies where—
  (a) the National Convener establishes an area support team under paragraph 12(1), and
  (b) the area of the area support team consists of or includes a new area.

(2) The National Convener must notify each relevant CPAC member of the National Convener's intention to transfer the member to the area support team.

(3) A notice under sub-paragraph (2) must state that the relevant CPAC member will become a member of the area support team unless the member notifies the National Convener within 28

days of receiving the notice that the person does not wish to become a member of the area support team.

(4) A relevant CPAC member is a person who—
[1] (a) at the time of the establishment of the area support team, is a member of a Children's Panel Advisory Committee whose area falls wholly within the new area concerned, and
(b) was nominated as such by the Scottish Ministers (or, as the case may be, by the Secretary of State) under paragraph 3 or 4(a) of Schedule 1 to the 1995 Act.

(5) The National Convener must appoint each relevant CPAC member as a member of the area support team unless the member notifies the National Convener in accordance with sub-paragraph (3).

(6) On appointment as a member of the area support team under sub-paragraph (5), a relevant CPAC member ceases to be a member of the Children's Panel Advisory Committee.

(7) In this paragraph—
"area", in relation to a Children's Panel Advisory Committee, means the area of the local authority (or authorities) which formed the Children's Panel Advisory Committee,
"Children's Panel Advisory Committee" includes a joint advisory committee within the meaning of paragraph 8 of Schedule 1 to the 1995 Act,
[2] "new area" means an area which has never previously been the area (or part of the area) of an area support team.

NOTES
1. As amended by the Children and Young People (Scotland) Act 2014 (asp 8) Pt 16 s.88(2)(b) (effective January 26, 2015).
2. Inserted by the Children and Young People (Scotland) Act 2014 (asp 8) Pt 16 s.88(2)(b) (effective January 26, 2015).

Area support teams: functions

14.—(1) An area support team is to carry out for its area the functions conferred on the National Convener by section 6.

(2) The National Convener may delegate to an area support team to carry out for its area—
(a) a function conferred on the National Convener by paragraph 1(1) of schedule 2,
(b) other functions of the National Convener specified for the purpose by the National Convener.

(3) The National Convener may not specify for the purpose of sub-paragraph (2)(b) the functions conferred on the National Convener by section 8.

(4) Before delegating a function under sub-paragraph (2) to be carried out by an area support team the National Convener must consult each constituent authority.

(5) A function to be carried out by an area support team by virtue of sub-paragraph (1) or (2) may not be delegated by the area support team to a person who is not a member of the area support team.

(6) Nothing in sub-paragraph (1) or (2) prevents the National Convener from carrying out any function mentioned in those sub-paragraphs.

(7) An area support team must comply with a direction given to it by the National Convener about—
(a) the carrying out of the functions mentioned in sub-paragraph (1),
(b) the carrying out of a function delegated to it under sub-paragraph (2).

(8) Before giving a direction to an area support team as mentioned in sub-paragraph (7) the National Convener must consult each constituent authority.

[1] (9) A constituent authority must provide an area support team with such administrative support as the National Convener considers appropriate.

[1] (10) In sub-paragraph (9), "administrative support" means staff, property or other services which the National Convener considers are required to facilitate the carrying out by an area support team of its functions.

NOTE
1. Inserted by the Children and Young People (Scotland) Act 2014 (asp 8) Pt 16 s.89(2) (effective January 26, 2015).

Committees

15.—(1) CHS may establish committees.
(2) The members of committees may include persons who are not members of CHS.

Schedule 1

(3) A committee must not consist entirely of persons who are not members of CHS.

(4) CHS must pay to a person who is not a member of CHS and who is appointed to a committee such remuneration and allowances as CHS may, with the approval of the Scottish Ministers, determine.

(5) A committee must comply with any directions given to it by CHS.

(6) In this paragraph, only sub-paragraph (4) applies in relation to area support teams.

CHS's supplementary powers

16.—(1) CHS may do anything that it considers appropriate for the purposes of or in connection with its functions.

(2) CHS may in particular—
  (a) acquire and dispose of land and other property,
  (b) enter into contracts,
  (c) carry out research relating to the functions conferred on it by virtue of this Act or any other enactment,
  (d) publish, or assist in the publication of, materials relating to those functions,
  (e) promote, or assist in the promotion of, publicity relating to those functions.

Procedure

17.—(1) CHS may determine—
  (a) its own procedure (including quorum), and
  (b) the procedure (including quorum) of any of its committees.

(2) An area support team may determine—
  (a) its own procedure (including quorum), and
  (b) the procedure (including quorum) of any of its sub-committees.

Delegation of CHS's functions

18.—(1) Any function of CHS (whether conferred by virtue of this Act or any other enactment) may be carried out on its behalf by—
  (a) a member of CHS,
  (b) a committee of CHS, or
  (c) a person employed by CHS.

(2) Nothing in sub-paragraph (1) prevents CHS from carrying out any function delegated under that sub-paragraph.

Financial interests

19.—(1) The Scottish Ministers must from time to time satisfy themselves that the members of CHS have no financial or other interest that is likely to prejudicially affect the performance of their functions as members of CHS.

(2) A member must comply with a requirement of the Scottish Ministers to give them any information that the Scottish Ministers consider necessary to enable them to comply with sub-paragraph (1).

Grants

20.—(1) The Scottish Ministers may make grants to CHS of amounts that they determine.

(2) A grant is made subject to any conditions specified by the Scottish Ministers (including conditions about repayment).

Accounts

21.—(1) CHS must—
  (a) keep proper accounts and accounting records,
  (b) prepare for each financial year a statement of accounts, and
  (c) send a copy of each statement of accounts to the Scottish Ministers by such time as they may direct.

(2) Each statement of accounts must comply with any directions given by the Scottish Ministers as to—
  (a) the information to be contained in it,
  (b) the manner in which the information is to be presented,
  (c) the methods and principles according to which the statement is to be prepared.

(3) The Scottish Ministers must send a copy of each statement of accounts to the Auditor General for Scotland for auditing.
(4) In this paragraph, "financial year" means—
  (a) the period beginning on the date on which CHS is established and ending—
    (i) on 31 March next occurring, or
    (ii) if that period is of less than 6 months' duration, on 31 March next occurring after that, and
  (b) each subsequent period of a year ending on 31 March.

Provision of accounts and other information to Scottish Ministers

22.—(1) The Scottish Ministers may direct CHS to give them accounts or other information specified in the direction relating to CHS's property and activities or proposed activities.
(2) CHS must—
  (a) give the Scottish Ministers accounts or any other information that it is directed to give under sub-paragraph (1),
  (b) give the Scottish Ministers facilities for the verification of the information given,
  (c) permit any person authorised by the Scottish Ministers to inspect and make copies of accounts and any other documents of CHS for the purposes of verifying the information given, and
  (d) give the person an explanation, reasonably required by the person, of anything that the person is entitled to inspect.

CHS's annual report

23.—(1) CHS must, as soon as is reasonably practicable after the end of each financial year, prepare and submit to the Scottish Ministers a report on the carrying out of its functions during the year.
(2) The report must include a copy of so much of the report made to CHS by the National Convener as relates to the year.
(3) CHS may include in the report any other information that it considers appropriate.
(4) The Scottish Ministers must lay before the Scottish Parliament each report submitted to them.
(5) In this paragraph, "financial year" means—
  (a) the period beginning on the date on which CHS is established and ending—
    (i) on 31 March next occurring, or
    (ii) if that period is of less than 6 months' duration, on 31 March next occurring after that, and
  (b) each subsequent period of a year ending on 31 March.

National Convener's annual report

24.—(1) The National Convener must, as soon as is reasonably practicable after the end of each financial year, prepare and submit to CHS a report on the carrying out during the year of the functions conferred on the National Convener by virtue of this Act or any other enactment.
(2) The National Convener may include in the report any other information that the National Convener considers appropriate.
(3) In this paragraph, "financial year" means—
  (a) the period beginning with the appointment of the first National Convener and ending—
    (i) on 31 March next occurring, or
    (ii) if that period is of less than 6 months' duration, on 31 March next occurring after that, and
  (b) each subsequent period of a year ending on 31 March.

Validity of proceedings and actions

25. The validity of proceedings or actions of CHS (including proceedings or actions of any of its committees) is not affected by—
  (a) any vacancy in the membership of CHS or any of its committees,
  (b) any defect in the appointment of a member of CHS or any of its committees, or
  (c) the disqualification of a person as a member of CHS after appointment.

Schedule 2

SCHEDULE 2

THE CHILDREN'S PANEL

(introduced by section 4)

Recruitment and tenure of panel members

1.—(1) The National Convener may make arrangements for the recruitment of persons as members of the Children's Panel (a person appointed as a member being referred to in this schedule as a "panel member").

(2) It is for the National Convener to appoint persons as panel members from those recruited under sub-paragraph (1).

(3) The National Convener must reappoint as a panel member a person whose appointment has ceased unless—
 (a) the person declines to be reappointed, or
 (b) the National Convener is satisfied that sub-paragraph (4) applies.

(4) This sub-paragraph applies if the person is unfit to be a panel member by reason of—
 (a) inability,
 (b) conduct, or
 (c) failure without reasonable excuse to comply with any training requirements imposed by the National Convener.

(5) The period for which a person is appointed or reappointed as a panel member is 3 years.

(6) The National Convener may, with the consent of the Lord President of the Court of Session, remove a panel member during the period mentioned in sub-paragraph (5) if satisfied that sub-paragraph (4) applies.

List of panel members

2.—(1) The National Convener must publish a list setting out in relation to each panel member—
 (a) the member's name,
 (b) the local authority area in which the member resides, and
 (c) if the member works, the local authority area in which the member works.

(2) The National Convener must make the list available for public inspection.

Training

3.—(1) The National Convener may train, or make arrangements for the training of, panel members and potential panel members.

(2) The National Convener must take reasonable steps to involve persons who are under 25 years of age and in respect of whom a children's hearing has been held in the development and delivery of training under sub-paragraph (1).

(3) The National Convener must, in training (or making arrangements for the training of) panel members under sub-paragraph (1), have regard to the need to provide training on how panel members may best elicit the views of a child to whom a children's hearing relates.

(4) The National Convener may monitor the performance of panel members.

Allowances

4.—(1) The National Convener may, with the approval of the Scottish Ministers, determine the allowances to be paid to—
 (a) panel members,
 (b) potential panel members.

(2) Different determinations may be made for different cases or different classes of case.

(3) The National Convener may pay to panel members and potential panel members allowances determined under sub-paragraph (1).

Children's Hearings (Scotland) Act 2011

SCHEDULE 3

THE SCOTTISH CHILDREN'S REPORTER ADMINISTRATION

(introduced by section 16)

Status

1.—(1) SCRA—
   (a) is not a servant or agent of the Crown, and
   (b) does not enjoy any status, immunity or privilege of the Crown.
(2) SCRA's property is not property of, or property held on behalf of, the Crown.

Membership

2.—(1) The members of SCRA are to be appointed by the Scottish Ministers.
(2) There are to be no fewer than five and no more than eight members.
(3) The Scottish Ministers may by order amend sub-paragraph (2) so as to substitute for the numbers of members for the time being specified there different numbers of members.
(4) A member holds and vacates office on terms and conditions determined by the Scottish Ministers.
(5) The Scottish Ministers may appoint a person to be a member only if satisfied that the person has knowledge or experience relevant to the functions of SCRA and the Principal Reporter.
(6) The Scottish Ministers may appoint a person to be a member only if satisfied that the person, after appointment, will have no financial or other interest that is likely to prejudicially affect the performance of the person's functions as a member of SCRA.
(7) The Scottish Ministers may reappoint as a member a person who has ceased to be a member.

Persons disqualified from membership

3. A person is disqualified from appointment, and from holding office, as a member if the person is or becomes—
   (a) a member of the House of Commons,
   (b) a member of the Scottish Parliament, or
   (c) a member of the European Parliament.

Resignation of members

4. A member of SCRA may resign office by giving notice in writing to the Scottish Ministers.

Removal of members

5.—(1) The Scottish Ministers may revoke the appointment of a member of SCRA if—
   (a) the member becomes insolvent,
   (b) the member is incapacitated by physical or mental illness,
   (c) the member has been absent from meetings of SCRA for a period longer than 3 months without the permission of SCRA,
   (d) the member is otherwise unfit to be a member or unable for any reason to discharge the functions of a member.
(2) For the purposes of sub-paragraph (1)(a) a member becomes insolvent when—
   (a) a voluntary arrangement proposed by the member is approved,
   (b) the member is adjudged bankrupt,
   (c) the member's estate is sequestrated,
   (d) the member's application for a debt payment programme is approved under section 2 of the Debt Arrangement and Attachment (Scotland) Act 2002 (asp 17), or
   (e) the member grants a trust deed for creditors.

Remuneration, allowances etc.

6.—(1) SCRA must pay to its members—
   (a) such remuneration as the Scottish Ministers may determine, and
   (b) such allowances in respect of expenses properly incurred by members in the performance of their functions as may be so determined.

Schedule 3

(2) SCRA must—
(a) pay to or in respect of any person who is or has been a member of SCRA such pension, allowances or gratuities as the Scottish Ministers may determine, or
(b) make such payments as the Scottish Ministers may determine towards provision for the payment of a pension, allowance or gratuity to or in respect of such a person.

(3) Sub-paragraph (4) applies where—
(a) a person ceases to be a member otherwise than on the expiry of the person's term of office, and
(b) it appears to the Scottish Ministers that there are circumstances which make it right for the person to receive compensation.

(4) SCRA must make a payment to the person of such amount as the Scottish Ministers may determine.

Chairing meetings

7.—(1) The Scottish Ministers must appoint one of the members of SCRA to chair meetings of SCRA (the "chairing member").

(2) The chairing member holds and vacates that office on terms and conditions determined by the Scottish Ministers.

(3) If a person is appointed as the chairing member for a period that extends beyond the period of the person's appointment as a member, the person's appointment as a member is taken to have been extended so that it ends on the same day as the period of appointment as chairing member ends.

(4) The chairing member may resign that office by giving notice in writing to the Scottish Ministers.

(5) If the chairing member is for any reason unable to chair a meeting of members, a majority of the members present at the meeting may elect one of those members to chair the meeting.

The Principal Reporter

8.—(1) The Principal Reporter is to be appointed by SCRA with the approval of the Scottish Ministers.

(2) SCRA must take reasonable steps to involve persons who are under 21 years of age in the process for selection of a person for appointment under sub-paragraph (1).

(3) The Principal Reporter holds and vacates that office on terms and conditions determined by SCRA and approved by the Scottish Ministers.

(4) The Scottish Ministers may by regulations prescribe qualifications that must be held by the Principal Reporter.

(5) A person is disqualified from appointment, and from holding office, as the Principal Reporter if the person is or becomes—
(a) a member of the House of Commons,
(b) a member of the Scottish Parliament, or
(c) a member of the European Parliament.

(6) The Principal Reporter may appeal to the Scottish Ministers against dismissal by SCRA.

(7) SCRA is the respondent in an appeal under sub-paragraph (6).

(8) The Scottish Ministers may by regulations make provision about—
(a) the procedure to be followed in appeals under sub-paragraph (6),
(b) the effect of making such an appeal,
(c) the powers of the Scottish Ministers for disposing of such appeals (including powers to make directions about liability for expenses),
(d) the effect of the exercise of those powers.

(9) Nothing in this paragraph affects any appointment in force on the commencement of this paragraph.

Supplementary powers of Principal Reporter

9. The Principal Reporter may do anything that the Principal Reporter considers appropriate for the purposes of or in connection with the functions conferred on the Principal Reporter by virtue of this Act or any other enactment.

Delegation of Principal Reporter's functions

10.—(1) The functions of the Principal Reporter conferred by virtue of this Act or any other enactment (other than the duty imposed by paragraph 22) may be carried out on the Principal Reporter's behalf by a person employed by SCRA who is—

Children's Hearings (Scotland) Act 2011

(a) authorised (whether specially or generally) by the Principal Reporter for the purpose, or

(b) a member of a class of person authorised (whether specially or generally) by the Principal Reporter for the purpose.

(2) Nothing in sub-paragraph (1) prevents the Principal Reporter from carrying out any function delegated under that sub-paragraph.

(3) The Scottish Ministers may by regulations prescribe the qualifications to be held by a person employed by SCRA to whom a function, or a function of a class, specified in the regulations is delegated.

(4) A function of the Principal Reporter may not be delegated to a person who is employed by both SCRA and a local authority unless SCRA consents to the delegation.

(5) The Principal Reporter may give directions about the carrying out of a delegated function.

(6) The persons to whom the function is delegated must comply with the direction.

Staff

11.—(1) SCRA may employ any staff necessary to ensure the carrying out of SCRA's functions.

(2) Staff are employed on terms and conditions determined by SCRA and approved by the Scottish Ministers.

(3) SCRA may—
  (a) pay a pension, allowance or gratuity, including by way of compensation for loss of employment, to or in respect of an eligible person,
  (b) make payments towards the provision of a pension, allowance or gratuity, including by way of compensation for loss of employment, to or in respect of an eligible person,
  (c) provide and maintain schemes (whether contributory or not) for the payment of a pension, allowance or gratuity, including by way of compensation for loss of employment, to or in respect of an eligible person.

(4) SCRA may, with the approval of the Scottish Ministers, determine—
  (a) who, of the persons who are or have ceased to be employees of SCRA, are to be eligible persons, and
  (b) the amount that may be paid or provided for.

(5) Sub-paragraphs (6) and (7) apply where—
  (a) a person employed by SCRA becomes a member of SCRA, and
  (b) the person was (because the person was an employee of SCRA) a participant in a pension scheme established and administered by SCRA for the benefit of its employees.

(6) SCRA may determine that the person's service as a member of SCRA is to be treated for the purposes of the scheme as service as an employee of SCRA whether or not any benefits are to be payable to or in respect of the person under paragraph 6.

(7) Any discretion which the scheme confers on SCRA as to the benefits payable to or in respect of the person is to be exercised only with the approval of the Scottish Ministers.

Appeals against dismissal

12.—(1) A person employed by SCRA who is of a description or class specified in regulations made by the Scottish Ministers may appeal to the Scottish Ministers against dismissal by SCRA.

(2) SCRA is the respondent in an appeal under this paragraph.

(3) Regulations under sub-paragraph (1) may make provision about—
  (a) the procedure for appeals under this paragraph,
  (b) the effect of making such an appeal,
  (c) the powers of the Scottish Ministers to dispose of such appeals (including powers to make directions about liability for expenses),
  (d) the effect of the exercise of those powers.

Committees

13.—(1) SCRA may establish committees.

(2) The members of committees may include persons who are not members of SCRA.

(3) A committee must not consist entirely of persons who are not members of SCRA.

(4) SCRA must pay to a person who is not a member of SCRA and who is appointed to a committee such remuneration and allowances as SCRA may, with the approval of the Scottish Ministers, determine.

(5) A committee must comply with any directions given to it by SCRA.

Schedule 3

SCRA's supplementary powers

14.—(1) SCRA may do anything that it considers appropriate for the purposes of or in connection with its functions.
(2) SCRA may in particular—
  (a) acquire and dispose of land and other property,
  (b) enter into contracts,
  (c) carry out research relating to the functions conferred on it by virtue of this Act or any other enactment,
  (d) publish, or assist in the publication of, materials relating to those functions,
  (e) promote, or assist in the promotion of, publicity relating to those functions.

Procedure

15. SCRA may determine—
  (a) its own procedure (including quorum), and
  (b) the procedure (including quorum) of any of its committees.

Delegation of SCRA's functions

16.—(1) Any function of SCRA (whether conferred by virtue of this Act or any other enactment) may be carried out on its behalf by—
  (a) a member of SCRA,
  (b) a committee of SCRA,
  (c) a person employed by SCRA,
  (d) any other person authorised (whether specially or generally) by it for the purpose.
(2) Nothing in sub-paragraph (1) prevents SCRA from carrying out any function delegated under that sub-paragraph.

Financial interests

17.—(1) The Scottish Ministers must from time to time satisfy themselves that the members of SCRA have no financial or other interest that is likely to prejudicially affect the performance of their functions as members of SCRA.
(2) A member must comply with a requirement of the Scottish Ministers to give them any information that the Scottish Ministers consider necessary to enable them to comply with sub-paragraph (1).

Grants

18.—(1) The Scottish Ministers may make grants to SCRA of amounts that they determine.
(2) A grant is made subject to any conditions specified by the Scottish Ministers (including conditions about repayment).

Accounts

19.—(1) SCRA must—
  (a) keep proper accounts and accounting records,
  (b) prepare for each financial year a statement of accounts, and
  (c) send a copy of each statement of accounts to the Scottish Ministers by such time as they may direct.
(2) Each statement of accounts must comply with any directions given by the Scottish Ministers as to—
  (a) the information to be contained in it,
  (b) the manner in which the information is to be presented,
  (c) the methods and principles according to which the statement is to be prepared.
(3) The Scottish Ministers must send a copy of each statement of accounts to the Auditor General for Scotland for auditing.
(4) In this paragraph, "financial year" means each period of a year ending on 31 March.

Provision of accounts and other information to Scottish Ministers

20.—(1) The Scottish Ministers may direct SCRA to give them accounts or other information specified in the direction relating to SCRA's property and activities or proposed activities.
(2) SCRA must—
  (a) give the Scottish Ministers accounts or any other information that it is directed to give under sub-paragraph (1),

(b) give the Scottish Ministers facilities for the verification of the information given,
(c) permit any person authorised by the Scottish Ministers to inspect and make copies of accounts and any other documents of SCRA for the purposes of verifying the information given, and
(d) give the person an explanation, reasonably required by the person, of anything that the person is entitled to inspect.

SCRA's annual report

21.—(1) SCRA must, as soon as is reasonably practicable after the end of each financial year, prepare and submit to the Scottish Ministers a report on the carrying out of its functions during the year.

(2) The report must include a copy of so much of the report made to SCRA by the Principal Reporter as relates to the year.

(3) SCRA may include in the report any other information that it considers appropriate.

(4) The Scottish Ministers must lay before the Scottish Parliament each report submitted to them.

(5) In this section, "financial year" means each period of a year ending on 31 March.

Principal Reporter's annual report

22.—(1) The Principal Reporter must, as soon as is reasonably practicable after the end of each financial year, prepare and submit to SCRA a report on the carrying out during the year of the functions conferred on the Principal Reporter by virtue of this Act or any other enactment.

(2) The Principal Reporter may include in the report any other information that the Principal Reporter considers appropriate.

(3) In this paragraph, "financial year" means each period of a year ending on 31 March.

Validity of proceedings and actions

23. The validity of proceedings or actions of SCRA (including proceedings or actions of any of its committees) is not affected by—
(a) any vacancy in the membership of SCRA or any of its committees,
(b) any defect in the appointment of a member of SCRA or any of its committees, or
(c) the disqualification of a person as a member of SCRA after appointment.

SCHEDULE 4

TRANSFER OF STAFF AND PROPERTY TO CHS

(introduced by section 24)

Interpretation

1. In this schedule—
"recognised" has the meaning given by section 178(3) of the Trade Union and Labour Relations (Consolidation) Act 1992 (c.52),
"trade union" has the meaning given by section 1 of that Act, and
"transfer day", in relation to a person, means the day on which a staff transfer order comes into force in relation to the person.

Staff transfer orders

2.—(1) The Scottish Ministers may by order (a "staff transfer order") make provision for or in connection with—
(a) the transfer of persons employed by SCRA to CHS,
(b) the transfer of persons employed by local authorities from authorities to CHS.

(2) A staff transfer order may in particular—
(a) prescribe rules by which the transfer of persons, or classes of person, specified in the order can be determined,
(b) require—
(i) in relation to persons employed by SCRA, SCRA and CHS acting jointly, or
(ii) in relation to persons employed by a local authority specified in the order, the local authority and CHS acting jointly,
to make a scheme in relation to the transfer of the persons to whom the order relates.

Schedule 4

(3) Sub-paragraphs (4) and (5) apply where—
   (a) an order includes a requirement of the sort mentioned in sub-paragraph (2)(b)(i) and SCRA and CHS are unable to comply with the requirement, or
   (b) an order includes a requirement of the sort mentioned in sub-paragraph (2)(b)(ii) and the local authority and CHS are unable to comply with the requirement.

(4) The Scottish Ministers may determine the content of the scheme.

(5) The scheme is to be treated as if made in accordance with the requirement imposed by the order.

Schemes for transfer of staff: consultation

3.—(1) Sub-paragraph (2) applies where a staff transfer order includes a requirement of the type mentioned in paragraph 2(2)(b)(i).

(2) SCRA must consult the persons mentioned in sub-paragraph (3) about the content of the scheme.

(3) Those persons are—
   (a) persons employed by SCRA,
   (b) the Principal Reporter,
   (c) representatives of any trade union recognised by SCRA.

(4) Sub-paragraph (5) applies where a staff transfer order includes a requirement of the type mentioned in paragraph 2(2)(b)(ii).

(5) The local authority must consult the persons mentioned in sub-paragraph (6) about the content of the scheme.

(6) Those persons are—
   (a) persons employed by the local authority,
   (b) representatives of any trade union recognised by the local authority.

Effect on existing contracts of employment

4.—(1) This paragraph applies where—
   (a) a person is to be transferred by virtue of a staff transfer order, and
   (b) immediately before the transfer day the person has a contract of employment with the relevant employer.

(2) On and after the transfer day the contract of employment has effect as if originally made between the person and CHS.

(3) On the transfer day the rights, powers, duties and liabilities of the relevant employer under or in connection with the contract of employment of the person are transferred to CHS.

(4) Anything done before the transfer day by or in relation to the relevant employer in respect of the contract of employment or the person is to be treated on and after that day as having been done by or in relation to CHS.

(5) If, before the transfer day, the person gives notice to CHS or the relevant employer that the person objects to becoming a member of staff of CHS—
   (a) the contract of employment with the relevant employer is, on the day immediately preceding the day that would, but for the objection, have been the transfer day, terminated, and
   (b) the person is not to be treated (whether for the purpose of any enactment or otherwise) as having been dismissed by virtue of the giving of such notice.

(6) Nothing in this schedule prejudices any right of the person to terminate the contract of employment if a substantial detrimental change in the person's working conditions is made.

(7) The person has the right to terminate the contract of employment if—
   (a) the identity of the relevant employer changes by virtue of the making of the staff transfer order, and
   (b) it is shown that, in all the circumstances, the change is significant and detrimental to the person.

(8) In this paragraph "relevant employer", in relation to a person, means—
   (a) where the person has a contract of employment with SCRA, SCRA,
   (b) where the person has a contract of employment with a local authority, the local authority.

Transfer of property etc. to CHS

5.—(1) The Scottish Ministers may make a transfer scheme.

(2) A transfer scheme is a scheme making provision for or in connection with the transfer to CHS of property, rights, liabilities and obligations of any of the following—
   (a) SCRA,

(b) a local authority,
(c) the Scottish Ministers.

(3) A transfer scheme must specify a date (the "transfer date") on which the transfer is to take effect.

(4) A transfer scheme may—
   (a) specify different dates in relation to different property, rights, liabilities and obligations,
   (b) make different provision in relation to different cases or classes of case.

(5) On the transfer date—
   (a) any property or rights to which a transfer scheme applies transfer to and vest in CHS,
   (b) any liabilities or obligations to which such a scheme applies become liabilities or obligations of CHS.

(6) A transfer scheme may make provision for the creation of rights, or the imposition of liabilities, in relation to the property, rights, liabilities or obligations transferred by virtue of the scheme.

(7) A certificate issued by the Scottish Ministers that any property, right, liability or obligation has, or has not, been transferred by virtue of a transfer scheme is conclusive evidence of the transfer or the fact that there has not been a transfer.

(8) A transfer scheme may in particular make provision about the continuation of legal proceedings.

(9) A transfer scheme may make provision for CHS to make any payment which—
   (a) before a day specified in the scheme could have been made by a person specified in sub-paragraph (2)(a) or (b), but
   (b) is not a liability which can become a liability of CHS by virtue of a transfer scheme.

(10) A transfer scheme may make provision for the payment by CHS of compensation in respect of property and rights transferred by virtue of the scheme.

(11) Before making a transfer scheme, the Scottish Ministers must consult—
   (a) CHS,
   (b) the person mentioned in sub-paragraph (2)(a) or (b) whose property, rights, liabilities and obligations (or any of them) are to be transferred by virtue of the scheme, and
   (c) any other person with an interest in the property, rights, liabilities or obligations which are to be so transferred.

SCHEDULE 5

MINOR AND CONSEQUENTIAL AMENDMENTS

(introduced by section 203(1))

Legal Aid (Scotland) Act 1986 (c.47)

1.—(1) The Legal Aid (Scotland) Act 1986 is amended as follows.

(2) In section 4 (Scottish Legal Aid Fund)—
   (a) in subsection (2)—
      (i) in paragraph (aza), after sub-paragraph (ii) insert—
         "(iia) children's legal assistance;", and
      (ii) after paragraph (aza) insert—
         "(azb) any sums payable by the Board under contracts made by virtue of section 33B;", and
   (b) in subsection (3), after paragraph (cb) insert—
      "(cc) any contribution payable to the Board by any person in pursuance of section 28K of this Act;".

(3) In section 4A (Scottish Legal Aid Board's power to make grants in respect of provision of civil legal aid etc.)—
   (a) in subsection (2)—
      (i) in paragraph (a) for the words from "aid" to "matters" substitute "aid, advice and assistance in relation to civil matters or children's legal assistance",
      (ii) in paragraph (b) after "matters" insert "or children's matters", and
      (iii) in paragraph (c) at the end add "or children's matters",
   (b) in subsection (13)—
      (i) for the words "aid or advice and assistance" substitute "aid, advice and assistance or children's legal aid", and
      (ii) at the end add "or children's legal aid", and
   (c) in subsection (14), at the end add "and
      "children's matters" means matters relating to children's hearings, pre-hearing

Schedule 5

panels (as defined in section 79(2)(a) of the 2011 Act) or proceedings under Part 10 or 15 of the 2011 Act".

(4) In subsection (1A) of section 31 (selection of solicitors and counsel)—
  (a) after paragraph (a), insert—
    "(aa) section 28M(3),",
  (b) after paragraph (d), insert—
    "(da) regulations made under section 33B(4),", and
  (c) in the full-out, after "assistance" insert "or children's legal assistance".

(5) In section 35A (Board's powers to obtain information from solicitors in certain cases)—
  (a) after subsection (1) insert—
    "(1A) The Board may, for the purpose of determining whether—
      (a) a solicitor, an employee of the solicitor or an employee of the solicitor's firm may be committing a criminal offence in connection with children's legal assistance,
      (b) a solicitor may be seeking, in relation to children's legal assistance, to recover from the Fund money to which the solicitor is not entitled, as, for example, by performing unnecessary work, or
      (c) a solicitor or firm whose name appears on the register maintained under section 28M(1) is or may not be complying with the code of practice under section 28N for the time being in force,
    require the solicitor or firm to produce such information and documents relating wholly or partly to the provision of children's legal assistance as it may specify, at such time and place as it may specify.", and
  (b) in subsection (2), after "(1)" insert "or (1A)".

(6) In section 35B (Board's powers of entry)—
  (a) in subsection (1), after paragraph (c) insert "or
    (ca) a solicitor whose name appears on the register maintained under section 28M(1) may not be complying with the code of practice under section 28N for the time being in force;",
  (b) in subsection (2)—
    (i) in paragraph (b), at the beginning insert "in the case mentioned in subsection (2A),", and
    (ii) after paragraph (b) insert—
      "(ba) in the case mentioned in subsection (2B), take possession of any documents which appear to him to relate, wholly or partly, to any children's legal assistance provided in or from those premises;", and
  (c) after subsection (2) insert—
    "(2A) The case mentioned in subsection (2)(b) is where the warrant is issued in pursuance of—
      (a) paragraph (a), (b) or (c) of subsection (1), or
      (b) paragraph (d) of subsection (1) where the requirement to produce the documents was made under subsection (1) of section 35A.
    (2B) The case mentioned in subsection (2)(ba) is where the warrant is issued in pursuance of—
      (a) paragraph (ca) of subsection (1), or
      (b) paragraph (d) of subsection (1) where the requirement to produce the documents was made under subsection (1A) of section 35A.".

(7) In section 37(2) (regulations under Act which require to be laid in draft and approved by the Scottish Parliament before being made), after "24(4)" insert ", 28C(3), 28K(2), 28L(1) or (8),".

(8) In section 41 (interpretation)—
  (a) after "requires—" insert—
    ""the 2011 Act" means the Children's Hearings (Scotland) Act 2011 (asp 1);",
  (b) after the definition of "the Board" insert—
    ""children's legal aid" has the meaning given to it in section 28B(2) of this Act;
    "children's legal assistance" means—
      (a) children's legal aid, and
      (b) advice and assistance in relation to children's hearings, pre-hearing panels (as defined in section 79(2)(a) of the 2011 Act) or proceedings under Part 10 or 15 of the 2011 Act;", and
  (c) in the definition of "legal aid"—
    (i) after "aid,", where it third occurs, insert "children's legal aid", and
    (ii) the words from "or", where it second occurs, to the end of the definition are repealed.

(9) In section 42 (disposable income and disposable capital: regulations), after subsection (3) insert—

"(4) Regulations under this section may make different provision for—
(a) children's legal aid and legal aid other than children's legal aid,
(b) advice and assistance in relation to children's matters and advice and assistance other than advice and assistance in relation to children's matters.

(5) In subsection (4)(b), "children's matters" has the meaning given by section 4A(14).".

Children (Scotland) Act 1995 (c.36)

2.—(1) The Children (Scotland) Act 1995 is amended as follows.
(2) In section 12 (restrictions on certain decrees)—
  (a) in subsection (1), for "or 54 of this Act" substitute "of this Act or section 62 of the Children's Hearings (Scotland) Act 2011",
  (b) in subsection (2)(a), for "or 54 of this Act" substitute "of this Act or section 62 of the Children's Hearings (Scotland) Act 2011".
(3) In section 16 (welfare of child and consideration of views)—
  (a) in subsection (1)—
    (i) the words "a children's hearing decide, or" are repealed,
    (ii) the words "their or" are repealed,
  (b) in subsection (2), the words "a children's hearing or as the case may be" are repealed,
  (c) in subsection (3)—
    (i) for "(4)(a)(i) or (ii) or (b)" substitute "(4)",
    (ii) the words "requirement or", in both places where they occur, are repealed,
    (iii) the words "the children's hearing consider, or as the case may be" are repealed,
  (d) for subsection (4) substitute—
    "(4) The circumstances to which subsection (2) refers are that the sheriff is considering whether to make, vary or discharge an exclusion order.",
  (e) in subsection (5)—
    (i) paragraph (a) is repealed,
    (ii) in paragraph (b), for "Chapters 1 to 3" substitute "Chapter 1 or 3".
(4) In section 17 (duty of local authority to child looked after by them)—
  (a) in subsection (6), for paragraph (b) substitute—
    "(b) who is subject to a compulsory supervision order or an interim compulsory supervision order and in respect of whom they are the implementation authority (within the meaning of the Children's Hearings (Scotland) Act 2011);",
  (b) subsection (6)(c) is repealed,
  (c) in subsection (6)(d), for "such responsibilities" substitute "responsibilities as respects the child".
(5) In section 19 (local authority plans for services for children)—
  (a) in subsection (2), after paragraph (a) insert—
    "(aa) the Children's Hearings (Scotland) Act 2011;",
  (b) in subsection (5)—
    (i) in paragraph (c), the words "appointed under section 127 of the Local Government etc. (Scotland) Act 1994" are repealed,
    (ii) for paragraph (d) substitute—
      "(d) the National Convener of Children's Hearings Scotland;".
(6) In section 33 (effect of orders etc. made in different parts of the United Kingdom)—
  (a) in subsection (1)—
    (i) the words "or to a supervision requirement" are repealed,
    (ii) the words "or, as the case may be, as if it were a supervision requirement" are repealed,
  (b) in subsection (2)—
    (i) paragraph (b) is repealed,
    (ii) in the full-out, the words "or requirement" are repealed,
  (c) subsection (4) is repealed,
  (d) in subsection (5)(b), the words "or to a supervision requirement" are repealed,
  (e) in subsection (5)(c), the words "or to a supervision requirement" are repealed.
(7) In section 38(4) (limited disapplication of certain enactments while child being provided with refuge), for "section 83 of this Act" substitute "section 171 of the Children's Hearings (Scotland) Act 2011".

Schedule 5

(8) In section 75 (powers in relation to secure accommodation)—
  (a) in subsection (1)(b), for "supervision requirement" substitute "compulsory supervision order, interim compulsory supervision order, medical examination order or warrant to secure attendance (all within the meaning of the Children's Hearings (Scotland) Act 2011)",
  (b) after subsection (2) insert—
    "(2A) In subsection (2), "relevant person" has the meaning given by section 200 of the Children's Hearings (Scotland) Act 2011 and includes a person deemed to be a relevant person by virtue of section 81(3), 160(4)(b) or 164(6) of that Act.", and
  (c) for subsection (4) substitute—
    "(4) A child may not be kept in secure accommodation by virtue of regulations made under this section for a period exceeding 66 days from the day when the child was first taken to the secure accommodation.".
(9) In section 76(8) (making of child protection order instead of exclusion order)—
  (a) in paragraph (b), for "section 57 of this Act" substitute "Part 5 of the Children's Hearings (Scotland) Act 2011",
  (b) in the full-out—
    (i) for "an order under that section" substitute "a child protection order",
    (ii) after "that" insert "Part".
(10) In section 93(1) (interpretation), in the definition of "children's hearing", for "section 39(3); but does not include a business meeting arranged under section 64, of this Act" substitute "section 5 of the Children's Hearings (Scotland) Act 2011".
(11) In section 93(2)(b) (meaning of "child"), for the definition of "child" substitute—
  ""child" means—
    (i) in relation to section 75, a person under the age of 18 years,
    (ii) in relation to any other section, a person under the age of 16 years;".

Antisocial Behaviour etc. (Scotland) Act 2004 (asp 8)

3. In section 12 of the Antisocial Behaviour etc. (Scotland) Act 2004 (sheriff's power to refer child to children's hearing where antisocial behaviour order made etc.), for subsection (1) substitute—
  "(1) This section applies where—
    (a) the sheriff makes an antisocial behaviour order or an interim order in respect of a child, and
    (b) the sheriff considers that a section 67 ground (other than the ground mentioned in section 67(2)(j)) applies in relation to the child.
  (1A) The sheriff may require the Principal Reporter to arrange a children's hearing.
  (1B) The sheriff must give the Principal Reporter a section 12 statement if—
    (a) the sheriff makes a requirement under subsection (1A), and
    (b) a compulsory supervision order is not in force in relation to the child.
  (1C) A section 12 statement is a statement—
    (a) specifying which of the section 67 grounds the sheriff considers applies in relation to the child,
    (b) setting out the reasons why the sheriff considers the ground applies, and
    (c) setting out any other information about the child which appears to the sheriff to be relevant.
  (1D) In this section—
    "compulsory supervision order" has the meaning given by section 83 of the Children's Hearings (Scotland) Act 2011,
    "section 67 ground" means a ground mentioned in section 67(2) of that Act.".

SCHEDULE 6

REPEALS

(introduced by section 203(2))

Enactment	Extent of repeal
Rehabilitation of Offenders Act 1974 (c.53)	Section 3. In section 5, in subsection (3), paragraph (b) and the word "and" immediately preceding it; in subsection (5), paragraph (f); and, in subsection (10), the words ", or a supervision requirement under the Children (Scotland) Act 1995,".
Legal Aid (Scotland) Act 1986 (c.47)	Section 29.
Tribunals and Inquiries Act 1992 (c.53)	In Part 2 of Schedule 1, paragraph 61(a) and the title ("Social work") relating to it.
Local Government etc. (Scotland) Act 1994 (c.39)	Sections 127 to 138. Schedule 12.
[1] Children (Scotland) Act 1995 (c.36)	Sections 39 to 74, except section 44. In section 75(1), paragraph (a) and the word "or" immediately following it. Section 75(5). Sections 75A and 75B. Sections 81 to 85. Section 90. Section 91(3)(a) to (c). Section 92. In section 93, in subsection (1), the definitions of "chief social work officer", "child assessment order", "child protection order", "compulsory measures of supervision", "education authority", "local government area", "place of safety", "the Principal Reporter", "relevant local authority", "supervision requirement" and "working day"; and, in subsection (2)(b), the definition of "relevant person". In section 101(1), in paragraph (a), the words "or under section 87(4) of this Act"; and paragraph (c) and the word "and" immediately preceding it. Section 101(4). In section 105, in subsection (8), the words "[...] 70(4), 74, 82, 83"; and subsection (10). Schedule 1. In Schedule 4, paragraph 23(2) and (3).
Vulnerable Witnesses (Scotland) Act 2004 (asp 3)	Section 23.
Antisocial Behaviour etc. (Scotland) Act 2004 (asp 8)	Section 12(2) to (5).
Legal Profession and Legal Aid (Scotland) Act 2007 (asp 5)	Section 72(4) to (6).

NOTE

1. As amended by the Children and Young People (Scotland) Act 2014 (asp 8) Sch.5 para.12(10) (effective 30 September 2015).

Appendix

Lord Advocate's Guidelines to the Chief Constable on the Reporting to Procurators Fiscal of offences alleged to have been committed by children:
Revised categories of offence which require to be Jointly Reported

This document contains guidance to police officers in Scotland on the categories of offence which require to be jointly reported to the Procurator Fiscal and the Children's Reporter. Children under the age of twelve years will, from the commencement of section 52 of the Criminal Justice and Licensing (Scotland) Act 2010, no longer be liable to prosecution in respect of any alleged criminal conduct and will therefore not be jointly reported to the Procurator Fiscal.

Category 1
Offences which require by law to be prosecuted on indictment or which are so serious as normally to give rise to solemn proceedings on the instructions of the Lord Advocate in the public interest.

Category 2
Offences alleged to have been committed by children aged 15 years or over which in the event of conviction oblige or permit a court to order disqualification from driving.

Category 3
Offences alleged to have been committed by people who are aged 16 or 17, and who are classified as children by section 199 of the Children's Hearings (Scotland) Act 2011.

In terms of section 199 of the Children's Hearings (Scotland) Act 2011, the definition of a child includes:
- A person aged 16 and 17 years who is subject to a compulsory supervision order; or
- A person over the age of 16 years who was referred to the Principal Reporter before they turned 16, but a "relevant event" has not yet occurred.

A "relevant event" is defined as being:
- The making of a compulsory supervision order;
- The notification to the person that the question of whether a compulsory supervisions order should be made will not be referred to a children's hearing, or
- The discharge of the referral to the Principal Reporter.

However, there is no requirement to jointly report the child to the Procurator Fiscal and the Children's Reporter if the offence falls within the Framework on the use of Police Direct Measures and Early and Effective Intervention for 16 and 17 year olds. Such offences should be submitted to the Children's Reporter alone.

EXPLANATORY NOTES

CATEGORY 1
Offences which require by law to be prosecuted on indictment. These offences fall under two heads:
(1) Common law offences which are within the exclusive jurisdiction of the High Court of Justiciary namely treason, murder and rape; and
(2) Statutory offences for which the statute only makes provision for prosecution on indictment or for a penalty on conviction on indictment—for example, contraventions of the:
- Firearms Act 1968 section 16, 17(1) and (2), and 18(1),
- Road Traffic Act 1988 section 1,
- Criminal Law (Consolidation) (Scotland) Act 1995 section 5(1), and
- Sexual Offences (Scotland) Act 2009 sections 1, 2, 18 and 19.

Offences Which Normally Give Rise to Solemn Proceedings

Offences which may be prosecuted on indictment on the instructions of the Lord Advocate in the public interest is a wider category of offences, which often depends on the facts and circumstances of a particular case.

Early discussion with the local procurator fiscal is advised where there is any doubt. Some common areas of offending which may fall to be considered under this heading are:

(1) Offences which are normally indicted in the High Court of Justiciary—these are offences of culpable homicide, attempted murder, assault to the danger of life, assault and robbery involving the use of firearms, attempted rape, incest and related offences (contrary to the Criminal Law (Consolidation) (Scotland) Act 1995 sections 1–2). This category also includes sodomy and contraventions of section 3 of Criminal Law Consolidation (Scotland) Act 1995 (intercourse with a child under 16 by a person in a position of trust) where the offence occurred on a date prior to 1 December 2010.

(2) Other offences which may fall into this category as being those normally prosecuted on indictment are assault to severe injury or permanent disfigurement, assault with intent to rape, serious assault and robbery (in particular involving the use of weapons other than firearms), assault with intent to rob involving the use of firearms, fire-raising and malicious mischief causing or likely to cause great damage to property or danger to life, all Misuse of Drugs Act 1971 offences involving possession of class a drugs and being concerned in the supply of any controlled drugs.

(3) The following sections of the Sexual Offences (Scotland) act 2009 contains offences that can be prosecuted on indictment:

- sections 3, 4, 5, 6, 7, 8, 9 and 11—offences capable of being committed against adults (aged over 16) and younger (aged under 13) and older (aged 13, 14 and 15) children who do not consent to the conduct.
- sections 20, 21, 22, 23, 24, 25 and 26—offences capable of being committed against a younger child (aged under 13) who consents to the conduct.
- sections 28, 29, 30, 31, 32, 33, 34, 35 and 36—offences only capable of being committed by a person who has attained the age of 16 against an older child (aged 13, 14 or 15) who consents to the conduct. These offences should only be considered for joint reporting where the offence has been committed by a "child" aged 16 or 17 who is subject to a supervision order or where a relevant event has not yet occurred.
- Section 37—offences involving older children engaging in sexual conduct with each other. See paragraph (4) below.

Offending behaviour which is covered by any of the aforementioned offences may fall to be jointly reported for consideration. The facts and circumstances of the offence are therefore vitally important when considering whether the offence is so serious in its nature as to merit being prosecuted on indictment.

Where there is any doubt at all that the offence may fall into this category, contact is to be made with the local area sexual offences team to discuss the facts of the particular case, either by telephone or by submission of an occurrence report for advice & direction prior to submitting a full report.

(4) Section 37 of the Sexual Offences (Scotland) Act 2009 creates the offence of older children engaging in sexual conduct with one another. This is not an offence which requires by law to be prosecuted on indictment but it may, depending on the facts and circumstances, be so prosecuted. When considering whether to report jointly allegations which are covered by this section, officers should pay regard to the following indicators:

- Age of the parties involved;
- Any power imbalance between the parties, for whatever reason;
- Overt aggression, manipulation, coercion or bribery;
- Misuse of substances as a disinhibitor, especially where this is at the instigation of the more dominant party;
- Whether the child's own behaviour, because of the misuse of substances, places

Appendix

him/her at risk so that he/she is unable to make an informed choice about any activity;
- Whether any attempts to secure secrecy have been made by the dominant party beyond what would be considered usual in a teenage relationship;
- Whether the either party is known to one of the agencies;
- Whether the parties deny, minimise or accept concerns;
- Whether the evidence is suggestive of grooming.

This is not an exhaustive list. Where, however, elements in this list or other circumstances are present which indicate that a young person may not have given free agreement to the activity concerned the matter should be jointly reported.

It should be re-emphasised that only offences which are normally prosecuted on indictment are to be reported jointly and that any cases of doubt should be discussed with the local procurator fiscal in advance of any report being submitted.

CATEGORY 2

This category applies exclusively to children aged 15 years or over.

Children will be prosecuted for this type of offence only if the procurator fiscal considers that it would be in the public interest to obtain a disqualification which would still be in force when the child became 16 and that in the event of conviction it was likely that the court would impose such a disqualification. Minor road traffic act offences carrying a liability to discretionary disqualification should not normally be reported.

CATEGORY 3

There is no restriction on the forum for the prosecution of children of or over 16 years of age who can be proceeded against in the justice of the peace court. However, where the child is 16 or 17 years old and subject to a supervision order (or a relevant event has not yet occurred) and the offence alleged to have been committed falls within the framework on the use of police direct measures and early and effective intervention for 16 and 17 year olds then there is no requirement for the case to be jointly reported. Such cases may be reported directly to the children's Reporter.

Frank Mulholland, QC
March 2014

INDEX

References are to paragraph number.

Absconding
  child absconding from person, C.549
  child absconding from place, C.548
  enforcement of orders, C.547
  offences related to absconding, C.550
  overview, C.379.17
Advice
  provision of advice to children's hearings, C.387
Age of child
  requirement to establish, C.503
Amendments
  generally, C.582, C.590
Ancillary provision
  generally, C.583
Annual reports
  compulsory supervision orders, C.560
Appeals
  appeals against children's hearing decisions
    appeals to sheriff principal and Court of Session, C.542
    determination of appeals, C.535
    generally, C.533
    procedure, C.534
    time limits for disposal, C.536
  appeals to sheriff principal and Court of Session
    contact and permanence orders, C.544
    generally, C.542
    relevant persons, C.543
  decisions affecting contact or permanence orders, C.540, C.544
  decisions to implement secure accommodation authorisations, C.541
  frivolous and vexatious appeals, C.538
  overview, C.379.16
  relevant person determinations, C.539, C.543
  requirements imposed on local authority, C.545–C.546
  suspension of CSOs pending appeal, C.537
Attendance
  child's duty to attend, C.452
  introductory note, C.451.5
  overview, C.379.8
  power to exclude relevant person, C.455
  power to exclude relevant person's representative, C.456
  power to proceed in absence of relevant person, C.454
  relevant person's duty to attend, C.453
  rights of certain persons to attend, C.457
  warrants to secure attendance, C.502
Child assessment orders
  consideration by sheriff, C.415
  generally, C.414
  implementation, C.437
  offences, C.438
  overview, C.379.6

Child protection orders
  ancillary measures
    contact directions, C.420
    information non-disclosure directions, C.419
    parental responsibilities and rights directions, C.421
  consideration by sheriff, C.417–C.418
  generally, C.416
  implementation, C.437
  local authorities' obligations, C.423
  notice, C.422
  offences, C.438
  other emergency measures
    application to justice of the peace, C.434
    constable's power to remove child to place of safety, C.435
    regulations, C.436
  overview, C.379.6
  review by children's hearings
    child in place of safety, C.424
    decision of children's hearing, C.426
    order preventing removal of child, C.425
  termination
    automatic termination, C.431
    Principal Reporter's powers, C.432
    termination after maximum of 8 working days, C.433
  termination or variation by sheriff
    applications, C.427
    children's hearing to provide advice to sheriff, C.429
    determination by sheriff, C.430
    notice of applications, C.428
  welfare of child, C.437
Children's advocacy services
  generally, C.501
Children's Hearings Scotland
  directions, C.392
  further provision, C.382, C.586
  generally, C.381
  independence of National Convener, C.391
  provision of assistance to National Convener, C.390
  transfer of staff, property, etc., C.403, C.589
Children's Panel
  generally, C.383, C.587
Commencement of Act
  generally, C.585
Compulsory supervision orders
  annual reports, C.560
  duty to consider including contact direction, C.408.5
  implementation
    applications for orders, C.526
    breach of duties, C.525
    duty where order requires child to reside in certain place, C.524

enforcement orders, C.527
further provision, C.528
general duties of implementation authority, C.523
interim compulsory supervision orders
  applications for extension or variation, C.477
  children's hearing to consider need for further order, C.475–C.476
  further extension or variation, C.478
  meaning, C.465
  sheriff's power to make orders, C.479
meaning, C.462
overview, C.379.14
Principal Reporter's duty to arrange children's hearing, C.516
review
  Antisocial Behaviour etc. (Scotland) Act 2004, C.508
  cases remitted under Criminal Procedure (Scotland) Act 1995 s.49, C.509
  child to be taken out of Scotland, C.513
  child transferred, C.515
  children's hearing's powers on deferral, C.518
  children's hearing's powers on review, C.517
  implementation authority's duty to require review, C.510
  interim variation of orders, C.519
  movement restriction conditions, C.504
  preparation of reports regarding permanence orders or adoption, C.520
  Principal Reporter's duty to initiate review, C.512
  relevant person determinations, C.521
  requirement to review, C.504
  right of child or relevant person to require review, C.511
  secure accommodation authorisations, C.514
suspension pending appeal, C.537
Consequential amendments
generally, C.582, C.590
Constitution of children's hearings
generally, C.384
selection of members, C.385
Contact directions
child protection orders, C.420
duty to consider inclusion, C.408.5
review, C.505
Contact orders
appeals, C.540, C.544
Criminal record certificates
generally, C.567
Deferral
children's hearings following deferral, C.498
grounds hearing's powers on deferral, C.471
powers of children's hearing on deferral, C.499

Disclosure of information
generally, C.557
panel members, C.559
prosecution, C.558
Enforcement of orders
child absconding from person, C.549
child absconding from place, C.548
generally, C.547
offences related to absconding, C.550
overview, C.379.17
Failure to provide education for excluded pupil
referral to children's hearing, C.506
Formal communications
generally, C.572
Forms
generally, C.573
Grounds hearings
applications to establish grounds
  child's duty to attend hearing, C.482
  grounds accepted before determination, C.484–C.485
  hearing of applications, C.480
  jurisdiction and standard of proof, C.481
  representation at hearing, C.483
child or relevant person unable to understand grounds, C.473
child's failure to attend, C.474
grounds hearing's powers, C.470
grounds hearing's powers on deferral, C.471
grounds not accepted, C.472
grounds to be put to child and relevant person, C.469
Principal Reporter's duty to prepare statement of grounds, C.468
review of grounds determinations
  applications for review, C.489
  child's duty to attend hearing, C.491
  introductory note, C.488.7
  new s.67 ground established, C.495
  no grounds accepted or established, C.494
  power to refer other grounds, C.493
  recall, C.493–C.494
  representation at hearing, C.492
  review or dismissal of applications, C.490
  sheriff's powers on review, C.493
Holding of hearings
generally, C.386
Implementation of orders
compulsory supervision orders
  applications for orders, C.526
  breach of duties, C.525
  duty where order requires child to reside in certain place, C.524
  enforcement orders, C.527
  further provision, C.528
  general duties of implementation authority, C.523
  movement restriction conditions, C.529
  overview, C.379.15
  secure accommodation authorisations
    implementation, C.530
    placement in other circumstances, C.531

Index

regulations, C.532
transfers in cases of urgent necessity, C.522
Independence of children's hearings
generally, C.388
Interim compulsory supervision orders
applications for extension or variation, C.477
children's hearing to consider need for further order, C.475–C.476
further extension or variation, C.478
meaning, C.465
sheriff's power to make orders, C.479
Interpretation provisions
generally, C.578–C.581
key definitions, C.462–C.467
Investigation and referral by Principal Reporter
cases remitted under Criminal Procedure (Scotland) Act 1995 s.49, C.450
child in place of safety, C.451
determinations
no referral to children's hearing, C.447
referral to children's hearing, C.448
generally, C.445
overview, C.379.7
provision of information to Principal Reporter
constables' duties, C.440
local authorities' duties, C.439
provision by constable where child in place of safety, C.444
provision by court, C.441
provision by other persons, C.443
provision from certain criminal cases, C.442
requirement under Antisocial Behaviour etc. (Scotland) Act 2004, C.449
s.67 grounds, C.446
Justices of the peace
applications, C.434, C.436
Legal aid and advice
generally, C.571
introductory note, C.569.4
overview, C.379.20
Medical examination or treatment
child's consent, C.565
Members of children's hearings
generally, C.384
selection, C.385
Minor amendments
generally, C.582, C.590
Movement restriction conditions
generally, C.529
Mutual assistance
generally, C.562–C.563
National Convener
annual report on CSOs, C.560
Children's Panel, C.383, C.587
further provision, C.382, C.586
generally, C.380
independence, C.391
overview, C.379.2
power to change functions, C.389

Orders made outwith Scotland
generally, C.569
Overview of Act
generally, C.379.1–C.379.21
Parenting orders
duty to consider application, C.507
Permanence orders
appeals, C.540, C.544
review of contact directions, C.505
Places of safety
constables' power to remove children, C.435, C.436
restrictions on use of police stations, C.568
Pre-conditions
making certain orders and warrants, C.407–C.408
Pre-hearing panel
appointment of safeguarder, C.461
determination of claim that person be deemed a relevant person, C.460
determination of matters referred, C.459
determination that deeming of person as relevant person to end, C.460.8
overview, C.379.9
referral of matters for pre-hearing determination, C.458
Principal Reporter
duty as respects location of children's hearings, C.396
duty to prepare statement of grounds, C.468
further provision, C.395, C.588
generally, C.393
introductory note, C.392.3
investigation and referral
cases remitted under Criminal Procedure (Scotland) Act 1995 s.49, C.450
child in place of safety, C.451
determinations (no referral), C.447
determinations (referral), C.448
generally, C.445
overview, C.379.7
provision of information to Principal Reporter, C.439–C.444
requirement under Antisocial Behaviour etc. (Scotland) Act 2004, C.449
s.67 grounds, C.446
overview, C.379.3
power to change functions, C.397
rights of audience, C.398
Procedural rules
generally, C.556
Publishing restrictions
generally, C.561
Rehabilitation of offenders
treatment of children's hearings disposals, C.566
Repeals
generally, C.582, C.591
Safeguarders
duty to consider appointment
children's hearing's duty, C.409
sheriff's duty, C.410
functions, C.412

325

overview, C.379.5
regulations, C.413
Safeguarders Panel, C.411
Savings provisions
generally, C.584
Scottish Children's Reporter Administration
assisting Principal Reporter, C.399
directions, C.402
further provision, C.395, C.588
generally, C.394
independence of Principal Reporter, C.401
provision of accommodation for children's hearings, C.400
Secure accommodation authorisations
appeals, C.541
implementation, C.530
placement in other circumstances, C.531
regulations, C.532
review, C.514
Selection of members
generally, C.385
Sharing of information
generally, C.557
panel members, C.559
prosecution, C.558
Sheriff court proceedings
application of provisions where CSO in force, C.497
applications for extension or variation of ICSO, C.477–C.478
applications to establish grounds
child's duty to attend hearing, C.482
grounds accepted before determination, C.484–C.485
hearing of applications, C.480
jurisdiction and standard of proof, C.481
representation at hearing, C.483
Court of Session power to regulate sheriff court procedure, C.564
determination of applications
grounds established, C.487
power to make ICSO, C.488
evidence
cases involving sexual behaviour, C.552–C.554

use of evidence obtained from prosecutor, C.551
vulnerable witnesses, C.555
overview, C.379.11, C.379.18
review of determinations
applications for review, C.489
child's duty to attend hearing, C.491
introductory note, C.488.7
new s.67 ground established, C.495
no grounds accepted or established, C.494
power to refer other grounds, C.493
recall, C.493–C.494
representation at hearing, C.492
review or dismissal of applications, C.490
sheriff's powers on review, C.493
sheriff's power to make ICSO, C.479
termination of orders by Principal Reporter, C.486
vulnerable witnesses, C.555
withdrawal of applications, C.486
Short title
generally, C.585
Statements of grounds
Principal Reporter's duty to prepare, C.468
Subordinate legislation
affirmative procedure, C.576
generally, C.574
negative procedure, C.575
super-affirmative procedure, C.577
Transitional and transitory provisions
generally, C.584
Urgent necessity
transfer of child, C.522
Views of child
confirmation that child given opportunity to express views, C.500
generally, C.406
Warrants to secure attendance
general power to grant, C.502
Welfare of child
child assessment orders and child protection orders, C.437
decisions inconsistent with welfare requirement, C.405
generally, C.404